HISTORICAL PRAGMATICS

Pragmatics & Beyond
New Series

35

Andreas H. Jucker (ed.)

Historical Pragmatics

HISTORICAL PRAGMATICS

PRAGMATIC DEVELOPMENTS IN
THE HISTORY OF ENGLISH

Edited by

ANDREAS H. JUCKER
Justus Liebig University, Giessen

JOHN BENJAMINS PUBLISHING COMPANY
AMSTERDAM/PHILADELPHIA

The paper used in this publication meets the minimum requirements of American National Standard for Information Sciences — Permanence of Paper for Printed Library Materials, ANSI Z39.48-1984.

Library of Congress Cataloging-in-Publication Data

Historical pragmatics : pragmatic developments in the history of English / edited by Andreas H. Jucker.

    p.   cm. -- (Pragmatics & beyond, ISSN 0922-842X ; new ser. 35)

    Includes bibliographical references and indexes.

    1. English language--Grammar, Historical. 2. Pragmatics. I. Jucker, Andreas H. II. Series.

PE1101.H49   1995

306.4'4--dc20   95-36115

ISBN 90 272 5047 2 (Eur.) / 1-55619-328-9 (US) (alk. paper)   CIP

John Benjamins Publishing Co. • P.O.Box 75577 • 1070 AN Amsterdam • The Netherlands

John Benjamins North America • P.O.Box 27519 • Philadelphia PA 19118-0519 • USA

Contents

Introduction

Part I: Pragmaphilology

Part II: Diachronic form-to-function mapping

Part III: Diachronic function-to-form mapping

Preface

Historical pragmatics is a very young field of scientific enquiry. It combines the methodologies of pragmatics, which is itself still quite young, and historical linguistics, which can look back on a long tradition. Pragmatics may be defined very crudely as the study of language in use, while historical linguistics is concerned with the investigation of earlier stages of particular languages and their diachronic development.

In recent years, pragmatics has witnessed an unprecedented upsurge in interest, while historical linguistics has experienced something of a renaissance after the sixties and seventies, which were dominated by Chomskyan linguistics. It seems only natural that pragmatics and historical linguistics should be combined in order to pose and perhaps even answer questions concerning the use of language at different stages of its development. And indeed there was an overwhelming response to my first call for papers. It appeared that historical pragmatics had been waiting to be constituted as a new field of scientific enquiry and only required a tiny push in order to get started and to gain momentum.

Few people could fall back on exisiting research. Most contributors had to start from scratch and carry out original research before they could write their contributions. This meant that I had to set a series of deadlines because each successive deadline came too soon for many people. Some people, regrettably, even had to withdraw their promises to submit a paper because of a lack of time.

The volume now contains 22 original papers that encompass a wide range of approaches. All but two of them use English language data, and therefore I have decided to subtitle this volume "Pragmatic Developments in the History of English". I do not believe that the papers by Onodera on Japanese discourse markers and by Fritz on dialogue forms in German reduce the overall coherence of the volume even though, strictly speaking, they fall outside the scope of the subtitle. Fritz uses data from a language that is very closely related to English, and Onodera uses a theoretical framework which is very similar to that used by Schwenter and Traugott. The papers by Fritz and Onodera may thus be taken as indicative of the wider relevance of the issues discussed in this volume. All 22 papers show, I believe, the great potential of this new and exciting area.

The opening paper by Jacobs and Jucker surveys the field of historical pragmatics and tries to distinguish and categorise several branches of historical pragmatics. We list some of the research interests and methodologies, and we relate the papers that appear in this volume to these branches. Our categorisation distinguishes between pragmaphilology and diachronic pragmatics. The former is concerned with pragmatic interpretations of historical texts while the latter compares pragmatic units at different stages in the development of a particular language.

The book itself adopts the same classification and starts with seven pragmaphilological papers. They all deal with historical English texts and their interpretation. And all of them endeavour to go beyond the traditional levels of analysis. In the words of Navarro-Errasti, they aim to review "historical texts in the light of pragmatic approaches", or they investigate the reliability of modern editions of old texts for pragmatic analyses. They pay close attention to the communicative context of these texts, which are not just seen as historical artefacts but as communicative acts with a sender who wrote for a particular audience with a particular purpose or intention. Who was the author, to whom was the text addressed, and what was the purpose of writing the text?

The second and the third part of this book comprise papers in diachronic pragmatics, in which the authors trace the development of a pragmatic unit across different stages in the development of English (or Japanese in the case of Onodera's contribution). Two broad classes can be distinguished within diachronic pragmatics. On the one hand, there are papers that take a linguistic form as their starting point, e.g. particular lexical items or syntactic constructions, and study their pragmatic functions at different times. These approaches are called diachronic form-to-function mappings (Part II). And on the other hand, there are papers that take a particular pragmatic function as their starting point, e.g. discourse strategies or politeness, and study their linguistic realisation at different times. These approaches are therefore called diachronic function-to-form mappings (Part III).

These two types of approaches can, of course, not always be easily distinguished. In many cases, changes in form coincide with changes or at least shifts in function. Thus, few papers are pure examples of the class into which I have put them, but I believe that the fundamentals of their approaches are different enough to justify the classification. Moreover, many papers are implicitly or explicitly concerned with more fundamental theoretical issues about the nature of language change in general. In these cases the mapping of form to function or vice versa is of course not an end in itself but only a crucial step in the analysis.

All the contributors deserve thanks for their unfailing cooperation and patience, and above all for the enthusiasm with which they have responded to my call for papers. I am convinced that this enthusiasm makes itself felt in the pages that follow, and I hope that it will spark off a lot of new research in historical pragmatics.

My greatest thanks, however, must go to my team of student assistants at the University of Giessen, without whom this volume would not have been possible. Annette Bergmann, Angelika Decker and Dorkas Kistler took over many of the practical tasks involved in editing this book such as transforming computer files into a unified format, scanning texts, proof-reading, and double-checking all the articles. They also compiled the indices. Needless to say that they are not to be held responsible for any remaining faults and infelicities. The blame for these must remain squarely with the editor.

List of Contributors

Cynthia Allen
Department of Linguistics, Arts
The Australian National University
GPO Box 4
Canberra ACT 2601
AUSTRALIA

Ulrich Bach
Institut für Englische Philologie
Universität Würzburg
Am Hubland
97074 Würzburg
GERMANY

Heinz Bergner
Institut für Anglistik und Amerikanistik
Justus-Liebig-Universität
Otto-Behaghel-Str. 10
35394 Gießen
GERMANY

Enrique Bernárdez
Departamento de Filología Inglesa
Universidad Complutense de Madrid
Ciudad Universitaria, s/n
28040 Madrid
SPAIN

Monika Fludernik
Englisches Seminar
Universität Freiburg
79085 Freiburg
GERMANY

Gerd Fritz
Fachbereich Germanistik
Justus-Liebig-Universität
39394 Gießen
GERMANY

Werner Hüllen
Literatur-und Sprachwissenschaften
Universität-Gesamthochschule Essen
Universitätsstr. 12
45117 Essen
GERMANY

Andreas Jacobs
Institut für Anglistik und Amerikanistik
Justus-Liebig-Universität
Otto-Behaghel-Str. 10
35394 Gießen
GERMANY

Andreas H. Jucker
Institut für Anglistik und Amerikanistik
Justus-Liebig-Universität
Otto-Behaghel-Str. 10
35394 Gießen
GERMANY

Roman Kopytko
School of English
Adam Mickiewicz University
Al. Niepodłosci 4
61-874 Poznań
POLAND

John Lennard
Trinity Hall
Cambridge CB2 ITJ
ENGLAND, U.K.

Mª Pilar Navarro-Errasti
Cesáreo Alierta, 6 10^0 D.
50008 Zaragoza
SPAIN

Barbara Kryk-Kastovsky
Perlhofgasse 17
2372 Giesshuebl
AUSTRIA

Noriko Okada Onodera
4-1-18-402, Nishi Ikuta
Tama-ku, Kawasaki-City
Kanagawa, 214
JAPAN

Terttu Nevalainen
Department of English
University of Helsinki
P.O. Box 4
00014 University of Helsinki
FINLAND

Helena Raumolin-Brunberg
Raatihuoneenkatu 17
06100 Porvoo
FINLAND

José Pinto de Lima
Faculdade de Letras, Departamento de
Estudos Germanísticos
Cidade Universitária
1699 Lisboa Codex
PORTUGAL

Scott A. Schwenter
Department of Linguistics,
Building 460
Stanford University
Stanford CA 94305-2150
USA

Gert Ronberg
Department of English
King's College
Aberdeen AB9 2UB
SCOTLAND, UK

Paloma Tejada
Departamento de Filología Inglesa
Universidad Complutense de Madrid
Cuidad Universitaria, s/n
28040 Madrid
SPAIN

Irma Taavitsainen
Department of English
University of Helsink‡
P.O. Box 4
00014 Helsinki
FINLAND

Tuija Virtanen
Department of English
Åbo Akademi University
Fänriksgatan 3 A
20500 Åbo
FINLAND

Elizabeth Closs Traugott
Department of Linguistics,
Building 460
Stanford University
Stanford CA 94305-2150
USA

Katie Wales
Department of English
Royal Holloway
University of London
Egham, Surrey TW20 0EX
ENGLAND, U.K.

Brita Wårvik
Department of English
University of Turku
Henrikinkatu 2
20500 Turku
FINLAND

Richard Watts
Department of English
Universität Bern
Länggaßstraße 49
3000 Bern 9
SWITZERLAND

Introduction

The Historical Perspective in Pragmatics

Andreas Jacobs and Andreas H. Jucker
Justus-Liebig-University Giessen

1.   Introduction

Pragmatics is at present one of the most active and most prolific fields of linguistics. It has grown at an enormous rate during the last fifteen years or so but it is still, as Verschueren (1987: 4) called it, a "large, loose, and disorganized collection of research efforts". It ranges from discourse analysis to speech act theory and from the study of presuppositions to relevance theory. Some approaches in pragmatics focus on communication in general and on the human cognitive processes that make communication possible, while others concentrate on specific languages and on the communicative meaning of specific elements (e.g. speech acts or discourse markers) in specific languages.

There are also pragmatic analyses that compare the linguistic inventory and how it is used by communicators in different languages, that is to say studies in contrastive pragmatics, e.g. Blum-Kulka *et al.* (1989), Oleksy (1988), and Wierzbicka (1991). However, there are as yet only few studies that focus on the linguistic inventory and its communicative use across different historical stages of the same language.

Diachronic studies have always had to rely on written data, while pragmatics has almost always preferred spoken data. It is therefore not surprising that few scholars have tried to integrate the two approaches. However, both historical linguistics and pragmatics have made a lot of progress recently in extending the scope of their databases. Historical linguistics has made some progress in investigating stylistic differences including approximations to spoken registers, while pragmatics has extended its field of analysis into the written language.

The step from contrastive pragmatics to historical pragmatics is not a conceptually difficult jump. Contrastive studies compare the realisation of linguistic units (be they semantic, functional, pragmatic, or something else) in different cultures, in different languages, or in different varieties of one language. Historical studies, on the other hand, compare the realisation of linguistic units at different stages in the development of one language. The historical dimension does not differ systematically from such other dimensions as the geographical, the social, the stylistic and so on (cf. Schlieben-Lange 1975: 87).

In this article we shall try to explore the field of historical pragmatics as we envisage it. We distinguish two different approaches that can be subsumed under the label of historical pragmatics: pragmaphilology and diachronic pragmatics. Our survey will take the form of a state-of-the-art report in that we will try to review the relevant literature in these fields. In spite of the scarcity of studies that deal explicitly with historical pragmatics, there are of course numerous studies that are more or less relevant to historical pragmatics as such.

It might be argued that historical pragmatics is just a new label for a range of research efforts that have existed for a long time. However, we feel that it is more than that. The label will give these research efforts a focus that has been lacking so far, and it sketches out the scope for future developments of the field.

2.   The nature of historical pragmatics

Theoretical discussions on the historical dimension in pragmatics have so far been conducted mainly, but not exclusively, in Romance and Germanic studies (cf. e.g. Apostel 1980; Bax 1981, 1983 and 1991; Cherubim 1980, 1984; Jucker 1994; Panagl 1977; Presch 1981; Schlieben-Lange 1975: 87, 1983; Schwarz 1984: 247-256; Stein 1985a). However, these theoretical discussions consist of no more than some programmatic remarks outlining the shape of a historical pragmatics in fairly broad terms. A far-reaching comprehensive debate on the historical perspective in pragmatics has not yet taken place. Those authors who have attempted to embark on this new discipline often fail not only to refer to each other but also to push the debate forward. So far, the potential of the historical dimension in pragmatics has been repeatedly touched upon, but the historical pragmatic plane has never really taken off.

Is this because linguists never felt a real need for such a new discipline? While some researchers (e.g. Cherubim 1980: 4) express that they have no doubts about the necessity and usefulness of a *historical* pragmatics, others (cf. e.g. Presch 1981: 213) ask what exactly a historically dimensioned pragmatics should be able to reveal. Obviously, when founding a science it is not enough to refer to its own value. We should have an idea about the feasibility of the new discipline. In the case of pragmatics it is reasonable to assume that communication in earlier periods can also be described in terms of pragmatic phenomena such as speech acts, implicature, politeness phenomena, or discourse markers.

However, not least because of the mismatch between theory and practice did attempts to lay the foundation for a comprehensive historical pragmatics misfire. Sitta's (1980) and Schlieben-Lange's (1983) arguments, for example, merely "combine broadly based programmatic comments with short practical applications" (Bergner 1992: 165). Thus a need for straightforward theoretical propositions which can be evaluated against results obtained by specific research efforts is imminent.

The lack of comprehensiveness is also due to problems arising in connection with the task of integrating a language-historical dimension and a pragmalinguistic dimension. One might think of two ways for such an integration: either historical linguistics becomes more pragmatic, or linguistic pragmatics becomes more historical (cf. Presch 1981: 230). In Sitta (1980) the new discipline under discussion is given two different labels. While in the title of his volume Sitta chooses *pragmatische Sprachgeschichte* (pragmatic historical linguistics), Cherubim picks the term *historische Sprachpragmatik* (historical linguistic pragmatics) for his programmatic article. The question then is whether both authors talk about the same thing (cf. Presch 1981: 230; Weigand 1988: 159). Are we dealing with a historical dimension in pragmatics or a pragmatic perspective in historical linguistics? .

To solve this dilemma one might first try to outline what the two disciplines are possibly about. If we apply a pragmatic perspective to historical linguistics, we are simply interested in describing the development of a language, or the language change, as social acts of communicators under shifting historical circumstances (cf. Cherubim 1984: 809). In this context, the conditions leading to altered types of speech acts are of particular importance, e.g. aims, motives, interests, public and private behaviour, institutions, formulae and rituals. Language change from a pragmatic point of view can thus be understood as a shift in (potential) human behaviour (cf. Weigand 1988: 159).

If we add a historical dimension to pragmatics, we try to investigate language use over time. In most programmatic remarks it is suggested that the task of historical pragmatics is to describe pragmatically how language was used in former times as transmitted in historical texts (cf. e.g. Weigand 1988: 159). What types of rules, conditions, and functions of social acts were effective in earlier language stages or processes of language change (cf. Cherubim 1984: 807)? In short, historical pragmatics focuses more on language use, pragmahistorical linguistics more on language change. The latter appears to be the more general approach (cf. also Cherubim 1984), while the former presents itself as a complementary subject and thus provides the raw material on language use relevant for the analysis of language change. As the title of this overview suggests, we shall here concentrate on the historical perspective in pragmatics, but this volume also contains articles that adopt a more pragmahistorical perspective, in particular the papers by de Lima, Bernárdez and Tejada, Schwenter and Traugott, and Allen.

Historical pragmatics deals with changes in the linguistic structure resulting from altered communicative needs which are due to changes in the social structure (cf. Stein 1985b), or, in other words, with changes in traditions of language use resulting from changes in the situational context, e.g. the institutionalisation or a medium change (cf. Schlieben-Lange 1983). Hence the aims of a historically conceived pragmatics include

(1) the description and the understanding of conventions of language use in communities that once existed and that are no longer accessible for direct observation, and

(2) the description and the explanation of the development of speech conventions in the course of time (Bax 1981: 425; cf. also Bax 1991: 200).

However, historical pragmatics can also be used as a philological tool to explain literary artefacts from the past (cf. Bax 1983: 3). In fact,

especially in the field of diachronic language development [...] it is pragmatics which could make important contributions to a linguistic solution of problems. This could be achieved by trying to illuminate the variety of relations between the respective linguistic signs, between linguistic sign and sign-user, as well as between the respective creator of the sign and its recipient (Bergner 1992: 163).

3.   The data problem

Pragmatics is predominantly concerned with spoken language. The most prominent problem for historical pragmatics, therefore, concerns the availability of historical natural language data (cf. e.g. Bax 1983: 3). Since electronic recording techniques were not available until the twentieth century, spoken language of the past cannot be investigated through direct observation. Contrastive studies of present-day languages and language varieties can rely on the whole range of data-gathering techniques developed for the description of living languages, such as recordings and transcriptions of spoken conversations, native speaker intuitions, questionnaires and the like. Except for the very immediate past, historical-pragmatic hypotheses can never be empirically supported (cf. Bax 1983: 18). The pragmatician has to rely on written records as approximate evidence for his or her claims on spoken language. Furthermore, if the linguistic researcher accepts that for a historical pragmatic analysis he or she needs data on the socio-historical environment, he or she has to face the problem that texts from earlier periods inform very sparsely about their situational context (cf. Sitta 1980: 32).

However, historical linguistics has recently refined its methodology to a considerable extent, and it is now possible to get an approximate picture of the spoken language of past centuries. For example, sociolinguistic methodologies have provided the means to compare and measure the styles of different texts in terms of their formality.

Moreover, there are some arguments which show that results obtained through the analysis of written records may support claims on spoken language as well (cf. Bax 1983: 18f.; Bax 1991: 212f.). First, types of verbal interaction may be recorded not only in literary but also in other contexts such as juridical or clerical. Analogy may thus help to support a hypothesis which otherwise would be based on a single data source only. Second, literary history has shown that literary texts from the Middle Ages tend to be more realistic than today's fictional works. Third, from a functionalist point of view the question arises whether specific types of verbal interaction may be imaginable not only in fictional but also under real life circumstances. Fourth, there are many types of verbal interaction, such as quarrels, children's games, non-verbal signals, routines, which can be readily understood on the basis of underlying behavioural patterns. Thus, if a specific type of verbal interaction appears in historical texts and is also easily understood, the text may be taken to reflect a real life situation.

It is plausible to suggest that written records of spoken language are closer to the actual spoken language of the time than written language not based on spoken language. Features that are consistently more frequent in records of spoken language than in written language proper can fairly safely be hypothesised to be even more frequent in the spoken language of that period (cf. Rissanen 1986). These points have also been treated by Biber and Finegan (1992) in their comparative diachronic analysis of three written genres – essays, fiction and personal letters – and two speech-based genres – dialogue from plays and from fiction. Speech-based genres are defined as

varieties originating in speech that have been permanently preserved in writing. These include various kinds of transcribed speech, such as court proceedings, political debates, town meetings, and some public speeches and sermons, as well as various literary representations of speech (Biber and Finegan 1992: 689).

The analysis takes place on three dimensions. Each one of them displays linguistic features that interact directly with the contrasts among 'oral' and 'literate' genres in English. Dimension A matches 'Informational vs. Involved Production'. Positive factors for this dimension include, for example, the type-token ratio and attributive adjectives, while negative factors cover, for example, contractions and discourse particles. On Dimension B they distinguish 'Elaborated vs. Situation-Dependent Reference'. Here positive factors involve WH-relative clauses on object positions and nominalisations. Time and place adverbials belong to the negative factors. Finally, Dimension C is concerned with 'Abstract style', which comprises conjuncts, *by*-passives or agentless passives. The analysis comprises 163 texts representing four periods from the 17th century up to 1950.

As a result, texts from the 17th and 18th century tend to be more literate while from the 19th century onwards there is a transition to more oral styles (Biber and Finegan 1992: 695ff.). As far as abstract style and situation dependence are concerned, there is a drift to more oral styles and to less variation between oral and written styles. This

> might be taken to indicate that authors capture the linguistic characteristics of conversation fairly accurately with respect to Dimension B [...] and Dimension C [...] and further that conversation itself has not changed much over these centuries (Biber and Finegan 1992: 699).

In order to test this hypothesis Biber and Finegan used present-day conversation data from the London-Lund corpus. They come to the conclusion that "literary dialogue is remarkably similar to actual conversation with respect to these two dimensions" (Biber and Finegan 1992: 699f.). In contrast, as far as Dimension A (Informational vs. Involved Production) is concerned, literary dialogue is markedly unlike modern face-to-face conversation. This is interpreted to be due to the high information load in literary dialogues. Nevertheless, Biber's and Finegan's study offers a way to determine the oral character of speech-based genres.

Letters, and in particular private letters, are a rich source of data for historical pragmatics. They may contain more intimate and more colloquial language than other text types. It is an empirical question whether they are therefore closer to the spoken language than other more formal texttypes, but they contain many interactional features such as address terms, directives, politeness markers, apologies, and so on. Kryk-Kastovsky (this volume) uses

Early Modern English letters to analyse the demonstratives *this* and *that*. Nevalainen and Raumolin-Brunberg (this volume) use the same type of data for their investigation of address formulae.

Many researchers have come to see written artefacts not just as imperfect renderings of the real thing. Written texts can be understood as communicative manifestations in their own right, and as such they are amenable to pragmatic analyses. Danet and Bogoch (1992a, 1992b), for instance, analyse the pragmatics of Anglo-Saxon wills; Bach (this volume) investigates English wills from the 16th and 17th century; and Fritz (1993b) explores the communicative strategies of early German newspapers. In all these cases there are no claims about the spoken language of that particular period of English or German respectively. Wills as well as newspapers are analysed as independent forms of communication that warrant a pragmatic analysis.

Literary texts, too, have been analysed as communicative acts. Watts (1981) and Brönnimann-Egger (1991) both concentrate on the cooperation between the author and the reader of literary texts. Watts develops his analysis on the basis of Charles Dickens' *Hard Times*, while Brönnimann-Egger uses eighteenth-century English poets. Sell (1985a and 1985b) analyses Chaucer and his relationship to his audience (cf. also several articles in Sell 1991), and Navarro-Errasti (this volume) studies the Middle English poem *Sir Gawain and the Green Knight*.

These approaches contrast with those that use literary texts as a source for simulated spoken interactions. Bax (1981), for instance, explores the ritual challenges among medieval knights on the basis of Middle Dutch romances, while Breuer (1983) and Kopytko (1993a and this volume) use the verbal interactions in Shakespeare's plays to analyse the use of address titles (such as *master*, *madam*, *your honour* or *goodman*) and the use of politeness formulae respectively.

It is also possible to deduce information about the conversational behaviour of earlier generations by closely studying what contemporary authors had to say about conversations of their time. Gloning (1993), for instance, analysed a whole range of sources including manuals on good behaviour, language teaching books, and literary references to conversational behaviour, and Fritz (this volume) uses extracts from Albrecht von Eyb's so-called *Ehebüchlein* – published in 1472 – which is a treatise on legal proof procedures on matters of marriage.

Burke (1993: 89-122), in a study of conversational behaviour in Early Modern Europe, looked at a large number of manuals which appeared between the 17th and 19th centuries in England, France and elsewhere. They typically have titles such as *The Art of Conversation* and tell their readers how to behave in conversations either generally or on particular occasions. They warn their readers, for instance, not to interrupt their interlocutors and not to talk about themselves.

Historical pragmatics will always have to rely on written material. However, this should no longer be seen as detrimental. There are many ways in which the written data can be used. Modern sociolinguistic methodologies can help to establish which texts may be used as rough approximations to the spoken language of that time. Literary texts may contain simulated spoken interactions. In the case of drama they actually consist almost entirely of simulated spoken interactions. And finally, written texts can be analysed as communicative acts in their own right.

In all cases it is of course crucial to use the most reliable editions available. Both Ronberg (this volume) and Lennard (this volume) argue very strongly for editions that stay as close to the original texts as possible. They show that the modernisation of punctuation has far-reaching consequences for the pragmatic interpretation of historical texts.

4.   The scope of historical pragmatics

Under the heading historical pragmatics various linguistic research efforts can be given a historical dimension (cf. Cherubim 1984: 807f.): e.g. a pragmaticalised semantics, speech act theory, the research into function words, the analysis of maxims of conversation, text analysis (text types, communication forms, text pragmatics; cf. Gumbrecht 1977), conversation analysis, language change, language norms and varieties.

In general, some pragmatic frameworks might be more suitable than others for research into historical pragmatics. Pragmatics comprises an extremely diverse range of research efforts not all of which seem equally suitable for contrastive pragmatics in general and for historical pragmatics in particular. Research efforts in pragmatics can be split up into general pragmatics, socio-pragmatics and pragmalinguistics (Leech 1983: 10-11). General pragmatics concentrates on the general conditions of the communicative use of language. Such frameworks do not lend themselves easily to contrastive studies because these general conditions are taken to be relatively language independent. Socio-pragmatics concentrates on the local conditions of language use. Grice's cooperative principle and Leech's politeness principle, for instance, operate variably in different cultures and in different language communities. This is amply demonstrated by the different ways in which politeness is interpreted in cultures such as Japan, Britain and India.

Pragmalinguistics analyses the linguistic (syntactic, lexical, etc.) means that a language makes available to fulfil certain functions and to realise particular speaker intentions. Speech act theory is one such framework. Both socio-pragmatic and pragmalinguistic frameworks should lend themselves not only to contrastive analyses but also to historical comparisons.

At the present state of research two approaches to the pragmatic study of earlier language states may be distinguished. We shall call them pragmaphilology and diachronic pragmatics. In the following we are going to introduce these approaches as we see them, review some of the existing literature, and indicate briefly how the articles of this volume fit into them.

4.1. *Pragmaphilology*

Traditionally, historical linguists have spent most of their efforts on sound changes and on the phonology and morphology of historical texts. Syntax and semantics have always been less popular among the language historians. Pragmaphilology goes one step further and describes the contextual aspects of historical texts, including the addressers and addressees, their social and personal relationship, the physical and social setting of text production and text reception, and the goal(s) of the text.

Bergner (1992) describes many of the relevant aspects of medieval text production and reception. From his article it emerges that the communicative environment of medieval texts is characterised by a preference for norm and typicality, and a tendency towards the formal and impersonal. Bergner (this volume) draws attention to the openness of medieval texts. He argues that all forms of human communication are open in that they may be unclear in various degrees or may allow for different interpretation. Medieval texts, in particuar, are characterised by a very considerable degree of openness because of the lack of linguistic standards, because of the specific character of textual communication in the Middle Ages, and because of the entire social and cultural political framework of these texts. Beetz (1990) concentrates on the standards and rules of interaction in earlier periods. Albeit from a linguistically unsatisfactory perspective, he analyses the discourse of Early Modern politeness, in particular the nature and the change of rituals and compliments in the Old German speaking world.

Since research into earlier language stages depends on written records, it is central to a pragmaphilological study to investigate the similarities and dissimilarities of written and spoken language (see also the discussion on the non-availability of historical natural language data in this article). For example, in the (written) language of the first German newspapers in the 17th century it can be shown how specific communicative tasks require different linguistic means: references are given in passive constructions, objects or persons are introduced by relative clauses without a finite auxiliary or by attributes, or appositions are used to ensure the appropriate interpretation of pronouns (cf. Fritz 1993b). Betten (1990) demonstrates that there is a considerable closeness of written language to spoken language. She refers to Luther's translation of the Bible and Early Modern High German prose which contain well recorded features of Medieval spoken language, especially when texts were conceived to be read aloud.

Ronberg (this volume) and Lennard (this volume) both show that an adequate (i.e. pragmatic) analysis of historical texts must study these texts in their entirety including the socio-historical context, their production process and – crucially – a faithful account not only of the syntactic/lexical level but also the physical and orthographic level.

Hüllen (this volume), Bach (this volume), Watts (this volume) and Navarro-Errasti (this volume) study Middle English or Early Modern English texts as communicative acts in their own right. This includes a careful consideration of the writers of these texts, their communicative intentions and their intended audiences as well as the entire socio-historical context in which these texts were written. Hüllen analyses William Caxton's *Dialogues in French and English*, that is to say a foreign language teaching book first published at the end of the Middle Ages. He subjects this book to a type of analysis that has been developed by Sinclair and Coulthard for the modern classroom. What is surprising is the high level of structural similarities between this late Middle English textbook and the oral interaction in a modern classroom.

Bach (this volume) explores the pragmatics of wills and will-making on the basis of a corpus of wills written in the 16th and 17th century by people connected to the University of Cambridge. He shows that these wills can only be adequately interpreted if they are seen in their legal and religious context, and if the beliefs and motivations of the testators are taken into consideration.

Watts (this volume) uses the prefatory sections of grammar books of English written between the 16th and 18th century to study the discourse strategies that the authors employed in order to define an audience for themselves. These grammars are seen as complex communicative acts that must be studied in their socio-pragmatic context.

The pragmatic analysis of literary texts also belongs to the category of pragmaphilology (cf. Watts 1981; Sell 1985a, 1985b, 1991; Brönnimann-Egger 1991). Navarro-Errasti (this volume) uses relevance theory to analyse the Middle English poem *Sir Gawain and the Green Knight*, in which she looks for communicative clues. She finds the stylistic value of words and the sound-based poetic properties to be of special significance, or to be – in the technical sense – relevant. The literary work is explicitly seen as a communicative act whose author chooses stylistic forms that yield sufficient cognitive effects to counterbalance the effort the reader needs to process them.

4.2. *Diachronic pragmatics*

While synchronic contrastive pragmatics compares the linguistic inventory and how it is used by communicators in different languages, diachronic pragmatics focuses on the linguistic inventory and its communicative use across different historical stages of the same language. Within the diachronic studies it is possible to distinguish two subtypes. Some studies may take a linguistic form (such as discourse markers, relative pronouns or lexical items) as a starting point in order to investigate the changing discourse meanings of the chosen element or elements while the other subtype takes the speech functions (such as a specific speech act or politeness) as their starting point in order to investigate the changing realisations of this function across time. We shall call the former approach *diachronic form-to-function mapping* and the latter *diachronic function-to-form mapping*.

One of the major problems of contrastive pragmatics – and hence also of diachronic pragmatics – is the *tertium comparationis*. Any comparison relies on an element that remains fixed. Krzeszowski (1984) suggests that formal, semantic, statistical, system or translation equivalence are inadequate concepts for contrastive analyses and that more subtle distinctions are required. A translation, for example, is not necessarily a good translation if it is formally equivalent to the original version. A good translation rather has to be pragmatically or functionally equivalent (Krzeszowski 1984: 303). Thus to analyse, for example, a particular discourse marker, i.e. the linguistic form, or a specific speech act, i.e. the speech function, at two stages of their development, we need to refer to the concept of *pragmatic equivalence* (cf. also Fillmore 1984; Kalisz 1986; Janicki 1990).

In both cases both the form and the function may change in the course of time, and therefore, there can be no hard and fast boundary between these two approaches (cf. Fritz this volume). It is the perspective that differs, rather than any fundamental methodological issue.

4.2.1. *Diachronic form-to-function mapping*

This approach traces individual linguistic items in their historical development. It considers (the emergence of) the pragmatic meaning of these elements. The *tertium comparationis* is here the linguistic form. It does not have to be constant but the more recent realisations must be seen as direct developments of earlier realisations.

The first four papers classified as diachronic form-to-function mapping in this volume (i.e. de Lima, Bernárdez and Tejada, Schwenter and Traugott, and Allen) adopt a perspective that has been described as pragmahistorical linguistic, rather than historical pragmatic, that is to say they are primarily concerned with pragmatic explanations of language change. Within this perspective, however, they analyse individual linguistic items and describe how these have changed in the course of the development of English or other languages. De Lima uses several examples of lexical change, mainly in German, in order to ascertain to what extent pragmatic maxims can be used to explain language change but he finds that language change induced by pragmatic principles is just a special case of change induced by norm-following, as he calls it; and norm-following is a special case of language change by rational behaviour. Bernárdez and Tejada (this volume) show how an economy principle and a communicative principle can be used to explain word-order changes from Old to Middle English, and thus to explain these changes from a pragmatic rather than a syntactic perspective.

Traugott has done a lot of pioneering work on the regularities of semantic change (e.g. Traugott 1989 on how *again* changed its meaning). She describes subjectification as a pragmatic-semantic process whereby "meanings become increasingly based in the speaker's subjective belief state/attitude toward the proposition" (Traugott 1989: 35). More precisely, Traugott relates subjectification to the process of grammaticalisation. *Subjectification in grammaticalisation* is

> a gradient phenomenon, whereby forms and constructions that at first express primarily concrete, lexical, and objective meanings come through repeated use in local syntactic contexts to serve increasingly abstract, pragmatic, interpersonal and speaker-based functions (Traugott in press prefinal draft: 2).

Grammaticalisation is defined as

> the process whereby lexical items or phrases come through frequent use in certain highly constrained local contexts to be reanalyzed as having syntactic or morphological functions, and once grammaticalized continue to develop new grammatical functions (Traugott in press prefinal draft: 2).

Thus, for example, the imperative *Let us go* developed into the hortative *Let's go*, or the temporal *Mary read while Bill sang* evolved into the concessive *Mary liked oysters while Bill hated them* (cf. Traugott in press prefinal draft: 1). Furthermore, in her analysis of the rise of epistemic meaning Traugott

(1989) emphasises the need for a theory of pragmatic inference controlled by principles of strengthening of informativeness and relevance to account for the semantic changes observed, i.e. the development of both lexical and grammatical items into expressions of epistemicity.

Schwenter and Traugott (this volume) work within grammaticalisation theory, which has its origins in work in historical syntax and morphology within a functionalist framework in which language change is seen as a process and not as a product. This line of research examines historical data in their discourse context and thus differs somewhat from the socio-pragmatic approaches adopted by many of the other contributors. In their contribution Schwenter and Traugott trace the development of three complex prepositional phrases in English expressing substitution, *instead of*, *in place of*, and *in lieu of*.

Allen (this volume) traces the history of the verb *please* in expressions such as *you can do as you please*, where the experiencer is the only expressed argument in the construction. She argues that the pragmatic function and text-typological evidence of the construction must be taken into account. Thus, one of the alternative constructions with the experiencer in object position, which remained common in *if*-clauses until the 18th century, is no longer used in everyday speech except for very specific speech acts in very specific settings such as *May it please the court, ...* in a courtroom setting.

Wales (this volume) analyses the generalising-possessive or generic-deictic pronoun *your*, as in the newspaper headline *Just your average French movie star*. She traces it from its first appearance in written English in the late 16th century to Modern English and analyses its function, its colligations and collocations, and its frequency of occurrence in a broad range of contexts.

Linguistic items which can be analysed within a framework of diachronic form-to-function mapping include deictic elements. Fries (1993) proposes a programme for the historical study of discourse deixis and offers a preliminary analysis of the Old English discourse deictic elements *hēr* and *nū* ('here' and 'now'). By means of discourse deictic elements the speaker or writer expresses in various combinations where he or she is at the moment of speaking or writing.

Kryk-Kastovsky (this volume) investigates the English demonstratives *this* and *that* in Early Modern English and compares these findings to the situation in Modern English. It turns out that most Modern usages were already present in Early Modern English, but with some notable exceptions as for instance in the dating of Early Modern English letters (*Alicant, this 31st of July, 1706*).

Wårvik (this volume) traces the development of the conjunctions/ adverbials *þa* and *þonne* from Old English to their Modern English counterparts *then* and *when* concentrating on the changes that these elements underwent in the Middle English period. In Old English these elements were ambiguous and could be used either as a conjunction or as an adverb. This is again a clear case of form-to-function mapping because the starting point is the linguistic item. The item itself changes too in the course of time; *þa* and *þonne* even conflate in Late Middle English to *then*. But Wårvik investigates the different discourse functions that these elements fulfil.

Discourse markers attracted a lot of interest in this field (cf. Brinton 1990; Stein 1985b; Taavitsainen 1994b; Burger 1980; Henne 1980; Fludernik this volume; and Onodera this volume). One of the major debates focuses on their historical status. In particular, it is not clear whether discourse markers can be characterised as ephemeral due to the fact that they are typical of linguistically transitional periods (cf. Stein 1985b: 300). Stein (1985b) investigates the choice between the two endings *s* and *th* of the third person singular present indicative and the use of *do* or the finite form in declarative sentences. In Stein's (1985b: 300) view the "discourse meanings of *s/th* and *do* have to be considered as instances of [...] ephemeral and transitional functionalisations of syntactic and morphological contrasts". He suggests a discourse structure explanation according to which in the *s*-passages "the circumstances, the agents and the places are described in more detail" (Stein 1985b: 284), "the use of direct speech makes for a more involved and vivid impression of the scene", and "much more descriptive, circumstantial, detailed individuating verbal effort" can be observed. The *th*-parts, on the contrary, are "distinctly more technical" (Stein 1985b: 288). Furthermore, the use of *do* seems to be "related to what is the high point of the content, the essential parts" (Stein 1985: 295).

The opposite view postulates that discourse markers "are characteristic of every period, no matter how stable" (Brinton 1990: 62). Accordingly, Brinton (1990: 63) concludes from his analysis of Old English *hwæt* and Modern English *you know* that the history of particular discourse markers is not as transitory as Stein suggests in his analysis of discourse markers in Early Modern English. For example, old English *hwæt* is similar to *you know* in Modern English, since

> it indicates knowledge shared by speaker and addressee or common to all; it presents new information as if it were old, it establishes either intimacy or distance between speaker and addressee; it solicits a favourable reception for the following information; it is an attention-getting device; it provides evaluation of the narrative point; and it makes explanatory material salient (Brinton: 1990: 56).

Hwæt disappeared after the Middle English period, but its function has been assumed by a Modern English equivalent. Brinton (1990: 62) interprets the development of *hwæt* "from interrogative in direct questions to complementiser in indirect questions to discourse marker of shared information" in Traugott's terms. Thus

> the development of the discourse meaning of shared knowledge from the simple interrogative meaning can be seen as the result of a pragmatic inference. Furthermore, it represents an increased emphasis on the speaker's attitude, from a questioning of what the hearer knows to an expression of the speaker's belief in, or confirmation of, what the hearer knows to an expression of what is known by both speaker and hearer (Brinton 1990: 62).

Therefore, discourse markers cannot simply be attested a temporary nature. They continue to exist beyond transitional periods through shifts in form or function.

Fludernik's paper (this volume) is devoted to the development of narrative discourse markers (in particular *þo*) in Middle English. The old *þo*-pattern, in which *þo* operates as a discourse marker, undergoes radical changes in Middle English. It becomes functionally ambiguous and has to compete with other discourse markers until it disappears in the late 14th and 15th century, when the *when-then* construction wins out over *þo* and other discourse markers. Her analysis traces both the shifts in form (from *þo/þa* to *then, than, thenne, thanne* and eventually to *then*) and the functional changes (from discourse marker to adverbial and finally to conjunction). Her starting point in this very complex series of functional and formal changes is the linguistic item *þo*, and in this sense her analysis is an example of a diachronic form-to-function mapping.

Onodera (this volume) works within the same general framework as Schwenter and Traugott. She starts out with the question of whether the discourse functions that have been postulated for various linguistic items are a recent phenomenon in the evolution of language – and in particular in the evolution of Japanese – or whether their earlier existence just has not been discovered yet. She analyses two Japanese discourse markers, *demo* and *dakedo*. The former was first used as a marker in the 16th century and the latter in the early 20th century.

Burger's (1980) article on German interjections (e.g. *ach, ey, ha*) in texts from the 17th century outlines a programme for tracing the frequency and functional diversity of interjections. In this context, he suggests to investigate the decrease in interjections and the increase in discourse particles (*Abtönungs-partikel*), and to ascertain whether this process can be regarded as a shift in written style or language change in both written and spoken communication.

From a more general perspective discourse markers, such as *apropos* or *kurz und gut*, can also be studied as linguistic items establishing the broader contours of conversational structure, e.g. as portrayed in Henne's (1980) study of dramas of the *Sturm und Drang* period.

Exclamations are another type of discourse marker which have already been under investigation from a historical perspective. The common assumption seems to be that exclamations were used much more widely and for a broader variety of functions in Late Middle English than in present-day English. Taavitsainen (1994b) outlines the use of exclamations in Late Middle English, e.g. *alas*, *ey*, *ah*, or *harrow*, and discusses their function with special reference to text types. Her analysis shows that exclamations act as markers of the fictional rather than the non-fictional mode. Their functions include personal affect, foregrounding, and the marking of turn-taking. In this volume, she continues her work with an analysis of interjections in Early Modern English.

She provides statistical evidence of the frequency of interjections in different Early Modern English text genres, and she analyses the functions that these interjections serve. In traditional accounts based on Present Day English, interjections have usually been relegated to the purely emotive level of language, as the speaker's reaction to the current situation. In her data, however, Taavitsainen found many interjections that were used to appeal to addressees, most commonly as vocatives.

Topic changers such as *well*, *now*, *by the way* or *anyhow* can also be studied from the perspective of diachronic form-to-function mapping. Their development from the mid-seventeenth century until the early 20th century suggests that they "are more common in informal discourse than in formal discourse" (Finell 1992: 731). In particular, topic changers express a communicator's attitude, his or her wish for interaction, and politeness. In her analysis of topic changers in informal letters, Finell (1992: 732) concludes that it seems that "in present day English there is, proportionally, a higher number of discourse markers that function as explicit topic changers than there was in Early Modern English". This may be taken to express a more urgent need for interaction and to be part of the process of a move towards the subjectification of language. In Modern English the functional specialisation and diversification of topic changers led to their conventionalisation. Topic changers thus underwent a shift from semantic explicitness to pragmatic explicitness. These results "attest Traugott's hypotheses concerning the direction of functional-semantic shifts (from propositional via textual to expressive); and the tendency towards the subjectification of language" (Finell 1992: 721).

4.2.2. *Diachronic function-to-form mapping*

This approach compares the realisation of specific speech functions (speech acts, politeness formulae, text types, forms of dialogue) at two or more specific points in the development of a language. Here the speech function is the *tertium comparationis*. Again it is possible, even likely, that not only the realisation of specific functions changed in the course of language history but that the functions themselves changed.

To take the example of speech act theory, one might hypothesise that speakers of different languages realise apologies, requests, or compliments differently, and then analyse the differences in these realisations. In this case the illocutionary force of the speech act would be the *tertium comparationis* (cf. the cross-cultural speech act realisation project, CCSARP, reported on in Blum-Kulka *et al.* 1989). However, declaring one's love is not the same for Sir Gawain and for a hip hop character in the 1990s. It is not only the linguistic (and non-linguistic) realisation that is different, but in a fundamental sense Sir Gawain and the hip hop character are not really doing the same thing (cf. Fritz this volume). Thus it is not clear that the illocutionary force is necessarily the best *tertium comparationis*, because different cultures, or one culture at two different points in history, may very well encode a different range of speaker intentions. Wierzbicka (1991) goes even further and advocates a kind of neo-Whorfianism, i.e. she believes that speech acts are so culture-specific that we cannot compare them across cultures.

For Stetter (1991: 74) speech act theory has no historical dimension, since it is impossible to grasp exactly what a speaker meant by his utterance. In his view, the historical description of linguistic phenomena cannot grasp the immediate situation-dependent subjective experiencing connected with speech acts unless the explicit performative becomes socially accepted (1991: 79).

To explain the use of speech acts in earlier periods, a thorough even though approximative analysis of all possible types of contextual factors, especially the conventions of language use in the period under investigation, is needed. Then it would not only be possible to elucidate what types of speech acts existed in former times and how they were expressed but also to identify the shifts in view of the socio-historical context. Thus, when performatives change their meaning, they express a different set of intentions and motives arising from changes in the socio-cultural environment (cf. Schlieben-Lange and Weydt 1979: 72).

In any case, the speech act is the pragmatic concept which has already gained most of the interest so far. In fact, speech act theory has often been proposed as the basis of any pragmatic description and as the main methodological tool in historical pragmatic analyses (cf. Weigand 1988: 160). Adding a historical dimension to speech act analysis means to focus on "the correlation of changes in the types of illocutions with changes in the society" (Stein 1985a: 350). For example, Cherubim (1980: 13) observes that in the wake of the secularisation, the German verb *fluchen* 'to swear' shifted from an explicit performative act to an expressive act.

Most contrastive analyses of speech acts, however, are non-historical and across different modern languages. Theoretical debates have focused on the universal vs. conventional nature of speech acts. These debates can also be given a historical dimension. In Schlieben-Lange and Weydt (1976), for example, the universalist view represented by Weydt puts forward the hypothesis that speech acts are possible in any language, while Schlieben-Lange supports the non-universalist view that there are only culturally differentiated speech acts. More precisely, Schlieben-Lange (1976: 114) suggests that speech acts are not universal, but historically determined, differentiated and conventionalised. Hence a universal act of 'promising', for example, does not exist; there are only historical forms of 'promising'. A corollary of this thesis is the proposition that speech acts can only exist if they can be verbally identified, though not necessarily by an explicit performative (cf. Schlieben-Lange and Weydt 1979: 67).

In general, as expounded above, problems in connection with explaining the semantic change of linguistic items can be tackled more promisingly by adding a pragmatic dimension. In the context of her analysis of speech act verbs and declarations of intention in the historiography of the French Middle Ages, Schlieben-Lange (1983: 148-161) suggests that shifts in the designations of the author's activities are indicators of changes in the author's self-experience and the function of historiography.

For the historical study of speech acts Schlieben-Lange (1976) proposes to begin with the search of conspicuous speech-act-like phenomena and continue with the delimitation of the analysis to a specific aspect, e.g. speech act (adjacency) pairs. Schlieben-Lange's investigation is based on, first, dictionaries to find out about the kind of performative and speech act denoting verbs; second, texts to examine how speech acts are executed and accepted; and, third, the history of institutions and the law to illuminate the conditions and forms of speech acts under different social contexts. Yet Schlieben-Lange's tendency to almost exclusively reconstruct the function of a (historical) text from the (historical) text itself has drawn criticism, e.g. from Presch (1981: 224). In fact, he postulates that more independent historical data on the text's functional context needs to be included. A problem in this context is that the functional context of the text itself also has to be explained. In addition, Cherubim (1980:

12f.) suggests that more detailed analyses of speech acts, speech act sequences and/or speech act fields can also be obtained through a broader analysis of language-related references, such as grammars or style books.

For a historical pragmatician it would be interesting to localise the genesis of a particular speech act (cf. Schlieben-Lange and Weydt 1979: 74). However, for lack of evidence this endeavour is difficult. In contrast, the explanation of why a speech act ceased to be used or has been replaced can take place against the background of shifting communication patterns or a changing value system (cf. Schlieben-Lange 1983: 141). The explanation of how a particular speech act developed entails the interpretation of present forms as the results of a process. The explanatory potential of a diachronic analysis is, of course, higher than that of a historical contrastive analysis. However, taking account of both the processual and the comparative perspective could prevent premature hypotheses on historical causes (cf. Presch 1981: 226f.).

Arnovick (1994) notes the differences in promises between the straightforward and direct formulations reported in Anglo-Saxon poetry and today's formulations which seem to require a fair amount of additional verbal work in order to convince the promisee of its sincerity. She explains the appearance of such pragmatically expanded promises in Present Day English on the basis of the semantic change of the modal auxiliaries *shall* and *will*.

Besides, a speech act analysis can also be carried out against the background of the pragmaphilological framework since

> the pragmatic basis for medieval texts and the particular conditions governing communication between author and audience connected with it are fundamentally different from those prevailing in modern times (Bergner 1992: 174).

In particular, the conditions governing communication are important factors for the fact that in the Middle Ages "the explicit, directly formulated illocutionary speech-act is often marked, and the performative verb is rather the rule than the exception" (Bergner 1992: 169). It may, however, be the case that this explicit speech act changes into an implicit speech act. The communicative status as an implicit speech act and thus the degree of conventionalisation can be regarded as conditioned by history. Again, in order to understand a speaker's intention expressed in the speech act, it is important to know as precisely as possible the historical circumstances of the utterance. For example, in former times communicators used implicit speech acts to avoid the use of explicit speech acts that were morally unacceptable or taboo (cf. Hartmann 1977: 50).

Within the general outline of how to comprehend old texts, Schwarz *et. al.* (1988) ask how it is possible to determine a text's function and, again, the intention of the speaker/writer. In fact, as exemplified in the context of reconstructing some speech acts in medieval *Vuchs Reinhart* (Schwarz *et. al.* 1988: 125-166), it is important to know what kind of action the text represents. Schwarz' (1984) pragmatic study of verbal courtship in medieval and modern Tristan poems is a more thorough historical speech act analysis presented as an example of 'speech act history'. The practical part investigates the speech act of declaring one's love by throwing light on questions about (1) the speaker's intention, (2) the situation, (3) the contents, (4) the manifestness, (5) the explicit performative and (6) the speech act's consequences.

Bax (1981, 1983 and 1991) investigates the speech event of verbal duelling as reported in medieval literary texts. Verbal duelling is a very widespread speech event. It has been described in many diverse societies, both historical and modern (for references see Bax 1991: 201-2 and list of references). Pragmatic analyses of the sequential structure of utterances in texts like the Old High German *Hildebrandslied* or the Old-Icelandic *Hárbardsljód* can change the interpretation of the verbal interaction.

Gloning (1993) deals with historical texts containing passages with instructions or reflections on language use. His study also shows that address formulae were used according to a subtly differentiated system of conditional factors such as social rank, membership of the clergy, or domicile (town or countryside). Deviations from the norm were interpreted as a lack of deference and often answered by ill-humour or laughter. Furthermore, turn-taking rules included the requirement not to interrupt women while they talk. On the other hand, men had the right to give instructions to women, while women were not allowed to resist. Further research into texts containing reflections on language use is faced with a scarcity of reliable evidence, and again, it is difficult to determine whether the written evidence really reflects oral communication. Therefore, references have to be studied with a very critical eye.

Historical differences in aggressive verbal behaviour such as swearing and insults can also be related to socio-cultural factors. In Lötscher's (1981) contrastive analysis of swearing and insults in the Swiss German of the 15th and 16th century, it emerges that today swearings and insults are less vulgar in terms of sexual and excretory language. In contrast, they are more differentiated and contain more allusions to physical and mental shortcomings. Religious and blasphemic features disappeared almost completely. As factors for this development especially the refinement of politeness rules and the process of secularisation have to be considered.

Cultural and anthropological aspects also have to be taken into account for the analysis of discourse strategies such as 'arguing' (cf. Geier *et al.* 1977). In fact, there is sufficient written evidence to show that the art of arguing has a long history stretching from so-called 'primitive' societies up to modern times via Ancient Greece and scholasticism in the Middle Ages.

A text's conversational structure as such can throw light on whether the text is orally or textually conceived. In her analysis of the *Nibelungenlied*, for example, Weigand (1988) concludes that the work contains both oral and written features but does not represent language as spoken in the 12th century. The work's formulaic nature of conversational structure reflects a principle of oral composition or literary orality.

Some authors take text types as their starting point. Görlach (1992), for instance, traces the history of the cookery recipe. He claims that "its content and function are well defined, so we can assume identity over the centuries – an identity that is much harder to prove in many other types of text" (Görlach 1992: 736). He can show that there is relatively little development in the actual realisation of cookery recipes over the centuries, and, at the same time, that this text type has not been standardised to the same extent as other text types have. The authors of cookery recipes still have a fair amount of freedom in the way they want to formulate a recipe. He is right, of course, to point out that the content and function of a particular text type may vary considerably over the centuries even if the name for the text type remains more or less the same.

Taavitsainen (1994a) traces the history of scientific writing from the late Middle English period to the Early Modern English period. Scientific writing is a fairly broad genre with many subgenres such as academic textbooks, lunaries, urinoscopies and remedy books. She concludes:

> Textual traditions, the audience parameter, and the macro-level of textual form are all important when assessing the evolution of early scientific texts. It is obvious that scientific texts of these periods may take various forms and deviate from one another greatly. Their evolution reflects the history of ideas, the scientific methods, and the linguistic and sociocultural conditions of the time (Taavitsainen 1994a: 341).

Fries (1986 and 1987) analyses German and English curricula vitae both contrastively and diachronically. He, too, delimits his text type on the basis of its content and its function because he concentrates on curricula vitae that appear in dissertations. He lists several structural elements of curricula vitae that are realised differently in modern German dissertations and in German dissertations written at the beginning of the 20th century, but he does not discuss potential differences in the function of this text type.

Text types, forms of dialogue, speech acts and politeness strategies all impose a functional perspective on historical pragmatics. The function is taken to be relatively stable, while the development of the actual linguistic realisation is at the centre of the researcher's interest.

Fritz (1993a) deals with aspects of a historical analysis of dialogue forms. Dialogues in present-day communication may take forms that are different from those in earlier periods. The standardisation of dialogue forms, such as in address formulae or greetings, arises from institutionalisation processes. Linguistically, the standardisation is most evident on the levels of syntax and lexis. Apart from that, dialogues may also differ as to the topics treated. Topics are different in their distribution among specific groups, in their relative importance or in their social acceptance (e.g. sexuality or death). While some principles of communication are universal, like Grice's Cooperative Principle or the Principle of Relevance, others, such as taciturnity or politeness, depend on the historical peculiarities of life-style or institutions.

In his contribution to this volume Fritz uses particular types of dialogue as the basic units of analysis. As a first example he considers a type of dialogue in legal procedures, viz. the elementary sequence of accusation and response to an accusation. The second example are declarations of ones love. These reflections lead Fritz to draw up an agenda of work to be tackled by historical pragmatists, or historians of forms of dialogue, as he would call them. "Special purposes of dialogues call for specialised dialogue forms." (18).

Virtanen focuses her attention on discourse strategies in Early Modern English travelogues. In particular she looks at temporal and locative discourse strategies on the one hand, and on participant/topic-oriented discourse strategies on the other. These strategies may appear globally or locally, and it turns out that they are associated with specific text types.

The problems faced by contrastive analyses of politeness phenomena are no less serious. It is not only the linguistic realisation of politeness that may differ between two speech communities (separated in space or time) but also what the two speech communities consider to be polite behaviour. Can we compare the realisation of politeness in English and in Japanese or are they so fundamentally different in their essence that a comparison is not possible?

Aspects of the history of politeness in language are dealt with in Watts *et al.* (1992: Part 1). Brown and Gilman (1989) applied Brown and Levinson's politeness theory to some of Shakespeare's tragedies. In particular, they checked the theory against the dimensions *Distance*, *Power*, and *Extremity*. They found that the dimension of *Distance* is strongly contradictory to the theory. In contrast to what the theory predicts, affect strongly influences politeness. The other two dimensions, *Power* and *Extremity*, however, were congruent with the theory, i.e. the person with less power is more polite, and the more extreme face threat is expressed more politely.

The use of particular greeting formulae and greeting rules can also be closely linked to contextual aspects. Lebsanft (1988) shows how in the Old French period specific events, states of mind, location, sex, age, religion or status of the addressee had a considerable effect on the linguistic structure of greetings.

Kopytko (1993a and this volume) analyses four tragedies and four comedies by Shakespeare, and he reaches the tentative conclusion that the interactional style of British society has developed from a predominantly positive politeness culture in which the expression of solidarity was paramount to a predominantly negative politeness culture with its stress on non-impositions.

Shakespeare's works were also analysed with respect to the use of titles and address formulae (cf. Breuer 1983). Social rank and power, age, and sex were found to be important factors in the selection of the appropriate formula. Titles may be categorised into five groups: social honorary titles, titles expressing respect due to a difference in power (e.g. *master, lady*), habitual titles (e.g. *neighbour, husband, child*) including titles used in embarrassment (e.g. *friend, gentle maiden*), professional and official titles (e.g. *captain*), as well as family titles (e.g. *father, sister*). The use of first names was still rare in Shakespeare's time. Finkenstaedt (1963) exemplifies the use of address formulae in relation to the historical and social context by the English pronouns *you* and *thou*. His analysis reveals that in Old English the existence of only one pronoun, *thou*, can be explained by the lack of class differences. The plural use of *you* in Middle English was introduced because there was a need to distinguish two social ranks. Thus *you* indicated a higher and *thou* a lower social rank.

Nevalainen and Raumolin-Brunberg (this volume) present a very comprehensive analysis of forms of address in letter salutations in Early Modern English. They trace these salutations from Late Middle English over a period of about two hundred and fifty years (1420-1680). They are thus able to present not only an historical but a truly diachronic analysis of address formulae. Their analysis pays close attention to the socio-historical context in which these letters were written both in general terms (i.e. concerning the social order, literacy and postal services in England at the time) and in more specific terms concentrating on the social distance between the letter writer and his or her addressee and their relative power over each other (i.e. Brown and Levinson's 1987: 76 parameters D and P).

5.   Conclusion

Historical pragmatics is not a new term, and even less does it describe an entirely new field of scientific enquiry. However, it is a term that so far has only been used sporadically. The research efforts that are potentially relevant for this field are scattered over various branches of pragmatics and historical linguistics. The use of the term historical pragmatics does not only delimit a field of scientific enquiry; it should also bring together researchers who share an interest in both language history and pragmatics. It should help to put a wide range of research efforts into a clearer focus. We have tried to give a rough and ready overview of the most important literature in this field.

It is no coincidence that the time seems to be ready now for a more rigorous application of the term historical pragmatics. Pragmatics has learnt to look for communicative behaviour beyond the limits of the spoken word, and historical linguistics has learnt to ask questions that go beyond the immediate sentence and text boundaries of historical texts. In this way both fields can make important contributions to the other field. The time has come for inter-disciplinary research efforts.

References

Apostel, Leo
    1980   "Pragmatique et linguistique diachronique." In: *Recherches de linguistique. Hommages à Maurice Leroy.* Bruxelles: Éditions de l'Université de Bruxelles, 8-19.
Arnovick, Leslie Katherine
    1994   "The expanding discourse of promises in Present-Day English: A case study in historical pragmatics." *Folia Linguistica Historica* 15.1-2, 175-191.
Bax, Marcel M. H.
    1981   "Rules for ritual challenges: a speech convention among medieval knights." *Journal of Pragmatics* 5, 423-444.
    1983   "Die lebendige Dimension toter Sprachen. Zur pragmatischen Analyse von Sprachgebrauch in historischen Kontexten." *Zeitschrift für germanistische Linguistik* 11, 1-21.
    1991   "Historische Pragmatik: Eine Herausforderung für die Zukunft. Diachrone Untersuchungen zu pragmatischen Aspekten ritueller Herausforderungen in mittelalterlicher Literatur." In: Dietrich Busse (ed.). *Diachrone Semantik und Pragmatik. Untersuchungen zur Erklärung und Beschreibung des*

Sprachwandels. (Reihe Germanistische Linguistik 113). Tübingen: Niemeyer, 197-215.

Beetz, Manfred

1990   *Frühmoderne Höflichkeit. Komplimentierkunst und Gesellschaftsrituale im altdeutschen Sprachraum.* Stuttgart: Metzler.

Bergner, Heinz

1992   "The pragmatics of medieval texts." In: Dieter Stein (ed.). *Cooperating with Written Texts. The Pragmatics and Comprehension of Written Texts.* Berlin: Mouton de Gruyter, 163-177.

Betten, Anne

1990   Zur Problematik der Abgrenzung von Schriftlichkeit und Mündlichkeit bei mittelalterlichen Texten. In: Betten, Anne (ed.). *Neuere Forschung zur historischen Syntax des Deutschen: Referate der internationalen Fachkonferenz Eichstätt 1989.* (Reihe Germanistische Linguistik 103). Tübingen: Niemeyer, 324-335.

Biber, Douglas, and Edward Finegan

1992   "The linguistic evolution of five written and speech-based English genres from the 17th to the 20th centuries." In: Matti Rissanen, Ossi Ihalainen, Terttu Nevalainen, and Irma Taavitsainen (eds.). *History of Englishes. New Methods and Interpretations in Historical Linguistics.* Berlin: Mouton de Gruyter, 688-704.

Blum-Kulka, Shoshana, Juliane House and Gabriele Kasper (eds.)

1989   *Cross-Cultural Pragmatics: Requests and Apologies.* Norwood, NJ: Ablex.

Breuer, Horst

1983   "Titel und Anreden bei Shakespeare und in der Shakespeare-Zeit." *Anglia* 101.1/2: 49-77.

Brinton, Laurel

1990   "The development of discourse markers in English." In: Jacek Fisiak (ed.). *Historical Linguistics and Philology.* (Trends in Linguistics, Studies and Monographs 46). Berlin: Mouton de Gruyter, 45-71.

Brönnimann-Egger, Werner

1991   *The Friendly Reader. Modes of Cooperation between Eighteenth-Century English Poets and Their Audiences.* Tübingen: Stauffenburg.

Brown, Penelope, and Stephen C. Levinson

1987   *Politeness. Some Universals in Language Usage.* Cambridge: Cambridge University Press.

Brown, Roger, and Albert Gilman

1989   "Politeness theory and Shakespeare's four major tragedies." *Language in Society* 18.2, 159-212.

Burger, Harald
    1980   "Interjektionen." In: Horst Sitta (ed.). *Ansätze zu einer pragmatischen Sprachgeschichte. Zürcher Kolloquium 1978.* (Reihe Germanistische Linguistik 21). Tübingen: Niemeyer, 53-69.

Burke, Peter
    1993   *The Art of Conversation.* Cambridge: Polity Press.

Busse, Dietrich (ed.)
    1991   *Diachrone Semantik und Pragmatik. Untersuchungen zur Erklärung und Beschreibung des Sprachwandels.* (Reihe Germanistische Linguistik 113). Tübingen: Niemeyer.

Cherubim, Dieter
    1980   "Zum Programm einer historischen Sprachpragmatik." In: Horst Sitta (ed.). *Ansätze zu einer pragmatischen Sprachgeschichte. Zürcher Kolloquium 1978.* (Reihe Germanistische Linguistik 21). Tübingen: Niemeyer, 3-21.
    1984   "Sprachgeschichte im Zeichen der linguistischen Pragmatik." In: Werner Besch, Oskar Reichmann und Stefan Sonderegger (eds.). *Sprachgeschichte.* Vol. 1. Berlin: Mouton de Gruyter, 802-815.

Danet, Brenda, and Bryna Bogoch
    1992a   "From oral ceremony to written document: The transitional language of Anglo-Saxon wills." *Language & Communication* 12.2, 95-122.
    1992b   "'Whoever alters this, may God turn his face from him on the day of judgment' Curses in Anglo-Saxon legal documents." *Journal of American Folklore* 105, 132-165.

Eder, Alois
    1973   "Pragmatik in der historischen Semantik: Zur Peiorisierung von 'gemein'." *Wiener Linguistische Gazette* 4, 37-62.

Fillmore, Charles J.
    1984   "Remarks on contrastive pragmatics." In: Jacek Fisiak (ed.). *Contrastive Linguistics. Prospects and Problems.* Berlin: Mouton, 119-141.

Finell, Anne
    1992   "The repertoire of topic changers in personal, intimate letters: a diachronic study of Osborne and Woolf." In: Matti Rissanen, Ossi Ihalainen, Terttu Nevalainen, and Irma Taavitsainen (eds.). *History of Englishes. New Methods and Interpretations in Historical Linguistics.* Berlin: Mouton de Gruyter, 720-735.

Finkenstaedt, Thomas
    1963   *You and thou. Studien zur Anrede im Englischen.* Berlin: Mouton.

Fries, Udo
    1986   "A textlinguistic analysis of German and English curricula vitae." In: Dieter Kastovsky and Aleksander Szwedek (eds.). *Linguistics across Historical*

and Geographical Boundaries. In Honour of Jacek Fisiak on the Occasion of His Fiftieth Birthday. Vol. 2. Descriptive, Contrastive and Applied Linguistics. (Trends in Linguistics, Studies and Monographs 32), Berlin: Mouton de Gruyter, 1203-1217.

1987   "Bemerkungen zur Textsorte Lebenslauf." In: Otto Rauchbauer (ed.). *A Yearbook of Studies in English.* Language and Literature 1985/86. Festschrift für Siegfried Korninger. (Wiener Beiträge zur Englischen Philologie 80). Wien: Braumüller, 39-50.

1993   "Towards a description of text deixis in Old English." In: Klaus R. Grinda and Claus-Dieter Wetzel (ed.). *Anglo-Saxonica. Festschrift für Hans Schabram zum 65. Geburtstag.* München: Fink, 527-540.

Fritz, Gerd

1993a   "Geschichte der Dialogformen." In: Gerd Fritz und Franz Hundsnurscher (eds.). *Handbuch der Dialoganalyse: Handbook of Discourse Analysis.* Tübingen: Niemeyer, 545-562.

1993b   "Kommunikative Aufgaben und grammatische Mittel. Beobachtungen zur Sprache der ersten deutschen Zeitungen im 17. Jahrhundert." *Sprache und Literatur in Wissenschaft und Unterricht* 71, 34-52.

Geier, Manfred, Gisbert Keseling, Marianne Nehrkorn and Ulrich Schmitz

1977   "Zum Beispiel: Argumentieren. Ein Beitrag zum Verhältnis von synchroner, ontogenetischer und historischer Rekonstruktion." In: Klaus Baumgärtner (ed.). *Sprachliches Handeln.* (Medium Literatur 7). Heidelberg: Quelle und Meyer, 69-108.

Gloning, Thomas

1993   "Sprachreflexive Textstellen als Quelle für die Geschichte von Kommunikationsformen." In: Heinrich Löffler (ed.). *Dialoganalyse IV. Referate der 4. Arbeitstagung, Basel 1992. Teil 1.* (Beiträge zur Dialogforschung 4). Tübingen: Niemeyer, 207-217.

Görlach, Manfred

1992   "Text-types and language history: the cookery recipe." In: Matti Rissanen, Ossi Ihalainen, Terttu Nevalainen, and Irma Taavitsainen (eds.). *History of Englishes. New Methods and Interpretations in Historical Linguistics.* Berlin: Mouton de Gruyter, 736-761.

Gumbrecht, Hans Ulrich

1977   "Historische Textpragmatik als Grundlagenwissenschaft der Geschichtsschreibung." *Lendemains* 6, 125-136.

Hartmann, Claudia

1977   "Implizite Äußerungen im Rahmen einer historisch-pragmatischen Analyse." *Linguistische Berichte* 48, 47-56.

Henne, Helmut
    1980   "Probleme einer historischen Gesprächsanalyse. Zur Rekonstruktion
            gesprochener Sprache im 18. Jahrhundert." In: Horst Sitta (ed.). *Ansätze zu
            einer pragmatischen Sprachgeschichte. Zürcher Kolloquium 1978.* (Reihe
            Germanistische Linguistik 21). Tübingen: Niemeyer, 89-102.
Janicki, Karol
    1990   "On the tenability of the notion 'pragmatic equivalence' in contrastive
            analysis." In: Jacek Fisiak (ed.). *Further Insights into Contrastive Analysis.*
            Amsterdam: John Benjamins, 47-54.
Jucker, Andreas H.
    1994   "The feasibility of historical pragmatics." *Journal of Pragmatics* 22, 533-
            536.
Kalisz, Roman
    1986   "More on pragmatic equivalence." In: Dieter Kastovsky and Aleksander
            Szwedek (eds.). *Linguistics across Historical and Geographical
            Boundaries.* In Honour of Jacek Fisiak on the Occasion of His Fiftieth
            Birthday. Vol. 2. Descriptive, Contrastive and Applied Linguistics. (Trends
            in Linguistics, Studies and Monographs, 32). Berlin: Mouton de Gruyter,
            1203-1217.
Kopytko, Roman
    1993a   *Polite Discourse in Shakespeare's English.* Poznan: Wydawnictwo
            Naukowe UAM.
    1993b   "Linguistic pragmatics and the concept of 'face'." *VIEWS (Vienna English
            Working Papers)* 2.2, 91-103.
Krzeszowski, Tomasz P.
    1984   "Tertium comparationis." In: Jacek Fisiak (ed.). *Contrastive Linguistics:
            Prospects and Problems.* (Trends in Linguistics, Studies and Monographs
            22). Berlin: Mouton, 301-312.
Lebsanft, Franz
    1988   *Studien zu einer Linguistik des Grusses. Sprache und Funktion der
            altfranzösischen Grußformeln.* (Beihefte zur Zeitschrift für romanische
            Philologie 217). Tübingen: Niemeyer.
Leech, Geoffrey N.
    1983   *Principles of Pragmatics.* London: Longman.
Lötscher, Andreas
    1981   "Zur Sprachgeschichte des Fluchens und Beschimpfens im Schweizer-
            deutschen." *Zeitschrift für Dialektologie und Linguistik* 48, 145-160.
Oleksy, Wieslaw (ed.)
    1988   *Contrastive Pragmatics.* Amsterdam: John Benjamins.

Panagl, Oswald
1977 "Pragmatische Perspektiven in der historischen Sprachwissenschaft." In: Gaberell Drachman (ed.). *Akten der 2. Salzburger Frühlingstagung für Linguistik.* Tübingen: Gunter Narr, 399-412.

Presch, Gunter
1981 "Zur Begründung einer historischen Pragmalinguistik." In: Josef Klein und Gunter Presch (eds.). *Institutionen – Konflikte – Sprache. Arbeiten zur linguistischen Pragmatik.* Tübingen: Niemeyer, 206-238.

Rissanen, Matti
1986 "Variation and the study of English historical syntax." In: David Sankoff (ed.). *Diversity and Diachrony.* Amsterdam: John Benjamins, 97-109.

Schlieben-Lange, Brigitte
1975 *Linguistische Pragmatik.* Stuttgart: Kohlhammer.
1976 "Für eine historische Analyse von Sprechakten." In: Heinrich Weber and Harald Weydt (eds.). *Sprachtheorie und Pragmatik. Akten des 10. Linguistischen Kolloquiums Tübingen 1975.* Vol. 1. Tübingen: Niemeyer, 113-119.
1983 *Tradition des Sprechens. Elemente einer pragmatischen Sprachgeschichtsschreibung.* Stuttgart: Kohlhammer.

Schlieben-Lange, Brigitte und Harald Weydt
1979 "Streitgespräch zur Historizität von Sprechakten." *Linguistische Berichte* 60, 65-78.

Schwarz, Alexander
1984 *Sprechaktgeschichte: Studien zu den Liebeserklärungen in mittelalterlichen und modernen Tristandichtungen.* Göppingen: Kümmerle.

Schwarz, Alexander, Angelika Linke, Paul Michel und Gerhild Scholz William
1988 *Alte Texte lesen.* Bern: Paul Haupt.

Sell, Roger D.
1985a "Tellability and politeness in *The Miller's Tale*: First steps in literary pragmatics." *English Studies. A Journal of English Language and Literature* 66.6, 496-512.
1985b "Politeness in Chaucer: Suggestions towards a methodology for pragmatic stylistics." *Studia Neophilologica* 57, 175-185.
1991 "Literary genre and history: Questions from a literary pragmaticist for socio-semioticians." In: Eija Ventola (ed.). *Approaches to the Analysis of Literary Discourse.* Åbo: Åbo Akademis Förlag, 1-38.
1992 "Postdisciplinary philology: culturally relativistic pragmatics." In: Francisco Fernandez, Miguel Fuster, and Juan Jose Calvo (eds.). *Papers from the 7th International Conference on English Historical Linguistics,* 29-36. Amsterdam: Benjamins.

Sell, Roger D. (ed.)
  1991   *Literary Pragmatics*. London: Routledge.
Sitta, Horst (ed.)
  1980   *Ansätze zu einer pragmatischen Sprachgeschichte*. Zürcher Kolloquium
            1978. (Reihe Germanistische Linguistik 21). Tübingen: Niemeyer.
Sitta, Horst
  1980   "Pragmatisches   Sprachverstehen   und   pragmatikorientierte
            Sprachgeschichte. Methodologische Probleme der Rekonstruktion von
            historischen Verständigungsakten." In: Horst Sitta (ed.). *Ansätze zu einer
            pragmatischen Sprachgeschichte. Zürcher Kolloquium 1978*. (Reihe
            Germanistische Linguistik 21). Tübingen: Niemeyer, 23-33.
Stein, Dieter
  1985a   "Perspectives on Historical Pragmatics." *Folia Linguistica Historica* 6.2,
            347-355.
  1985b   "Discourse markers in Early Modern English." In: Roger Eaton, Olga
            Fischer, Willem Koopman, and Frederike van der Leek (eds.). *Papers from
            the Fourth International Conference on English Historical Linguistics*.
            Amsterdam: John Benjamins, 283-302.
Stetter, Christian
  1991   "Text und Struktur. Hat die Sprechakttheorie eine historische Dimension?"
            In: Dietrich Busse (ed.). *Diachrone Semantik und Pragmatik.
            Untersuchungen zur Erklärung und Beschreibung des Sprachwandels*.
            (Reihe Germanistische Linguistik 113). Tübingen: Niemeyer, 67-81.
Taavitsainen, Irma
  1994a   "On the evolution of scientific writings from 1374 to 1675: Repertoire of
            emotive features." In: Francis Fernández, Miguel Fuster and Juan José
            Calvo (eds.). *English Historical Linguistics 1992*. Amsterdam: John
            Benjamins, 329-442.
  1994b   "Interjections in the late Middle English period." Paper read at the
            International Conference on Middle English Language. Rydzyna, 13-16
            April 1994.
Traugott, Elizabeth Closs
  1982   "From propositional to textual and expressive meanings: Some semantic-
            pragmatic aspects of grammaticalization." In: Winfred P. Lehmann and
            Ykov Malkiel (eds.). *Perspectives on Historical Linguistics*. Amsterdam:
            John Benjamins, 245-271.
  1985   On regularity in semantic change. *Journal of Literary Semantics* 14.3, 155-
            173.
  1989   "On the rise of epistemic meanings in English: An example of
            subjectification in semantic change." *Language* 65.1, 31-55.

in press   "Subjectification in Grammaticalization." In: Dieter Stein and Susan Wright (eds.). *Subjectivity and Subjectivization*. Cambridge: Cambridge University Press.

Verschueren, Jef
1987   "The pragmatic perspective." In: Marcella Bertuccelli-Papi and Jef Verschueren (eds.). *The Pragmatic Perspective: Selected Papers from the 1985 International Pragmatics Conference*. (Pragmatics & Beyond Companion Series 5). Amsterdam: John Benjamins, 3-8.

Watts, Richard J.
1981   *The Pragmalinguistic Analysis of Narrative Texts. Narrative Co-operation in Charles Dickens'* Hard Times. (Studies & Texts in English 3). Tübingen: Gunter Narr.

Watts, Richard J., Sachiko Ide and Konrad Ehlich (eds.)
1992   *Politeness in Language. Studies in its History, Theory and Practice*. Berlin: Mouton de Gruyter.

Weigand, Edda
1988   "Historische Sprachpragmatik am Beispiel: Gesprächsstrukturen im Nibelungenlied." *Zeitschrift für deutsches Altertum und deutsche Literatur* 117, 159-173.

Wierzbicka, Anna
1991   *Cross-Cultural Pragmatics. The Semantics of Human Interaction*. Berlin: Mouton de Gruyter.

Part I: Pragmaphilology

The Openness of Medieval Texts

Heinz Bergner
Justus-Liebig-University Giessen

1. Introduction

Oral or written texts, which are unclear in various degrees, which allow for different interpretations and which lack comprehensibility, should, in general, be referred to as "open". On the grounds of this definition it becomes obvious that the openness of texts can basically concern any kind of linguistic utterance and that it is not confined to a particular era or age.

This is, first of all, due to the possibilities and basic characteristics of human communication. Human communication can be disturbed in various ways with regard to its process, both in horizontal and in vertical direction. The constituents relevant for this communication process can be involved in it, i.e. the text itself, its author(s), its recipient(s) and the communicative path(s) leading to both of them. All of them can be affected by disturbances, irregularities and discrepancies; the persons involved may lack the necessary understanding and background knowledge. This is also true, among other things, for scientific discourse, in which transparency and clarity should actually prevail (Selzer 1993; Schüttler 1994). However, this turns out to be a misconception if the people involved in this discourse do not possess the specialized knowledge required (Gibbons 1994; Munsberg 1994: 46-49). Of course, a lack of clarity can result on different levels: on the phonological, on the morphosemantic as well as on the syntactic level.

Likewise, it is generally true that the openness of texts can be intended and planned in many ways. It occurs spontaneously whenever encoding, intended secrecy, disguise, mystification, pretended quasi-openness (Scott 1990: 126-31) are the objectives of an utterance. The same result occurs when linguistic material and its conventions are dealt with in a consciously playful and associative way. This can also apply to informative utterances, e.g. in advertising (Fritz 1994: 64-81). Openness can occur in any text, as long as it lacks acceptability and coherence or as long as the propositions which constitute the text are not intentionally controlled by linguistic illocutions and thus turn out to be ambiguous. It is known that free oral speech is generally characterized by a considerable degree of uncertainty, i.e. openness, which explains well-known features such as variability, corrections, change of construction, repetition, and redundancy (Ong 1982: 31-77; Barton 1994: 83-94). The phenomenon presents itself particularly in oral dialogue, which usually appears to be unplanned and is thus frequently hypothetical and full of modal verbs (Langford 1994: 19-30; Schwitalla 1994, Biere 1994). Studies of everyday dialogues have confirmed this phenomenon impressively (Stempel 1984). Ultimately, all of this is also connected with the important question as to how and to which degree the normal linguistic utterance is characterized by vagueness and openness. So far, this problem has hardly been studied. It seems, however, that vagueness, which can be traced both in written and in oral discourse, is often a natural form of utterance, not to be attributed to a deficient speaker competence and is thus an element of linguistic pragmatics (Channell 1994).

As far as openness of linguistic utterance is concerned, a literary or poetic text is a domain of its own (Pallotti 1990; Sell 1991). Its nature consists precisely in resisting the orderliness usually typical of texts, in revealing content structure and in planning often only sporadically, in diminishing the intensity of elements such as coherence and cohesion, i.e. factors characterizing the continuity of a discourse. Instead, it often employs means such as multiple perspective, aporia and ambiguity, complex metaphors and symbols, and its descriptions and accounts often refer to non-existent referents and situations. This implies a more or less high degree of uncertainty. The process indicated can reach relatively far, as there is indeed an art school extending from Antiquity to Baroque which chose *obscuritas* as its stylistic and structural ideal. In general, such an open way of conceptualization actually provokes the free imagination of the recipient, who is thus confronted with several possibilities of interpretation and has to rely on the subjectivity of his reading because the text denies an unequivocal explanation. Within the field of literary criticism this phenomenon has, for a long time, been studied by hermeneutics. Iser (1987 and 1991), as one of its many representatives, should be mentioned in this context. There is still a large potential for linguistic studies in this area, which is revealed particularly by Blake (1990).

2.   The Medieval context

Apart from the openness that is intrinsic to every era, the kind of linguistic openness dealt with here is a specific and restricted vagueness typically only found in medieval texts. First, a well-known truth needs to be pointed out: medieval discourse, which will be mainly discussed here on the basis of Old English and Middle English texts, is only accessible through the written medium; the oral dimension can at best be revealed by questionable reconstructions and will never be completely accessible. Reflecting, in addition to this, on the openness of medieval utterances, we have in mind a certain openness that presented itself to the speaker/writer or listener/reader of that time as an entirely natural accompanying phenomenon of his linguistic environment. To the present-day beholder this appears rather odd. In any case, it is recommendable to distinguish the medieval perspective from the present-day one. In general, it can be stated that the Middle Ages had no concept of itself, neither of its temporal nor of its notional dimension. This is shown by the extremely discrepant notions of world and history of this era. Thus, it is also generally true that the Middle Ages do not know unequivocal categories (Borst 1979; Duby 1984; Gerhards 1986; Boockmann 1988), which is documented not only by medieval institutions and philosophic principles but also by artistic and linguistic utterances of this period. This can be briefly explained with the help of two examples. In the English Middle Ages, there is, for instance, no political order that could claim the quality of a general political system in connection with universally accepted theoretical foundations. The same fact is supported by another example. It is known that the church service is, among other things, the centre of medieval religious experience. The essential text of the mass liturgy, however, is reflected in a variety of fairly different versions, which resulted in completely different mass liturgies being used often in the very same place.

Another condition for the basic openness of medieval linguistic utterances requires explicit mentioning. The medieval way of thinking and talking is used to perceiving each detail of existence not in an isolated way, but always in its relation to spiritual values, this, however, often in free decision and with a choice of certain second, third and other meanings. In this way, it is true that the individual linguistic sign refers to a known every-day referent, but usually also to another referential dimension which is not predetermined and only vaguely related to spiritual conventions. This referential dimension is shown in allegorical, tropological and anagogical interpretations (Lubac 1959-64). In this context the etymologicalizing procedure of medieval thinking and talking can be subsumed. In a free etymological decision of analysis – etymological not from a modern viewpoint, but only in the sense of general theological concepts – this procedure consists in creating a relationship between the *signifiant* of a linguistic sign and a similarly sounding word that spiritually elevates the former (Schwarz *et al.* 1988: 207-260; Harms 1993). In the Middle Ages there is no binding system regulating this procedure for all persons involved, at best there are different theological hints and practices. Consequently, however, this results in a strange amorphousness of the individual linguistic sign, both with regard to its phonetic structure as well as to its content.

3.   Schooling and literacy

As will be illustrated in greater detail later, almost all elements of form and content that constitute the individual medieval text have a certain indefiniteness or openness that do not appear in this fashion in modern times (Milroy 1992). This is clearly linked to the lack of linguistic standards in the Middle Ages, which can fundamentally only be mediated if the vast number of those involved in the communication process have access to schooling and a reading culture. Generally, it must be pointed out that the great majority of medieval laymen did not have any opportunity to educate themselves in reading and writing. Their productive share in literary culture is therefore infinitesimally small. Even today it is not easy to estimate the number of those in the Middle Ages who were able to read or write. However, the number probably may not have exceeded more than 1% of the population. The medieval *illiteratus*, found among the higher nobility as well as among country folk, can, then, in no way be compared with the illiterates of today (McKitterick 1990; Clanchy 1993). Wherever education was reserved for the few, and indeed only desired by a few, and where a book was still a precious rarity because of the conditions of its production, knowledge of a language could only be acquired by listening and by approximate imitation, thus immensely increasing the importance of memory (Carruthers 1990). Schooling was reserved for the younger generation of the monastic clergy and was only later offered to a certain extent to the urban middle class in the late Middle Ages. But as long as this was possible only by means of handwritten books or manuscripts, the learning process itself turned out to be a procedure subject to immense obstacles, as will be shown later.

Especially important in this connection is the fact that there are no clues to whether instruction in the vernacular was given in medieval schools, whatever type of schools they might have been. The first primers of standard English usage are known to us only from the early modern period (Hughes 1988: 92-124). Beyond that there are hardly any indications of any standardization of English in the Middle Ages. It seems that some type of linguistic norm had developed at some stage in the late West Saxon court of Winchester (Hofstetter 1987), which then, however, declined in the Middle English era since the Middle English of this period, due to political conditions, split once again into different non-standardized variants and sub-variants. In view of this, it is not surprising that the vernacular, acquired without recourse to written texts and teachers, possessed a great degree of openness and alternatives inconceivable today. Surprisingly, the same is moreover true of Latin, a type of *lingua franca* for those who could read and/or write. To be sure, there were popular primers, especially those of Donatus and Priscianus, but the Latin of the Middle Ages, depending on the nation, country or region, the situations and the time in which it was used, is just as multi-faceted, manifold and open to linguistic possibilities as the native or vernacular languages (Langosch 1988; Hunt 1991).

4.   Dialects

The situation described is further corroborated by the fact that both variants of medieval English, Old English and Middle English, occur in the form of dialects just as in other languages of that age. It is characteristic of the state of research that no one has succeeded in presenting reliable and detailed treatises on the dialectal features, even though an abundance of individual observations have been published especially in the past (Toon 1992: 409-451). On the one hand, this stems from the linguistic contours of these dialects, which were certainly never standardized anywhere at that time. But, in particular, today we see the reason for this in the fact that many manuscripts are copies, whereby the original and the copy probably often greatly differed from a dialectal perspective. The most complicated case is certainly that of an original text found in the region where two dialects border. The confusing situation can be demonstrated by the paradigm of *Beowulf*, handed down to us in a very typical mixed dialect like many other works of Old English poetry. The manuscript forming the basis (MS Cotton Vitellius A. XV) dates from the late 10th Century and was probably compiled in the region where late West Saxon was spoken. We can, however, conclude from what we know about Old English dialects that a number of linguistic forms found in *Beowulf* refer rather to an earlier place of origin of the text in Anglia or Mercia (Jack 1994: 1-7). Linguistic inconsistency and general openness can thus be found.

   The situation in regard to Middle English presents itself in a similar way with its considerably larger wealth of manuscripts. The *Linguistic Atlas* (McIntosh *et al.* 1986) certainly represents a very helpful instrument for the study of dialects of individual Middle English texts and their regional classification – at least for the period between 1350 and 1450. But even then it is evident that a localization of individual texts is extremely difficult. The reason for this is not only that dialectal features overlap in these manuscripts due to the special processes of their production, but also because simple, clear linguistic structures are lacking. "Variation in written Middle English is so extensive that it is reasonable to ask in what sense we are dealing with a single state or stage of language" (Milroy 1992: 157).

5.   Syntactic and morphological disparity

It is symptomatic of the state of affairs that present-day descriptions of Old English and Middle English stress disparity and inconsistency in contrast to earlier idealizing portrayals, which emphasized linguistic uniformity and unity (Hogg 1992; Blake 1992). This is certainly not because linguistic evidence of both periods belongs to a linguistic transitional epoch in which language norms and categories are normally weakened and in part fail, thus raising questions for both the reader of that day as well as the present. Lass (1994: 244) quite correctly points out that late Old English manuscripts are virtually chaotic in appearance on all grammatical levels. Referring to the linguistic appearance of Wulfstan's *Sermo Lupi ad Anglos* (ca. 1013), Whitelock talks, for example about "confusion" (1977: 21). This is quite certainly not to be explained by a lack of writing traditions. For Old English is by far the best known and documented idiom among all the old Germanic languages, which means that the situation described here more likely indicates a fundamental situation.

The same findings are also true of the Middle English handed down to us in a wealth of manuscripts. Middle English begins to take on a somewhat homogeneous shape from the second half of the 15th Century. Apart from that, however, as Fisiak maintains (1992), it should rather be pointed out that no linguistic reality as such exists for Middle English. There is, of course, no uniform linguistic frame for Middle English; it does not even exist for the individual work or manuscript, neither in the early or late periods of Middle English. This is also a matter of the particular political situation of an age which at first did not even accept Middle English as the official vernacular. In addition, a number of fundamental linguistic changes influenced Middle English that were then integrated in different ways. Finally, it is quite difficult to establish the range, extent and date of any linguistic change in Middle English. It is often only reflected in a limited way in manuscripts and then leads to controversial interpretations especially in regard to the question to what extent such language changes are to be judged as individual in nature or as part of a greater development. All of this makes it extremely difficult to establish universal, unambiguous linguistic rules and structures for Middle English, which would in turn facilitate a clear decoding of Middle English texts.

If one browses through the English literature of the Middle Ages with regard to this aspect, each of these observations will be confirmed. Both Old English poetic and prose texts are characterized by the instability of verbal and nominal endings, which sometimes applies even to the very same text. Texts of Northumbrian provenance are particularly affected by this phenomenon. Old English nouns can alter both declination class and gender relatively easily, which results in a certain syncretism in favour of frequently used paradigms. Accordingly, this also applies to Old English verbs~ (Hogg 1992: 122-167). Inflections in Old English can vary depending on the context and thus those cases that are combined with prepositions are also not unequivocal in Old English (Mitchell 1995: 15-54). This morphological ambiguity implying the openness of texts can be observed to an even greater extent in Middle English. In Middle English grammatical morphemes are still discernible in written texts, yet they are often linguistically without function. Frequently they are not obligatory, but in many cases only optional and, besides, not clearly marked (Lass 1992).

Certainly the degree of openness was lower in the oral discourse of the Middle Ages as it could be reduced more or less strongly by extralinguistic indicators. However, in our case, without being able to have recourse to native speakers, we have to rely solely on the written basis. Unfortunately, the syntactic relations resulting from Old English and Middle English texts do not contribute to clarification either. Relations between sentences were not clearly marked in those times. It is true that word order in Old English is not free, yet neither for prose nor for poetry can generally valid rules be formulated (Mitchell 1995: 61). Likewise, it is impossible to register syntactic regularities in a consistent and uncontradicted way, which could have been considered as part of a superordinate system (Fischer 1992: 207-209).

6. Semantic opacity

The most important dimension in this respect undoubtedly concerns the semantics of words. The situation in this case is, as a whole, even more opaque due to the constraints of the given linguistic conditions. Thus, it is indicative that so far there has been no reliable dictionary for the Old English age. The extensive *DOE* (1986 pp.) has just been initiated and, therefore, for the time being we still depend on the quite unspecific *MCOE* (1980), i.e. we have to rely on our own investigations. The semantic openness which is revealed here, first of all, concerns the present-day reader and linguist, as one can easily imagine the difficulties in finding the exact meaning of Old English words if one considers that the semantic investigation of words basically works only with the help of context analysis and that comparative etymological observations or cross-connections to words which possibly exist in modern English can often give only approximate, if not dangerous support.

Moreover, there have been no comprehensive surveys of Old English vocabulary so far. In contrast to this, a number of studies have been presented on individual words or lexical fields, which are, however, based on doubtful methodological grounds (Kastovsky 1992: 400-408). It is even very difficult to determine the exact content of frequently occurring expressions such as *wyrd*, *dōm* or *lof* (Mitchell 1995: 246). This is certainly also due to the fact that these and similar basic concepts in Old English are subject to different ideological connotations (heathen or Christian or a mixture of both). Another difficulty arises from the fact that the use and the content of Old English words in prose texts on the one hand and in poetic texts on the other hand often seem to differ fundamentally, as can be shown by a word like *lēod* in *Beowulf* (Jack 1994: 48). In addition to this, there are quite a number of words of which evidence can only be found in Old English poetry (Jack 1994: 18). The special character of Old English poetry, whose formal character is, among other things, expressed by the so-called "variation", needs to be regarded in this context. This device consists in paraphrasing the nature of an object, person or the like in ever new ways, in conveying a total impression which is generally difficult to determine, as it is full of allusions and associations, sometimes repetitive, sometimes synonymically or semantically progressive, yet hardly ever referring to contents which can be exactly described. A well-known example is Caedmon's hymn of creation, which lists the name of God in nine lines in a total of seven different ways, but which are semantically difficult to determine: *heofonrīces Weard* (1), *Meotodes meahte* (2), *Wuldorfæder* (3), *ēce Drihten* (4, 8), *hālig Scyppend* (6), *moncynnes Weard* (7), *Frēa ælmihtig* (9) (Mitchell 1995: 264). This procedure is reinforced and thus becomes semantically more open by the fact that the unknown poets consistently contrive an abundance of new compounds, which are not always transparent. In this context, a special problem arises primarily in Old English poetry by the quite frequently occurring "hapax legomena". These are words which are recorded only once and, of course, are thus very difficult to interpret. The reasons for the occurrence of such words can never be completely established, yet they may have been caused by faulty or deficient tradition or often by a conscious procedure aiming at the use of archaic and opaque sounding words. Such expressions occur, for example, again and again in *Beowulf*. What is the meaning of *ealuscerwen* (769), *lemede* (905), *unhlitme* (1129), *woroldrǣdenne* (1142), *hēafodsegn* (2152), *æppelfealuwe* (2165) (Jack 1994)? Considering this general linguistic situation, it is not astonishing that even famous works of Old English poetry are still awaiting their comprehensive edition. This is true, for instance, for *Beowulf*, which was last authoritatively edited by Klaeber (1950).

If one keeps in mind that the users of Middle English were never aware of their linguistic identity, that English at that time was virtually a language without a past, that even the great literary heritage was never fostered with just a few exceptions in the Late Middle Ages (e.g. the works of Chaucer), then one can understand why the Middle English word also lacked firm contours (Blake 1977: 80-100). At the same time typical problems for Middle English vocabulary~ ensue as a consequence of the particular political circumstances. It is known that the official language culture in England was dominated by Latin and French, languages that slowly infiltrated the indigenous idiom. What follows from written sources proves that a very different degree of integration and knowledge of the new vocabulary prevailed with Middle English speakers or writers. Native words possessed contents very difficult to determine, especially when they were in a synonymous relationship to French and/or Latin loan-words. In addition, the question arises in individual cases as to how far these loan-words were congruent in meaning to the original meaning of the borrowed words. This holds all the more considering that only a fraction of the Middle English population had a basic command of Latin and French, and in view of the fact that numerous loan-words, moreover, sounded similar in both Latin and French, confusion was always possible here. Usually, the only reliable lexicon of Middle English, the rather far-advanced *MED* (1952ff.), can scarcely help in overcoming these difficulties. We can illustrate this situation with many examples. What does Chaucer mean, for example, in his famous *General Prologue* of the *Canterbury Tales*, when he talks of *licour* (l. 3) in connection with the beneficial qualities of spring rain? The circumstances in other texts are far more complicated, for instance the texts of the *alliterative revival*. Whoever looks closely at the elaborate and in part very sophisticated vocabulary, for example of *Sir Gawain and the Green Knight*, will confirm this observation (Davis 1967: 138-143). It is highly questionable whether the small elitist circle, for whom this poetry was written, was aware of all the different meanings of the words used. Finally, it is very difficult to identify clearly particular semantic connotations of Middle English~ words, especially when they are borrowings.

As a compensation and corrective for the semantic indefiniteness of Middle English words~ and their comparative lack of precision in regard to their use, Blake observes (1977: 97-100) a tendency toward repetition in Middle English (also Old English texts), which is not to be overlooked even if this phenomenon has still other causes.

From the middle of the 14th Century on, the so-called *aureate diction* begins to make headway in Middle English texts. It includes large parts of the literature of the time and involves the use of polysyllabic, rare and artificial words of Latin and French origin, and is to be detected among almost all the writers and poets of the era. This style intensifies the foreignness and indefiniteness of many texts and words, which must have confronted the reader/listener of that time with the same problems of understanding as the present-day reader. A stanza from Lydgate's *Balade in Commendation of Our Lady* may illustrate this (Norton-Smith 1966: 25-29, l. 57-63):

> Of alle Cristen protectrix and tutele,
> Retour of exilid, put in proscrypcyoun,
> To hem that erryn, the path of her sequele,
> To wery wandrid, the tente, pavil[i]oun,
> [The feynte to fresshe, and the pawsacioun,]
> Vnto deiecte rest and remedye,
> Feythfull unto all that in the affye.

The quite incomprehensible mode of expression here is a convention of the time found everywhere. A corresponding development can even be traced in Middle English prose, especially in technical prose texts on law, administration, theology and medicine that are interspersed with many Latinisms. For Middle English, then, the same state of research now arises as for Old English: with the exception of scattered studies focusing on individual words, there is a lack till now of an overall account of Middle English vocabulary. This is not surprising in view of the great extent of semantic openness and indefiniteness of Middle English words~ .

7.   Text structure

Macro- and micro structures of medieval texts are, furthermore, fundamentally open if one considers that these texts are available primarily in the form of hand-written manuscripts. There are, indeed, also writing and script traditions of that time (Bischoff 1986), but it is exactly one characteristic of medieval manuscripts that the scribes allow themselves a fair deal of freedom. How extensive this liberty is can be measured wherever a text is available in several manuscripts, at that time the only possibility of duplication. As can be expected, popular works have been handed down in numerous manuscripts. Chaucer's *Canterbury Tales* (ca. 1387-1400) are preserved in 83 manuscripts (and six early printed copies), Langland's *Piers Plowman* (1362-93) in 51 manuscripts, and the moral-theological tractatus *Prick of Conscience* (ca. 1350) in as many as 117 manuscripts (Brown and Robbins 1943; Robbins and Cutler 1965). The situation in the rest of Europe is no different. Just two examples: Wolfram's *Parzival* (ca. 1200) exists in 90 manuscripts and the extremely popular Old French prose novel *Tristan* (ca. 1230) in 80 manuscripts. At the same time one can easily observe that the individual versions differ from each other sometimes more, sometimes less, thus confronting modern editors with the most difficult alternatives.

It is also clear that in this situation one can hardly speak of an original text. Medieval texts were never authorised versions, were copied and changed according to need, and in the process were often adapted to the personal or prevailing taste of the time. When being copied, they were abridged or expanded with diverse changes, variations, improvements and impairments as the result. Here, of course, the intellectual ability of the scribe played a great role. For this reason the final version of a medieval work is not conceivable from either a medieval or modern perspective. The *Variorum Edition* of the individual works of Chaucer shows, for example, how open the single text is in this respect (Ruggiers and Ransom 1979ff.). In the end, in view of the numerous text variations in existence, the editor of a medieval text is dependent on subjective decisions if he wants to choose, in his opinion, a plausible version. The problem has caused diverse reactions among scholars in this field (Morse *et al.* 1992; Scragg and Szarmach 1994).

But the openness of medieval texts or manuscripts goes even further. It also affects those texts, of course, which, like Old English poetry, are only available in one manuscript version. For the medieval manuscript hardly shows signs of structuring and is devoid of ordered orthography, paragraphs and punctuation. Often, just as in the Old English period, it does not clearly emerge from the arrangement of lines whether we are dealing with prose or poetry. Naturally, parts of medieval manuscripts can be distorted to the point of incomprehensibility owing to the poor education of the scribe. Finally, modern editors are also confronted with a phenomenon, which is not to be blamed on the Middle Ages, but on the material conditions of handing down manuscripts. These are often to be made responsible for the gaps and partial destruction of manuscripts, which then in the reconstruction of the text must necessarily give cause for much speculation. *Beowulf*, 1. 3150-55, is an exemplary case (Westphalen 1967).

8. Medieval intertextuality

In addition to all of this, specific elements of communication occur, which strengthen the impression of the openness of medieval texts even more (Hahn and Ragotzky 1992). It is fundamentally true of these texts that they are very strongly dominated from outside in their subject matter as well as thematically and aesthetically. A very restricted creativity is typical of the medieval author. His originality is a limited category in every respect, moving within a narrow sphere. It is steered by the knowledge of other texts. In order to ascertain the semantic potential of a medieval text fully, it is therefore necessary to have a knowledge of the text or texts that served the text at hand as a guideline and model. In every medieval text one pretext or even several of these are hidden, and in order to be able to assess the semantic achievement of the former correctly, the modern interpreter must trace, as it were, the text within the text and uncover the intertextual references (Morse 1991: 231-248). Here, the present-day reader and researcher enters a field full of incalculable risks, because in general one has to be satisfied here with conjecture, which still applies even if the author names or intimates his source or sources in the text, as for instance in *Sir Gawain and the Green Knight* (Davis 1967: 1.1-36). This uncertainty is true almost without reserve for the most common type of text of the Middle English period, the "romance" (Severs 1967). But also in respect to such a renowned work as *Beowulf*, researchers puzzle over the background texts (Newton 1995).

The text-communication process is, moreover, further laden with indefiniteness because the medieval author and consequently his pragmatic contexts, intentions and prerequisites are normally a dimension with many unknown elements. Most medieval works cite no author whatsoever; many names are associated with uncertainties and lack of clarity (e.g. Cynewulf, Caedmon, Wulfstan, Layamon, William Langland, Robert Henryson, Thomas Malory). There is a certain amount of information concerning just a few (for instance Ælfric, John Gower, Geoffrey Chaucer, John Lydgate, William Dunbar). The same also applies to the class of recipients, who are mostly unknown to us and about whom we must rely on assumptions and reconstructions. The medieval text as a potential for meaning promoting understanding or insight between author and recipient must then, however, remain to a great extent open. And therefore, the important questions of author motivations that lie behind the texts and of the receptive expectations and reactions associated with them can only be answered with great difficulty, even for well-known authors such as Chaucer.

In addition, a further fact must be considered, referred to briefly at the beginning. The medieval texts we read today, especially the literary texts, were not received in this way in the Middle Ages (Tristram 1992). The reader devoted to his/her private, personal inspirations is a phenomenon only of modern times. From what we know about medieval texts, poetic texts especially, they were not read, probably also not read aloud. They were recited to a listening public and were performed in certain cases, be it in free rendition and realisation, be it in a form that more or less came close to the text or one of its versions depending on the situation. The vocal quality of this communication process, whose details completely elude the modern reader and thus leave many possibilities of interpretation, might be one reason for the different degrees of stereotyped nature, for the oral-formulaic character, which mark the medieval text in many ways (Zumthor 1987; Richter 1994).

9. Conclusion

To summarise briefly, the openness of medieval texts is of a quite specific quality. It results from the social and cultural political framework of these texts, from the lack of standards in the linguistic area, which can be clearly seen in respect to morphology, syntax and semantics. It is produced by the formlessness of the manuscripts and by the indefiniteness of the textual communication process, which in the end is based on orality and vocality.

References

Barton, David
    1994   *Literacy. An Introduction to the Ecology of Written Language.* Oxford: Blackwell.

Biere, Bernd Ulrich
    1994   "Verstehen und Beschreiben von Dialogen." In: Gerd Fritz und Franz Hundsnurscher (eds.). *Handbuch der Dialoganalyse.* Tübingen: Max Niemeyer Verlag, 155-175.

Bischoff, Bernhard
    1986   *Paläographie des römischen Altertums und des abendländischen Mittelalters.* 2nd ed. Berlin: Erich Schmidt Verlag.

Blake, Norman
    1977   *The English Language in Medieval Literature*. London: Methuen.

Blake, N. F.
    1990   *An Introduction to the Language of Literature*. London: MacMillan.

Blake, Norman (ed.)
    1992   *The Cambridge History of the English Language. Vol. II: 1066-1476*. Cambridge: Cambridge University Press.

Boockmann, Hartmut
    1988   *Das Mittelalter*. München: Verlag C. H. Beck.

Borst, Arno
    1979   *Lebensformen im Mittelalter*. Wien: Ullstein.

Brown, Carleton, and Rossell Hope Robbins
    1943   *The Index of Middle English Verse*. New York: Columbia University Press.

Carruthers, Mary
    1990   *The Book of Memory. A Study of Memory in Medieval Culture*. Cambridge: Cambridge University Press.

Channell, Joanna
    1994   *Vague Language*. Oxford: Oxford University Press.

Clanchy, Michael T.
    1993   *From Memory to Written Record. England 1066-1307*. 2nd ed. London: Arnold.

Corner, John, and Jeremy Hawthorn (eds.)
    1993   *Communication Studies. An Introductory Reader*. 4th ed. London: Edward Arnold.

Davis, Norman (ed.)
    1967   *Sir Gawain and the Green Knight*. 2nd ed. Oxford: Clarendon Press.

DOE 1986ff. = Cameron, Angus *et al.*
    1986ff.   *Dictionary of Old English*. Toronto: Pontifical Institute of Mediaeval Studies.

Duby, Georges
    1984   *L'Europe au Moyen Age*. Paris: MA Editions.

Fischer, Olga
    1992   "Syntax." In: Blake, 207-408.

Fisiak, Jacek
    1992   "Linguistic Reality of Middle English." In: Francisco Fernandez, Miguel Fuster, and Juan José Calvo (eds.). *English Historical Linguistics*. Amsterdam: John Benjamins, 47-61.

Fritz, Gerd, and Franz Hundsnurscher (eds.)
    1994   *Handbuch der Dialoganalyse*. Tübingen: Max Niemeyer Verlag.

Fritz, Thomas
    1994   *Die Botschaft der Markenartikel. Vertextungsstrategien in der Werbung.* Tübingen: Stauffenberg Verlag.

Gerhards, Agnès
    1986   *La Société Médiévale.* Paris: MA Editions.

Gibbons, John (ed.)
    1994   *Language and the Law.* London: Longman.

Hahn, Gerhard, and Hedda Ragotzky (eds.)
    1992   *Grundlagen des Verstehens mittelalterlicher Literatur.* Stuttgart: Alfred Kröner Verlag.

Harms, Wolfgang
    1993   "Funktionen etymologischer Verfahrensweisen mittelalterlicher Tradition in der Literatur der frühen Neuzeit." In: Wolfgang Harms and Jean-Marie Valentin (eds.). *Mittelalterliche Denk- und Schreibmodelle in der deutschen Literatur der frühen Neuzeit.* Amsterdam: Radopi, 1-17.

Hofstetter, Walter
    1987   *Winchester und der spätaltenglische Sprachgebrauch.* München: Wilhelm Fink Verlag.

Hogg, Richard M. (ed.)
    1992   *The Cambridge History of the English Language. Vol. I: The Beginnings to 1066.* Cambridge: Cambridge University Press.

Hogg, Richard M.
    1992   "Phonology and Morphology." In: Hogg, 122-67.

Hughes, Geoffrey
    1988   *Words in Time. A Social History of the English Vocabulary.* London: Blackwell.

Hunt, Tony
    1991   *Teaching and Learning in Thirteenth-Century England.* 3 vols. Cambridge: D. S. Brewer.

Iser, Wolfgang
    1987   *The Act of Reading.* Baltimore: Johns Hopkins University Press.
    1991   *Das Fiktive und das Imaginäre.* Frankfurt: Suhrkamp.

Jack, George (ed.)
    1994   *Beowulf. A Student Edition.* Oxford: Clarendon Press.

Kastovsky, Dieter
    1992   "Semantics and Vocabulary." In: Hogg, 290-408.

Klaeber, F. (ed.)
    1950   *Beowulf and the Fight at Finnsburg.* 3rd ed. Boston: D. C. Heath and Company.

Langford, David
    1994   *Analysing Talk. Investigating Verbal Interaction in English*. London: MacMillan.

Langosch, Karl
    1988   *Lateinisches Mittelalter*. 5th ed. Darmstadt: Wissenschaftliche Buchgesellschaft.

Lass, Roger
    1992   "Phonology and Morphology." In: Blake 1992: 103-15.
    1994   *Old English. A Historical Linguistic Companion*. Cambridge: Cambridge University Press.

Lubac, Henri de
    1959-64   *Exégèse Médiévale. Les Quatre Sens d l'Écriture*. 4 vols. Paris: Aubier.

McIntosh, Angus, M. L. Samuels, and Michael Benskin
    1986   *A Linguistic Atlas of Late Mediaeval English*. 4 vols. Aberdeen: Aberdeen University Press.

McKitterick, Rosamund (ed.)
    1990   *The Uses of Literacy in Early Medieval Europe*. Cambridge: Cambridge University Press.

MCOE 1980 = Venezky, Richard L. and Antonette diPaolo Healey
    1980   *A Microfiche Concordance to Old English*. Toronto: Pontifical Institute of Mediæval Studies.

MED 1952ff. = Kurath, Hans and Sherman H. Kuhn (eds.)
    1952ff   *Middle English Dictionary*. Ann Arbor: University of Michigan Press.

Milroy, James, and Lesley Milroy
    1991   *Authority in Language. Investigating Language Prescription and Standardisation*. 2nd ed. London: Routledge and Kegan Paul.

Milroy, James
    1992   "Middle English Dialectology." In: Blake, 156-206.

Mitchell, Bruce
    1995   *An Invitation to Old English and Anglo-Saxon England*. Oxford: Blackwell.

Morse, Charlotte C., Penelope R. Doob, and Marjorie C. Woods (eds.)
    1992   *The Uses of Manuscripts in Literary Studies. Essays in Memory of Judson Boyce Allen*. Kolamazoo: Medieval Institute Publications.

Morse, Ruth
    1991   *Truth and Convention in the Middle Ages. Rhetoric, Representation, and Reality*. Cambridge: Cambridge University Press.

Munsberg, Klaus
    1994   *Mündliche Fachkommunikation. Das Beispiel Chemie*. Tübingen: Gunter Narr Verlag.

Newton, Sam
    1995   *The Origin of Beowulf and the Pre-Viking Kingdom of East Anglia.* Woodbridge: Boydell and Brewer.

Norton-Smith, John (ed.)
    1966   *John Lydgate. Poems.* Oxford: Clarendon Press.

Ong, Walter J.
    1982   *Orality and Literacy. The Technologizing of the Word.* London: Methuen.

Pallotti, Donatella
    1990   *Weaving Words. A Linguistic Reading of Poetry.* Bologna: Cooperativa Libraria Universitaria Editrice.

Richter, Michael
    1994   *The Oral Tradition in the Early Middle Ages.* Turnhout: Brepols.

Robbins, Rossell Hope, and John L. Cutler
    1965   *Supplement to the Index of Middle English Verse.* Lexington: University of Kentucky Press.

Ruggiers, Paul G., and Daniel J. Ransom (eds.)
    1979ff   *The Variorum Edition of the Works of Geoffrey Chaucer.* Norman: University of Oklahoma Press.

Schüttler, Susanne
    1994   *Zur Verständlichkeit von Texten mit chemischem Inhalt.* Frankfurt: Peter Lang.

Schwarz, Alexander, Angelika Linke, Paul Michel, and Gerhild Scholz
    1988   *Alte Texte lesen.* Bern: Paul Haupt.

Schwitalla, Johannes
    1994   "Gesprochene Sprache – dialogisch gesehen." In: Gerd Fritz und Franz Hundsnurscher (eds.). *Handbuch der Dialoganalyse.* Tübingen: Max Niemeyer Verlag, 17-36.

Scott, W. T.
    1990   *The Possibility of Communication.* Berlin: de Gruyter.

Scragg, D. G., and Paul E. Szarmach (eds.)
    1994   *The Editing of Old English.* Woodbridge: Boydell and Brewer.

Sell, Roger D. (ed.)
    1991   *Literary Pragmatics.* London: Routledge.

Selzer, Jack (ed.)
    1993   *Understanding Scientific Prose.* Madison: University of Wisconsin Press.

Severs, J. Burke (ed.)
    1967   *A Manual of the Writings in Middle English, 1050-1500.* Facs. 1: *Romances.* New Haven: Connecticut Academy of Arts and Sciences.

Stempel, Wolf-Dieter
    1984   "Bemerkungen zur Kommunikation im Alltagsgespräch." In: Karlheinz
            Stierle and Rainer Warning (eds.). *Das Gespräch*. München: Wilhelm Fink
            Verlag, 151-69.

Toon, Thomas E.
    1992   "Old English Dialects." In: Hogg, 409-51.

Tristram, Hildegard L. C. (ed.)
    1992   *Medialität und mittelalterliche insulare Literatur*. Tübingen: Gunter Narr
            Verlag.

Westphalen, Tilman
    1967   *Beowulf 3150-55. Textkritik und Editionsgeschichte*. München: Wilhelm
            Fink Verlag.

Whitelock, Dorothy (ed.)
    1977   *Sermo Lupi ad Anglos*. 2nd ed. Exeter: University of Exeter.

Zumthor, Paul
    1987   *La Lettre et la Voix de la "Littérature" Médiévale*. Paris: Editions du Seuil.

They Had Their Points
Punctuation and Interpretation in English Renaissance Literature

Gert Ronberg
University of Aberdeen

The advent and expansion of printing in the 15th century coincided with the spread of Humanist ideas, from which derived the essential principles and conventions of punctuation practice.

The Humanists reacted to a large extent against the medieval Scholastics, who promoted a form of rational thinking with precise formulation and expression of thought. The Humanists were of course not opposed to rational thinking and precise linguistic formulation; but they did emphasise the importance of the *persuasive* function of language: language, according to Humanist thinking, was not there solely to demonstrate; it was also there to persuade. This emphasis resulted in a rebirth of rhetoric, which is clearly reflected not only in literary texts but also in pragmatic ones.

In punctuation the Humanists therefore attempted to strike a balance between the logical relationships in syntactic structures and the rhetorical structure of a period. To some extent we still try to achieve that kind of balance, but the rhetorical element was much more to the fore in Renaissance texts. Our punctuation system is essentially logical and grammatical, as in the following piece of text:

(1)   Shakespeare's work falls into three main periods: an initial period dominated by comedy, both lighthearted and serious, and history plays; a middle period including the great tragedies, the Roman plays, and the so-called 'problem plays'; and a final period consisting of the late comedies, sometimes called the 'romances'.

In that passage essential qualifications are not separated by a comma: there is not one before *dominated, including* and *consisting*. But the phrase *both lighthearted and serious* and the clause *sometimes called the 'romances'* are preceded by commas since those qualifications are non-essential and non-defining. Note also how the semicolons separate the larger units from the smaller ones within these, and how the colon, as is typical of today's usage, has been employed to introduce a particularising explanation. As we shall see shortly, the Renaissance use of the colon was quite different. Renaissance pointing is essentially rhetorical and elocutionary,[1] as can be seen in the next passage (2) from Francis Bacon's *The Advancement of Learning*. For comparison it is followed by a modern version (3).

(2)   For as knowledges are now delivered, there is a kinde of Contract of Errour, betweene the Deliuerer, and the Receiuer: for he that deliuereth knowledge, desireth to deliur it in such fourme, as may be best beleeued; and not as may be best examined: and hee that receiueth knowledge, desireth rather present satisfaction, than expectant Enquirie, & so rather not to doubt, than not to err: glorie making the Author not to lay open his weaknesse, and sloth making the Disciple not to knowe his strength.

(3)   For as knowledges are now delivered, there is a kind of contract of error between the deliverer and the receiver. For he that delivereth knowledge desireth to deliver it in such form as may be best believed, and not as may be best examined; and he that receiveth knowledge desireth rather present satisfaction than expectant inquiry; and so rather not to doubt than not to err: glory making the author not to lay open his weakness, and sloth making the disciple not to know his strength. (Wright 1973: 170-171)

First of all note the generally heavy punctuation of (2). The many commas often emphasise contrastive units: *there is a kinde of Contract of Errour, betweene the Deliuerer, and the Receiuer.* Similarly in the rhetorical *parison* of *rather present satisfaction, than expectant Enquirie.* What is perhaps even more noteworthy is the use of the colon. Passage (3) has only one, signalling the particularising conclusion, whereas (2) has three, separating persuasively and elegantly the steps of the argument in a single sentence:

Step 1: Introduction of *Deliuerer* and *Receiuer.*
Step 2: Deliuerer.
Step 3: Receiuer.
Step 4: Conclusion: the kind of contract of error that exists between deliverer and receiver results in glory for the author (deliverer) since by delivering his knowledge in such a way as it may be best *believed*, not *examined*, he does not lay himself open to weakness (by the receiver objecting). The 'contract' also results in sloth for the receiver since he does not employ his strength, i.e. the force of argument he might

adduce against the deliverer if the argument or statement had been examined properly.

Bacon's semicolon stresses the antithetical *parison* of *best beleeued* and *best examined,* i.e. a contrast within the antithesis of *deliuereth* (line 2) and *receiueth* (line 4), marked by the second colon, a heavier rhetorical punctuation mark than the semicolon. There is no semicolon before & *so rather not to doubt* because we have already had the antithesis in *rather present satisfaction, than expectant Enquirie.* That is why the semicolon in that position in text (3) is too heavy, distorting Bacon's more subtly persuasive use of that punctuation mark. On the other hand, full stops would be too heavy for Bacon. They would not have the connective force that the colons retain, for although they separate, they also connect the steps in argument. The punctuation in the modern version ruins this rhetorically parallel balance by having three *different* marks for Bacon's three colons, viz. full stop, semicolon and colon.

Let us now move to an example from fictional literature in order to illustrate briefly how a return to Renaissance punctuation in editions of Renaissance texts can be beneficial to the reading of a passage. The following lines are from Book V, lines 86-92, of Milton's *Paradise Lost.* The first quotation (4) is from Beeching's edition of 1914, which follows faithfully that of 1667; the second (5) is from Douglas Bush's 1966 version. We have examples of Milton's own punctuation in his manuscript of Book I of *Paradise Lost,* and when this is compared with Book I of the 1667 edition, we note that the printers made hardly any changes to Milton's pointing practice. We are thus justified in assuming the same to be the case in the rest of the poem as it appears in the 1667 (and Beeching's) edition:

(4) Forthwith up to the Clouds
     With him I flew, and underneath beheld
     The Earth outstretcht immense, a prospect wide
     And various: wondring at my flight and change
     To this high exaltation; suddenly
     My Guide was gon, and I, me thought, sunk down,
     and fell asleep;

(5) Forthwith up to the clouds
     With him I flew, and underneath beheld
     The earth outstretched immense, a prospect wide
     And various. Wond'ring at my flight and change
     To this high exaltation, suddenly
     My guide was gone, and I, methought, sunk down,

> And fell asleep;

Being relatively heavy, the colon before *wondring* in (4) foregrounds by subtle *rallentando* Eve's suspended amazement. This delightful effect would be impossible if modern practice were followed, and it is certainly absent from Bush's version. His full stop has too much separating force, particularly since he elects to place only a comma before *suddenly,* thereby creating an unattached participial clause preceding it: it can hardly be the guide (Satan) who is wonderstruck at being airborne.

Pausal reasons for punctuation are particularly significant in drama, where, during the Renaissance, they were closely connected with the effects of rhetoric in stage performance. The remaining examples are from Heminge and Condell's First Folio edition (1623) of Shakespeare whose own pointing practice is unknown, except perhaps for the punctuation in a section of *Thomas More*, the manuscript of which may be Shakespeare's. However, we do know what general Renaissance practice was, although we must be on our guard: some printers could be highly idiosyncratic or even incompetent. All the same, close examination of the First Folio and of the good quartos gives us a positive picture of elocutionary pointing, frequently serving as a guide to the actor in ways considerably different from today's. By the 18th century the punctuation we find in Elizabethan plays may be described as a lost art, clearly not appreciated or understood by Samuel Johnson when, referring to his editorial work on Shakespeare, he said: "In restoring the author's works to their integrity, I have considered the punctuation as wholly in my power; for what could be their care of colons and commas, who corrupted words and sentences" (Sherbo 1968).

From Dr Johnson onwards editors of Shakespeare have been generally contemptuous of Elizabethan punctuation. It is important to realise that much of it was geared towards highlighting rhetoric (which, it may be noted in passing, did not find much scholarly favour and attention after the 18th century until the 1970s) and suggesting to the actor how to speak his lines. Percy Simpson's pioneering book *Shakespearian Punctuation* (1911) shows quite unambiguously that what could not be done in Johnson's day and cannot be done in ours (if we keep adhering rigidly to the present logico-grammatical system), could be done in Shakespeare's, before the advent of Cartesian rationalist formalism, which changed considerably occidental views of language.

The First Folio having no line numbers, line references to quotations from it have been added for the reader's convenience and follow the complete-works edition by Peter Alexander (1951). We shall start with four typical examples of emphatic pointing

(6)   *Cel.* Was, is not is: (*As You Like It*, First Folio, III.iv.28)

(7)   *Rom.* Loue, is a smoake made with the fume of sighes,
      (*Romeo & Juliet*, First Folio, I.i.188)

(8)   *Macb.* Will all great *Neptunes* Ocean wash this blood Clean from my
      Hand? no: this my Hand will rather
      The multitudinous Seas incarnadine,
      Making the Greene one, Red.
      (*Macbeth*, First Folio, II.ii.60ff)

(9)   *Surrey.* Dishonourable Boy;
      That Lye, shall lie so heauy on my Sword,
      That it shall render Vengeance, and Reuenge,
      Till thou the Lye-giuer, and that Lye, doe lye
      In earth as quiet, as thy Fathers Scull.
      (*Richard II*, First Folio, IV.i.65ff)

(10) *Surrey.* Dishonourable boy!
      That lie shall lie so heavy on my sword
      That it shall render vengeance and revenge
      Till thou the lie-giver and that lie do lie
      In earth as quiet as thy father's skull.
      (Peter Alexander (ed.))

Commas in (6), (7) and (8) illustrate the mark being used to emphasise or stress
a preceding word. In (6) it shows that Celia's remark is metalinguistic: "'Was'
is not 'is'". Quotation marks did not become current until the 18th century. The
comma in (7) tells the actor playing Romeo to dwell on a word particularly
prominent in this scene; and the last line of (8) should tell editors that only one
interpretation is likely here, viz. the reading that takes *one* as a stressed modifier
of *Red* ('completely red') and not as a headword with *Greene* as a modifier,
seen as a possible interpretation by, for instance, Hunter in his Penguin edition,
1967. The heavy pointing of (9), which can usefully be compared with (10),
clearly draws rhetorical attention to the *ploce* and *antanaclasis* of *Lye/lie/lye*,
and to the *epanalepsis* of *Venge-/-uenge* in the third line. The next passage
shows light pointing:

(11) *Rob.* The King doth keepe his Reuels here to night,
      Take heed the Queene come not within his sight,
      For *Oberon is* passing fell and wrath,

Because that she, as her attendant, hath
A louely boy stolne from an Indian King,
She neuer had so sweet a changeling,
And iealous *Oberon* would haue the childe
Knight of his traine, to trace the Forrests wilde.
(*A Midsummer Night's Dream*, First Folio, II.i.18)

The light punctuation is particularly marked in the use of only commas at the end of the first and fifth lines. This and the rhymed verse are in perfect keeping with the otherworldly, fleet-footed spirit of Robin Goodfellow (=Puck), the passage following hard on his famous 'Over hill, over dale'.

The final extract is Portia's famous speech from *The Merchant of Venice*, first from the First Folio, then from Alexander's edition by way of comparison:

(12)

Por. The quality of mercy is not strain'd,
It droppeth as the gentle raine from heauen
Vpon the place beneath. It is twice blest,
It blesseth him that giues, and him that takes,
5 'Tis mightiest in the mightiest, it becomes
The throned Monarch better then his Crowne
His Scepter shewes the force of temporall power,
The attribute to awe and Maiestie,
Wherin doth sit the dread and feare of Kings:
10 But mercy is aboue this sceptred sway,
It is enthroned in the hearts of Kings,
It is an attribute to God himselfe;
And earthly power doth then shew likest Gods
When mercie seasons Iustice. Therefore Iew,
15 Though Iustice be thy plea, consider this,
That in the course of Iustice, none of vs
Should see salvation: we do pray for mercie,
And that same prayer, doth teach vs all to render
The deeds of mercie. I haue spoke thus much
20 To mitigate the iustice of thy plea:
Which if thou follow, this strict course [sic] of Venice
Must needes giue sentence 'gainst the Merchant there.

The quality of mercy is not strain'd;
It droppeth as the gentle rain from heaven
Upon the place beneath. It is twice blest:
It blesseth him that gives and him that takes.
'Tis mightiest in the mightiest; it becomes
The throned monarch better than his crown
His sceptre shows the force of temporal power,
The attribute to awe and majesty,
Wherein doth sit the dread and fear of kings;
But mercy is above this sceptred sway,
It is enthroned in the hearts of kings,
It is an attribute to God himself;
And earthly power doth then show likest God's
When mercy seasons justice. Therefore, Jew,
Though justice be thy plea, consider this -
That in the course of justice none of us
Should see salvation; we do pray for mercy,
And that same prayer doth teach us all to render
The deeds of mercy. I have spoke thus much
To mitigate the justice of thy plea,
Which if thou follow, this strict court of Venice
Must needs give sentence 'gainst the merchant there.

This famous speech has all the hallmarks of judicial rhetoric and can be divided into the classically rhetorical units of *exordium, narratio, refutatio* and *conclusio*. The Folio pointing highlights the considerable effect of this.

The first sentence covers the introduction (*exordium*) of the key concept of mercy with only the lightest of punctuation marks used. Then follows the *narratio,* which is in two parts, each with a climax: the first *narratio* section ends on the climactic *Crowne* (line 6) and moves there swiftly with light pointing to give the full stop its maximum crowning effect, which is lost completely in the modern version with its semicolon after *mightiest* slowing down the flow and without the culminating force of the stop after *crown.*

The second part of the *narratio* – stopping equally climactically with another key word, *Iustice,* in line 14 – has two subtle uses of the heavier marks. The first of these, the colon after *Kings* in 9, signals a rhetorical pause before the significantly contrastive *But* in the argument. Here Alexander makes do with a semicolon because of the much narrower, particularising use of our colon (as in 3, holding up the steady flow towards the first climax), which would therefore be confusing here in modern punctuation. The semicolon in 12 (the only one in the passage) eloquently emphasises *God himselfe.*

The *refutatio* follows until the next full stop in 19. Note how the comma in 16 rhetorically stresses both *Iustice* and *none of vs.* Even more prominent and expressive is the colon's highlighting of the word *salvation,* a very significant concept in the argument because of its relation to the key issues of the whole speech: justice *versus* mercy. Considering only justice does not lead to salvation, but considering mercy does. The comma after *prayer* (18) eloquently draws attention to the thematic *polyptoton* with *pray* in the preceding line; and the horror of Antonio's possible fate, expressed in the last two lines of the *conclusio,* is foregrounded by a final rhetorical colon. No such foregrounding is suggested by the modern version.

Although it may sometimes be dangerous to rely fully on Renaissance punctuation as an indication of the author's usage, there is enough evidence to suggest that without a close study of Renaissance pragmatic pointing practice we do ourselves a serious disservice. Especially during the latter part of the 16th century and a good part of the 17th, punctuation helps us to understand the Renaissance reception of text, giving us a clearer picture of how linguistic structures were used in tandem with rhetorical principles for persuasion, both in logical argument (*logos*) but also, and perhaps above all, within the other two fields of the famous Aristotelian rhetorical triad, viz. *ethos* and *pathos.* Perhaps now, with the considerable upsurge of interest in rhetoric, it is time for editors of Renaissance drama, at least, to present their texts in accordance with the original views of rhetorical syntax, suggested so powerfully by the original punctuation. In the words of Pollard: "The only rule for dealing with these supra-grammatical stops is to read the passage as punctuated, and then consider how it is affected by the pause at the point indicated. In the same way, if there is no stop where we expect one, or only a comma where we should expect a colon or even a full stop, we must try how the passage sounds with only light stops or none at all, and see what is the gain or loss to the dramatic impression" (Pollard 1917).

Notes

1.   See Renaissance accounts of the marks in, for instance, Mulcaster (1582), Puttenham (1589), Daines (1640), Simpson (1911), Pollard (1917), Banks (1927), Simpson (1928), Ong (1944), Treip (1970), McKenzie (1987), Salmon (1988). For a more general view, see also Parkes (1992).

References

Alexander, Peter (ed.)
    1951   *The Complete Works of Shakespeare*. London & Glasgow: Collins.
Bacon, Francis
              Of the Proficience and Aduancement of Learning, Second Booke, MS fol. 62.
Banks, Theodore H.
    1927   "Miltonic rhythm: A study of the relation of the full stops to the rhythm of *Paradise Lost*." *Publications of the Modern Language Association of America* 42, 140-5.
Beeching, Henry C. (ed.)
    1912   *The Poetical Works of John Milton*. London: Oxford University Press.
Bush, Douglas
    1966   *Milton: Poetical Works*. Oxford: Oxford University Press.
Daines, Simon
    1640   *Orthoepia Anglicana*. Meston facsimile (ed.). London, 1967, 69-75.
Hunter, George K. (ed.)
    1967   *Macbeth*. Middlesex: New Penguin Series, 153.
McKenzie, Donald F.
    1987   "Shakespearian punctuation: A new beginning." In: V. Salmon and E. Burness. *A Reader in the Language of Shakespearean Drama*. Amsterdam & Philadelphia.

Mulcaster, Richard
 1582 *Mulcaster's Elementarie.* Edited by E.T. Campagnac. Oxford: Tudor and Stuart Library, 1925, 166.

Ong, Walter J.
 1944 "Historical backgrounds of Elizabethan and Jacobean punctuation theory." *Publications of the Modern Language Association of America* 59, 349-60.

Parkes, M. B.
 1992 *Pause and Effect: An Introduction to the History of Punctuation in the West.* Aldershot.

Pollard, Alfred W.
 1917 *Shakespeare's Fight with the Pirates and the Problems of the Transmission of his Text.* London.

Puttenham, George
 1589 *The Art of English Poesie.* G. Willcock and A. Walker (eds.). Cambridge: Cambridge University Press, 1936, 74.

Salmon, Vivian
 1988 "English punctuation theory 1500-1800." *Anglia* 106, 285-314.

Sherbo, Arthur (ed.)
 1968 "Johnson on Shakespeare." *The Yale Edition of the Works of Samuel Johnson* 7, New Haven.

Simpson, Evelyn M.
 1928 "A note on Donne's punctuation." *Review of English Studies* 4, 295-300.

Simpson, Percy
 1911 *Shakespearian Punctuation.* Oxford.

Treip, Mindele A.
 1970 *Milton's Punctuation and Changing English Usage 1582-1676.* London.

Wright, William A. (ed.)
 1973 *The Advancement of Learning.* Oxford: Clarendon Press, 170-171.

Punctuation: And – 'Pragmatics'

John Lennard
Trinity Hall, Cambridge

PUNCTUATION is to written language as cartilage is to bone, bearing stress and allowing articulation. To make a text readable, to create a *mise-en-page*, is of necessity to impose lineation on the text, and then pagination, and so to demand from the reader the regular movements of eye and hand which punctuate the act of reading. Until the later seventh century scribes rarely went any further, and produced texts without word-separation, in the classical *scriptio continua*, where a stringoflettersrepresentingastringofsoundsappeared withneitherspacingnoranymarksofpunctuation. Faced with such a text the process of reading must begin with the necessary addition of spaces, marks, capitals, etc.; but confronted with a fully punctuated text, a host of clues are apparent, not only in the visual clarity of the words themselves, but also in cues to pauses, to stress! pitch, and tone-contours – and from these cues gesture will develop as well, the movements of body and hands which orchestrate the cadences of voice. Yet punctuation is little studied, its historical development and usage as much as its contemporary importance and variation systematically omitted from practical criticism, period scholarship, editorial attention and theoretical consideration. In English letters, at least, there are historical and ideological reasons for this omission, and in recent years it has become possible to see the lacuna, and to begin to chart it; and though there are very different ways of trying such (d/r)econstruction a concern with the pragmatic has been common to most of them. My brief here, especially given the European authorship and readership of this volume, is to advertise the approaches that seem most useful, and the new questions that seem most interesting; but I have found it worth beginning with a very brief schema of what little is known about the historical development of punctuation.[1]

Besides the line and the page (or scroll) the earliest unit of punctuation in the West is the paragraph, which dates from at least the second century BCE (cf. Müller 1964; Gordon 1957); but until the seventh century CE it was unaccompanied by any other division or mark. Before that, readers must (I assume) have divided the *scriptio continua* that they read into words, and organised the words into what Cicero called *membra* (*cola* and *commata* or their equivalents),[2] but scribal texts did not offer them any authoritative punctuation to follow: hence Augustine's warning[3] about the danger of committing heresy by misconstruing/mis-punctuating John 1:1, to produce "et Deus erat. Verbum ..." (and God was. The Word ...) rather than "et Deus erat Verbum." (and the Word was God.), and so to deny the divinity of the Word. Where (as in Rome and Alexandria) most readers were citizens, but many scribes were slaves or freedmen (Kleberg 1967: 22-68), it may even have been the case that for a scribe to punctuate a text that a citizen would read would have been regarded, in imposing a slave's authority on a citizen, as an infringement of civil liberty.

The two pressures which seem to underlie the development of scribal and authorial punctuation are the desire of the church to control sacred and exegetical texts (Parkes 1978), and the need to teach Latin as a second language. These pressures came together in Christian evangelism in Ireland: for whereas in Old Irish verbs are usually initial, in Latin they are usually terminal, and the difficulty which Irish-speaking novices might have had in learning to construe the Vulgate both grammatically and orthodoxly can readily be imagined. Word-separation begins to be found in Irish manuscripts in Latin in the late seventh century CE (Parkes 1991a), and once established in Latin the technique of glossing led to the extension of word-separation into the Celtic and Germanic vernaculars, and then into the Romance languages.[4]

Once written punctuation had begun, it developed fairly rapidly by applying the analysis *per cola et commata*, which was known through the works of Cicero and Quintilian. Marks were created and disseminated principally through the European network of monastic scriptoria, but the single greatest contribution came from the Carolingian scribes who devised, for use with Caroline minuscule, systematic and conventional indications of periodic boundaries (Parkes 1991b). Until at least the eleventh century, however, there are a great variety of and variation in written marks, and it is most helpful to regard these as sometimes overlapping repertoires of marks that are associated with a particular scriptorium or geographical area; but between the twelfth and fourteenth centuries there existed a general repertoire with a wide European distribution. In addition to the paragraph and the word as units indicated principally by spacing (though the paraph [¶] and paragraphus [§] could also be used), the marks of this general repertoire were the *punctus, punctus elevatus, punctus interrogativus*, and *virgula*, which approximately correspond in function (but not in shape) to the modern full-stop [.], colon [:], question-mark [?], and comma [,].

Three further marks were added by Italian humanists: the *punctus admirativus*, or exclamation-mark [!], claimed by Iacopo Alpoleio da Urbisaglia in the 1360s to be his invention (Novati 1909); round brackets, or more properly lunulae[5] [()], are first found as probably autograph corrections to a 1399 MS of Colluccio Salutati's *De Nobilitate Legum et Medecine* now in Paris;[6] and the semi-colon [;] was invented by Pietro Bembo, expressly as a half-way house between the comma and the colon, during the 1490s (Parkes 1992: 86). All three marks were disseminated in print: lunulae, for example, are first found in England in Richard Pynson's 1494 edition of the *Opus Grammaticum* of Sulpitius,[7] but are not found in script until a Wells Psalter of 1514 copied by Petrus Monoculus (Parkes 1969: xxix, n.1); and semi-colons remain relatively rare in England in both print and script until after their proliferation in the roman and italic fonts widely adopted as basic by English printers during the later 1570s and 1580s[8] (they seem particularly to have been popularised by their extensive use in sonnet sequences).

To speak now strictly of English (where the intensely analytical grammar and almost complete absence of inflection privilege both word-order and punctuation in the production of meaning) the early modern period begins with a rapidly expanding language increasingly subject to the discipline of a general repertoire of punctuation which the humanists had made both supple and subtle. The effect of print is patently to accelerate dissemination and to standardise. The evolution of English prose between the fourteenth and seventeenth centuries has received little attention since R. F. Jones (1951, esp. 75-160), but in a forthcoming study Ian Robinson (1996) argues that a conceptual change from the 'period', defined aurally and rhetorically, to the 'sentence', defined visually and syntactically, should be dated to the mid-to-late seventeenth century, and maps the difference between the prose styles of Sir Thomas Browne and John Dryden. Certainly the other marks of punctuation which we now deploy within and around sentences – dashes, hyphens, inverted commas, and apostrophes – are in their current uses largely creations of the modern period,[9] and those uses broadly accord with the conceptual change Robinson suggests, serving to increase visual specificity and to clarify the syntactical relations of words within the sentence. The invention of these marks, and the further development of earlier marks, make for a complex (if still very sketchy) picture: inverted commas, for example, originated (as did their French equivalent, the *guillemets* [«»]) as a mediæval *nota*, or marginal mark, called the 'diple', which could indicate lemmata (such as scriptural phrases quoted for exegesis) or *sententiæ* (received maxims or epigrams, often pious or classical), but inverted commas do not seem to reach their exact modern usage, in conjunction with *alinéa* (the convention of according each new speaker a new line), until 1857 (Parkes 1992: 93-94). I have attempted elsewhere to chart the history of lunulae in English printed verse from 1494 to the present, and took more than 300 pages to do so (Lennard 1991). In general it may be said, though, that modern punctuation is of more recent origin than many scholars and critics realise, and that throughout the early modern and modern periods it is more complex and variable than is usually allowed.

Two further points are worth making. The first is that the history I have been talking about is not a history that may be obtained by reading the grammarians, past or present. In their work one may find, both advertently and inadvertently, a history of theory; but this history of theory is in no way a simple description of the history of practice, and the theoretical prescription or proscription of a given epoch is likely to be in conflict with its historical practice. Ben Jonson's *English Grammar* of 1640, for example, which has quite a lot to say about punctuating, neither reflects nor adequately describes the practice of Jonson's own first folio of 1616; the practices of Swift and Pope are not accounted for by the rules of Bishop Lowth (1762), nor those of Coleridge and Byron by Cobbett's *Grammar of the English Language* (1824). In consequence it is unfortunately the case that while we may have, as professional or scholarly readers, impressions about the history of practice which we believe reliable, there is a lot of work to be done, a widespread re-examination of many texts of many kinds, before any of us can be sure about the history of practice; and the widespread post-war habit of modernising the punctuation of older texts, often with only the briefest general statement of the editor's reasons and methodology, does not help.

The second thing is that the history of theory offered by the grammarians has shown since about the sixth century CE two broad tendencies of argument: that all punctuation is 'elocutionary', a guide to rhetorical construction and phrasing, or, conversely, that all punctuation is 'syntactical', a guide to logical construction and interpretation.[10] I would take it as a basic and necessary assumption for the pragmatic investigation of punctuation that the mutually exclusive opposition of the elocutionary and syntactical functions of punctuation is misguided, and that most if not all punctuation can and does normally function in either mode, or in both: one principal determinant being whether the reader is reading silently or aloud. With this approach it is also clear that the search for grammatical or other rules of punctuation is also misguided, and has more to do with ideological and social linguistic prescription than with any linguistic 'laws'. Grammarians and theorists are not the lawgivers of punctuation, but only its lawyers, and there is one to be found on both sides of every question. There are no 'rules' of punctuation; rather, there are *conventions*: and throughout the early modern and modern periods, what is visible in the punctuation of English printed texts is not writerly obedience to or deviation from 'rules', but the observance and disregard, deliberately or otherwise, by authors, scribes, editors, and compositors, of very complex sets of conventions. The need for agreed typographic conventions is basic to the existence of a printed literature, and neither Sterne nor Joyce could have written as they did without drawing on a huge body of typographical conventions; but it is equally true that *Tristram Shandy* and *Ulysses* generate their meanings in part by bending, breaking, and flouting certain typographical conventions. The same thing is true of *Don Juan*, and *The Waste Land*, to choose only examples in which the 'unorthodox' punctuation is obvious: and what is true of these extreme cases is just as true, though less obvious, of all cases. In other words, the significance of any mark, space, or unit of punctuation is in the end relative, not determined by an absolute value which every ., , or , must have, but interpreted by the reader with greater or lesser regard for convention and for the contexts of writing and reading.

The question of most immediate concern to pragmatists is the relations of gesture and punctuation. The absence from spoken language of any voiced equivalents of marks or spaces of punctuation makes whatever punctuation of spoken language is necessary a matter of pragmatics: pauses and tone can function in obvious ways as equivalents of spaces and question- and exclamation-marks, but in common speech (as opposed to reading aloud, when the speaker-reader's movement may be inhibited) the greater rôle is that of gesture.

The most direct (and almost certainly the most recent) international gesture is the waggling in parallel of the index and/or middle fingers of both hands to indicate inverted commas: the gesture may be accompanied by the spoken words "quote unquote", in which case it signals direct quotation; or may be accompanied by a specific variation in stress and/or pitch, in which case it usually signals the partial suspension or qualification of the sense of a word or words. This distinction may be made in print between the functions of double and single inverted commas, but that printed distinction is recent, and (as I mentioned above) the set of conventions which govern the uses of inverted commas in contemporary English printing do not come together until 1857. The marginal use of the diple to indicate *sententiæ*, quotations, and speech survives until at least the early eighteenth century (Gildon 1701: 315), and the first editions of Jane Austen, for example, use sets of double inverted commas around paragraphs of indirect speech. It seems very unlikely, therefore, that the finger-waggle could have come to signify inverted commas much before 1857, but of the origins and dissemination of the gesture I know nothing, nor can I suggest with any conviction a date for its emergence more precise than 1850-1975.

I have not found in contemporary English or European use any other gesture which appears to correspond so precisely to a mark of punctuation, though there are at least two arguable possibilities. One is the clucking of the tongue several times after the last word of a phrase which has trailed away into silence or thought, where in print suspension marks [...] would be used; and the other jabbing gestures with hand or index finger, which when they indicate finality (rather than simple emphasis) resemble the dramatic placement, with the finger as pen, of the last full-stop. However, it is, I suspect, a mistake to look primarily for such exact correspondences, which it seems probable are only an interesting subset {gestures of punctuation modelled on pre-existing conventional printed marks} of the gestures which function as spoken punctuation. More interesting possibilities are raised, for example, by the complex stage gesture used by the cloaked villains of melodrama to indicate an aside, the upper body angled to the left (or right), and the left (or right) hand brought up to the right (or left) side of the mouth, with the voice lowered or hissing.[11] In Western dramatic manuscripts and printed dramatic texts (including Elizabethan and Jacobean quartos) asides may be indicated by, in any combination, italicisation, parenthesisation, setting to the right margin, dashes, and the stage direction "aside", and there would appear to be basic correspondences of, for example, the relative positionings of words and actor[12] on page and stage, of the actor's use of body angle and the printer's use of italics, and of {the actor's use of a hand held vertically as a barrier between the ears of other actors and the words of the aside} and {the printer's use of lunulae to isolate an aside from the other words on the page}. Mulcaster declared in 1582, in the *Elementarie*, that "Parenthesis ... in reading warneth us, that the words inclosed by them, ar to be pronounced with a lower & quikker voice, then the words before or after them",[13] and there are some contemporary examples from printed song-lyrics which suggest that this convention is still current:[14] so there may also be a correspondence of the actor's use of a hissing or lower tone and the printer's use of parenthesisation. This cat's-cradle of interactions between printed and oral-gestural ways of conveying information to a reader/auditor-spectator reveals a much denser and richer field of pragmatic historical semiotics than the specificity of the finger-waggle or tongue-clucking would suggest.

It is no surprise that this richness is most readily apparent in the context of drama, and specifically in the relations of staged and printed 'texts' – nor, conversely, that it is hardest to find (with the great exception of *Tristram Shandy*) in the novel, the most silent and still of printed genres. The obvious premium on successful communication which drama demands, the constant repertory production of texts preserved in printed (and so punctuated) editions, and the basic elocutionary interpretation of punctuation when reading aloud shared by all Western literates, together ensure that all theatrical production except that of wholly devised 'texts' must constantly exhibit, examine, and develop the relations of printed punctuation and gesture, as a single, if important, component of the pragmatics of the printed dramatic text. Moreover, this must have been as true for any Elizabethan company working from a printed text (or even from scribal part- and prompt-books, if they had been professionally prepared) as for a modern company presented with a new (typewritten or word-processed) script or staging a revival from printed copies; and it seems at least possible, therefore, that the punctuation of early printed plays – and especially those which, like Shakespeare's first Folio, are believed to preserve acting (rather than reading) texts – records evidence about the historical use of stage gestures, which may in turn help to construct histories of other non-dramatic and common gesture.

Consider, for example, this exchange between Terrill and Cælestine, from the 1602 quarto of Dekker's *Satiro-Mastix*:

> *Ter.* The king
>   Sat heauy on my resolu[t]ion
>   Till (out of breath) it panted out an oath.

> *Cæl.* An oath? why, what's an oath? tis but the smoake
>   Of flame and bloud; the blister of the spirit,
>   Which rizeth from the Steame of rage, the bubble
>   That shoots vp to the tongue, and scaldes the voice,
>   (For oathes are burning words) thou swor'st but one,
>   Tis frozen long agoe: (Dekker 1602: k1ʳ)

"out of breath" is a parenthetical clause, and its parenthesisation with lunulae is unproblematic; but "(For oathes are burning words)" requires more explanation. It is, in fact, also conventional, in that the emphatic indication of *sententiæ* by lunulae is widespread in English printed texts of 1575-1700, but the convention is no longer current, and the quarto punctuation is likely to be unfamiliar to a modern reader. What matters here is that such *sententiæ* functioned as the cruces of argument by authority: this one caps Cælestine's argument by developing his highly rhetorical and dynamic metaphor of heat ("smoake ... flame ... blister ... Steame ... scaldes") into a received and quasi-biblical phrase[15] which retrospectively validates the metaphor; the identity of the *sententia* is pointed by the lunulae, and the typographical unit {parenthesis = *sententia*} then becomes the compact target which Cælestine's last eight words – "thou swor'st but one / Tis frozen long agoe:" – hit and effectively deflate. To put it another way, the bathetic deflation which Cælestine uses to finish depends on the preceding rhetorical inflation, and that inflation culminates in the invocation of the *sententia* which the lunulae visually emphasise.

How, then, did a Jacobean actor respond to the punctuation of this quarto text?[16] The rhetorical and gestural style associated particularly with Edward Alleyn, though clearly challenged by Burbage, would still have been a strong part of many actors' training. Abraham Fraunce had argued that gesture "must followe the change and varietie of the voyce, answering thereunto in euerie respect";[17] and Heywood, in the *Apology for Actors*, defined "speaking well" as "with iudgement to obserue his comma's, colons and full poynts, his parenthesis, his breathing spaces, and distinctions" (Heywood 1612, quoted in Joseph 1952: 76). Fraunce was not a theatre practitioner, and his grand certainty may be only that of the deskbound theorist; but Heywood certainly was a practitioner, and if he seems understandably to show an authorial bias, it is nevertheless true that he had as a successful playwright worked closely with actors, and very much to the professional requirements of a company. His demand that actors observe punctuation carefully also makes good sense, especially with regard to the periodic (rather than logical) construction of Elizabethan and Jacobean prose and verse – a matter readily proved by reading aloud the same biblical passage in the King James and New English translations, or by experimenting with readings aloud of the poetry of Donne.[18] Clearly, however, while Mulcaster's idea that words in parenthesis should be pronounced in a "lower & quikker" voice might work on stage for "(out of breath)", it cannot possibly work for "(For oathes are burning words)". In an actor's delivery, as much as on the page, the orotund and sententious magniloquence which culminates in the *sententia* must be riding for the bathetic fall, and on stage such rhetorical inflation surely calls for volume and heavy stress, and so for slower (rather than "quikker") delivery. It also calls for gesture, to emphasise and express both the magniloquence and the deflation. A casual shrug, palms turned briefly and enquiringly upward, could well accompany "thou swor'st but one", and a flap of the hands "Tis frozen long agoe", and the actor must modulate into that (or an equivalently dismissive) gesture from the posture/gesture accompanying "(For oathes are burning words)", perhaps a more sweeping movement of the arms and a greater pouting inflation of the chest. It seems likely (after some experimentation, which readers are encouraged to try for themselves) that this more exaggerated gesture would include the extension of the actor's arms forwards and sideways, positioning the hands somewhat as the compositor of the quarto positioned the lunulae; and it is in practice immediately and startlingly clear that a gesture specifically mimicking with hand movement the curves of the lunulae is neither absurd nor pedantic, but fits rather well. The quarto text can therefore be taken as representing a moment written both for the eye of a reader and for the eye of a spectator, a moment as readily imaginable on the Jacobean stage as a modern actor waggling index fingers when speaking a word placed within inverted commas by a character of Pinter's or Stoppard's. A theatrically educated and literate member of the Jacobean audience could, in other words, have turned from the stage performance to the previously unconsulted quarto with a strong suspicion, intended by the actor, that the phrase "For oathes are burning words" was printed within lunulae, just as a modern spectator of a stage finger-waggle would not be surprised to find the spoken word(s) indicated by that gesture printed within inverted commas in the text sold in the foyer. Unless a Jacobean diary or journal detailing an actor's gesture turns up the gestural dimension of the moment in Dekker's quarto must remain a matter of imagination; but I believe that scholars alerted to the possibility of such moments, and willing to look for them in their readings of Elizabethan and Jacobean texts, may find a fair number – there are certainly several in Jonson's quartos and 1616 folio[19] – which would in itself tend to confirm the possibility as substantial. It is also a pragmatic imagination, rooted in the demonstrable possibilities of human anatomy and the known meaning of specific historical typographical conventions, modelled on a widespread contemporary gestural practice, and offering a rich entry to a historical field largely unmapped by scholarship.

The conventional typographical indications of *sententiæ* with lunulae (Lennard 1991: 28-36) has at least two implications: that, because *sententiæ* functioned (*inter alia*) as the cruces of arguments by authority, the lunulae (or any other mark conventionally used for this purpose) can become a typographical register of argument; and that the lunulae must in that case be read as visually emphasising their contents, and not as grammatically subordinating them. The Elizabethans had several typographical conventions for indicating *sententiæ* (including diples, indical hands, and italics, as well as lunulae) which often serve to make embedded *sententiæ* readily findable, simply by paging through a volume, probably for purposes of reference and extraction.[20] In consequence, no one typographical convention could be held to be co-extensive with the printed use of argument by authority; but it seems probable, nevertheless, that an accurate plotting of this conventional use of lunulae, in a large number and variety of texts, would provide a typographical sketch of the use of argument by authority. The decline in the use of lunulae in this convention (which in English books is to be dated $c.1640 - c.1700$) might be of particular value in achieving a more exact and detailed account of the emergence of empirical argument than has hitherto been possible.

I choose the convention using lunulae rather than another mark because they are implicated in a second conventional use, the indication of comparisons (including similes and metaphors), which may be read as marking the cruces of arguments by analogy. As a brief example, consider these lines of Antonio's from the 1623 quarto of Webster's *The Dutchesse of Malfy*:

> *Ant.* It then doth follow want of action
> Breeds all blacke male-contents, and their close rearing
> (Like mothes in cloath) doe hurt for want of wearing.
>
> (Webster 1623: B2ʳ)

The analogy with moths eating cloth is not a parenthesis, for both the grammar and the meaning of the following phrase, "doe hurt for want of wearing", depend upon the moths (it must be the clothes that suffer from "want of wearing"): and if the parenthesis is removed – to produce 'and their close rearing doe hurt for want of wearing' – the sense is irretrievably lost. The simile is serving as a grammatically (and by Jacobean standards logically) integral metaphor, without which Antonio's argument about the creation of malcontents by idleness cannot be understood, and is therefore properly distinguished, typographically, for the convenience and instruction of the reader. In conjunction with the lunulaic indication of *sententiæ* a most suggestive picture of the relations between lunulae and modes of argument begins to emerge; and a further parallel is visible in the modern 'parenthesisation' in scholarly argument of page-numbers, bibliographical data, and other references. In conference or lecture delivery such 'parentheses' would doubtless be omitted, and they are clearly grammatically subordinate; but not argumentatively so, for if the reference is wrong the damage to the argument is potentially very great; and the common demand by universities that submitted typed work use standard conventions (including the use of lunulae) to signpost references is certainly in part to assist examiners in finding and checking them. In this sense, as on any occasion when a modern academic book is consulted for a reference, lunulae around page-numbers or bibliographical data can be understood visually to distinguish (or emphasise) their contents, much as do the lunulae around the *sententia* in the Dekker and around the analogy in the Webster.

These apparently parallel conventions raise especially intriguing issues about 'authority', whether a classical author in quotation as a *sententia* or a simple reference/citation by page-number, and suggest a degree of continuity in modes of argument to be set against the common representation of the *Aufklärung* as a powerful discontinuity. In English the most striking representative of that (supposed) discontinuity is probably Dr Johnson, and one particular misunderstanding of Johnson's is for me very instructive. In the famous and influential *Preface to Shakespeare* (1765) Johnson contended that a "quibble", or pun, was for Shakespeare "the fatal Cleopatra for which he lost the world"[21] – an argument that Shakespeare marred his writing because he was unable to resist unnecessary wordplay (which he thought ornamental) of one or another kind. Implicit in all that Johnson says (and his treatment, in the 'Life' of Cowley, of metaphysical conceits is similar)[22] is the idea that Shakespeare could have done without these puns if he had had the will to do so; the wordplay, in other words, is not in any way constitutive of essential meaning. But that is not the lesson of Hamlet's "A little more then kin, and lesse then kinde" (1.2.65),[23] nor of the Webster speech I quoted: those kinds of wordplay, rhetorical and metaphorical as well as overtly punning, are both integral and necessary to their arguments. In both cases there is a momentary 'elimination of distance', to reveal as if by superimposition the 'kin' in 'kind' and the moth-eaten origins of malcontentment; and without that superimposition (or 'meta-phoria', 'carrying above') *there is no argument* – for the arguments are arguments by analogy. If the reader does not compare "kin" and "kind", or does not see the parallelism of moth-eaten clothes and idle malcontents, Hamlet's and Antonio's arguments remain unread. It is that argumentative value of Shakespearean quibbling (and of metaphysical conceits) to which Johnson's *Aufklärung*-modernity appears to have blinded him.

I would like now to suggest that there is a parallel blindness from which we still suffer, and which explains, with much else, the old critical contention that there is no irony to be found in English metaphysical poetry. Dan Sperber and Deirdre Wilson (1981: 302; 1986: 239) have suggested a "pragmatic-rhetorical" definition of irony, in which it is viewed as a form of quotation or allusion, an idea that ironic statements are, as it were, wearing inverted commas, but are not adequately signalled as such (a dry tone of voice, perhaps, but no finger-waggle). One says, for instance, what one might say if circumstances were otherwise, or what another might say if they were present: a gap is created between the apparent fact (what one has actually said) and a further datum, the act of quotation, of speaking within 'inverted commas' (which alter the whole sense, by altering the mode of sense). Irony is in this way a 'preservation of distance' directly opposed to the 'elimination of distance' that radically defines metaphor; and it is also connected to the idea of quotation, which is the basic necessity for argument by authority: for a *sententia* must be quoted (or at least made to appear to be quoted ...) for it to function as a vehicle of suprapersonal authority. At its bluntest the underlying pattern here may be expressed as an aphorism: that irony was to argument by authority as metaphor was to argument by analogy, a vehicle or mode of argument and not an optional ornament of empirical argument.[24] This, if true, has at least two crucial consequences: that 'irony' in the modern sense only emerged clearly with the seventeenth- and eighteenth-century decline of argument by authority; and that in argument by authority the 'ironic gap', the distance preserved between the one who speaks/writes and the one who is quoted, need not be in the modern sense underminingly 'ironic', but can instead reinforce and substantiate argument – backing it up, even if at a distance.

I find it interesting to measure this idea against, for example, Eliot's famous notion about the seventeenth-century "dissociation of sensibility", or against much of the older critical work (from Johnson to A. J. Smith) which found such recurrent difficulty with the idea of Metaphysical irony. There has, for example, been much ink spilt about Donne's use in his apparently penitential 'Hymne to God the Father' of the repeated pun on his own name and on the maiden name of his wife (Ann More)[25] – "When thou hast done, thou hast not done,/ For, I have more.":[26] is it irreverent? and how are we to understand a 'quibbling' and 'ironic' 'sincerity'? It seems to me a great strength of the pragmatic-rhetorical approach that it can easily account for these lines (and for earlier critical difficulties with them) on the basis that Donne is deploying arguments by authority ('irony') and by analogy (homophony) simultaneously. The authority is partly Donne's own, properly so as the actual author and as the husband of Ann More, but improperly so as one imagining the condition of God; and partly the authorities of the Roman Catholic church, whose priests could not marry but to which Donne had not been obedient for many years, and of the Church of England, whose priests, including Donne, could marry. The principal analogy is the theologically traditional one between secular marriage and the mysterious union of Christ and his church, and by extension between Donne's piety and his uxoriousness as the husband of Ann More. Previous critical difficulties arose from the confusion of the two modes of argument, or from a Johnsonian misunderstanding of quibbles, with the result that 'irony' was supposed to be generated by the 'inappropriate' presence of 'puns'; but such 'irony' was both misconceived as ornamental, and misunderstood as 'ironic' in the modern sense. In contrast, the new reading would locate a 'proto-irony' in the assertion by Ann More of sexual authority over Donne, a blissful but perhaps damnable inversion of order which distances Donne from God, and would recharacterise the modern 'irony' as Donne's witty manipulation of his arguments by authority and analogy, his impossibly but imaginably simultaneous preservation with irony, and elimination with homophonic metaphor, of the distances between {Donne and God} and {Donne and Ann Donne (undone)}. The older critics ran into difficulties because the postulations of 'irony' and 'punning' supplied too few axes to accommodate Donne's method;[27] but if four axes are maintained – each of the arguments, by authority and by analogy, both vertically (Donne/God – marriage-on-earth/marriage-in-heaven) and horizontally (Donne-More/ piety-uxoriousness), plus the crucial diagonal (More~God) which was Donne's *donnée* – a reading granting Donne a far more complex and profound control can readily be sustained.

This particular instance did not attract or require, in its various surviving manuscripts or in the 1633 *Poems*, any lunulae, but the possibility remains of learning to read certain uses of lunulae as a typographical indication of (proto-) irony. An interesting test is offered by the First Folio text of *The Winter's Tale*, whose 369 pairs of lunulae[28] mark it as having been transcribed for the compositors by Ralph Crane. Crane's well-known proliferations of lunulae arise from his unusually consistent observation of nine or so conventions using the mark, including the indication of comparisons and of *sententiæ*; but even so, the Folio *Winter's Tale* is an extreme case,[29] and makes me wonder why Crane should have been so on his mettle.

At least 155 of the pairs of lunulae (more than 40%) indicate vocatives, overwhelmingly the conventional honorifics '(My lord)', '(Sir)', and '(Madam)', and the familiar '(Boy)'. Crane's consistency in applying the conventional lunulae makes the near-ubiquity of these vocatives visually apparent to a reader of the Folio text; and the inconsistent and irregular use of the convention in other Folio texts may inhibit a reader from becoming aware of vocatives in the same way: but my own impression (without attempting to count all the vocatives in the First Folio) is that there genuinely are more of them in *The Winter's Tale* than elsewhere, and that Crane's particular thoroughness in marking them here was in part a response to a quality (and I assume, a Shakespearean quality) of *his* copy-text. Whether that was so, the marked vocatives of the Folio text bring to *The Winter's Tale* an almost incessant signalling of relative social authority, much of it centred on Leontes.

There is a moment in the play which engaged Anne Barton to produce her wonderful essay 'Leontes and the spider: language and speaker in Shakespeare's last plays' (1980; in: Barton 1994: 161-81). Upstage, Hermione listens in tableau to Mamillius's "sad Tale ... of Sprights, and Goblins" (2.1.25-6);[30] downstage, Leontes begins his public denunciation of her for adultery:

> *Leo.* How blest am I
>   In my iust Censure? in my true Opinion?
>   Alack, for lesser knowledge, how accurs'd,
>   In being so blest? There may be in the Cup
>   A Spider steep'd, and one may drinke; depart,
>   And yet partake no venome: (for his knowledge
>   Is not infected) but if one present
>   Th'abhor'd Ingredient to his eye, make knowne
>   How he hath drunke, he cracks his gorge, his sides
>   With violent Hefts: I haue drunke, and seene the Spider.
>   *Camillo* was his helpe in this, his Pandar:
>   There is a Plot against my Life, my Crowne;
>   All's true that is mistrusted: that false Villaine,
>   Whom I employ'd, was pre-employ'd by him:
>   He ha's discouer'd my Design, and I
>   Remaine a pinch'd Thing; yea, a very Trick
>   For them to play at will: (2.1.36-52)

Professor Barton adduces in comparison a speech of Othello's – "I had beene happy, if the generall Campe, / Pyoners and all, had tasted her sweet Body, / So I had nothing knowne." (3.3.345-47) – and comments:

> Leontes' speech ... is very different from Othello's. The little inset story of the spider is palpably an old wives' tale: a piece of unnatural natural history which Leontes trots out as part of his self-defeating effort to make something out of nothing, to give substance to a bad dream. As such, it functions in ways of which the speaker himself is unaware, tells a truth he consciously rejects. If Leontes sees himself as being in Othello's situation, we do not. Othello, with some excuse, could not distinguish between Desdemona's truth and Iago's cunning falsehood. He was not the only person in the play to make this mistake. Leontes, on the other hand, inhabits a world of clear-cut black and white, one in which there is no Iago, and even the herd of anonymous gentlemen at the court always know that Hermione is innocent. Leontes' mind, as his words involuntarily but explicitly inform us, has poisoned itself, breeding madness from an illusory evil, even as the minds of people doomed by voodoo or black magic are supposed to

do. Whether visible or not, the spider in the cup is itself innocuous: it is the human imagination that is destructive and deadly. This is the most important thing Leontes has to tell us. It is characteristic, however, of the last plays, that the speaker should be quite unconscious of what, for the theatre audience, is the primary meaning of his own words.   (Barton 1994: 163)

This thought leads Professor Barton (perhaps prompted by Leontes's reference to Camillo as a "Pandar") to a further comparison with Pandarus's speech in *Troilus and Cressida*:

Pand. Go too, a bargaine made: seale it, seale it, Ile be the witnesse here I hold your hand: here my Cousins, if euer you proue false one to another, since I haue taken such paines to bring you together, let all pittifull goers betweene be cal'd to the worlds end after my name: call them all Panders; let all constant men be *Troylusses*, all false women *Cressids*, and all brokers betweene, Panders: say, Amen.

Troy. Amen.

Cres. Amen.

Pan. Amen.   (3.2.197-207)

This Folio typography is interestingly precise in italicising "*Troylusses*" and "*Cressids*", but neither of the "Panders": which effectively registers a distinction between the two names which (unimportantly) did not become eponyms, and the one name which (crucially) did. The audience's knowledge of the term 'a pandar' and of the received Trojan story, and their consequent understanding that Pandarus prophesies the truth unwittingly and against his own intentions, creates a tension of audience-speech-character which clearly parallels the theatrical situation produced by Leontes and his spider; but, as Professor Barton implies in the comparison with Othello, there is also an important distinction between Pandarus and Leontes. In *Troilus and Cressida* the authority which, unwittingly self-invoked and recognised by the theatre audience (but not by Troilus or Cressida), trumpets the vanity of Pandarus's hopes is the authority of received history and historiography, and is located outside both the play and Shakespeare; but in *The Winter's Tale* the only authority by which Leontes convicts Hermione is his own, self-willed and -wielded. Not even the "herd of anonymous gentlemen at the court" think their rightful king a cuckold; his own words turn in upon themselves to display their false centres; and the dramatic tension generated by the audience's knowledge of justice not miscarried but procured and aborted leads directly from this moment to the crisis of Hermione's trial, and the revelatory moment (3.2.140-48) when Leontes maligns the oracle, Mamillius is reported dead, and Paulina pronounces Hermione dead. In the theatrical comparison of Pandarus and Leontes undone there is an object lesson in the modulation of irony by the manipulation of authority.

Leontes may not know that he is lying to himself, but he does know that he has to convince other people. It is to that end that he consults the oracle and stages the trial; and the spider is pressed to the same service by way of distractingly emotive and false analogy. An image-cluster of some kind may be implicated, for of Shakespeare's thirteen other uses of 'spider' and its compounds, at least nine occur with a similar association. In *Richard III* Anne declares that she likes spiders more than Richard at the beginning of the scene in which he successfully woos her (R3, 1.2.19), and Queen Margaret twice calls Richard a "Bottel'd Spider" (R3, 1.3.241 & 4.4.81), and on both occasions the words accompany the phrase "painted Queen" (R3, 1.3.240 & 4.4.83); Thersites invokes a spider (TRO 2.3.16) four lines before calling Helen a "placket" (TRO 2.3.20); Cloten's reaction to being told by Guiderius that a spider would frighten him more is to assert that Guiderius "shalt know/ I am Sonne to'th'Queene" (CYM 4.2.90-92); and the Duke uses "ydle Spiders strings" to substitute Mariana for Isabella in Angelo's bed (MM 3.2.275). "Weauing Spiders" are warned away from "our Fairy Queene" (MND 2.2.20), the "smallest Spiders" turn up in Mercutio's 'Queen Mab' speech (ROM 1.4.64), and Bassanio discovers an artistic one with the portrait of Portia in the leaden casket (MV 3.2.121) – so there may well be in the spider itself an element of borrowed authority, the old wives' tale that Professor Barton finds, associating spiders with women, rule, and sexual duplicity. Besides the habit which some female spiders have of eating their mates, this association may be, in part, of classical origin (from Ariadne via Penelope, perhaps), a potent authority for Leontes to claim; but there is, I think, something more:

> There may be in the Cup
> A Spider steep'd, and one may drinke; depart,
> And yet partake no venome: (for his knowledge
> Is not infected) but if one present
> Th'abhor'd Ingredient to his eye,

I would suggest as companion to the false analogy of the spider a false authority, the 'parenthesised' *sententia* of lines 41-42. The use of a colon to introduce the 'parenthesis', and the centrality of the 'parenthesised' words to Leontes's argument, both promote a reading of the lunulae as signalling a rhetorical crux; but as the lunulae do not indicate a comparison, they ought in that case to be indicating a *sententia* – for Leontes is arguing formally and in public. The phrase "for his knowledge is not infected" is not a *sententia*, but considered in isolation it does have a biblical ring which might allow it, delivered with gravitas, to serve as one; and the speech as a whole, including the spider and its Shakespearean associates, draws on powerful biblical conjunctions of imagery. Consider, for example (in the King James Bible of 1611), Job 8.13-16:

> So *are* the paths of all that forget God; and the hypocrite's hope shall perish: / Whose hope shall be cut off, and whose trust *shall be* a spider's web. / He shall lean upon his house, but it shall not stand: he shall hold it fast, but it shall not endure. / He is green before the sun, and his branch shooteth forth in his garden.

Proverbs 30.20, 28, 31 and 31.4-5:

> Such *is* the way of an adulterous woman; she eateth, and wipeth her mouth, and saith, I have done no wickedness. / ... The spider taketh hold with her hands, and is in kings' palaces. / ... A greyhound; an he goat also; and a king, against whom *there is* no rising up. / ... It is not for kings, O Lemuel, it is not for kings to drink wine; nor for princes strong drink: / Lest they drink, and forget the law, and pervert the judgement of any of the afflicted.

and Isaiah 59.3-5:

> For your hands are defiled with blood, and your fingers with iniquity; your lips have spoken lies, your tongue hath muttered perverseness. / None calleth for justice, nor *any* pleadeth for truth: they trust in vanity, and speak lies; they conceive mischief, and bring forth iniquity. / They hatch cockatrice' eggs, and weave the spider's web: he that eateth of their eggs dieth, and that which is crushed breaketh out into a viper.

If the spider found its way into the company of adulterous women and false justicers via an old wives' tale it did so with biblical precedent; and if the readers of the First Folio (and before them, perhaps, members of Shakespeare's audiences) were familiar with and were led by Leontes's speech, including the pseudo-*sententia*, to recall these passages (in the Vulgate or translation), the profound and self-betraying falseness of his arguments both by analogy and by authority would be made scripturally plain. The contrast between the ironies of Leontes and Pandarus undone would then appear as one between the consequences of wrongly invoking sacred (Christian) and secular (Trojan) history as authorities for one's own actions.

The First Folio (and almost certainly, Ralph Crane) typographically prompts one further comparison, within *The Winter's Tale*, of Leontes undone with Leontes at last done up, by Paulina in the final scene:

> *Paul.* It is requir'd
> You doe awake your Faith: then, all stand still:
> On: those that think it is vnlawfull Businesse
> I am about, let them depart.
>
> *Leo.* Proceed:
> No foot shall stirre.
>
> *Paul.* Musick; awake her: Strike:
> 'Tis time: descend: be stone no more: approach:
> Strike all that looke vpon with meruaile: Come:
> Ile fill your Graue vp: stirre: nay, come away:
> Bequeath to Death your numnesse: (for from him,
> Deare Life redeemes you) you perceive she stirres:
> Start not: her Actions shall be holy, as
> You heare my Spell is lawfull: doe not shun her,
> Vntill you see her dye againe; for then
> You kill her double: Nay, present your Hand:
> When she was young, you woo'd her: now, in age,
> Is she become the Suitor?
>
> *Leo.* Oh, she's warme:
> If this be Magick, let it be an Art
> Lawfull as Eating.   (5.3.95-109)

The Christian reference that helped show Leontes as unlawful now helps in New Testament guise to legitimate Paulina's resurrection of Hermione, a moment which (given audience belief in the possibility of diabolical statuary vivification) must have posed some risk for a Jacobean company. Paulina's grammatically compressed but quite passable *sententia* can be read as 'the Dear [Lord of] Life redeems you from death', so an auditor could "heare", and a reader see, that her "Spell is lawfull". The analogy with Jesus' redemption and resurrection devolves upon her the authority necessary simultaneously to raise the dead and remit sins. The only potentially troublesome 'irony' arises from readings of Paulina as, like Prospero, a figure of Shakespeare, but such metatheatrical reference is common in Shakespeare, and cannot prevent this scene from appearing to enact a fairly precise reversal of the moment when Leontes began to make his nightmare real. His immediate return to an image of consumption[31]

("Lawfull as Eating") marks the banishment of the spider, and the moments when Hermione, in frozen tableau upstage, is called downstage to be accused by and to forgive Leontes demand a parallelism of staging to match their careful Folio punctuation.

At the most general level, the reconsideration of what a pragmatic approach to punctuation might mean can usefully begin with the appointment of Jerome McGann, in the early 1970s, as the editor of the now complete 7-volume Clarendon edition of Byron's *Complete Poetical Works*. Beginning without much editorial experience, McGann set about acquiring and applying the *soi-disant* traditional craft of editing, as represented by Fredson Bowers, then at the pinnacle of the profession; but as he got into the work (which eventually took some twenty years) McGann grew increasingly dissatisfied with the received wisdom of the Bowers school. In 1983 he codified and published his objections in *A Critique of Modern Textual Criticism* (McGann 1983), which specifically challenged the notions of copy text and authorial intent.

McGann's argument, though theoretical and wholly to do with the understanding of text, was firmly grounded in a historical narrative which may be biographically summarised as Lachmann-Greg-Bowers. It is the history in gross of editorial principles and formalised methodologies, which originated in the eighteenth century as a way of dealing with scriptural and classical texts which have polygenous stemmata (i.e. they exist in multiple early copies which appear to be independent of one another). The method by which the relations, and hence the relative authorities, of these variant texts may be established has come to be known as the Lachmann method after the great German philologist, successively professor at Königsberg and Berlin, who by the time of his death in 1851 had brought the theory into a coherent exactitude. Our basic notion of the 'eclectic' text, which takes a given text as copy text but may adopt variant readings, and which collates all known texts with possible authority and presents them via textual and critical apparatuses, is inherited wholesale from Lachmann. With Lachmann's method itself McGann has no quarrel, but he makes two observations: that it is a method developed to deal with classical and scriptural texts whose surviving versions are far removed from their putative authors, and in more or less flat conflict with one another; and that it assumes that there is a single authoritative text to be hypothetically reconstructed, an original correct version now lost. As in one test case the putative author was God, and in the other case Homer, this assumption of a single and transcendent authority is not surprising.

The next link in McGann's history is the application, by Sir Walter Greg, of the Lachmann method to Shakespearean texts. Though the volume of his reservations increased, and he noted that Shakespeare was being quite explicitly treated as a secular national scripture, McGann did not in his *Critique* fundamentally object to Greg's development of Lachmann. There seems no getting away from Shakespeare's relative disinterest in printed versions of his work (especially in comparison with Jonson, and probably Marston), and the multiple quarto and folio texts of Shakespearean plays therefore present a problem which is in one way soluble by the Lachmann method, albeit with certain refinements and alterations, notably those consequent on the shift from treating manuscripts to treating printed books. Chief among these was a distinction which has come to be of great importance, between the *substantives* of a text, which supposedly constitute its meaning, and the *accidentals* of that text, which are held not to be constitutive of meaning.

McGann's real target was the third link, Fredson Bowers, who applied Lachmann's method as modified by Greg, and with further modifications, to nineteenth- and twentieth-century texts. Bowers also enshrined the notions of copy text and authorial intent. McGann's basic ground in attacking Bowers was that the Lachmann method was fundamentally inappropriate to the editing of works whose authorial manuscripts, proofs, and revises survived, and that its application to these works required Bowers to treat the normal process of publication as analogous to the scribal corruption of manuscript texts over centuries. The result is to make the author a transcendental source of meaning, and to promote the use of authorial manuscripts as copy text in preference to first editions. This, says McGann, is rabid Romanticism, preferring sweeter unheard melodies to anything that anyone ever actually read or was influenced by. It is, for instance, a method which would suggest that Byron's manuscripts of *Don Juan* should be preferred to the final corrected proofs of the first edition, which Byron had read, marked-up, and authorised, and which authorise the first edition, and are the authority from which the millions of pirated copies ultimately descend. Bowers, in other words, does not allow that an author's intention be other than single, nor that the source of authority (author-ity) be other than individual. This McGann rejects in favour of a theory that texts are socially constructed, and exist in complex radial forms extending through time and subject to continuous interferential development. This position has been elaborated in McGann's recent sequel to *Critique*, *The Textual Condition* (McGann 1991).

McGann has retheorised the text as being constituted by two distinct but profoundly and constantly intertwined codes, the lexical codes – in bluntest shorthand the words – with which Lachmann, Greg, and Bowers were almost exclusively concerned, and the bibliographical codes – in bluntest shorthand the page, and the book of which it is a part – with which almost no-one has been concerned. It is possible, in almost all cases, to argue for the rôle of authorial intent in determining the lexical codes, and, in some cases, in influencing the bibliographical codes; but it is not possible, in McGann's theory, to argue that authorial intent can solely determine either the lexical or the bibliographical codes of any published work. In other words there may of course be a single author, in the traditional sense, but authority cannot legitimately be invested in a single person; or indeed, invested wholly in people, for physical, technological, financial, and social constraints will influence the process of publication, and will again (though not in identical ways) influence the process of each and every republication. The entry of any reader into what I would call the 'sphere' of any given text, the text imagined not as an object but as an area extended through time, will be through one or another of these acts of publication or republication, and – whether or not the reader is conscious of it – their particular point of entry into the sphere of the text will determine what aspect or version of the text they first encounter, which will not be the only possible or the only legitimate aspect or version. For example, any reader coming to Shakespeare's *Antony and Cleopatra* in any modern paperback edition, is presented with a play printed in five acts, as if between the reader and the text there were a five-barred window; but a reader of *The Tragedie of Anthony, and Cleopatra* in the First Folio of 1623 is presented with a play in 42 scenes, but without act division: and the perspective on the text which the Folio allows is thus signally and significantly different from that allowed by the modern edition. So far, so good: I agree with McGann that retheorisation is needed, and that his distinction of lexical and bibliographical codes is a very sensible and useful tool. What I want to do is to set that tool against Sir Walter Greg's distinction of substantives and accidentals.

In his seminal essay on *The Rationale of Copy-Text* Greg distinguished between:

> the significant, or as I shall call them "substantive", readings of the text, those namely that affect the author's meaning or the essence of his expression, and others, such in general as spelling, punctuation, word division and the like, affecting mainly its formal presentation, which may be regarded as the accidents, or as I shall call them "accidentals", of the text.   (Greg 1966: 376)

As is made clear above, I regard "word division and the like" as aspects of punctuation, and I am made immediately suspicious by the offhand brevity of Greg's list, and by his apparent failure to consider either the *mise-en-page* or the material book. Nearly fifteen years ago Don McKenzie (now Professor of Bibliography at Oxford) pointed out that "In its application by others, Greg's practical distinction has been utterly divisive" (McKenzie 1981: 84); but I would go further, for I am not persuaded, and increasingly dissuaded, that it is either a practical or a practicable distinction. I note in the first place that Greg is not concerned at all with what I would call true accidentals, i.e. turned or pulled letters, letters set incorrectly as a result of incorrectly distributed type, incorrect imposition, folding, gathering, or binding, and so on. He is instead concerned to distinguish two categories which for the compositors and readers of the book are equally deliberate, and thus quite intentionally present. If a published text has received authorial sanction then Greg's accidentals and substantives alike will have received such sanction. This Greg does not dispute, and it is treated in his theory of copy text; but the issue becomes problematic again if the text is reconceived as a social construct with plural authorities.

Second, I note Greg's use of the word 'essence', which, even more tellingly than 'accidentals', reveals a profoundly Platonic conception of the text. In Greg's view any number of changes in what he calls the accidentals will not affect the essence of the meaning, a view like that of Plato with regard to, say, an oak tree. Oak-tree-ness inheres in each and every oak tree, regardless of whether it is a one-month sapling or a thousand-year old giant on the verge of death; cup-of-coffee-ness does not specify the size or colour of the cup, nor the brand of coffee, nor the milk and sugar; and in the same way, apparently, *Countess of Pembroke's Arcadia*-ness does not vary at all between the 1590 edition, a facsimile of the 1590 edition, and Maurice Evans's modernised Penguin edition based on the 1590 edition. However ludicrous this idea of an immaterial plane sporting *Madame Bovary*-ness as much as *Moby-Dick*-ness may seem, it would appear to be the basic theoretical legitimisation of the act of modernising, and that must be so whatever the particular reasons for modernising a given text may be: for one cannot hold that one is presenting the same essential text in a modernised edition unless one holds that those features which are being modernised are not constitutive of the essential meaning.

Looking again at the distinction that Greg made between substantives and accidentals it strikes me as not only fundamentally misconceived, but also as having been effectively superseded by the distinction that McGann makes between lexical and bibliographical codes. McGann's distinction, however, reaches much further than Greg's, and applies to materials which in Greg's view would have been outside and disconnected from the text; and the point of distinction between the lexical and bibliographical codes is not clear, in that punctuation, a component equally of the lexical string and the *mise-en-page*, would appear to straddle it nicely. But this is not for McGann's model a problem, as it is for Greg's; and McGann's arguments since his articulation of the distinction between lexical and bibliographic codes have effectively used that distinction to dismiss Greg's Platonic conception of texts and to assert instead a culturally and socially constructed dynamic textual identity which replaces the metaphysical and theoretically hypothesised static identity. He has never, though, so far as I am aware, made explicit either the Platonic character of his target nor the effects of his attack on Greg's substantives and accidentals – a distinction which in the *Critique* McGann appears at least partly to countenance.

I am arguing therefore that to accept McGann's position, and his lexical and bibliographical codes, is to dismiss textual essence and with it Greg's distinction; and that this has practical and pragmatic consequences which have not much been addressed. The first is the complete loss of the principal theoretical justification of modernising, leaving only the practical justification, that without modernisation a given text is, for the purposes of teaching or commercial sale, unacceptably inaccessible. I accept that there are texts of which this may be true, but do not accept that for the purpose of university teaching it is true of any English text written after about 1500 (though I will enter a mild caveat about blackletter texts predating 1580, on the grounds of eyestrain).

The second consequence of McGann is that all texts which have been edited by editors who did accept Greg's distinction – and that is almost all scholarly editions of the last eighty years – must now be consulted with the untenability of that distinction (more bluntly, with that *error*) in mind. This does not mean that they should not be used – quite the opposite, in fact; it does mean that they should never be assumed to reproduce an essential version, but only another version. One scholarly edition may supersede another, but none may close the process, and all, whether printed books or CD-ROMs, intrinsically include their own bibliographical codes which they cannot but impose upon the inset edited text: so more than one should be consulted, as should, wherever possible, facsimiles and/or originals. In the bluntest and most immediate terms we should not work as if meaning is confined to lexical codes; and textual work attending to bibliographical codes must commonly involve comparative reference to editions. In such work attention to punctuation will be problematic, because so many recent editions have been modernised, and because the apparently lexical *and* bibliographical status of punctuation suggests that both as practice and system it remains elusive to theorisation, at least until more and more accurate historical data can be gathered.

It is here that the work done in pragmatics may prove of the greatest value, for the dissatisfaction with philology and linguistics with which pragmatics began is closely parallel to the dissatisfaction we now have with the older editorial method and with textual theorising which has confined itself to lexical codes. Linguistics, shearing away from an utterance the circumstances in which it communicates, was unable adequately to theorise its production of meaning; and critical approaches which similarly shear a text of its material embodiment (as well as its author and reader) are equally wanting. Many elements of that materiality correspond closely to the subjects of pragmatic study. Spaces and marks may indicate pauses; marks, fonts, or layouts may indicate tone, status, and other determinants of meaning; marks may be habitually associated with gesture (especially finger-waggling and shrugs); layouts and bindings may confer upon particular copies an authority of vestment or function; and there is also the influence of the place in which a text/book is read. The particular meaning which a scriptural passage has for an individual reader at a specified time, for example, does not depend (even in a given translation) solely on grammar, nor on some theological or dogmatic pronouncement, but also on the reader's theology (or lack of it), on the edition, and on the context of reading. To read the scriptural passage by chance in an empty church, in one of the great bibles designed for brass-winged ecclesiastical lecterns, is very different than for a scholar hurriedly to consult a small, personal reference copy, or for a priest to encounter the passage while dipping and browsing when a sermon must be written. The grossest contextual and bibliographical conditions – the reader's identity, the location of reading, and the paper-size of the edition, for instance – will have the grossest effects; and more subtle elements of the bibliographical codes will correspond to what a pragmatist analysing an utterance of the scriptural text would call its pragmatics. Punctuation exists as the fine points of this correspondence, recording (in the *King James Bible*) the pauses and indicating the cadences of a largely ecclesiastical mode of oration which complements the bibliographical 'vestments' of the lectern bible, visually declaring and symbolising its special authority. Nor need such authority be sacred: one has only to think, for example, of how Oxford University Press use the light-blue dust-jackets of their hard-cover and very expensive Clarendon editions, and of the trust which scholars grant those editions in accepting as an assurance of the Clarendon imprimatur that the lexical codes of the inset text (the punctuated alphanumeric string that has been edited) will be authoritative; – or of the world-wide recognition of Penguin's colophon and former colour-coding (black for classics, green for crime, and so on), and the authority in matters of orthography and punctuation which Penguin editions of handbooks (and Penguin's own house-style) have accrued through the sheer size of their distribution network and from their hard-won reputation. As always, things are more obvious on the larger scales, but the approach I am outlining cannot stop short of punctuation, especially if the term is understood both generously (so that word-division, line-, stanza-, and paragraph-breaks, and distinguishing fonts are included as well as marks) and conceptually – the application of the idea of punctuation (the separation and articulation of the component words of a text) to the processes of writing and reading as well as to the text/book that is written or read.

Critics will also need to think again, as some scholars of pragmatics have done, about intentionality, the extent to which authors seeking to impose intentional meaning either lexically or bibliographically can or do control the contexts and materiality of reading, and the extent to which those factors influence readers by persuading them of, or leading them to suppose, a particular intention. In writing this article I have the definite intention of prodding readers to think hard about punctuation, and to re-think their present theories and nostra; to further that intention I have in writing deliberately employed certain devices (theomissionofspacestoillustrate *scriptio continua*, for example, or the use of an actual   , instead of the word 'space') which directly encode my meaning, and which cannot be correctly read if they are seen as printers' errors or as "accidentals"; and by the time you the reader read this sentence (if you do) I will in all probability also have fought a minor but lengthy battle with the editor, and with the house-stylists at the publishers, to keep both the original devices and these repetitions in my text. If I have succeeded, the victory will probably have had much to do with the new wordprocessing technology which enables me to submit, if not camera-ready copy, then at least a text on disk which is *supposed* to need little editorial or compositorial jiggery-pokery. To that (increasing) extent I can as the author include and try to maintain a degree of unconventionality which I believe to serve my purpose; but there is not a great deal more which I can control (the format and *mise-en-page* of the volume which you now hold, for example, or your identity and location), and I remain at the mercy of market forces and misreaders. The crucial point though is not simply, it seems to me, what my intention actually was, but that the reader cannot read my text without attributing to me, consciously or unconsciously, an hypothesised and projected intention.

To return to the example of Byron, no-one could now commercially reproduce the sumptuous binding and elegant layout of some of Byron's first editions, but there is a cost to forgetting the calfskin and the facsimiles in Arnâout, to reducing the leading and the price, and to increasing the number of stanzas per page from two to four (cf. Lennard 1991: 147-65). Byron was an aristocrat: his first books were privately printed, and his first publications sumptuous and expensive; but even so, with a little help from John Murray, his first publisher, they sold – yet in 1815 Byron sold his library rather than accept the royalties (of more than £1500) which Murray offered (cf. Lennard 1991: 286, n. 40, and 287, n. 48). Such data suggests a man to whom his imagination of his readers, and the material object through which he communicated with them, were of central importance; but Steffan, Steffan, and Pratt, the editors of the Variorum and Penguin texts of *Don Juan*, thought nothing of Byron's bibliographical codes, and also supposed that his inconsistent autograph manuscripts justified wholesale editorial interference with the text of the first edition. Moreover, the Penguin edition of their text cramps four stanzas to the page, and is of a quality and price designed for student pockets. In consequence it reproduces neither lexically nor bibliographically the text/book that Byron authorised. McGann restored the authorised lexical code, and while his Clarendon edition was only available in hardback (at about £350 for a full set of seven volumes) it could be argued that something of Byron's authorised bibliographical codes were also reproduced. The interesting thing is that the contemporary clash of the Clarendon hardback and Penguin editions itself repeats (and in part reverses) the earlier history of *Don Juan*, for, as William St Clair has shown, the readership of the poem was dramatically enlarged by cheap pirate editions, some priced at as little as one shilling; he has also shown how sharply political that shift of readership was, and that Byron's influence on Chartism is a demonstrable fact. Comparing the Penguin and Clarendon editions in St Clair's light, the questions raised include how we can relate our own editions and readings of *Don Juan* to those of, say, a Tory aristocrat in the 1820s, possessed in a palace of the first edition, and a Chartist artisan in the 1840s, selecting from a cheap piracy a Byronic motto to be made into a banner.[32] What kind of identity is there between the text/s that produce/s these variants? between it/them and our own variant/s? What kinds of intentions did the aristocrat and the artisan suppose Byron to have harboured? and how were their understandings of those intentions influenced by the similarity of lexical and dissimilarity of bibliographical codes in the editions that they read or possessed? At the moment we cannot even assume that the Tory and the Chartist had a common understanding of what and how the bibliographical codes signified, although we tend to make the assumption anyway, just as we assume that they shared an understanding of the lexical codes. But if Byron's extraordinary and creative punctuation is to be considered as lexical (and he continued to care about and to correct it in proofs and revises after the average price and material quality of his printed works had begun to decline) that second assumption is itself mistaken: for just as McGann has quite a different understanding of Byron's punctuation from Steffan, Steffan, and Pratt (because they all have, as human beings, scholars, and editors, different theories, beliefs, ideologies, and experiences) so it strains belief that the Tory and the Chartist, with their respective births, educations, social status, in all probability distinct religious beliefs, and differing practices of both sacred and secular literacy,[33] should have identically understood Byron's sometimes complex, unorthodox, and original punctuation. Byron created his authorised punctuation by imposing deviations and corrections upon the systematic punctuation supplied (at Byron's request) by employees of the publisher; when I come now to some unorthodox moment in *Don Juan* I must – in order to read what is printed – hypothesise Byron's intent, as satirical, perhaps, or comical, or lyrical, and test that hypothesis against what I know of the conventions that are breached and of the man who caused them to be breached. Not least, I must think about the tones of voice which I find in Byron's poems, letters, and life, about the poses that he struck and the attitudes that he held: the pragmatics that once attended his voice and which he sought to encode in his punctuation.

If an historical and contemporary pragmatics of reading is to be developed it must attend to punctuation, and not only to such interesting and unorthodox punctuators as Byron. The ubiquitously cavalier dismissal of first-edition punctuation by modernising editors, and the brevity of their methodological comments, begin to draw attention to themselves as protesting too much, and work by a number of scholar-critics, particularly Professor Mackenzie and Dr Parkes at Oxford, has begun strongly to suggest that the importance of punctuation is indeed in proportion to the scale on which it has been censored and silently emended. With punctuation you can force a heresy, reverse or emphasise a meaning, and make or unmake the sense; with the *mise-en-page* and the grosser bibliographical codes it forms the pragmatics of the written text, and we ignore it to our detriment and in peril of unending confusion. The whole function of punctuation is to clarify, organise, and display the meaning of the words, and we cannot theorise about that meaning without it; but besides the specific questions about this or that practice of punctuation, of the kinds I have suggested, there are also the larger conceptual issues I have tried to suggest: the punctuation of reading as an activity, for example, and the consequent reconception of the page/page-break as a unit of narration/ punctuation. Such a reconception seems to me a necessity for the critical reading of graphic novels such as Spiegelman's *Maus* and *Maus II*, or Moore's and Gibbons's *Watchmen*,[34] where the use of larger or smaller frames (and so a variable number of frames per page), and the non-linear *mise-en-page*, demand that both the graphic and alphanumeric texts be read page-by-page (or even opening-by-opening) as well as frame-by-frame and word-by-word. The reunderstanding of how far-reaching a tool a workable theory of punctuation might be, and of how much could be brought together by applying it, may well prove more important in the end than the visual and typographical details needed to generate that theory.

We are only beginning, and there are fascinating and tantalising views of what should prove possible in marrying pragmatics and the study of punctuation – but a new and very substantial obstacle to such study has emerged, for just as the combined efforts of concerned scholars have begun to concentrate on the material book, and to end the practice of wholesale modernisation of the 'accidentals' of older texts in scholarly and student editions, the same damnable practice has returned in the Chadwyck-Healey and other CD-ROM databases of literature. The inclusion of font and layout information is (supposedly) beyond even the storage capacity of CDs if databases are to be priced competitively, but that cannot excuse the extent to which increasingly suspect, or even discredited, eclectic and modernised editions have been used as the copy-texts for databases,[35] and the extent to which even information about the pagination of copy-texts may be lost in the creation on CD of the text as an immaterial alphanumeric string, the computerised version of *scriptio continua*. *Plus ça change* ... . Such databases are, as a result, virtually useless for the purposes of research into both historical pragmatics and the history of punctuation, and, as things stand, if that work is to be done, it will have to be done in libraries, on microfilm, and by the direct consultation of first editions or facsimiles. My point, therefore, is

¡¡ B E W A R E   C Ds !!

And I will end with that warning, but having done enough, I hope, to convince pragmatic readers who have never turned their attention to punctuation that they would do well to do as Heywood asked, and "with iudgement to observe his comma's, colons and full poynts, his parenthesis, his breathing spaces and distinctions" as well as 'his' fonts, layouts, bindings, and words.

Notes

1.   The seminal work on the history of punctuation is Parkes 1992; and beyond that the most useful account is by Brown 1989, in the *Encyclopædia Brittanica*. My summary

account here, and some other parts of this essay, draw freely on passages and footnotes in Lennard 1991.

2. There is a distinction between the italicised terms *colon/cola* & *comma/commata* and their roman homographs, which form plurals in *-s*: colon/colons & comma/commas. Colons and commas are simply the marks [:] [,], but a *colon* is the clause indicated by two colons, or by a colon and a full-stop; and a *comma* the (sub-)clause indicated by two commas, or by a comma and a heavier stop. Semi-colons and *semi-cola* may similarly be distinguished. In classical use, therefore, *cola* (or *commata*) should be understood to mean clauses within *scriptio continua* which would be indicated by colons (or commas) if the text were to be provided with written punctuation.

3. Augustine, *De Doctrina Christiana* III.2-5.

4. See the " Palæographical Commentary" in Bischoff *et al.* 1988: 13-25.

5. A term coined by Erasmus which usefully avoids the confusion of having 'parentheses' indicated by 'parentheses'; see Erasmus 1530: n5^v.

6. Bibliothèque Nationale, MS Lat 8687; 55.

7. Duff 388; Pollard & Redgrave, *Short Title Catalogue* (2nd edn) 23425.

8. William Herbert, editing Aymes's *Typographical Antiquities* in the 1780s, identified Henrie Denham's edition of Thomas Rogers, *A golden chaine* (London: H. Denham, 1579; *STC* 21235), as the first English book " to use the semi-colon with propriety". See Parkes 1992: 216-17.

9. *Signes de renvoi* are older, but their conventions of use have evolved considerably within the modern period, in Northern Europe at least.

10. These arguments usually correspond to two underlying (and quasi-philosophical) positions: that writing may signal to the eye, but does so via the mouth and a (silent but nevertheless) oral construction of meaning; and that writing can convey meaning to the mind through the eye alone and autonomously.

11. This gesture (which I believe now to be more common in amateur theatricals than professional productions, at least in the UK) does not appear to be illustrated or discussed by Barba and Savarese 1991: but with no index of any kind it is hard to be sure. The gesture I have in mind is, however, similar to the left image of illustration 5, p. 177 (" A[n] example of opposition"), and interestingly resembles illustration F, p. 149, a detail from an engraving of Pantalone now in the Fitzwilliam Museum.

12. The word 'actor' is used throughout as gender neutral, male and female actors being specified if necessary. This usage is increasingly widespread, in response to the pejorative and sexual associations of the word 'actress'.

13. *The first part of the Elementarie which entreateth of right writing of our English tung* (London: T.Vatroullier, 1582; *STC* 18250), ch. xxi.

14. See/hear, for example, Elvis Costello, 'Let Him Dangle' on *Spike: the Beloved Entertainer* (Warner Brothers, 1989; catalogue no. 925 848-1). The lyrics are printed on the inner sleeve.

15. Cf. esp. Proverbs 26: 21-28.

16. I have in mind specifically a revival, where a printed quarto supplied the copy for part-books; the standard of punctuation in original part-books or promptbooks, before any copy had been prepared for the press, remains very uncertain because so few originals survive. Quarto texts must, however, often have been the cheapest and quickest source for a revival.

17. Fraunce 1582, quoted in Joseph 1952: 53. Fraunce was later supported by Bulwer in the *Chironomia* (London: T. Harper, 1644; Wing B5465; pp. 138, 133) and by the unknown author of MS Ashmole 768 (p. 541).

18. Richard Burton's recordings of Donne, available in various cassette packages and recently re-released in the UK (1990s), are particularly helpful: he reads very rapidly, indicating punctuation (with pause and tone-contour) far more clearly than lineation, and in so doing makes the poems far more grammatically comprehensible than any other style of delivery, professional or amateur, that I have come across – so much so that I have come to believe the commonest reason for difficulty with Donne is reading too slowly, and privileging the printed line over the grammatical clause. That, I suspect, is what Jonson meant by his remarks to Drummond of Hawthornden about Donne's " not keeping of accent" – that he abused prosody with enjambment.

19. See Lennard 1991: 49 and 260, n. 99. Valuable work on Jonson's folio, the typographical practice of which Jonson personally supervised, is being done by Mark Bland, of St John's College, Oxford.

20. One of the best examples is the first edition of Sidney's *Arcadia* (London: J. Windet, 1590; *STC* 22539) (available in several facsimile editions) in which marginal diples and textual lunulae are both used to indicate *sententiæ*, and it is immediately apparent that a prime effect of this double notation is to make rapid reference possible. Dictionaries of *sententiæ* were also compiled for this purpose.

21. Samuel Johnson, *Preface to Shakespeare*, para. 44.

22. Samuel Johnson, 'Abraham Cowley', paras 52-107, in *Lives of the English Poets*.

23. The quotation gives the Folio text, from Hinman 1968, but for readers' convenience the reference is to the Riverside text.

24. The argument of this and the following paragraphs was briefly adumbrated towards the end of my review of Sitter 1991, in *Essays in Criticism* XLIV.2 (April 1994): 140-47.

25. The vast majority of the ink has in fact been spilt about the Donne/done pun alone, an astonishing number of editors and commentators failing even to mention the typographical presence of Ann More: in which case their confusions are well-deserved.

26. I quote from Patrides 1985: 490.

27. Much as the cartographic plane offers too few axes for the undistorted representation of the earth's spherical surface.

28. The figure is Ashley Thorndike's (see Lennard 1991: 13). My own count, using the *Norton Facsimile* of the Folio, came to 364, of which (in a rough classification) 155 indicated vocatives, 9 attributions of speech, 7 oaths and exclamations, 13 conditional clauses, 136 relative clauses, 4 questions, 3 asides (Autolycus), 17 comparisons, 16 *sententiæ*, and 4 'other'.

29. The next largest number of pairs of lunulae in any Folio text of Shakespeare is 259 (Thorndike's figure) in *2 Henry IV*, almost certainly also transcribed by Crane.

30. As above, quotations are from the Folio text, but references to the Riverside.

31. Or even of communion, given the repetition of Paulina's " lawfull".

32. St Clair 1991. A useful summary of St Clair is more readily available in Barton 1992: 91-93.

33. Some of my findings (Lennard 1991: 245-46) suggest that in England the division between Anglicans and Nonconformists may have had, and may still have, a considerable effect on practices of punctuation. The initial crux would seem to have been the Nonconformist stress on reading the bible for oneself rather than listening to a priest read it aloud to you, and the most important consequence the later emergence of dissenting academies. For the purpose of the example, my point is that as many Chartists but few aristocratic Tories were Nonconformists, the readers I hypothesise would probably have been taught to read in quite different ways, and so would not perceive the same page of text identically, let alone the same passage in quite different editions.

34. Spiegelman 1987, 1992; Moore and Gibbons 1987; see also van der Wetering and Kirchner 1986, Keiji Nakazawa's *Barefoot Gen* series, and the Tintin books of Hergé, a pioneer of the graphic page-as-unit.

35. See Sutherland 1994. " When in Rom", his damning review of the Chadwyck-Healey *English Poetry Full-Text Database*, in the *London Review of Books* 16.11 (9 June 1994): 7-8.

References

Barba, Eugenio, and Nicola Savarese
    1991   *The Secret Art of the Performer: A Dictionary of Theatre Anthropology*. Translated by Richard Fowler. New York, NY., & London: Routledge.

Barton, Anne
    1992   *Byron: Don Juan.* Cambridge: Cambridge University Press.
    1994   *Essays, Mainly Shakespearean.* Cambridge: Cambridge University Press.

Bischoff, B., M. Budny, G. C. Harlow, M. B. Parkes and J. Pfeifer (eds.)

1988   "Palæographical Commentary". *The Épinal*. Erfurt, Werden, & Corpus Glossaries. Copenhagen & Baltimore, MD.: Rosenkilde & Bagge, 13-25.

Brown, T. J.

1989   "Writing, adjuncts to." In: *Encyclopædia Brittanica,* 15th ed, 32 vols, Chicago, IL.: Encyclopaedia Brittanica Inc., xxix. 1071. 1b - 1073. 2a.

Dekker, Thomas

1602   *Satiro-Mastix.* London: E. Allde, *STC* 6521.

Erasmus, Desiderius

1530   *De Recta Latini Græcisque Sermonis Pronuntiatione.* Basel: Frobenius *et al.*, March 1530.

Fraunce, Abraham

1582   *The Arcadian rhetorike: or the præcepts of rhetorike made plaine by examles, Greeke, Latin, English.* London: T. Orwin, *STC* 11388.

Gildon, Charles (ed.)

1701   *A New Miscellany of Poems.* London.

Gordon, J. S., and A. E. Gordon

1957   *Contribution to the Palæography of Latin Inscriptions.* (University of California Publicatons in Classical Archaeology .3), Berkeley, CA.: University of California Press.

Greg, W. W.

1966   "The Rationale of Copy-Text." In: J. C. Maxwell (ed.). *Collected Papers.* Oxford: Oxford University Press.

Heywood, Thomas

1612   *Apologie for Actors.* London: N. Oakes, *STC* 13309.

Hinman, Charlton (ed.)

1968   *The Norton Facsimile: The First Folio of Shakspeare.* London, New York, NY., Sydney, & Toronto: Paul Hamlyn.

Johnson, Samuel

'Abraham Cowley', paras 52-107, in *Lives of the English Poets.*

Jones, Richard F. *et al.*

1951   *The Seventeenth Century: Studies in the History of English Thought and Literature.* CA. & London: Stanford University Press.

Joseph, B. L.

1952   *Elizabethan Acting.* Oxford: Oxford University Press.

Kleberg, J. V. B. T.

1967   *Buchhandel und Verlagswesen in der Antike.* Darmstadt: Wissenschaftliche Buchgesellschaft, 22-68.

Lennard, John
 1991 *But I Digress: the Exploitation of Parentheses in English Printed Verse.* Oxford: Clarendon Press.
Lowth, Robert
 1762 *A Short Introduction to English Grammar: with critical notes.* London: J. Hughs.
McGann, J. J.
 1983 *A Critique of Modern Textual Criticism.* Chicago, IL.: University of Chicago Press; repr. Charlottesville, VA., & London: University Press of Virginia, 1992.
 1991 *The Textual Condition.* Princeton, NJ.: Princeton University Press.
McKenzie, D. F.
 1981 "Typography and meaning: The case of William Congreve." In: Giles Barber and Bernhard Fabian (eds.). *Buch und Buchhandel in Europa im achtzehnten Jahrhundert.* (Wolfenbütteler Schriften zur Geschichte des Buchwesens, no. 4). Hamburg: Hauswedell.
Moore, Alan, and Dave Gibbons
 1987 *Watchmen.* London: Titan Books.
Müller, R. W.
 1964 *Rhetorische und syntaktische Interpunktion, Untersuchungen zur Pausenbezeichnung im antiken Latein.* Dissertation. Tübingen.
Novati, F.
 1909 *Di un Ars punctuandi erroneamente attribuita a Fr. Petrarca.* Rendiconti del Reale Instituto Lombardo di Scienze e Lettere, ser. 2, xlii, 83-118.
Parkes, M. B.
 1969 *English Cursive Book Hands 1250-1500.* Oxford: Clarendon Press, xxix n. 1.
 1978 "Punctuation, or, Pause and Effect." In: James J. Murphy (ed.). *Mediæval Eloquence: Studies in the Theory and Practice of Mediæval Rhetoric.* Berkeley, CA.: University of California Press, 127-42.
 1991a "The contribution of insular scribes of the seventh and eighth centuries to the 'Grammar of Legibility'." In: *Scribes, Scripts and Readers: Studies in the Communication, Presentation and Dissemination of Mediæval Texts.* London: Hambledon, 1-18.
 1991b "The palæography of the parker manuscript of the chronicle, laws and sedulius, and historiography at Winchester in the late ninth and tenth centuries." In: *Scribes, Scripts and Readers: Studies in the Communication, Presentation and Dissemination of Mediæval Texts.* London: Hambledon, 143-70.

1992   *Pause and Effect: An Introduction to the History of Punctuation in the West*. London: Scolar Press.

Patrides, Constantinos A. (ed.)

1985   *The Complete English Poems of John Donne*. London: Dent.

Robinson, Ian

1996   *The Foundations of English Prose: The Art of Prose Writing from the*
(forthc.)   *Middle Ages to the Enlighenment*. Cambridge: Cambridge University Press.

Sitter, John

1991   *Arguments of Augustan Wit*. Cambridge: Cambridge University Press.

Sperber, Dan, and Deidre Wilson

1981   "Irony and the Use-Mention Distinction." In: Peter Cole (ed.). *Radical Pragmatics*. New York, NY.: Academic Press.

1986   *Relevance: Communication and Cognition*. Cambridge, MA.: Harvard University Press.

Spiegelman, Art

1987   *Maus: A Survivor's Tale*. Harmondsworth: Penguin.

1992   *Maus II: And Here My Troubles Began*. Harmondsworth: Penguin.

St Clair, W.

1991   "The impact of Byron's Writings." In: A. Rutherford (ed.). *Byron: Augustan and Romantic*. London: British Academy.

van der Wetering, Janwillem, and Paul Kirchner

1986   *Murder by Remote Control*. New York, NY.: Ballantine Books.

Webster, John

1623   *The Dutchesse of Malfy*. London: N. Okes, *STC* 251176.

A Close Reading of William Caxton's *Dialogues*
"... to lerne Shortly frenssh and englyssh"

Werner Hüllen
University of Essen

1. The original and its derivates – interest of topic

"Monarchs and magnates apart, William Caxton (ca. 1420-1491) is today probably the best-known and most widely honored Englishman of his century. All of Caxton's fame depends on the activities of the last two decades of his life" (Needham 1986: 15). His was the first printing shop in England, in which he carried out an extremely varied programme. These activities resulted in the incredible output of 80 printed books within 14 years (DNB 3: 1293). Indeed, William Caxton's fame appears to rest much more on the fact *that* he printed books in English than on *what* he printed.

In 1483 he issued a book without any title which has become known as *Dialogues in French and English* or *Vocabulary in French and English* according to its designation in diverse academic papers and editions (Bradley 1900; Gessler 1931; Oates/Harmer 1964). Needham (1986: Appendix B) lists all pertinent entries in the STC and similar censuses. In their introductions, Gessler (1931) and Oates/Harmer (1964) trace Caxton's book back to its origins and describe the manuscripts as well as their passage through the centuries.

Behind Caxton's book is the original work called *Livre des Metiers* which must have originated around 1340 in Bruges and which has not survived. It was a manual of conversations in French and Flemish, obviously written by a schoolmaster using the linguistic varieties of northern Picardy, more precisely of Hainaut, and of Bruges. The only transcription still extant and now kept at the *Bibliothèque Nationale* in Paris was printed for the first time by Michelant (1875). The topography of its dialogues is without any doubt the topography of Bruges, as can be seen from a map of the town drawn in 1562 by Marc

Gheeraerdts. "...en effet, tous les noms qu'il cite étaient connus à Bruges ou le sont encore..." (Gessler 1931: 14). Besides the transcription used by Michelant, there is an adaptation of about 1420 in which the Flemish part of the original was replaced by a Dutch version in the dialect spoken between Limburg and the German border. The only example, entitled *Gesprächsbüchlein*, can now be found in Cologne (Stadtarchiv). It was published by Hoffmann von Fallersleben (1854). There must have been another adaptation, of which no copy has been preserved and which became the source of Caxton's French-English version of 1483 as well as of a French-Dutch version in the dialect of Antwerp published by Roland Vanden Dorp shortly before 1501. All published versions have been reprinted by Gessler, who also worked out the filiation (1931: 47) by scrupulous comparisons.

The age of the lost prototype has been established on linguistic as well as on general historical grounds and on the basis of political geography (Grierson 1957). Scholars are fairly unanimous on this score. There is less common agreement about the date of the French-English version and even about its author-translator. Grierson (1957) concludes on numismatic grounds that it must have been written in 1465-66. As Caxton lived in Bruges as a mercer between 1446 and 1476, it is, however, difficult to find reasons why he should have done the translating precisely within these two years. Blake (1965) argues that it was not Caxton at all who translated, because the admittedly many mistakes of the English part are different in kind from the mistakes he made when translating *The History of Reynard the Fox* in 1481, and for this book Caxton's authorship of the translation is beyond doubt. If this is correct, the English translation of the French-Flemish dialogues could have been written in 1465-66 by somebody else, perhaps by a mercer of Caxton's acquaintance, and handed over to him much later, when he printed it in his own shop, not so much out of interest in the translation but as a matter of business. All this sounds quite artificial. Oates and Harmer (1964) accept the theory of Caxton being the translator when he lived at Bruges.

There is consensus that the translation deviates frequently from its source. Oates and Harmer even call it "grossly inaccurate" (1964: XXVIII). Sometimes the semantic correspondence between French and English is lacking, sometimes the English is incomprehensible. It is irregular in a way which is regarded as typical for Caxton when he was translating, and it is obviously influenced by Flemish. As Caxton would, consciously or unconsciously, be subject to interference from the Flemish language in his translations quite frequently, this is another argument for his translatorship (Oates/Harmer 1964: XXVI).

Much philological work has been devoted to the *Livre des Metiers* and its derivates. Interesting as its findings are in every single case, it seems irrelevant vis-à-vis the fact that the original manual of conversation in two languages, written in Bruges around the middle of the 14th century, obviously exercised no little influence on the people of that time. In the region of its origin, there must have been a lively interest in foreign language teaching and learning. French and Flemish, Dutch in various dialects, German as spoken in the western part of the lower Rhineland and, via trade connections, English were in competition with each other. The *Livre* may have answered this interest quite well. This is the assumption which will guide the following chain of deliberations, and to prove this is the interest of the present analysis. Caxton's *Dialogues* are taken as an example of foreign language teaching at the end of the Middle Ages. As such, it stands in a long tradition of texts devoted to that goal, and perpetuates old techniques. But as is usually the case with a particularly successful link in a traditional chain, it must also have added or at least supported new ideas and new techniques.

To make the old and the new visible, the *Dialogues* will be subjected to a linguistic analysis. The guidelines for this are the rules of text analysis as worked out by Sinclair and Coulthard (1975) and elaborated with reference to dialogue in the foreign language classroom by Lörscher (1983). However, since the text under analysis is not oral performance with all its intricate pragmatic signs, but, if at all, oral performance streamlined, as it were, and turned into print, the Sinclair/Coulthard and Lörscher models of analysis can be stripped down to a few basic ideas and terms. Their essential linguistic assumptions are the following: A teaching text like the *Dialogues* conforms to the general definition of 'text' insofar as it is a large unit consisting of smaller sub-units whose central obligatory part is a so-called 'nucleus'. There are optional boundaries either preceding or succeeding the nucleus or both. Their function is the opening and closing of such speech as constitutes the central part. Before and after the teaching text, we find a frame introducing and rounding off the text as a whole, together with so-called 'pre-units' and 'post-units' which are rather loosely connected with the main body of the text. All these textual differentiations can be kept apart on the basis of their diverging functions.

2. A close reading of Caxton's *Dialogues*

Caxton's *Dialogues* can be broken down into the following linear sequence of units:

(1)   invocation of the Holy Trinity;
(2)   formulae for greetings;
(3)   objects: house and furniture;
(4)   objects: food;
(5)   objects: commerce and trade ;
(6)   offices, social ranks;
(7)   proper names together with professions, trades, and crafts;
(8)   pilgrimage;
(9)   counting, money;
(10) a final religious invocation.

As will be shown later, these units have fairly clear boundary markers, but the strongest criterion for their delimitation is their semantic cohesion, which discloses itself right away. This is even stronger than the table of contents which is given at the beginning for the benefit of the learner: "For to fynde all by ordre / That whiche men wylle lerne" (1.3-4)$_1$.

2.1.

The first sub-unit[2] (2) contains rules of behaviour, of what to do and what to say when meeting people in the street. Then follow routine formulae for the opening and closing parts of conversations which give an interesting insight into oral speech conventions at that time. More interestingly, these routine formulae are at least partly arranged in the sequence of a natural conversation with people greeting each other, inquiring after each other's health, their whereabouts in the recent past, mutual compliments, saying good-bye etc. As the voice of the teacher giving introductory rules for proper linguistic behaviour is clearly recognisable, the subsequent conversations can also be understood as spoken by him in both parts, i.e. the teacher performs a short role-play, thus illustrating his rules of behaviour given at the beginning.

Something similar happens in the sub-unit dealing with items of food (4). To begin with, there are somewhat moralising rules on how married people should talk to each other, how they should talk to their children and to their servants. They are followed by a dialogue (10.7-11.15) in which a fictitious landlord orders a servant to buy food, using the vocabulary for various sorts of meat. Again, we have a role-play with both parts of the dialogue spoken by one person, obviously the teacher, in order to illustrate at least some of the rules he has previously told the learner to observe.

An outstanding instance of this method is to be found in the following sub-unit (5), which deals with trade and commerce. The learner is first told where to go in order to buy cloth in different colours (14.25-15.4). Then we find a long conversation full of addresses, question-answer sequences, adjacency pairs, all of which would deserve an analysis in their own right using the method of conversational analysis. We would find routine formulae, instances of the cooperation principle etc. (15.5-19.16). The conversation centres around the price, the yardstick to be used, the currency available and, finally, other places and markets for different kinds of business. This lively exchange of speech is, again, obviously produced by one person, the teacher. One proof of this is that the parts of direct speech are introduced by an author-voice which, in doing so, refers to other parts of the book: "So may ye beginne / By suche gretyng / As it is in the first chapitre" (15.2-4) or "Ye shall ansuere / Also as it is wreton els where" (19.17-18). The conversation itself is quite lively and deictically correct. It is dramatic in the technical sense of the theory of drama.

A last instance of fictitious dialogue is to be found in the sub-unit containing exchanges with reference to a pilgrimage (8). Rather extensive religious admonitions by the teacher merge into a conversation obviously conducted during a pilgrimage to Boulogne. It deals with asking the way, looking for accommodation, and the departure of a ship.

2.2.

Besides the technique of giving rules for acting and then staging a fictitious conversation in a role-play, the sub-units on houses and furniture (3), food (4), commerce and trade (5), and finally on offices and social ranks (6) contain long lists of semantically related words which are scantily embedded in syntactical structures whose only function is obviously to couch them somehow in speech. This technique can be very clearly illustrated by examples, of which the sub-unit on houses and furniture gives a wide choice. After a description of how a house should be built, a long list of furniture and household goods is introduced by "Now must you have beddes..." (etc.) (6.33), enumerating all the things a bedroom should be furnished with, followed by a list of vessels introduced by "Yf ye haue wherof (i.e.bedroom furniture), / Doo that ye haue / Werkes of tynne ...(etc.) (7.14-16). Next comes a list of plates and cutlery introduced by "Now must ye haue..." (etc.) (7.29). Sometimes, lists of names for things are not only introduced but also closed by remarks that place them in a context. For example: "Cuppes of silver, / Cuppes gylte, / Couppes of goold, / Cuppes with feet; / Thise things set ye / In your whutche or cheste; / Your jewellis in your forcier / That they be not stolen" (8.15-22). Finally, some rather long lists of names of objects are patterned by remarks in between, which establish a loose but clearly discernible semantic cohesion over many lines. There is, for example, the introductory line "The names of trees:" (13.10), followed by 15 such names. Then the linking lines "Vnder thise trees / Ben herbes suete smellyng" (13.16-17) lead to 8 more names, followed by "In wodes ben the verdures, / Brembles, bremble beries, / Ther is founden ofte / In gardyns on the mottes. / Within the medewis is the grasse / Whereof men make heye; / So ben ther thistles and nettles; / Yet ben in the gardynes..." (13.22-29). This leads to 19 more names of garden plants.

In the sub-unit devoted to house and furniture, the syntactic embeddings of word lists are comparatively elaborate and even have a background of common experience, as the remark on the jewels, which are prone to be stolen, shows. In other sub-units (e.g. 4), introductory or finalising remarks as boundaries are much briefer, for example, "Of fruit shall ye here named..." with 14 names following (13.3-9) or "The names of trees:..." with 15 following (13.10-15).

It would be no trouble at all to sift the learning vocabulary out of these presentations and to arrange it in lexical fields, as indeed the text already does. Naturally, the choice of words is of tremendous interest for the historiographer of general cultural development. By and large, this choice agrees with the many topical word-lists that have come down to us and which the author or the translator could easily consult. Houses and furniture, plants, animals and food, objects of trade, oils and paints, finally grains and metals belong to the usual store of nominals and other lists (Hüllen 1989, 1992). However, our attention focuses on the method of presentation rather than on semantics. The teacher obviously starts from given word lists, wherever he found them or however he collected them himself. He then integrates them into his teaching by creating a minimal context which presupposes some knowledge of the world in which and for which the teaching is done.

2. 3.

The boundaries around sub-units and, within them, even around smaller sub-sub-units, serve a function which is obviously different from giving rules for behaviour, staging role-plays, and delivering syntactically embedded word-lists. They explain beforehand what the teacher is going to do. If we think of the three functions mentioned as 'teaching the foreign language in the narrow sense', we can say that it is the function of such boundary remarks between teaching sub-units to organise the teaching itself. Learners are obviously told what they have to expect, and in doing this the teacher imposes a clear order on his own activities.

The sub-unit on houses and furniture (3), for example, is introduced by "Now standeth me for to speke / Of othir thynges necessarie" (6.16-17). It closes with the line: "Here endeth the thirde chapitre" (9.10). The greater number of such remarks are short and matter-of-fact, as "Yet I haue not named the metals / Whiche folowe" (21.19-21) or even "Thise ben marchandises" (21.30). Others are longer and more personal, such as "For that I am not / Spycier ne apotecarie / I can not name / All maneres of spyces; / But I shall name a partie " (19.33-36). But they all have the same function: they announce the beginning or announce the end of a teaching phase and are thus not part of the teaching itself but of its internal organisation.

2.4.

Quantitatively speaking, the sub-unit on proper names together with professions, trades, and crafts (7) is of course most noteworthy. But it also seems remarkable in its way of presenting the foreign language. The names are introduced in alphabetical order and are made a pivot for various examples of everyday speech by which the bearer of the name is addressed. In spite of differing names, some of the speeches are connected with each other. The general context is the departure for a journey and having dinner at an inn. In a few cases, the bearer of the name is not addressed directly, i.e. in the 2nd person singular, but information is given about him in the 3rd person singular. We must assume that this information is addressed directly to the learner of the foreign language with the aim of rendering the ensuing dialogue intelligible. The following example mixes both procedures: "Agnes our maid / Can well name / All the grete festes / And the termes of the yere. / 'Damyselle, name them.' / 'I shall not, so god helpe me ! / Agace shall name them'" (28.5-11). And then Agace indeed does.

Following this, we have the many characterisations of professions, trades, and crafts which give a singular overview of the activities of people in a town like Bruges in the 15th century. Each is tied to a proper name. They proceed alphabetically in an unbroken line from the beginning of the long sub-unit on names, professions, trades, and crafts to its end. Unlike the addresses to the persons whose proper names are given, the characterisations of professions, trades, and crafts are directed by the speaker, i.e. the teacher, towards the learner, and refer to the bearer of a name and his or her doings. For example: "David the bridelmaker / Is a good werkman / For to make sadles, / Bridles, and spores, / And that thereto belongeth" (33.21-25). The number of details mentioned differs considerably. Thus, the speaker needs only four lines for *Colard the fuller* (32.9-12), but 36 lines for *Geruays the scrivener* (36.35-

37.30). Frequently, personal incidents and pieces of information are mentioned which betray that the speaker is talking of persons of his acquaintance. Even here, the tendency to slip into a dialogue is at work. It showed already in the example of Agnes and Agace. Of the following example, the first six lines are descriptive, the last four, however, belong to a dialogue between the speaker as customer and Gabriel the linen-weaver as shop-owner: "Gabriel the lynweuar / Weueth my lynnencloth / Of threde of flaxe / And of touwe. / My lacketh woef / And of warpe. / Is it ended? / Ye, sith thursday / Hit is wouen / For to doo white" (38.9-18) All these texts are highly informative and a great store of knowledge for social historiography. Sometimes vignettes of impressionistic charm are produced. Apart from the naturalness of speech and of the fictitious dialogues, they give plenty of opportunities to mention words which semantically belong to one field.

2.5.

Finally, mention must be made of the frame around everything described and explained so far, i.e. the teaching text *in toto*. At the beginning (1), after the overview of the chapters, we have an invocation of the Holy Trinity followed by a self-appraisal of the book, "By the whiche men shall mowe / Reasonably vnderstande / Frenssh and englissh" (3.22-24). Moreover, the usefulness of knowing foreign languages for successful business is pointed out. At the end (10), we have an invocation of the Holy Ghost again with a self-appraisal of the book, this time pointing out that it facilitates learning French and English *shortly*. This frame binds the whole text together. In addition, there are quite a number of cross-references which serve the same function.

Summing up, we can say that, apart from the table of contents, there are five functionally distinguishable kinds of speech in Caxton's *Dialogues*: (i) framing utterances situating the whole text, (ii) boundary utterances opening and rounding off sub-units, (iii) informing utterances on what to do with the foreign language, (iv) teaching utterances of two kinds, *firstly* descriptive vocabulary containing long lists of semantically related words in syntactic embeddings, and *secondly* such vocabulary in connection with direct addresses to imaginary people, and (v) fictitious dialogues which serve as illustrations for language use. The utterances under iii, iv, and v form the nuclei of the sub-units.

A full sub-unit consists of an opening boundary, a nucleus, and a closing boundary. However, the closing boundary is obviously optional. It is quite frequently missing (see appendices A and B). There are two cases in sub-units 6 and 7 where two nuclei follow each other without a boundary. This is why they have not been counted as separate sub-sub-units.[3]

The pre-unit, i.e. the table of contents, has its clear function, which is even stated in its opening boundary. The post-unit is a kind of appendix which does not conform to the otherwise lucid structure of the whole text.

3.   Performance in the classroom

It is not difficult to imagine this printed text as actually spoken in class. The teacher explains what he is going to do and how the language to be learnt should be used. He teaches its vocabulary, he addresses imagined people whose names and occupations he supposes to be well known to his learners, and he stages role-plays in dialogues. As far as the teacher is concerned, all important functional elements of foreign language teaching in a classroom are present. The linguistic analysis of present-day classroom discourse, as carried out by Sinclair and Coulthard (1975) and by Lörscher (1982), yielded quite similarly structured dialogues. This is the great surprise of this analysis of an old text with the help of a modern analytical technique. Of course, we cannot know whether Caxton's *Dialogues* are real lessons orally performed and then turned into print, or whether they are just imagined lessons. Some anaphoric remarks point to the latter possibility. Here the author of the book refers to a previous chapter, where a performing teacher would speak of "what he said before". But even so, the *Dialogues* are characterized by what could be called their scholastic realism, which contains many features of orality, even if we admit that many pragmatic signals would be omitted and stylistic shifts would probably be effected by turning the imagined dialogues into performed speech. But there is no reason to assume that such shifts were particularly drastic.

Unfortunately, we have no trace of the learners' performance in Caxton's *Dialogues*. If it is right to see them as a mirror of classroom reality, it seems plausible to assume that the actual teaching was done by the teacher presenting the text as we have it and by the learner repeating and/or translating it, either in chorus or individually, with the intention of learning it by heart. For the book, the same procedure has to be envisaged. The reader-learner, who would act as his own teacher, would have to pronounce the texts and translate them, thus turning into a twofold speaker-learner. We must not forget that everything said/printed in the *Dialogues* is done in the two languages, utterances facing each other as a sign of their assumed translatory equivalence. Framing and boundary utterances are possibly to be exempted from repetition. Nothing is discernible about the teaching of grammar and of pronunciation.

Thomas Wright in his *Volume of Vocabularies* (...) *from the Tenth Century to the Fifteenth* (1857) suggests that, for teaching and learning Latin, word-lists were dictated by the teacher and written down by the learner. However, this procedure seems to be unimaginable under the conditions prevailing during the centuries in question with writing utensils and paper much too costly and rare to be in everyday use for a large number of people. Besides, in the Middle Ages learning meant learning by heart and, thus, teaching was almost certainly an entirely oral process (Hüllen 1992). Even with a printed text-book in class, teaching would still be oral and learning would still mean learning by heart. The advent of printing did not mean that this habit changed right away. For almost two more centuries, books were looked upon as sources for memorising, and only then did they start to adopt the function which they have today, i.e. relieving the obligation to store knowledge in one's memory (Borst 1983: 505-512). Only slowly did the mnemonic culture of the Middle Ages (Carruthers 1991), incredible as it sometimes seems to us, turn into the culture of written and printed texts as we have it today.

If the reading and explanation of Caxton, as unfolded so far, is plausible, the title *Dialogues in French and English* turns out to be at least as inaccurate as the title *Vocabulary in French and English*. The whole book is in fact a monologue with role-play dialogues inserted. On the other hand, it seems understandable that the fictitious dialogical part should have been so impressive for the first editor. It is indeed *the* outstanding feature of the book. And, again, it seems understandable that the vocabulary part should have been so impressive, for example, for the editor of the French-Dutch version, because the text often reads like a contextualised word-list.

4.   Dialogue as a traditional principle of foreign language teaching

Caxton's *Dialogues* must be seen within the tradition of the teaching of French in England. Its general background is, of course, the spreading of French there after 1066, though only in narrow circles and for special communicative functions (Lambley 1920, Kibbee 1991). Not English, but French succeeded Latin in certain registers, most notoriously in law and court procedures, but there was never a chance (or danger) of it taking over as a general means of communication. This is why French had to be *taught*; at least for most people it could not simply be acquired in their families or in the streets. However, for quite a number of people its knowledge was important. French was more prestigious than any other language in Europe, and besides all the feudal connections between England and France there developed a lively wool and wine trade between England and Flanders from the middle of the 13th century which made a command of French (and Flemish) important.

Teaching French in England brought forth five types of manuals, viz. nominals, orthographical treatises, grammars, model letters, and dialogues. Only the last are dealt with here. In their treatment, William Caxton's *Dialogues* with their linguistically demonstrable scholastic realism will appear as the culmination point of a long-standing tradition in foreign language teaching.

Dialogues between teachers and learners are supposed to have been an outstanding feature of foreign language teaching from its very beginning. The dialogical procedure between teacher and learner is useful for guaranteeing a fairly natural communicative situation such as also prevails in normal contact between a sender and a receiver. The dialogical procedure also guarantees semantically coherent contents and, thus, makes teaching and learning meaningful. Moreover, many linguistic rules like anaphora, cataphora, pronominalisation then come into play quite naturally. Already many of the *Hermeneumata* (Goetz 1888-1923), the oldest foreign language teaching manuals for Greek and Latin still extant, contain colloquies (Dionisotti 1982: 87). But there is something unnatural about them. They are hard to understand as dialogues in a classroom or similar teaching situations and the term 'colloquy' seems to be a misnomer. Such so-called colloquies "... are exercises in the vocabulary and idiom of everyday life, including dialogue, of course, but only as a component, not as their overall form" (Dionisotti 1982: 93). And this component can be very small indeed as, for example, in the colloquy written down by Conrad Celtes in 1495 on the basis of a much older manuscript where it does not actually amount to more than the learner saying "ave, domine, avete; bene tibi sit" (Dionisotti 1982: 98, line 16). The bewildering thing about the *Hermeneumata* is that in their colloquies the roles of teachers and learners seem to be unduly exchanged in that most of the utterances are clearly spoken by the learner. It is he who gives a report about getting up, going to school, having dinner, going to bed, etc.

A somewhat similar case is *The Colloquy* by Ælfric the grammarian (Wright-Wülcker 1884/1968), consisting of Latin sentences with Anglo-Saxon interlinear glosses. It has a clear dialogical structure. The teacher asks and the learners answer by giving details of their trades and crafts. This, however, again makes their part in the dialogue much more extensive and elaborate than the teacher's, who does not do much more than raise short questions.

The reason for this arrangement could be that such colloquies are in fact vocabularies in disguise. This didactic purpose is stronger than anything else, above all stronger than any wish for a realistic imitation of the teaching procedure.

There are three works (Wright 1857) which are generally thought to be important milestones for the teaching of French in England. Towards the end of the 12th century, Alexander Neckham published his Latin nominal *De Utensilibus* which was glossed in Anglo-French. About 1220 John of Garland compiled his *Dictionarius*, which gave Latin words together with occasional translations into French and English. Both works compile words referring to the parts of the human body, parts of houses, life in the country as well as to occupations and callings of men (Lambley 1920: 5-25, Hunt 1992). Lastly, Walter de Bibbesworth's rhymed narrative, published towards the end of the 13th century, contains a collection of words and phrases of a very practical character, beginning with the nursing and feeding of a new-born child, followed by a description of objects which are important for the child's upbringing together with actions to be performed in daily life, domestic arrangements and a feast (Lambley 1920: 14). It was the most successful of the three texts mentioned. However, none of these works employed a natural dialogical principle.

Neckham, Garland and Bibbesworth are not really forerunners of Caxton's *Dialogues* because they deal with Latin and a vernacular, and therefore they serve a teaching situation which was different from that of the 15th century, which in the case of Caxton involved two vernaculars. Although Latin was then not a 'dead' language as it is today, it was not a natural one, which could be heard in the streets, either. The three works make the tradition on which Caxton's work rests visible. It is the tradition of topical glosses and dictionaries which, for various purposes, collect words in order to present them in an arrangement which was thought to be the natural one (Hüllen 1989, 1992). For teaching and learning purposes this arrangement also included dialogical and narrative sequences.

One of the derivatives of Bibbesworth is a text of 1415 called *Femina* (Kibbee 1991: 75-78), "quia sicut femina docet infantem loqui maternam sic docet iste liber Iuvenes rhetorice loqui gallicum..." (Wright 1909: 1). It contains rhymed couplets in French followed by their English translations. Thus, the principle of a complete translation is established as different from the occasional glossings of earlier texts. This part is followed by an alphabetical glossary of French words in three columns, of which the first column gives their spelling, the second their pronunciation and the third their meanings in English.

The subjects of *Femina* are mainly the same as in Bibbesworth, though in a different order. But, more importantly, the text acquires a different style with a definite teaching tone. A teacher addresses a learner. The first lines are telling: "Beau enfaunt pur apprendre / En franceis deuej bien entendre / ffayre chyld for to lerne / in frensh je schal wel vnderstande / Coment vous parlerej bealment / Et deuaunt lej sagej naturalment / How je schal speke fayre / And afore thyje wyjemen kyndely" (1.1-8). The sixth chapter, for example, speaks of 'De proprietatibus campi' and starts with a small introductory remark [4] : "Now go we to mede and feld / ffor to norshe oure chyldren" (27.24-28.1). Something similar is to be read at the beginning of the eleventh chapter. "the day by cometh fayr & cleer / Go we in somer to pleye / In erber wher ben thyje flourus / Wher of gon out thyje swete odourus / Erbej al so for medicine / And here namej y wylle deuine / fflour of rose flour of lilie..."(49. 16-17, 20-21, 24 - 50.1,3). Such remarks, mostly with opening but some of them with closing function, delimit certain chapters of the text clearly and give it the kind of inner organisation we will find later and much more perfectly done in Caxton.

The early 15th century also sees the appearance of a type of conversation book which prefigures Caxton even more. It is the *Manière de Langage*, "intended for the use of travellers, merchants, and others desiring a conversational and practical rather than a thorough and grammatical knowledge of French" (Lambley 1920: 35).[5] There are three versions, which go under the generalising title of *Manière* (Baker 1989), the earliest dating from 1396 (Meyer 1903). Three years later appeared *Un petit livre pour enseignier les enfantz de leur entreparler comun francois*, which employs very much the same means of teaching as the *Manière*, geared however to the needs of children. Finally, *Dialogues* were composed late in 1415, precisely datable because of their references to the battle of Agincourt (Kibbee 1991: 81-82). They come very near to Caxton's scholastic realism (Meyer 1903), mainly because a voyage is imagined with fictitious dialogues (Gessler 1934: 9-42). Contrary to the dialogues in *La Manière*, a voyage through Britain (not through France) is imagined in *Dialogues* with persons conversing in French. Similar to Caxton, the conversations start with a religious invocation, but are followed by an enumeration of the parts of the human body. The various types of greetings are then added. There are dialogues between a host and his guest, between the master and his servant. A little drama is even created when the guest unexpectedly recognises a friend in the hostel. The dialogues are dramatic and direct, sometimes developing into pure lists of words. However, this does not happen too often, indeed less frequently than in Caxton's *Dialogues*. There are short narrating texts between the dialogues, which create natural scenes of communication and even some action. After a conversation during a meal we read, for example: "Après vient le signeur et se monte à chival, et s'en vait chivalcher sur son chemyn; et quant il venra à boute de la ville, il demandera ... à un pute veile ou à un aultre ainsi ..." (Gessler 1934:52), and then another dialogue follows. These dialogues arouse the same general interest that some of Caxton's stimulate, because they are not loaded with word-lists. 'Ils sont plus courts et offrent moins d'intéret pour la lexicographie, parce qu'ils sont moins riches en listes de poissons, de comestibles divers, d'objets d'habillement ou d'ameublement" (Meyer 1903: 47). Indeed, some parallels with Caxton are so close that a detailed comparison seems worthwhile. It cannot be given here; it should, however, not be confined to comparing vocabulary and scenes. It is the teaching with the help of fictitious dialogues that marks the *Manière*-texts just as it does Caxton.

This quick march through several centuries of foreign language teaching, as far as the texts allow us to conjecture on what actually happened, is not really meant to show a linear development in time. It is mainly meant to show that two principles were at work through the centuries, viz. semantic cohesion of vocabulary, which often takes on the form of narrative, and dialogue. The former is easily recognisable in all the texts mentioned and it is also easy to assess its didactic function. The latter however, though present from the beginning, integrates only reluctantly and with some difficulties into a normal teaching procedure. It is with *La Manière* and with Caxton that we obtain a first fairly clear view of how fictitious dialogues were used in class as a teaching procedure.

The question arises of why teaching texts which employ natural dialogues seem to originate at the beginning of the 15th century. There may be two answers. Either earlier teaching was different or it was not different but its oral performance was not thought fit to be written down. If it was different it may very well be that new ideas about natural, i.e. practical, teaching came into being because the learners demanded them. The goal of teaching French in England may have changed towards the realistic and the practical during the 15th century. As regards Caxton's book, a happy coincidence seems to have prevailed. Out of a regional linguistic situation around Bruges and in Flanders a whole family of books for foreign language teaching originated, which Caxton (or somebody else) adapted to English needs as they had already surfaced in earlier texts (*Femina* and *Manière*) and made available for many learners in print. Anybody who cared (and had the money to buy a book) could now read what teachers would say in class by role-playing what native speakers would say in the streets or at the market. Caxton (or the technique of the *Dialogues*, which he printed) "extended language learning beyond the classroom, creating a new ideal of the pedagogical text, the manual that replaced the master, an ideal which extended the learning of French to a new clientele" (Kibbee 1991: 94).

5.   Caxton and the new medium

The early 15th century was not a time when the printing of oral speech could be considered a normal thing. It needed a man with linguistic ambition, enthusiasm for printing, and an interest in spreading a knowledge of useful foreign languages. This is the set of conditions that probably caused William Caxton to become involved. He had a lifelong interest in translations and became England's first printer after learning the art on the Continent. Moreover, he had spent 30 years in a country with a (for him) foreign language. As governor of the Mercers' Company, which held a royal charter and controlled the wool-trade with the Low Countries, he knew about the importance of learning foreign languages. However, in order to be successful as a printer Caxton needed a public whose members were interested and literate enough to read printed texts and who shared so much common knowledge that they could understand them (Giesecke 1980). This was not too difficult in the case of literature and theology. But it must have been difficult in the case of foreign language teaching and learning. Perhaps Caxton found such people among the Mercers' Company, whose members resided in London as well as in Bruges. Such companies would establish a system of communication among their members, which might include foreign language teaching. In the special case of the Mercers' Company there is no proof of this. Still, the *Zeitgeist* of the 15th century would support this assumption. At that time, literacy, which had up to then been a privilege of the clergy, of administrators, who were often clerical, and of lawyers, was also adopted by merchants, craftsmen and artisans (Orme 1973: 48-49). Besides the usual grammar schools with their Latin curriculum, studies in trade and business were set up, which not only included accounting and the drafting of contracts but also the teaching and learning of French as a foreign language (Orme 1973: 68-79). In 1459, a merchant named Simon Eyre bequeathed the huge sum of 2000 pounds for the establishment of a school under the auspices of the Drapers' Company in London.

It is quite plausible that Caxton's teaching texts were meant for the teachers of mercers and for the mercers themselves in Bruges and in London and were specially geared to their needs. This is supported by the choice of vocabulary and the method of characterising professional activities. Typically, word-lists for the parts of the human body, which are almost indispensible in similar texts before and after Caxton, are absent here, because they were obviously more suitable for children learning a foreign language than for grown-ups.

There is currently a wide debate on the way in which spoken texts were turned into written ones and later into print, and what this meant for the linguistic features of orality. Text tokens are, as a rule, taken from literature, religion, natural history, and law (Schlieben-Lange 1983), not however from the teaching of foreign languages. Our discussion will have shown that this is a mistake. Teaching is a wide-spread oral activity in any society. There is almost no culture known where foreign language teaching did not play an important role. Texts which document it can give us a lively insight into the way it may have been done.

Against this general background, the question of who translated the *Dialogues* loses its importance, although its answer remains biographically interesting. The important thing is that William Caxton recognised their potential as teaching and learning texts outside Bruges. A knowledge of similar enterprises in the *Femina* and *Manière* dialogues may have been helpful. Even if we accept that such productions as the *Dialogues* were needed to keep Caxton's press going (Blake 1969: 65-66), we need not assume that his decision to print them was made without careful deliberation. Too many details suggest that he knew what he was doing. Caxton's historical role seems to lie in the fact that he printed the right text at the right time.

Notes

1. Bradley's reprint of 1900 has become the most frequently quoted one, in spite of severe criticism. See Oates/Harmer 1964: XXXV: "Bradley's text is very faulty and, according to Gessler (Introduction, pp. 36-9), diverges unwittingly from Caxton's text exactly 162 times. Gessler himself has diverged from it rather more often, but wittingly (ibid. pp. 24 n.I.42)". As the facsimile edition is very difficult to read and the Gessler edition is difficult to come by, I will stick to quoting from Bradley. I only give the English utterances, and not their juxtaposed French versions.

2. The following analysis should be checked against Appendices A and B. The terms 'sub-unit', 'unit', 'boundary' etc. are used in the sense defined above. For better orientation, the numbers of the tentative groups in linear sequence, as given above, are placed after the first mention of a sub-group etc., because our analysis will follow their textual functions, but not their linear sequence. Numbers after quotations refer to pages and lines in the Bradley reprint.

3. The table of contents is different in this case. I give linguistic criteria priority.

4. From now on I only quote the English lines in a spelling which is adapted to modern technical means. Page numbers follow the Wright edition, line numbers are my own.

5. There is almost no historiographical treatment of these texts. A recent and noteworthy exception is Kaltz 1995. She treats the *Manière de langage* as a genre in its own right besides dictionaries, topical and alphabetical, and grammars.

6. In both appendixes letters and numbers to the left (A, B, C1, C2, etc.) have been added to show the arrangement of pre-unit, frame, sub-units, sub-sub-units, etc. The numbers give page and line according to the Bradley edition. Descriptive passages on the right (in capitals) are my own, the other lines are quotations.

7. Lines 3.11-3.13 do not strictly belong to the table of contents, but I think it is justified to ignore this, because they are a direct continuation of the lines 3.9 and 3.10. They read: "Doo diligence for to lerne./ Flee ydlenes, smal and grete,/ For all vices springen therof."

Appendix A[6]

Caxton's Dialogues: *the boundaries within its textual structure*

A	*1.1 - 3.16*	PRE-UNIT: TABLE OF CONTENTS
	1.1	Hier begynneth the table
		Of this prouffytable lernynge,
		For to fynde all by ordre
	1.4	That whiche men wylle lerne.
	1.5 - 3.13	TABLE OF CONTENTS[7]
	3.14	Ryght good lernyng
		For to lerne
	3.16	Shortly frenssh and englyssh
B	3.17 - 4.7	FRAME: INVOCATION AND SELF-APPRAISAL
C1	*4.8 - 6.15*	SUB-UNIT 1: FORMULAE FOR GREETINGS
	4.8	Now knowe what behouet
	4.9	That he haue of alle a partie.
	4.10 - 6.13	RULES FOR BEHAVIOUR, FICTITIOUS DIALOGUE
	6.14	Thus enden the salutations
	6.15	And the ansueris.
C2	*6.16 - 9.1u*	SUB-UNIT 2: OBJECTS: HOUSE, FURNITURE
	6.16	Now standeth me for to speke

Of othir thynges necessarie:
That is to saye of thinges
That ben vsed after the hous,
Of whiche me may not be withoute.
Of the hous first I shall saye,

6.22		On auenture, if it be to doo.
6.23 - 9.9		DESCRIPTIVE VOCABULARY
9.10		Here endeth the thirde chapitre.

C3	9.11 - 14.24	SUB-UNIT 3: OBJECTS: FOOD
	9.11	Now understande, litell and grete,

I shall saye you right forth
Of an othir matere

	9.14	The whiche I wyll begynne.
	9.15 - 11.15	RULES FOR BEHAVIOUR, FICTITIOUS DIALOGUE
	11.16	Yet ben ther othir bestes
	11.17	Whereof men recche not to ete:
	11.18 - 11.32	DESCRIPTIVE VOCABULARY
	11.33	Now hereafter shall ye here of fissh.

Of the fisshes may ye here
The names of somme,
Not of alle,
For I ne wote not
How alle to knowe;
Also ne doo not the maroners.

	11.40	First of fisshes of the see:
	11.41 - 12.9	DESCRIPTIVE VOCABULARY
	12.10	Of othir fishes
	12.11	Of the river, etc:
	12.12 - 12.20	DESCRIPTIVE VOCABULARY
	12.21	Who knoweth more, name he more;
	12.22	For I ne knowe no more to speke.
	12.23	Now name we the white mete
	12.24	And that wherof is made.
	12.25 - 13.2	DESCRIPTIVE VOCABULARY
	13.3	Of fruit shall ye here named
	13.4 - 13.9	DESCRIPTIVE VOCABULARY
	13.10	The names of trees:
	13.11 - 13.37	DESCRIPTIVE VOCABULARY
	13.38	These ben the potages:
	13.39 - 14.2	DESCRIPTIVE VOCABULARY
	14.3	Thise ben the drynkes :
	14.4 - 14.24	DESCRIPTIVE VOCABULARY

C4	14.25 - 22.13	SUB-UNIT 4: COMMERCE
	14.25	Of othir thinge withoute taryeng,

Whiles that I remembre,

14.27		I wyll to you deuise and teche.
14.28 -15.1		RULES FOR BEHAVIOUR
15.2		So may ye beginne
		By suche gretyng
15.4		As it is in the first chapitre.
15.5 - 19.16		FICTITIOUS DIALOGUE, DESCRIPTIVE VOCABULARY
19.17		Ye shall asuere
19.18		Also as it is wreton els where.
19.19		Yet shall I not leue it
		That I ne buye
		Hydes of kyen ,
19.22		Whereof men make lether.
19.23 -19.31		DESCRIPTIVE VOCABULARY
19.32		Alle in one chapitre.
19.33		For that I am not
		Spycier ne apotecarie
		I can not name
		All maneres of spyces;
19.37		But I shall name a partie:
19.38 -20.8		DESCRIPTIVE VOCABULARY
20.9		Now shall we saye of the oyles.
20.10 - 20.14		DESCRIPTIVE VOCABULARY
20.15		I shal bye thinges
20.16		Wherof ben made paintures
20.17 - 21.18		DESCRIPTIVE VOCABULARY (NOT HOMOGENEOUS)
21.19		Yet I have not
		Named the metals
21.21		Which follow:
21.22 - 21.29		DESCRIPTIVE VOCABULARY
21.30		These ben marchandises:
21.31 - 22.5		descriptive vocabulary
22.6		Here I shall make an ende,
22.7		And shall saye of graynes:
22.8 - 22.11		DESCRIPTIVE VOCABULARY
22.12		Of these thinges I am wery,
22.13		So that I shall reste me.
C5	*22.14 - 25.9*	SUB-UNIT 5: OFFICES, SOCIAL RANKS
	22.14	But the grete lordes I shall name;
		The prelats of holy chirche;
		The princes, the grete lords.
	22.17	Fyrst of the hyest:
	22.18 - 24.11	DESCRIPTIVE VOCABULARY
	24.12	Now comen the names
	24.13	Of dukes, of erles
	24.14 - 25.9	DESCRIPTIVE VOCABULARY

C6	25.10 - 47.30	SUB-UNIT 6: NAMES, PROFESSIONS, ARTS, CRAFTS
	25.10	For this that many wordes
		Shalle fall or may falle
		Which ben not playnly
		Here tofore wreton,
		So shall I write you
		Fro hens forth
		Diuerse maters
		Of all thynges
		Syth of one sith of anothir
		In which chapitre
		I wyll conclude
		The names of men and of wymmen
		After the ordre of a.b.c.,
		The names of craftes,
	25.24	So as you may here.
	25.25 - 31.32	NAMES, PORTRAITS, DIALOGUES
	31.33 - 47.25	NAMES, (PORTRAITS), PROFESSIONS, ARTS, CRAFTS
	47.26	I am all wery
		Of so many names to name
		Of so many craftes,
		So many offices, so many seruises;
	47.30	I wyll reste me.
C7	47.31 -50.31	SUB-UNIT 7: PILGRIMAGE
	47.31	Neuertheless, for to lengthe
		That whiche I haue begonne,
	47.33	I shall saye the beste:
	47.34 - 48.40	RELIGIOUS ADMONITIONS
	49.1 - 50.24	FICTITIOUS DIALOGUE
	50.25	Lordes, who wolde,
		This boke shold neuer be ended,
		For men may not so moche write
		Me shold fynde alway more:
		The parchemen is so meke;
		Hit suffreth on hit to write
	50.31	What someuer men wylle.
	50.32 -51.31	POST-UNIT 8: NUMBERS
	50.32	Here after I shall deuise you
		A litell book that men calle
		The nombre, the which is
	50.35	Moche prouffytable,
	50.36 -51.31	DESCRIPTIVE VOCABULARY, NUMBERS
D	51.32 -52.5	FRAME: INVOCATION AND SELF-APPRAISAL

Appendix B

Caxton's Dialogues*: a textual overview*

A	pre-unit	
	1.1-1.4	boundary: opening
	1.5-3.13	nucleus: table of contents
	3.14-3.16	boundary: closing

B	frame	
	3.17-4.7	invocation and self-appraisal

C	teaching unit	
C1	sub-unit 1	
	4.8-4.9	boundary: opening
	4.10-6.13	nucleus: rules, fictitious dialogue
	6.14-6.15	boundary: closing

C2	sub-unit 2	
	6.16-6.21	boundary: opening
	6.22-9.9	nucleus: descriptive vocabulary
	9.10	boundary: closing

C3	sub-unit 3	
C31	9.11-9.14	boundary: opening
	9.15-11.15	nucleus: rules, fictitious dialogue

C32	11.16-11.17	boundary: opening
	11.18-11.32	nucleus: descriptive vocabulary

C331	11.33-11.40	boundary: opening
	11.41-12.9	nucleus: descriptive vocabulary

C332	12.10-12.11	boundary; opening
	12.12-12.20	nucleus: descriptive vocabulary
	12.21-12.22	boundary: closing

C34	12.23-12.24	boundary: opening

	12.25-13.2	nucleus: descriptive vocabulary
C35	13.3	boundary: opening
	13.4-13.9	nucleus: descriptive vocabulary
C36	13.10	boundary: opening
	13.11-13.37	nucleus: descriptive vocabulary
C371	13.38	boundary: opening
	13.39-14.2	nucleus: descriptive vocabulary
C372	14.3	boundary: opening
	14.4-14.24	nucleus: descriptive vocabulary
C4	sub-unit 4	
C411	14.25-14.27	boundary: opening
	14.28-15.1	nucleus: rules
C412	15.2-15.4	boundary: opening
	15.5-19.16	nucleus: fictitious dialogue, descriptive voc.
	19.17-19.18	boundary: closing
C42	19.19-19.22	boundary: opening
	19.23-19.31	nucleus: descriptive vocabulary
	19.32	boundary: closing
C43	19.33-19.37	boundary: opening
	19.38-20.8	nucleus: descriptive vocabulary
C44	20.9	boundary: opening
	20.10-20.14	nucleus: descriptive vocabulary
C45	20.15-20.16	boundary: opening
	20.17-21.18	nucleus: descriptive voc.(not homogeneous)
C46	21.19-21.21	boundary: opening
	21.22-21.29	nucleus: descriptive vocabulary
C47	21.30	boundary: opening
	21.31-22.5	nucleus: descriptive vocabulary
	22.6	boundary: closing

C48	22.7	boundary: opening
	22.8-22.11	nucleus: descriptive vocabulary
	22.12-22.13	boundary: closing
C5	sub-unit 5	
C51	22.14-22.17	boundary: opening
	22.18-24.11	nucleus: descriptive vocabulary
C52	24.12-24.13	boundary: opening
	24.14-25.9	descriptive vocabulary
C6	sub-unit 6	
	25.10-25.24	boundary: opening
	25.25-31.32	nucleus: names, portraits, dialogues
	31.33-47.25	nucleus: names, (portraits), professions etc.
	47.26-47.30	boundary: closing
C7	sub-unit 7	
	47.31-47.33	boundary: opening
	47.34-50.24	nucleus: rules ,fictitious dialogue
	50.25-50.31	boundary: closing
D	post-unit	
	50.32-50.35	boundary: opening
	50.36-51.31	nucleus: descriptive vocabulary (numbers)
E	frame	
	51.32-52.5	invocation and self-appraisal

References

Baker, John H.

    1989   " A French vocabulary and conversation guide in a fifteenth century legal notebook." *Medium Aevum* 58: 80-192.

Blake, N. F.

    1965   "The vocabulary in French and English." Printed by William Caxton. *English Language Notes* 3: 7-15.

    1969   *Caxton and His World.* London: André Deutsch.

Borst, Otto
    1983   *Alltagsleben im Mittelalter.* Insel Taschenbuch 513. Frankfurt: Insel.

Bradley, Henry (ed.)
    1900   See Caxton, William (~ 1483)

Carruthers, Mary
    1990   *The Book of Memory. A Study of Memory in Medieval Culture.* Cambridge: Cambridge University Press.

Caxton, William
    ~ 1483   " Dialogues in French and English." Ed. from Caxton's printed text with Introduction, Notes, and Word-Lists by Henry Bradley. *Early English Text Society Extra Series* LXXIX. London: Kegan Paul, Trench, Trübner & Co. 1900.

Dictionary of National Biography
    1917ff.   " William Caxton." Sir Leslie Stephen and Sir Sidney Lee (eds.). Reprint: Oxford: Oxford University Press, 1973, vol.3, 1290-1298.

Dionisotti, A. Carlotta
    1982   " From Ausonius' schooldays? A schoolbook and its relatives." *The Journal of Roman Studies,* LXXII: 83-125, 3 plates.

Gessler, Jean (ed.)
    1931   *Les Livres des Metiers de Bruges et ses derivés. Quatre anciens manuels de conversation.* Bruges.

    1934   *La Manière de Langage qui enseigne à bien parler et écrire le francais. Modèles de conversations composés en Angleterre à la fin du XIVe siècle.* Nouvelle édition -avec Introduction et Glossaire- publiée par... Bruxelles/Paris: L'Edition Universelle / Librairie Droz.

Giesecke, Michael
    1980   " 'Volkssprache' und 'Verschriftlichung des Lebens' im Spätmittelalter - am Beispiel der Genese der gedruckten Fachprosa in Deutschland." In: Hans-Ulrich Gumbrecht (ed.). *Literatur in der Gesellschaft des Spätmittelalters.* Heidelberg: Winter, 39-70.

Goetz, Georg (ed.)
    1965   1888-1923 *Corpus Glossarium Latinorum.* Begonnen von Gustav Loewe. Vol. 1-7. Leipzig: Teubner. repr. Amsterdam: Hakkert.

Grierson, Philip
    1957   " The dates of the 'Livre des Metiers' and its derivatives." *Revue Belge de Philologie et d'Histoire* XXXV: 778-83.

Hüllen, Werner
    1989   " Von Glossaren und frühen Lehrbüchern für den fremdsprachlichen Unterricht." In: Eberhard Kleinschmidt (ed.). *Fremdsprachenunterricht*

zwischen Sprachenpolitik und Praxis. Festschrift für Herbert Christ. Tübingen: Narr, 112-122.

1992 " Der 'Orbis sensualium pictus' und die mittelalterliche Tradition des Lehrens fremder Sprachen." *Beiträge zur Geschichte der Sprachwissenschaft* 2.2-3, 149-171.

Hunt, Tony (ed.)

1992 *Teaching and Learning Latin in Thirteenth-Century England.* 3 vols. Cambridge: D. S. Brewer.

Kaltz, Barbara

1995 " L'enseignement des langues étrangères au XVIe siècle." *Beiträge zur Geschichte der Sprachwissenschaft* 5. 1:79-105.

Kibbee, Douglas A.

1991 *For to Speke Frenche Trewely. The French Language in England, 1000-1600: Its Status, Description and Instruction.* Amsterdam: Benjamins.

Lambley, Kathleen

1920 *The Teaching and Cultivation of the French Language in England during Tudor and Stuart Times.* Manchester/London: Manchester University Press/Longman, Green & Co.

Lörscher, Wolfgang

Linguistische Beschreibung und Analyse von Fremdsprachenunterricht als Diskurs. Tübingen: Narr.

Meyer, Paul

1903 " Dialogues français composés en 1415." *Romania* XXXII: 47-58.

Michelant, Henri

1875 *Le Livre des Metiers: dialogues francais-flamands composés au XIV siècle par un maitre d'école de la ville de Bruges.* Paris: Librairie Tross.

Needham, Paul

1986 *The Printer and the Pardoner. An Unrecorded Indulgence.* Printed by William Caxton for the Hospital of St. Mary Rounceval, Charing Cross. Washington: Library of Congress.

Oates, J. C. T., and L. C. Harmer

1964 *Vocabulary in French and English. A Facsimile of Caxton's Edition ca. 1480. With Introductions by...* Cambridge: The University Press.

Orme, Nicholas

1973 *English Schools in the Middle Ages.* London: Methuen.

Schlieben-Lange, Brigitte

1983 *Traditionen des Sprechens. Elemente einer pragmatischen Sprachgeschichtsschreibung.* Stuttgart: Kohlhammer.

Sinclair, John McH., and R. Malcolm Coulthard
      1975   *Towards an Analysis of Discourse.* London: Oxford University Press.
Wright, Thomas (ed.)
      1857   *A Volume of Vocabularies, Illustrating the Condition and Manners of our*
                  Forefathers, as well as the History of the Forms of Elementary Education
                  and of the Languages Spoken in this Island, from the Tenth Century to the
                  Fifteenth. Edited from mss. in Public and Private Collections by Thomas
                  Wright. Privately Printed.
      1884/1968*Anglo-Saxon and Old-English Vocabularies.* Second edition. Edited and
                  collated by Richard Paul Wülcker. Vol.1: Vocabularies. London: Trübner,
                  repr. Darmstadt: Wissenschaftliche Buchgesellschaft, 89-103.
Wright, William Aldis (ed.)
      1909   *Femina.* Now first printed from a unique ms. in the Library of Trinity
                  College, Cambridge. Cambridge: The University Press.

Wills and Will-Making in 16th and 17th Century England
Some Pragmatic Aspects

Ulrich Bach
University of Würzburg

> "Let's choose executors and talk of wills"
> *Richard II*, III, ii, 148

1. Introduction

In the 16th and 17th centuries, a period largely characterised by the turbulent and controversial consequences of the Reformation, wills and will-making in England reached a peak in terms of linguistic flexibility and structural complexity accompanied by a broader range of use of this text type. For many testators, will-making involved more than the foresighted disposal of their property after death, i.e. more than the traditional double-function of providing for the welfare of one's surviving dependants as well as for the health of one's soul (by making bequests of alms). Particularly during the hundred years or so from the accession of Elizabeth I in 1558 and the first stirrings of dissatisfied, radical Puritans until the restoration of the monarchy in 1660 and the firm re-establishment of the Anglican Church, testators sounded out the potential of this written instrument for purposes typical of a period of fierce religious controversy, i.e. purposes involving the expression of one's own religious beliefs and often also the attack of those of others. This applies to literate and illiterate testators alike. For the latter, the will (dictated to a scribe) represented a unique occasion to make known and record at least once in their lives their religious beliefs and opinions in writing. Thus, making a will often included defining, asserting, demonstrating, confessing, justifying and defending one's religious beliefs, hopes and knowledge as well as denouncing particular unwanted rites in the bewildering landscape of competing doctrines of belief. For example, of the 25 manuscript lines of the last will of Henry Cockrofte

(1566), fellow of Trinity College, Cambridge, and a Protestant exile during the rule of Mary, only three and a half lines are devoted to short bequests of his goods; the rest, after the opening formula that he is making his will, is given over to religiously motivated considerations.[1]

This extended use of wills – to make them a platform of religious belief and controversy – also determined the content and form of the bequests themselves (thus, instead of giving money to the church and alms to the poor, a testator could feel more inclined to further the spread of Protestantism by founding a scholarship for a promising student with detailed educational precepts),[2] but essentially it added to and thereby changed the traditional schematic macrostructure of this text type. Still, the will of Henry Cockrofte and others like it were granted probate not less readily than the conventional wills.

If we fail to treat the elements briefly mentioned above as serving a deliberate and in their time recognised historical function of will-making, then many wills of this period would represent, in Gricean terms, gross floutings of the maxims of relevance and of quantity, violations otherwise hard to explain in the context of making bequests of property which were meant to be clearly understood and performed to the letter by one's chosen executor.

In this paper, I will therefore attempt to determine and discuss the beliefs and motivations of testators as well as the legal and religious institutional conditions for wills and the typical situational context including the roles of persons involved, all of which served as principal factors influencing and determining the way in which testators expressed their 'wills', and how these private records were used in the period under consideration.

The discussion of language use in historical wills within the pragmatic framework of the role of the functions, religious motivations, and situational context of will-making requires some notes of caution, however. First, not all of the elements, motivations, or functions briefly mentioned above are found in or hold for every will of the period. Those most likely to use the will for their particular purposes were the numerous groups of radical Protestant testators, but it should be kept in mind that even during the Civil Wars and Cromwell's rule they represented a minority in England (Coward 1991: 3, 161f.). Then, some testators obviously preferred to keep religious utterances in their wills to an inoffensive minimum. Furthermore, it is highly probable that a considerable number of testators of lesser means made wills of which we have no knowledge because they were not officially registered and filed in order to save the costs of obtaining grant of probate. Finally, as very many wills were dictated to a literate person of trust (mostly the parish priest or minister) because the testator was illiterate or seriously ill, there can be no absolute certainty whether or to what extent the written will represents the original words of the testator. For many (but by no means all) villagers' wills in Cambridgeshire it has been shown that the wording represents either well-tried testamentary formulae or that it was fashioned to the personal style of identifiable scribes (Spufford 1971; 1974: 319-44).

Examples in this article are quoted from a corpus of registered wills of members of the University of Cambridge, which, as indeed the whole region of East Anglia, was known for its radical Protestant, 'Puritan' leanings (Porter 1958, Spufford 1974, Leedham-Green ed. 1991). The testators represent a broad spectrum of different social levels and trades, because in addition to the masters, fellows and students themselves, certain privileged persons (servants, cooks, gardeners, bricklayers, launderers, inn-keepers, bakers, printers, etc. and "the man who times the University clock") living in 16 parishes in and around Cambridge, also came under the jurisdiction of the Court of the Vice-Chancellor of the University of Cambridge for probate of their wills.[3]

So far, last wills have only rarely been studied from the point of view of pragmatics including discourse analysis;[4] much rarer still are historically oriented pragmatic studies of English wills and the act of making a will in England in the past.[5] This is surprising not only because historical wills – a rich field of dated and localised documents which have survived in their hundreds of thousands (Camp 1974, France 1965) – offer a good example of the 'functional explosion' of a commonly used private record under specific historical conditions, but also because the last will and will-making, i.e. acting as a testator, *per se* have some pragmatically challenging, if not 'peculiar' (Finegan 1982: 119) distinctive properties, imposed by the social institutions of the law and (in former centuries) the church.

2.   Will-making and the legal function of wills

The English will is a private, generally written document containing the wishes of a testator concerning the disposal of his property after his death (cf. *OED will* n[1], sense IV.23.a.). As such, a will (including the act of making one) represents the testator's attempt to reach, by verbal means, beyond the limits set to his individual right by physical death (Spreckelmeyer 1977: 91). A general consequence of this legal, institutional condition is that a testator has no chance of explaining his meaning further when the will is examined as to its validity and executed after his death. This calls especially for the testator's words to be clear and understandable and also stresses the importance of fixing the will in writing (as distinct from *making* the will). Awareness of the pressing need to make their meaning clear and of the distinction between the acts of making a will and putting it down in writing is often made explicit in the wills studied:

> I [...] have ofte considered the greate stryffes and busines that here to fore have rysen and may ryse of vncertayn and undelyberated wylles and testamentes eyther by false wrytinge or elles by vntrew surmysinge of thynges contrary to the deades wyll and purpose Therfor, I the seyde Edmunde perpoynte clarke to avoyde all dowtes and cauillacions do make ordeyne and protest and with myne owne hand have here wryten this my last wyll and testament as folowethe (Edmund Perpoynte, clerk, 1556, I, 101v).

Here, the testator distinguishes by the use of tenses the ongoing act of making his will on the date stated earlier in the will (present tense of *do, make, ordain, protest*) from the act of writing it in the same situation (present perfect of *write*). Combining *have here wryten* with the cataphoric *as folowethe*, he seems to anticipate, in the manner of deictic projection, the future situation of someone reading the completed will for probate and execution after his death.

The 'after-death' condition also means that the testator himself cannot perform his bequests nor check whether they are correctly performed by the executor to whom the power to act is delegated by appointing him in the will. Again, it is a feature of many wills that the implicit trust involved in choosing an executor is made explicit by the expression of this trust and often an appeal to his honour:

> whom I [...] nominate, and appoynte my sole Executor of this my will, not doubtinge that he will reserve, and ymploy the same to the best benifitt he can, and that the same may redounde to the good of my sayd godson" (Richard Anguish, fellow of Corpus Christi, 1615, III, 316v).

> I do make master Bovell felow of our college and myne old frend the only doer and minister for me of my goods to dispose the same as well and as truly as charytye and conscience dothe requyre knowing assuredlye that he wyll doo for me on this case as I wolde doo for hym in the lyke moreouer he knoweth my mynde best bothe how I wolde and also wysshe that all thynges [...] pertayning to me shulde be ordered in my behalfe, not dowtyng but that he will deale vpryghtlye here in [...] I trust for owlde acquayntance specyally that master bovell yf he be alyve wyll do so myche at this my last request bothe for our owlde former famylyarytie and allso for charytye sake [...] but specyally I truste to see and speke with master bovell that he may know more of my mynde herein er I dye for his honestye doo I myche credytt and therefore I looke assuredlye that he

wyll satisfye my desyre herin. (Henry Dylcocke, fellow of Christ's College, 1551, I, 92r-92v)

The will of Henry Dylcocke offers in addition an example of incorporating into the will a brief mention of (intended) accompanying verbal acts which were meant to ensure that the testator's wishes were correctly understood: *but specyally I truste to see and speke with master bovell that he may know more of my mynde herein* may even make one think of a kind of second, oral version of the original written will (which was not dictated, but written by Dylcocke himself). Writing may be useful to fix the testator's words beyond doubt in the case of the will being disputed after his death, but the spoken word was, for Dylcocke, the obvious means to make his meaning quite clear.

Finally, as in each occurrence of the common bequest *formula I give/will and bequeath X to Y*, the utterance is necessarily made with the implication 'after my death'; the use of these verbs cannot be interpreted, in terms of speech acts, as explicitly performative; to utter this formula in the context of a will does not in itself perform the act of bequeathing. (In Dylcocke's will above, there is an indication of the testator's awareness of this in the use of the verb *dispose* not for the testator's act, but for that of the executor.) Here, the second basic institutional condition of wills, their free *revocability*, comes into play. Thus, bequests can only be performed by the executor after the testator's death, when there can be no new will. The changeability of a testator's opinions and wishes – and its legal recognition – is made strikingly clear by the valid second will of William Lewes (1584) which reads: *Now I am otherwise mynded, uppon some good consideracion not to bestowe upon my sister Rose alone my ringe or the remaynder of my gooddes* (II, 92r). Wills could be revoked by simply making a new will without referring to prior wills, or by explicitly performing the act of revoking in the new will, making thereby the abstract concept of *revocability* more palpable:

I william bosome [...] do make and ordayne this my last wyll and testament in maner and forme Folowing; hereby revokyng and disanullyng all former wylles and testamentes by me made. (William Bosom, apothecary, 1582, II, 87v)

I [...] do therfore renownce revoke and vtterlye disalowe all wyllis and testamentes heretofore by me made spokyn wryton or declaryd and make and declare [...] (George Crede, gentleman, 1559, II, 24r-24v)

In the second example, the testator makes excessive use of a strategy common in legal language, i.e. clustering more or less synonymous terms of the same wordclass to name the performance of a single speech act. It seems that testators who explicitly revoked former wills were well aware of the non-performative nature of uttering a bequest: they felt free to 're-allot' their property, and they did so not by expressing a revocation of the particular bequest, because a bequest had not been performed; it is the will which is revoked.

It is highly indicative of the 'peculiar' pragmatic aspects of will-making (or rather the conditions of the act of bequeathing and the use of the verb 'bequeath') that, in the few relevant pragmatic discussions there are, this verb is varyingly classified as a "postponing performative" (Finegan 1982: 119) and a (mere) "declaration of intention" (Kurzon 1986: 42), but also as a "declaration" in the sense of "saying makes it so" (Searle 1976) as well as an "exercitive" (Austin 1962: 142, 156) and alternatively as one of those expressions which are "used in naming the act which, in making such an utterance, I am performing" (Austin 1962: 32) – the last of which it is clearly not. Apart from the institutional revocability of a will, there is linguistic evidence in the form of variants of the formula *I will/give and bequeath*, e.g. *my will, and entente is that her child or Children shall have that legacye porcion, which* [...] (Swithin Butterfield, gentleman, 1611, III, 24v), which supports the view that, instead of performing the act of bequeathing, a testator merely declares his wish (i.e. his 'will').

There is a difference, then, between making a *will* (as a testator's declaration of his wishes, including the written record of it), which legally counts as a will from the moment the testator declares it to be his will: *I do (hereby) make and constitute this my present testament and last will in manner and form following,*[6] and making the *individual bequests* contained in the will, where no transfer of the right of property is effected at the moment of uttering them. Occasionally, this future aspect of the execution of a bequest is explicitly referred to in the wills: *my will is that he consider my poore schollers with some of my overworne apparell which shall **then** be attendinge vppon me*; [...] *to be payed within twoe monthes after my Deathe* (Robert Landesdale, fellow, 1602, III, 16v-17r; my emphasis).

The third basic institutional condition is that will-making is strictly *unilateral*, which means that the language of wills lacks any contractual quality. The three conditions mentioned are closely interrelated: because a will is unilateral, i.e. not binding upon the testator, it may be revoked; revoking means to make another will, which in turn is related, as we have seen, to the 'after death' condition: bequests can be performed only when the testator can no longer revoke his will.

In pragmatic terms, this property of being a unilateral legal act also means that the first person present tense use of the verbs *give, will, bequeath*, etc. in a will cannot count as having the force of a promise or indeed of any speech act at all by which the testator commits himself to the performance of a future action. As a consequence of this, the act of revoking a will cannot be seen as breaking a promise.

A particular linguistic feature of wills mirrors their status as a unilateral act; this is the absence of the use of second person pronouns. Wills have no addressee.[7] It is extremely rare that a testator betrays a different understanding of the situation by using a direct form of address. If we discard for the moment an instance in which Christ himself is addressed (where no second person pronoun is used: *Come Lord Jesus, come quickly*, John Allen, fellow of Gonville and Caius, 1625, III, 154r.), there is only one case in the corpus of 325 wills studied: *Edwarde I make you the disposer of that sum of money* (John Roper, fellow of Peterhouse, 1549, I, 87v).

The lack of an addressee raises, of course, the weighty question of the recipient(s) of wills. This touches directly upon the pragmatic problem of the uses and functions of wills in the 16th and 17th century with their occasional pieces of educational advice and exhortation as part of individual material bequests, but especially with their distinctive additional elements of confessing sinfulness, professing faith, quoting doctrines and the Bible, etc. For whom, or in the presence of whom, i.e. for which audience, were the acts of confessing, professing, demonstrating knowledge and 'correct' beliefs, etc. made?

The heirs (i.e. family members) and legatees are, legally speaking, the recipients only of the goods bequeathed, but not of the testamentary record itself (Spreckelmeyer 1977: 105). But instances of educational advice and exhortation expressed in several wills of the corpus seem to indicate that the testator himself thought of the heirs as being *somehow* the recipients not only of his material bequests of property and rights, but also of his 'last words'; yet he does not address heirs directly and therefore must have meant his 'last words' to be passed on to them by the will's 'real' recipient(s). Who can be thought to have fulfilled that role?

A competent person to admonish people and thus also to pass on testamentary (parental and husband's) advice and last words was the parish priest (or the minister). Very often, he was in a position to do that, as it was he who was commonly called upon to act as scribe for orally delivered wills (being a literate person close at hand, but also because wills were often made during the testator's last illness), and thus was at once audience and recipient of the dictated version and co-producer of the final, written version of the will.

Doubtless, the court of probate may also count as a recipient of the will insofar as it had to prove the will's validity. In the period under consideration, it is, however, highly probable that many wills were not submitted for probate at all to save the legal fees. For these wills, usually lost in the course of time, no answer can be given. In the case of the corpus of University wills, the Vice-Chancellor's court was authorised to prove, and retain (after 1540) the original will, of which it had two copies made, one for registration and one to be handed over to the executor together with the grant of probate. This copy served the executor as written authorisation and simultaneously as a basis or the list of instructions for his task of performing the bequests. Insofar as the copy of the will gave him the necessary information about what to give to whom, when, and under which conditions, the executor had an even greater claim to being considered as the legal recipient of the will. Is, then, the expression of a bequest to be performed (which is a declaration of his 'will' as far as the testator is concerned) a directive for the executor once the will was proved after the testator's death? Here again, the problem lies in the consistent avoidance of direct forms of address. An explicit directive, however, may be assumed to have accompanied the act of a court official handing over a copy of the will to the executor. I will come back to the question of the recipient of the will in the context of discussing the historical religious function of the will.

The three basic features of wills briefly illustrated and discussed here – in technical terms, that they are ambulatory, unilateral and revocable – all refer to the *legal* function of wills as an instrument to dispose of one's property after death. They have constituted the permanent distinctive legal properties of the English will since the 13th century, following the adoption of canonical law in this domain of individual right (Sheehan 1963: 140). As such, they distinguish the will proper (discussed here) more or less clearly from the earlier, Anglo-Saxon 'wills', i.e. various forms of the final disposition of property which were largely effective at the moment of making them, definitely contractual in nature, and to a certain extent irrevocable (Sheehan 1963: 140).

Whilst these legal properties themselves have remained the constant features of the English will, they nevertheless stimulated changes in some other factors of will-making in the past. Thus, after the vernacular began to make its appearance in wills at the end of the 14th century,[8] occasional explicit justifications of the use of English in wills point unmistakably towards the need for clarity on the part of the testator's words demanded by the 'after death' condition discussed above: *I ordeyne and make my testament in Englisshe tonge for my most profit, redyng and undirstanding.*[9] English finally superseded Latin as the language of wills in the Cambridge corpus in the first half of the

16th century, mirroring the rising status of English as an all-purpose language.[10] Or, to take a later example, the diffuse element of orality inherent in the frequent process of dictating wills rather than writing them with one's own hand faded with the growing expansion of literacy and the slow decline of the custom, still common in the 16th and 17th centuries, of making a will only when one was ill and felt death to be near.

The more conspicuous changes in the complexity and the range of use of wills in the post-Reformation period, however, cannot be traced to the influence of the permanent legal function of wills but to that of their second basic function, the historical religious function of wills.

3.   Will-making and the religious function of wills

The religious function of will-making originated with the interest of the church as the traditional guardian of a dying man's last words to look after his pious bequests and deathbed alms for the health of his soul. This combination of alms-giving and providing for the salvation of one's soul characterised will-making as a ritual act, which is strengthened by the fact that it was usually a cleric who wrote the wills of illiterate and seriously ill testators. Claiming that will-making was the duty of every true Christian according to the word of God: "put thine house in order: for thou shalt die and not live" (II Kings 20: 1), the church had a strong interest in securing and asserting authority in testamentary matters including the probate of wills in ecclesiastical courts. This control was gained before the end of the 12th century (Sheehan 1963).

Thus, after its emergence in the 13th century, the English will proper fulfilled two basic functions: the legal function of the disposal of property after death, and a distinct religious function. The Wills Act of 1857, which transferred the granting of probate from ecclesiastical courts to secular *district probate registeries*, eventually marked the formal termination of this second function of wills in England (after it had in practice already become less important in the century before).

The church's strong interest and also the testamentary control which it had won by the end of the 12th century account for the development of two legally effective conditions of will-making, which in turn had far-reaching pragmatic consequences for the astonishing development of the will and of will-making in the 16th and 17th centuries.

(1) The right to make a will was not the prerogative of people of a particular status or social class but, with the exception of married women and minors, insane people and certain categories of felons and heretics, persons

from all domains and levels of society were principally free to make a will (Swinburne 1590: f.34r-67v).

(2) In the interest of (1), formal requirements for making a valid will were kept to a minimum, including the linguistic form of the will: "Words and sentences are not required for the forme" (Swinburne 1590: f.190r-192v). Testators were not compelled to use particular testamentary formulae: "Much lesse ought it to bee preiudiciall to the testament, where in steede of the wordes omitted, other wordes of the same sense to such purpose are vsed and expressed" (Swinburne 1590: f.190r).

Both conditions are of pragmatic consequence insofar as they determine who was allowed to make a valid will and how free the testator was in expressing his last will individually.

In the 16th and 17th century, the effects of these conditions can clearly be seen. First, it shows in the broad range of the social status of testators and the number of wills made.[11] A quick succession of publications and reprints of law guides and of manuals on dying well, which included making one's will, did their own part in spreading the idea and the requisite knowledge of will-making, notably Thomas Becon's *The Sycke Mans Salue* (London 1561). This book, which in its subtitle addresses the familiar contemporary association of sickness and will-making (*wherein the faithfull Christins may learne both how to behaue themselves paciently and thankefully in the tyme of sickenes, and also vertuously to dispose their temporall goodes*), saw ten editions between 1561 and 1619 alone.[12]

Literary reflexes of the will and of will-making offer a more indirect indicator of the position which the matter of wills and testaments occupied in the minds of the contemporary public: not only did testamentary law play a conspicuous role in Elizabethan drama (Clarkson and Clyde 1942: 231ff.), but fictitious wills (or *testaments*) also constituted a recognisable poetic genre (Perrow 1914, Bach 1977, Bach 1982). The form of the will was also familiar and popular enough to serve as a vehicle for satirical and polemical writings, notably within the vast corpus of 17th century mass-distributed broadsides and pamphlets (Bach forthcoming).

The second effect I wish to mention is that the minimum of formal requirements allowed the insertion of additional elements like those emphasised by radical Protestant testators. This particular church-imposed condition of will-making was therefore an institutional prerequisite for the development of the will into the flexible instrument of fervent post-Reformation testators, just as the religious function as a whole served as the basis from which the changes of post-Reformation wills ultimately derived. Some of the changes mentioned above, which were promoted by these preconditions, are discussed in the following.

Like the use of the legal 'disposal of property' function, which expresses the testator's wish to make provisions for the welfare of his surviving dependants, the use of the religious function of wills was also strongly motivated by the testator's considerations of the time after his death. They found their commonest, most familiar expression in the testator's initial bequest of his soul to God. The development of the will to the stage represented by the bulk of the Cambridge corpus can already be seen in the different treatment of this single bequest of the soul by testators of traditional wills and by radical Protestants. Traditional testators usually follow a formulaic model of the bequest: first I bequeath my soul to almighty God my maker and to all the holy company of heaven.[13] Radical Protestant testators usually expand this formula to include the demonstration of biblical knowledge, the confession of and repentance for their sins, the profession of their faith, the expression of their assured hope of salvation and a prayer for strength of faith as in the will of Robert Landesdale, fellow, 1602:

> First I commende my soule to God the father God the sonne, and God the holye Ghoste; all is one God the glorie aequall the majestie toe eternall, from whence cometh Jesus Christ the immortable sonne of God the saviour of me, and all mankinde that beleeve in him whose blood was shedd and hath made an attonement for me, and synns with God the Father and for all mankinde that beleeve in him, as the holy writinges of the Bible given vnto vs do playnely show, soe that I am heartelye sorrye for my Sinns, and transgressions committed against him, and his holye word, Thus fixed to have a glorius resurrection when he shall come in his great glorye to Judge the quicke, and the deade, and his is my true, and vndoubted fayth, wherin god for his greate mercye sake stregthen me duringe this my naturall lyfe (III, 16v).

This raises again, as in the case of educational advice and exhortation discussed above, the questions of purpose and of recipients: with which intention, for whose ears and for which occasions are these speech acts made? They are different from educational advice and exhortation. These refer explicitly, by naming, to individual heirs as members of the familiy of the testator, and they are commonly integrated into the context of material bequests of household chattels, money, and titles to legal rights. This 'secular' or 'legal' part of the will was, moreover, commonly separated from the preceding religious part by a formulaic expression which marked the transition from the one to the other by containing expressions for both: *Concerninge my earthly goodes wherwith God hath blessed me I giue* [...] *to* [...] (William Fulke, Master of Pembroke, 1589, I, 112r).

The relevance of the questions asked becomes still more evident when the elements which expand the bequest of the soul are expressed not as a more or less integrate part of that bequest but as more clearly defined entities, almost constituents of the will in their own right, as the following examples from wills of the Cambridge corpus illustrate:

(1)   the profession of faith as a separate prayer:

I beleeve in god the father, god the sone, and god the holie ghost three persons but one eternall and ever-lyvyng god and I do fullie looke to be saved by thys my beleiff (Thomas Merburie, fellow-commoner, 1571, II, 62r)

(2)   the confession of having been a sinner:

the damnable pyt of Idolatry wherin I was plonged [...] I was most vnworthie yea which well deserved to have been 10 000 tymes vtterly reiected from him [...] all my stynkynge synnes [...]. (Robert Beaumont, Master of Trinity, Vice-Chancellor, 1567, II, 45r)

(3)   the display of theological knowledge:

everye man is of thees two partes soule and bodye the soulle being from heaven hevenly / the bodie made of the earthe and is earthlie. (Thomas Merburie, 1571, II, 62v)

(4)   quoting from the Bible:

When shall I heare that Joyfull voyce / come the blessed of my father inherite yee the kyngdome prepared for yow before the begynnynge of the worlde [...] acording to that saying of the profet David what man is he that lyveth and shall not see deathe [...] there is nothyng more vncertayne than the vncertayn howr of deathe, for whose cause we are admonished in the 24 of matthew continuallie to watche. (Thomas Merburie, 1571, II, 62r-63r)

(5)   joining in polemical controversy: assertion, refusal, and attack:

withowt all vayne opinion of any mans merites which I do vtterly reiecte, deteste and abhorre as mervellous Iniurious to the blude of my savior Jesus [...]. (Thomas Merburie, 1571, II, 62v)

Provyded that my buryall nor after there be no vayne Jangelynge of belles nor any other popishe ceremonyes or mystrustfull prayers as though my happye state with god were doubtefull. (Robert Beaumont, 1567, II, 45r-45v)

A rough, non-technical and idealised synopsis of the relevant parts of both the conventional will and the radical will shows their typical order within this type of private record:

conventional last will	radical last will
1) *preamble*	1) *preamble*
invocation of God	invocation of God
initial date	initial date
self-identification	self-identification
justification (= death close)	justification (=death close)
assertion of capacity to act	assertion of capacity to act
(= sound mind)	(= sound mind)
declaration of making will	declaration of making will
2) *'religious part'*	2) *'religious part'*
bequest of soul	bequest of soul
	profession of faith
	assertion of hope
	confession of sinfulness
	Bible quotations
	theological doctrines
	[polemical attack]
bequest of body	bequest of body
burial instructions	burial instructions
(elaborate)	(plain)
(RC) intercession and	
requiem mass	
3) *'secular bequests'*	3) *'secular bequests'*
	transitional formula incl.
	thanksgiving for
	possessions
individual bequests	individual bequests
[advice and admonition]	[advice and admonition]
appointment of executor	appointment of executor
[expression of trust]	[expression of trust]

4) *assertion and*	4) *assertion and*
confirmation of	*confirmation of*
authenticity	*authenticity*
scribal statement	scribal statement
signature	signature
end date	end date
witnesses	witnesses

The best approach, probably, to an explanation of the linguistic choices of radical Protestant testators is to consider will-making an art. Indeed, much of the pragmatics of will-making in 16th and 17th century England can be better understood with the conceptualisation of the testator *performing* an art.

To talk of will-making as an art does not mean, of course, that wills were governed by poetic principles: as far as the legal function was concerned, the foremost linguistic requirement asked of the testator was simply to express his bequests as clearly and unambiguously as possible (Swinburne 1590: 244v-248v, 261, Sheehan 1963: 177). The making of a will, i.e. of a personal document *mortis causa*, was an art because of its close association with the deathbed situation – will-making being typically postponed until the last sickness[14] – and hence with the traditional *Art of Dying Well* in the presence of witnesses.[15]

'To die well' in the turbulent age of the Reformation and its aftermath in England meant the demonstration of whatever behaviour – *verbal* behaviour – was expected by one's brethren within a particular Protestant group or sect (Duffy 1992: 322ff.). 'Dying well' presupposes the presence of witnesses, which gave will-making the quality of being part of the procedure of dying. Thomas Becon's *The Sycke Mans Salue*, the influential, strongly Protestant manual of conduct in times of illness and dying, expressly shows this in a fictitious dialogue. His model character Epaphroditus prepares for making his will only when he feels that he will not recover. He then begins, in the presence of neighbours, to demonstrate in an exemplary way his belief, emphasising these elements: the confession of his sins, a prayer for mercy, the expression of assured hope of belonging to the elect of God, the profession of faith, and repentance, and concluding with dictating his last will: *neighbours all, I think it best even out of hand to dispose my temporal possessions, and to set an order in such worldly goods as God hath lent me* (Becon 1561: 116).

Does practice, i.e. the wills themselves, in any way confirm what Becon sets forth as an ideal model? In the Cambridge wills studied, a semi-public function of will-making is indeed made clearly evident by the expressions which testators choose in the religious parts of their wills. Edmund Perpoynte, B.D., clerk, and Master of Jesus College, begins his will after the invocation of God with: *Be it knowen to all chrysten people that I* [...] (1556, I101v). Thomas Merburie states public demonstration as a function of his will explicitly:

> [I] deliberatelie do ordeyne and make this my present testament conteynyng my last wyll wherbye god wyllynge yt shalbe evident to all that duryng my lieffe I held the profession and beleif of a trew christian man. (1571, II, 62r-62v)

How should the testator's explicit wish of publicly demonstrating and professing his faith by his will come true if not through an *audience* either at his will-making or at a public reading of his will? The same question is provoked by the presence of the other elements of radical Protestants' wills listed above: quoting the Bible, quoting doctrines, etc. Who should benefit from this? The number of persons present at the will-making, whose names are listed at the end of a will, usually surpasses the conventionally required two witnesses and is thus evidence of at least one kind of potential audience. The will of the fervent Protestant Richard Robynson, barber (1569), contains the wish for an audience to be exhorted and taught on the occasion of the testator's death and burial; it is evidence of propagating, by will, those doctrines especially embraced by the godly:

> And within the same churche a sermon to be made by some godly learned man which at my buryall wyll teache and exhorte the people vnto the feare of god / repentaunce of the former lyeffe / faythe / and trust in the bloude of Jesus Christ (II, 56v-57r)

Further evidence has been adduced in a study of Puritan wills from the cognitive point of view (Bach 1992). There it is argued that the particular structuring and the linguistic choices of the religious parts of Puritan wills facilitate the comprehension and retention of their contents by a listening audience.

The combination of demonstrating the art of dying well with the act of making a will underlines the ritual character of will-making mentioned earlier. If this is taken together with the conventional invocation of God at the beginning of virtually all wills and the inclusion of prayers in many of the radical Protestant wills, then this indicates that for these testators, the audience also included an invisible witness, especially if there is a directly addressed request as in the will of John Allen, 1625 (III, 154r): *come Lord Jesus come quickly*.

4.   Conclusion

To conclude the discussion of some of the more conspicuous pragmatic aspects of will-making in the post-Reformation period in England, I want to turn briefly to the question of the relation, as it becomes evident in the texts themselves, between the two basic functions of wills, which in this discussion were treated under the separate headings of 'legal' and 'religious' functions.

The pragmatic approach to will-making, for one thing, throws light upon a basic difference between the two functions. Whereas the essential speech act expressed within the frame of the legal function, the act of *bequeathing*, has been shown to be a 'postponing' act, an act not performed by uttering it, this postponing quality does not apply to the speech acts expressed within the frame of the religious function. Here, expressing gratitude towards God, asking God for mercy, professing one's faith, asserting one's assured hope of belonging to God's elect, etc. are all acts which are in this context performed by making the utterance. The power to perform these acts cannot readily be delegated and thus postponed, because they are essentially personal. This argument holds especially for the beliefs of Protestant testators with their strict refusal of, e.g., invoking the intercession by saints of requiem masses (having others pray for their souls), and finally of their understanding of the office of the *pastor* as shepherd: not as ordained and consecrated priests, bishops and the pope, but ministers (see Davies 1970). It was an essential part of their practised belief to stress the individual, personal and direct nature of man's relationship to God, which also becomes visible in their demand that everybody read the Bible for themselves in the vernacular, which in turn was one reason for their emphasis on furthering education and literacy, and which had no place for the idea of *locum tenens* and intermediary.

However, it is also clear from many expressions in the wills studied that the testators did not emphasise the distinction between the 'legal' and the 'religious' parts of their wills, but on the contrary, established linguistic links. One of these is the transitional formula mentioned above, which mediates between the religious part and the series of material bequests of possessions to heirs and legatees. These latter worldly possessions are, in the radically Protestant wills of the corpus, invariably attributed to the grace of God shown towards the individual testator. This is done by explicitly thanking God for them, drawing God into the legal affairs of the law of property.

In a similar way, reference to God establishes a link between both functions at the beginning of wills. It is a common feature of the wills studied that the testator refers to situational factors of the act of will-making not only by naming the persons present, but also, in an act of self-reference, by making statements on his bodily and on his mental condition at the time of making his will. The statement of being of 'sound mind' has in this context the illocutionary force of asserting that one of the institutional conditions of making a valid will is fulfilled. It is thus a matter of the legal function of wills. Yet here, too, we find reference to God in the usual formula of expressing gratitude for the healthy state of mind.

These examples may not seem weighty evidence, but acts of reference to God are especially telling in this context, because it was in the many references to God – in prayers, in even directly addressing him – that the ritual aspect of will-making (i.e. being considered part of the *Art of Dying Well*), which was perhaps the most spectacular manifestation of the will's religious function, found its verbal expression.

Notes

1. Probate Records of the Vice-Chancellor's Court, University Archives, University Library, Cambridge, *Wills* II, 46v.
2. See, e.g., the will of Sir Andrew Perne, Master of Peterhouse, 1589, II, 116v-117r.
3. Probate records of the Vice-Chancellor's Court, University Archives, Cambridge (*Wills* I-V). The complete archives index of trades, professions and status of testators contains 77 different terms. See also Roberts 1927.
4. Danet (1985), Fisher and Todd, eds. (1986), Finegan (1982), Kurzon (1984), (1986). Both Austin (1962) and Searle (1976) briefly mention the performative use of *bequeath*.
5. Bach (1992), Spufford (1974), Danet and Bogoch (1992).
6. This is a typical formula. Expressions vary in the wills, e.g. *I* [...] *do make, and ordeine this my present Testament, and last will* (Robert Landesdale, fellow, 1602, III, 16v). The argument also holds, of course, for the act of 'un-making' a will, i.e. revoking it.
7. Spreckelmeyer (1977: 96, 105); Finegan (1982: 115).
8. The earliest English-language wills which have been published are of 1383 (*Testamenta Eboracensia or Wills Registered at York* [...], *I* (Surtees Society IV). London 1836: 185) and 1387 (*The Fifty Earliest English Wills in the Court of Probate, London, A.D. 1387 - 1439*, ed. F. J. Furnivall, London 1882 (EETS 78)).
9. Anne, countess of Stafford, 1438 (quoted after Jacob, ed. 1938: 596).
10. Of the 315 wills registered there between 1502 and 1596, 22 are in Latin; of these, 21 were made before 1527, the last Latin will is of 1549.

11. Thus, in London, Cambridge, Lincoln and Norwich alone, some 125.000 wills from the end of the 14th to the end of the 16th century have survived in archives (Bach 1977: 30).
12. Others are by Swinburne (1590), Perkins (1595), Sutton (1601).
13. See, for instance, the wills of Henry Veesy, apothecary, 1503, I, 4r and of Oliver Aynesworth, fellow, 1546, I, 78r.
14. This is proved by the conventional self-reference which overwhelmingly included the statement of *being sick in body*. The comparison of the dates of making the testament and of granting probate further confirms this: this time-span for the Cambridge wills is only a matter of weeks and months, with few exceptions.
15. See, e.g., Beaty (1970). Distinctly Protestant books of advice are Becon (1561), Perkins (1595), and Sutton (1601).

Manuscript Source

Probate Records of the Vice-Chancellor's Court. University Archives, Cambridge. *Wills* I-V.

References

Austin, John L.
　　1962　　*How to do Things with Words.* 2nd ed., repr. Oxford: Oxford University Press.
Bach, Ulrich
　　1977　　*Das Testament als literarische Form. Versuch einer Gattungsbestimmung auf der Grundlage englischer Texte.* (Düsseldorfer Hochschulreihe 3). Düsseldorf: Stern.
　　1982　　*Kommentierte Bibliographie englischer literarischer Testamente vom 14. bis zum 20. Jahrhundert.* (Anglistische Forschungen 163). Heidelberg: Winter.
　　1992　　"From private writing to public oration: the case of Puritan wills: Cognitive discourse analysis applied to the study of genre change." In: Dieter Stein (ed.). *Cooperating with Written Texts: The Pragmatics and Comprehension of Written Texts.* (Studies in Anthropological Linguistics 5). Berlin/New York: Mouton de Gruyter, 417-436.
　　forthc.　　*Titelstruktur und Rezipientenwissen bei englischen Flugtexten des 17. Jahrhunderts: Linguistische Untersuchungen zu Strategien der Verstehenslenkung bei einem frühen Massenkommunikationsmittel.* Heidelberg: Winter.

Beaty, Nancy L.
1970   *The Craft of Dying. A Study in the Literary Tradition of the "Ars Moriendi"*
           in England. New Haven/London: Yale Universtiy Press.

Becon, Thomas
1561   *The Sycke Mans Salue. Wherin the faithfull Christians may learne* [...] *to*
           dispose their temporal goodes [...]. London.

Camp, Anthony J.
1974   *Wills and their whereabouts*. 4th edn., revised and extended. London: The
           Author.

Clarkson, Paul S., and T. Warren Clyde
1942   *The Law of Property in Shakespeare and the Elizabethan Drama*.
           Baltimore: Johns Hopkins Press.

Coward, Barry
1991   *Cromwell*. (Profiles in Power). London: Longman.

Danet, Brenda
1985   "Legal discourse." In: Teun A. van Dijk (ed.). *Handbook of Discourse*
           Analysis, I. London: Academic Press, 273-291.

Danet, Brenda, and Bryna Bogoch
1992   "From oral ceremony to written document: the transitional language of
           Anglo-Saxon wills." *Language and Communication* 12, 95-122.

Davies, Horton
1970   *Worship and Theology in England: From Cranmer to Hooker 1534-1603*.
           Princeton, N. J.: Princeton University Press.

Duffy, Eamon
1992   *The Stripping of the Altars: Traditional Religion in England 1400-1580*.
           New Haven/London: Yale University Press.

Finegan, Edward
1982   "Form and function in testament language." In: Robert J. Di Pietro (ed.).
           Linguistics and the Professions. (Advances in Discourse Processes VIII).
           Norwood, NJ.: Ablex, 113-120.

Fisher, Sue, and Alexandra D. Todd (eds.)
1986   *Discourse and Institutional Authority: Medicine, Education, and Law*.
           (Advances in Discourse Processes XIX). Norwood, NJ: Ablex.

France, R. Sharpe
1965   "Wills." *History* 50, 36-39.

Jacob, Ernest F. (ed.)
1938   *Wills proved before the Archbishop or his Commissaries. The Register of*
           Henry Chichele: Archbishop of Canterbury 1414-1443, II. Oxford:
           Clarendon Press.

Kurzon, Dennis
    1984   " Themes, hyperthemes and the discourse structure of British legal texts."
            Text 4, 31-55.
    1986   *It is hereby performed ...: Explorations in Legal Speech Acts.* (Pragmatics
            & Beyond VII: 6). Amsterdam: John Benjamins.
Leedham-Green, Elizabeth S. (ed.)
    1991   *Religious Dissent in East Anglia.* Cambridge: Cambridge Antiquarian
            Society.
Perkins, William
    1595   *A Salve for a Sicke Man: or, A Treatise Containing the Nature, Differences,
            and Kindes of Death; as also the Right Manner of Dying Well* [...].
            Cambridge.
Perrow, Eber C.
    1914   " The last will and testament as a form of literature." *Transactions of the
            Wisconsin Academy of Sciences, Arts and Letters* 7, 682-753.
Porter, Henry C.
    1958   *Reformation and Reaction in Tudor Cambridge.* Cambridge: CUP.
[Roberts, H.]
    1927   *Calendar of Wills proved in the Vice-Chancellor's Court at Cambridge,
            1501-1765.* Cambridge.
Searle, John R.
    1976   "A classification of illocutionary acts." *Language in Society* 5, 1-23.
Sheehan, Michael M.
    1963   *The Will in medieval England: From the Conversion of the Anglo-Saxons to
            the End of the Thirteenth Century.* (Studies and Texts 6). Toronto:
            Pontifical Institute of Medieval Studies.
Spreckelmeyer, Goswin
    1977   " Zur rechtlichen Funktion frühmittelalterlicher Testamente." In: Peter
            Claassen (ed.). *Recht und Schrift im Mittelalter.* Sigmaringen: Thorbecke,
            91-113.
Spufford, Margaret
    1971   " The Scribes of Villagers' Wills in the Sixteenth and Seventeenth
            Centuries, and their Influence." *Local Population Studies* 7, 28-43.
    1974   *Contrasting Communities.* Cambridge: CUP.
Sutton, Christopher
    1601   *Disce Mori. Learne to Die.* London.
Swinburne, Henry
    1590   *A briefe Treatise of Testaments and last Willes.* London.

Justifying Grammars
A Socio-Pragmatic Foray into the Discourse Community of Early English Grammarians

Richard J. Watts
University of Berne

1.   Introduction

The heyday of English grammar writing began in the late sixteenth century, reached its peak at the end of the seventeenth and the first half of the eighteenth century to tail off slowly throughout the second half of the eighteenth century. The motivation for writing grammars of the English language did not, of course, remain stable throughout these two centuries.

Would-be grammarians in the sixteenth century were concerned just as much with general pedagogical principles in the spirit of Richard Mulcaster and Roger Ascham[1] as they were with codifying the vernacular so that it could compete not only with Latin but also with other European vernaculars such as French, Italian and Spanish. Indeed, the major problem for those writing on English during this century was to achieve some form of standardisation of the orthography.[2]

Some of the pedagogical predilections of the sixteenth century grammarians are echoed in the work of those writing in the first two decades of the seventeenth. However, as the century progressed, grammar writing became more involved in the search for universals,[3] in the formulation of 'rules' for English which would, at the same time, retain what was felt to be 'universal' in the grammatical description of Latin and yet be appropriate to the very different structures of English,[4] and in the writing of grammars which would be accessible to non-native speakers of English.

Grammar writing from around 1720 on concentrates once again on the presumed excellence of the classical languages, in particular Latin, and follows the Enlightenment trend towards the propagation of classical, Latinate prose to which learners should aspire as a standard model of written English.[5] The trend towards exemplifying 'good' structure and style by quoting from well-known authors, which has its tentative beginnings in the seventeenth century, now becomes a regular feature of grammar writing and culminates in Bishop Lowth's tendency to exemplify not only what is 'good' from well-known authors, but also what he considers 'bad'. Grammar writing, in a word, becomes well and truly prescriptive and, at least within the educational framework, has remained so, explicitly or implicitly, ever since.

Yet despite these rather significant shifts in perspective, there remain very interesting and, from the point of view of discourse analysis and pragmatics, very illuminating similarities which lead me to posit that grammar writers in English during this period represent a discourse community reflecting an increasing degree of social institutionalisation within education and the academic world which remained unchallenged until the twentieth century in Britain. The first similarity is that all of the grammars during the period from the end of the sixteenth to the end of the eighteenth century, with the possible exceptions of Ben Jonson's and John Wallis' grammars, are explicitly addressed either to the learners or to the teachers (universally in this case 'schoolmasters'). The second similarity consists in the belief that learning the principles of English is a pedagogical prerequisite for learning Latin. The third similarity is that all the grammars, although not always to the same extent, are concerned with extolling the excellence of the English language compared with other European vernaculars or even with Latin and Greek. In the sixteenth and seventeenth centuries this need appears to be greater than in the latter half of the eighteenth, and this fact can be correlated with the increase in Britain's imperial power during that century.

Undoubtedly, the writing of grammars for English has been a major component in the codification of modern standard written English, but it has to be studied within the wider historical framework of the rise of the idea of the nation-state in Britain and the political and educational processes which helped to form that idea. In other words, studying the writing of grammars of English is not simply a study in linguistics. Looked at from that point of view only, it becomes almost trivial. It is rather part of a wider socio-historical study of those processes through which the uniquely European idea of a nation develops.[6] Despite the differences in perspective over the two centuries which I am considering in this paper, the discourse community of grammar writers possesses a common set of socio-communicative objectives and uses a common core of discourse strategies.

During this paper I shall consider one of the major problems for grammar writers, all of whom (at least to my knowledge) were male, which was to define an audience for themselves. Who were they addressing, the potential 'learners' of English grammar, those whose sons needed instruction in English grammar, schoolmasters, etc.? Why were they addressing them and what did they imagine gave them the right to do so?

Most of the grammars during this period contained letters or addresses to the reader, which were frequently, but by no means always, labelled 'preface' and many also contained a dedication to a patron who supported the grammar writer or whose support he hoped to obtain. They were all given lengthy expository titles. It is in these prefatory sections and lengthy titles that the common core of discourse strategies can be identified, and it is these which I shall examine in more detail in this paper. Some of those discourse strategies were of course part of other written genres of the period, but certainly the parts of the prefatory sections dealing with the nature of grammar, the excellence of the English tongue, the reading public envisaged for the grammars, etc., are, I shall argue, symptomatic of the sense of a discourse community of grammar writers.

In the following section I shall list those grammars I have consulted, which represent only a subsection of all the grammars of English written from around 1580 till around 1780, and shall discuss what kinds of prefatory material are to be found in them. I shall restrict myself only to these sections and refrain from commenting on the texts of the grammars themselves, since I believe that there are various levels of communication involved in the writing, publishing and reading of any text which are realised in other textual sections than the body of the text itself. In section 3 I shall therefore elucidate the discourse analytical and pragmalinguistic principles on which my analysis of a reduced selection of four examples from the corpus will be undertaken in section 4. In section 5 I shall summarise the results of the analysis. In particular I shall argue that we cannot properly understand the nature of our work as linguists, discourse analysts, literary critics, etc. if we do not carry out a dispassionate socio-historical analysis of how the object of our research came to look the way it does to us today. In the last resort, the paper is thus a study of the historicity of the social institutionalisation of our own academic disciplines.

2.   Data base of grammars

Strictly speaking, not all of the works published between 1580 and 1780 which purport to be 'grammars' of the English language can really be considered

grammars if we take a grammar to represent as full a description as possible of
the structures of the English language. Some are termed 'grammatical essays',
others are surveys of certain points of English which cause the learner of Latin
problems when translating from English into Latin, others are in effect
grammars of Latin which begin with a survey of grammatical problems in
English, and still others deal in detail with certain specific areas of English
grammar.

In addition, it is wise to move away from the notion of grammar during
the historical period under discussion as a 'description' of structures. Most
grammars were constructed on the model of Latin grammars, in particular that
of Lily's influential school grammar of 1549, beginning with a list of
pronunciations for the various graphemes of English,[7] continuing with two
lengthy sections on the noun and the verb and shorter sections on what were
then taken to be the six other parts of speech (adjectives, pronouns, participles,
prepositions, conjunctions and interjections), and often, but certainly not
always, ending with a brief section on 'syntax', this term relating far more to
morphological problems and certain quirks of complex sentence structure than
what present-day linguists understand by the term.

The richest source for writings on the English language in the period from
1500 to 1800, including grammars of English, is Alston's *English Linguistics
1500–1800: A Collection of Facsimile Reprints* (1967-1972). My observations
have been drawn from a selected subset of 16 grammars taken from this series.
The selection is a fairly random subset of those available to me at the time of
writing this paper, except that I have deliberately left out Bullokar's grammar of
1580, Charles Butler's grammar of 1633, which is written entirely in a revised
morphemic orthography for English, John Wallis' *Grammatica Linguæ
Anglicanæ* (1653), which was written in Latin under the auspices of the Royal
Society, and Lindley Murray's influential grammar of 1810. The grammars I
have chosen are perhaps less well-known (with the exception of Lowth's), but
they offer a fairly good picture of the discourse strategies common to grammar
writers during the seventeenth and eighteenth centuries.

In chronological order of publication, the 16 grammars studied are listed
as follows:

John Hewes. 1624. *A Perfect Survey of the English Tongue*.
Ben Jonson. 1640. *The English Grammar*.
Joshua Poole. 1646. *The English Accidence*.
Guy Miège. 1688. *The English Grammar*.
Joseph Aickin. 1693. *The English Grammar*.
Richard Johnson. 1706. *Grammatical Commentaries*.

Charles Gildon and John Brightland.1711. *A Grammar of the English Tongue.*

James Greenwood. 1711. *An Essay towards a Practical English Grammar.*

Michael Maittaire. 1712. *The English Grammar.*

Hugh Jones. 1724. *An Accidence to the English Tongue.*

John Entick. 1728. *Speculum Latinum.*

Daniel Duncan. 1731. *A New English Grammar.*

anonymous. 1733. *The English Accidence.*

Samuel Saxon. 1737. *The English Scholar's Assistant.*

James White. 1761. *The English Verb.*

Robert Lowth. 1762. *A Short Introduction to English Grammar.*

In these works there are 8 types of prefatory material, a title page which tends to become shorter in the second half of the eighteenth century, a dedication to a patron, a dedication to the reader or possible user(s) of the work, comments on the work by third persons, various quotations generally in Latin, complimentary verse in praise of the author, a preface, the approbation of the censor. The order in which these appear is as follows:

1. Approbation of censor
2. Title page
3. Dedication to a patron *or* dedication to the reader/user
4. Comments on the work by third persons *or* various quotations *or* complimentary verse
5. Preface

No author indulges himself to the extent of using all five types of prefatory material. However, if we discount the approbation of the censor, which only occurs in the Gildon and Brightland work and is in any case rather exceptional, there are only two authors who make use of the remaining four categories, John Hewes (title page, dedication to the Bishop of London, various verses [largely Latin], and a preface), Richard Johnson (title page, testimonials on Johnson by third persons, a dedication to the schoolmasters who are expected to use the work entitled *Ludorum in Anglia Magistris* and a preface). Only 6 authors make use of two categories, Joshua Poole (title page and address to the reader), Michael Maittaire (title page and preface), Hugh Jones (title page and dedication to a patron), John Entick (title page and address to the possible users, which is in effect rather like a preface), the anonymous author of *The English Accidence* (1733) (title page and preface), Samuel Saxon (title page and preface) and Robert Lowth (title page and preface). Hence, 10 of the 16 authors make use of three or more kinds of prefatory material. 13 of the 16

Richard J. Watts

authors make use of a preface of some kind (14 if we count John Entick's address to the possible users).

Table 1 gives an overview of the kinds of prefatory material used by each author:

Table 1: *Types of prefatory text per author*

Author	Appro-bation of censor	Title page	Dedica-tion to patron	Dedica-tion to reader	Com-ments on work	Various quota-tions	Compli-mentary verse	Preface
Hewes		x	x			x		x
Jonson		x				x		x
Poole		x		x				
Miège		x		x				x
Aickin		x					x	x
Johnson		x		x	x			x
Gildon/Bright-land	x	x	x					x
Greenwood		x	x					x
Maittaire		x						x
Jones		x	x					
Entick		x						x
Duncan		x	x					x
anonymous		x						x
Saxon		x						x
White		x	x					x
Lowth		x						x

The table shows quite clearly that, apart from the title page, the most important type of prefatory text is the preface, and that, within at least 5 of the texts from 1711 on, some form of dedication to a patron is thought to be necessary; in the case of Hugh Jones it replaces a preface. Throughout the seventeenth century and the first decade of the eighteenth we meet only one case of a dedication to a possible patron (John Hewes). In three cases, however, we do see a dedication to the reader or possible user of the work (Poole, who like Jones omits a preface, Miège and Johnson). It is also significant that all other forms of prefatory material (comments on the work and testimonials by third persons, various quotations, complimentary verse) are not to be found beyond 1706.

The three most important forms of prefatory text are therefore, in order of their frequency of occurrence, the title page, the preface and the dedication to a patron or the reader/user. It is within these texts that common discourse strategies are to be found, indicating that we are in fact dealing with a discourse community, but it is also within these texts that changes in perspective and point of view are revealed which indicate significant changes in the socio-cultural role that grammar writers fulfil and the socio-political function that the writing of grammars of English has. Since it is not possible to analyse all 16 texts in detail, I have chosen 4, which I consider illustrative of different periods in the two hundred years of grammar writing that I am considering. The grammars I have chosen are those by Hewes (1624), Miège (1688), Jones (1724) and White (1761), and in section 4 I shall explain my reasons for choosing this subset. In the following section, however, I shall discuss the communicative significance of the three kinds of prefatory text from the point of view of a socio-pragmatic model of the writer-reader relationship in printed book-length texts.

3.   A socio-pragmatic model of prefatory texts

The normal procedure in reading a printed book-length text is to ignore, or perhaps pay only scant attention to, any printed information prior to the introductory chapter and after the final concluding chapter. The impression is often that we are in some sense communicating with the author, or at least s/he with us, through the language printed on the pages that make up the book.

Depending upon our idea of the concept 'communication', we will interpret what we think is going on in the reading process in rather different ways. The conduit metaphor of communication, which is still commonly accepted and propagated, might lead us to believe that there are messages, intentions, ideas, etc., which the author wishes to transfer to potential readers by putting them in the form of written language. If we look at language in terms of dialogic structure, i.e. that all language implies an utterer and a hearer, we might prefer to think of the writing/reading process in terms of a social contract (cf. Grice's cooperative principle), in terms of deriving inferences which most closely fit the cognitive patterns we are forming during the reading, etc.

Whatever we are doing as readers, however, is embedded in a very complex socio-communicative process involving the author, critics to whom the author may have sent preliminary drafts of the manuscript, the publisher, the printer, some notion of the 'ideal' readership which the author may have in mind, a patron, who lends her/his moral weight to the efforts of the author to have the manuscript published, possibly also a financial sponsor, and, today at least, an advertiser and/or public relations expert. What we read is the end product of a long and often complex process in which the author's original 'voice' has been modified, edited, changed, etc. so that finally it is really only a figment of the reader's imagination, a fiction. It might therefore be necessary for the original author to address other people than merely the imagined reader, or to allow others to address her/him or the potential readership; hence what is included between the covers of the printed work represents a number of different communicative levels.

Work on oral narratives has criticised the tendency to isolate the narrative from the rest of the discourse and to analyse it as if that discourse in which it is embedded fulfilled no further function in relation to our understanding of the narrative itself. We need to know where a narrative occurs in the total verbal interaction so that we can relate it to topics that have preceded it and those which spring from it. We need to know what role a narrative plays for the narrator and the narratee(s). Is it simply for entertainment? Is it used to exemplify some aspect of the topic, to support an argument position? Is it a flashback into the personal past experiences of the narrator? And if so, why is that flashback necessary? Is a narrative really only told by one person, the unique narrator her/himself, or is the narratee not also just as much a co-creator of the narrative? The narratee may actually contribute significantly to the creation of the narrative by taking over the narrative line at certain points, or by adding important background information, or simply by encouraging the narrator to continue.

Work of this kind can show that narratives do not just occur in verbal interaction out of the blue. Something that has been said may remind a potential narrator of an event which deserves to be told as a relevant contribution to the overall discourse. The potential narrator may then put in a bid for floor space to tell the narrative, but only get to tell it at a later stage in the interaction. Narratives have to be introduced by various types of conversational gambit to give the other participants a chance to reject the offer. They thus have to be presented briefly and in an interesting way. At the conclusion of a narrative the participants have somehow to return to the normal give and take of verbal interaction, and this can be achieved in a variety of ways, including an assessment of the discourse validity of the narrative by the narrator her/himself. The narrative may be commented on or assessed by other participants.

My argument here is that an analogous process is at work in the publishing world. The wider discourse within which a published grammar of English has to be evaluated in the discourse of education at the time the work is published and the place that the grammar can be seen to have in relation to other previous grammars and works on language are important factors in interpreting it.

Beyond that, of course, the discourse of education is always a socio-political form of discourse which will have greater or less value in the language market-place from one culture to the next and from one age to the next. At the beginning of the seventeenth century educational issues were still very much in the minds of writers on the English language, but those issues were seen to have more to do with the codification of English and its status in relation to Latin than with using English as a conscious symbol of social excellence and a way of unifying the 'nation' and justifying its imperial expansion.

I shall argue that the title page of the grammar is the type of prefatory text which embeds it within this wider discourse and that as the period progresses we can identify certain significant changes in this part of the prefatory discourse which reflect changes in attitudes towards language in education away from the pedagogical concerns of the sixteenth and early seventeenth century, through the didactic concerns of the late seventeenth century towards the imperialist concerns of the second half of the eighteenth century.

The dedication to a patron does not appear to have an analogy in the oral situation discussed above, although it is perfectly logical if we consider the complexity of the publishing process. To appear in print and be seen by the reader to enjoy the patronage of a socially important person can help to enhance the prestige and authority of the author and may even boost the sales. The communication with the patron is generally in the form of a letter and is for the benefit of the reader even if s/he is not addressed directly.

The address to the reader(s) or potential user(s) of the work is equivalent to remarks made by the would-be narrator to the potential narratee(s) such as conversational gambits, preemptive bids for floor-space, etc. But although the addressee is presumed to be the same at this point and during the text of the grammar, the levels of address are different. In the case of the prefatory address to the reader, the author is attempting to make his text appear important and readable to the reader. The reader can, of course, discontinue the reading process after reading the address; s/he can consider that reading the text of the grammar is not going to be worth the effort in much the same way as the potential narratee can indicate to the would-be narrator that the conversational gambit used to gain 'permission' to tell the narrative does not warrant its telling. In effect, this very rarely happens, and in much the same way the address to the reader is either not read or does not generally prevent the reader from continuing. Nevertheless, the discourse strategy of giving the addressee at least an opportunity to reject the offer is a tactically clever move. It places the responsibility into the addressee's hands, i.e. it appears to turn over the power of decision making to the addressee. On the other hand, rejecting the offer is a very face-threatening move to make, and will thus hardly ever be made.

Testimonials and comments by third persons which are presented as prefatory material are equivalent in the oral situation to comments made during and after the narrative by the narratee(s). They also serve the purpose of testifying to the quality of the work in much the same way as the advertising blurb on the dust-covers of present-day books. It is in this functional category that various lines of verse chosen by the author (or perhaps even by the printer and/or publisher?) and complimentary verses on the author also belong. The point that needs to be explained in the case of grammars of English in the period from c.1580 to c.1780 is why none of this sort of prefatory material appears in grammars printed after 1706. The answer that readily springs to mind is that during the eighteenth century grammar writers do not consider it necessary to justify what they are doing by advancing the good opinions of third persons, i.e. that grammar writing has become a necessary and generally accepted part of educational discourse. However, since I shall not be concerned with analysing this type of prefatory material in the present paper, I shall leave the question open for the time being.

Apart from the title page, the most common type of prefatory text in the corpus of grammars looked at (14 out of 16) is the preface itself, and it is at this point that the comparison with oral narratives does not offer us a clear analogue. As we shall see in section 4, it is in the preface that the author goes to great lengths to justify the effort of writing a grammar of English and expecting it to be read and possibly even used regularly as a basis for instruction. Statements are made about the need for a grammar, and particularly about the need for one which is structured in the way that the grammar being presented is structured. Time is spent indicating the target group of learners for whom the grammar has been constructed, and suggestions of a didactic kind are often made. The ultimate goals of writing a grammar of English are spelt out for the potential reader. If we consider the large number of English grammars written in the period under consideration – and the 16 studied are only a small subset – it becomes obvious that each new grammar needed to be seen as offering something uniquely different from the others. The potential readership was, after all, considerably smaller than today's. In one way, therefore, the preface fulfils an advertising function.

Apart from these didactic and pedagogical aspects, however, the underlying discourse topic is always admiration and praise for the English language. Time and again its supposed virtues over other languages are extolled, its history is recounted (often wrongly), its positive attributes are listed, etc. The basic discourse is in reality political in that English is being moulded into a standard 'language'. It is being shaped into a monolithic, supposedly perfect and therefore unchangeable unit in order to serve as a potent symbol representing what was (and still is) a mythical socio-political unit and the values of those in control of that polity.

My argument here is, therefore, that in much the same way as a narrative needs to be looked at in terms of the overall discourse in which it is embedded, so too do the different sections of a printed book relate in different ways to different aspects of the overall discourse in which it is embedded. The different sections of a printed work must be looked at on different communicative levels and the totality of the text seen in terms of a core and different levels of periphery, the latter ensuring connections with other significant discourses beyond the work.

In section 4 I shall analyse in more detail the title pages, dedications to patrons and readers, and prefaces of four grammars of English, those by Hewes, Miège, Jones and White. Apart from showing how these differ through time, I shall also be concerned to indicate features of this basic discourse which are common to all four grammars and which emerge more clearly as we move towards the latter half of the eighteenth century.

4.   An analysis of the prefatory texts in four selected grammars

In this section I shall examine the prefatory texts of the four grammars chosen in more detail to determine where the differences between them lie, but, more importantly, what similarities they display over a time span of almost two hundred years. I shall not take each grammar separately, but shall concentrate in the first subsection on differences and similarities in the title pages. I shall then move on to a detailed analysis of the dedicatory texts in all four grammars, in Hewes, Jones and White the dedication to a supposed patron and in Miège the dedication to the reader.

The analysis will focus on the kinds of illocutionary act made by the author and, where different, the underlying illocutionary force in each 'utterance', the propositional content of the utterances, their participant design and discourse function. These terms will be briefly explained at the beginning of the second subsection. In the third subsection I shall then extract certain salient points from the prefaces of Hewes, Miège and White to support my contention that grammar writers during this period of time constitute a discourse community despite the differences between them that are bound to exist. I shall leave out of the discussion the brief selected passages of verse (mainly in Latin) from the Hewes text.

4.1. *Title pages*

In section 3 I argued that the title page of the grammar is that type of prefatory text which embeds the grammar within the wider discourse of education. However, it is also the first part of the overall text that the potential reader sees. On the assumption that it was as important for marketing reasons in the seventeenth and eighteenth centuries to attract a readership as it is today, the title page can be expected to give more 'information' about the nature of the text and the credentials of the author than simply the title.

Modern books contain other types of prefatory material of this nature which are printed, often on the dust cover, in the form of a brief résumé of what the text is about and a 'bioblurb' on the author.[8] The title page of the grammars generally indicates not only the title of the work but also its overall goal(s), what additional material it contains, the methodology employed by the author, the credentials of the author, the intended audience, the printer and the time and place of the first imprint, etc.

I have adopted a term that is common in high-point narrative analysis (cf. Labov and Waletsky 1967; Watts 1981; Peterson and McCabe 1983) to refer to the kind of material presented in the title pages of books in the seventeenth and eighteenth centuries (and not just those on English grammar), viz. the 'abstract'. This is one of a set of functional categories postulated by Labov and Waletsky to account for the high degree of structural similarity in the oral narratives in their data corpus. My criticism of those categories is that they are presented as if they were structural building blocks constituting a discourse genre 'narrative'. In effect, at least two of the categories, the abstract and the coda, provide the discoursal frame for the narrative text itself and need not actually occur. If and when they do occur, however, they allow the narrator to move out of and back into the non-narrative discourse (cf. the points made in section 3).

I shall argue that the title page of a grammar of English (as indeed the title page of any book, together with other forms of introductory material such as a brief résumé of the content, bioblurb, etc.) is equivalent to an abstract and that the abstract in the printed book form of verbal communication is always necessary.[9] The title pages, in reduced font size, are given in Appendix 1.

All four title pages make use of the conventional 'by'-phrase to indicate the agent, i.e. the author, responsible for the text to follow. The only evidence we have that the agent responsible for the text on the title page is in fact the author, whose identity is veiled by this implicit passive structure, is the subtitle (e.g. in the Miège text), the elaborate information concerning the intended use to which the grammar should be put (e.g. Hewes and in particular Jones) and the explanatory clause beginning with 'being' in the Jones text.

The next problem concerns the identity of the addressee. Bell (1984) makes a neat distinction between the addressee, who is known, a ratified group member and referred to directly, the listener, who is known, a member of the group involved in verbal interaction but is not the participant being directly addressed, the overhearer, who is known, hears what is being said, is a ratified participant of the group, but is not at that point in time participating in the activity, and the eavesdropper, who is unknown, not a ratified group member, who is not participating in the activity, but who hears what is said. It would seem to me that the modern reader is in the position of an eavesdropper.

The person at whom the text is directed, i.e. in Bell's terms the addressee, is for Hewes someone who is in need of a "more plaine exposition of the Grammaticall Rules and Precepts, collected by LILLIE, and for the more certaine Translation of the *English* tongue into *Latin*", i.e. a schoolmaster striving to get his pupils to understand Latin grammar and to translate more fluently into Latin, for Miège, someone who is in need of the "True *Spelling* and *Pointing*, the usual *Abbreviations*, the several *Hands* used in *Writing*, and *Characters* in *Printing*, the Variety of *Styles*, and the Method of *Books*, &c.", i.e. a learner of English, rather than of Latin, probably a foreign learner, and for Jones, someone who needs to know about "the true Manner of *Reading*, *Writing*, and *Talking* proper *English*" so that he can teach this to three categories of learner, "such BOYS and MEN, as have never learnt *Latin* perfectly" (cf. Hewes), "the FEMALE SEX", and "for the *Welch*, *Scotch*, *Irish*, and *Foreigners*" (cf. Miège). White's title page is strikingly simpler than the other three and is in this respect typical of texts written in the second half of the eighteenth century. Nevertheless, the tell-tale phrase 'in the didactive form' indicates that its purpose is for use in teaching and that the real addressee is therefore a schoolmaster.

This brief analysis of the intended addressees in the four title pages reveals a number of important common elements which become even clearer in the other prefatory texts:

1. The primary addressee is a schoolmaster, presumably one working in the grammar schools and public schools.

2. The secondary addressees are learners, either young native speakers enrolled as pupils, or non-native speakers of English. Note how Jones (despite his own Welsh name) lumps the Welsh, Scots and Irish together with 'foreigners'.

3. Explicitly or implicitly English is compared with Latin.
4. The teaching of English grammar is directly related to specific written tasks, such as translating into Latin, spelling, punctuation, learning about written styles, the 'true manner' of writing and reading, etc.
5. The impression is given that there is a perfect grammar of English (Hewes), that there is a 'true' way of spelling English (Miège), that there is a 'true' way of writing, reading and speaking English (Jones), etc. In other words, the attitude towards teaching English grammar is prescriptive from Hewes through to White, and the author always conveys the impression that he is an authority on the subject of what to do or say and what not to do or say.

The similarities display a common set of assumptions which grammarians of English in the seventeenth and eighteenth centuries shared and a common set of discourse strategies to achieve their goals through the print medium.

There are significant differences, however. Whereas Hewes at the beginning of the seventeenth century was pleading that the grammatical rules of English should be taught to pupils to enable the latter to acquire Latin on a more solid foundation, Jones assumes that those 'boys and men' who have learnt Latin 'perfectly' will have less trouble in understanding the rules of English. In other words adjusting the grammar of English to facilitate the learning of Latin has developed into the assumption, which is borne out by analysis of the grammars of the eighteenth century, that the grammar of Latin is fundamentally the same as that of English – despite Wallis's warnings (unfortunately in Latin!) to the contrary.

A second major difference concerns the social significance of grammar teaching/learning. Whereas in both Hewes and Miège the motivation for writing the grammar is largely practical, by the time we reach Jones an implicit distinction is made between 'proper' and 'improper' English. Proper English is linked to the acquisition of a classical education, and the text to follow makes it abundantly clear what this implies, viz. the socially appropriate use of ornate Latinate syntax in English prose, the abundant use of vocabulary derived from Latin, a proper command of linguistic etiquette, or what Jones calls 'polite language', etc. White's title page no longer displays the same pressing concern to present credentials and to state the goals of the grammar and the intended readership. It is almost as if, by 1750, grammar writers have become respectable guardians of proper, polite English, so much so that there is no need to state the fact and, as Lowth's grammar shows, that it is even incumbent on the grammarian to point out to the learner where famous authors have slipped up.

The text of White's 'grammatical essay', however, is very similar in the sort of socio-political assumptions he makes to Jones' text.

4.2. *Dedications to patrons*

The texts of the three dedications to patrons, by Hewes, Jones and White, are given in Appendix 2 with a brief summary of four different levels of pragmatic and socio-pragmatic analysis. The texts are looked at first on the level of the speech act to see what illocutionary act the grammar writer is carrying out in his utterance and whether there is also an underlying illocutionary force in addition to and different from the illocutionary act. This level corresponds to Schiffrin's (1987) discourse level of action structure. The propositional content of the utterances is then given in an informal, brief way to indicate what meanings, explicit or implicit, are expressed through the utterances (cf. Schiffrin's ideational level of discourse structure).

The third level of analysis concerns what I have called 'participant design'. The term is derived from Goffman's notion of participation framework (Goffman 1981), which is the term used by Schiffrin to categorise a further level of discourse structure. It concerns the orientation of hearers (in our case readers) to the interaction and the ways in which speakers orient towards their audience. Goffman splits this into production and reception formats, but since we do not know how (or indeed whether) the intended addressee ever responded to the dedication, I have decided to refer simply to the way in which utterances are designed with respect to the intended addressee, and to call this the participant design.

The fourth and final level of analysis concerns the total discourse rather than the individual utterances or the local participational nature of the interaction. It does not correspond exactly to any one level of discourse structure posited by Schiffrin (1987), but it is in some respects similar to what she calls 'exchange structure'. I have used the term 'discourse function' in the analysis, since I refer to the various interactional functions which utterances may have during the discourse. The units that I posit at this level have to do with the tabling of topics, the opening and closing of discourse sections and the putting and supporting of what Schiffrin (1987) calls a position, which she defines as "descriptive information about situations, events, and actions in the world" together with a commitment to that information on the part of the speaker (in our case the author).

One level of discourse structure which Schiffrin posits, the information state, has not been used in the analysis of the three dedicatory addresses for two reasons. In Watts (1991) I describe the information state as encompassing "the shared knowledge of the participants, the knowledge and meta-knowledge that they display or can be presupposed to possess". I go on to suggest that "it concerns the expectations which participants hold with respect to shared knowledge and will thus guide how utterances are structured and propositions are generated" (1991: 32). Firstly, in written communication it is not possible to know whether the reader actually shares knowledge or meta-knowledge with the writer, since the readers are in any case always potential figures who do not usually show that knowledge to the writer. Secondly, however, if grammar writers during these two centuries can be considered to be members of the same discourse community, it should be possible for the researcher to piece together evidence which will help us to postulate hypotheses about the kinds of 'expectations which participants [in this case the grammar writer, the patron and the potential reader of the text] hold with respect to shared knowledge'. This is the aim of the present subsection.

The first impression gained on reading through the three dedicatory texts is that the Hewes text (1624) is rather different from and yet shares certain similarities with the Jones text (1724) and the White text (1761). An analysis of the three texts along the lines of the four socio-pragmatic levels of communication outlined above bears out this impression (cf. Appendix 2).

I have divided the three texts into nine speech acts in the Hewes' text, and seven each in the Jones and White texts. The decision as to the length of utterance constituting a speech act is always problematic in written texts. Should one take two clauses conjoined with the logical connector *and* to be two speech acts, or two parts of the same speech act? If a term of address occurs periphrastically, should it be listed as a secondary speech act within the framework of the utterance in which it occurs? What does one do with complex utterances which balance one set of clauses logically against another? In the case of conjoined clauses I have only considered these to represent two speech acts if the one stands in opposition to the other or is used to illustrate or explain the other. I have generally omitted terms of address, even though they ought really to be included as speech act types. However, since their communicative significance is also covered in my analysis by the level of participant design, I have not felt it to be necessary to complicate the level of action structure unnecessarily. However, in a number of cases, in particular the first complex utterance of the Hewes text, I have considered it important to distinguish between different speech acts, each supporting the other to create a larger semantic-pragmatic effect. My division on this level is nevertheless controversial.

The dominant form of illocutionary act in all three texts is the statement, of which there are 8 out of a total of 9 speech acts in the Hewes text, 6 out of a total of 7 speech acts in the Jones text and 4 out of a total of 7 speech acts in the White text. However, if one looks at a deeper level of speech act analysis and asks whether or not the statements correspond with the intended illocutionary force of the writer, there are great differences between the early seventeenth century text and the two eighteenth century texts. In Hewes only two indirect speech acts realised as statements occur, the illocutionary force of one being in effect a request to the addressee and that of the second an offer to the addressee. In the Jones text of the six statements five are in effect compliments paid to the addressee and one is an apology. In the White text every single speech act, whether statement or not, has a different illocutionary force. All four statements are in effect compliments; an apparent request for information turns out to represent two illocutionary forces, a compliment and an exclamation, and the two explicit exclamations realise two compliments. White thus spends the whole of his dedicatory address complimenting his patron, the Earl of Bute, while Jones uses five of his seven speech acts to compliment his patron, the Queen Consort, Wilhelmina Charlotte.

On the level of action structure, therefore, there are indeed significant changes between the early seventeenth century text and the two texts from the eighteenth century. This could be explained by the social status of the writer compared to that of the patron. Hewes dedicates his text to the then Bishop of London, whereas Jones dedicates his to the Queen Consort and White dedicates his to the Earl of Bute, one of the king's 'Principal Secretaries of State'. I believe, however, that there is a more subtle explanation which presents itself on comparing the three texts at other discourse levels.

If we consider the propositional content of the speech acts, i.e. if we look at the texts at the level of ideational structure, we might derive the following three summaries:

Hewes: The writer creates and attempts to sustain a metaphorical comparison between teaching schoolboys and gardening. The teaching profession is 'poor' and not well respected despite the fact that the number of schoolmasters is large. The writer wishes to help schoolmasters with his text. He has collected his own 'seeds' and 'plants' on the structure of English and Latin, which have proved profitable, and suggests that they can help schoolmasters. He presents the seeds and plants to his patron in the form of the book and requests the patron's protection and help in propagating his ideas. He concludes by anticipating the patron's help and wishing him well.

Jones: The writer asks for protection of the treatise by the patron since she is well-known and well respected as a protectress of the English language. The patron deserves the noblest expressions of praise that are in the language because she is renowned throughout 'all the British dominions'. The accomplishments of the patron are the constant subject of praise in Britain and America and are eagerly transmitted from one hemisphere to the other. He begs to be excused for dedicating the treatise to her, but he does so because of his veneration of her.

White: The writer explains why he submitted the work to the patron. He had fully expected it to be accepted in such a way as to add glory to and esteem for British imperial power. He was not disappointed in this expectation. He praises the patron for his greatness in supporting works of art and science and thanks him for deeming to consider his own work. Again he praises the greatness and innate generosity of his patron and conveys his humble greetings to him.

Both the Jones and the White texts display great differences in pragmatico-semantic content from the Hewes text. Jones and White both refer, although in different ways, to the notions of 'Britain' and British imperialism. Both writers lavish public praise on their patrons for protecting the English language (Jones) and generously supporting various works of art and science (White). The Hewes text refers explicitly to the low esteem in which schoolmasters are held and praises his own ideas as being one possible antidote to the problems he elucidates later. There is no mention of a link between the language and the state, nor any hint of a connection with imperialist expansion.

I shall posit that, even though the writing of grammars of the language has become progressively more a part of the educational establishment, it has also become associated, and is therefore intended to bolster up, ideas that the greatest protection for the standard language is to be found in the upper echelons of the social order, i.e. the aristocracy, and that the language has reached a degree of 'excellence' that matches, and indeed is made to match, the assumed 'glory' of the nation in creating a world empire. In this situation patrons are naturally sought at the level of the aristocracy and the language used to address them has, firstly, to correspond to the assumed superiority of a classical style and, secondly, to contain the elaborate expressions of admiration, praise and respect that such a style demands. It is for this reason that the overwhelming illocutionary force of Jones's and White's texts is that of the compliment, which can most effectively be expressed indirectly and elaborately.

In terms of participant design, the three texts display certain interesting similarities and differences. In the analyses (cf. Appendix 2) I have concentrated on the relationship expressed between the writer and his patron and the writer and the content of his utterances. There are several points in all three texts in which the writers display deference towards and respect for the addressee, in which they show admiration of the addressee and belittle, or denigrate, themselves, in which they praise the addressee and enhance his/her public image, etc. In the Hewes text there is even an example of the writer praising his own work.

All three writers are deferent towards their patrons, although, while 30% of Hewes's and Jones's utterances show signs of deference, only 15% of White's show similar signs. All three writers display degrees of self-denigration and humility, Hewes 20%, Jones 20% and White 30%. However, only Hewes indulges in self-praise. The degree to which the writers indulge in enhancing their patrons' public image ('public' since the dedication has been published as prefatory material to a grammar of English) is extensive in Jones (40%) and White (53%) but non-existent in Hewes, which ties in with the analysis of speech acts and propositional content given above.

Finally, the discourse functions evident in the three texts show that the authors proceed in fairly similar ways in structuring their dedications. A lot of time is spent in setting up positions, either concerning the value of the material to be presented or, in the case of Jones and White, in making elaborate compliments to their patrons. However, only Hewes sets up an argument from which the value of what he offers can be deduced. The argument is set up through the metaphor comparing teaching to gardening and is concluded on a note of self-praise on Hewes' part. Hewes then uses the argument to persuade his patron to protect the treatise and propagate the ideas contained in it.

In general the dedication to a patron serves the purpose of indicating to the reader that the writer enjoys prestigious support. It enhances his value in the discourse market of education. From this point of view he clearly hopes that the reader will be more inclined to read the text if a dedication to a renowned patron is included. Given the analysis of the material so far, we can posit that patronage among the aristocracy is a crucial hallmark of whether or not the grammar has any value in the educational market, and this will be more significant for authors in the period from around 1710 on than for authors in the seventeenth century. The table presented in section 2 bears out this hypothesis.

4.3. *Miège's address to the reader*

In place of a dedicatory address in Miège's grammar, we find an address to the reader, which is altogether different in a number of ways. The text, divided in a similar way to the three dedications, is as follows:

1. The Want of an *English Grammar* for the Use of this Nation, and the fair Opportunity I had in the Composing of my late Dictionary, to find out the Genius of the English Tongue, did easily prevail with me to gratify the Publick with this Service.

2. But, lest I should be Tedious, I studied how to be Short, and yet to leave out nothing that were Material.

3. It required Time to do so.

4. And herein I took my Measures from the pertinent Answer of an Orator; who, being twitted with a long Speech he had made, alledged this Excuse, That he had not had Time enough to make it shorter.

5. Thus you have it in a small Compass, considering the Variety and Largeness of the Subject.

6. My Aim in it is to satisfy the Curious, and to advance the Illiterate into the Knowledge of the Grounds of their Language, so as to be able to give an Account thereof.

7. The Matter is easy, if but minded a little; and the Book, of so small a Price, that there can be no Discouragement pretended on that side.

8. Could I have my Option, all Young People that are designed for any Thing of good Education should begin with the Grounds of their Language.

9. And, as it is fit for Travellers to be capacitated first to give an Account of their Native Country before they lanch into forein Parts, I think it were very proper, before a Young Man be turned over to the Latine Tongue, to know the Nature and Principles of his own.

10. 'Twould be in a manner a Prelude and Introduction, which would facilitate unto him the Learning of other Languages.

11. And, for a young Learner that is not yet thorough-paced either in Reading or Spelling of English, there's Nothing fitter than this Book to bring him up to it, such is the Variety of Matter herein contained.

12. 'Tis the Judgement of several Judicious Persons, that have incouraged me very much to this Design. Neither will it be improper for the Use of Forreiners, especially the French, that have already got some Smattering of the English Tongue.

13. Whether or no I am mistaken in my Measures, a little Time will shew.

14. My Design is good, and the Reasons on which it is grounded perhaps not to be rejected.

As in the dedications the dominant speech act type is the statement, except that in this text there is little or no indirectness; the illocutionary force corresponds with the illocutionary act. This lends the text an impression of straightforwardness and openness which is lacking in the three texts examined in the previous section. No attempt is made to frame the propositional content either in metaphorical terms (cf. Hewes) or in ornate pseudo-classical syntax (Jones and White). What is stated is stated directly and unpretentiously (cf. the brevity of 3. and 13. and the relative brevity of 5. [main clause + modifying non-finite clause], 10. [main clause + modifying restrictive relative clause], and 13. [main clause with a finite nominal clause in the topicalised object position]).

The propositional content of the first five speech acts focuses on the assumed need for an English grammar, the reason why he decided to take on the task and his efforts to make it as brief as possible without leaving out anything essential. The statement that there was at the time a 'want of an English grammar' ignores the fact that several had already been published within the seventeenth century, although later in the text from 8. to 12. he suggests that, apart from making it easier for the learner to learn Latin, it will also make it easier to learn other foreign languages, to give an 'account' of English when travelling in foreign countries and for foreign learners of English. It should perhaps be mentioned that Guy Miège was a native speaker of French who was born and educated in Lausanne. He was thus a non-native speaker of English and had already published a popular French-English dictionary. In 6. and 7. he states his general aims, viz. "to satisfy the curious" and "to advance the illiterate into the knowledge of the grounds of their language", and then elucidates these aims in more detail in the rest of the text.

However, despite the clear differences between this address and the three dedications looked at in the previous subsection, there are a number of unifying

elements which are evidence that Miège is also a member of the discourse
community of grammar writers. The first point is the connection of grammar
with the written language, e.g. 'to advance the illiterate into the knowledge of
the grounds of their language' and 'for a young learner who is not yet
thorough-paced either in reading or spelling English'. Part of the dynamic of
grammar writing was its influential contribution to the creation of a written
standard English, and towards the end of the seventeenth century the goal of
standardising the orthography and those structures acceptable within the
standard had almost been completed. The second point is the belief that a
knowledge of the grammar of English was a necessary prerequisite for the
acquisition of Latin, which, as we have seen, was reversed during the eighteenth
century so that only those with a classical education were considered able to
write 'correct' standard English. The third point concerns the assumed 'genius'
or 'excellence' of the English language, which was stressed in different ways
and to different degrees by virtually all grammar writers during this period.

The Miège text is also different from the three dedications in its
participant design. The addressee, the potential reader, is not complimented
(although s/he is also not criticised negatively), the author does not constantly
display deference and respect towards the addressee and is not concerned to
enhance the addressee's public status (the addressee is, after all, the public!),
and, significantly, the author does not indulge in false modesty, humility, even
self-denigration. On the contrary, he praises the book ("my design is good",
"there's nothing fitter than this book to bring him up to it") without, however,
praising himself.

The most significant clause in the address, however, is "and the Book [is]
of so small a Price, that there can be no Discouragement pretended on that
side". The address to the reader thus fulfils a rather different communicative
function from the dedication to a patron. It is included to convince the potential
reader that it will be worth her/his while to read the grammar, not only in terms
of the quality of what is offered but also in terms of the price.

4.4. *The prefaces*

The analysis of the prefaces in the Hewes, Miège and White texts will not be as
detailed as the analyses of the other forms of prefatory material considered. It is
my intention to extract from these texts information which will support the
hypotheses advanced so far in this paper. The prefaces are generally much
longer than the dedicatory texts or the address to the reader and a full analysis
would exceed the scope of the paper. Nevertheless, many of the points of view
expressed briefly or hinted at on the title page or in the dedication/address to

the reader recur in more detail in the prefaces themselves and provide us with a fuller picture of those elements which lead to my major hypothesis. Despite differences between grammar writers over the two-hundred year period, the similarities are striking enough to justify considering them to be a significant discourse community which was a major force in moulding the view of the socio-political functions of the standard language within the framework of educational discourse which was prevalent at the end of the eighteenth century (cf. on this point Smith 1984) and lasted until well into the twentieth.

The first point to note is that not all the prefaces are labelled as such. Hewes, for example, appends the following heading to this part of his work:

> To all Teachers of the Art of Grammar in the Latine tongue, and what other his louing Countrey-men and Friends, who are desirous to finde a more easie and speedie way thereto: IO: HEVVES *wisheth all Happiness to their good and laudable Endeauours.*

Guy Miège uses the following heading for his preface:

> A Prefatory DISCOURSE Concerning the Original, and Excellency of the English Tongue.

James White, however, simply calls it "ADVERTISEMENT TO THE PUBLIC, Concerning this ESSAY."

Hewes explicitly addresses in his preface "all teachers of the art of grammar in the Latine tongue". He suggests that potential readers of the book who are fully conversant with Latin grammar and usage will not need to continue unless they are concerned with teaching others. In this case, he argues, they will find here a new method of approaching the task by first teaching the pupils the principles of English grammar. He criticises the tradition of teaching the art of Latin grammar only "in the Latine tongue" and suggests that, because of the differences in structure between the two languages, pupils should be first trained "in the right knowledge or censure of their owne Mother tongue". The idea that a knowledge of the structures of English must precede a knowledge of the structures of a foreign language is a pervasive theme in all three prefaces.

The main perspective adopted by Hewes throughout the preface is that of the educationalist in the tradition of the great educational theorists of the sixteenth century, Ascham and Mulcaster. Ascham is in fact mentioned explicitly in the text. Hewes' main criticism in fact echoes a point made by Ascham in that he suggests that "Pupils learne much without the Booke ... then that they make any good or profitable vse of what they doe learne". Although he hastens to exonerate teachers by admitting that they are very poorly paid and that the size of their classes are very large, he goes on to develop his criticism of this method of learning.

The learning of Latin grammar and use must therefore be preceded by the learning of English grammar, and this can only be done through and with the appropriate books. We can note here the connection between the learning of grammar and the written language, which becomes one of the major tenets of language learning into the eighteenth century. The learning of a language is the learning of its grammar, and the translation of structures from the mother tongue (whose grammar is also learnt abstractly through written texts) into the L2 is that activity which gives the learner practice in using the L2. It is in precepts such as these that we can recognise the beginnings of the deductive, grammar-translation method of L2 learning.

Miège's 'prefatory discourse' on the English language starts from a very different angle from Hewes, although both authors are concerned with the practical issues of teaching language. Miège concentrates on persuading the potential reader that the English language is worth learning simply because of what he calls 'the original and the excellency' of the language. In order to do this he gives a brief and, in the circumstances, quite creditable historical outline of English tracing it back to the 'languages' of the Saxons and the Angles. Other grammar writers of the late seventeenth century had done the same, notably John Wallis in the preface to his *Grammatica Linguæ Anglicanæ*, and it was these authors in particular who set the stage for what Crowley (1989) calls the early nineteenth century obsession for the history of *the* language, i.e. English, rather than the history of language (cf. the work of early comparative philologists on the continent) and the subsequent piecing together of a body of texts which show the development of English from Old to Modern English that was then used as the basis of the literary canon.

Miège considers that the 'excellency' of the English language consists of four qualities, 'facility' (i.e. English has a minimum of inflections and is therefore 'easy' to learn), 'copiousness' (i.e. English has borrowed liberally from a number of different linguistic sources such as French, Latin and Greek), 'significancy' (i.e. the flexibility of English in adapting to poetic and scientific registers), and 'sweetness' (i.e. his own subjective impression of English as combining all the positive affective attributes of other languages such as Italian, French, Dutch and Spanish). Miège's purpose, of course, is to argue for the superiority of English over other European vernaculars.

He concludes his argument by suggesting that "now the *English* is come to so great Perfection, now 'tis grown so very Copious and Significant, by the Accession of the Quintessence and Life of other Tongues, 'twere to be wished that a Stop were put to this unbounded Way of Naturalizing forein Words and that none hereafter should be admitted but with Judgement and Authority". This is an early example of what Milroy and Milroy (1985) call the 'complaint tradition'. One might justifiably wonder who Miège sees as a possible 'authority' given the fact that there was never an English equivalent to the Académie Française. It probably implied that the grammar writers themselves represented authoritative views on the language, and this is precisely how the grammarians of the eighteenth century tended to see things (cf. Lowth's and Lindley Murray's grammars in the second half of the following century and the first decade of the nineteenth).

Commentators on the English language, whether grammarians or not, and today as much as in the seventeenth century, frequently perceive it to have reached a state of perfection from which any further movement must be movement for the worse. Change in language is considered by the complainers to be undesirable and merely a degeneration of the language, a linguistic fall from grace.

This attitude results from a conceptualisation of language as moving towards a standardised state of perfection. If the complainer feels that perfection has already been reached at the time when the complaint is made, his/her feeling reflects an attitude that the socio-political structure of the ethnic group has also reached a state of perfection. Change in language is deplored precisely because it reflects a change away from that perfect social state, and any change is by definition change for the worse. Here we see a grammar writer explicitly underwriting this attitude in a text which is, after all, aimed at teachers and learners of English. Indeed, Miège goes on in his next sentence, the last but one of his preface, to say the following:

> Were this Nation contented to improve what Grain they have already, without over-stocking themselves from other Parts, and putting their Language on a perpetual Motion, it would be much for the Credit of it.

The language is seen here as the property of the 'nation', although it is not quite clear exactly what Miège means by the 'nation' in this context. One suspects that it is indeed an early reference to the country, the state, as a nation, although almost a further twenty years went by until the Act of Union between England and Scotland officially created the entity that was then referred to as Britain.

This point leads us directly into White's 'Advertisement to the Public', the first clause of which reads as follows:

> As Grammatical knowledge, when introduc'd into any language, greatly contributes to the embellishment, perfection, and preservation of it ...

We can infer from this that White assumes that languages can exist without grammar, that 'grammatical knowledge' exists apart from any individual language and that once this 'knowledge' is applied to a language, the latter is 'embellished', 'perfected' and 'preserved'. The duty of a grammar writer, therefore, has been extended quite considerably from the time that Hewes wrote his grammar. Whereas Hewes simply wanted to provide some written help for poorly paid overworked teachers of Latin, White, almost 140 years later, implies that the grammar writer's duty is to embellish the language – which does not mean changing it! –, to perfect it, i.e. to standardise it, and to preserve it, i.e. to prevent it from changing. He goes on to suggest that the writing of grammars for English is no longer "merely the amusement of a few speculative Persons among the learned", but that it is now "a real and necessary part of BRITISH education". It has truly found a firm place within the discourse of education in the second half of the eighteenth century, and this discourse is 'British', not 'English'. The nation that Miège did not name in 1688, is now named, several times in White's text, as Britain. Britain has become the polity, the socio-political unit, for which the language 'standard written English' is being turned into a symbolic nationalistic rallying point.

White justifies his own grammar, which in fact only deals with English verbs, by stating that "our Essays towards forming an English Grammar, have not been very many". This is totally erroneous when we consider the spate of grammars that were written for English starting in the late sixteenth century and increasing throughout the seventeenth in addition to the two he mentions, viz. Ben Jonson's grammar and John Wallis's grammar. At this point, therefore, we have to exercise great care in suggesting the existence of a discourse community of grammar writers. This does not, of course, mean that every writer was fully aware of all the previous work on the subject. It simply suggests that those few works that were familiar to the grammar writer contained a set of beliefs and discourse strategies that were generally taken over and, possibly, modified to suit the purposes of the present writer. This would account for the similarities that exist between grammars that are 150–200 years apart but also for the development and change of attitude and perspective that took place over that period.

White states that the theory of English verb structure that he will shortly present is not the product of "Abstract Erudition" but "the natural and gradual result of ten years various experience, in a Practical Course of Education", from which we may gather that he has had experience at teaching languages. Certainly, like Miège, he pleads for an increased understanding of and esteem for English which would "render the attainment of other Languages much more pleasant and easy", sentiments which we find echoed in various ways through the grammars, and "the judgement with respect to their Comparative value, much more precise and certain", which echoes the subjective assessment of English as against other European languages made by grammarians like Miège.

I shall close this discussion of White's preface with the following paragraph:

> But however slow our progress has been in forming the Grammar of our Language, we have no reason to despair of success in it. – This is an Acquisition that seems to have been reserv'd by Providence to adorn the happy reign of that Illustrious Monarch, in whom the ROYAL LINE again becomes BRITISH, and who glories in being a Native.

The illustrious monarch is George III, and the royal line again becomes British by speaking English as its native language. This is a clear indication of the connection between language and nation-state which was to reach its full development in the second half of the nineteenth century (cf. Hobsbawm 1990). One becomes British and is able to glory in being a native of Britain by speaking and writing (particularly writing!) standard English, which meant mastering the embellishments of neo-classical Latinate prose in English and the elaborate, ornate forms of polite discourse. This was the discourse of those educational establishments (public schools and universities) through which one had to pass to gain access to a 'good' education and to be eligible for social advancement. It was the discourse we see presented in Lowth's grammar, which set itself higher than and acted as a moral judge of many of the best contemporary authors. Grammar writing had indeed achieved a powerful position within the educational discourse community.

5. Conclusion

My hypothesis in this paper has been that grammar writers of English from the beginning of the seventeenth to the end of the eighteenth century show sufficient similarities in terms of their discourse strategies and cognitive assumptions to justify their being considered a discourse community. This does not exclude the existence of a number of differences, of course, but these can be explained by showing that the writing of grammars, which was always carried out for the English language with practical rather than theoretical aims, gradually achieved for itself a firm position within the discourse of public education.

In a way, this is an obvious point to make if we consider that grammar writing is one of those areas through which a standardised written form of language develops out of what Joseph (1987) calls a "synecdochic dialect". It is one of the major areas in which a standard language becomes codified. What is not quite so obvious, however, is the way in which the discourse conventions of grammar writing were themselves instrumental in shifting the status of grammars from early attempts to standardise orthography and to provide solutions to the didactic problems of learning Latin, which were illustrated very clearly by Roger Ascham, through attempts to present the structures of English in as clear a way as possible for the benefit not only of learners who would be going on to learn Latin (but also for non-native learners of English), to a codex of what was 'proper' and 'correct' in English.

My argument has also been that rather than study the actual texts of the grammars themselves, it is just as instructive, possibly more so, to study the various types of prefatory text. In order to do this, however, it is necessary to develop a model of communicative levels. We need to know who is the intended addressee of the text and to assess how the particular type of prefatory text ties the actual grammar into the world of publishing in the seventeenth and eighteenth centuries, the world of patronage, and even the world of marketing. Each grammar arises out of the discourse of grammar writing and out of written, published discourse. If these different levels are not considered, the prefatory texts themselves become almost meaningless. However, if we assume that the different types of prefatory text correspond to different combinations of writer-reader relationship and represent different types of communicative function, an analysis of those texts reveals a number of significant points which allow a set of hypotheses to be formulated.

The analysis of the dedicatory texts and Miège's address to the reader has been carried out using my adaptation of Schiffrin's levels of discourse structure. The analysis shows that when we move from the seventeenth to the eighteenth century, grammar writers are more concerned to show deference towards their patrons and to enhance the latter's public image to the detriment of their own. The principal method used to achieve this effect is the indirect speech act in which the dominant speech act of the statement in fact realises other types of illocutionary force, above all that of compliment. The discourse-structural level of the participation framework (what I have called 'participant design') in which explicit reference to the writer or reader is made supports this analysis.

The brief analysis of the actual prefaces shows that many of the discourse strategies and cognitive attitudes which are explicitly or implicitly evident in the title pages and dedications/addresses to the reader recur there, often in more detail. When these are put together, they form a revealing picture of a discourse community whose overall aims remained fairly similar, while the significance of grammar writing itself changed. Grammar writers became 'authorities' on what was 'proper' and 'correct' in English. They related an eloquent command of the standard written language with the expression of patriotism and national feeling. We see the beginnings of the link between standard language and the nation-state which was to dominate educational discourse until well into the twentieth century.

It is imperative that, as linguists, sociolinguists and educationalists working at the end of the twentieth century, we recognise some of the problems confronting our own disciplines as having a historicity of their own. This is particularly important in the present debate on the national curriculum for English within Britain. That debate can only be properly understood within the historical context. At present the British government policy on English language education seems determined to take teachers and pupils back into the nineteenth century, and it is important that teachers and linguists should understand this.

I am not convinced that this paper has been an exercise in historical pragmatics, although I have attempted to exercise eclecticism in my use of pragmatic principles and discourse analytical methods. But pragmatics can be understood in very broad terms indeed, taking one all the way through from the derivation of speaker's meaning in language use to various forms of sociolinguistics and anthropological linguistics, and that is the way the concept has been taken here.

Notes

1. Mulcaster (1582) and Ascham (1570).

2. The two most important works on the orthography during the Tudor period are John Hart (1569/70) and Thomas Smith (1568). Hart's work was written in English, rather than Latin, and shows how amazingly inconsistent writers were during the sixteenth century in their orthographic habits, even those who were pleading for a standardised orthography.

3. Wallis's grammar of English in 1653 is clearly influenced by the Port Royal grammarians' concern with language universals. John Wilkins' *Mercury: or, The Secret and Swift Messenger* (1641) was an attempt to develop an artificial language which would directly represent the writers' thoughts and ideas and avoid the criticism made by Bacon that the vernacular was good for the marketplace but not for the purposes of scientific enquiry.

4. This is particularly marked in John Wallis' *Grammatica Linguæ Anglicanæ*, which was probably the most influential of the seventeenth century grammars.

5. A good critical analysis of the ways in which Latinate prose were taken to be the hallmark of learning and education and used to discriminate against political adversaries is given in Olivia Smith (1984).

6. One might of course argue here that the notion of nation-state was not confined to Europe alone. The United States of America would probably be put forward as the prime counter-example. However, given the fact that the USA was forged by those of European provenance, the argument still holds.

7. Note the inadequate way in which the sixteenth-century arguments for an orthographical standardisation of English were later resolved in the grammars.

8. Indeed a bioblurb is even requested today from the contributors to a number of important academic journals.

9. This does not mean that the abstract or any of the other categories posited by Labov and Waletsky are universal structural (or in this case functional) categories. The points that I am making here are restricted to communication genres in the Western European/North American cultural framework. I am arguing here for cultural relativity rather than cognitive universality, although it may still be possible, on the basis of a more rigorous analysis of communication genres in other cultures, to discover a set of universal core concepts. That, however, is an enormous and probably impossible task on which I will not venture here.

Appendix 1: Title pages of the four grammars examined

John Hewes (1624)

A
PERFECT
SVRVEY OF THE
ENGLISH TONGVE,
TAKEN ACCORDING TO
THE VSE AND ANALOGIE
of the LATINE.

And serueth for the more plaine
exposition of the Grammaticall Rules and
Precepts, collected by LILLIE, and for the more
certaine Translation of the *English* tongue into *Latine*.

*Together with sundry good
demonstrations, by way of Sentences in
either tongue.*
Written and collected by *Io : Hewes*,
Master of Arts.

---

*Principiis cognitis, multo faciliùs
extrema intelligentur.* Cic. *pro* Cluentio:

LONDON.
Printed by *Edw : All-de*, for *William
Garret*. 1624.

Guy Miège (1688)

THE
ENGLISH
GRAMMAR;
OR, THE
GROUNDS, and *GENIUS*
OF THE
English Tongue.

WITH A
PREFATORY DISCOURSE,
Concerning Its
Original, and Excellency;
And, at the End, a Collection of
The *ENGLISH MONOSYLLABLES;*

Being the Radical Part of the
Language. Wherein True *Spelling*
and *Pointing*, the usual
Abbreviations, the several *Hands*
used in *Writing*, and *Characters* in
Printing, the Variety of *Styles*, and
the Method of *Books,* &c. are
Explained

By GUY MIEGE,
*Author of the Great French
Dictionary.*

London, Printed by *J. Redmayne*, for
the *Author*, at his House next to the
Nag's head, in *James Street,* Covent-
Garden. 1688.

Hugh Jones (1724):   James White (1761):

AN

A C C I D E N C E
TO THE
ENGLISH TONGUE,

CHIEFLY

FOR THE USE OF SUCH **BOYS** AND MEN
AS HAVE NEVER LEARNT *LATIN*
PERFECTLY, and for the Benefit of the
FEMALE SEX: Also for the *Welch,
Scotch, Irish*, and *Foreigners*.

BEING A
Grammatical Essay
UPON OUR
LANGUAGE,

Considering the true Manner of
Reading, *Writing*, and *Talking*
proper *English*.

By HUGH JONES, A.M. lately Mathematical Professor at the College of William
and Mary, at Williamsburgh in Virginia, and
Chaplain to the Honourable the Assembly
of that Colony.

Si quid novisti rectius Candidus
imperti; si non, his utere mecum

LONDON :
Printed for JOHN CLARKE, at the *Bible*,
under the *Royal-Exchange*.
MDCCXXIV

T H E
ENGLISH VERB;
A
GRAMMATICAL
E S S A Y
In the DIDACTIVE FORM.

By Mr. W H I T E.

Negata tentat iter via.   HOR.

Μάρτυρα ἔλαβον καὶ θεατὴν τὸν ἄριστα
κρῖναι τὸ κατορθούμενον, καὶ μάλιστα
ἀμείψασθαι δυνάμενον. PLUTARCH

L O N D O N :
Printed for A. MILLAR, in the Strand.
MDCCLXI.

Appendix 2: Analysis of the dedications to patrons

Hewes (addressed to 'the Right Reverend Father in God, George by the Diuine prouidence, Bishop of London')

1. As it happeneth to the skilfull Gardener, when hee hath committed his Seedes and Plants to the Earth, that still as the same begin to spring vp to open shew, so fast againe doth his labour and toyle increase vpon his hands:

   ILLOCUTIONARY ACT: **statement**

   PROPOSITIONAL CONTENT: **the more successful the gardener is, the more work he has**

   PARTICIPANT DESIGN: **neutral**

   DISCOURSE FUNCTION: **setting up a point of comparison**

2. So fareth it (Right Reuerend good Lord) with the like poore and vnrespected, yet necessary state of Schooling and managing of Youth, that all the labours of the Teacher, are little enough to order, polish and refine, that once hee hath taken in hand to performe and execute.

   ILLOCUTIONARY ACT: **statement**

   PROPOSITIONAL CONTENT: **similar situation holds with the work of a teacher + that work is not respected and 'poor'**

   PARTICIPANT DESIGN: **respect to the addressee**

   DISCOURSE FUNCTION OF 1. + 2.: **tabling the topic by putting a position**

3. Many Gardeners hath this Land had, and now hath at this instant (thankes bee vnto the Lord)

   ILLOCUTIONARY ACT: **statement**

   PROPOSITIONAL CONTENT: **large number of teachers in the land**

   PARTICIPANT DESIGN: **neutral**

   DISCOURSE FUNCTION: **putting a position to support 4.**

4. and as their hands are now full of worke, so would I (as my small Mite may bee accepted) shew my selfe in dutie prest to help, or in some part to further their godly industry.

   ILLOCUTIONARY ACT: **statement**

   ILLOCUTIONARY FORCE: **wish**

   PROPOSITIONAL CONTENT: **expression of desire to help teachers**

   PARTICIPANT DESIGN: **self-denigration, praise of teachers**

   DISCOURSE FUNCTION: **support for 1. + 2., new position**

5. Some seedes or plants haue I also by no lesse tedious search in my time
    collected, and such as to the younger or weaker Students shall not be
    vngratefull;
    ILLOCUTIONARY ACT: **statement**
    PROPOSITIONAL CONTENT: **has collected 'seeds' and 'plants'; will be to the
    benefit of less proficient students**
    PARTICIPANT DESIGN: **self-praise**
    DISCOURSE FUNCTION: **support for new position in 4.**

6. for well I know their proofe in more barren plots.
    ILLOCUTIONARY ACT: **statement**
    PROPOSITIONAL CONTENT: **knows qualities of 'seeds' and 'plants'**
    PARTICIPANT DESIGN: **self-praise**
    DISCOURSE FUNCTION: **support for position in 5.**

7. Those, as I wish them some place within the Garden of his our Common-
    Wealth, and whereof your Lordship holdeth in part a most respectiue &
    vigilant eye; so haue I made bold first to subiect them to your onely censure
    & defence.
    ILLOCUTIONARY ACT: **statement**
    ILLOCUTIONARY FORCE: **offer**
    PROPOSITIONAL CONTENT: **presents the seeds and plants to the patron for
    censure or defence**
    PARTICIPANT DESIGN: **deference to the addressee and self-denigration**
    DISCOURSE FUNCTION: **conclusion of topic**

8. And though to your wisedome now in farre greater affaires and designes
    imployed (I confesse) they shall not be worthy the note, yet if the same (as
    in your wonted and great clemency to others) shall vouchsafe them the
    meanest fauour or applause, I doubt not, but that you shall thereby incite
    many and diuers, to seeke and finde herein, what may, and that most
    necessarily import them, and the common state, whereof they are particular
    members.
    ILLOCUTIONARY ACT: **statement**
    ILLOCUTIONARY FORCE: **request**
    PROPOSITIONAL CONTENT: **protection and propagation of the author's
    work by the patron**
    PARTICIPANT DESIGN: **deference to and implicit praise of addressee**
    DISCOURSE FUNCTION: **request to patron to propagate the author's work**

9. And as it behooueth herein euery man for his part to be a Labourer, so I
    beseech the Lord, that what we sowe, plant or water, in a godly zeale, hee
    will giue vs an ample increase thereof to his glory, and preserue your

Lordship with a long and happie life, to the good of the Church, and the comfort of all true and vpright hearts in the same. *Your Lordships most devoted:* Io: HEVVES.

ILLOCUTIONARY ACT: **plea**

PROPOSITIONAL CONTENT: **God should grant ample increase to the author's and the addressee's labours and give the addressee a long and happy life**

PARTICIPANT DESIGN: **self-denigration; deference to addressee**

DISCOURSE FUNCTION: **closing the interaction**

Jones (addressed to 'Her Royal Highness Wilhelmina Charlotte, Princess of Wales'):

1. MADAM, With the utmost Humility I entreat *Your Royal Highness*'s Protection of this Treatise concerning the Order, Use, and beautiful Graces of the *English* Language.

   ILLOCUTIONARY ACT: **plea**

   PROPOSITIONAL CONTENT: **protection of the treatise**

   PARTICIPANT DESIGN: **deference to addressee, self-denigration ('with the utmost humility')**

   DISCOURSE FUNCTION: **tabling the topic**

2. For *You (Madam)* may well be deem'd the Protectress of our Language; nay it may even claim that Right of *You,*

   ILLOCUTIONARY ACT: **statement**

   ILLOCUTIONARY FORCE: **compliment**

   PROPOSITIONAL CONTENT: **protection of the language**

   PARTICIPANT DESIGN: **respect to addressee ('Madam')**

   DISCOURSE FUNCTION: **support for the plea in 1.**

3. since *You* are so justly entitl'd to its noblest Expressions in extolling *Your Many, and Eminent Virtues*; which have gained *You an universal Renown* throughout *all the British Dominions.*

   ILLOCUTIONARY ACT: **statement**

   ILLOCUTIONARY FORCE: **compliment**

   PROPOSITIONAL CONTENT: **noblest expressions of language deserved by addressee; addressee universally renowned**

   PARTICIPANT DESIGN: **enhancing public status of addressee**

   DISCOURSE FUNCTION: **support for the compliment in 2.**

4.   This I can *particularly* affirm, with Respect to the *American Plantations* (where I have several Years resided) that the *numerous and inimitable Accomplishments*, wherewith *You* highly adorn *Your Royal Station*, are the constant Subject of Praise, in *That*, as well as *This*, Part of the *World*:
     ILLOCUTIONARY ACT: **statement**
     ILLOCUTIONARY FORCE: **compliment**
     PROPOSITIONAL CONTENT: **accomplishments of addressee are constant subject of praise in America and Britain**
     PARTICIPANT DESIGN: **enhancing public status of addressee**
     DISCOURSE FUNCTION: **position supporting 2. and 3.**

5.   So that it may be almost said, that Men never cease to applaud *Them*; alternately transmitting the Grateful and *most Illustrious Topick*, with the *bright Meridian* of the Revolving Sun, from One *Hemisphere* to the Other.
     ILLOCUTIONARY ACT: **statement**
     ILLOCUTIONARY FORCE: **compliment**
     PROPOSITIONAL CONTENT: **accomplishments of addressee are applauded and transmitted from one hemisphere to the other**
     PARTICIPANT DESIGN: **enhancing public status of addressee**
     DISCOURSE FUNCTION: **position supporting 4.**

6.   I shall only add, that I hope to obtain *Your* Excuse for my Presumption, in inscribing this mean Performance to *Your* Royal Highness;
     ILLOCUTIONARY ACT: **statement**
     ILLOCUTIONARY FORCE: **apologising**
     PROPOSITIONAL CONTENT: **dedicating the treatise to the addressee is a presumption for which he hopes to be excused**
     PARTICIPANT DESIGN: **enhancing public status of addressee, deference to addressee, self-denigration**
     DISCOURSE FUNCTION: **repairing potential face damage**

7.   since I flatter my self, (with Reliance upon *Your Royal Highness*'s great Condescension) that it will be solely imputed to the fervent Zeal, and respectful Veneration, with which I am, MADAM, *Your Royal Highness's most devoted, and most obedient humble Servant*, Hugh Jones.

ILLOCUTIONARY ACT: **statement**
ILLOCUTIONARY FORCE: **compliment**
PROPOSITIONAL CONTENT: **author's presumption springs from fervent zeal and respectful veneration for addressee**
PARTICIPANT DESIGN: **enhancing public status of addressee, deference to addressee**
DISCOURSE FUNCTION: **support for 6.**

White (addressed to 'the Right Honourable John, Earl of Bute, One of His Majesty's Principal Secretaries of State; &c.'):

1. My LORD, The High and Amiable Character in which your LORDSHIP so distinguishedly shines, of being the most Eminent Judge and Impartial Patron of Literary Merit, imbolden'd the Author of this Tract, adventurously, to lay a Specimen of it, together with the Plan, before you;
   ILLOCUTIONARY ACT: **statement**
   ILLOCUTIONARY FORCE: **compliment**
   PROPOSITIONAL CONTENT: **the reason why the author gave a specimen of the work to the addressee**
   PARTICIPANT DESIGN: **enhancing the public status of the addressee; deference to the addressee; humility of author**
   DISCOURSE FUNCTION: **narrative**

2. which you receiv'd with that indulgence and candour, whereby, like another MÆCENAS, whilst you rear and support every Elegent or Useful Work of Art and Science, You add fresh and unfading grace to the sway of the BRITISH AUGUSTUS.
   ILLOCUTIONARY ACT: **statement**
   ILLOCUTIONARY FORCE: **compliment**
   PROPOSITIONAL CONTENT: **manner in which the patron received the work adds to the esteem in which British imperial power is held**
   PARTICIPANT DESIGN: **enhancing the public status of the addressee**
   DISCOURSE FUNCTION: **narrative + a discourse position tabling a topic**

3. In this behaviour of Yours, my LORD, there is something so Extraordinary, so Great, and so Generous; that it far exceeds all the

expression that I am master of, to describe or represent it in any suitable degree.

ILLOCUTIONARY ACT: **statement**

ILLOCUTIONARY FORCE: **compliment**

PROPOSITIONAL CONTENT: **extolling the greatness of the addressee's reactions and the author's incapacity to describe it**

PARTICIPANT DESIGN: **deference to addressee, enhancing the public status of the addressee, humility**

DISCOURSE FUNCTION: **position supporting discourse position in 2.**

4. For what Instance can there be produc'd in our times, or any other, of a Person of your High Rank and Elevated Sphere, who hath ever condescended to look into a Work of Literature, let what Merit soever belong to it, that came to him without any other Circumstance to recommend it?

ILLOCUTIONARY ACT: **request for information**

ILLOCUTIONARY FORCE: **compliment; exclamation**

PROPOSITIONAL CONTENT: **the greatness of the patron for looking into what the author considers below the accepted level of merit**

PARTICIPANT DESIGN: **enhancing the public status of the addressee; self-denigration**

DISCOURSE FUNCTION: **support for position in 3.**

5. Yet what real Unrival'd greatness is there, in having the Spirit to act thus!

ILLOCUTIONARY ACT: **exclamation**

ILLOCUTIONARY FORCE: **compliment**

PROPOSITIONAL CONTENT: **the greatness of the patron**

PARTICIPANT DESIGN: **enhancing the public status of the addressee**

DISCOURSE FUNCTION: **position supporting position in 3.**

6. And how noble that Generosity, which arises from an Internal Principle so strong, that it needs no Impulse from without!

ILLOCUTIONARY ACT: **exclamation**

ILLOCUTIONARY FORCE: **compliment**

PROPOSITIONAL CONTENT: **innate generosity of the patron**

PARTICIPANT DESIGN: **enhancing the public status of the addressee**

DISCOURSE FUNCTION: **position supporting position in 3.**

7. *I am, With the profoundest Esteem,* My LORD, *Your most obedient, and most humble Servant,* JAMES WHITE.
    ILLOCUTIONARY ACT: **statement**
    ILLOCUTIONARY FORCE: **compliment**
    PROPOSITIONAL CONTENT: **author conveys his greetings to addressee**
    PARTICIPANT DESIGN: **self-denigration; deference to the addressee; enhancing the public status of the addressee**
    DISCOURSE FUNCTION: **closing the interaction**

References

Aickin, Joseph
   1693   *The English Grammar*. London.
Alston, R. C.
   1967–72   *English Linguistics* 1500-1800. A Collection of Facsimile. Reprints. Menston: The Scolar Press.
anon.
   1733   *The English Accidence*. London: Roberts.
Ascham, Roger
   1570   *The Schoolmaster*. L.V. Ryan (ed.). Ithaca, NY: Cornell University Press.
Bell, Allan
   1984   "Language style as audience design." *Language in Society* 13.2, 145-204.
Bullokar, William
   1580   *Booke at Large for the Amendment of Orthographie for English Speech*. London.
Butler, Charles
   1633   *The English Grammar, or the Institution of Letters, Syllables, and Words in the English Tongue*. Oxford.
Crowley, Tony
   1989   *The Politics of Discourse*. London: Macmillan.
Duncan, Daniel
   1731   *A New English Grammar*. London: Prevost.
Entick, John
   1728   *Speculum Latinum, or Latin Made easy to Scholars by an English Grammar only*. London: Tookey.
Gildon, Charles, and John Brightland
   1711   *A Grammar of the English Tongue*. London.

Goffman, Erving
    1981   *Forms of Talk.* Oxford: Blackwell.
Greenwood, James
    1711   *An Essay towards a Practical English Grammar.* London: Tookey.
Grice, H. Paul
    1975   "Logic and conversation." In: Peter Cole and Jerry L. Morgan (eds.).
             Syntax and Semantics 3: Speech Acts. New York: Academic Press, 41-58.
Hart, John
    1569/70 *An Orthographie, conteyning the due order and reason, howe to write or
             painte thimage of mannes voice, most like to the life or nature.* London.
Hewes, John
    1624   *A Perfect Survey of the English Tongue.* London: William Garret.
Hobsbawm, E. J.
    1990   *Nations and Nationalism since 1780: Programme, Myth, Reality.* London:
             Cambridge University Press.
Johnson, Richard
    1706   *Grammatical Commentaries.* London.
Jones, Hugh
    1724   *An Accidence to the English Tongue.* London: Millar.
Jonson, Ben
    1640   *The English Grammar.* London.
Joseph, John
    1987   *Eloquence and Power.* London: Francis Pinter.
Labov, William, and Joshua Waletsky
    1967   "Narrative analysis." In: June Helm (ed.). *Essays on the Verbal and Visual
             Arts.* Seattle: University of Washington Press, 12-44.
Lily, William, and John Colet
    1549   *A Short Introduction of Grammar.* Menston: The Scolar Press Limited.
Lowth, Robert
    1762   *A Short Introduction to English Grammar.* London: Millar.
Maittaire, Michael
    1712   *The English Grammar.* London: Clements.
Miège, Guy
    1688   *The English Grammar.* London: Redmayne.
Milroy, James, and Lesley Milroy
    1985   *Authority in Language.* London: Routledge and Kegan Paul.
Mulcaster, Richard
    1582   *Mulcaster's Elementarie.* Edited by E.T. Campagnac. Oxford: Oxford
             University Press.

Murray, Lindley
>   1810   *An English Grammar: Comprehending the Principles and Rules of the Language.* New York.

Peterson, Carole, and Alyssa McCabe
>   1983   *Developmental Psycholinguistics: Three Ways of Looking at a Child's Narrative.* New York: Plenum Press.

Poole, Joshua
>   1646   *The English Accidence.* London.

Saxon, Samuel
>   1737   *The English Scholar's Assistant.* London.

Schiffrin, Deborah
>   1987   *Discourse Markers.* London: Cambridge University Press.

Smith, Olivia
>   1984   *The Politics of Language 1791–1819.* Oxford: Clarendon Press.

Smith, Sir Thomas
>   1568   *De recta et emendata linguæ anglicanæ scriptione dialogus.* Paris.

Wallis, John
>   1653   *Grammatica Linguæ Anglicanæ.* London.

Watts, Richard J.
>   1981   *The Pragmalinguistic Analysis of Literary Texts: Narrative Co-operation in Charles Dickens' Hard Times.* Tübingen: Gunter Narr.
>   1990   "The Role of Early Grammar Writers in Creating a Linguistic Tradition." In: R. Liver, I. Werlen and P. Wunderli (eds.). *Sprachtheorie und Theorie der Sprachwissenschaft.* Tübingen: Gunter Narr, 299-315.
>   1991   *Power in Family Discourse.* Berlin: Mouton de Gruyter.

White, James
>   1761   *The English Verb.* London: Millar.

Wilkins, John
>   1641   *Mercury: or, The Secret and Swift Messenger.* London.

Communicative Clues in
Sir Gawain and the Green Knight

Mª Pilar Navarro-Errasti
Universidad de Zaragoza, Spain

This is an amalgamation of quite an ancient piece of literature with quite a modern piece of theoretical framework. The father of the former is unknown and vanished. The latter has a lot more parental support and family relations, and newcomers to the clan spring up every day. My most basic intention in joining this well-known orphan with such an innovative approach is in line with the widely shared aim of reviewing English historical texts in the light of pragmatic approaches.

The text I have in mind is *Sir Gawain and the Green Knight* (GGK from now on), and the pragmatic approach within which I would like to work is the relevance-theoretic framework such as presented by Sperber and Wilson in 1986. As is well known, this is a very comprehensive model and, if it is right, probably many of its insights could throw light on many aspects of our linguistic heritage. So far very little has been done within the frame of this all-embracing theory, and consequently, a lot is still left to be explored. Although I am a very enthusiastic believer in this pragmatic approach, I do not want to argue about the superiority of this model over others. Here I will just assume it and work within it.

This work will be more tentative and experimental than conclusive since it is my intention to apply some aspects of the theory as criteria for a diachronic analysis rather than to conclude on features of GGK. However, in the course of the work, I may make some points about the validity of the theory as a tool for historical studies, and eventually, our knowledge of this medieval text may increase.

Relevance theory is a theory of human communication. Thus, to be coherent with this approach, we must assume that a literary work is a communicative act. It can be seen either as a single entity or as set of communicative acts – this distinction is not relevant now – and consequently

organised by the principles underlying communicative acts, i.e. the author
(addresser) has a communicative and an informative intention to communicate
to the reader (addressee).

Relevance theory is to be considered somehow within the Gricean
mainstream (inferential approach), although it departs from the most orthodox
view in that the recovering of information is not achieved by the obedience to
some principles and maxims, which would organise communication, and that
might turn out to be useful for the analysis of texts. Relevance theory selects
one of the Gricean maxims to make it the main principle of the whole model, in
fact the basic principle of communication. Consequently, if a literary work is
considered an act of communication, it must be organised by this very principle.

As is well known, relevance theory approaches communication from
cognitive standards. The cornerstone of relevance theory is the principle of
relevance: "Every act of ostensive communication communicates the
presumption of its own optimal relevance" (Sperber and Wilson 1986: 158).
The presumption of optimal relevance is defined by the authors as follows:

> a) The set of assumptions {I} which the communicator intends to make manifest
> to the addressee is relevant enough to make it worth the addressee's while to
> process the ostensive stimulus.

> b) The ostensive stimulus is the most relevant one the communicator could have
> used to communicate {I} (Sperber and Wilson 1986: 158).

Relevance is defined in terms of contextual effects and processing effort. The
greater the contextual effects, the greater the relevance. But the greater the
processing effort needed to obtain these effects, the lower the relevance.
Occasionally the cost may be higher than expected by the addressee because the
communicator (the writer) intends the reader to attain greater effects. The cost
is evaluated in terms of the effort needed in the inferential processes, the benefit
in terms of the modification of the reader's cognitive environment. An utterance
is a stimulus that modifies the reader's cognitive environment so that he
entertains thoughts similar to those the author entertained when he was writing
the utterance. This is true at utterance level but probably also at higher levels.

The cost is related to the number of assumptions the reader has to activate
in order to form the appropriate context. These assumptions are either retrieved
from memory or acquired by perception. Those assumptions originated in
perception will undergo an inferential process of non-demonstrative logical
deduction. The cost of those recovered from memory will depend on how
remotely these old assumptions are stored in the audience's memory.

One of the most promising points of relevance theory is that language is not primarily used as a code but as an ostensive stimulus: Language conveys meanings by means of linguistic codification, and it also activates thoughts as a result of its ostensive potential. An artist makes use of many devices to carry out his project. As a matter of fact, in a literary composition the most basic means is linguistic codification. But, paradoxically, linguistic codification is not the primary medium for communication. Codification is only a convenient "commodity" for communicative behaviour. Linguistic communication is primarily ostensive. The writer can play with the code as an object to attain linguistic communication as much as non-linguistic communication (ostensive-inferential) like in any other communicative situation. The total effect of the reading of the work will be the whole set of thoughts elaborated by the reader. Some of them will come from the effect caused by codification, others by the effect caused by ostentation.

Gutt (1991) describes the existence of communicative clues within the relevance theoretic framework.[1] These are linguistic options selected by a writer by means of which he wants to communicate something that is not necessarily encoded in the language. They are to be understood as stimuli the reader has to perceive in order to wholly comprehend the communicative and informative intentions of the author. Gutt implements these features in order to analyse translations. My intention in this paper is to extend Gutt's proposal and prove the validity of these features as criteria for the analysis of historical texts so as to arrive at new conclusions or, at least, to provide old ones with formal explanations.

Among the possible communicative clues, Gutt quotes: type of words, syntactic structures, semantic representations, syntactic properties, semantic constraints on relevance, formulaic expressions, phonetic properties, onomatopoeia, stylistic value of words, and sound-based poetic properties. This list is not necessarily complete and new features may be taken into account. It can be argued that communicative clues, or at least part of them, are highly connected with features that traditionally have been considered stylistic properties. There is no problem in this. The interesting point is that from the relevance-theoretic framework the importance of these features does not lie in their "intrinsic value, but rather in the fact that they provide *clues* that guide the audience to the interpretation intended by the communicator" (Gutt 1991:127, his emphasis). And, at the same time, as stimuli provided by the communicator, they must enter the effort/effect mechanism or, to put it in a more appropriate terminology, they must be in agreement with the principle of relevance.

Be they stylistic features or communicative clues, the fact is that they are present in literary compositions and they are stimuli the reader has to capture. These stimuli are ostensive. Ostension embraces the communicative intention of the author. The reader has to recover the stimulus by means of an inferential process. Inferential processes are prior to linguistic decoding. Sperber and Wilson maintain that linguistic codification is more precise than non-linguistic communication; on the other hand, ostensive non-linguistic communication allows for a certain vagueness that the communicator can use to produce certain poetic effects. These effects can be intended by the writer of a literary composition who may brightly use them to call forth certain responses in the reader.

The author of GGK made use of communicative clues too. His most elementary choice was the selection of a poetic pattern. From the beginning this option conditioned the selection of other clues, even some of the most basic ones, such as semantic representations or syntactic properties. He chose alliterative poetry which, in turn, limited the choice of other clues and greatly imposed constraints on possible explicatures that might have codified the meanings he wanted to convey in a much easier way. Most likely the poem is full of communicative clues that I am not going to consider here. My intention is to concentrate on a couple of them which will suffice in attaining my aim in writing this paper: to prove their usefulness in historical studies. These two clues are the *stylistic value of words* and *sound-based poetic properties* which seem particularly relevant in the case of an alliterative poem. Let us consider them briefly.

We do have concepts about concrete objects but we also have concepts about abstract objects. Thus we can have concepts about words themselves. Gutt argues about the English word *cow*. We have a concept labelled with the English word *cow*. But we also have concepts about the English word *cow*. In other languages the users of the word will have concepts about their word, too. In relevance theory, concepts are regarded as having a logical entry, a lexical entry, and an encyclopaedic entry. Thus, each lexical item is connected to an encyclopaedic entry. In this entry it is reflected what we know about each word, and this knowledge helps us build the concept about it. A portion of this concept is the potential stylistic value of the word. This encyclopaedic information about words contributes to the interpretation of utterances. In this way words provide communicative clues for the interpretation intended by the communicator.

The fact that GKK is included in the English alliterative renewal of the fourteenth century makes it particularly attractive to analyse the presence of the above-mentioned communicative clues. Taking into consideration the first type, *sound-based poetic properties*, it is clear that they gear the linguistic realisation of alliterative poems, and that is also the case in GGK. In the light of relevance theory, these properties are stimuli that the reader must process and contextualise as poetic effects. Other things being equal, one might conclude that GGK is one more alliterative poem within the Anglo-Saxon tradition.

But things are not so simple. We know very well that we cannot speak of a true Anglo-Saxon tradition in those days: To begin with, there is very little written material to be able to trace back the continuity of the tradition. Secondly, we do not even know whether there was any oral counterpart which is, in origin, the true *raison d'être* of alliterative compositions. Thirdly, the patterns in the fourteenth century were sensibly different from those in previous periods. But we cannot tell whether this is the result of evolution or of individual attempts to revive old traditions. And finally, new literary tendencies were already flourishing in other parts of the country. In the middle of this doubtful panorama, there appears the unknown author of some skilfully elaborated poems.

This conjunction of factors raises a lot of questions. Why does this writer make use of alliterative patterns? Does he want to make up a well designed story in an alliterative structure or does he want to do alliteration and include some fragments at random so as to make up a coherent plot? What is prior, alliteration or plot?

It has been extensively discussed that content was very important for this author as is shown by the fact that the three poems he left us have very well-worked-out plots. It is not so clear why he delivered his stories in alliterative patterns. And it is still less clear what importance he conferred to the use of alliteration. Did he want to use alliterative patterns at any rate? Did he have to give up other devices in favour of alliteration? Was he geographically conditioned? Did he ostensibly decide in favour of an opposition to London and its innovative techniques? Did he feel more at his ease with the Anglo-Saxon traditions? It is hard to believe that he did not know what type of literature there was being written in London at the time. His works show signs that this man was highly educated and had an extensive culture; the poem itself shows the author's knowledge about the classical world, his acquaintance with older plots composed in French and other languages.

In *Pearl*, he makes use of more innovative devices such as rhyme and number of syllables. Did he not want to be innovative in this poem or, at least, did he not want there to be an additional cost from that side? Did he only want to invest in the cost of alliteration? What is his leading interest here? Can we find an answer to these questions from relevance theory?

Utterance interpretation is sensitive to processing effort. In the case of an alliterative poem, which in turn may make use of other poetic devices, the author has to decide constantly on what type of makeshift he selects so that the poem may attain the intended contextual effects at the lowest cost. When an author embarks on a poetic piece of writing he, at least, has two aims: to communicate some message and to achieve a certain degree of artistic architecture. As a matter of fact, a poet must always search for a certain poetic building as, otherwise, he must have decided on prose writing. Thus, one of the author's primary intentions must have been to make the reader entertain thoughts about the artistic quality of the poem similar to those he entertained when he was writing it. The most basic artistic features in a poem are instanciated in the type of words the writer selects and also in the way he arranges them to attain rhythm, rhyme, sequence of sounds, etc. All these features are chances the writer offers himself when embarking on such a work, but at the same time they impose limits to his possibilities of conveying thoughts in the most appropriate linguistic devices, in the most economic display. If relevance theory is right, the author's choice should always be geared by the search for relevance, and this is the result of the cost-benefit balance: largest contextual effects at the lowest processing effort. This must have been the choice of GGK's author, too.

It is time to turn to the *stylistic value of words*, the other communicative clue I want to consider. The existence of a large number of loan words is a striking feature of GGK. In my opinion, the presence of French words is particularly curious, taking into account that these words are used to produce alliteration. There are lines in which there are more native words:

Hit is þe worchyp of yourself þat noȝt bot wel conneþ

For were I worþ al þe wone of wymmen alyue

And ay þe lady let lyk as hym loued mych

but there are many lines in which there are lots of French words

Vnder couertour ful clere, cortyned aboute

Of bewté and deborneté and blyþe semblaunt

And, soberly your seruaunt, my souerayn I holde yow

As it were, French words seem to attract the use of more French words. In this respect it is interesting to remember *The Brut*. In this older alliterative poem, somehow a rendering of a French writing, the absence of French loan words is a feature of the poem. Certainly, at the end of the fourteenth century, large numbers of French words were part of the everyday vocabulary. In this way GGK is not necessarily innovative. However, taking into account Gutt's ideas, the concept one has about French words should be different to that one has about native words. This is very frequently the case now, and it must have been more so in the fourteenth century. The encyclopaedic entry of French words offers wider information than that of more common native words. This information provides certain words with a connotative and stylistic potential that other words lack. However, the recovering of all this knowledge represents a bigger cost. The processing effort is greatly increased, and consequently, the relevance of the utterances in which these words are included decreases proportionally. With his choice the author lowered his communicative standards.

My point is that he did not: he increased the processing effort because it was worthwhile to do so in order to attain greater contextual effects. However, French words were not used in a well-designed distribution in search of wider contextual effects of their own. That is, the writer did not want the reader to spend the greater effort needed to process words with wider encyclopaedic information in order to attain the contextual effects they might call forth. Probably that would be too high a price for a poem with a more valuable craft. The author did not mind using words that necessarily increased the reader's processing effort because his interest lay in the construction of a well-designed alliterative structure attending to the sound-based poetic properties provided by the arrangement of lexical items, no matter whether they were native, French or even Danish. That was his leading interest. It was worthwhile to increase the cost.

His aim was to maintain the alliterative patterns no matter how difficult or remote the items selected were. No matter how high the processing effort might be, his intention was to achieve alliterative effects. To this, we add the fact that he made up his plot out of chunks extracted from stories of non-native origin. We may, then, hypothesise that the author's primary intention was to build an alliterative architecture where he could fancifully include chunks drawn from varied stories, words of all types and arrangements at ease. In other words, plot, constituent fragments and all types of linguistic and poetic devices were subsidiary to the author's primary intention. The poem was not just casually another alliterative poem within a vanishing native tradition. What the poet wanted above all was to intentionally construct a well-designed alliterative mold. And that was probably the most highly intended communicative clue.

As said at the beginning, this paper has tried to be exploratory rather than conclusive. However, as a final point I would like to emphasise that if a literary work is to be considered an act of communication, it can be approached from the relevance-theoretic framework. It is to be regarded as a piece of ostensive behaviour where linguistic codification as such is not the only stimulus to modify the reader's cognitive environment. Linguistic communication is primarily an instance of ostensive behaviour and has to be evaluated as such.

The presumption of relevance will also apply to literary compositions. If relevance is to be attained, it will have to be so in terms of cost and benefit, that is, in terms of processing effort and contextual effects. Perhaps this is the masterly formula to create one of those works that time styles as classical or the formula to build up a bestseller. Maybe this statement is too daring or even too simple. It has not been my intention to state great assertions. I have been more interested in taking smaller issues of the theory and proving their usefulness to formally explain features of a historical literary work.

Notes

1.   Gutt studies communicative clues in relation to translation. My point here is to apply
      the concept.

References

Gutt, Ernst-August
      1991   *Translation and Relevance. Cognition and Context*. Oxford: Blackwell.
Sperber, Dan, and Deirdre Wilson
      1986   *Relevance. Communication and Cognition*. Oxford: Blackwell.

Part II: Diachronic form-to-function mapping

Pragmatic Maxims in Explanations of Language Change?

José Pinto de Lima
University of Lisbon

1. The introduction of the concept of a pragmatic maxim in explanations of language change

In the second edition of his excellent book on historical and comparative linguistics, Raimo Anttila mentions maxims as a factor to be reckoned with in explaining how a certain language state, or language order, comes about:

> An order is explained as the causal consequence of intentional actions performed according to similar rationality principles (maxims) (Anttila 1989: 409).

The reference to maxims was motivated by Anttila's consideration of Rudi Keller's work on the so-called *invisible-hand mode of explanation* of language change, as one can infer from both the title and the bibliography of the section of the book where maxims are mentioned.

Let us therefore turn to Keller to understand better why maxims should be appealed to in explanations of language change. In numerous articles (Keller 1982, 1984, 1985, 1987, 1989a, 1989b, 1992) and a book (Keller 1990), Keller has suggested that language change is an *invisible-hand process*. The expression 'invisible-hand' is intended to call attention to the fact that this process is neither purely causal (involving natural causes only) nor purely final (involving only intentions directed towards ends), but is of a mixed type, where both causes and intentions play a role. A brief definition that might enhance the interplay of the causal and the intentional factors might be that language change is an invisible-hand process in so far as it is the *causal* effect of the cumulation of individual speakers' actions whose individual *intentions,* however, were not directed at the production of such an effect, which appears at the *social* level.

Language change would thus be a social phenomenon of the same kind as inflation or traffic-jams. Inflation is also the causal consequence (at the macro-level) of a cumulation of individual actions of the most varied economic agents (at the micro-level), whose intentions were not directed at the production of inflation; and a traffic-jam may be the causal result of drivers' actions in this way: in order to avoid collision with a putative obstacle, a driver slows down, and every driver behind him slows down, too. As prudence recommends that each driver should reduce speed to a value inferior to that of the driver in front, the cumulation of this kind of (intentional) attitude eventually (and causally) results in a standstill, which, however, was not intended by any driver.

An invisible-hand explanation of language change can be conceived as consisting of several steps, which I will try to present on the basis of an example by Keller:[1]

(1)   *The situation before the change.* At the beginning of the 19th century, the German form *englisch* had two meanings: $englisch_1$ meant 'angelic' (from German *Engel*, 'angel') and $englisch_2$, meant 'english'. It was a case of homonymy, which, however, did not give rise to significant conflict (i.e. misunderstandings) in communication.

(2)   *Change in ecological conditions:* industrial progress in England led to an ever-increasing introduction of English products into German territory, so that the occasions for using $englisch_2$ became more and more frequent.

(3)   With the increase in use of $englisch_2$, the danger of homonymic clashes with $englisch_1$ became real.

(4)   Those who wanted to avoid these clashes and consequent misunderstandings had the possibility of using – instead of $englisch_1$ – another word derived from *Engel*, namely, *engelhaft*. The German derivation rules, however, did not provide an alternative for $englisch_2$.

(5)   *Following of pragmatic maxims.* In avoiding $englisch_1$ and using *engelhaft* instead, speakers were following the pragmatic maxims:

(A) "Speak in such a way as to avoid being misunderstood as much as possible!"
(B) "Speak in such a way as to be understood!"

(6)   *The invisible-hand process:* this process begins with the avoidance of $englisch_1$; but as words which are less frequently used are also more difficult to remember, $englisch_1$ gradually ceased to be part of the memorised vocabulary of an ever-increasing number of speakers; on top of this – as words which cannot be recalled cannot be taught either – the

number of speakers of the younger generations who were taught *englisch*₁
progressively decreased; after a certain point, even those speakers who
still knew the meaning of *englisch*₁ tended to avoid it — even in those
contexts where there would be no risk of a homonymic clash — simply
because their chance of being understood was slight.

(7)   *The explanandum*, i.e. the fact that *englisch*₁ disappeared from German
      can now clearly be seen as the causal consequence of the invisible-hand
      process just described.

As we can see, the process which the form *englisch*₁ underwent can properly be
called an *invisible-hand process* because it satisfies the definition given above:

(a)   there are both intentional and causal factors involved: speakers avoid the
      form *englisch*₁ with the intention of not being misunderstood, and the
      cumulation of these intentional acts of avoidance causally results in the
      disappearance of the form;

(b)   the individual intentions were, however, *not directed* at the production of
      the effect obtained: in avoiding the form *englisch*₁, speakers simply
      intended not to be misunderstood, and they did not for a second have the
      intention of making *englisch*₁ disappear from the language; in spite of this,
      the form in fact disappeared.

2.   Trying to locate maxims amidst norms

From this illustration of the invisible-hand process of language change, the role
of pragmatic maxims stands out clearly: pragmatic maxims are appealed to in
order to account for the individual speakers' intentional behaviour. Pragmatic
maxims enter invisible-hand explanations at the *micro-level*: the level of the
individual and of the intentional. These maxims are a fundamental element in the
explanation, in so far as it is Keller's contention that it is the fact of their being
repeatedly followed by many speakers that gives rise to language change in the
long run.

In what follows, I will raise some questions about the relevance of this
appeal to maxims. I will, first of all, ponder over the concept of a maxim itself;
then, I will try to make the idea plausible that language change through maxims
is just a very special case of change through rational behaviour and, beyond this,
that there can also be language change without the intervention of rational
behaviour.

Let us then begin by asking whether the notions of a *maxim* and of *following a maxim* are well suited to describe the kind of linguistic behaviour that gives rise to change. What is a maxim, after all?

On one point there seems to be general agreement among authors, and this is that the word 'maxim' stands for a normative concept, just like 'rule', 'norm', 'principle', and others. On the question of how the concept should be delimited in relation to other normative concepts, however, there is no absolute consensus. Some authors who have written about norms do not even mention maxims specifically: these include von Wright in *Norm and Action* (1963) and Bartsch in *Norms of Language* (1987). But an important philosopher such as Max Black does – in his article on "The Analysis of Rules" (Black 1962: 95-139) – and we will take him as a starting point. Black distinguishes four main kinds of rules:

(a) *regulations*: these include traffic regulations and laws; they have definite historical moments of birth and death, have authors, are enforced by authorities, and infraction to them involves sanctions;

(b) *instructions* or *directions*: Black's examples are "In solving quartic equations, just eliminate the cubic term" and "Do not plant tomatoes until after the last frost"; instructions have neither authors nor histories, and they are assessed in view of a practical purpose: one is supposed to achieve better results by following them, so that they are typically qualified as "effective / ineffective", "confirmed / unsupported by experience", "easy / hard to follow", etc.;

(c) *precepts* or *maxims:* "It is a sound rule to pay one's debts promptly" and "A good rule is: to put charity ahead of justice" are formulations of rules of this kind (the first a prudential, and the second a moral rule); again, unlike regulations, it makes no sense to talk about anybody enforcing, rescinding or reinstating precepts, nor do they have histories or authors; they might, however, be considered similar to instructions in so far as they may be taken as expressing means for achieving purposes (e.g. to be a morally good person, or successful in social life);

(d) *principles* or *general truths*: examples are "Cyclones rotate clockwise, anticyclones anticlockwise" and "years that are divisible by 4 are leap years"; these seem to be far away from other rules, because there is no question here of something obligatory, forbidden or permitted and, besides, truth values can be ascribed to them; although they can be said to be a 'degenerate' case, it is justifiable to call them rules because they can function in an instruction-like manner as mnemonic devices in the activity of problem-solving.

In a more recent work, *Language, Sense and Nonsense* by Baker and Hacker (1984), a classification of normative phenomena is put forward in which maxims integrate a group that does not seem to have been established along lines significantly different from Black's:

> The term 'rule' belongs to a large class of expressions ramifying in many directions. We can characterize the centre of this 'semantic field' by reference to five related groupings of each of which we give a representative sample: (l) law, statute, regulation; (2) practice, code, convention; (3) standard, canon, model, paradigm; (4) maxim, principle, precept, recipe; and (5) prescription, direction, directive, instruction. Though the boundaries are not sharp, and the groupings imprecise, this list reveals distinctive focal points around which diverse normative concepts cluster, viz. (1) formal rules, voluntarily created according to rule-governed stipulations, and (2) informal rules, which exist in the practices of a social group and which are not created by norm-creating acts. Such concepts as in group (3) focus on the *evaluative* role of rules; those in (4) highlight the guiding role of 'impersonal rules', i.e. rules not addressed to anyone in particular but 'available' to anyone who wishes to adopt them. The final group emphasizes rules *issued* by individual authorities, often *to* individual subjects. (Baker/Hacker 1984: 250; my italics on *maxim*)

What Max Black and Baker/Hacker say about maxims, being in general accordance with the common everyday conception, makes it easier for us to propose a plausible characterisation of their main features. A *maxim* might thus be a rule such that:

(i)   It guides human behaviour.

(ii)   It has neither definite and public authorship nor history (it makes no sense to speak of dates of creation, or of rescission, as far as maxims are concerned).

(iii) There is no authority to enforce them or to apply sanctions in cases of infraction; actually, the categories of enforcement, infraction and sanction do not apply to maxims, although it makes sense to speak of following / not following / failing to follow a maxim.

(iv)   A maxim is a rule that *an individual adopts,* such as "Never drink before evening!" or "In cases where you cannot follow both prudence and courage, choose courage!". They are rooted in the individual and therefore are not the property of a whole community or of a definite group. In this, maxims differ from customs, whose mode of existence is eminently social: customs exist only as long as there is general and (at least relatively) frequent compliance: otherwise, we say that the custom is dying, or is dead. Not so with maxims, which may live on as long as there are individual followers. Baker and Hacker call our attention to this point (as well as to the one under (iii) – that there is no authority for 'maxim enforcement') in the following passage:

> Rules may originate in very different ways. They may or may not emanate from an authority. [...] If they are not so created, the rules may exist in so far as they are generally accepted as rules in a social group, followed, alluded to in criticism, and invoked in justification – as are normative customs, practices, and conventions. Or, like maxims, principles, and precepts, their existence may not depend upon *general* acceptance but upon individual use, citation, and guidance. (Baker/Hacker 1984: 251)

Of course, a custom can also be adopted by an individual, but this adoption presupposes a *community* where the custom has its place and from which the individual adopts it. Such presupposition does not apply to maxims, in so far as, in the case of a maxim, the individual adopts it from other individuals, or – an even more extreme case – adopts a maxim he has coined for himself.

(v)   A point related to the previous one is that maxim adoption is an intentional and conscious act, reached after thoughtful deliberation; in opposition to this, one can become the follower of a custom simply because one 'went along with the others', or 'did what was given': normally, the custom of greeting by shaking the right hand enters into a person's life without the person ever having deliberately *decided* to share in the custom. But, on the contrary, a maxim is what an individual adopts for *himself*: it is common to hear the expression "my maxim is ..." or even "the maxim of *my life* has been ...".[2]

(vi)   Maxims are at the service of more or less clear purposes; it is in this feature that maxims come close to instructions, as Black rightly notices. The ends to be achieved can be varied: either to be healthy, or wealthy, or a good person (or, more specifically, a good father, a good student, etc.); however, I agree with Black when he says that maxims tend to be prudential or moral in character.

(vii) Maxims may clash: being a matter of individual use, it may happen that two individuals of the same community, having different opinions, may follow incompatible maxims: one may, for instance, follow the maxim formulated above that puts courage before prudence, while the other follows the inverse maxim. This is not possible with a custom or a convention: a convention to the effect that people are to drive on the right excludes a possible convention to the effect that people are to drive on the left. Given a community, there cannot exist two customs or conventions, valid for that community, that are incompatible at the level of their *formulations* (i.e. at the conceptual level), although two customs may conflict at the level of application (i.e. it may be impossible for an individual, in a concrete situation, to comply with both: this is the case of the dilemma).

(viii) Maxims are regulative, not constitutive, rules. In the spirit of Searle's definition (1969: 33-42), we may say that a rule is constitutive of a social fact when it is unthinkable that the fact may obtain without the existence of the rule: the rules of chess are constitutive of chess, because it cannot be said that the game of chess exists in a society if no member of it is acquainted with any rule of chess. Again, semantic rules are constitutive of the social fact we call 'natural language', because no natural language is conceivable without semantic rules. Constitutive rules are said to *constitute* the kind of behaviour they are relevant to, and this means that such behaviour would not be available in a community, and could not even be referred to, if no such rules existed. Constitutive rules, therefore, may be said to make that behaviour possible, or to create it. The rules of chess constitute chess behaviour, because there can be no talk of chess-playing behaviour where no rules of chess are available. On the other hand, regulative rules apply to already existent behaviour and merely modify it in one direction or other.

Now, it is obvious that maxims are regulative: the maxim "Never drink before evening!" does not make drinking behaviour (im)possible (unlike the checkmate rule in chess, which makes checkmating possible), but simply sets limits to drinking habits.

(ix) Maxim-oriented behaviour differs from *habitual* behaviour in significant respects:

(a) Maxim-oriented behaviour is *mnemonic*, while habitual behaviour is not. A maxim is something one *keeps in mind* and then *recalls* when the appropriate occasion arises. One can *fail* to recall a maxim, be *reminded* of a maxim, or *incorrectly recall* a maxim, while it makes no sense to say of someone that he failed to recall his habit, has to be reminded of it or incorrectly recalls it.

(b) Behaviour according to a maxim never corresponds to what one would do *out of habit* or *in the normal course of events*. Therefore, maxim following does not have to be a regular affair. It takes place only when an unusual situation requires unusual actions, or when one has to fight against propensities or habits. Someone who drinks only in the evening *out of habit* cannot be said to be following the maxim "Never drink before evening!"; on the other hand, of somebody who has a tendency to drink during the day and does not do so on a certain day, one may say that he *witfully keeps to* this maxim.

3.   Do maxims play a role in language change?

After this characterisation of maxims, we turn now to the question of whether maxims are in fact, as Keller (1990) defends, involved in the process of language change. Let us come back to Keller's own example of *englisch₁*, given in section 1, and ask whether the injunctions Keller puts forward as playing a role in the disappearance of *englisch₁*, namely

(A)   "Speak in such a way as to avoid being misunderstood as much as possible!"
(B)   "Speak in such a way as to be understood!"

can properly be called 'maxims'.

My answer is that, basically, they cannot. Of course, it looks as if speakers who avoided the form *englisch₁*, for fear of confusion with *englisch₂*, were following a maxim with the formulation (A). But, certainly, a more plausible (and empirically more adequate) way to describe what went on would be to say that speakers avoided *englisch₁* simply in order *to avoid being misunderstood*. That a speaker may act thus does not mean that he is under the compulsion of a maxim, but simply that he has a *reason* to act the way he does. "To avoid being misunderstood" is, therefore, not the content of a maxim, but the content of a reason. In fact, injunction (A) does not satisfy some important requisites for maxims given in section 2, namely (iv) and (v).

As far as requisite (iv) goes, it is to be noticed that injunction (A) is not something an *individual adopts* for himself, because homonymic clashes of the type *englisch₁ / englisch₂* do not occur so often in communication as to lead a speaker into creating a maxim that would guide him in his behaviour. The facts are better described by saying that, when confronted with the possibility of a homonymic clash, a speaker chooses *on that occasion* to avoid the clash. And we may add that, on many other occasions, the same choice is made – simply because it is the *rational* thing to do – giving rise to a process of language change.

Concerning requisite (v), we may say that, even if it may look *as if* a speaker, in avoiding *englisch₁*, were following an explicit injunction whose formulation would be "Speak in a such a way as to avoid being misunderstood as much as possible!", it is more or less obvious that this formulation cannot be looked upon as having been in any way adopted at a given historical moment after *deliberation.* It is certainly a distortion of the language facts to consider that the matter of avoiding the homonymic clash *englisch*$_1$ / *englisch*$_2$ was ever thoughtfully pondered and deliberated upon by the speakers of German. As if this were a matter of life or death! Certainly, the clash between the two senses of *englisch* may have been noticed by some attentive linguists of that time, but this fact by itself is neither sufficient nor necessary to explain the disappearance of *englisch*$_1$, because this disappearance was a consequence of the behaviour of millions of speakers who were perfectly unaware of the opinions and even of the existence of these hypothetical linguists.

Finally, let us notice that requisite (ix (a)) is obviously not satisfied by injunction (A) either. When, in the course of communication, a speaker comes across a possible clash like *englisch*$_1$ / *englisch*$_2$, or any other source of misunderstanding, and accordingly chooses his words or sentence frames in such a way as to avoid being misunderstood, he certainly does not act so because the possibility of misunderstanding has caused him to recall a previously memorised injunction. The reason for this is simply that no injunction has been memorised in the first place. That when we try to avoid a misunderstanding, we do not act on the grounds of previous memorisation, I take to be an obvious fact, which anyone can confirm by looking at his own experience. Besides, if we consider the reason why an injunction has to be memorised, it immediately becomes clear why injunction A is no candidate for memorisation: an injunction is memorised when what it says, i.e. its contents, goes against what one would do by tendency or habit. As our tendency would lead us to act in a certain way, an injunction has to be memorised that will help us fight against our propensity at the right moment (remember the example given above of the maxim "Never drink before evening"). However, in the case of communication, there is no attested propensity on the part of speakers to express themselves misleadingly, and thus to give rise to misunderstandings; at least, as far as I know, no linguist has ever pointed to such a fact. The truth of the matter seems to be that speakers are neutral as to misleading speech behaviour: they have neither a propensity to fall prone to it nor to avoid it.

4.   What categories, normative or not, are involved in language change?

From the argumentation so far expounded, we may conclude that we have found no decisive evidence in favour of the thesis that maxims, in the central sense of the word, are present in the kind of linguistic behaviour that gives rise to language change. Instead of appealing to maxims of communication, the case of *englisch*₁ / *englisch*₂ – we maintain – is better explained simply by saying that *rational behaviour* has led speakers to avoid *englisch*₁, thus giving rise – by an invisible-hand process – to its disappearance from the language. The expression 'rational behaviour' is meant to signify that speakers had a *reason* for acting as they did; but the reason does not have to be that there is a maxim that ought to be followed, for, as a matter of fact, such a maxim does not exist.

Rational behaviour does not only play a role in the disappearance of *englisch*₁, but is also present in all similar cases of homonym disappearance and, in fact, in many other instances of language change. It is indeed a pervasive element in phenomena of this kind. However, one should not overgeneralise. Some phenomena about communication which look like cases of rational behaviour are in fact better explained in different terms. A case in point is behaviour according to the so-called 'principle of least effort': the passage of Latin *octo* to Italian *otto,* although an example of change due to ease of articulation, cannot, however, be said to be the result of rational behaviour. The reason is that this process of change involved millions of speakers through many occasions of use during a considerable stretch of time, so that it cannot be said, of any particular speaker, on any particular occasion, that he pronounced *octo* with a lax articulation out of a *reason.* As it has been frequently pointed out by linguists, the speaker is not aware of having spoken laxly: he is not conscious of any degree of laxness. Therefore, it cannot be said that he was lax out of a reason: he would be unable to name one. This is very different from the *englisch*₁ case, where a speaker – if asked why he had favoured *engelhaft* instead of *englisch*₁ – might very well point to a reason by saying that he wanted to avoid being misunderstood. The change from *octo* to *otto* is a piecemeal process, distributed over many years and millions of speakers, where minute, and mainly unconscious, deviations from a standard pronounciation have all, or mostly, gone in the direction of laxness; this laxness, having 'piled up' along the time line, has ultimately led to the elimination of the velar plosive.[3] It makes no sense, in this case, to characterise the speakers' behaviour as rational (or irrational, for that matter). All that may be said is that speakers followed a *tendency* to minimise effort, which is to be located more on the *natural* than on the cultural and rational side of their being.[4]

Therefore, it would be clearly inadequate to speak, as Keller (1990: 135) does, of a maxim like "Speak in such a way as to avoid unnecessary effort" being at work in this case. Even the term 'principle' can be misleading, since we are not dealing here with norms, or rational behaviour. The best terminology is simply to speak of a *tendency to least effort*.

But the fact that we have not so far found cases of change where principles have been involved does not mean that such cases do not exist. Rudi Keller (1989a: 119; 1990: 103-104) gives an example that, I think, rightly belongs here. He defends that there is a permanent semantic change in the vocabulary for women in German (and other languages), and that this change is ultimately caused by the western principle of gallantry ~ . This courtly principle compels speakers to be exquisite in their choice of terms for women. Constantly, terms are chosen which are higher in register than the concrete speech situation would demand. In this way, for instance, in many situations where *women* would be alright, the word *ladies* is nevertheless preferred and, in German, where *Frauen* would be appropriate, the word *Damen* is uttered or written. If this preference for the exceptional is followed by many, the exceptional "becomes the norm, and exactly for that reason, it ceases to be gallant" (Keller 1989a: 119). In this way, by an invisible-hand process, abidance by the principle of gallantry leads in the long run to unintended pejoration of the terms for women. Again, we cannot truly say that a maxim is at work here. There is no maxim of gallantry if by a maxim we understand the type of norm that has been defined above in section 2. I will abstain from a thorough demonstration of this point, as the concept of a maxim has already been extensively dealt with and as the main characteristics of the norm involved in gallantry are common knowledge, but I will nevertheless point to the fact that the principle of gallantry is not individual-bound (it is indeed the principle of whole communities), it is not adopted as the result of conscious deliberation, it is not mnemonic in kind, and it is doubtful whether it can be said to be behaviour-dissuasive. The principle of gallantry might be better classified as a *custom* in the way this concept is generally conceived.[5] We can, however, continue calling it a 'principle' if it is clear that 'principle' is being used as another term for 'norm'.

The principle of gallantry is the first example we have seen so far that goes to show that norms can be a factor of language change. More generally, it can easily be seen that customs relating to *politeness* are apt to be factors of linguistic change. More generally still, it is plausible to admit that any custom that may imply restrictions on what can be said, or on how what can be said is to be said, on given occasions, is the kind of norm whose following may give rise to language change.

Arguments in favour of this thesis can be gathered from religious norms. Some of these compel speakers to avoid uttering sacred expressions on many occasions, namely those on which their utterance would be felt as futile, and hence instances of profanity (remember Deuteronomy 5, 11: "Thou shalt not take the name of the Lord thy God in vain"). This religious taboo has been responsible throughout the centuries for many language changes, such as the creation of terms like *parbleu* and *morbleu* in French (where *bleu* respectfully replaces *Dieu*).[6] The following of religious norms is also responsible for the coinage of new terms for taboo realities: the German word *Gottseibeiuns* has begun its career as an euphemism for the Devil.

Not only religious norms, but any norms relating to taboos are likely to induce linguistic, and particularly semantic, changes: it is well known that the Germanic words for 'bear' are derived from a term which originally only meant 'the brown one': the word began as a euphemism for the name of the animal, which was considered taboo. Again, it is clear that these norms which restrict the use of taboo expressions are not maxims, but social customs.[7]

5.   Language change with no normative origin

Besides cases of language change that have speakers' norm-following at their origin, we have seen that there are cases in which the changes in language are not attributable to speakers' following norms, but to other factors of which we mentioned two: rational behaviour (example: the disappearance of *englisch*₁ from German), and natural tendency (example: the 'principle of least effort').

We seem to be heading towards a taxonomy of kinds of language change. It would be preposterous, however, to try to offer one in a paper this size. We will therefore limit ourselves to point to some basic facts which, we think, any acceptable taxonomy will have to contemplate. In a nutshell, they are the following:

(a)   Although examples of maxims originating changes are hard to come by, examples of norm-following behaviour giving rise to changes are conspicuous; thus, changes may be the product of speakers' following norms of social politeness, religious norms, and still others we have had no occasion to touch on in this article.

(b)   Some changes have no norms at their origin: some are simply the result of speakers' *natural tendencies*, others are the result of speakers' *rational behaviour.*

About this last factor, rational behaviour, some further remarks have to be made. The first thing to stress is, of course, that the cases of norm-following behaviour are also cases of rational behaviour. This is because we define rational behaviour as behaviour where a reason can be traced back to the person behaving. For the person who acts by following a norm, the norm can surely be given as the reason for his or her action.

The second thing that is important to stress about rational behaviour is the way it relates to those language changes referred to in the literature as having a *metaphorical* or a *metonymical* basis. It is generally accepted that metaphor and metonymy are the two great sources of semantic change. But our question is this: Where are they to be located in a classification such as the one that emerges from this article, i.e. a classification that takes norm-following as its basic criterion? Is there norm-following involved in changes resulting from metaphor or metonymy? And if there is not, can it at least be said that rational behaviour is involved?

I think the answer is different depending on whether we are talking of the metaphorical or the metonymic processes. I would say that changes introduced by metaphors are basically cases where either norm-following or, at least, rational behaviour is involved. Take the case of the word for *weasel* in Italian and Portuguese: the animal is called respectively *donnola* and *doninha* in these languages, which literally means 'little lady'. At the beginning, then, these words were euphemistic metaphors that speakers had recourse to in order to comply with a taboo norm according to which direct reference to the animal was to be avoided, as it was commonly believed that the beast (or reference to it) was a bad omen. We see that a norm relating to a superstition gives rise to the metaphorical use of a word which in the course of time becomes the common term for the referent. This example shows that norms relating to taboo, religion, etc. may lie behind the introduction of the metaphor. But other words that have originated in metaphors were introduced simply because of similarity between referents as for instance in the case of the word for a tailor's dummy, *mannequin*, which ultimately derives from a middle Dutch word for 'little man' *(mannekijn)*. In this case, no norm is involved, but rational behaviour is: resemblance between referents together with the lack of a word in the language to designate the 'new' referent make up a good reason for the introduction of the metaphor.

When it comes to metonymically-based semantic changes we have to be more careful, as many cases that are considered in the literature as having to do with metonymy really have not, in my opinion. The cases that *have* to do with metonymy follow a simple pattern: a metonymy is introduced into the language by a speaker or some speakers who then are followed in their use by many other speakers, so that, after a more or less long period of time, the original metonymic expression becomes the neutral one for the referent in the whole community (and this independently of whether the original metonymic link with the old referent is recoverable by the speakers or not). A much cited example is the word *bluestocking* ('learned woman'), which began its history as a true metonymy introduced into English in the 18th century by Admiral Boscawen, who thus meant a literary society, a member of which wore blue stockings instead of the appropriate black ones. Other examples are words for physical standard measures, such as *ampere, volt* and *ohm,* which received the names of their inventors.

But some cases of apparent metonymic change do not have a truly metonymic origin. The French word for 'workers' strike', *grève,* for instance, comes from the name of a place in Paris, *Place de Grève,* where workers used to meet when they had no work. This example is frequently cited as a case of metonymic change.[8] In spite of this, the differences to the above-mentioned cases of *true* metonymic change should not be overlooked. The most striking one is that in this example no word or expression was introduced by some speaker with the intention that it be taken as a metonymy. In opposition to the *bluestocking* example, where we find the name of a garment *used to* refer to a member of a society (and to the society itself), what we have here is not an utterance of *Je vais à la (Place de) Grève* or *Je fais la (Place de) Grève* taken to mean by the speaker that he is striking or going to strike. The expression *faire la (Place de) Grève* has *not* been introduced at a certain moment in the history of French *as a metonymic expression* for striking. The facts of the matter are a bit more complex. All we basically have at the beginning is the simple material coincidence between a place and workers in a certain situation: when they had no work, they had the habit of going to the Place de Grève. As a consequence, going to the Place and not working came to be linked. When, later in the course of history, workers lost the habit of going to the Place de Grève when they didn't work, the use of the expression *faire la Grève* was nevertheless retained because of its high probability of being understood. This understanding, however, was not the understanding of the expression as a metonymy, since it was merely based on historical antecedents. At no moment do we find a metonymy in this case, but a different pattern: a material coincidence first, and a subsequent continuous tradition of designating a certain activity with a certain routine expression.

Semantic changes that have their origin in true metonymies are similar to the ones induced by metaphors: recourse to metonymy is either triggered by the need to comply with a norm (this is the case of the word *bear*, which originally meant 'the brown one': the metonymy was introduced to comply with a taboo norm), or when no norm is involved but rational behaviour is, because it is rational to designate a 'new' referent by the term for another referent which is somehow contiguous to the 'new' one (this is what happens in the *bluestocking* case).

Pseudo-metonymic cases like *faire la grève*, on the other hand, do not seem to have anything to do with rationality, for we cannot say that any speaker was, at any historical moment, ever confronted with the question of describing a new reality 'striking' with the name of a contiguous referent – (*Place de*) *Grève*. The truth of the matter is simply that two realities, having coincided for a time, gave rise to a constant association between them, so that the assertion that the first one obtained came to be taken as equivalent to the assertion that the second one also obtained, and eventually to a situation where the simple expression *faire la Grève* was no longer taken as an assertion concerning a certain place in Paris, but as an assertion about striking. There was thus a change of reference, but one that came about *due to historical fortuitous circumstances*, and not one having its origin in any *rational* speech act of intended displaced reference (as is the case in true metonymy). Since rationality plays no part in this type of language changes, we will call them changes by *material coincidence*.

According to Anttila (1989: 141-143), metaphor and metonymy are processes of change by iconicity and indexicality as far as the *meaning* of linguistic units goes. He also mentions two other mechanisms of change concerning the *form* of linguistic units, so that the following pattern obtains (Anttila 1989: 142):

	Iconicity (similarity)	*Indexicality* (contiguity)
Meaning	metaphor	metonymy
Form	folk etymology	ellipsis

In order to complete our classification of the origins of change, we have to ask ourselves where we should locate folk etymology and ellipsis. Again, the answer is that, basically, they are changes produced by *rational behaviour*. Folk etymology, for instance, is responsible for the appearance of the German word *Sündflut* ('deluge') after the original *sinvluot,* which meant 'general flooding'. In the course of time, however, speakers became ignorant of the fact that *sin* meant 'general', and thus were led to the (wrong) idea that it was a variant of *Sünde* 'sin'. This eventually caused a change in the form of the word and also in its meaning: it began to be pronounced *Sündflut* and to be interpreted as meaning a flooding which is a punishment for humans' sins. We might be tempted to attribute this change to sheer ignorance of a more erudite form, but there is more to it than this, since plain ignorance might simply see in *sinfluot* an opaque form (as far as the element *sin* is concerned) and people might thus continue to use it; the new form *Sündflut*, however, results from a *rational* endeavour to find a motivation behind opacity. In general, I think we may say that a rational attitude always lies behind changes by folk etymology.

Finally, changes by ellipsis are also the product of rational behaviour. What leads a speaker to say *a daily* instead of *a daily newpaper* or even *a paper* instead of *a newspaper*, is that, other things being equal, shorter forms are to be preferred to more complex ones, as they require less effort. Something like a 'principle' of least effort is present here. However, contrary to what goes on in the phonological cases of the *octo > otto* type, this cannot be called a 'natural tendency to least effort'. The expression 'natural tendency' was used above to characterise a process of very slow change which goes on unnoticed by the individual speaker, so that reason plays no part in the process. But this is not what happens in the evolution from *daily newspaper* to *daily*. Here, introducers of the shorter expression are very well aware of behaving elliptically and may forward easiness of expression as their reason for their preference.

6.   A summarising diagram

Having begun by inquiring into the correctness of appealing to maxims in order to explain the origins of changes in language, we were brought to the conclusion that such changes can get triggered off in a number of ways that are more varied than the 'maxim-hypothesis' would let us suppose. Language change induced by maxim-following is just a special case of change by norm-following, which in turn is a case of change by rational behaviour. The first distinction to be made, in fact, is that between language changes that occur as consequence of rational choices of speakers, and those in which reason plays no part. In this last class, a dichotomous distinction is to be observed between changes by natural tendencies and those by material coincidence. As far as changes resulting from rational behaviour are concerned, we ought to keep apart those in which norm-following is involved from those in which it is not. Finally, changes attributable to norm-following can be of various kinds, which are as many as the types of norms involved: general principles, customs, laws, religious norms, taboo norms, and others. (An exhaustive classification of norms is, understandably, beyond the scope of the present paper.) These distinctions are represented in the following diagram, where reference is made to examples given along the text:

Language change...	... as the ultimate result of rational behaviour:	as the result of norm following: custom (ex: terms for women in German), religious norms (ex. Fr. *parbleu*), taboo norms (ex: Engl. *bear*, Ger. *Bär*), etc.
		unconnected to norm following: (ex: the disappearance of Ger. *englisch* 'angelical')
	... unconnected to rational behaviour:	as the result of natural tendency: (ex: Lat. *octo* > It. *otto*)
		as the result of material coincidence: (ex: Fr. *faire la grève*)

Notes

1. What follows is a slightly simplified version of the description in Keller (1990: 125-127).

2. It is interesting to note that dictionaries reflect precisely this facet of maxims as being "individual rules of life". The *Wahrig Deutsches Wörterbuch* (1986) registers under the German word *Maxime*: "[...] Grundsatz, Lebensregel; die ~ seines Lebens war [...]". *The New Shorter Oxford English Dictionary* (1993) registers as the third sense of the word: "A rule or principle of conduct [...]"; and defines *maximist* as "[...] a person who makes or coins maxims [...]". This definition is in accordance with our conception of maxims as rules that may be the creation of an individual, in opposition to customs, which are by necessity products of communities.

3. Heringer (1985: 269) also stresses that language changes possess this peculiar feature of involving a great number of speakers over relatively long stretches of time.

4. Explaining the workings of the 'principle of least effort' in terms of a natural tendency towards simplification is in accordance with what Raimo Anttila says about language

change. Anttila claims that multiple factors of varied nature are responsible for change, but acknowledges "the psychological factor to be the strongest one – that is, the general *tendency* toward simplicity and symmetry" (Anttila 1989: 193; my italics). Later on, he connects the principle of least effort – as well as its counterpart, the principle of perceptual differentiation – to naturalness: "The principle of perceptual differentiation maximizes the degree of perceptual contrast, and the principle of least effort minimizes articulatory expenditure. The balance between these two factors keeps the phonology *natural*, 'easy-to-hear' and 'easy-to-say'" (Anttila 1989: 198; my italics).

5.   On custom, see section 2 above and references given there.

6.   The terms chosen, here and throughout the article, to exemplify the role of normative behaviour in language change do not claim to be original: on the contrary, common examples were sought, so that the plausibility of our theses might be more easily assessed. Most of these exemplifying terms can be found in Ullmann (1962) and in Anttila (1989). Whether these authors would agree with my explanations and classifications is, of course, another matter.

7.   They are, therefore, community-dependent, as can be seen from the fact that the list of animals (and other objects) which are considered taboo changes considerably from one society to another (see Ullmann 1962: 205-206).

8.   Ullmann (1962: 218-219), for instance, takes it to be so.

References

Anttila, Raimo
    1989   *Historical and Comparative Linguistics.* Amsterdam: John Benjamins.
Baker, George P., and Peter M. S. Hacker
    1984   *Language, Sense and Nonsense. A Critical Investigation into Modern Theories of Language.* Oxford: Basil Blackwell.
Bartsch, Renate
    1987   *Norms of Language. Theoretical and Practical Aspects.* London: Longman.
Black, Max
    1962   "The analysis of rules." In: Max Black (ed.). *Models and Metaphors.* Ithaca / London: Cornell University Press, 95-139.
Heringer, Hans Jürgen
    1985   "Not by nature nor by intention." In: Thomas T. Ballmer (ed.). *Linguistic Dynamics. Discourses, Procedures and Evolution.* Berlin / New York: Mouton de Gruyter, 251-275.
Keller, Rudi
    1982   "Zur Theorie sprachlichen Wandels." *Zeitschrift für Germanistische Linguistik* 10, 1-27.

1984   "Zur Theorie des Sprachwandels." *Zeitschrift für Germanistische Linguistik* 12, 63-81.

1985   "Towards a theory of linguistic change." In: Thomas T. Ballmer (ed.). *Linguistic Dynamics.. Discourses, Procedures and Evolution.* Berlin / New York: Mouton de Gruyter, 211-237.

1987   "Der evolutionäre Sprachbegriff." In: Rainer Wimmer (ed.). *Sprachtheorie.* Düsseldorf: Schwann, 99-120.

1989a   "Erklärung und Prognose von Sprachwandel." *Zeitschrift für Phonetik, Sprachwissenschaft und Kommunikationsforschung* 42, 383-396.

1989b   "Invisible-hand theory and language evolution." *Lingua* 77, 113-127.

1990   *Sprachwandel.* Tübingen: Francke.

1992   "Zeichenbedeutung und Bedeutungswandel." *Zeitschrift für Semiotik* 14, 327-366.

Searle, John R.

1969   *Speech Acts.* London / New York: Cambridge University Press.

Ullmann, Stephen

1962   *Semantics. An Introduction to the Science of Meaning.* Oxford: Blackwell.

Wright, Georg H. von

1963   *Norm and Action. A Logical Enquiry.* London/Henley: Routledge and Kegan Paul.

Pragmatic Constraints to Word Order and Word–Order Change in English[1]

Enrique Bernárdez and Paloma Tejada
Universidad Complutense, Madrid

1. Introduction

As is well known, the order of sentential constituents changed in a significant way during the transition from Old English (henceforth OE) to Middle English (ME). Whereas ME word order is basically coincident with that of Present-Day English (PDE), OE word order was significantly different, and, according to many scholars, it still kept some of the main features of the Common Germanic word order. A lot of research has been devoted to the understanding, description, and explanation of this important change. Many other studies examine the word-order changes in various languages, so that this is one of the types of syntactic change that has enjoyed the greatest popularity among linguists. The same also holds for the synchronic studies on word order, and after so much work done we should expect to know a lot about linguistic ordering in general and about the causes of its change, so that the issue could be considered as settled.

But this does not seem to be the case. On the one hand, the mechanisms responsible for word order are still poorly understood. On the other hand, there are very few valid *explanations* for the changes affecting the order of words, both within the history of a particular language and in languages belonging to the same family. The aim of this paper is to make a proposal for the understanding of these changes in general and in the history of English in particular. We shall first review some of the main current ideas on the issue and then put forth a proposal which should serve as the basis on which an interpretation of the word-order changes from OE to ME could be attempted. Its main tenet is that word order can only be explained in pragmatic terms;

moreover, the same (pragmatic) principles responsible for historical change are also responsible for synchronic ordering.

We shall use the term *pragmatic* to mean 'the relationship between linguistic structures and the 'world', including the communicative setting or situation, the speaker(s) and listener(s) involved, etc.' As a linguistic message or utterance is always part of an act of communication, viz. the means used by the speaker to set up a relation with the listener(s), the conditions of that act of communication will necessarily influence the product itself. This view is, of course, very close to the cognitive and functional-cognitive approaches to language, as will be clear from what follows.

We shall not consider those explanations that can be termed 'autonomously syntactic', i.e. mainly those due to Generative Grammar; in spite of the appeal of their proposals, we shall focus our attention on the phenomena observable in language use and ultimately on the cognitive principles underlying them.

2.   Some methodological prerequisites

Most scholars trying to analyse word order from a pragmatic or functional perspective agree that word-order studies require an explanation on cognitive principles[2] as well as greater empirical and methodological precision, including a quantification of the principles identified.

The explanation searched for must be based on the cognitive principles that play a part in the processing of discourse information and which are also eventually responsible for the syntax, which is taken to respond to functional semantic and pragmatic principles determined by the cognitive component. As we shall see when we come to consider the issue of *Basic Word Order*, a view like the one purported here allows an interpretation of the same facts explained in the autonomous syntax approach, which at the same time seems coherent with the explanation of non-syntactic facts, especially discoursive ones.

From this stance, the need for empirical analysis and quantification need not be emphasised: if the real texts of a language are to be the centre of our attention, only the analysis of a great number of them can confirm or disconfirm the hypotheses advanced; and this analysis cannot be but quantitative, due to the stochastic nature of textual organisation. The need for statistical methods is obvious, but more refined mathematical tools might also be used (see Altmann 1988, Köhler 1986, Altmann *et al.* 1983).

Something will be regarded as an *explanation* if it sets up a cause-effect relationship so that other causes are not needed in order to understand the effect. This relationship may be probabilistic, even if it does not provide us with a fully deterministic explanation, which, in fact, seems out of place in historical linguistics (Lass 1980; on this theoretical, epistemological issue, see Bernárdez 1995). From this point of view, the usual autonomous syntactic descriptions of word order and word-order change cannot be regarded as explanations, as they can only be fully understood if the mental processes involved in syntactic structures are included in the picture; but these are not part of syntax, whose limits have then to be abandoned in order to be able to explain syntactic phenomena. In our (pragmatic, functional or cognitive) view, however, those mental processes are an integral part of the communication process, and as such they can be used in our explanation of linguistic facts.

Our view enables us then to take into account the structure of the reality transmitted via linguistic means; essential concepts such as *iconicity* and *markedness* can only be understood in these terms. The 'problem of word order' can be seen as a part of the general 'problem of communication' in the terms sketched above: a certain reality – not only exterior: mental realities, too – is processed in the mind of the speaker and translated into linguistic elements, which are then transmitted to a listener who translates them again into a mental image of the original reality.[3] Now chronological sequencing and spatial organisation are two aspects of reality. Speakers face the problem of mapping non-linear meanings abstracted from a linearly ordered reality onto a highly constrained linear medium. A chain of events is always (chronologically) ordered, as is the spatial distribution of objects within a space; but linearity and spatiality are lost in part during the process of categorisation, to be then re-created for its linguistic transmission with the aim of enabling the listener to identify the original ordering of the elements of the reality conveyed by the message. This can be seen in the usually chronological ordering of the events told in a narrative ('iconic ordering'). At the same time, the states, processes, etc. which occur in that reality include simultaneous elements which have to be linearised for its linguistic transmission.[4]

The problems posed by the communication process are solved differently in human language, certain more economic and effective solutions being more widely adopted. The same happens in word order, which can be taken to be the solution to the particular problem discussed above. These solutions may vary historically, so that the most effective solution at a certain point of time may prove unusable at a later stage, thus leading to changes which can spread through the community (see Keller 1990 for the approach to the spread of change we are following here).

This is in fact what happens in the word-order changes from OE to ME: the solutions for the ordering problem – we shall call them *ordering strategies* – which could be considered as optimal in OE ceased to be so and were superseded by alternative strategies. This new solution was based on some of the old strategies – a high degree of continuity does exist, even up to PDE – and this can probably mean that the conditions regulating the use of those OE strategies would have become more influential than before. The change, therefore, lies ultimately much more in the *conditions determining the selection of ordering strategies* than in any internal syntactic structuring principles, or than in some not very plausible changes in the cognitive organisation of the individual. Myhill's (1992b: 186) opinion is not very different from ours: "Word-order changes do not consist simply of one order being used more and another being used less. Rather they can consist of certain constructions, involving particular verbal forms and particular word order's expanding their functions while others become more restricted."

To summarise, we can say that an explanation of word order and of word-order change has to take into account:

1.   The structure of the reality transmitted through language.
2.   The cognitive organisation of human beings (what is simpler and more complicated to process, i.e. accessibility, the order in which linguistic processing takes place, the general cognitive principles, etc.; everything related to the naturalness of linguistic change should be included here).
3.   The conditions determining the selection of comprehension strategies.
4.   The 'institutionalisation' or prototypicalisation of strategies, usually understood in syntactic terms (syntactic rules, structuring principles and the like).

Not all of these aspects are going to be discussed in this paper, of course. It shall be limited to a general consideration of part of one of the changes affecting the position of S(ubject) and V(erb) in the history of English, but we hope that it will allow us to set up the base for future empirical studies and for the refinement of our theoretical foundations. We shall be facing this problem against the background sketched in these pages and shall try to put forth a proposal which can be confirmed or not confirmed by further, more detailed studies.

3. A view of linguistic change

We take linguistic change to be due to the existence of conflicting factors which disrupt stability. Human language tends towards a state of maximum stability, which can be termed the *optimal functional state*. But no language stays for a long time in that state, if it ever reaches it, as many factors affect its stability and finally upset it. The conflicts between competing principles may also be considered responsible for the synchronic organisation of the linguistic messages, i.e. the texts (see in this respect Enkvist's 1987 view of the conspiracy and conflict of strategic principles in text-formation).

From a pragmatic and cognitive perspective these opposing principles leading to instability can be understood in terms of an *economy principle* (EC) opposing a *communicative principle* (CP) that can not be satisfied simultaneously. EC can be understood as the optimum for the speaker, as it reduces his/her effort to a minimum; CP, on the other hand, favours the needs of the listener, as it enhances the possibility of easy understanding.[5] This was also René Thom's proposal over twenty years ago (1973) in one of his first attempts to approach linguistic phenomena from the point of view of Catastrophe Theory.

We are here in the realm of the functional interpretation of linguistic change: a change serves certain aims of the language users. This is an interpretation which has been subjected to criticism, not only by Lass (1980) but also, much more recently, by Labov (1994). This criticism is indeed valid in its main traits; but recent developments both in the natural and social sciences provide us with a new way of understanding the teleology underlying all functional changes, and it is René Thom's concept of teleology which seems especially useful for the explanation of this type of process (see Bernárdez 1992; 1995). A very brief interpretation of the way of acting of our two principles (EC and CP) could be as follows: the speaker tends to use those forms which are easier to code and produce, and communication would be impossible in the last term if EC were the only acting principle; if CP prevails, understanding and decoding would be very easy for the listener but would lead to an excessive effort on the part of the speaker; according to the situations in which communication takes place, the degree in which one or the other of these principles has the leading hand will vary.

This is, so we think, a valid explanation for both the synchronic functioning of language *as it is used* and for linguistic change; CP will usually be fully favoured in the most formal situations, while EC will prevail in extremely informal communication, let us say between people who know each other very well and who are dealing with a subject equally known to all of them.

The explanation of word-order change may seem to lie in the consideration of a set of parameters responsible for ordering and which do not lead to a fully stable situation; i.e. they should contain a principle of conflict within themselves. The different ways of solving these conflicts would lead to: (a) the different orderings in different languages, (b) the synchronic dynamics of word order, and (c) the historical changes affecting word order. In this way we could reach a view of change of the ordering of the linguistic elements coherent with the most plausible of all ways of looking at change, viz. that it is based on the existence of internal conflicts.

Incidentally, we may point to the similarity of this way of looking into the dynamics of language and especially of linguistic change, and the explanation of abrupt, non-gradual changes in systems with an otherwise gradual dynamics, as put forward by Catastrophe Theory (Bernárdez 1992): a relatively stable state determined by a set of parameters can be destabilised by the action of one or more of them. Both Catastrophe Theory and Synergetics can prove their usefulness for the explanation of dynamic phenomena, especially of language use and including linguistic change.

4.   Word-order studies

We shall first analyse some of the main ideas in current word-order research in order to locate our own proposal against this background and identify the main difficulties and possible shortcomings encountered in this area of research.

Word-order typologies are a fundamental tool for the understanding of many syntactic features, and they have proved extremely useful. However, no convincing explanation has yet been found for the low frequency or even the inexistence of certain types of ordering in spite of the various proposals put forward in literature.

Word order is usually explained in terms of certain *principles*. They may range from only one, as Dryer's (1992) *branching direction theory*, to many, as in Simon Dik's Functional Grammar (1989).[6] Givón (1988) proposes two pragmatic-functional principles that probably "underlie much of what we know about the organisation of perception, cognition and behaviour": *informational predictability* and *task importance*, with a macro-principle he states in this way: *Attend first the more urgent task*. The importance of the linear organisation of processing is acknowledged by many other scholars; Payne's (1992) *focal principle* coincides also with proposals by Firbas (1987a, 1987b), Wårvik (1990), and partially Tomlin (1986) and Mithun (1992), who see the thematic information as closely related to the selection of a focus of attention. Anna

Siewierska (1988) also considers linearisation to be based on the psycholinguistic need for specifying the amount of attention required for the processing of salient information.

The point in these principles is to explain the primacy of the initial position in statements, which may range from the sentence to the full text. This primacy of the initial position, also recognised by Dik (1989),[7] was not challenged in the history of English, so that it cannot play a major role in the explanation of the changes. It seems to correspond to a fundamental cognitive principle and not to any pragmatic constraints, and it explains so much that it practically cannot be used to explicate matters of detail.

The principle stating that heavy elements are located at the end of the clause or sentence is also probably based on general human cognitive abilities and is equally too vague to be of much use. There is a clear continuity from OE (and earlier) to ME (and beyond) in this respect.

The *iconicity principle* is probably more useful, although still too abstract and based on general cognitive principles; Givón's (1985: 189) *Iconicity Meta-Principle* is formulated in these terms: "All other things being equal, a coded experience is easier to *store, retrieve* and *communicate* if the code is maximally isomorphic to the experience."[8]

More precise are Tomlin's (1986) three principles: the *Topic First Principle* (TFP) has been referred to above as one version of the *Focus Principle*, but his *Verb-Object Bonding* (VOB) is more syntactic in nature; it states that the relation of an object with a transitive verb is syntactically and semantically closer than the one tying the verb and its subject together. This is in fact a functional principle ("Semantic concepts which are closely related to one another are realised syntactically through close proximity"; Tomlin 1986: 135) which has been criticised because the term *proximity* is difficult to define in a precise way. This principle raises the issue of the structural independence of S(ubject), V(erb), and O(bject). The verb is frequently believed to be the most independent of the three, but it is far from clear whether it is the object or the subject which is the least independent. In both the generative and some functional views of language, V+O form a unity that S is somehow external to (an 'external argument'); this may be confirmed by the existence of *Object-Incorporation* and the absence of *Subject-Incorporation*. Myhill (1992b) and Moreno (1990) see a close relation between incorporation and specificity, so that it is non-specific objects which are incorporated; theirs is a functional view, but Baker (1988) has shown that incorporation can equally well be explained on the basis of formal, syntactic principles, so that its simple existence cannot be taken as evidence of a communicative-functional tie between Verb and Object.

On the other hand, the autonomous status of S and O is by no means as straightforward as it could seem. According to Dik (1989, see also Siewierska 1991), a language may lack *Subject* or *Topic Assignment*, or both, i.e. it may not have grammaticalised the syntactic functions of Subject and/or Object. *Subject Assignment* seems to be more frequent interlinguistically than *Object Assignment*, probably as a consequence of the role of the Subject as the 'primary perspective' vs. the 'secondary perspective' represented by the Object.[9] OE seems to have had the first, but not the second, as the following examples may show:

(a) Wulfstan (AgSubj) ageaf þæm preoste (Rec) þæt boc (GoObj)
     Wulfstan gave the book to the priest
(b) Wulfstan (AgSubj) ageaf þæt boc (GoObj) þæm preoste (Rec)

According to Dik (1989: 222),

> a necessary condition for the recognition of distinctive Obj-assignment in a language is the existence of an opposition such as between English:
> a. John gave the book (GoObj) to Peter (Rec)
> b. John gave Peter (RecObj) the book (Go)

where the Object function can be assigned to the semantic functions of *Recipient* and *Goal*; in OE, however, the semantic function *Recipient* cannot be assigned the syntactic function of Object and, in general, the semantic functions, as marked by the surface case endings, are kept unchanged irrespective of their NPs' position in the sentence. On the other hand, "Subject function [...] is relevant to a language if and only if that language has a regular opposition between active and corresponding passive constructions" (1989: 219), which does exist in OE.

If Dik's proposals are accepted, one additional change from OE to ME (and PDE) would be the assignment of syntactic Object, due perhaps to the loss of a clear correlation between surface cases and semantic functions or more probably to the generalised loss of the semantic and pragmatic 'transparency' of OE. It would presumably have an effect on word-order change as part of the passage from a semantic-pragmatically to a syntactically organised language (already proposed by Givón and others), which could be seen in many phenomena in the historical evolution of English: re-organisation of pronominal references,[10] specification of the relation between a main clause and its dependent clauses, clearer fixing of text-type distinctions, and also word order.

If we accept Dik's proposal, moreover, the position of the *syntactic* Object would play no role. We should be able to define the possible positions occupied by Subjects and NPs with a certain semantic function, which would bring them closer to a phenomenon usually considered separately, viz. the position of adverbials. Bean (1983) already recognised word-order patterns with three elements: S, V, and X, which she defines as everything apart from S and V, thus including the Object, the adverbials, etc.

The traditional acceptance of the existence of S and O as clearly defined entities is perhaps incompatible with a pragmatic stance, as we should be using purely syntactic concepts in a pragmatic/semantic framework. However, it is probably necessary to consider the syntactic and pragmatic aspects of word order together, as in Siewierska's proposal (1993), and this is the line we shall be following in these pages.

Tomlin's *Animated First Principle* (AFP) is also probably pragmatic, although semantic factors may play a more important role. It is not just coincidental that these three principles should correspond to the three main components of language (syntax: VOB, semantics: AFP, and pragmatics: TFP). Moreno (1991) also posits principles corresponding to the three components, his *formative* principles being rather syntactic in character, while his *informative* principles are pragmatic and semantic. But the usefulness of Tomlin's principles for the explanation of historical change seems doubtful.

Languages may be classified in groups according to the principles which are satisfied: in the SOV and SVO languages all three principles are fulfilled, while VSO languages only satisfy TFP and AFP. The VOS languages only satisfy the syntactic principle VOB, and the OSV languages satisfy none of them. The SVO and SOV languages are at the 'best' end of the continuum of 'functional optimality' while the OSV languages, on the contrary, occupy the opposite, 'worst' position. As could be expected, most languages belong to the 'optimum' group, while the existence of OSV languages (the 'least functional') still seems doubtful. The statistical correlation of the world's languages supports Tomlin's three principles, but how can we use them to explain changes in ordering? If both SOV and SVO are at the best side of the optimality continuum, why should a language change from one type to another, as seems to have been the case in the passage from Common Germanic to OE and ME (SOV → SVO)? Only changes leading to optimisation (say VOS → SVO) would be understandable from this perspective. But although SVO and especially SOV seem to be the most stable of all language-types, there are enough attested cases of change from one type to the other or even from these 'optimum' types to the 'worse' ones (e.g. SOV → VSO), as seems to have been the case in the evolution from Common Indo-European to Celtic. Moreover, why should a language NOT implement one or more of these principles?

Steele (1975: 243) puts forth two principles which she considers responsible for the ordering changes of modals: a (pragmatic) tendency similar to the *focal principle,* which reserves the initial position for certain communicative purposes, and a (syntactic) principle relatively equivalent to VOB (the grammatical elements tend to cluster around the verb), which is viewed as responsible for the disruption of stability and therefore of change: if an element has to leave the vicinity of the verb in order to receive focus, a conflict between both principles will arise. Steele's view of word-order change as a consequence of the conflict of two opposing principles coincides then with the view exposed in section 3.

Other principles proposed may seem syntactical but are in fact liable to a cognitive and functional interpretation.[11] So the clause seems to have a favoured role in ordering, as Gergely 1991 points out. It has a special perceptual status in sentence processing by the listener. According to him, the end of the clause shows an increase of local processing load, and after the clause the accessibility of lexical material decreases.

As Mallinson and Blake (1981) pointed out, the elements tend to occupy a fixed position within the sentence. This can be understood as the institutionalisation of a certain strategy, and Dryer's (1992) *branching direction theory* would fit in this picture. For reasons of simplicity of processing (economy; see below), there is a tendency for the speakers to rely on those strategies which may prove effective in most (non-marked) situations.

5. Basic Word Order and a proposal

A major issue in word-order studies is whether all languages have a *Basic Word Order.* As for the history of English, the current opinion is that OE was an SOV language which changed to SVO in ME, although the issue is still far from settled. There is widespread agreement that no language has a fully free word order, although some doubts have recently been raised in this respect (Mithun 1992); so the idea that some form of basic word order exists, although it may be altered by certain factors – which may ultimately be termed 'functional' (see Rögnvaldsson 1990) – seems attractive. Moreover, languages show differences in word order which could then be explained in these terms. In addition to all this, the word-order correlations studied by linguistic typologists (see Croft 1990) seem to reinforce this view.

Within Generative Grammar, for instance, word order is explained einerseits durch sprachspezifisch festgelegte Unterschiede in syntaktischen Repräsentationen [...] (in einigen (OV-) Sprachen stehen Köpfe hinter und in anderen (VO-) Sprachen vor ihren Komplementen) und andererseits durch sprachspezifische Variation in der syntaktischen Derivation der Strukturen: eine Bewegung findet in einer Sprache statt und in einer anderen nicht (vgl. V-nach-C Bewegung in deklarativen Hauptsätzen in V2-Sprachen, die im Englischen nicht zu beobachten ist). (Wilder and Ćavar 1994: 11).

Dik (1989) and others also accept the existence of some language-specific principle favouring a certain word-order pattern.[12] Moreover the explanation of word-order change seems easier if we accept a basic order which is then changed; in English for instance, SOV should have changed to SVO, what can be understood as a restructuration process also frequent in other types of change (see Lightfoot 1991, who includes an interesting proposal on how this restructuration could have taken place). This SOV → SVO change should have brought about other changes in word order and in other parts of the grammar.

There are several different definitions of *basic word order* (see Mithun 1992), but we shall mainly be concerned with Siewierska's (1988: 8): the order found in stylistically neutral, independent, indicative clauses with full NP participants, where the subject is definite, agentive and human, the object is a definite, semantic patient and the verb represents an action. Alternatively, it may be defined as the prototypical order in transitive clauses.[13]

This definition is not free from problems. First, there seems to exist a contradiction between the necessary presence of full NP participants and the non-marked character of the basic word order. Transitive clauses with full NPs are rare, and as such they could as well be regarded as *marked*. Normally, one or more of the NPs in a transitive clause in real texts consist of pronouns or Ø. In an OE or ME text, for example, up to 50 % of the clauses (transitive or intransitive) can have a non-overt subject-NP.[14] It is practically only in isolation that we can find this type of clause with overt NPs, and it is probably in this sense that 'unmarked' has to be understood. But if we are to deal with real texts, can this notion of basic word order be of any use? Moreover, the stylistically unmarked character of these clauses is also doubtful because, as Traugott and Romaine (1985) point out, every linguistic form is stylistically marked. In historical studies the problem is still more acute, because the texts we have to rely on can belong to stylistically (and pragmatically) very marked types. The way out of this difficulty could be to ignore these texts and pay attention only to the structural principles and the correlations between types of basic order and lower level orderings, such as those holding between SOV languages and postpositions, preposed adjectives, etc. But these correlations are not always free from problems either, as Dryer (1991, 1992) has shown.

When considering real texts in OE and ME from a pragmatic perspective, then the basic word order should yield its place to the *dominant order*, which can be defined as the most frequent order found in texts (see Siewierska 1988: 8-9). Usually it does not coincide with the basic order(and never necessarily), and is much closer to our own view of ordering, as it is dependent on pragmatic and communicative factors and is the one really found in discourse. But the dominant order may thus be different according to the text type a particular text belongs to.

A short statistical analysis of a few OE and ME texts allows us to confirm this. Six OE and six ME excerpts from texts belonging to three different types were analysed in order to identify the percentage of the two possibilities of ordering of V and S. Although the sample is too small to have any real statistical significance, the results show a clear distribution in both periods.[15] The following table shows the percentage of VS order in the sample; only those verbs were considered which had an overt subject.

Table 1: *VS order in OE and ME*

	NARRATIVE	DESCRIPTIVE	ARGUMENTATIVE
OE	18,49%	30,40%	22,37%
ME	12,34%	16,29%	6,38%

Although the standard deviation is rather high in some cases (9.32 for the OE descriptive texts, 9.91 for the OE narratives analysed), these results may illustrate a small aspect of the interrelation between text type and word order. The pragmatic and cognitive paramaters responsible for text-type distinctions could also be taken as at least partly responsible for the selection of certain orderings.

Text types are probably organised on the basis of the particular needs posed by the 'type of problem' they try to solve; the criteria regulating the information that has to be foregrounded is different in the various text types; temporal sequencing and specification of the agent may be important in narrative, but not in argumentative texts, as Wårvik (1990: 532) points out. Bernárdez and Tejada (1991) offer an analysis of the strategies used in OE documentary texts, including some remarks on word order, which are clearly not valid for other texts, e.g. for narratives.

The importance of text types for word order has also to be considered in a historical perspective. Although, as can be seen from the table above, there is a clearly lower percentage of VS order in all our ME texts, the argumentative texts show an especially significant drop (from 22.37% to a mere 6.38%). Could this mean that we are dealing with a change affecting the definition of the text type as such? Therefore, the study of the historical evolution of text-types might also be important for the study of word-order changes. Much more research is needed, of course, in order to try to confirm this hypothesis.

An alternative view to seeing word-order changes as a substitution of one basic order by a new one would be to identify the (pragmatic) parameters determining the presence of several possible orderings *and* the changes which lead to the change in word-order preference. That is, instead of positing an (underlying) basic word order in OE –SOV– which can be functionally or pragmatically altered and which disappears in ME substituted by the new SVO-order, we can understand the process along the following lines:

In OE *and* ME there exist several pragmatically determined orderings; certain factors – which have to be identified – favour certain orderings in OE; a change *in these factors* brings about a change in the ordering preferred in ME. This would enable us to *explain* both synchronic ordering and its changes, as the same parameters would be used to both effects. If we posit a basic order which is then changed or substituted by a different, new one, we should still have to find a reason for the existence of that basic order *and* for the change itself. And an idiosyncratic principle, being rather *ad hoc*, would not be a sufficient explanation. A dynamic, instead of a structural approach to word order could then enhance our knowledge of the phenomenon (see also Kindt (1994) for a rather similar view).

In OE, ME and even PDE, in fact, we find practically the same ordering possibilities; what has changed is the preference towards one or more of them in the different periods, so that what was once a usual although not statistically fully predominant order was restricted to limited contexts in ME and even more so in PDE. The data of our analysis show this clearly in spite of the small size of the sample: both SV and VS exist in both stages of English; there is a descent in the frequency of VS which goes together with the corresponding increase of SV, as can be seen from the following figures:[16]

Table 2: *Percentage of SV*

	NARRATIVE	DESCRIPTIVE	ARGUMENTATIVE
OE	81.52 %	69.60 %	77.63 %
ME	87.67 %	83.72 %	93.63 %

As in the previous table, text type seems to be a decisive factor in explaining the frequency of a certain ordering both synchronically and diachronically. Although this table does not show it, some OE texts have even a higher frequency of SV than certain of our ME texts. Ælfric's *Life of St. Oswald* has 88.52 % of its verbs following their subjects, even more than *The Book of Margery Kempe*. The difference is especially meaningful in the non-narrative texts; let us now have a look at the individual percentages for the argumentative texts:

Table 3: *SV and VS in argumentative texts*

	SV	VS
OE: *Sermo Lupi*	78.79 %	21.21 %
OE: *Cura Pastoralis*	76.47 %	23.53 %
ME: Richard Rolle	96.77 %	3.23 %
ME: Wycliff	90.48 %	9.52 %

Both OE texts show a clear preference for SV but with a high percentage of VS; that is, the *variability* of word order is rather high, but it has been greatly reduced in ME. It may be useful to examine the variability found in our texts according to their type. Variability was calculated as the standard deviation of the means of both word-order types. For a larger corpus the method has to be refined, but the results are illustrative for the purpose of this paper. The lower the figure obtained, the higher the variability.

Table 4: *Word-order variability*

TEXT TYPE	OLD ENGLISH	MIDDLE ENGLISH
Narrative	44.57%	53.27%
Descriptive	27.72%	47.68%
Argumentative	39.07%	61.70%

The narrative texts have a rather high variability both in OE and ME, but it is the descriptive texts which show the highest variability. The argumentative texts, on the contrary, have a very low value in ME, as we have already seen.

The high degree of variability in the narrative texts is perhaps a consequence of their being centred on the actions and events more than on the agents themselves. But it is necessary to confirm the relation between importance of the agent and position of the subject. Since these texts have a high degree of iconicity, variability is expectedly high. The descriptive texts, on the other hand, are less iconic in character and therefore more heavily narrator-oriented. This would lead predictably to the high degree of variability observed. As for the argumentative texts, iconicity plays only a minor role, the arguments reflecting rather the narrator's own mental activity. This would lead to high variability, but we can speculate that the lack of an external reality which might be recovered through the text, as in the narrative and descriptive text types, will make the understanding of the text more difficult for the reader. The writer then limits the possibilities of variation, reducing them to a minimum level. This can be confirmed empirically by considering a larger corpus of argumentative texts and taking into account the particular level of abstractness of each text. We should expect more abstract texts to have a lower degree of variability.[17]

This measure of the variability of word order can be interpreted in pragmatic terms: the higher the accessibility of a text, the higher its variability. This means that the variability will depend, as we have seen, on the type of text, but not in an absolute way; that is, more accessible texts belonging to a certain type (say argumentative) can have greater variability than less accessible texts of another, usually more accessible type (say descriptive). This is also Solà's (1994: 238-9) view on the higher variability of word order in Catalan colloquial texts as compared with formal, written discourse:

> Catalan is probably a remarkable language as regards the possibility of altering the order of elements; but this alteration, when it exceeds certain limits, can easily be felt as typical of the colloquial, less elaborated language, as more impressionistic. We could perhaps say that there are several ordering possibilities corresponding to the degree of formality. The "lowest" would be that of everyday colloquial language [...]. The "highest" or coldest could be the one specifically used in the scientific language [...]. This language would probably make a very reduced use of the alterations in element order [...] [Our translation].

Assuming this proposal could lead to an explanation of synchronic word-order variability, we still have to explain its changes, as it is clear that from OE to ME there was a decrease in word-order variability or, as it has always been stated, 'word order became fixed in ME'. Although it is still too early to propose an explanation, it may lie in the progressive formalisation of written English (as opposed to the spoken language) during the ME period. Many OE written texts were still close to the spoken language, although there is a progressive splitting of the two. It is in Middle English that the autonomy of the written language cuts it drastically off from the spoken form. Being less accessible to the listener than the spoken texts, variability could be expected to fall.

We can put this in relation to René Thom's proposal (1973); (see also Bernárdez (1992)) to consider SV order as 'listener-oriented' and VS as 'speaker-oriented' orders. This proposal is perhaps confirmed by facts such as the higher frequency of VS in very informal conversation in languages with variable word order, as Spanish, and even in languages which allow less variation, as Modern French. Some word-order changes in widely different languages might support the French mathematician's proposal, as VS has yielded to SV in certain Austronesian languages which have been in close contact with other languages for a long period (Malay for instance; cf. also the relatively high frequency of SV in an otherwise VS language like Tagalog), but not in other more isolated languages of the same group. In situations where the accessibility of a text to its listener or reader is not easily predictable (as is the case in situations of strong language contact), the speaker is likely to adopt a more listener-oriented form of speech. Note also that Creoles usually prefer a more fixed, SV-based order,[18] as could be expected.

We can draw the following provisional conclusions:

word order works differently according to the text types;
there existed a clear preference for the order SV in OE;
this preference for SV increases in ME;
OE had a relatively large variability of ordering;
this variability diminishes in ME.

That changes in English word order are in fact a shift in the preference for some of the orders allowed can also be seen when the patterns in OE and PDE are compared. Of the various word-order patterns described by Bean (1983) for OE, the following also exist in ME and PDE: X'VS,[19] SVX, X'SV, OSV, OVS, SXVX:

X'VS: *Þa eode se here to hiera scipum.*
          then the army went to their ships
          Into the stiffling smoke plunged the desperate mother
          (Quirk *et al.* 1985: 18.21).

SVX: *And þa Deniscan ahton sige.*
          and the Danes won the victory
          The children won the prize.

X'SV: *Her Cyneheard ofslog Cynewulf cyning.*
          Here (in this year) C. killed king Cynewulf
          Almost to a man they said they were sorry.
          (Bean 1983: 62).

OSV: *And his broþur Horsan man ofslog.*
And his brother Horsa was killed
Relaxation you call it.
(Quirk *et al.* 1985: 18.20).

OVS: *And hiene ofslog an eofor.*
And he was killed by a boar
'Please go away' said one child.
(Quirk *et al.* 1985: 18.23).

SXVX: *And Mierce friþ namon wiþ þone here.*
And the Mercian agreed on a truce with the army
The child then went back home.

Of these, SVX (35%) and X'VS (28%) are the most frequent patterns in Bean's corpus, but they also have the highest frequency in PDE. The difference is therefore not one of existence vs. non-existence but of the conditions determining these patterns and the changing restrictions on their use.[20] This would also be simpler than trying to explain the (surface) presence of orderings corresponding to the already abandoned basic word order which, in our opinion, would be difficult to justify in purely syntactic terms.[21]

Let us have a quick look at some ordering phenomena in OE and their changes, so that we can try to confirm what has just been said. As is well known, even inside the clausal constituents there existed a certain amount of ordering variability. The following are some word-order correspondences in clausal constituents in OE and ME/PDE (those marked with a star (*) are not meaningful for word-order typologies according to Dryer 1991, 1992)

AN/NA	————————	AN*
GN/NG	————————	NG/GN
DemN/NDem	————————	DemN*
Nrel	————————	NRel
NumN	————————	NumN
PrepN	————————	PrepN

When two possibilities are given, the first is the more frequent one. Only the presence of prepositions and the order of a Relative Clause and its governing Noun (NRel) are inconsistent with SOV order. The only really significant change appears to be the possibility of postposing a Genitive Noun to its governing N; but this possibility also existed in OE:

in leornunge haligra gewrita
in the learning of the Holy Writs (Rot 1982: 279).

The principle of the postposing of heavy elements could be responsible for a construction like this, but the fact remains that NGen was a possible order in OE, as GenN also is in PDE. The change, then, consists in its generalisation, the loss of the constraints that limited its use in OE. We might remind the reader that exactly the same applies to Old Norse; the only significant change affecting these correlations is that from a preferred order GenN to a preferred NGen order in the modern Scandinavian languages including, as in English, its substitution by Prepositional Phrases (of the type *táin á pabba*, 'daddy's toe', lit. 'the toe on daddy').

6.   Conclusion

We have seen that the general change, which we can term 'shift in preferred order', is identifiable both at the level of the sentence and the clause, and probably also at the textual level. We have also seen that text types could also have been affected by the same tendency responsible for word-order change, viz. to ease the reader's work of processing. On their turn, the text types so altered (and 'fixed', as word order also was) exerted an influence on the development and spread of the new preference for more 'listener-oriented' orderings.

Although we have only been able here to offer a rather superficial analysis of a few of the changes in word order that took place in English during the Middle Ages, we think that the theoretical and methodological grounding put forward constitutes a proposal which may be developed and, if confirmed, be used for the unified explanation of the synchronic functioning of word order, as well as for the word-order changes in English and other languages. We believe to have shown that it is possible – and convenient – to try to explain word-order change from a pragmatic, not a syntactic perspective, without losing the results obtained by previous research in the field.

NOTES

1. This paper has been partly financed by DGICYT Research Contract PS 91/0026.
2. This is also one of the main aims of the autonomous syntax approach to word order, although the interpretation of 'cognitive' is probably different.
3. We are following here a view of the process of linguistic communication due to some works by René Thom and his followers; see Thom (1980).

4.   Cf. Firbas (1983: 22): "The existence of a relation between linguistic phenomena and extralinguistic reality can hardly be doubted. The language user's experience of the natural order of extralinguistic phenomena cannot stay unreflected in language. Only the language user is free to view the extralinguistic phenomena in different perspective and language is a pliant tool to function accordingly."

5.   On the theory of language and of linguistic change behind this approach, see Altmann (1988), Bernárdez (1995), Bichakjian (1987), Köhler (1986), Lüdtke (1980), Nöth (1983), Ronneberger-Sibold (1987).

6.   He proposed 8 general assumptions, 9 general principles and 12 specific principles to explain word order. See Dik (1989: 336ff.).

7.   "There is a universally relevant clause-initial position P1, used for special purposes, including the placement of constituents with Topic or Focus functions. [...] All languages may be supposed to use P1 for special purposes, though not necessarily in the same way" (Dik 1989: 348f.).

8.   On word order and the iconicity principles, see Myhill (1992a), Tai (1985) and other papers in Haiman (ed., 1985). A useful review of iconicity can be found in Larsen (1993). See also Bernárdez (1994) for the relationship between iconicity and word-order change in English.

9.   This was already recognised by René Thom (1980), see also (1973).

10.   Pronouns could be identified in OE by pragmatic means; in ME and PDE it is mainly their position in the sentence which decides the selection of their referent. All these changes probably point to the increasing independence of the written language, to which we shall come back later.

11.   This is also Rögnvaldsson's (1990) opinion on the formal (generative) structuring principles he defines for Modern Icelandic.

12.   Cf. Dik's *specific principles* of ordering, numbers (1) and (3): "A language makes a basic choice between Prefield or Postfield ordering of dependents with respect to their heads"; "Relators have their preferred position".

13.   Incidentally, the *prototypicality* of word order is another way of posing the already mentioned 'institutionalised' character of certain ordering strategies. Prototypes, in fact, are just the most effective strategies for the solving of cognitive problems, which have spread socially.

14.   In our sample, the percentage of verbs without an overt subject ranges from 1.92 % (*Mandeville's Travels*) to 42.5 % (*The Beggar and the Usurer*) in ME, and from 22.78 % (*Life of St.Oswald*) to 5.71 % (*Sermo Lupi*) in OE. See below, Note 15.

15.   The fragments submitted to this analysis are the following: (1a) lines 1-69, *The Life of Saint Oswald* (Ælfric); (1b) lines 1-52, entries for the years 892-3 of the *Anglosaxon Chronicle*; (1c) lines 1-32 of *The Beggar and the Usurer*; (1d) lines 82-112, *Book of Margery Kempe*; (2a) lines 103-162 from *The Voyage of Wulfstan*; (2b) lines 2-54 of

Bede's *Historica Ecclesiastica*; (2c) lines 1-64, Trevisa's translation of the *Polychronicon*; (2d) lines 12-36 of *Mandeville's Travels* (XXI: Lamary); (3a) lines 1-58 from Wulfstan's *Sermo Lupi*; (3b) lines 88-121, King Alfred's *Cura Pastoralis*; (3c) lines 1-52, Richard Rolle's *The nature of the bee*; (3d) lines 39-85 of Wyclif's *The great sentence of curs expounded*. Numbers 1c, 1d, 2b, 2d, 3b, 3d were taken from Kaiser (1954); 2c and 3c from Sisam (1921); the others from Sweet (1967). (1a-d) are considered as 'narrative', (2a-d) as 'descriptive', and (3a-d) as 'argumentative'. Needless to say, the results of this extremely elementary analysis are only illustrative, and few consequences can be drawn from them. Moreover, all instances of VS order are counted in the analysis, irrespective of possible semantic, communicative or syntactic factors as the presence of an adverbial in the initial position of the clause, etc. As neither in OE nor in ME was verb-subject inversion automatic, our procedure can be tolerated. In a deeper analysis of a larger sample, however, these factors have to be taken into consideration.

16.   Only cases of overt S have been counted, i.e. the S of two co-ordinated verbs is only counted once.

17.   Although our corpus is too small to draw any clear conclusions, the fact that Richard Rolle's text is much more abstract than any of the other three and that it has a variability of only 66.14 % may be significant in this respect. In contrast to it, the *Cura Pastoralis* has a variability of 37.43 % and it is rather non-abstract, even including a dialogue.

18.   To mention only one example, Papiamento, a Spanish-based Creole spoken in the Netherlands Antilles, favours SV order to the point of exclusivity, whereas Spanish uses VS nearly as frequently as SV, and even more in certain text types and in many informal conversational situations. VS accounts for 25 % of all subjects, according to Meyer-Hermann (1987); see also Meyer-Hermann (to appear).

19.   X is any constituent except S and V; X' is any adverbial.

20.   This appears obvious from our examples: OVS seems only possible with verbs like *to say* in PDE, and the syntactic correspondence between the OE and the PDE sentences is sometimes only superficial.

21.   This is also Reinhard Meyer-Hermann's view (1991: 101): "Es wäre daran zu denken, Sprachen nicht durch eine einzige 'Basis'-Abfolge zu charakterisieren, sondern durch die Hierarchie der Satztypkonstruktionen". He identifies 7 types of order of sentential constituents in Old Castilian, with varying degrees of frequency, which are directly comparable with Bean's results for Old English. The percentages for the *Crónica General* which are of interest for our discussion are the following: SVO 44.7 %; VS 29.3 %.

REFERENCES

Altmann, Gabriel
    1988   *Wiederholungen in Texten*. Bochum: Brockmeyer.
Altmann, Gabriel, H. v . Buttlar, W. Rott., and U. Strauss
    1983   "A law of change in language." In: B. Brainerd (ed.). *Historical Linguistics*. Bochum: Brockmeyer, 104-115.
Andersen, Henning, and Konrad Koerner (eds.)
    1990   *Historical linguistics 1987*. Amsterdam: Benjamins.
Baker, Mark C.
    1988   *Incorporation*. Chicago: The University of Chicago Press.
Bean, Margaret C.
    1983   *The Development of Word Order Patterns in Old English*. London: Croom Helm.
Bernárdez, Enrique
    1992   "Can catastrophe theory provide adequate explanations for language change? An application to syntactic change in English." In: F. Fernández *et al.* (eds.). *English Historical Linguistics 1992*. Amsterdam: John Benjamins, 1994, 17-27.
    1994   "Cambios de orden de palabras en inglés. ¿Cambio de perspectiva del hablante al oyente?" *Estudios Ingleses de la Universidad Complutense* 2.
    1995   *Teoría y epistemología del texto*. Madrid: Cátedra.
Bernárdez, Enrique and Paloma Tejada
    1991   "Strategy and tactics in Old English documentary texts." *Atlantis* XIII, 121-130.
Bichakjian, B. H.
    1987   "The evolution of word order: A paedomorphic explanation." In: A. G. Ramat et al. (eds). *Papers from the 7th International Conference on Historical Linguistics*. Amsterdam: John Benjamins, 87-108.
Croft, William
    1990   *Typology and Universals*. Cambridge: Cambridge University Press.
Dik, Simon
    1989   *The Theory of Functional Grammar*. Part I: The Structure of the Clause. Amsterdam: Foris.
Dryer, M. S.
    1991   "SVO languages and the OV:VO typology." *Journal of Linguistics* 27, 2, 443-482.
    1992   "The Greenbergian word order correlations." *Language* 61, 1, 81-132.

Enkvist, Nils Erik
    1987   "Text strategies: single, dual, multiple." In: R. Steele and T. Threadgold
                (eds). *Language Topics*, Vol. II. Amsterdam: John Benjamins, 203-212.
Firbas, Jan
    1983   "On some basic issues of the theory of functional sentence perspective.
                Comments on Alexander Szwedek's critique." *Brno Studies in English* 15,
                9-35.
    1987a   "Thoughts on functional sentence perspective, intonation and emotiveness."
                Brno Studies in English, 17, 9-48.
    1987b   "On some basic issues of the theory of functional sentence perspective II.
                On Wallace Chafe's view on new and old information and communicative
                dynamism." *Brno Studies in English*, 17, 51-59.
Gergely, György
    1991   *Free Word Order and Discourse Interpretation*. Budapest: Akadémiai
                Kiadó.
Givón, Talmy
    1985   "Iconicity, isomorphism and non-arbitrary coding in syntax." In: J. Haiman
                (ed.), 187-219.
    1988   "The pragmatics of word-order: predictability, importance and attention."
                In: M. Hammond *et al.* (eds). *Studies in Syntactic Typology*. Amsterdam:
                John Benjamins, 243-284.
Haftka, Brigitta (ed.)
    1994   *Was determiniert Wortstellungsvariation?* Opladen: Westdeutscher Verlag.
Haiman, John (ed.)
    1985   *Iconicity in Syntax*. Amsterdam: John Benjamins.
Kaiser, Rolf
    1954   *Medieval English*. Berlin.
Keller, Rudi
    1990   *Sprachwandel. Von der unsichtbaren Hand in der Sprache*. Bern: Francke.
Kindt, Walther
    1994   "Wortstellung als Problem einer dynamischen Grammatik." In: B. Haftka
                (ed.), 49-62.
Köhler, Reinhard
    1986   *Zur linguistischen Synergetik: Struktur und Dynamik der Lexik*. Bochum:
                Brockmeyer.
Labov, William
    1994   *Principles of Linguistic Change. Internal Factors*. Oxford: Blackwell.

Larsen, Mariann
  1993   "Between text and grammar: the principle of iconicity." *Estudios Ingleses de la Universidad Complutense* 1, 111-126.
Lass, Roger
  1980   *On explaining language change*. Cambridge: Cambridge University Press.
Lightfoot, David W.
  1991   *How to Set Parameters. Evidence from Language Change*. Cambridge, Mass.: MIT Press.
Lüdtke, Helmut
  1980   "Auf dem Wege zu einer Theorie des Sprachwandels." In: H. Lüdtke (ed.). *Kommunikationstheoretische Grundlagen des Sprachwandels*, Berlin: de Gruyter, 182-252.
Mallinson, Graham, and Barry J. Blake
  1981   *Language Typology*. Amsterdam: North Holland.
Meyer-Hermann, Reinhard
  1987   "La posición del sujeto en español antiguo y moderno (en comparación con el francés)." In: M. Ariza *et al.* (ed.). *Actas del I Congreso Internacional de Historia de la Lengua Española*. Madrid: Arco, 541-562.
  1991   "Theorie und Empirie der Wortfolge im Spanischen." *Zeitschrift für Romanische Philologie* 107, 1/2, 58-103.
  in print *Es el español una lengua V-S-O?* (To appear in Iberoamericana, 1995).
Mithun, M.
  1992   "Is basic word-order universal?" In: D. L. Payne (ed.), 15-61.
Moreno, Cabrera J. L.
  1990   "Polarización: ensayo de sintaxis universal." In: C. Martín Vide (ed.). *Lenguajes Naturales y Lenguajes Formales* V. Barcelona: Universitat, 217-231.
  1991   *Curso Universitario de Lingüística General I: Teoría de la gramática y sintaxis general*. Madrid: Síntesis.
Myhill, John
  1992a   "Word-order and temporal sequencing." In: D. L. Payne (ed.), 265-278.
  1992b   *Typological discourse analysis*. Oxford: Blackwell.
Nöth, Winfried
  1983   "Systems theoretical principles of the evolution of the English language and literature." In: M. Davenport, E. Hansen and H. F. Nielsen (eds.). *Current Topics in English Historical Linguistics*. Odense: Odense UP, 103-122.
Payne, Davis L.
  1992   "Introduction." In: D. L. Payne (ed.), 1-13.

Payne, Davis L. (ed.)
1992   *The pragmatics of word-order flexibility.* Amsterdam: John Benjamins.
Quirk, Randolph, Sidney Greenbaum, Geoffrey Leech and Ian Svartnik
1985   *A Comprehensive Grammar of the English Language.* London: Longman.
Rögnvaldsson, Eiríkur
1990   *Um orðaröð og færslur í íslensku.* Reykjavík: Háskóli Íslands.
Ronneberger-Sibold, Else
1987   "A performance model for a natural theory of linguistic change." In: Ramat *et al.* (eds.), 517-533.
Rot, Sándor
1982   *Old English.* Budapest: Tankönyvkiadó.
Siewierska, Anna
1988   *Word-order rules.* London: Croom Helm.
1991   *Functional Grammar.* London: Croom Helm.
1993   "Subject and object order in written Polish: Some statistical data." *Folia Linguistica* XXVII/1-2, 147-170.
Sisam, Kenneth (ed.)
1921   *Fourtheenth Century Verse and Prose.* Oxford: Oxford University Press.
Solà, Joan
1994   *Sintaxi normativa: estat de la qüestió.* Barcelona: Empúries.
Steele, Susan
1975   "On some factors that affect and effect word order. In: Ch. N. Li (ed.). *Word Order and Word Order Change.* Austin & London: Croom Helm, 197-268.
Sweet's Anglo-Saxon Reader.
1967   Rev. by D. Whitelock. Oxford: Clarendon Press.
Tai, James H.-Y.
1985   "Temporal sequence and Chinese word order." In: J. Haiman (ed.), 49-72.
Thom, René
1973   "Sur la typologie des langues naturelles: essai d'interprétation psycho-linguistique." In: M. Gross *et al.* (eds.). *Formal Analysis of Natural Languages.* The Hague: Mouton, 233-248.
1980   "L'espace et les signes." *Semiotica* 29-3/4, 193-208.
Tomlin, Russell S.
1986   *Basic word-order.* London: Croom Helm.
Traugott, Elisabeth Closs, and Suzanne Romaine
1985   "Some questions for the definition of 'style' in socio-historical linguistics." *Folia Linguistica Historica* 6/1, 7-40.

Wårvik, Britta
1990   "On the history of grounding markers in English narrative: style or typology." In: M. Andersen and K. Koerner (eds.), 531-542.
Wilder, Chris, and Damir Ćavar
1994   "X0-Bewegung und Ökonomie." In: B. Haftka (ed.), 11-32.

The Semantic and Pragmatic Development of Substitutive Complex Prepositions in English

Scott A. Schwenter and Elizabeth Closs Traugott
Stanford University

1. Introduction[1]

The study of historical pragmatics in the United States originated largely in work in historical syntax and morphology within a functionalist framework, e.g. Li and Thompson (1976a,b), Givón (1979), Bybee (1985), Haiman (1985), Hopper and Martin (1987). In the last decade or so it has become centrally associated with two closely related lines of research. One is the theory of diachronic grammaticalization as developed in e.g. Fleischman (1982), Traugott (1982), Bybee (1985), Brinton (1988), Traugott and Heine (1991), Hopper and Traugott (1993), and Bybee, Perkins and Pagliuca (1994), where influences from pragmatics and from discourse analysis defined as the study of competence for language use in context often play a major role. Grammaticalization is concerned with the development of such grammatical material as tense, aspect, mood markers, case markers, clause connectives, and discourse markers out of non-grammatical (lexical or phrasal) or less grammatical material. The central question is what semantic-pragmatic motivations and constraints there are on such developments, and solutions tend to be found in the domain of context-induced inference or metonymy. The second line of research is cognitive linguistics, as developed in e.g. Langacker (1990), Sweetser (1990), Heine, Claudi and Hünnemeyer (1991). Cognitive linguistics is concerned with the systematic relation between language and cognition, particularly as evidenced by mapping from one semantic domain to another, polysemies, and *gestalt* phenomena such as figure and ground (cf. Talmy 1988, Croft 1994), and solutions tend to be found in the domain of metaphor. Taking as our starting-point a possible analysis from the point of view of cognitive linguistics, we will argue in this paper for an analysis that takes functional textual discourse into account as well, and exemplify one way in which the two strands of work can be fruitfully combined.

As Jucker (1994) points out, the framework used for analysis tends to severely restrict the range of topics tackled. Given its origins in historical syntax, grammaticalization theory as practiced in the first line of research mentioned above is concerned primarily with linguistic contexts and not with socio-pragmatics. Given that the data are to be found exclusively in texts, except where the present century is concerned, discourse analysis that focuses primarily on linguistic competence is ultimately not suitable, because we cannot tap linguistic intuitions of speakers several hundred years ago. Therefore, the approach needed must look to competence for use, and for different genres. A useful frame of reference for historical pragmatics, modified in ways outlined below, is articulated by Clark as follows:

> Discourse is language use in the large (...). It is extended activities that are carried out by means of language. (...) including stories, novels, newspaper articles, speeches, lectures – any extended but circumscribed piece of language use created for a coherent purpose (...).
>
> Discourse (...) can be viewed as a product, as an object that gets produced by people speaking (...). It can also be viewed as a process, what the people speaking actually do (...). The first view, in its simplest form, is that a discourse is a text or sequence of sentences that is coherent by virtue of its internal linguistic structure (...). The second view is that a discourse is a joint activity carried out by an ensemble of two or more people trying to accomplish things together (...). The idea is that conversations, stories, and other discourses are not created by speakers acting autonomously. Rather, they are the emergent product of an ensemble of people working together (Clark 1994: 985-986).

However, there are still methodological problems. We have no direct access to speech (though trials and drama give us some insights, and synchronic discourse strategies can be used to hypothesize possible historical developments, cf. Herring 1991 on question tags in Tamil oral performance narratives). We certainly have no direct access to joint activity in interaction in earlier history. Ultimately we can only attempt to reconstruct what some elements of such possible interactions might have been (see for example Brinton 1990 on discourse markers in Old English, Dasher in progress on the development of honorifics in Japanese). Always, we need to keep in mind that we are dealing with the production of written text (see Fleischman 1992), in particular genres which require particular rhetorical strategies (see Justus 1993 on topic continuity and clause cohesion in Indo-European prayers; also Wright in press on the development of the experiential progressive in 18th century women's letters, e.g. *I am talking to you*). As we do so, we need to recognize that "it is absolutely necessary to distinguish between language traditions and text traditions" (Schlieben-Lange 1992: 353).

One way of making this distinction is to remind ourselves that, although historical linguistics within the generative tradition has focused on the question of how language is transmitted to children across the discontinuity of generations, there is little or no direct relationship between changes in the language of the texts that remain to us and child language acquisition. The data for historical pragmatics are primarily written genres often of a religious, pedagogical, or legal sort, in other words genres usually not used by small children. Furthermore, they are written, and therefore, although we can use the theories and methodologies of spoken discourse analysis, we must use caution in doing so. Being written, they are often the products of or for the upper strata of society, so once again we must use caution in using the theories and methodologies of sociolinguistics (cf. Romaine 1982, Ebert 1992).

One final caution is the nature of the data that we use. Almost all studies suffer from being based on editions that add punctuation, etc. For example, Old English punctuation, in as far as it existed, seems to have been based on the prosodic unit, not on anything we think of as sentence structure punctuation. Nevertheless, we have been blessed within the last few years by the development of a number of computerized data bases. The study of English has been revolutionized by such on-line data bases as the *Diachronic Part of the Helsinki Corpus of the English Language* (hereafter HC) (Rissanen and Ihalainen 1991), the *Toronto Corpus of Old English* (Healey and Venezky 1980, hereafter TC), and the on-line *Oxford English Dictionary* (*OED*). Without these, the study of historical pragmatics in English from a discourse analysis perspective would still be in its infancy.

The present study investigates the development of three complex prepositional phrases expressing substitution, but originally meaning literally "in place of" in the history of English: *instead of, in place of,* and *in lieu of.*[2] We will show how a detailed discourse analysis approach serves as a check on some of the more global claims about semantic-pragmatic change made without attention to such detail.

"Substitution" as used here refers to the process whereby an entity X replaces another entity Y, where Y is a token of a certain type, and X is a new token of the same type. On a conceptual level, substitution involves the "moving out" of Y followed by the "moving in" of X. Typically, X and Y are represented syntactically as noun phrases, such that "X (an NP) *in stead/place/lieu of* Y (an NP)" (but see metalinguistic examples such as (12) below, where X and Y can be tensed verbs in the context of *instead of*).

The constructions share certain semantic-pragmatic and syntactic properties. All three start out as structures consisting of $NP_1 - P - NP_2 - P - NP_3$, where the first NP (=X) is semantically relatively free, the first P is *in*, the second NP names a location (*stead, place, lieu*), the second P is a genitive inflection or *of*, and the third NP (=Y) is of the same semantic type as the first NP (as we will see below, this is more accurately described in pragmatic terms as "expected to serve the same general function"). All three have come to have substitutive meaning, though with different lexical and temporal constraints to be discussed below. One contemporary example is:

(1)   S. was appointed by U.S. Bankruptcy Judge B.L. in April to run Eastern *in place of* parent Continental Holdings, formerly known as Texas Air Corp. (1991 *UPI*)

They are examples of grammaticalization (Hopper and Traugott 1993), in that they have become fixed phrases in which the article is no longer available in the locative NP (**in the stead/place/lieu of*).[3] Furthermore, they are examples of renewal (what Meillet 1915-16 called "renouvellement"): *stede* appears first, then *place*, then *lieu* (the latter two borrowed from French). As is to be expected of older forms (Bybee, Pagliuca and Perkins 1991), *instead of* has also come to be more fully grammaticalized than the others, for example it occurs in a wider number of environments: like *rather than*, but unlike *in place/lieu of*, it can be used with a gerund as in *Sam watched TV instead/*place/*lieu of studying* (Thompson 1972: 241), metalinguistically, as in *I sang instead/ *place/*lieu of danced* (Thompson 1972: 242), and as an adverb as in *Instead/ *place/*lieu, she went to Chicago*. All three have undergone semantic shifts from more concrete to more abstract meaning, in that a concrete locative expression has given rise to a more abstract meaning based on concepts of similarity. All three are also examples of pragmatic subjectification in the sense of Traugott (1989: 35): "Meanings tend to become increasingly based in the speaker's subjective belief state/attitude toward the proposition". The classes of lexical referents that can be treated as instances of substitution require pragmatic access to assessments of appropriateness of fit between referents, as well as attitudes based in experience, expectation, and other types of temporal distance (Fleischman 1989).

On first glance the changes might also be said to illustrate what Heine, Claudi and Hünnemeyer (1991) have characterized as a unidirectional metaphorical shift from PLACE > QUALITY. However, close inspection suggests that although the lexical items *stead, place,* and *lieu* can be said to exemplify these changes, the constructions themselves, as complex phrases used in discourse, evidence a less clearly unidirectional path of change. We must therefore be cautious in projecting metaphorical mappings that occur in lexical items onto changes undergone by the larger constructions in which they participate, in other words, onto grammaticalization. This issue will be discussed in section 7.

2. *Instead of*

The ancestor of *instead of* is to be found in early Old English (OE) in the construction *in stede* 'place' + genitival NP,[4] and developed the substitutive meaning by late OE. The word *stede* is presumably a Germanic word, since it is also found in Gothic and Old Norse as *staðr*. It now survives only as a derivative suffix as in *homestead*, and though *in his/her/its stead* occurs occasionally, it is largely considered archaic; in essence the structure has become grammaticalized, fixed as an indivisible phrase (the *OED* notes that the spelling *instead* became common in the sixteenth century).

Already in the earliest texts, OE *stede* was polysemous between place as region/general location (2a), individual location (2b,c), and location with which one identifies (home, fortress) (2d) (for a study of the conceptual structure of spatial relations as expressed in language, see Svorou 1993):

(2) a. manega menn siððan gesohton þone *stede* heora hæle feccende.
　　 many　　 people then　 sought　 that　 place　 their　 health seeking
　　 'many people then sought the place, looking for their salvation'.
　　 (Ælfric *Lives of Saints* P.III,140 [HC])[5]

　 b. uncnyte ðin gescy hræðe of ðinum fotum
　　 untie　　 thy shoes quickly from thy　 feet
　　 for ðam ðe se *stede* is halig.
　　 be-cause that place is holy
　　 'remove your shoes quickly from your feet, because the place is holy'.
　　 (Ælfric *Old Test* P.V,1 [HC])

　 c.　 sume heaflcwice flugon on fæsten ond feore burgon
　　　 some half:alive fled　 in　 fortress and life　 hid
　　　 æfter stanclifum, *stede* weardedon ymb　 Danubie.
　　　 behind rocks,　　 places defended around Danube
　　　 'some half-alive fled to safe places and hid behind rocks,

defended their strongholds in the region of the Danube'.
(*Fates of Apostles* P69 [HC])

d.   ne gelyfe ic buton ic geseoðæra nægela fæstnunge on his handa
      not believe I unless I see those nails' fixing   in his hands
      & ic do minne finger *on ðære nægela stede.*
      & I put my   finger in those nails'   place.
      'I will not believe unless I see the holes made by the nails in his hands,
      and put my finger in the place of those nails'.
      (*Gospel John* WSCp [TC])

Stede is also used in the sense of 'rank, position, function, job', as terms for
location often are (cf. the words *position, rank* themselves), as in (3):

(3)   Gif ealle menn on worulde rice wæron,
       If   all   men in world   rich were,
       ðonne næfde   seo mildheortnyss nænne *stede.*
       then   neg:have:SUBJ that compassion no   place
       'If everyone in the world were rich,
       there would be no place/role for compassion'.
       (*Ælfric Hom* 11, 7 [TC])

The role sense of *stede* is an abstract one. The place in which compassion exists
is not a physical one, but is (synchronically[6] conceived as) a figurative one:
metaphorically, compassion occupies a space in the mental world of values or
functions.

The Helsinki Corpus has one example from later OE of the substitutive
stede, and it is used in the sense of substituting one person for another in a role
(that of disciple):

(4)a. Mathias bodode   on Iudea lande seþe wæs gecoren
      Mathias preached in Judea land who was chosen
      on Iudan stede.
      in Judas' place
      'Mathias, who was chosen in Judas' place, preached in the land of Judea'.
      (*Ælfric Letter Sigeweard* P60 [HC])

This too is an abstract sense of place: the place out of which Judas is "moved"
and into which Mathias is put is not one of physical location, but rather a
figurative space or "rank" for preachers. As noted above, the crucial factor in a
substitutive expression is that some entity Y (Judas) is "moved out" and
replaced by some entity X (Mathias). Additional examples in the Toronto
Corpus include the following, where the role of warden is implied:

(4)b. Nu grete ic wel mine leofne mæi Wigod on
      Now greet I well my dear cousin Wigod in
      Wallingeforde & ic beode ðe ðat ðu *on minre*
      Wallingford & I ask thee that thou in my
      stede beride ðas land ðam hælge to hande
      place ride-around these lands that:DAT saint:DAT to possession
      'Now I greet you well, my dear cousin Wigod in Wallingford, and I ask
      you to ride around these lands as my deputy and to take them in the name
      of the saint'.
      (Charter 1148 (*Harm* 104) [TC])

In Middle English (ME) all the OE uses continue. The locative typically occurs
with an article, or some other operator, but does not necessarily do so, whereas
the substitutive phrase typically occurs without. It is important to note,
however, that strictly speaking, there were no articles in OE, only the numeral
an 'one' and demonstrative *se, seo, þæt* 'that' (see (2a,b)). Although the use of
articles began in very late OE, the use of articles as we know them did not
develop until Early Modern English (EModE). In particular, head nouns that are
further specified by *of*-phrases tend in ME not to have articles: "[i]t is very
likely that the determiner is left out in these cases in Middle English because the
of-phrase functions like a determiner just as the pronominal possessive does"
(Fischer 1992: 220). Therefore we cannot rely on the use of articles to identify
the substitutive construction during the earlier periods.

By the later ME period we begin to find the substitutive construction
extended from persons to concrete objects (5a) and to terms for abstract
activities (5b):

(5)a. he may right lyghtly ben disceyued For men sellen a gomme tat men
      clepen Turbentyne *in stede of* bawme.
      'A person may very easily be deceived, for people sell a gum called
      turpentine instead of balsam'. (*c.* 1400 Mandeville P 32 [HC])

   b. For many a man so hard is of his herte,
      He may nat wepe, althogh hym soore smerte.
      Therfore *in stede of* wepynge and preyeres
      Men moote yeve silver to the povre freres.
      'For many a man is so hard of heart that he cannot weep
      although his heart hurts. Therefore instead of weeping and
      prayers, people should give silver to the poor priests'.
      (*c.* 1388 Chaucer *ProlCant. Tales* P 27.C1 [HC])

In the EModE period there is one example with the article, showing that the construction was still not fully grammaticalized:

(6)   And Abraham went and tooke the Ramme, and offered him vp for a burnt offering, *in the stead of* his sonne.
       (1611 Bible *OldTest* P XXII,1G [HC])

However, the substitutive construction reveals considerable increase in frequency and also expansion of its role to constructions not attested earlier. For example, syntactically *instead of* becomes readily available with gerunds. Although out of context it is ambiguous between a nominalization and a gerund because 'weep' is intransitive, *wepyng* in (5b) *in stede of wepynge and preyeres* is presumably a nominalization because of the coordination with *preyeres*. However, in EModE we find constructions like those in (7), which suggest the more strongly verbal character of the gerund:

(7)a. studies, [...] which will corrupt and hurt *in stead of* doing good. And therefore all filthy places in the Poets would be wisely passed over, or wearily expounded. (1627 Brinsley *Ludus Literarius*: P 45 [HC])

b.   medicines [...]; have a great care of tampering that way, least *instead of* preventing you draw on diseases. (1693 Locke *Education*: P 48 [HC])

c.   by experience we find [...] those who are least able to judge, to be frequently the most [...] peremptory and perverse: and *instead of* demeaning themselves with the submission of Learners, to assume to themselves the authority of Judges. (bef. 1671 Tillotson *Sermons*: P II: ii 451 [HC])

Examples (5b) from later ME and (7b,c) from EModE involve topicalization of the substitutive phrase. Indeed, of nineteen EModE examples of substitutive *instead of* in the Helsinki Corpus, ten are topicalized. In the earliest examples the syntax suggests that the *instead of* NP phrase has been fronted leaving the syntax intact, as in (7a), but at other times the syntactic constraints seem fairly loose:

(8)a. Some out of curiosity *instead of* Clay when they graff Trees, cover the Heads of the Stocks with Lime mix'd with Hair.
       (1699 Langford *FruitTrees*: P 121 [HC])

b.   was glad to [...] bee a chare-Woman ['maid'] in rich mens houses, her softhand was now hardened with scowring, and *in steade of* gold rings vpon her lillie fingers, they were now fild with chaps, prouoked by the sharpe lee and other drudgeries. (1619 Deloney *JackofNewbury*: P 74 [HC])

For (8a) we can hypothesize a paraphrase such as 'some cover the heads of stocks (for the tree grafts) with lime instead of clay', with the prepositional phrase extracted out of an assumed oblique *with* phrase, and for (8b): 'her lily fingers were filled with chaps instead of having gold rings on them', with a non-parallel passive (*fild* 'filled') and an assumed active verb like *have*.

In terms of discourse functions, substitutive *instead of* comes to be used in extended metaphors, as in:

(9)   so that the Fable and fiction of Scylla seemeth to be a liuely Image of this kinde of Philosophie or knowledge, which was transformed into a comely Virgine for the vpper parts; but then, "Candida succinctam, latrantibus inguina monstris". So the Generalities of the Schoolmen are for a while good and proportionable; but then when you descend into their distinctions and decisions, *in stead of* a fruitfull wombe, for the vse and benefite of mans life; they end in monstrous altercations and barking questions. (1605 Bacon *Adv. of Learning*: P 20V [HC])

Here the idea of language as a spatial system based in the body is elaborated upon, a system in which large-scale issues are lodged in the upper part of the body, and detailed analysis in the lower part, specifically the womb. This kind of context may be the motivation for metalinguistic uses. The first example available in HC is:

(10)   But if that which Beza says in his notes on this place be well observed, there is none that will not see, that *instead of* pains, it should be bands; and then there is no further cause to seek for purgatory in this text. (1651 Hobbes *Leviathan* Pt. 4, Ch. 44, p. 605)

Clearly Hobbes is writing about the written word, so *pains* and *bands* can be thought of as concrete objects (signs) that simply happen to be linguistic. A present-day English (PDE) example is:

(11)   Sen. Orrin Hatch, R-Utah, said supporters of the bill were seeking an edge "under the guise of civil rights to force businesses to go to proportional hiring – which is quotas."
       "This bill should be called the quota bill *instead of* the civil rights bill," Sen. Jesse Helms, R-N. C., said.
       Kennedy said the charge was "spurious", adding, "It is a mockery of civil rights and the fundamental principles of equal justice ... to raise the false hue and cry of quotas." (1990 *UPI*)

Recently there has been a shift to truly metalinguistic examples like (12):

(12) It rained instead of snowed. (Thompson 1972: 242)

The main changes that the data demonstrate concern grammaticalization and semantic-pragmatic changes. The original phrases concerning location or rank continued to allow full NPs following *in*, and indeed some variation in preposition, e.g. ME (1250-1350) *MPsalter* P. 53, *in-to þe stede of purgatorij* 'in-to the place/state of purgatory'. The substitutive construction, by contrast, shows decategoralization of the first NP (loss of the article) and syntactic generalization from strictly nominal to increasingly deverbal constructions (gerunds, as in (5b)) and ultimately to tensed verbs (the metalinguistic type as in (12)). And it shows semantic generalization from substitution of one individual for another in a certain role to substitution in general, and concomitant semantic bleaching of *stede*. We will return to the pragmatic issues in sections 6 and 7.

3.   *In place of*

In (the) place of (< Fr. *place*) was borrowed as a locative construction from French in the ME period, and has continued to be used as a locative. The ME locative construction *in (the) place of* X (where X is a name ('place of John'='John's place'), or concrete object located in the place) is illustrated in (13):

(13)a.for the same Nichol sayd bifor mair. Aldermen. & owre craft bifor hem gadred *in place of* recorde. that xx. or xxx. of vs. were worthy to be drawen & hanged.
'for the same Nicholas said in the presence of the mayor, aldermen, and our guild, who were gathered before them in the place of record, that twenty or thirty of us were worthy to be drawn and hanged'. (1388 *Appeal London*: P195 [HC])

b.And he turnede aȝen bi the weye in which he cam fro the south in to Bethel, til to the place, in which bifore he hadde sett tabernacle, bitwixe Bethel and Hay, in the place of the auter which he made bifore, and inwardli clepide there the name of the Lord.
(*c*. 1384 WBible *OldTest*: P XIII, 1G [HC])

As noted in the case of *stede*, the PDE usage with respect to articles was not yet well established in earlier ME, so the absence of the article in (13a) is not to be regarded as significant.

The Helsinki Corpus gives no examples of *place* in the sense of rank or role, or of use in substitutive *in (the) place of* in ME. However, *MED* cites the following as an example of *place* under sense 4d: 'social position, station, rank; role, status; spiritual status; also, office, post...':

(14) Jonathas resceyuyde the princehod, and rose *in the place of* Judas, his brother. (*c.* 1384 WBible[1], 1 Mac.9.31, *c.* 1384) [*MED* 'place' 4d])

OED and *MED* suggest that this kind of extended use of the term postdates locative uses by about one hundred years, as does the substitutive use. An example of the latter is:

(15) As Judas was among þe apostelis. [...] as a candel newe queynt þat synkeþ al þe hous in stede of a lyȝt lanterne, and as a smoke þat blendeþ mennys eiȝen *in place [vr. stede] of* clier fier, ȝif þou contrarie þus þe forme of lyuynge þat Crist and his apostelis leften to prestis [...]
'Just as Judas was among the apostles [...] like a candle newly extinguished that sinks the whole house into darkness instead of a bright lantern, and just as smoke blinds mens' eyes *in place of* clear fire, so, if you defy in this way the form of living that Christ and his apotles left to priests [...]' (?1387 *Wimbledon Serm.* [*MED* 'place' 4d])

The parallelism with *in stede of,* and the fact that other MSS have *in stede* suggests that *in place of* is used for stylistic purposes in the particular MS cited, to avoid using the same construction in successive clauses.

Examples (14) and (15) are particularly interesting because they pre-date the French development of the rank and substitutive uses of *en (la) place de.* Wartburg (1928-65) cites *en la place de* 'in the place of, in replacement of' as dating from approximately 1538, a form itself later replaced by *à la place de* (*c.* 1665). If this dating is correct, then the semantic development occurred sporadically in English prior to the French.[7]

The Helsinki data attest to the use of *place* in EModE, with the article and other noun modifiers, in locative and rank/role uses. An example of the latter is:

(16) Next if you have any discreet servant capable of it and has the *place* of governing your childe I thinke it is best the smart should come more immediately from another hand though by the parents order, who should see it donne, whereby the parents authority will be preservd. (1693 Locke *Conc. Education*: P 59 [HC])

There is a potentially ambiguous example of *in the place of*, in which either a locative or a substitutive sense can be construed. The general admonishing tone of the passage, however, suggests that this is indeed the substitutive use:

(17) hee is found to be seduced, and wrapped in blinde errours of the deuill, in infidelitie, and euill works, in which he fulfilleth the will of Satan, and honoureth him *in the place of* God: (1593 Gifford *Witches*, P B3V [HC])

If so, the place out of which God is 'moved' and into which Satan is put and honored is not one of physical location, e.g. the house of God, but rather a figurative space for supreme beings that guide the lives of people; in this case, those that are under the control of the devil.

Indeed, the substitutive construction generally appears in the later EModE period with the article *the*. We find not only substitutive uses with inanimate NPs (18a), but also explicit association with substitution (18b):

(18)a.his counsellors serve him *in the place of* memory, and mental discourse. (1651 Hobbes *Leviathan* Pt. 2, Ch. 25, p. 245)

   b.And lest you think these Phaenomena proceed from some peculiarity in the piece of Amber I employed, I shall add, that I found uniformity enough in the success, when, *in the place of* Amber, I substituted another Electrick, and particularly a smooth mass of melted Brimstone. (1675-6 Boyle *Electricity & Magnetism*, p. 34 [HC])

By the mid-eighteenth century, the substituted entity can be linguistic:

(19) and I add the following note, *in place of* the following paragraph: (1741-2 Hume *Essays* Pt. 2 E. 11 gp. 424)

This is reminiscent of *instead of*, e.g. (10); however, unlike *instead of*, *in place of* cannot be used for truly metalinguistic correction of the type in (12).

The modern-day *in place of* construction, with substitutive meaning, is found in the Helsinki EModE corpus with the definite article only, as *in the place of*. However, near the end of the EModE and into the PDE period, examples without the definite article are found with regularity in other texts. The examples in (20) and (21) demonstrate the loss of *the*:

(20) For I have been credibly informed that a bitch will nurse, play with, and be fond of young foxes, as much as, and *in place of*, her puppies; if you can but get them once to suck her so long, that her milk may go through them. (1690 Locke *Ess. Conc. Hum. Und.* Bk2 Ch.11 p.205)

(21) I was perfectly right in being guided by the friend whom you will love
      better than you do now. To me, she was *in place of* a parent. Do not
      mistake me, however. I am not saying that she did not err in her advice.
      (1818 Austen *Persuasion* Vol.II, p.246)

As examples (20) and (21) show, the absence of the definite article is paralleled
by an extension of the construction to a different set of discourse contexts,
dealing with more abstract conceptions of *place*. Whereas in the periods up to
and including EModE, the substitution of one entity is into the pre-existing
position of another, e.g. Jonathas taking over the 'slot' held previously in the
real world by Judas in (14), and thus conceptually involving both movement out
and into some 'space', these later examples do not refer to such a pre-existing
position, but rather to generic, non-unique 'slots' that are present or anticipated
in the writer's construal of the world (cf. Chafe 1976: 39; Givón 1984: 399).
Both the 'place' of the puppies in (20) as well as that of a parent in (21) are
potential slots that are regarded as filled or fillable by other entities; however,
they do not necessarily entail the prior moving out of another entity before
being filled. Rather, the X entities that fill these potential slots are considered
suitable replacements for the expected (and 'normal') Y entities.

      Indeed, during this early PDE period it may be that the distinction
between referential 'places' that can be recovered from preceding context and
non-referential ones that cannot is marked by the definite article, even though
both undeniably have substitutive meaning:

(22) When he does this by words, or by such actions as have no other effect
      than in as far as they stand *in the place of* words, the offence may be
      styled vilification. (1780 Bentham *Principles of Morals and Legislations*
      Ch.16, p.225)

Here, the act of doing things through 'words' – using them to carry out some
task or duty – has already been evoked in the context, and thus these 'words'
have a metaphorical 'place' that can be substituted by actions which carry out
the task of the 'words'.

      Like *instead of*, substitutive *in place of* has become grammaticalized. This
is manifested by the restriction to the construction without the article; in other
words, the noun *place* has become decategoralized. It is also manifested by the
generalization of the lexical classes of nouns that can fill the third (=Y) NP slot.
However, it is not yet available in metalinguistic uses with tensed verbs, and
thus is less grammaticalized than the older *instead of* (see section 2 above).[8]

      Although *place*, *stead* and *lieu* all originated as spatial terms, *place* alone
has maintained its locative meaning. It appears that the continued coexistence of

the locative sense of *place* has imposed constraints on the substitutive *in place of*. The fact that *place* still conserves the locative uses accounts for the observation that one place cannot be moved into that of another, since a location cannot be moved out of its own location. Consider the unacceptable constructed example in (23):

(23)   *We flew to L.A. *in place of* San Francisco.

However, *instead of* is perfectly acceptable in (24):

(24)   We flew to L.A. *instead of* San Francisco.

Since *stead* has lost its locative meaning in PDE (except in frozen compounds like *homestead*), it allows the substitution of one place for another. Further changes, namely the weakening of the locative element in *place*, could extend the *in place of* construction to contexts like (24).

The continued locative force of *place* in the substitutive connective also accounts for the fact that the items that are substituted for each other also occupy or potentially occupy the same physical or metaphorically abstract location. Thus:

(25)   We flew to L.A. *in place of* our friends.

implies that we occupied the site that our friends would have if they had been able to make the trip, that is, we used their tickets for seats on the plane. On the other hand, the same example with *instead*:

(26)   We flew to L.A. *instead of* our friends.

does not necessarily imply that we used our friends' tickets or sat in their seats, in other words, that we took their reserved 'place'. We could have gone for them (for example to an event that some representative of a group needed to attend) (for the pragmatic force of expectation particularly with *instead of*, see section 6).

Another interesting case involving expectations is provided by:

(27)   By day, R. L. is a serious attorney. But Wednesday night, he unwound and arrived at the 7th Annual Save the Pun Foundation dinner with an electrical cord *in place of* his neck-tie. L. was one of about 180 pun-lovers who dressed as "visual puns" and played mind-stimulating, wit-provoking word games for hours at the April Fools Day affair. (1992 *UPI*)

Here the main inference that we draw may be (counter)expectation, since an electrical cord is not normal neckwear. Note, however, that the cord was being worn in the same physical location as a tie. This example would also be acceptable with *instead of*. The difference between the two constructions becomes clear when the substituted entities do not share the same physical location:

(28)   But Wednesday night, he unwound and arrived at the 7th Annual Save the Pun Foundation dinner with polka-dot socks *instead of* (*in place of) his neck-tie. (constructed example)

Again, the non-acceptability of *in place of* in (28) reflects the locative PDE meaning of the noun *place*. Apparently, the noun acts as a kind of 'leash' on the construction of which it forms part, by not allowing the latter to stray too far from the meaning of the former.

4.   *In lieu of*

In lieu of (< Fr. *lieu* 'place') first appears in EModE.[9] Like *instead of*, in PDE it has become fixed as a complex prepositional phrase. In PDE *lieu* also occurs in a few lexical items such as *lieutenant*, but the historical connection is synchronically lost for most speakers. According to Wartburg (1928-65), French *en lieu de* was used from 1200 on in Middle French in the sense 'instead of (a person)' (not attested in English, perhaps because *in stead/place of* already existed in this sense), 'instead of something' (see (30)), or 'in compensation' (see (31)).
Lieu occurs with the meaning 'place':

(29)   *In the lieu* and place of Goddes innumerable, all their song is now of Jesus Christe alone.
'In the location and place of (erstwhile) innumerable Gods, all their song is now only of Jesus Christ'.
(1548 Udall *Erasm. Par. Luke Pref.* ii b [*OED*])

but for the most part it appears to have been used much like *instead of* and *in place of*, in constructions in which X is inanimate, as in:

(30)a. present other related ideas, *in lieu of* that which the mind desired at first to survey. This change we are not always sensible of; but continuing still the same train of thought, make use of the related idea
(1757 Hume *Treat. Hum. Nat.* Bk. 1, Pt. 2, p. 60)

b.For the nonce, however, he proposed to sail about, and sow his wild oats in all four oceans. They had made a harpooneer of him, and that barbed iron was *in lieu of* a sceptre now.
(1851 Melville *Moby Dick*: Ch. 12, p. 56)

It appears that substitutive *in lieu of* was calqued into English with the substitutive meanings since from the earliest times *in lieu of* as a substitutive construction has been used without an article, as in French.

The meaning of 'compensation' or, as the *OED* says "payment, penalty, or reward for", appears to have gained ground, so that *in lieu of* is now often found in contexts referring to financial and legal dealing, e.g. *hold a person in lieu of taxes/bond/bail*, etc.:

(31)a.introduced into the finances, by substituting an universal poll-tax, *in lieu of* almost all the tithes, customs, and excises, which formerly composed the revenue of the empire.
(1741-42 Hume *Essays* Pt. 2 E. 8, p. 358)

b.Probation is a set of restrictions given to convicted criminals *in lieu of* jail time, while parole is the supervised early release of an inmate from prison.
(1990 *UPI*)

c.Adding salt to the wound for Democrats was the last-minute inclusion in the package, *in lieu of* a capital gains cut, of a series of tax breaks for venture capitalists investing in small-growth companies. (1991 *UPI*)

A difference between *in place of* and *in lieu of* that appears to derive directly from the sense of 'compensation' is the tendency for the two constructions to occur in different temporal contexts in PDE. Whereas *in place of* typically refers to a realis past event in which one entity is in effect 'replacing' another, *in lieu of*, when used in the context of institutional practices, often refers to anticipated irrealis future events, in which the expected Y is to be preempted by something that deviates from the norm:

(32) With Kaifu at his side on a diplomatic fence-mending mission, Bush lauded Japan at a joint news conference for its role in the gulf war: A promised $13 billion in cash, services and support *in lieu of* military forces barred by its constitution. (1991 *UPI*)

Note that here, rather than future military aid, the promised sum of money is to be contributed to the war effort at some later time. But the military aid is not being substituted for; in fact, it was not even a possible contribution since the

Japanese constitution banned such aid. Since this is so, *in place of* would be pragmatically odd in (32).

5.   Summary of the changes

A summary of the changes in the *in stead/place of* constructions discussed above is given in Tables 1 and 2. Since there is no discernible progression of changes in the development of *in lieu of* in English, no table is included for this construction. Each 'stage' is incremental and overlaps with the prior stage, except in the case of *instead of*, where the original locative meanings have been lost.

Table 1: *Stages of development of* instead of

STAGE	DESCRIPTION
0 (preOE)	locative (ex. 2)
I (OE)	role (ex. 3, 36)
II (lOE)	slot Y = person/being in an abstract social or spiritual position (ex. 4)
III (lME)	slot Y may be inanimate object in a functional slot (ex. 5a); loss of constraint that X must be in same physical location as Y (ex. 5b)
IV (EModE)	slot Y may be gerund (ex. 7)
V (PDE)	slot Y may be tensed clause (ex. 12)

Table 2: *Stages of development of* in place of

STAGE	DESCRIPTION
0 (French, ME)	locative
I (ME)	slot Y = person/being in an abstract social or spiritual position (ex. 14)
II (EModE)	slot Y may be inanimate object in a functional slot; inference that X and Y also occupy the same physical location (ex. 18b).

Similar changes have occurred with *instead of*, but have gone even further. The contexts for '(counter)-expectations' are greatest for *instead (of)*, which can be used as a discourse marker to contrast expected and unexpected propositions (Thompson 1972), as in this constructed example, where the speaker and/or hearer expected that Jamie would go home for the summer:

(35) Jamie didn't go home for the summer. *Instead*, she took classes.

In the case of *in lieu of*, the disparity between expectations is typically less than with *instead of* and *in place of*. As we have seen, the Ys are frequently of an institutional sort: jail time for criminals, taxes for citizens, capital gains cuts for tax payers in an election year, flowers at funerals, and the substituted elements are frequently sanctioned by the community (or a part of it).

7.   Implications for historical pragmatics

If we consider the data in the light of theories associated primarily with cognitive linguistics and metaphorical analyses of change, we might as a first approximation argue that the changes in the nouns *stead*, *place*, and *lieu*[10] from physical location to social position follow the concrete-to-abstract directionality of metaphorical abstraction that is often reported in semantic-pragmatic change. The development of the substitutive constructions might then be said to be based on a fairly straightforward case of a conceptual category SPACE – one person being put into the physical location of another – being transferred metaphorically into the domain of QUALITY – one person being put into the social (or other) role of another. Such change has been made explicit by the model of semantic-pragmatic change in grammaticalization put forth by Heine *et al.* (1991), who see the semantic development of grammatical items from lexical source concepts as following the unidirectional path:

PERSON>OBJECT>ACTIVITY>SPACE>TIME>QUALITY

This path is unidirectional in that each category on the right is more abstract than the one to its left. Thus, an abstract category like QUALITY will be conceptualized in terms of a more concrete one like SPACE. None of the conceptual domains is a necessary step in the development of a particular lexical item. In the case of *stead*, *place*, and *lieu*, the main steps involve SPACE > QUALITY. Because it is based primarily on lexical items, this putative analysis fails to distinguish the development of the lexical meaning of role/position from the substitution meaning.

The history of the substitutive constructions suggests that a richer analysis is needed to account for the changes involved. For one, as we have suggested, it is not so much the lexical items themselves that are at issue, but rather the whole construction: *X in stead/place/lieu of Y*. From this perspective, Sweetser's (1990) account of metaphorical transfer from concrete to abstract across three worlds (rather than conceptual domains) might bring us closer to the empirical facts of the data. She proposes that unidirectionality is based on transfer from the socio-physical (image-schematic) world to the mental world of reasoning and belief, and thence to the communicative (metalinguistic) world. From this perspective one could say that in the three cases the socio-physical world of social status (X in the social role of Y) is transferred to the mental world of substitution generally (when X or Y can be gerunds), and finally in the case of *instead of* to the metalinguistic world. But this analysis too appears to fail to give us an adequate way to distinguish the transfer from the strictly locative construction to the social role construction since both are in the socio-physical world.

An approach that allowed for iterative processes of change, rather than the more step-wise changes suggested by Heine *et al.* and Sweetser, was proposed in Traugott (1989) and Traugott and König (1991). This was an approach from Semantic-pragmatic Tendencies, specifically Tendency I: "[m]eanings based in the external described situation [shift to] meanings based in the internal (evaluative/perceptual/cognitive) described situation"; Tendency II: "[m]eanings based in the described external or internal situation [shift to] meanings based in the textual and metalinguistic situation"; Tendency III: "meanings tend to become increasingly based in the speaker's subjective belief-state/attitude toward the proposition" (Traugott 1989: 34-35). This approach, while similar in many respects to Sweetser's, did not assume that metaphorical transfer was the prime motivating process for meaning change. It too, however, fails to capture the changes in the substitution construction adequately because the ordering of the Tendencies is too specific. As has been noted in Traugott (in press), these proposals do not correctly account for changes across a large variety of conceptual domains – as Sweetser 1990 suggested and Powell 1992 demonstrated, metalinguistic meanings tend to arise last, at least in some domains. *Instead of* shows that this is true of the substitutive domain.

All of these approaches in essence fail to take into consideration the discourse processes that lead to meaning change. If we think of discourse as proposed in Section 1, not as product, but as process and activity carried out by speakers and hearers, then we can shift our focus from the stages of change, which are products, to the processes that lead to the development of each stage.

From this perspective, the dominant process whereby lexical items and constructions change is the conventionalizing of inferences (see Grice 1975). Such inferences arise in Speaker-Hearer interactions, most especially interactions using such conversational principles as "Say no more than you must and mean more thereby" (for discussion of the implications of conversational principles to meaning change see Horn 1984). One of the best-known inferences of this type is the inference of causality from temporal succession, as in the case of *since* 'after/from the time that' > 'because'. Such inferences occur synchronically. Over time they may be drawn upon with greater and greater frequency and may eventually come to be conventionalized as a new polysemy, in other words to be semanticized (Hopper and Traugott 1993: 72-77). These types of meaning changes are known as conceptual metonymic changes and occur via context-induced inferences which arise out of contiguity in linguistic (and pragmatic) contexts (Hopper and Traugott 1993: 81).

Among conceptual metonymies, the dominant one for meaning change is subjectification. This is the general process (identified as Tendency III above) whereby meanings gradually shift from a more 'objective' possibility based in general beliefs and attitudes to a more 'subjective' possibility based in the individual speaker's belief or attitude (see Lyons 1977, Wright and Stein in press, and, for a narrower definition focusing on argument structure, most especially conceptual subjecthood, Benveniste 1966, Langacker 1990). It involves the development of polysemies in which the speaker's perspective is an essential element. For example, the initial shift from locative constructions to substitutive constructions is a case of subjectification, because it encodes the speaker's expectation. Subjectification also plays a major role in relating structure to rhetorical function. This is clearest in cases of subjectification that involve the development of discourse markers such as sentential adverbs (e.g. *probably*, 'in a provable/believable manner' Hanson 1987, or *well*), stance adverbs (e.g. *roughly speaking*, Powell 1992), evidential quotatives (e.g. *like*, Romaine and Lange 1991), or epistemic parentheticals (e.g. *I think*, Thompson and Mulac 1991), but it is also evidenced by the development of prepositional phrases into connectives (e.g. *while* 'for the time that' > 'during' > 'although', Traugott and König 1991) in that they take on a clause combining and therefore textual function. In the cases under discussion, the prepositional phrases take on the function of expectation marker.

What then is the role of metaphor in change? Briefly, the proposal here[11] is that metaphor is predominantly a product where meaning change as opposed to individual, often creative innovations, is concerned. By contrast, metonymy, being associative and pragmatically involving context-induced inferencing, is an ongoing process which may result in a new product (Heine *et al.*'s term for it is "context-induced reinterpretation"), but is potentially present in all language use. This is because, as Anttila (1989 [1972]: 141-42) points out, metonymy is basically indexical and continuous. Indexicality is a major property of language viewed as process – indexing speaker-hearer, topic-continuity, attitude to what is said, and most especially indexing context.[12] By contrast, metaphor is basically analogical, discontinuous (and indeed not omni-present).

The distinction being made here between metonymy (including subjectification) and metaphor can be thought of as follows. Let us assume that at some point in time t_1, speaker and hearer (child or adult) have acquired a grammar (rules of syntax, morphology, phonology, lexicon) and pragmatic principles such as "Say no more than you must and imply more thereby", "Make what you say or hear relevant to the situation". These rules or 'products', which may include synchronically available conceptual metaphors, can be thought of as frames on which discourse is built (Fillmore 1984). The condition for meaning change can be thought of as the indexical process whereby innovative inferences and practices occur in real time t_2, constrained by the prior products in t_1. Over time they acquire new weightings as the applicability of an inference is strengthened by local on-line repetitions and contextual discourse effects. The change can be said to have occurred at t_3, when semanticization of an inference occurs, that is, when inferences have become fixed or conventionalized with the result that a new structure emerges. This new product may look like metaphor (hence the intuitive appeal and validity of metaphorical approaches as espoused by Heine *et al.*, Sweetser, and others), but has resulted from the process of context-induced reinterpretation.

To illustrate with the history of *instead of*, in Pre-OE at t_1 (Stage 0), *stede* meant 'place, region'. In certain contexts a person's location can be associated with their rank (e.g. if one knows the protocol, one can surmize individuals' role/rank/standing based on where they sit at table, for example at a royal dinner, committee meetings), as illustrated by:

(36) þu   ȝeearnast   [...] þone *stede*   þe   se
       you   earn   [...] the   seat   that   the
       deofol of   afeoll   þurh   unȝehyrsumnysse.
       devil from   fell   through   disobedience.
       (Ælfr *Hom* 9 [*OED stead* 11])

This association presumably came through time (t_2) to gain weight and eventually led at t_3 to such unambiguous role uses as are illustrated in (3) (Stage I). Synchronically the relation between location and role is metaphorical (role is conceptualized in terms of location). Once this change had occurred, in locative prepositional phrases there must have been not only the possibility of the role meaning but also an inference at work due to the original locative meaning: that for any expression of the form X in the place of Y, it is no more possible for one person to have exactly the same role as another than it is possible for one place to be exactly where another is. Hence the speaker using that expression implies a mismatch (something more than is said), and the hearer is invited to make the construction relevant by drawing a subjective inference. Out of repeated uses the expectation (i.e. substitution) meaning was semanticized as in (4) by context-induced reinterpretation (Stage II). At first these are expectations based on norms of a general societal sort, and therefore represent weak subjectification. The expectation meaning came to gain ground and became the predominant meaning of the phrase, and speakers began to use the construction to imply broader and broader areas of expectation, leading to new conceptual and syntactic possibilities (Stages III-V). In other words, subjectification was strengthened.

Turning now to *in place of*, a very similar process of change involving increased subjectification occurred during its first three stages (see Table 2 above). However, the changes between Stages III and IV, in which the degree of functional disparity between X and Y was increased, may be a counterexample to unidirectional subjectification, since subjectification does not increase between these Stages (for a counterexample involving the Spanish Perfect, see Schwenter 1994). Although the original subjectification at Stage II is maintained, since all substitution expressions involve the speaker's subjective internal evaluation of what "expected to serve the same general function" entails, the pragmatic factor of expectation present in Stage III is eroded in Stage IV. Here, the construction comes to mark substitution between entities in the same physical location, that is, the external situation (see (34b) above). The strengthening of the locative element at the expense of the functional one is testament to how the PDE meaning of *place* acts as a 'leash' and affects the development of the whole construction.

This segment of change in the history of *in place of* also shows how the notions of semantic generalization and abstraction, conflated in Heine *et al.*'s unidirectional path, may need to be uncoupled in order to account for changes resulting from context-induced inferencing. Semantic generalization in grammaticalization has to do with the extension of grammatical forms to more and more contexts of use. The generalization of substitutive *in place of* to locative contexts does not seem to involve increasing abstraction, but rather an extension to a context involving a concrete sense of *place* that is still present in PDE. Thus, although evidence from many different cases of grammaticalization in a variety of the world's languages shows that generalization is often toward greater abstractness (as in the case of *instead of*), it appears that when such context-induced inferences are strong enough, changes leading to more concrete senses (in Heine *et al.*'s terminology) may also occur.

The theoretical point of importance here is that as historical discourse analysis and pragmatics progress, we need to examine carefully the different levels of analysis that contribute to change. At the lexical level we must be cautious about projecting changes occurring in individual items onto constructions that contain those items. At the same time, however, we must also consider that the lexical level may affect the development of a construction, e.g. *in place of*. At the level of the construction, we must attend both to the function of the construction type (e.g. locative, substitutive, etc.) and to the types of lexical items that can fill the X and Y slots during the grammaticalization process. Finally, we must look to the wider discourse level (or context) for the pragmatic conditions that underlie the use of forms and help to shape their subsequent development.

It is only through detailed examination of historical data in their discourse context, with focus on change as process rather than product, that a better understanding can be reached of how meanings change.

Notes

1.   Thanks to participants in Elizabeth Traugott's class on semantic change for comments on material in this paper. On-line corpora and searcher applications were made available by Academic Text Services at Stanford University.

2.   The periods of English are as follows: Old English (OE) *c.* 600-1125, Middle English (ME) *c.* 1125-1500, Early Modern English (EModE) *c.*1500-1750, Present Day English (PDE) *c.* 1750-.

3.   In the process of grammaticalization, there has also been a syntactic reanalysis such that [[in stead/place/lieu] [of Y]] > [X [in stead/[place/lieu of] Y], a change similar to that which occurred in constructions like attributive binominals such as *a hell of a problem* (Aarts in progress) (cf. *a big problem*), and degree modifiers like *kind of* (Tabor, in press) (cf. *somewhat large*). The nature of this syntactic change will not concern us here.

4.   OE had only inflectional genitive in this construction. The obligatory replacement by *of* in the context of non-human lexical nouns and optional replacement of it with human lexical nouns is independent of the semantic development of *instead of.*

5.   This and all other OE examples are from the later period, around 950-1050 A.D.

6. See section 7 for a proposal that metaphor is primarily the result of change, rather than a process of change itself.
7. The question remains whether the French meaning was borrowed from English or an independent development, or whether the materials available to us on French are inadequate to provide a definitive answer to the question of which language influenced the other.
8. There is only one example of *in place of* with a gerund: (22) *In place of* immediately entering into business, he continued to reside for some time with his parents (1844 *Herschel Ess.* (1857) 556 [*OED*]). Such structures seem to us to be only marginally acceptable in PDE and thus are further evidence that *in place of* is less grammaticalized than *instead of*.
9. The *OED* cites "And nouþe *in liue of* Aungels ane man ich i-seo" (1290 *S. Eng. Leg.* I.237); however, there is no entry in the *MED* for *lieu*, and no examples were found in HC.
10. The change in *lieu* presumably occurred in French, see section 4.
11. The discussion builds on Traugott and König (1991), Heine *et al.* (1991), and Hopper and Traugott (1993: Chap. 4).
12. Thanks to Mark Durie for comments leading to the formulation of the relationship between indexicality and language use.

References

Aarts, Bas
 (in progress) *The Syntax of Binominal Noun Phrases in English*. University College London. MS.
Anttila, Raimo
 1989 [1972] *Historical and Comparative Linguistics*. (2nd ed.) Amsterdam: John Benjamins. [first edition 1972, New York: Macmillan].
Benveniste, Emile
 1966 *Problèmes de linguistique générale*. Paris: Gallimard (trans. by Mary Elizabeth Meek as *Problems in General Linguistics*, Coral Gables, FL: University of Miami Press).
Brinton, Laurel
 1988 *The Development of English Aspectual Systems*. Cambridge: Cambridge University Press.
Bybee, Joan L.
 1985 *Morphology: A Study of the Relation between Meaning and Form*. Amsterdam: Benjamins.

Bybee Joan L., and William Pagliuca

   1985   "Cross-linguistic comparison and the development of grammatical meaning." In: Jacek Fisiak (ed.). *Historical Semantics. Historical Word-formation*. Amsterdam: John Benjamins, 59-83.

Bybee, Joan L., William Pagliuca, and Revere D. Perkins

   1991   "Back to the future." In: Traugott and Heine (eds.) Vol. 2: 17-58.

   1994   *The Evolution of Grammar: Tense, Aspect and Modality in the Languages of the World*. Chicago: University of Chicago Press.

Chafe, Wallace

   1976   "Givenness, contrastiveness, definiteness, subjects, topics, and point of view." In: Charles N. Li (ed.). *Subject and Topic*. New York: Academic Press , 27-55.

Clark, Herbert H.

   1994   "Discourse in production." In: M. A. Gernsbacher (ed.). *Handbook of Psycholinguistics*. San Diego: Academic Press, 985-1021.

Croft, William

   1994   A Gestalt Analysis of Complex Sentences and its Typological Consequences. MS.

Dasher, Richard

   in progr.   Grammaticalization in the System of Japanese Predicate Honorifics. PhD dissertation, Stanford University.

Ebert, Robert Peter

   1992   "Internal and external factors in syntactic change in an historical speech community." In: Gerritsen and Stein (eds.), 201-228.

Fillmore, Charles J.

   1984   "Remarks on contrastive pragmatics." In: Jacek Fisiak (ed.). *Contrastive Linguistics: Prospects and Problems*. Berlin: Mouton, 119-41.

Fischer, Olga

   1992   "Syntax." In: Norman Blake (ed.). *The Cambridge History of the English Language*. Vol. 2. Cambridge: Cambridge University Press, 207-408.

Fleischman, Suzanne

   1982   *The Future in Thought and Language: Diachronic Evidence from Romance*. Cambridge: Cambridge University Press.

   1989   "Temporal distance: A basic linguistic metaphor." *Studies in Language* 13: 1-50.

   1992   "Discourse and diachrony: The rise and fall of Old French SI." In: Gerritsen and Stein (eds.), 433-473.

Gerritsen, Marinel, and Dieter Stein (eds.)
    1992   *Internal and External Factors in Syntactic Change.* Berlin: Mouton de Gruyter.

Givón, Talmy
    1979   *On Understanding Grammar.* New York: Academic Press.
    1984   *Syntax: A Functional-typological Introduction,* Vol. 1. Amsterdam: John Benjamins.

Grice, H. Paul
    1975   "Logic and conversation." In: Peter Cole and Jerry L. Morgan (eds.). *Speech Acts.* New York: Academic Press, 41-58.

Haiman, John
    1985   *Natural Syntax: Iconicity and Erosion.* Cambridge: Cambridge University Press.

Hanson, Kristin
    1987   "On subjectivity and the history of epistemic expressions in English." *Chicago Linguistic Society* 23, 132-147.

Healey, Antonette diPaolo, and Richard L. Venezky
    1980   *A Microfiche Concordance to Old English.* University of Toronto: The Dictionary of Old English Project, Centre for Medieval Studies. [Available in electronic form: Angus Cameron, Ashley Crandell Amos, Sharon Butler, Antonette diPaolo Healey, *The Dictionary of Old English Corpus in Electronic Form.* University of Toronto: Dictionary of Old English Project.]

Heine, Bernd, Ulrike Claudi, and Freiderike Hünnemeyer
    1991   *Grammaticalization: A Conceptual Framework.* Chicago: University of Chicago Press.

Herring, Susan
    1991   "The Grammaticalization of Rhetorical Questions in Tamil." In: Traugott and Heine (eds.), Vol. 1. Amsterdam: Benjamins, 253-284.

HC. See Rissanen and Ihalainen 1991.

Hopper, Paul J., and Janice Martin
    1987   "Structuralism and diachrony: The development of the indefinite article in English." In: Anna Giacalone Ramat, Onofrio Carruba, Giuliano Bernini (eds.). *Papers from the 7th International Conference on Historical Linguistics.* Amsterdam: John Benjamins, 295-304.

Hopper, Paul J., and Elizabeth Closs Traugott
    1993   *Grammaticalization.* Cambridge: Cambridge University Press.

Horn, Laurence R.
    1984   "Toward a new taxonomy for pragmatic inference: Q-based and R-based implicature." In: Deborah Schiffrin (ed.). *Meaning, Form, and Use in*

Context: Linguistic Applications. GURT 84. Georgetown University Press, Washington D.C., 11-42.

Jucker, Andreas H.

1994   " The feasiblility of historical pragmatics." *Journal of Pragmatics* 22, 529-547.

Justus, Carol

1993   "Dislocated imperatives in the Indo-European prayer." *Word* 44, 273-94.

Langacker, Ronald W.

1990   "Subjectificat ion." *Cognitive Linguistics* 1, 5-38.

Li, Charles N., and Sandra Thompson.

1976a   " Subject and topic: a new typology of language." In: Charles N. Li (ed.) *Subject and Topic*. New York: Academic Press, 457-90.

1976b   "Development of the causative in Mandarin Chinese: Interaction of diachronic processes in syntax." In: Masayoshi Shibatani (ed.). *The Grammar of Causative Constructions*. (Syntax and Semantics 6). New York: Academic Press, 477-92.

Lyons, John

1977   *Semantics*. Cambridge: Cambridge University Press.

MED: The Middle English Dictionary

1956   Ann Arbor: University of Michigan Press.

Meillet, Antoine

1915-16 Le renouvellement des conjonctions. Annuaire de l'École pratique des Hautes Études; repr. in Antoine Meillet. *Linguistique historique et linguistique générale*. Paris: Champion, 1958, 159-74.

OED: The Oxford English Dictionary

1989   Oxford: Clarendon Press, 2nd ed. [Available in electronic form on CD-ROM].

Powell, Mava Jo

1992   " The systematic development of correlated interpersonal and metalinguistic uses in stance adverbs", *Cognitive Linguistics* 3, 75-110.

Prince, Ellen

1988   "Discourse analysis: A part of the study of linguistic competence." In: Newmeyer (ed.). *Linguistics: The Cambridge Survey*. Cambridge: Cambridge University Press, 164-182.

Rissanen, Matti, and Ossi Ihalainen

1991   *The Diachronic Part of the Helsinki Corpus of English Texts*. Helsinki: University of Helsinki Department of English.

Romaine, Suzanne
    1982   *Socio-historical Linguistics: Its Status and Methodology*. Cambridge: Cambridge University Press.
Romaine, Suzanne, and Deborah Lange
    1991   "The use of *like* as a marker of reported speech and thought: a case of grammaticalization in progress." *American Speech* 66, 227-79.
Schlieben-Lange, Brigitte
    1992   "The history of subordinating conjunctions in some Romance languages." In: Gerritsen and Stein (eds.), 341-354.
Schwenter, Scott A.
    1994   "The grammaticalization of an anterior in progress: Evidence from a peninsular Spanish dialect." *Studies in Language* 18, 71-111.
Svorou, Soteria
    1993   *The Grammar of Space*. Amsterdam: Benjamins.
Sweetser, Eve E.
    1988   "Grammaticalization and semantic bleaching." *Berkeley Linguistics Society* 14, 389-405.
Sweetser, Eve E.
    1990   *From Etymology to Pragmatics: Metaphorical and Cultural Aspects of Semantic Structure*. Cambridge: Cambridge University Press.
Tabor, Whitney
    in press   "The gradual development of the degree modifier *sort of*: A corpus proximity model." *Chicago Linguistic Society* 29.
Talmy, Leonard
    1988   "Force dynamics in language and cognition." *Cognitive Science* 2, 49-100.
TC: see Healey and Venezky 1980.
Thompson, Sandra Annear
    1972   "*Instead of* and *rather than* clauses in English." *Journal of Linguistics* 8, 237-49.
Thompson, Sandra, and Anthony Mulac
    1991   "A quantitative perspective on the grammaticization of epistemic parentheticals in English." In: Traugott and Heine (eds.), Vol. 1, 313-329.
Traugott, Elizabeth Closs
    1982   "From propositional to textual and expressive meanings: some semantic-pragmatic aspects of grammaticization." In: Winfred P. Lehmann and Yakov Malkiel (eds.). *Perspectives on Historical Linguistics*. Amsterdam: Benjamins, 245-271.
    1988   "Pragmatic strengthening and grammaticalization." *Berkeley Linguistics Society* 14, 406-16.

1989   "On the rise of epistemic meanings in English: An example of subjectification in semantic change." *Language* 65, 31-55.

in press   "Subjectification in grammaticalization." In: Wright and Stein (eds.).

Traugott, Elizabeth Closs, and Bernd Heine (eds.)

1991   *Approaches to Grammaticalization*. 2 Vols. Amsterdam: Benjamins.

Traugott, Elizabeth Closs, and Ekkehard König

1991   "The semantics-pragmatics of grammaticalization revisited." In: Traugott and Heine (eds.),Vol. 1., 189-218.

Wartburg, Walther v.

1928-65   *Französisches etymologisches Wörterbuch*. Basel: R.G. Zbinden & Co.

Wright, Susan

in press   "Subjectivity and experiential syntax." In: Wright and Stein (eds.) *Subjectivity and Subjectivisation in Language*. Cambridge: Cambridge University Press.

Wright, Susan, and Dieter Stein (eds.)

in press   *Subjectivity and Subjectivization in Language*. Cambridge: Cambridge University Press.

On Doing as You Please

Cynthia L. Allen
Australian National University

1. Introduction

Since the introduction of the 'Government and Binding' (also known as the 'Principles and Parameters theory') by Chomsky (1981), explanations for syntactic changes which involve a change in the parameter-setting of some part of the grammar have become very popular among formal syntacticians. To give a simple example, Fischer and van der Leek (1983) suggest that the 'impersonal' constructions such as *me thinks* disappeared in Middle English (ME) because the loss of case-marking morphology triggered a syntactic change; that is, the lexical case-marking of objects, which was involved in the generation of 'impersonal' constructions, became impossible, and English was left with only structural case-marking for objects. This meant that it was no longer possible to generate expressions like *me thinks* because the NP in the subject position was no longer able to get object case marking by lexical case-marking by the verb; rather, an NP in this preverbal position would be assigned nominative case marking structurally.

Although details of the proposed analyses vary considerably, the idea that impersonal constructions had to be replaced by personal ones because the loss of case-marking morphology triggered a change in parameter-setting (i.e. having lexical case-marking versus not allowing it) is a widely accepted one; see for example Lightfoot (1991: Chapters 5 and 6). But however well this sort of analysis deals with the loss of the impersonal constructions as structural possibilities in English, it is quite clear that a purely syntactic explanation of this sort cannot be expected to account for the development of each old 'impersonal' verb; such accounts attempt to explain why at a particular point the argument which I will refer to as the 'Experiencer'[1] should either have to behave like a normal subject (that is, be before the verb and have nominative case marking when pronominal) or like an ordinary object (that is, be postverbal), but no attempt is made to explain why a particular verb should have adopted the Experiencer subject option while another one should have adopted the Experiencer object option, since such explanations must go beyond the realm of pure syntax, which seeks only to describe and explain the structural possibilities of the grammar as a whole. However, a detailed examination of the changes which took place to the syntax of individual verbs should not be neglected, as such studies raise many puzzles which cannot be solved by syntactic theory on its own but offer an opportunity to learn more about how syntax, semantics, and pragmatics interact.

In this paper, I examine the history of the verb *please* in expressions such as *you can do as you please*. In this construction, the Experiencer of *please* is the only expressed argument of the verb; the other argument is a proposition which is not expressed. I will refer to this construction as the UNPROP construction, short for 'unexpressed proposition'.

The UNPROP construction is of particular interest for a number of reasons. First, the verb *please* has a different link-up of semantic and grammatical roles here from what is normally found with the verb. *Please* ordinarily requires its Experiencer to be the object. This is true whether the other argument is an NP or an expressed proposition:

(1)   The plan pleased the children
(2)   It pleases me to see him working so hard

I will refer to the construction of (1) as the 2NP construction, and to that of (2) as the PROP construction. The UNPROP construction is different from these two constructions in that the Experiencer is assigned instead to the role of subject; it has the preverbal position of a subject and is in the nominative case when it is a declinable pronoun, as in *I'll do as I please*.

A second interesting feature of *please* in the UNPROP construction is that it shows what seems like a rather peculiar restriction compared with other verbs which appear in the UNPROP construction. It is odd to use *please* in this construction with an Experiencer which is not co-referential to the subject of the matrix clause:

(3) a. I can stay as late as I please
    b. ?I can stay as late as you please[2]

In contrast, the UNPROP construction is completely felicitous with non-coreferential subjects when the verb *like* is used:

(4)   I can stay as late as you like

Section 2 of this paper argues that the explanation usually forwarded for the introduction of the Experiencer subject in the UNPROP construction is inadequate. The traditional explanation also fails to explain why the Experiencer subject construction, once introduced, should have ousted the Experiencer object construction, which was never under serious threat in the PROP construction and has always been the only structural possibility in the 2NP construction. Section 3 discusses the introduction of the Experiencer subject construction. Although this event, as well as the eventual favouring of this option over the Experiencer object construction, cannot be explained in terms of a syntactic reanalysis, a consideration of the semantics of the UNPROP construction makes it clear why there should have been pressure towards treating the Experiencer of this particular construction as a subject, although the Experiencer of *please* remained an object in other constructions. Section 4 looks at the period in which the Experiencer subject and Experiencer object were in variation and demonstrates that the variation was not random, but was patterned. Section 5 traces the later development of the UNPROP construction, and my conclusions are summarised in section 6.

2. The UNPROP construction as a reanalysis

The development of the Experiencer subject in the UNPROP construction is normally treated as the result of syntactic reanalysis caused by structural ambiguity because of the loss of case-marking distinctions. This idea was first expressed by Jespersen in volume 3 of his *Modern English Grammar* (1927). Jespersen (§11.2, p. 209) suggested that expressions like *if you please* and *if you like* were ones which have retained their outward form, but whose syntactic analysis has changed. That is, the Experiencer of the verb was fronted, but in the objective case. With the pronoun *you* the case marking was unclear, because by ME *you* was no longer unambiguously non-nominative. Nouns also lost the morphological distinction between nominative and objective[3] case in ME, with the result that a fronted Experiencer in this construction was now liable to reanalysis as a subject, instead of as some sort of fronted object. Thus Jespersen was proposing a progression something like this:

(5)a. I'll do as me pleases
  b. The king can do as the king pleases
  c. I'll do as I please

At stage (a), the pronoun has clearly objective case and the verb does not agree with anything, since there is no nominative subject. At stage (b), the fronted

Experiencer frequently had no distinctive case marking to show that it was an object. For this reason, it becomes reanalysed as a subject, since preverbal position was usually reserved for subjects, and we get stage (c), in which a pronoun shows up in the nominative case whenever it is capable of showing distinctive nominative case and the verb agrees with the Experiencer.

This analysis is easily converted into a principles and parameters framework by assuming that earlier English had some sort of parameter-setting which permitted (indirect) objects to occur before the verb. The exact nature of this parameter-setting does not matter here. Then at some point this parameter-setting changed so that objects could not appear directly before the verb. At this point, a language-learner hearing sentences like (5b) would be forced to interpret the Experiencer as the subject, since the grammar that the language-learner had constructed did not allow for the generation of objects in this position.

This reanalysis hypothesis seems at first to be very plausible, but it cannot stand up to a scrutiny of the data concerning the introduction of the Experiencer subject option in the UNPROP construction. The cornerstone of the hypothesis is the assumption that the Experiencer was structurally ambiguous in the UNPROP construction because it was frequently both ambiguous in case marking and preposed. That is, it assumes that when the UNPROP construction was first introduced into English, the Experiencer of the construction was normally placed before the verb (as in (5a)). Then as case marking deteriorated, the preposed Experiencer became structurally ambiguous and was reanalysed as a subject.

This cornerstone crumbles, however, when we realise that at the time when *please* began to be used in the UNPROP construction in English, the object status of this Experiencer was quite unambiguous. To see that this reanalysis hypothesis cannot account for the facts, it is necessary only to consider some basic facts about how *please* was introduced into English (in all constructions) and how the UNPROP construction developed.

The verb *please* was introduced into English from French in the 14th century. In that century, examples of the verb in the 2NP construction are fairly numerous. In this construction, the Experiencer was always some sort of object. It was most commonly a bare NP object as in (6):

(6) *and   they   may   nat   plese   hym*
     and   they   may   not   please   him
     'And they cannot please him'
     (Chaucer CT. Pars. I. 225, MS c1400-1410)

The Experiencer could also appear as the object of a preposition (normally *to* or *unto*); this construction was particularly common in translations from French or Latin, as in (7), where *plesen* translates Latin *complaceant*:

(7)   ...*þat   hii   plesen   to   þe*
      that   they   please   to   thee
      'That they may be pleasing to you'
      (MPPsalter 18.15, c1350; example taken from *MED*)

The use of the preposition presumably stems from the fact that the verb *plaisir* was normally subcategorised for an indirect object in French.[4] The treatment of an Experiencer as an indirect object was not alien to English syntax, and so some English writers followed the French pattern in this respect, substituting *(un)to* for *à*). However, it was more usual for the Experiencers of such verbs to be treated as a simple object in English, and so the pattern with bare NPs was used by all speakers and became dominant, although the more typically French pattern was for a time popular both in translations from French and in original English works by authors such as Malory who were strongly influenced by French.

Examples of the PROP construction with *please* in this period are harder to find than examples of the 2NP construction, but there are a few from near the end of the 14th century. I have not found any convincing examples of the UNPROP construction in the 14th century, so it is the use in the 15th century which we must start with when we look at whether the Experiencer was typically preposed or not. I have detailed the position of the Experiencer of *please* in the UNPROP construction in selected texts of the 15th century in Table 1.

Table 1: Please *in UNPROP construction: 15th century*

	AMB V	NOM V	DAT V	it V (to) EXP	V (to) EXP
Capgrave (b.1398)	0	0	0	0	0
Caxton (b. 1422)	0	0	0	8	0
Marg.K (a1450)	0	0	0	11	0
Kn.TL (?1450)	0	0	1	6	0
Malory (fl. 1470)	0	0	0	35	0
Paston (1425-61)	0	0	0	0	0
Paston (1461-92)	0	0	0	2	1
Cely (1472-88)	0	0	0	8	3
TOTAL	0	0	1	70	4

This table demonstrates quite clearly that at the time when the UNPROP construction first became common, there was no possibility whatsoever that the Experiencer could be misinterpreted as a subject. The Experiencer behaved like an object not only in taking object case marking (if it was a pronoun), but also in being overwhelmingly in a postverbal position. It is also of considerable interest to note that even when the Experiencer was a pronoun, it was normally postverbal in this period. For example, in Malory's writings, we find 35 examples of *please* in the UNPROP construction, and all but 4 of them have a pronominal Experiencer. These were precisely the sort of objects which we would expect to precede the verb, if any could, and so the facts indicate that by Malory's period, postverbal position had become fairly fixed for all types of objects. In this respect, even fairly 'Frenchified' authors like Malory rejected the French pattern of placing pronominal objects before the verb. Although the treatment of an Experiencer as the object of a preposition was not alien to English syntax, the preposing of object pronouns clearly was by this time.

It is also worthy of note that the single example in this table of a preposed Experiencer in the UNPROP construction does not come from the period when the UNPROP construction was first used. It is quite impossible to argue that preposed Experiencers in the UNPROP construction with *please* antedated postposed (i.e. object-like) Experiencers, and in fact it seems rather doubtful that the postposed Experiencer with object case marking was ever a really idiomatic English construction. The single example in Table 1 comes from the *Knight of the Tour Landry*, a close translation of the French work *Le Livre du Chevalier de la Tour*. This example is given here as (8):

(8) *for*   *God*   *yeuith*   *and*   *sendithe*   *where*   *hym*   *plesith*
     because   God   gives   and   sends   where   him   pleases
     'because God gives and sends where it pleases him' (or: 'where he pleases')
     (Kn.TL. 111.2, Chap. LXXXVI)

Unfortunately, it is impossible to demonstrate that this particular example is a direct calque on the French original, because the only published edition of the French text (Montaiglon's) is based on a different version from the one which was used for the English translation, and this particular sentence is not found in the French version. However, French influence seems quite probable here.

It is only in the 16th century that examples of preposed Experiencers become reasonably numerous in the UNPROP construction with *please*. The position and case marking of the Experiencer in this construction in several texts of the 16th and early 17th century is detailed in Table 2.

Table 2: Please *in UNPROP construction: 16th and early 17th century*

	AMB V	NOM V	DAT V	it V (to)EXP	V (to) EXP
Fisher (b. 1469)	0	0	0	3	1
Berners (b. 1469)	2	0	0	34	2
More (b. 1478)	0	0	0	6	0
Elyot (b. ?1490)	0	0	0	0	0
Ascham (b. 1515)	0	0	1	1	0
QEI (b. 1533)	1	3	0	1	0
Shkspre (b. 1564)	43	21	1	50	6
Donne (b. 1572)	0	1	0	1	0
TOTAL	46	25	2	96	9

Tables 1 and 2 make it clear that preposed Experiencers in this UNPROP construction only become common when it was also possible for the Experiencer to be nominative. That is, it seems that subject Experiencers did not become possible because preposed object Experiencers were possible and were liable to reanalysis as subjects; rather, it seems that for some reason the subject Experiencer option was simply added to the grammar at a time when there was no possibility that speakers could have misanalysed the object status of the Experiencer. Looking at Table 2, it seems possible that there were a few examples of ambiguously marked preposed Experiencers in the UNPROP construction just before clearly nominative Experiencers appeared. However, it should be noted that although this table does not show it, it seems that in fact ambiguously marked preposed Experiencers do not antedate clearly nominative Experiencers. I have found one example from the Paston letters from 1462 with what looks like a clearly nominative Experiencer:[5]

(9) *Ye may excuse yow by me, if ye please, tyl the next terme*
     'You may excuse yourself on my account, if you wish, until next term'
     (Paston letter 662.15)

Given that the nominative Experiencer seems to have been introduced by this time, it seems better to assume that the two ambiguously marked preposed Experiencers in Berners were in fact subjects, and that the lack of clearly nominative Experiencers is a data gap,[6] caused by the fact that subject Experiencers, although now possible, were not yet used nearly as frequently as object Experiencers in the UNPROP construction.

In summary, it seems quite clear that the development of the subject Experiencer in the UNPROP construction with *please* cannot be treated as a syntactic reanalysis. Rather, it appears that the subject Experiencer was for some reason introduced as an option for the lexical entry of *please*. This new syntactic option alternated with the older one (the object Experiencer) but eventually gained favour.

3.   Introduction of the subject Experiencer

The reanalysis hypothesis does not explain why this new option should have been introduced, and it does not explain why the Experiencer subject option should have gained favour once it was introduced. Let us now consider possible explanations for these developments.

     One possibility which must be examined is that *please* was influenced by *like*. In OE, *lician* took a nominative Experiencer and a dative Theme, as in (6):

(10) *gif   hit   ne   licað   þam   mode*
      if   it   not   pleases the(D)   mind(D)
      'If it does not please the mind' or 'If the mind does not like it'
      (ÆlS (Lucy) 84)

In examples such as (10), there is no reason to regard the Experiencer of *lician* as anything other than an object. However, matters are not so clear in examples like (11):

(11) *ac   gode   ne   licode   na   heora   geleafleast*
      but   God(D)   not   liked   not   their   faithlessness
      'But God did not like their faithlessness' *or*
      'But their faithlessness did not please God'

Examples of this sort are usually analysed as having a preverbal object, but there is reason to believe that the Experiencer behaved syntactically like a subject when it was in preverbal position, despite its object-like morphology (for a discussion of the subject-like properties of these preposed datives in OE, see Allen (forthcoming: see especially sections 4.4-4.8). If we accept the notion of dative subjects, we can say that their purpose was to signal the importance of the Experiencer by assigning it to the subject role but to indicate the non-agentivity of the Experiencer by giving it dative case marking. But whether we treat these preposed datives as syntactic subjects in OE or as fronted objects, it is at any rate clear that these preposed Experiencers had quite different properties from 'ordinary' preposed dative objects, and that the movement toward (nominative) Experiencer subjects with *like* (the only option for Contemporary English) had begun by the OE stage.

Given that *like* developed nominative Experiencers at some point, it is reasonable to ask whether these nominative Experiencers in the UNPROP construction might not have influenced *please*. Let us therefore take a brief look at the situation with *like* in the UNPROP construction before and during the period when *please* was developing nominative subjects in this construction.

Nominative Experiencers first appear with *like*, both in the 2NP and the UNPROP construction, in the 14th century, but are not common in either construction even by the end of the 14th century, as table 3 indicates. In fact, a glance at table 4 shows that nominative Experiencers had not become really common with *like* in the UNPROP construction even by Shakespeare's period (early 17th century).[7] However, there can be no doubt that the nominative Experiencer was a real option by the mid-15th century at least, and so there is some possibility that this construction with the nominative Experiencer could have played a role in the introduction of nominative Experiencers with *please*.

Table 3: Like *in UNPROP construction: 14th and 15th century*

	AMB V	NOM V	DAT V	it V (to) EXP	V (to) EXP
Trevisa	0	0	1	0	0
Chaucer	5	0	25	18	4
WP	4	1	35	0	0
Wycliffe	0	0	4	0	0
Piers P	10	0	20	0	0
Capgrave	0	0	1	0	0
Caxton	0	0	0	0	0
Marg.K	0	1	10	7	0
Malory	1	3	10	6	0
TOTAL	20	5	106	31	4

It is of considerable interest to note that although nominative Experiencers were not very common in the 14th or 15th century with *like* in the UNPROP construction, preposed Experiencers with objective case marking were quite common. There is, for example, a striking contrast in this respect between *like* and *please* in Malory's writings. As discussed above, not one of the Malory examples with *please* had a preverbal Experiencer. On the other hand, Malory frequently used preverbal Experiencers with *like* in the UNPROP construction. Given that Malory normally did not front objects in subordinate clauses in general and given that there is independent evidence that some non-nominative Experiencers had subject-like properties in OE and ME, it seems best to analyse the preposed dative Experiencers of authors such as Malory as subjects with objective case marking, rather than as fronted objects. That is, Malory used both Experiencer subjects (with either nominative or dative case) and Experiencer objects (the postverbal Experiencers) with *like* in the UNPROP construction, but only Experiencer objects with *please*. By the time *please* began to allow subject Experiencers in the UNPROP construction, dative subjects had pretty much died out as an option for any verb, and so we do not get preposed dative Experiencers with *please* as a real option at any stage.

Table 4 *Like* in UNPROP construction: 16th century

	AMB V	NOM V	DAT V	it V (to) EXP	V (to) EXP
Fisher (b. 1469)	0	0	0	2	0
Berners (b. 1469)	0	0	0	0	0
More (b. 1478)	1	1	4	0	0
Elyot (b. ?1490)	0	0	4	0	0
Ascham (b. 1515)	0	1	0	0	0
Shkspre (b. 1564)	1	3	0	18	0
TOTAL	2	5	8	20	0

There is therefore some plausibility to the idea that *like* influenced the syntax of *please* in the UNPROP construction. It is important to note, however, that no such influence is detectable in the 2NP construction; in that construction *please* never showed the slightest tendency to develop nominative Experiencers. It seems, in fact, that if *like* influenced the syntax of *please* in the UNPROP construction, it only did so because the use of Experiencer subjects suited the semantics of this construction particularly well. And in fact, it is not difficult to see why the Experiencer subject should have been introduced and, once introduced, should have gained favour in the UNPROP construction when we go beyond pure syntax and consider the typical use of this construction. The essence of the UNPROP construction (whether with *please* or any other verb) is to say that whether something happens or not will depend on the Experiencer's attitude toward the event. The construction is, in fact, saying that the Experiencer is in control of things. It is hardly surprising that speakers of English would feel some pressure toward assigning the Experiencer of *please* to the role of subject in the UNPROP construction, because this was a construction in which the Experiencer had semantic attributes normally associated with subjects.

Support for the idea that it was the emphasis on control on the part of the Experiencer of *please* in the UNPROP construction which led to the introduction of the subject Experiencer in this construction comes from an examination of examples from the period when the Experiencer subject and the Experiencer object were both options for the UNPROP construction. Let us now turn to this period of variation.

4.   Variation between subject and object Experiencers

Given the hypothesis that Experiencer subjects were introduced because they indicated control of the situation on the part of the Experiencer, we can make a prediction about the period of variation between Experiencer subjects and Experiencer objects in the UNPROP construction: in general, we should find Experiencer subjects when the Experiencer was most in control of events, and objects when the Experiencer was least in charge. The period when the Experiencer subject option was first introduced does not supply enough examples to allow us to draw any firm conclusions about what controlled the choice between the two options, but abundant examples of both options are found in Shakespeare's work; furthermore, a concordance of Shakespeare's works is available, which makes the task of studying his usage much easier. These works are also particularly suitable because they contain representations of the speech of people of different walks of life. I will therefore first consider the question of what determined Shakespeare's choice of the constructions, and then return to the earlier period of variation to show that the very earliest examples of Experiencer subjects with UNPROP *please* fit nicely into the explanation given.

4.1. *Shakespeare*

It is particularly interesting to look at the Shakespearean data in the light of the following rather frustrated-sounding entry for *please* **II.6.** *intr.* in the *Oxford English Dictionary* (*OED*):

> To be pleased, to like; to have the will or desire; to have the humour; to think proper. (In sense, exactly = the passive in 4, 4b.) The history of this inverted use of *please* (observed first in Scottish writers) is obscure. But exactly the same change took place in the 14th c. in the use of the synonymous verb *like*, where the impersonal 'it liked him', 'him liked' became 'he liked' c 1430. It may therefore be assumed that 'I please' was similarly substituted for 'me pleases' (c 1440 in 3c). ...The remarkable thing in the case of *please* is that the sense was already logically expressed by the passive *to be pleased* (sense 4), and that the new idiom was therefore not needed, 'he pleases' being simply = 'it pleases him', and 'he is pleased'. Shakespeare uses the three forms indifferently.

More than one problem with the *OED*'s discussion should now be apparent; for example, it does not seem plausible that *I please* comes from *me pleases*, as discussed. But of particular interest at this point is the *OED*'s claim that Shakespeare used the three forms *he pleases, he is please,* and *it pleases him* "indifferently". It is in fact not difficult to show that the choice between the two active[8] forms was far from random, although this is not to claim that every single example could be explained. In trying to find a method to the apparent madness of variation in Shakespeare's use, I soon realised that one powerful predictor of the choice of the subject or object role for the Experiencer was whether the UNPROP clause began with the word *if* or with a wh-word like *when, what,* etc. In clauses beginning with *if,* the Experiencer was usually assigned to the role of object of that clause, as in (8):

(12) If it please your honor, I am the poor duke's constable
       (MM II.1.47)

On the other hand, when the UNPROP clause was introduced by a wh-word, the Experiencer was likely to be the subject:

(13) I may say so when I please
       (ADO 2.01.92P)
(14) It rested in your grace to unloose this tied up justice when you pleased
       (MM 1.04.32)

Semantically, the gross difference between these two types of clauses is that the clauses introduced by *wh-* words (other than *whether*) contain variables; they are similar to open questions. In contrast, clauses introduced by *if* refer to yes-no situations. Accordingly, I will refer to the two types as 'variable clauses' and '*if-clauses*'. Table 5 details the assignment of the Experiencer of *please* to the subject or object role in the two types of clauses in Shakespeare's works. It should be noted that under '*if-clauses*' I have also included clauses beginning with *and,* which was used in the meaning of 'if' in this period, as well as *whether.* I have excluded the expressions *so please EXP* and *please it EXP,* but have included *an' it please EXP.*

     Table 5 clearly shows a very marked preference for Experiencer subjects in variable clauses. On the other hand, *if-clauses* were likely to have object Experiencers, although the preference here is less marked. This sort of patterning is not difficult to understand when we consider general differences between the variable clauses and the *if-clauses.* The essence of a variable UNPROP clause is that something about an event, such as when it will happen, will depend on the Experiencer's pleasure; thus the Experiencer always has at least some degree of control, making it more agentive than the normal

Experiencer and therefore a good candidate for the role of subject. In comparison, the Experiencer in an *if-clause* was most frequently not in control at all in the Shakespearean examples, because the most common use of these clauses was simply to introduce information, as in (12), where the speaker is the duke's constable whether the addressee likes it or not.

Table 5: If *and Variable Clauses in Shakespeare's Works*

A. *If-clauses*

If AMB V	If NOM V	If DAT V	If V EXP	If it V EXP
20	5	0	4	47

Total *If-clauses* = 76
Preposed EXP = 25 (33%)
Postposed EXP = 51 (67%)

B. Variable Clauses

Var AMB V	Var NOM V	Var DAT V	Var it V EXP	Var V EXP
23	16	1	3	2

Total *If-clauses* = 45
Preposed EXP = 40 (89%)
Postposed EXP = 5 (11%)

If the hypothesis that the subject option was chosen because of control by the Experiencer is correct, then we should find that object Experiencers are found in variable clauses only when the Experiencer is less in control than is usual in such clauses and that subject Experiencers in *if-clauses* are only found when the *if-clause* involves more control on the part of the Experiencer than in the more typical clause which is used simply to introduce information. And as a broad generalisation, this is true. However, it is clear that control on the part of the Experiencer is not the whole story. Looking at *if-clauses* particularly, we find that the type of speech act and the social relationship between the speaker and the addressee is also important. Let us now look more closely at different kinds of variable clauses and *if-clauses*.

Because of the very small number of variable clauses which do not conform to the generalisation that they take Experiencer subjects, it is very difficult to make any convincing claims about what might have brought on the use of Experiencer objects in such clauses. However, it is worth noting that the 'exceptional' examples exhibit a higher than normal frequency of Experiencers which are not coreferential to the main clause subject. The subject of the variable UNPROP clause is usually coreferential with the subject of the main clause in the Shakespearean examples, as in (13) and (14). Sentences like (15), in which the Experiencer is not coreferential with the main clause subject, account for only 10 out of the 40 examples in which the Experiencer is preposed:

(15) and be it moon, or sun, or what you please;
      (AWW 4.05.13)

But in 3 out of the 5 variable clause examples in which the Experiencer is postverbal, the subject of the main clause is not coreferential with the Experiencer, as in:

(16) Her hair shall be of what color it please God
      (ADO 2.03.35P)

Clearly, we cannot simply say that the Experiencer must be the subject when it was coreferential with the main clause subject and must be the object when it was not, but it does seem that the subject role was especially strongly preferred for Experiencers which were coreferential with the actor of the main clause. It is also clear that 'non-matching' Experiencers were also normally assigned to the subject role, but it looks like they were more likely to be assigned to the object role than were the matching Experiencers. It might be that further examination of subtle semantic factors in the exceptional examples would yield some explanations, but given the small number of examples the explanations would not be very convincing. It is worth noting, however, that *please* in the UNPROP construction does not only refer to the Experiencer's actual wishes, but also can refer to what the Experiencer finds acceptable or suitable. Perhaps the reason for the Experiencer object in (15) was that God was not being portrayed as actually having a real desire for the hair to be of a particular colour, but was merely presented as choosing some colour as suitable, and that Experiencer subjects were more likely when what was being discussed was actual desire on the Experiencer's part, rather than acceptability to the Experiencer.

These remarks about Experiencer objects in variable clauses are quite speculative, because by Shakespeare's time, Experiencer objects were unusual in variable clauses. However, when we turn to the *if-clauses*, it is easy to make some general statements about the choice of subject or object Experiencers. It is important to note that UNPROP clauses introduced by *if* covered quite a wide semantic and pragmatic range. One very common use was simply to introduce new information, as in (12). In this function, the Experiencer was *always* assigned to the object role. It seems likely that the reason for this is that in this use, the addressee has absolutely no control over the situation. It seems likely that the social inferior used the verb *please* in this situation because although the Experiencer had no control over the situation, nevertheless the reaction of the Experiencer was extremely important. The formula is used to convey the hope that the addressee will not take the information or interruption amiss.

A rather similar use of UNPROP *please* is its use in polite contradictions:

(17) Fal.   Good morrow, goodwife.
     Quick.   Not so, and't please your worship
     (WIV 11.ii.35)

Here, the speaker is contradicting the assumption of the addressee (her social superior) that she is a wife. Another example, in which a social inferior disagrees with a statement by a superior:

(18) Sir, if it please your honor, this is not so
     (MM 2.01.85P)

In such examples, the speaker is disagreeing with the addressee, but uses *please* because although the Experiencer is not in control of the truth or otherwise of the contradicted statement, the use of *please* makes the contradiction less blunt by expressing a concern for the addressee's reaction. Once again, the expression has a deferential cast to it, because it was most frequently used by social inferiors, who had the most to fear from a bad reaction by the addressee.

Contradictions by social equals (or near equals, such as aristocrats contradicting the king) can also use Experiencer objects:

(19) My lords, and please you, 'tis not so
     (1H6 5.04.10)

However, such contradictions were frequently couched in terms of a polite command, and in this situation, the Experiencer took the subject role:

(20) Let me say no, my liege, and if you please;
     I only swore to study with your grace
     (LLL 1.01.50)

In this example, the speaker is contradicting the king's assertion that he had sworn to study, fast, and eschew the company of women. Such polite commands were also used to introduce criticisms made by speakers of high social standing to equals or superiors:

(21) O my liege, pardon me, if you please
     (R2 2.01.187)

This sentence directly precedes a criticism by York of the king (his nephew). In fact, polite commands by people of high social standing nearly always had Experiencer subjects:

(22) Pray, sir, put your sword up, if you please
      (TN 3.04.321P)

It is interesting that the Experiencer subject is used here, because in this situation the Experiencer was not really in control; the speaker expects compliance with the command. In fact, there are no examples of commands or requests in which the speaker has a right to expect compliance which have an object Experiencer. It is clear that the degree of control by the Experiencer is far from the whole story in the choice of subject or object. The use of the Experiencer subject in commands seems to result from a polite fiction that the Experiencer's wishes have something to do with the matter. Furthermore, structural parallelism between the main and subordinate clause may have increased the tendency to use an Experiencer subject in commands, since the understood subject of the command was always coreferential to the UNPROP Experiencer. While the Experiencer was not completely in control of the situation, they were nevertheless carrying out the action of the matrix clause.

While the use of the Experiencer subject was an absolute rule in commands (in which the speaker could expect compliance), it was not quite universal with the imperative *form*:

(23) Isabella (kneeling): Most bounteous sir: look, if it please you,
      on this man condemn'd As if my brother lived
      (MM 5.01.44)

This sentence, uttered by a woman of high social standing, is better considered an *entreaty*, not a request. Isabella is here pleading for a man's life, and it seems probable that she used the Experiencer object to make the entreaty more deferential.

Related to imperatives are jussive clauses, in which the subject is third person but the addressee is being asked to allow an event to happen. I have found only two *if-clauses* used with a construction which I would consider jussives in Shakespeare's works. In one, the Experiencer is the object:

(24) and please your majesty, let his neck answer for it
      (H5 4.08.43P)

In this sentence, the speaker wishes something to happen and asks the addressee to allow it to happen, not because the addressee necessarily wishes it to happen, but because he (hopefully) finds it acceptable or suitable. Thus, this sentence is similar to the entreaty of (19). In the other example, the Experiencer plays the role of subject:

(25) Oth.:   Most humbly, therefore bending to your state,
                 I crave fit disposition for my wife...
                 With such accommodation and besort
                 As levels with her breeding.

      Duke: If you please, Be't at her father's.   (OTH 1.3.240)

This example differs from the preceding one in that the speaker is not asking the addressee to allow something to happen because the speaker wishes it to happen. Here, the speaker has no need to be deferential and is merely suggesting a solution to a problem, if it is agreeable to the addressee.

The remaining *if-clauses* of the corpus are all used to indicate that a situation will happen if the Experiencer thinks that would be good (or would have happened had the Experiencer thought it would have been good). In such examples, it is frequently difficult to judge whether what is being talked about is actual desire on the Experiencer's part or merely the Experiencer's judgement that an event or situation would be suitable. That is, the Experiencer may judge that a situation would be good because they would derive some personal benefit or satisfaction from it, or may simply judge a situation which someone else desires to be acceptable or suitable. In sentences which clearly have a 'desire' meaning, the Experiencer is always in the subject role:

(26) This young maid might do her a shrewd turn, if she pleas'd
      (AWW 3.05.68)
(27) My daughter shall be Henry's, if he please
      (1 H6 5.03.127)

In (26), it is stated that the maid could do someone a shrewd turn if she wished to do so. In (27), the meaning is 'if he wishes to have her'. We can make the generalisation that in all the sentences in which we could confidently substitute *wish* without changing the meaning very much, the Experiencer is the subject of the UNPROP *if-clause*. This fact is consistent with the idea that the Experiencer subject is used when the Experiencer has a high degree of control; the situation happens because the Experiencer wishes it to happen.

On the other hand, all of the examples with an Experiencer object are consistent with the interpretation that the Experiencer is allowing the situation to happen simply because they judge it to be suitable or acceptable for some reason, not necessarily because they actually desire it:

(28) D. John: If your leisure served, I would speak with you.

> D. Pedro: In private?
>
> D. John: If it please you.
>
> (ADO 3.2.87)

(29) Whither, if it please you, we may now withdraw
      (R3 5.05.11)

Thus, the Experiencer is the subject when the meaning is clearly that the Experiencer personally wishes something to happen, but is the object when the Experiencer is doing something or allowing something to happen because someone else wants something to happen, and the Experiencer finds this good or acceptable.

It should be noted, however, that the Experiencer subject is not limited to situations in which the Experiencer would derive personal benefit from the situation. There are several examples like (30):

(30) I did not, sir. These lords, my noble fellows, if they please,
      Can clear me in't
      (WT 2.03.143)

If the lords take the trouble to clear the speaker, it will not be because of any personal benefit, but because of a wish to do so because they consider it to be proper. In these examples in which the meaning is intermediate between the meaning of real desire because of personal benefit and acceptance of a situation which someone else desires, either the subject or object Experiencer may be used, and it is not always clear what motivates the choice, although it seems likely that such factors as the degree of personal intervention by the Experiencer (which could be expected to bring on an Experiencer subject) played a role.

To sum up Shakespeare's usage, we can say that the Experiencer subject was in general used when the Experiencer was most in control of events: something is depicted as happening *because the Experiencer wishes it to happen that way*. The Experiencer subject was also used in polite commands. Here, the Experiencer is politely depicted as doing something because they wish to. On the other hand, the Experiencer was given the object role when the Experiencer was in control of whether something happened or not, but was either doing something or allowing it to happen because it seems suitable rather than actually beneficial to the Experiencer. The Experiencer object was also used when the Experiencer was the addressee and was not in the least in control of events, but was a person whose opinion or reaction was important.

4.2. The earliest Experiencer subjects

I have deferred discussion of the nature of the earliest Experiencer subjects until after the discussion of Shakespeare's use because when the number of examples is small, a number of hypotheses could fit the data, and it is not possible to be confident that the proposed explanation is the correct one. But now that we have seen that the Experiencer was highly likely to be the subject when the Experiencer was most in control in Shakespeare's works, we can note that the degree of control by the Experiencer seems to have played an important role in the very first examples: in all the early examples, not only does the event take place because the Experiencer wishes it to happen that way, but it is also the case that the Experiencer is the actor in the event. The first examples that I have found with a clearly nominative Experiencer, as indicated in table 2, come from the letters of Queen Elizabeth I. I present these examples here:

(31) We ... will do things as we please, and when we please
      (QEI Letter 5.xxix)
(32) for the pursuits of any of his malicious purposes at such time
      as he shall please
      (QEI Letter 5.xxxiii)

In both examples, the Experiencer of *please* is not only the arbiter of whether or how an action is carried out, but the actor of the action. It is also of interest to note that the same situation is found in the two examples of a preposed but ambiguously cased-marked example in Berners' writings which have been mentioned above:

(33) pylgryme, enter when you plese
      (Berners, Duke Huon p. 546.15)
(34) with the whiche, if you please, stryke of my hede
      (Berners, Duke Huon p. 202.10)

Sentence (34) is not a request; the speaker is telling the king that he realizes that he has deserved to die, and that the king has every right to execute him if that is his desire, although the speaker goes on to beg for mercy. The fact that these ambiguously marked examples conform to the type of the earliest examples with an indisputably nominative subject lends support to the suggestion made above that the preposed Experiencer of these examples is to be construed as the subject, despite the lack of clear case marking.

It is also of interest to note that the few examples in which the Experiencer is preposed but in the dative case are similar to these examples in that the Experiencer is coreferential to the matrix clause subject. However, as has already been noted, the number of examples is so few as to make it seem doubtful that these preposed datives were ever a genuine grammatical option. At any rate, the small number of examples makes it impossible to make generalisations about possible differences between this construction and the construction with a nominative Experiencer.

It is finally important to note that the introduction of the Experiencer subject in the UNPROP construction appears not to have increased the pragmatic range of this construction. All the speech act types which have been identified for the UNPROP construction in Shakespeare's works are also present in earlier works which have only object Experiencers. In the works of Malory, for example, we find this construction used in commands:

(35)   Therefore, and hit please you, tell me your name
       (Malory 659.17)

The construction was also used to convey a meaning of real desire on the Experiencer's part:

(36)   ye shall have her...to do with hir what hit please you
       'You shall have her to do with her what you please'
       (Malory 411.32)

As we have seen, both of these uses required an Experiencer subject in Shakespeare's usage. Thus it does not appear that the introduction of the Experiencer subject heralds new uses or meanings; rather, it seems that the Experiencer subject construction was particularly suited to expressing the idea that something would happen because the Experiencer wished it to happen, and once introduced, it was quickly adopted for this particular use. It then spread into other uses where the degree of control was not so great.

4.3. Comparison with the PROP construction

Before moving on to the later development of the UNPROP construction, let us briefly compare this construction with the PROP construction. As mentioned above, *please* never showed any tendency whatsoever to develop an Experiencer subject in the 2NP construction. This fact should now be easy to understand; in the 2NP construction there is no meaning of control at all on the part of the Experiencer, and so no pressure toward the development of an Experiencer subject. It should be noted, however, that Experiencer subjects were in fact an option for a period for *please* in another construction, the PROP construction, which differed from the UNPROP construction in that a proposition was explicitly mentioned. As with the UNPROP construction, the

PROP construction is first found with Experiencer subjects in the 16th century. An example from Shakespeare's works will suffice to illustrate the construction:

(37) If thou please to take me to thee
      (ANT 5.01.9)

There can be little doubt that this Experiencer subject was a real grammatical option for a period in English; examples are still found in the 18th century. However, this construction was never used as frequently as the older construction in which the Experiencer was the object. For example, in Shakespeare's works, we find a total of 109 examples of the PROP[9] construction with *please*, but in only 29 of them is the Experiencer the subject; in the other 80 examples the older construction, with an Experiencer object, is used:

(38) Come, come, will't please you go?
      (TGV 1.02.137)

Nor do we find a greater proportion of Experiencer subjects in the works of any other author. A detailed examination of the history of the PROP construction is beyond the scope of this paper. However, it seems very likely that the reason why the Experiencer subject was introduced is that the Experiencer was often in control of the event mentioned in the subordinate clause, as in (37). In such examples, the Experiencer was not only in control of whether the event took place, but was the actor in the event. In this respect, the PROP construction was similar to the UNPROP construction. But an important difference is that the notion of control on the part of the Experiencer was not built into the PROP construction, as it was in the UNPROP construction. With the PROP construction, the Experiencer is frequently merely reacting to the event, as in *it pleases me to see you working so hard*. It is no surprise that the Experiencer subject is found in the PROP construction in Shakespeare's works only when there is a great deal of control by the Experiencer. It is interesting to note, however, that there was never a period when the Experiencer subject was the only option for sentences with such a high degree of control. With the UNPROP construction, a meaning of control was built into the construction when it was introduced by a variable, and the Experiencer subject quickly became the only option with variable clauses. No formally recognisable variety of PROP clause ever had a built-in meaning of control, however, and perhaps this is why the Experiencer subject never became the preferred option.

5.   Later development of the UNPROP construction

Having looked at the use of the Experiencer subject in the very earliest
examples and at its variation in Shakespeare's period, we can now trace the
further development of the UNPROP construction through the 19th century.

Table 6: Please *in the UNPROP Construction in the 17th century and 18th
century*

A. *If-clauses*

	If EXP V	If V EXP	If it V EXP
Donne (b. 1572)	0	0	0
Walton (b. 1593)	0	0	0
Behn (b. 1640)	7	0	2
Defoe (b. 1660)	8	0	0
Fielding (b. 1707)	19	0	8
Cleland (b. 1710)	2	1	0
TOTAL	36	1	10

B. Variable Clauses

	Var EXP V	Var it V EXP	Var V EXP
Donne (b. 1572)	1	1	0
Walton (b. 1593	0	0	0
Behn (b. 1640)	13	0	0
Defoe (b. 1660)	21	0	0
Fielding (b. 1707)	36	0	0
Cleland (b. 1710)	10	0	0
TOTAL	81	1	0

Part B of Table 6 clearly suggests that by the end of the 16th century, the
Experiencer object had become restricted to *if-clauses* in the UNPROP
construction with *please*. The Experiencer object is no longer found in any
variable clauses in the works of writers born after 1600. The Experiencer object
remains fairly common in *if-clauses* in the 17th century, but it appears to have
lost ground even here; the Experiencer subject seems to be preferred even in *if-
clauses*. When we look at the variation between the subject and object option in
the *if-clauses*, it becomes apparent that the variation is not simply random, but
correlates with the speech act type. We have seen that the Experiencer object
construction already had a deferential ring to it by Shakespeare's time; by the
mid-17th century (at least) the deferential nature of the construction is

impossible to miss. For example, in the writings of Aphra Behn (born in 1640), I have found only two examples of Experiencer objects:

(39) ...it would be very much against her inclinations, and if it pleased her
      father, she had rather...
      (Behn, p. 343)
(40) May it please your majesty!
      (Behn, p. 357)

In both examples, the speaker is asking an addressee of higher status to *allow* a situation or event, and in both cases it is a situation which the speaker knows that the addressee does not really want.

While the number of examples in Behn's work is not large enough to make us very confident of our conclusions, these conclusions are strengthened by a consideration of the examples from the later 17th century and 18th century texts. In these texts, we find that the Experiencer object is particularly characteristic of the speech of servants and of lower-class people in general:

(41) May it please your worship, there never was a poor woman so injured
      (Fielding, *Tom Jones*, p. 105)
(42) ... but I live with him, an't please your honour
      (Fielding, *Tom Jones*, p. 830)
(43) Sweet heart, do you want a place? Yes! and please you!
      (with a curtsy down to the ground)
      (Cleland, *Fanny Hill*, p. 45)

In short, the Experiencer object was restricted to situations in which a lower-class speaker was softening a bit of information given to an addressee of higher status; it was used especially when the speaker was causing an interruption (e.g. by announcing a bit of news) or presenting information which might be thought unpalatable to the addressee. In both these situations, it was possible for the subject (*it*) to be left out, as in (43). By the time of Jane Austen (b. 1775), the Experiencer object has practically disappeared. I found 25 examples of *if-clauses* with Experiencer subjects in Austen's works (in all cases, the Experiencer is *you*), but only one example which might be interpreted as an UNPROP clause with an Experiencer object:

(44) '... and I should at this time have been in possession of a most valuable
      living, had it pleased the gentleman we were speaking of just now
      (Austen, *Pride and Prejudice*, 16 79 13)

This example is obviously quite different from the examples given in (41) through (43), since *please* is used here in a sense in which it could be used in any simple sentence, while the sense of *please* in (41) through (43) could only be used in an UNPROP construction. It is arguable that (44) should be treated as a 2NP construction in which the *it* refers to a proposition; this *it* is more clearly referential than the *it* of the typical UNPROP example. At any rate, it is clear that the Experiencer object was no longer used in the function of simply introducing a bit of information in a polite way. We do find in Austen's works examples of speech acts by servants similar to those of (41) through (43), but they have a simple *please*:

(45)   The Thrush is gone out of harbour, please, sir...
       (Austen, *Mansfield Park*, 7.377.7)

Here the (lower-class) speaker is simply conveying a piece of information. It seems likely that this usage originated from an UNPROP construction which was reduced by leaving out both the subject and the object.

It is also interesting to note that the usage of the 17th and 18th century differed from contemporary speech in its use of the Experiencer subject in *if-clauses*. In contemporary usage, *if you please* is very restricted. In particular, it can never be replaced by 'if you wish'. We can imagine a sales clerk saying 'step this way, if you please', but it would not mean 'step this way, if you wish'. In the 17th century and 18th century, however, *if you please* could still be used to convey that whether the action of the matrix clause took place or not depended on the Experiencer's attitude towards it. The Experiencer's attitude might involve actual personal desire for the situation to happen (as in (46)) or simple acceptance of the suitability or appropriateness of the action (as seems to be the case in (47)):

(46)   You may punish me if you please
       (Fielding, *Tom Jones*, p. 355)
(47)   if the reader please, therefore, we chuse rather to say she resigned
       (Fielding, *Tom Jones*, p. 328)

By the early 19th century, however, the Experiencer subject construction with *if-clauses* had become very restricted. For one thing, the Experiencer is always *you* in the 19th century texts studied here (including Austen's works). Furthermore, *if you please* is no longer used to convey the idea that something will happen only if the Experiencer allows it to happen. Rather, the construction has become a formula restricted to polite commands and contradictions or corrections:

(48)   We will take the volume up-stairs – and the pencil, if you please.
       (George Eliot, *Middlemarch*, p. 517)

(49) We will, if you please, say no more on this subject.
(George Eliot, *Middlemarch*, p. 317)
(50) Imprudent, if you please – but not mad
(Austen, *Emma*, 8 225 73)

(48) and (49) are polite commands, and in (50) the speaker politely disagrees with the addressee's previous statement. Such sentences are still possible in contemporary usage, but to my ear they have a rather condescending sound to them.

While the use of *please* in *if-clauses* has changed quite significantly within the modern period, its use in variable clauses has not changed very much from the 17th century, when the object Experiencer disappeared from these clauses. Notably, *please* still retains the 'wish' meaning in these clauses in contemporary English. However, there was one notable difference between the variable clauses of the 17th century and 18th century and contemporary usage. As mentioned in the introduction to this paper, it is my own judgement that the UNPROP construction is distinctly odd when the Experiencer (subject) of the UNPROP clause is not coreferential with the actor of the main clause.[10] Not all native speakers of English may agree with this judgement, but (admittedly not very extensive) examination of 19th century texts suggests that it was at least the normal situation (if not the only possibility) for this coreferentiality to hold. Since I have only studied two lengthy novels from authors born in the 19th century, my conclusions are merely suggestive, but it seems significant that in the total of 19 variable UNPROP clauses, only one has non-coreferentiality of the UNPROP subject with the matrix actor:

(51) Bulstrode's earlier life was, for some mids, melted into the mass of
mystery, as so much lively metal to be poured out in dialogue and
to take such fantastic shapes as heaven pleased
(Eliot, *Middlemarch*, p. 775)

The works of Jane Austen, who was born in 1775 but wrote in the early 19th century, similarly yield 9 variable UNPROP clauses with subjects coreferential to the subject of the matrix clause, but none with non-matching subjects. In contrast, although such examples with non-matching subjects are much less common in 18th century texts than ones with matching subjects, they are nevertheless not particularly difficult to find:

(52) We are prevented from making him mean what we please ourselves
(Fielding, *Tom Jones*, p. 138)

It appears that even if non-matching subjects have not become impossible for all speakers in variable *please* UNPROP clauses, there has nevertheless been a shift towards a preference for using a different verb, such as *like*, when the subject of the UNPROP clause is not coreferential with the actor of the matrix clause.

A really convincing explanation of why *like* should allow non-matching subjects in the UNPROP construction but *please* should prefer matching subjects would require a thorough analysis of semantic differences between these two verbs. Nevertheless, I would like to speculate briefly on why the preference for matching subjects should have developed. As already noted, the (variable) UNPROP construction always conveys the meaning that something happens *because the Experiencer thinks it is good*. However, with *please*, the Experiencer must not only be in charge of whether the action takes place or not, but must be actively involved in the action. That is, an even greater degree of control is involved. It does not seem unreasonable to suggest that this has come about because of the fact that the assignment of the Experiencer of *please* to the subject role puts special emphasis on the agentivity of the Experiencer. In all other constructions, the Experiencer of *please* is assigned to the object role, and is not at all agentive. In the UNPROP construction, however, it is in control and (unusually) assigned to the subject role. Speakers of English know that the Experiencer of *please* is usually a non-agentive object, and so it seems plausible that when this Experiencer was assigned to the subject role, the unusual agentivity of this argument would be particularly noticeable. Perhaps this obvious agentivity of the Experiencer subject with *please* led to a situation in which the meaning of *please* in this construction shifted subtly. I suggest that at an earlier stage, the variable clauses conveyed the meaning that something happens because the Experiencer wishes it to happen. But later, the meaning conveyed that the event happens *only* because the Experiencer wishes it to happen, and *not for any other reason*. To me, at least, the use of a variable clause UNPROP with *please* seems to emphasise that the Experiencer need not take anyone else's opinion into account.

In contrast, the Experiencer of *like* is the subject in all constructions, whether it is in control of events or not. Thus the Experiencer of *like* in the UNPROP construction did not acquire a stronger degree of agentivity, or an emphasis on the Experiencer's control of the situation.

5.1. *Summary of modern developments*

To summarise, the UNPROP construction with *please* in the post-Shakespearean period underwent structural, semantic, and pragmatic changes. An important structural change was the loss of the Experiencer object as a grammatical option. The Experiencer object disappeared from variable clauses by the late 16th century but lingered on until the late 18th century in *if-clauses*. This asymmetry in the two types of clauses is apparently not due to any structural difference, but rather a result of the fact that the variable clauses necessarily involve a high degree of control on the part of the Experiencer, whose attitude determines whether (or how) an event happens and who was furthermore most frequently the actor in the event. In *if-clauses*, however, the Experiencer was most frequently not in any sort of control.

The Experiencer object remained common in *if-clauses* up until the mid-18th century, but the construction had changed in meaning by this time, having become highly deferential. It had also become quite limited pragmatically by the mid-18th century, being used only for very specific speech acts. It is interesting to note that although the Experiencer object is no longer used in everyday speech, it is still used in some situations in which highly deferential language is required, such as the courtroom, e.g. *if it please the court, the prosecution wishes to introduce this evidence to prove motive.*

The meaning of *please* has not changed radically in variable clauses since the introduction of the UNPROP construction with this verb, although the increasing restriction of the construction to being used only when the Experiencer is coreferential to the actor of the main clauses perhaps points to the addition of an element of meaning which emphasises that something happens only because the Experiencer wants it to happen, and *not for any other reason*. In contrast, the meaning of *please* in *if-clauses* has changed quite appreciably; the meaning that something happens because the Experiencer wishes it to happen has disappeared entirely. The pragmatic range of the *if-clause* has undergone progressive restriction, to the point where the construction has all but disappeared in contemporary speech, although it is not impossible in polite requests or contradictions.

6.   Conclusions

One very important conclusion of this study is that the introduction of the Experiencer subject in the UNPROP construction with *please* cannot plausibly be attributed to a reanalysis of the grammatical relation of a fronted Experiencer which was caused by the loss of case-marking distinctions in the ME period. It is possible that the influence of the semantically similar *like* played a role in the introduction of the Experiencer subject. However, the *introduction* of this new grammatical option is to be explained, it is quite clear that the rapid adoption of the Experiencer subject construction can only be explained as a result of the fact that this assignment of grammatical roles to semantic roles was particularly suited to the UNPROP construction. The UNPROP construction conveys the meaning that the action of the matrix clause depends on the attitude of the Experiencer, resulting in an Experiencer with a high degree of agentivity. This high degree of agentivity made the Experiencer an especially suitable subject, particularly for variable clauses.

There can be little doubt that the loss of case-marking distinctions had important effects on the general syntax of English. However, this study suggests that general syntactic change (i.e. a change in parameter-setting) is the wrong place to look for explanations of change in the syntax of specific verbs.

Another important conclusion is that however we are going to explain the introduction of the Experiencer subject option, it is quite clear that variation between the subject and object options were not random, even at the earliest stage of variation. In the earliest stage, there was a good deal of overlap in the function of the two options, but variation was nevertheless not random because although it was apparently always possible to use the Experiencer object option, the Experiencer subject option could only be used when the Experiencer was not only in control of whether an event took place but was also the actor in the event. The Experiencer subject quickly became the preferred option in this situation and spread to situations where the Experiencer was not really in control but the speaker nevertheless found it appropriate to use the UNPROP construction because the addressee's reaction to what the speaker said was very important.

Our knowledge of the pragmatic functions of a construction which can be gleaned from written texts only in the absence of native speakers is necessarily limited. Nevertheless, it is encouraging to find that we are in fact able to discern particular functions for the Experiencer subject and Experiencer object options in texts which have a reasonable number of both constructions. It is reasonable to hope that an examination of the passive *be pleased* in Shakespearean texts, for example, would further dispel the notion that variation in the type of UNPROP construction used in this period was simply random.

Notes

1.   My adoption of this term does not indicate the adoption of a theory in which a limited
       number of semantic roles can be distinguished for arguments or an assumption that the
       semantic role of this particular argument is identical in all uses of the verb *please*. It
       will serve as a useful label for the argument in question, however.

2.   Not all English speakers might reject this sentence. However, my investigation of English texts suggests that the use of Experiencers not coreferential with the matrix subject becomes less and less usual in the Modern English period. See section 5 for details. While the construction with non-matching subjects may not be totally impossible for all speakers, it certainly has a different status than the same construction with *like*, which appears frequently with non-matching subjects in 19th century texts.

3.   Since this general objective case was (except with *it*) the reflex of the dative case, I will refer to the general objective case of ME and Modern English as 'dative'.

4.   See Tobler-Lommatzsch's (1969) entry for 'plaire', 'plaisir' *vb*, which offers numerous examples of the verb in its different uses. In the French equivalent of the UNPROP construction (the construction which Tobler-Lommatzsch characterizes as *unpersön.* 'impersonal'), the object status of the Experiencer is frequently made quite clear by the addition of a formal subject *il* 'it', as in *Ch. lyon* 5247 *Deus, s'il li plese* 'God, if it pleases him'. However, the formal subject was not obligatory in French, as examples such as *Karls R* 405 *Plöst al rei de gloire* 'may (it) please (to) the King of Glory!' demonstrate.

5.   There could be some doubt that *ye* is to be regarded as unambiguously nominative here, because by this time the syncretism of *ye* (the old nominative) and *yow* (the old object form) had begun, and in some writings of this period we find *ye* hypercorrectly used for objects. However, I consider this particular instance nominative because the writer of this particular letter used the two forms in the historically correct way in the rest of this letter.

6.   Note that we would have to assume a data gap even if we wanted to say that the preposed Experiencers were objects: if they were objects the fact that we have no preposed Experiencers clearly in the object case in this text is coincidental.

7.   Interestingly, nominative Experiencers seem to have been less prevalent with *like* in the UNPROP construction than in the 2NP construction by the 16th century. By Shakespeare's period, Experiencer subjects were considerably more common than Experiencer objects with *like* in the 2NP construction.

8.   I will have nothing to say here about the use of the passive form, but will merely note that it seems likely that a closer examination making the right sort of distinctions of types (pragmatic, syntactic, etc.) would yield some patterning, given the fact that patterns can be found for the active types.

9.   I have combined infinitival and tensed subordinate clauses in this count. Infinitival clauses are by far the more common with *please* in Shakespeare's works than are tensed ones.

10.   This actor would normally be the syntactic subject of the matrix clause, but not
       necessarily; for example, I find the UNPROP construction of example (32) quite
       acceptable, although the use of *shall* is somewhat archaic.

Appendix: Texts examined in this study

This appendix details the texts examined in this study. Besides the specific texts and
concordances listed here, I have also checked the entries for *please* and *like* in the *OED* and
the *Middle English Dictionary* for examples of the different constructions used with these
verbs and for possible counterexamples to claims made on the basis of my own investigations
of texts.

The OE examples in this paper use the citations found in Healey and Venezky's (1980)
Microfiche Concordance to Old English (see References). The following is a list of texts and
concordances used in this study for the 14th century through 19th century. I have listed the
texts by the author's name or an abbreviation for the author's name or the title of the work.
The information given here about dates of 14th century and 15th century MSS comes either
from the edition used, from the *MED,* or from the Severs-Hartung *Manual.*

The Fourteenth Century

Chaucer = Geoffrey Chaucer, d. 1400. I have checked the entries for all forms of *like* and
        please in Tatlock and Kennedy's (TK) concordance (see References). The
        abbreviations used here are those used in TK. Examples are cited from *The Riverside
        Chaucer.* Larry D. Benson, general editor, third edition, Boston, Houghton Mifflin,
        1987 (although this is not the edition upon which TK is based). It should be noted that
        not all of the works concorded in TK are considered to be Chaucer's work by the
        majority of scholars, but this fact is not of importance to this investigation. These texts
        are found in numerous MSS which cannot be described here, but it can be noted that
        the MS which the Riverside edition used as the base MSS for the *Canterbury Tales* is
        dated 1400-1410. The base MSS for most of the other texts come from the first part of
        the 15th century, while a few of the texts are found only in MSS from the later 15th
        century. These works were written between 1368 and 1400.
PiersP = *Piers Plowman.* Composed by William Langland (d. by 1387). This poem is found in
        many MSS, and there is more than one version of the text. The edition used in this
        investigation is A. V. C. Schmidt's *The Vision of Piers Plowman,* London, Dent, 1978.
        This is a version known as the B-text. MS Trinity College Cambridge B 15.17.
        According to Schmidt, the MS is dated c. 1400.
Trevisa = *The Properties of Things,* by John Trevisa. This is a translation of Bartholomaeus
        Angelicus' *De Proprietatibus Rerum* made in Gloucestershire in 1398/9. Edited by M.

C. Seymour, Oxford, Clarendon Press, 1975. The base MS used is British Museum Additional 27944, dated c. 1410. This investigation was limited to pages 40-91.

WP = *William of Palerne*. Edited by G. H. V. Bunt, Groningen, Bouma's Boekuis bv, 1985. MS King's College Cambridge 13. Date: c. 1360-75 , according to Dunn (in Severs-Hartung *Manual* vol. 1: 34) Translated from French between 1335-61) (Bunt, p.15).

Wyclife = *The English Works of Wyclif Hitherto Unprinted*. Edited by F. D. Matthew, EETS 74, 1880, rev. 1902. I examined only texts III, V, X, XI, XV, XVIII, XXII, XXIII, XXV. The remaining texts are either found only in a late MS, or likely not to have been composed by Wycliffe himself.

The Fifteenth Century

Capgrave = *John Capgrave's Lives of St. Augustine and St. Gilbert of Sempringham and a Sermon*. Edited by J. J. Munro, EETS 140, 1910. Capgrave b. 1398. MS Additional 36704, Capgrave's holograph. The MS was completed c. 1451.

Castle Pers. = *The Castle of Perseverance*. Edited by Mark Eccles in *The Macro Plays*, EETS 262, 1969. MS Folger V. a. 354. Date: Date of MS is c. 1440; composition c. 1400-1425.

Caxton = *The History of Reynard the Fox Translated from the Dutch Original by William Caxton*. Edited by N. F. Blake, EETS 263, 1970. Caxton b. 1422. This translation was finished in 1481 and probably printed the same year.

Cely = *The Cely Letters 1472-1488*. Edited by Alison Hanham, EETS 273, 1975.

Kn. TL = *The Book of the Knight of the Tour Landry*. Edited by Thomas Wright, EETS 33, 1868, rev. 1906. MS British Museum, Harleian 1764. Date: ?c. 1450.

Lon.Eng = *A Book of London English 1384-1425*. Edited by Majorie Daunt and R. W. Chambers, Oxford: Clarendon Press, 1967 (rpt. of 1931 edition).

Malory = *The Works of Sir Thomas Malory*. Edited in three volumes by E. Vinaver, Oxford, Clarendon Press, 1947. Malory fl. 1470. Citations used are those given in Kato's concordance (see References).

Marg.K = *The Book of Margery Kempe*. Edited by Sanford Meech and Hope E. Allen, EETS 212, 1940. Unique privately owned MS. Date: before 1450.

Paston = *Paston Letters and Papers of the Fifteenth Century*. Edited by Norman Davis, Oxford, Clarendon Press, 1971. This is a very large collection of letters, and I have restricted my counts to letters which were written by the Pastons (for whom birth dates are known) during selected specific periods. The numbers here cover pages 1-100, 215-30, 390-415, 519-44 and 649-61.

The Sixteenth Century

Ascham = three selections from the writings of Roger Ascham (b. 1515), found in *Roger Ascham: English works,* edited by William Wright, Cambridge: Cambridge University Press, 1904. The selections read are *Toxophilius Part A, A Discours of the Affaires and State of Germany,* and book one of *The Scholemaster.*

Berners = *The Boke of Duke Huon of Bordeux,* by Lord Berners (b. 1469). Edited by S. L. Lee, EETS 40 and 41, 1882 and 1883.

Donne = John Donne (b. 1572). The edition used is *John Donne Selected Prose,* edited by Evelyn Simpson, Oxford, Clarendon Press, 1967.

Elyot = *The Boke Named the Governour, by Sir Thomas Elyot.* Elyot b. ?1490. The editon used was the Everyman's Library edition edited by Ernet Rhys, London, 1907. However, I have checked all examples used in my counts against the facsimile of the 1531 edition published by Scolar Press (Menston, England, 1970) to ascertain that the syntax had not been changed in the Everyman edition, which has regularized spelling.

More = Sir Thomas More (b. 1478). The texts examined for this study were *The Apology* (The Complete Works of St. Thomas More 9), edited by J. B. Trapp, New Haven, Yale University Press, 1979 and *The Confutation of Tyndale's Answer* (in two vols, The Complete Works of St. Thomas More 8), edited by Louis A. Schuster, *et al.,* New Haven, Yale University Press, 1973.

Fisher = *The English Works of John Fisher.* Edited by John Mayor, EETS e.s. 27, 1876. John Fisher b. 1469. Only pages 1-250 of this volume were read for this investigation.

QEI = *The Letters of Queen Elizabeth.* Edited by G. B. Harrison, London, Cassell and Company, 1935. Queen Elizabeth I b. 1533. Most of these letters were not in Queen Elizabeth's own hand, but they serve to show the usage of the period.

Shkspre = William Shakespeare (b. 1564). Figures given for Shakespeare are based on examinations of entries in Spevack's concordance (see References). The citations given in the examples used in the text are taken from this concordance.

The Seventeenth Century

Behn, Aphra (b. 1640). *The Novels of Mrs Aphra Behn.* Edited by Ernest A. Baker, Westport, Connecticut, Greenwood Publishers, 1969.

Defoe, Daniel (b. 1640). *Moll Flanders.* Edited with an introduction by G. A. Starr. London, Oxford University Press, 1971. Cited by page number.

Etherege, Sir George (b. 1635?). *Letters of Sir George Etherege.* Edited by Frederick Bracher. Berkeley, University of California Press, 1974.

Walton, Isaac (b. 1593). *Lives: John Donne, Sir Henry Wotton, Richard Hooker, George Herbert, and Robert Sanderson.* London: T. Nelson and Sons, Ltd., 1926.

The Eighteenth Century

Austen, Jane (b. 1775). I have used De Rose's concordance to Austen's works (see References).

Cleland = John Cleland (b. 1710). *Fanny Hill.* Edited by Peter Wagner, New York, Penguin Books, 1985.

Fielding, Henry (b. 1707). *The History of Tom Jones.* Edited by R. P. C. Mutter, New York, Penguin Books, 1966).

The Nineteenth Century

Brontë, Charlotte (b. 1816). *Villette.* Edited by Sandra Kemp, Everyman, J. M. Dent, London 1993.

Eliot, George (Mary Ann Evans, b. 1819). *Middlemarch.* Edited by W. J. Henry. Penguin Books, Harmondsworth, Middlesex, England, 1965.

References

Allen, Cynthia L.
    In progr. *Case Marking and Reanalysis: Grammatical Relations from Old to Early Modern English.* To be published by Oxford University Press.
Chomsky, Noam
    1981   *Lectures on Government and Binding.* Dordrecht: Foris.
De Rose, Peter L.
    1982   *A Concordance to the Works of Jane Austen.* New York and London: Garland Publishing.
Fischer, Olga C.; and Frederike van der Leek
    1983   "The demise of the Old English impersonal construction." *Journal of Linguistics* 19: 337-368.
Healey, Antoinette, and Richard Venezky
    1980   *A Microfiche Concordance to Old English.* Toronto: Centre for Medieval Studies, University of Toronto.
Jespersen, Otto
    1927   *A Modern English Grammar on Historical Principles.* Vol.3. London: Allen and Unwin.

Kato, Tomomi
> 1974   *A Concordance to the Works of Sir Thomas Malory.* Tokyo: University of Tokyo Press.

Kurath, Hans et al.
> 1954–   *MED = Middle English Dictionary.* Ann Arbor, Michigan: University of Michigan Press; London: Geoffrey Cumberlege, Oxford University Press.

Lightfoot, David
> 1991   *How to Set Parameters.* Cambridge, Mass: MIT Press.

Lommatzsch, Erhard (ed.)
> 1969   *Altfranzösisches Wörterbuch.* Based on work by Adolf Tobler. Wiesbaden: Franz Steiner Verlag

Montaiglon, Anatole de (ed.)
> 1854   *Le Livre du Chevalier de la Tour Landry pour l'Enseignement de ses Filles.* Paris: Bibliothèque Elzevirienne.

Murray, James A. H. et al. (eds.)
> 1989   *OED = Oxford English Dictionary.* VII (second edition). Oxford: Clarendon Press.

Severs, J. Burke, and Albert Hartung (eds.)
> 1967–   *A Manual of the Writings in Middle English 1050-1500.* Based upon *A Manual of the Writings in Middle English 1050-1400* by John Edwin Wells, New Haven 1916 and Supplements 1-9, 1919-51. Vols. 1 and 2 were edited by Severs, and the remaining vols. which have appeared to date were edited by Hartung. New Haven, Connecticut: Connecticut Academy of Arts and Sciences.

Spevack, Marvin
> 1970   *A Complete and Systematic Concordance to the Works of Shakespeare.* Hildesheim: Georg Olms Verlagsbuchhandlung.

Tatlock, John S.P., and Arthur G. Kennedy
> 1963   *A Concordance to the Complete Works of Geoffrey Chaucer and to the 'Romaunt of the Rose'.* Gloucester, Massachusetts: Peter Smith.

Your Average Generalisations
A Case-Study in Historical Pragmatics

Katie Wales
Royal Holloway University of London

1. Introduction

About 60 years ago the Russian linguist and critic Mikhail Bakhtin was urging broader socio-stylistic and pragmatic frames and contexts of reference for the study of language, in his stressing of language's 'heteroglossic' nature, its stratification into "social dialects, characteristic group behaviour, professional jargons, generic languages, languages of generations and age groups, tendentious languages, languages of the authorities, of various circles and passing fashions, languages that serve the specific sociopolitical purposes of the day." (*Discourse in the Novel*, repr. 1981: 262-3) With the impact since the 1970s of such studies as discourse analysis, sociolinguistics and pragmatics on linguistics and English grammar, now more than ever before Bakhtin's vision can be realised, and something also of what he terms the "three-dimensionality" (p. 417) of language can be appreciated. This applies equally to the English of earlier periods, as well as of the present day: as Rydén (1979: 41-2) similarly argues, "the actual usage of a period is a multilayer phenomenon [...] the historical syntactician must be something of an exegete, trying to get under the skin of his [sic] texts". But as Bakhtin further argues, for historical study we "cannot rely for support on a living feel for language [...] as a consequence of our distance from it [the language] seems to lie on one and the same plane [...] we cannot sense in it [...] any distinction between levels and distances" (p.417).

Lack of evidence, of sufficient material, is one of the reasons why students and scholars are often frustrated in their efforts to grasp 'a living feel' of earlier English. It is the lack of spoken material in particular that is often commented on. Deductions about colloquial usages in the sixteenth and seventeenth centuries, for example, are usually made on the basis of secondary or derived material, such as private correspondence, court records, plays, etc. Yet the fact remains that the Early Modern period is very rich in a variety of material of different genres, styles and degrees of formality directed to different kinds of audiences and readers, and I would agree with Kytö and Rissanen (1983: 472-3), who argue that much material has not yet been sufficiently explored. Moreover, even material that is well known from this period (e.g. Shakespeare's plays) has not itself been probed in sufficient depth from the kind of broader perspectives and contextualisations mentioned at the beginning. In general, most histories of the English language have the drawbacks of either a very narrow focus on main linguistic changes or the broadest perspective of sociocultural trends.

My own awareness of the deficiencies in traditional accounts both of the history of English generally and of the EModE period in particular, and my own feeling of the need for a more 'three-dimensional', pragmatic and context-sensitive approach arose out of my recurring interest in developments in English pronouns. One particular usage, the generalising-possessive, or generic-deictic YOUR, as in Hamlet's "*your* worm is *your* only emperor for diet" (*Hamlet*, IV.3) or in *The Guardian*'s obituary headline "Just *your* average French movie star" (2.5.94), is especially interesting from the point of view of historical pragmatics, but it has received rather perfunctory treatment in grammatical histories. Originating in the EModE period (first sighted in the 1550s),[1] your generalising YOUR (or YOUR 2 for short) has persisted until the present day but, on the one hand, with significant variations in its colligations and collocations and, on the other hand, with illuminating variations of contexts of use and fluctuations of popularity. The closer this pronominal usage is studied, and especially in the EModE period itself, the more the researcher has to take into account such factors as the socio-stylistic context, dialect, genre, speech act type, degree of formality, attitude and stance, etc. What follows then is a modest attempt at a contrastive approach to historical pragmatics.

2.   YOUR 2 and generic reference: Early Modern English and the present-day English

In general YOUR 2, originating as a possessive determiner, combines features relevant both to its referential (generic) and discourse (deictic) meaning, features which are themselves interdependent. The notion of 'possessive' had to be extended from something like 'that which you have' to (i) 'that which you know' and thence to (ii) 'that which you and I and everybody know'. And the notion of 'second person' itself had to be widened, as happened with *you*-forms generally, to the more 'impersonal' reference whereby (i) the addressee is but one of a group or class of people, and thence (ii) a larger group includes speaker as well as addressee. Not surprisingly, there are ambiguities. So, in *Hamlet* again, in III.2 Hamlet enters giving generalising advice to the players on how to pronounce their part: "but if you mouth it, as many of *your* players do, I had as lief the town-crier spoke my lines". A reading of this as 'the players like you/the profession to which you all belong' seems plausible; yet Abbott (1872) paraphrases it to give the more generalising meaning: 'the players whom you and everybody know'.[2]

The metaphorical shift, as it were, from the immediate context-of-utterance to the wider contexts of knowledge and culture is matched by a deictic shift. If personal *your* is non-proximal in relation to the speaker, YOUR 2 inclines to the distal, matching distance of subject matter, whether physical or emotional. In spoken or declaimed utterances, even today, speakers often wave their hands away from the body, beyond the addressee, as if what they are referring to they wished 'out of sight', and hence 'out of mind'. Modulations of contempt or dismissal are indeed characteristic features of many examples of YOUR 2 utterances, both in the EModE period and today.

In both periods, but especially in ModE, certain particular kinds of negative constructions are popular in this respect, in contexts of generalising comparisons. The tone of dismissal is heightened by the post-verbal (chiefly *be*) or end-focus position of the YOUR 2 phrase, especially in present-day English:

(a)   neg.+ pronominal quantifier *one* + of + YOUR 2 + NP, as in

he's *not one of your* fat Citty chuffes (*Northward No*, V.1, Dekker and Webster 1607)

She's *none of you*r ramping cannibals that devour men's flesh (*The Dutch Courtesan*, I.2, Marston 1605)

The naming of cats is a difficult matter,/It isn't *just one of your* holiday games (opening lines of T. S. Eliot's *The Naming of Cats* 1939)

'I wasn't *one of your* grand fashion designers, nothing like that', she laughs.. (*Woman*, 2.5.81)

[...] a football match – *not one of your* namby-pamby World Cup games. (*The Guardian*, 6.7.82)

(b) Also popular with this modulation in ModE is the structure of neg. + YOUR 2 + post-deictic + NP, as in:

Alan Price is *not your average* singing star (*The Observer*, 27.4.80)

As parties go it was smart; *not your average* cheese and plonk do [...] (*Woman's Own*, 21.5.83)

Average is by far the commonest such evaluative postdeictic in present-day English in such contexts (for another connotation see below); but *ordinary, usual*, etc. also occur:

Now, these aren't *your ordinary* Sweet Williams [...] (*London Evening News*, 16.4.80)

[...] it's *not just your usual* cop-shop. But then, Helen Mirren is not *your usual* TV star [...] (*Ms London*, 20.12.93)

'Oh, it's *not your usual* glamorous West End opening, it's not your glitterati', snapped the PR man at the Almeida Theatre. 'It's much more intelligent – much more highbrow than that' (*The Guardian*, 8.9.93)

'It is *not your* bog standard concrete bridge', boasted the city's [Peterborough's] conservation officer [...] (*The Guardian*, 3.12.91)

Semantically speaking, as I have said above, what all these examples illustrate is the kind of generalisation involving comparison and evaluation; and there are corresponding syntactically 'positive' examples with the same or similar adjectives, to indicate what is 'ordinary', 'not special' (or down-grading as in the "*Just your average* French movie star" headline cited above); or "better than ordinary" (or up-grading), as in

Much better than *your average* American TV movie (*The Guardian*, 18.6.85)

In EModE, such up-grading and down-grading similarly occur, although the syntactic frame is most usually subject NP. Down-grading is expressed by dismissive or derogatory adjectives like *foul, whoreson, vulgar* and *four-penny*, and generalisations are directed to worthless people like fools, cuckolds and 'chuffs', low-status occupations like whores, punks and bawds, and foreigners (cf. "*your* sag-bellied Hollander", *Othello*, II.3) (See further (3) below.) Up-grading is commonly expressed by YOUR 2 + superlative adjectives, as in

Your best poet is he that rails grossest (*All Fools*, II.l, Chapman 1599)

Your smallest arrows fly farthest (*Northward Ho*, II.1).

Such generalisations have the quality of aphorisms or proverbs. Another possibility is YOUR 2 + *only*, as in the example from *Hamlet* cited above ("*Your* worm is *your only* emperor for diet"); and

> *Your only* deadly sin's adultery (*A Mad World My Masters*, I.2, Middleton 1608)

> *Your only* smooth skin is your Puritan's skin (*Eastward Ho*, II.2, Chapman, Marston and Jonson 1605).

What can be noted, moreover, is that such constructions appear not only to stress uniqueness in value, but also uniqueness of class as a type; cf. "your smoothest [type of] skin is your Puritan's skin", or "only your Puritan [as a class of people] has a smooth skin". Indeed, what can be noted with all the examples of YOUR 2 utterances quoted so far is that, for the purposes of generalisation or comparison, they are implicitly sorting people, objects, actions, etc. into 'typical' groups, both proto-typical and stereo-typical, and nontypical, whether these be holiday games, fashion designers, bridges, American TV movies, poets, arrows or Puritans. As such, YOUR 2 functions as a generic determiner along with the articles: cf.

> *The* Italian is a good singer
> *An* Italian is a good singer
> *The* Italians are good singers
> Ø - Italians are good singers
> *Your* Italian is a good singer.

It is important to stress, what is very obvious from all of my examples so far, that pragmatically speaking, YOUR 2 generic statements or gnomic propositions are undoubtedly more vivid or immediate, more colloquial than those with the articles. YOUR 2 preserves, as it were, the vestige of its 'second person' origins.[3] Yet these generalisations have the same truth values as those with the articles; and, as noted by Quirk *et al.* (1985: 5,55[a]), YOUR 2 resembles *the* in particular, with its focus on the 'typical specimen' of its class:

> *Your* [typical] Italian [as a kind/type of nationality] is [typically] a good singer.

In this example from Goffman, YOUR 2 has a useful deictic and discourse-friendly tone, suitable for the 'lecturing' mode:

> Take *your* auctioneer. He proves to be a 'character' [...] So, too, *your* air stewardess [...] (*Frame Analysis*, Penguin, 1974: 574)

Such examples occur frequently in Elizabethan and Jacobean drama, as we shall see in the section 3 below. In these examples, the typicalness of the 'representative' is made explicit:

> [...] the particular, and distinct face of every *your* most noted *species of persons*, as *your* marchant, *your* scholer, *your* souldier, *your* lawyer (*Cynthia's Revels*, II.3, Jonson 1600).

> There is not a more fearful *wild-fowl* than *your* lion living (*A Midsummer Night's Dream*, III.1)

> I'm more *your* Man Friday *type* (*London Evening News*, 6.8.80)

> [...] to another, the principle is that your better *type of person* says /njuw/ where ordinary people say /nuw/ (C. J. Fillmore, 1973, cited J. B. Pride, *Sociolinguistic Aspects of Language Learning and Teaching*, O.U.P. 1980, p.12).

> 'He's a genius', says Sean. 'A temperamental genius. *Your typical* flamboyant madman [...]' (*Woman's Own*, 12.12.82)

> Jimmy Carter didn't come up with *your stereotypical* business executive when he plucked Werner Michael Blumenthal from Bendix Corp [...] (*National Observer*, 1.1.77)

In present-day English YOUR 2 commonly colligates with *average* in the (statistical) sense of 'typical' or 'as the norm', and occurs freely in subject or post-verbal slots:

> Just the sort of story *your average* Fleet Street man likes to get his teeth into (*The Guardian*, 13.8.82)

> *Your average* person in the street [...] may well refer to our campaigning activities (*Times Higher Educational Supplement*, 25.2.83)

> It is quite extraordinary how thick *your average* bankmanager can be [...] (*Private Eye*, 11.2.83)

3.   YOUR 2 and discourse distribution from 1588-1608

On the evidence of my reading of a large number of texts and of different genres, it seems that YOUR 2 starts to appear significantly only in written texts towards the end of the sixteenth century, and dramatic rather than prose or poetic. Moreover, within any play, YOUR 2 is most likely to occur in prose dialogue, not verse, the switch from verse to prose, of course, indicating a shift of formality, from 'high' to 'low'. This might simply suggest that YOUR 2 was strongly associated with the contemporary colloquial idiom. Certainly, from the analysis of over 300 examples in over 50 different texts, it can be noted that sentences or utterances in which YOUR 2 occurs are frequently quite loosely structured. Parentheses and afterthoughts are common (as in present-day English), and so too is ellipsis of conjunctions and relative pronoun subjects; anacoluthon is also found. cf.

> She is the prettiest [...] ape under the pole. A skin *your* satten is not more soft, nor lawn whiter (*The Honest Whore* pt.1, III.1, Dekker and Middleton, 1604)

> There are a number of thy coat resemble *your* common post-boys (*The White Devil*, III.2, Webster 1613).

YOUR 2 may well have originated in the colloquial 'nonstandard' speech of the uneducated or working classes. (For its sociolinguistic implications in present-day English, related I feel, see section 4). It is perhaps significant that the earliest examples I found in Shakespeare (7 in *A Midsummer Night's Dream*, 1595) are used by Bottom the comic weaver. In many plays of the period YOUR 2 is associated with 'ordinary' skilled and unskilled trades like the apprentice, carrier, nurse, captain and simply 'the Clown': the notoriously slowwitted workman or rustic. Such characters are prone to speech acts of proverbial folk-wisdom, like the Clown in *All's Well That Ends Well*, I.3 (1603-4):

> For I the ballad will repeat
> Which men full true shall find:
> *Your* marriage comes by destiny,
> *Your* cuckoo sings by kind

YOUR 2 figures prominently in folk humour: 'I am like *your* tailor's needle, I go through', says Sogliardo the 'Clown' in Jonson's *Every Man Out of His Humour* (1600). It also figures in stereotypical jokes and satirical comments about foreigners and certain occupations:

> Malevole: I am in haste, be brief.

> Passarello [The Fool]: As *your* fiddler when he is paid. He'll thrive I warrant you, while *your* young courtier stands like Good Friday in Lent: men long to see

it, because more fatting days come after it [...] (*The Malcontent*, I. 7, Marston
and Webster 1604)

Given the kinds of speech act types mentioned so far, it is not easy to explain,
however, YOUR 2's relative scarcity in certain types of discourse and text.
While we might not expect it to appear in the elaborately rhetorical romances of
Sidney, we might expect it in the 'Euphuistic' prose of Lyly, since the subject-
matter – the generalisations and analogies drawn from nature and popular
wisdom – seems precisely the kind of field to favour gnomic utterance. In this
period also, it can be noted that the cultivation of epigrams and 'sententiae' in
common-place books was popular, which provided valuable source material,
whether about lawyers or tobacco, for playwrights like Chapman, Jonson and
Webster, who compiled their own. YOUR 2 does not appear in such
compilations, yet, as we shall see, it occurs very frequently in these writers' own
plays. Nor is it easy to explain YOUR 2's absence from the ballads and jest-
books of Tarlton and Armin, for instance, from which the dramatists most
probably derived their stock jokes. Stock 'types' also appear in the so-called
'character'-writing of Hall, Overbury and Webster again: whether a 'drunken
Dutchman in England', or a 'divilish usurer'.

It is in pamphlet-writing, particularly the kind that deals with the different
'types' of vagabonds and villains in the Elizabethan underworld, that we might
particularly expect a closeness of tone and informality to the colloquial speech
of the period. Many of the authors were also dramatists (e.g. Greene and
Dekker). In the texts I sampled before 1600 I found only one example (in
Nashe's *Pierce Penilesse*, 3rd ed. 1592); but by 1604 I had found 10 examples
in Thomas Middleton's *Father Hubbard's Tales*. It is during these early years
of the seventeenth century that YOUR 2 becomes increasingly popular in
dramatic usage, as we shall see. It may be that YOUR 2 had hitherto been
regarded by prose-writers, even pamphleteers, as being too informal, even
dialectal, for the medium of print.

One factor in its infrequency in prose, surprising as it may seem, may well
be due to its trace of 'second person-hood', of 'vocativeness', gesturing back
from the generalisations of common knowledge to the immediate situation.
There is a hint of addressee-awareness always there; YOUR 2 is a discourse
marker comparable to 'as you know' or 'have you got that' in present-day
English, and also provides discourse emphasis in anecdotes and narratives. As I
have noted elsewhere (1985), YOUR 2 is similar in this respect (and others) to
the so-called 'ethic datives' noteworthy at this period: In this example ethic *you*
and YOUR 2 occur together, in the Clown's generalisations drawn from his
occupational knowledge:

> [...] he [a corpse] will last *you* some eight year or nine year; a tanner will last *you* nine year [...] and *your* water is a sore decayer of *your* whoreson dead body. Here's a skull now; this skull hath lain *you* i' the earth three and twenty years [...] (*Hamlet*, V.1.)

Hence YOUR 2 would be most likely to be found in those kinds of discourse where the writer or speaker would either be very aware of an addressee or would wish to establish a particular and direct relationship with them. Not all prose-writers are concerned to do this, preferring to keep explicit reader-references to a minimum in a straightforward factual or descriptive narration, with only the occasional use of *I* or generalised *we*.

Associated with this discourse-awareness is the characteristic feature of emphasis, closely identified with the deictic and focusing function of YOUR 2. It 'points' prosodically, and it gives 'point' to a proposition. Frequently YOUR 2 clauses in the EModE examples are prefixed by markers of attention or emphasis: e.g. *aye, why, O, troth*, or terms of address. Moreover, a significant number of YOUR 2 phrases appear as 'marked themes' or 'topicalisations', sometimes explicitly introduced by (*as*) *for*. Note, for example,

> [...] Again, for *your* cuckold, what is it but a mere fiction? [...] (*All Fools*, III. 1, Chapman 1599)

Despite YOUR 2's apparent infrequency in prose of the period, there is, however, one particular text I have recently studied where it occurs extremely frequently: George Puttenham's handbook of rhetoric, *The Arte of English Poesie* (1588). This text was written much earlier than the main 'corpus' for the rest of my examples below; and altogether I have found about 80 examples in its 65 chapters/3 Books (50 of the examples are found in the second Book which deals with 'proportion', i.e. principles of metre). It is not easy to estimate the exact number, for it is sometimes difficult to distinguish YOUR 2 proper from other, more personal usages. Puttenham is certainly very conscious of his reader or readers. Sometimes he writes as if he is addressing a practising poet, sometimes Queen Elizabeth, sometimes the courtly circle of attendant ladies and gentlemen. He is not only keen to describe but also to teach and to inform; he is keen to present his material in a lively and dramatic manner. Directive speech acts are common: as if he is instructing the reader; or as if he is speaking of what all 'modern' poets should do, or both. Interesting is the combination of YOUR 2 with a kind of 'existential-*have*' construction (Quirk *et al.*, 1985: 18.51), with *you* + *have*, commonly thought of as being very informal in present-day usage. Like YOUR 2 phrases, it allows for focusing (on the complement in this case) and provides an 'immediate' connotation. Such sentences as these occur frequently in Chapter 13:

> for *your* Trocheus of a long and short *ye have* these English words 'maner', 'broken' [...] for *your* anapestus of two short and a long *ye have* these words but not many moe [...].

These sentences provide a good illustration of how Puttenham uses YOUR 2 as part of a 'catalogue' device: here a listing of the different types of classical metrical feet: '*the* foote spondeus' (sic); '*your* Trocheus'; '*your* Iambus', '*your* foote pirrichius', etc. We can note also the chapter heading which follows this chapter: "Of *your* feet of three times [...] ". This itself is part of a classification of feet: chapter 13 discusses "feet of two times". What the YOUR 2 phrases do is to point to the nominals in colligation, focus on them, to help the reader in the assimilation of quite complex information. (The marked theme position of the YOUR 2 phrases cited above can also be noted in this connection.)

It is possible that many YOUR 2 phrases in Puttenham are used with anaphoric reference (see footnote (3) above) or could have both generic and anaphoric reference. The very first sentence, for example, which follows the heading of Chapter 14 ("Of your feet of three times [...] ") begins: "*Your* feete of three times by prescription of the Latine Grammariens [...] ", and so could mean 'which I have already spoken of to you'.

Puttenham's consistent use of generic YOUR 2 is noteworthy, not only because the book was probably composed over a period of nearly 20 years (begun in the late 1560s), but also because he appears to be the only critic of rhetoric and poetry of the same period who uses YOUR 2 in this way, at least the only critic I have myself been able to find. The schematisation and classification of figures of speech was extremely popular, but many writers make only occasional acknowledgement of the reader's presence (e.g. Richard Mulcaster's *Elementarie* 1582; Thomas Blunderville's *The Arte of Logicke* 1599). There may be a couple of examples in John Hoskyn's *Directions for Speech and Style* (1598-1603), which uses the *you* of direct address, but they are not clear. But this work does resemble Puttenham's in its use of the framework of directive instruction and a vigorous style.

It is known that Puttenham's work was not originally intended for publication, but for private dissemination at Court. Perhaps Puttenham otherwise would have reframed his discourse completely and elevated his tone. But his courtly audience presumably accepted YOUR 2's presence, despite its probable 'lowly' origins, as a structural and rhetorical device in itself: a discourse marker of a distinctive kind.

Bearing its function in Puttenham in mind, I should now like to turn to an examination of the occurrences and distribution of YOUR 2 in dramatic texts of the period, by far the largest body of relevant material. We should, perhaps, not be puzzling over why so few occur in prose, but why so many occur in certain plays. Chronologically speaking, appearances are scattered in plays before 1599 and after 1608 (with the exceptions of Webster's *The White Devil* and Jonson's *The Alchemist* (both 1612)), when they decline rapidly. More interesting is the fact that, within this narrow short period, only certain kinds of plays and only certain playwrights seem to favour YOUR 2:

(I) 1598-1605: the satirical comedies of chiefly Jonson and also Chapman: mostly witty academic plays arising out of the so-called 'War of the Theatres'

(II) 1603-1608: the satirical city comedies and tragicomedies chiefly written in collaboration and popular with the rising middle class.

So in (I) I have found 29 examples in Jonson's *Every Man In his Humour* (Italian version acted 1598) and 22 in the English version (1600); 22 in his *Every Man Out of his Humour* (printed 1600); over 40 examples in *Cynthia's Revels* (pr. 1600); 15 in *The Poetaster* (1601) and almost 30 in *Volpone* (1605) (mostly in the 'sub-plot' involving the sententious Politick Would-Be's and Peregrine the traveller). Chapman has fewer examples, but they are to be noted: 7 in *All Fools* (1599); 11 in *May Day* (1601-2); 9 in *The Widow's Tears* (1605) and 6 in *Monsieur D'Olive* (1606).

The examples from Chapman well illustrate the kind of contexts in which YOUR 2 tends to occur in these plays. These are really 'set-pieces', witty or satirical orations or analogies, spoken by witty or satirical characters. So the 11 examples in *May Day* are all found in one speech where a banquet is described as a battle (IV.3) and the 6 examples in *Monsieur D'Olive* in an oration on the topical (or stereo-topical, to coin a phrase) subject of tobacco. This kind of context is found in the Jonson plays also, including *The Alchemist*. Amorphous, the scholar-poet, is responsible for half of the 40 examples in *Cynthia's Revels*. In the illustration which follows, partly quoted in section 2 above, we can note the very conscious posturing, the 'setting up' of his speech in the first five lines, as well as an awareness of his addressee:

Plant yourself there, sir; and observe me. You shall now, as well be the ocular, as the ear-witness [...] for instance; I will now give you the particular and distinct face of every *your* most noted species of persons, as *your* merchant, *your* scholar, *your* soldier, *your* lawyer, courtier, etc. [...]. First, for *your* merchant or city-face, 'tis thus; a dull plodding face [...] Then *have you your* student's, or academic face [...] The third is *your* soldier's face, a menacing and astounding face [...] The anti-face to this is *your* lawyer's face [...] Next is *your* statist's face [...] But now, to come to *your* face of faces, or courtier's face; this of three sorts [...] *your* courtier theoric, is he that hath arrived to his farthest [...] *Your* courtier practic, is he that is yet in his path [...]. *Your* courtier elementary, is one but newly enter'd [...]. (II.1)

There is the same Puttenhamish tendency to sub-division within sub-division, following the traditional rhetorical practice of discussing a topic of argument in terms of *genus* and *species*; and the same overlap, in some occurrences, with possible anaphoric function. Its popularity in such 'dramatic' contexts suggests the possibility that YOUR 2 was favoured as an oratorical device in public lecturing, accompanying the 'striking off' of the different subdivisions on the fingers, and that this is the model of discourse that Puttenham himself was drawing on. It is tempting to see a link between oratory and drama via the university buffoon or *terrae filius* described by John Evelyn later in the century in his diary: the orator privileged to make satirical strictures on public occasions. Educated witty dramatists like Jonson and Chapman may have seen the potential of using this oratorical YOUR 2 on the stage, in the harangues of the declaiming actors, while also aware of the presence, or origins, of YOUR 2 in the colloquial London speech around them. Jonson's own use of YOUR 2 is very much in harmony with his prevailing lively and vigorous style.

However, what must be stressed is the strong association of YOUR 2 in this group of plays, and also in group II in particular, with satire: the tone of contempt strongly associated with YOUR 2 generally (see section 2 above) extended, as it were, to the modulation of a subgenre. Fools, cuckolds and whores are held up for dismissive generalisations in these plays in group II, but also ordinary citizens and mercers, reflecting the centres of interest for these city comedies which take London's rising middle classes as their frame of reference. Although there can be found the same lively sententiousness as in group I, the pitch of the satire is generally harsher and bawdier. The most noteworthy plays are: Shakespeare's *All's Well That Ends Well* (1603-4) (16 examples); *Measure for Measure* (1603-4) (12); Marston and Webster's *The Malcontent* (pr. 1604) (17); Dekker and Webster's *Westward Ho* (pr. 1605) (12); Dekker and Webster's *Northward Ho* (pr. 1607) (30); and Dekker's *The Honest Whore* pt.2 (?1608) (11 examples).

That there does seem to have been a dramatic 'fashion' for using YOUR 2 in these years between 1603-1608, and in a particular kind of play, appears to be confirmed by other noteworthy details. In a masque by Thomas Dekker, *The*

Whore of Babylon (pr. 1607), there are 7 examples, all confined to the prose part of the allegorical character 'Plain-Dealing', whose moralistic sermons punctuate the play. YOUR 2 thus appears to be emblematic of this dramatic sententious-satirical role. For example:

> [...] for *your* Ordinary [tavern] is *your* Isle of Gulles, *your* ship of fools, *your* hospital of incurable madmen [...] (II.1).

Dekker's own romantic comedies, from *The Shoemaker's Holiday* (1600) onwards, are not conspicuous for YOUR 2 phrases. With collaborators, especially Webster, and in satirical comedy, the numbers rise as the figures above indicate. I shall return to Webster below. Moreover, one play written during these years actually has YOUR 2 in its title, which reinforces the idea of a dramatic fashion: *Your Five Gallants* by Thomas Middleton (1606). As the title suggests, it is about five types of men-about-town, but the title also points them out in order to ridicule them (There are about 6 examples of YOUR 2 in the play itself).

Shakespeare's own plays seem to testify to a dramatic fashion in several ways. YOUR 2 does not figure in his plays significantly at all, apart from those written between 1603-8. Elsewhere YOUR 2 phrases are distinctly colloquial: from their first appearance with Bottom the weaver in *A Midsummer Night's Dream* to their last appearance with the drunken Lepidus in *Antony and Cleopatra* (1608), talking about *your crocodile*. The occurrences of YOUR 2 in the plays between 1603-8, however, have all the appearance of being associated with fashionable and satirical dramatic speech-acts. So in *All's Well*, for example, YOUR 2 appears in the mouth of the 'Clown', emblematic of the ordinary man; but also in the mouth of Parolles, the witty courtier with his strong sexual undertones. In *Measure for Measure* usages are again divided between the bawd Pompey and Abhorson the hangman, also a clownish character, but all in the contexts of whores, bawds and thieves. In Hamlet again (1603-4) its 7 clear examples are divided between the Clown/grave-digger and Hamlet in his 'pose' as sententious cynic after Polonius's death (IV.3).

If Jonson dominates group I and the plays of the turn of the century, it is Webster who dominates the second group and the plays until the end of the first decade of the seventeenth century. (In his *Duchess of Malfi* (acted by 1617) there are only 2 examples of YOUR 2, suggesting perhaps that the fashion had waned.) As is well known, Webster's dramatic style is characterised by its colloquial vigour and its proverbial sententiousness. Many examples in *The White Devil* are aphoristic:

Camillo:[...] *your* silkworm useth to fast every third day, and the next following spins the better (I.2)

Francisco: *Your* flax soon kindles, soon is out again,
But gold slow heats, and long will hot remain (IV.1)

It is interesting that Dekker's plays written in collaboration with Webster contain more YOUR 2 phrases than the plays he wrote alone; and certainly, in these plays they tend to be concentrated in particular scenes that have often been attributed to his hand. The identification of idiolectal traits in plays written in collaboration is notoriously difficult, but I do wonder if Webster's influence in this respect is discernible in a play by John Marston he contributed to, *The Malcontent* (1604). Marston's earlier plays, *Antonio and Mellida* (1601), and *Antonio's Revenge* (1601) have only 2 examples of YOUR 2 each and are virtually identical: occurring in variants of the same aphorism, e.g.:

O, *your* foole is *your* only servant (Antonio and Mellida, II)
O, *your* unsalted fresh fool is *your* only man (III.1)

The scarcity of examples could be explained by the fact that the plays are tragedies, from which, generally, YOUR 2 phrases are absent. But there are only 2 examples in his *The Dutch Courtesan* (1605), a city comedy about prostitution, which could easily have fitted into my group II. There are 6 in the lighthearted comedy *Eastward Ho* (1605) he wrote with Chapman and Jonson – surprisingly few in view of his collaborators – but perhaps because it was not a satirical piece. Marston wrote sharply satirical verse, but there are no examples in his 'character' sketches, for example in *The Scourge of Villainie* (1598).

Webster's contributions to *The Malcontent* are a matter of some controversy because of the ambiguity of the title of the revised third edition:

The Malcontent. Augmented by Marston. With the Additions played by the Kings Maiesties servants. Written by Jhon [sic] Webster.

The 'Additions' would appear to be the Induction, which appears for the first time in the 3rd edition, and which is headed:

"The Induction to *The Malcontent*, and the additions acted by the Kings Maiesties servants. Written by John Webster."

The question is whether the 'additions' could include the scenes added to the first Quarto, or whether these are the 'augment[ations]', and whether these scenes in any case could have been wholly or partly written by Webster. Critics are hesitant and divided, and stylistic grounds remain vaguely defined. But it is noteworthy nonetheless that the 17 YOUR 2 phrases occur only in the

Induction (4), which is generally regarded as Webster's, and in some of the other scenes added after the first Quarto (13), mainly involving the 'new' character, Passerello, a 'fool' (I.8; II.1). In the Induction, the YOUR phrases emphasise the naturalness of the ordinary actors, as they prepare for the play; in the other scenes they are part of what appears to be stock jest material of the sort that a dramatist might well be pleased to resort to, for the replacement of the original musical intervals. Yet, in the context of the play overall, the jests against knights and courtiers – the allusions to Scotch barnacles and Puritans – act out in a low key the prevailing theme of corruption.

In general, the ready occurrence of YOUR 2 in certain plays written in collaboration was perhaps encouraged by this very process of composition, which was due to the strong pressure to produce a steady output of plays to satisfy popular demand. The general pattern of innovation, assimilation and conventionalisation of material and themes, which has generally been associated with Jacobean dramatists, nicely describes also the fortunes of YOUR 2. And as the fashion for dramatic sententiousness and city satire declines, so does YOUR 2, quite dramatically. The plays of this period typify and stereotype society and its 'humours', and YOUR 2 provides a most fitting symbolic marker.

What I have tried to suggest, therefore, is that there is in the late 16th century and early 17th century a 'layering' of usage of the kind mentioned in the Introduction, a Bakhtinian heteroglossic three-dimensionality which could easily be missed by superficial readings. Plucked from the colloquial speech of the London area, YOUR 2 becomes both an academic oratorical device and a trendy dramatic discourse marker for sententious cynics.

4.   Conclusion: Linguistic change and trends in contemporary usage

In sociolinguistic and pragmatic terms, the general issue of the 'fashionability' of certain constructions, expressions or idioms is well worth serious investigation, even in present-day usage, where material for investigation and knowledge of (types of) users is plentiful, especially in relation to language change. What Hudson terms "centres of influence" (1982: 41) are important in linguistic change, and it is possible to see Elizabethan and Jacobean academic oratory and drama, if only for a short time, as one such centre of influence giving rise to the significant redistribution of YOUR 2 noted above. What might also be relevant here is YOUR 2's 'expressivity', arising from a combination of its deictic force, discourse awareness and dismissive sententiousness.

Expressivity, too, has been seen as an underrated factor in linguistic change (cf. Lightfoot,1979: 385).

After 1610 it would appear that what has become a formula now becomes a fossil, and the contextual spread of YOUR 2 recedes back to colloquial speech and informal writing. That YOUR 2 is found in present-day American English and Hiberno-English, for example, testifies to its established position in the colloquial idiom of the colonists. Similarities and differences between present-day YOUR 2 phrases and those of EModE in respect of colligation and syntax I have noted in section 1 above; but what is particularly interesting, however, from the perspective of fashion and linguistic change, is the appearance in late 20th century usage of potential 'centres of influence' again.

One such particular centre I described in detail in 1985, since it seemed to afford a striking parallel to that of Jacobean drama. But it is also different in some respects. From the late 1960s onwards appeared a television comedy series *Till Death Us Do Part* by Johnny Speight, featuring a Cockney character, Alf Garnett from Wapping in the East End of London. *Your/yer* is certainly distinctive in his generalising diatribes, often more than one per utterance and around 20 per script: There is the same artistic licence or over-kill as in the 17th century plays. Alf is your modern-day cynical preacher, based on your modern day 'ordinary' or 'average' London citizen:

> I mean, a dog barks but it's not language. I mean, *yer* Jocks and *yer* Irish they've got that, they've got sounds. *Yer* Gaelic- but it's no good to 'em 'cept for talking among themselves [...] (20.9.72).

Although the series did not inspire a dramatic trend, there is no doubt that YOUR 2 between 1967-72 became associated with this TV character, a marker of a 'stage idiolect' as well as stage-dialect. When one of the original episodes was rescreened in 1982, *The Guardian* commented: "It's *yer actual* original Alf Garnett, innit?" (3.8.82). And when the character was relaunched in a new series in 1985, the headline in the *London Evening Standard* (30.8.85) read: "Golden Moments with *yer actual* author".

Speight, the author, was himself born in the East End of London, and there is no doubt that to many ears, YOUR 2 is strongly associated with Cockney (although, strangely, popular books on Cockney make no mention of it) and is thus stigmatised, marked as 'non-standard' in the evaluative sense:

> Now look here mate, wack or Jimmy, if you gonna get on you gotta talk proper. And that don't mean talkin' posh like *yer* famous Prince Charles, or *yer* equally illustrious Roy Jenkins. And it certainly don't mean talkin' common like *yer* Eric Heffer [...] (*The Times*, 20.8.81)

In Bakhtin's terms, all words have the 'taste' of a particular group (1981: 293); hence one might assume that 20 years ago Alf Garnett's idiom was unlikely to be a model of imitation for many educated people, except in parody, and that YOUR 2 was brought into the spotlight only to be thrust back-stage again; or so it might seem. Certainly, in journalism in particular, YOUR 2 has often been used in silent or 'intonational' quotation marks, in Bakhtin's terms again, as a borrowed or parodic accent, to suggest an East End stereotype:

> 'Look', he says, reclining in the private bar of Whitechapel's Skull and Trowel, a favourite resort of East End prehistorians, '*your actual* palaeontologist is a middle class bloke, right? [...]' (Miles Kington: *The Times*, 19.8.80)

> '*Your old* East End villain would always accept that if he was done fair and square, he was done', reflected a chief superintendant [...] looking back on his 20 years' service in the East End of London [...] (*The London Evening Standard*, 15. 12.82)

Nonetheless, it can be argued that features of social stigma, just as much as those of prestige, are still salient (cf. Dines 1980: 16). Dialect borrowing, even in quotation marks or parody, is one way in which usages actually do spread. And it is very clear that YOUR 2 has not simply confined itself to the East End of London, but is increasingly since the 1970s to be found in many general registers of informal standard English writing and speech, as the examples in section 1 above illustrate. Stigma itself is but the other face of covert prestige. There is, as with non-standard usages generally, a positive image or connotation of 'solidarity' and of friendliness in this YOUR 2 (cf. "All of the old – words and *none of your mateyness*": headline, *London Evening Standard*, 14.2.83, referring to the perennial debate about modernising the language of the liturgy). YOUR 2, like Estuary English in general, seems increasingly street-wise, appealing to the young and trendy:

> Transvestites like Eddie Izzard may be the darlings of the media, but *your average* cross-dressing *man-on-the-street* still has to weather a fair amount of abuse (*The Big Issue*, 14.5.93)

There is a noteworthy parallel to be drawn here between YOUR 2 and other 'Cockney' features such as glottal stops which have been borrowed by the RP speakers of the younger generations. What has been dubbed 'Estuary English' (cf. Coggle 1993), the English of Essex and Kent as well as of the East End of London, is fast replacing 'the Queen's English' as a centre of influence on standard English speech. Not surprisingly then, this trendy YOUR 2 is increasingly found in journalistic headlines, as examples in section 1 above illustrate, and also in advertising slogans:

> The Volkswagen Boulevard. More stylish than *your old* cul-de-sac (*The Guardian*, 7.8.85)

The evaluative comparison noted in section 1 is a particularly appropriate speech act in such a register, and the personal hint of reader-awareness is a bonus (cf. "A cut above *your* average tights"; "Not *your* traditional lager", etc).

There is another dimension to YOUR 2 that seems to be having an impact on its current popularity, which, interestingly, is foreshadowed in some of the usages of Alf Garnett in the late 1960s. YOUR 2's general 'pointing' function in the prosodic and discourse contexts of focus, emphasis and addressee-awareness has already been noted; in Alf's impassioned orations YOUR 2 itself often seems to be functioning merely as a deictic intensifier ~ . Many of the colligated nouns have unique reference rather than generic (*yer Buckingham Palace, yer God, yer Harold Wilson, yer BBC*), and accompanying post-deictic adjectives are not always in evidence. In this connection, *actual*, as in the examples quoted in East End 'dialect' above, and frequently found with YOUR 2, can itself be seen simply as an intensifying modifier. (In this respect, 'It's *your actual* real ale' is not easily replaced by 'It's *the actual* real ale'.) The combination of intensifier and addressee-awareness, but without the gnomic pretensions, probably accounts for the increasing popularity of YOUR 2 as a bare deictic in popular (London) radio broadcasting, e.g. for weather reports ("*Your* high today 72 degrees [...]" *Capital Radio*, May 94). What Simpson (1993: 127) would term its "pragmatic presuppositions" appear, to be shifting, i.e. the meanings that attach conventionally to items, derived from their normal contexts of use. Your media is certainly one of your likely centres of influence on standard English in the future.

Notes

1. The *OED's* first mention is Roger Ascham (1568); I have noted three clear examples in Gilbert Walker's pamphlet (1552), "A manifest detection of the most vile and detestable use of dice-play". However, as I note in section 2 below, YOUR 2 is not frequent in pamphlet-writing. It can also be noted that Puttenham's *Art of English Poetry*, which I discuss at length in section 3 because of its numerous examples of YOUR 2, was actually begun in the late 1560s, but he may have revised it later. The *OED's* earliest reference to impersonal *you* is in 1577, but it must have certainly developed earlier: see section 2 below.

2. There is another kind of 'intermediary' meaning for YOUR 2 that is detectable at this period: 'that which you have' extending to 'that which you have (just) mentioned' or 'that which you have (just) heard'. Consider: "[Mistress Justiniano:] What's the forepart? [Mistress Birdlime:] A very pretty stuff, I knowe not the name of *your forepart*" (*Westward Ho*, I. 2, Dekker and Webster 1605).

    Here the *your* phrases are characteristically anaphoric, the speaker referring back to a previous utterance in a kind of 'echo' structure, which is sometimes also a dismissive riposte. In utterances by the same speaker, as in the examples from Puttenham in section 3 below, it suggests a concern for coherence and emphasis. A modern example from a text book, with an additional touch of irony, is provided by Paul Simpson (1993: 152) in his analysis of an advertisement: "[...] *The plants and herbs* used for the remedies are 'wonderful', interest in the properties is 'tremendous' and the formulae used are simply 'superb'. *In short, your herbal remedies* look like a panacea capable of dealing with every conceivable ailment".

3. It is noteworthy that in indirect speech, YOUR 2 is not normally transposed into the definite article: "[...] he planted all the clues first and decided whodunnit afterwards, a process which, they all agreed, was the boring thing about *your* straight whodunnit [...]" (*The Guardian*, 21.10.82) [+ anaphoric]

    "Thwaites admits that the broad theme will not be unfamiliar to *your average* conference-goer [...]" (*Times Educational Supplement*, 16.7.82). Just occasionally, however, YOUR 2 and *the* are found within the same sentence: "'Can you imagine'", he asked, "all *your* compositors and all *the* broadcasting technicians happily catching their usual trains to work [...]" (*The Times*, 26.2.80).

References

Abbott, Edwin
    1872   *A Shakespearian Grammar*. London: Macmillan.
Bakhtin, Mikhail
    1981   *The Dialogic Imagination: Four Essays*. Austin: University of Texas Press.
Coggle, Peter
    1993   *Do You Speak Estuary?* London: Bloomsbury.
Dines, Elizabeth
    1980   "Variation in discourse – and 'stuff like that'." *Language in Society* 9, 13-31.
Hudson, Richard
    1981   *Sociolinguistics*. Cambridge: University Press.

Kytö, Merja, and Matti Rissanen
    1983   "The syntactic study of Early American English." *Neuphilologische Mitteilungen* 4, LXXXIV, 470-89.

Lightfoot, David
    1979   *Principles of Diachronic Syntax*. Cambridge: University Press.

Quirk, Randolph, Sidney Greenbaum, Geoffrey Leech, and Jan Svartvik
    1985   *A Comprehensive Grammar of the English Language*. London: Longman.

Rydén, Mats
    1980   "Syntactic variation in a historical perspective." In: Sven Jacobson (ed.). *Papers from the Scandinavian Symposium on Syntactic Variation 1979*, Stockholm: Almqvist & Wiksell, 37-45.

Simpson, Paul
    1993   *Language, Ideology and Point of View*. London: Routledge.

Wales, Katie
    1985   "Generic 'your' and Jacobean drama: the rise and fall of a pronominal usage." *English Studies* 66, 7-24.

Demonstratives in Early Modern English Letters

Barbara Kryk-Kastovsky
Adam-Mickiewicz-University, Poznań

1. Introduction

The present paper is a contribution to a new field emerging at the crossroads of pragmatic and historical studies, i.e. historical pragmatics. On the one hand, the inclusion of social and cultural context in its widest sense has long been felt a necessary enrichment of the methodologies employed by the historians of language (cf. Romaine 1982; Traugott 1982, 1990; Stein 1985 and the articles in the special issue of *Folia Linguistica* 1985: VI/1).[1] On the other hand, pragmatists have recently been searching for new perspectives which became apparent in the intercultural/anthropological or the cognitive slant of the topics of conference papers (cf. 4th International Pragmatics Conference Kobe, Japan, July 25-30, 1993) and some most recent publications (cf. Mey 1993 and most of the articles in *Journal of Pragmatics* as well as in IPrA Quarterly *Pragmatics*). Despite these new developments, the dissatisfaction with purely synchronic explanations in pragmatics, which has been in the air for some time, has not, to the best of my knowledge, found an overt expression so far. It is, however, covertly present in what the practitioners do. Indeed, while the term *historical pragmatics* has been lingering in linguistic writings for a decade or so (cf. Faarlund 1985, Stein 1985), it is only recently that pragmatic issues have been more systematically approached from a historical perspective, e.g. the history of English promises (Arnovik 1993); text deixis in Early Modern English (Fries 1994); forms of address in English and Polish (Kiełkiewicz-Janowiak 1992); politeness in Shakespeare (Kopytko 1993).

In this paper I am going to address the problem of the English demonstratives as used in selected Early Modern English private letters. That deixis is a pervasive phenomenon in natural language has long been agreed upon in many studies.[2] Some of these authors, notably Brugmann and Greenberg, have attempted a historical explanation of the present deictic systems in various languages; however, as I discovered in the course of my own studies on deixis, many links are still missing, and therefore, many questions are still left unanswered. As a small step towards filling this gap, I would like to compare the present-day pragmatic meanings of the English demonstrative pronouns *this* and *that* with their ancestors in EModE. The reason why the most immediate ancestors of the two demonstratives have been selected here is that much has been written on their more remote history. For instance, Greenberg (1978) shows that the demonstrative is the most common origin of the definite article, whereas Traugott enumerates the definite article *the,* which derives in EME from the non-proximal demonstrative *that* of OE, among "one of the well-known examples of grammaticalization in English" (Traugott 1982: 250).[3] In view of this, it might be worth investigating whether *this/that* had already assumed their ModE functions in EModE times. As to the choice of the corpus, letters seem to be most appropriate for the present purpose since this kind of written records is regarded as the most reliable source of socio-pragmatic data, cf. Romaine (1982: 167): "It is generally felt that letters and diaries are an excellent source of colloquialisms which existed at earlier stages of the English language". Apart from this opinion, I here also adopt one of Romaine's methodological tools, i.e. what she calls *uniformitarian principle*: "we accept that the linguistic forces which operate today and are observable around us are not unlike those which have operated in the past" (Romaine 1982: 122). It will become apparent from my analysis below that no serious investigations of historical data could be possible if this principle were not accepted. One more remark concerning the corpus concerns the choice of private rather than official letters. It should be obvious from our discussion so far that if letters in general abound in colloquialisms, it is certainly private letters that are likely to be the closest approximation of impromptu speech, so that even such typical impromptu speech categories like pragmatic particles should occur in them.[4]

The analysis will be organised as follows. In section 2 the theoretical framework will be outlined, i.e. the main usages of the demonstratives *this* and *that* will be enumerated, which will later serve as points of reference for various occurrences of the two demonstratives in my EModE corpus (section 3). Finally, section 4 will be devoted to conclusions and future research prospects.

2.   Theoretical framework

For reasons of brevity, the discussion of different usage of the English demonstratives will be organised under separate headings, which will include:

a) a description (context of occurrence) of a particular usage;
b) an illustrative example (along with its source);
c) additional references to other sources (if any).

Such an organisation of the theoretical framework should constitute good grounds for drawing potential parallels between the pragmatic meanings of *this/that* in ModE and their ancestors in EModE. The historical data have been drawn from a concordance based on *The Helsinki Corpus of English Texts*.

2.1. *The main deictic usages of* this *and* that[5]

2.1.1.

Gestural usage (Fillmore 1975, Levinson 1983) occurs along with pointing to an object (Bühler's "demonstratio ad oculos", cf. Bühler 1934):

(1) *This print* is good, but *that one* from Hawaii is better, Kryk (1987:54)

2.1.2.

Anaphora (Bühler 1934, Fillmore 1975, Levinson 1983, Lyons 1977) is used to point to an entity previously mentioned in a text:

(2) I cut a finger: *this one*, Levinson (1983: 67)

Lyons (1977: 676) has noticed that a deictic term can often be used both deictically and anaphorically:

(3) I was born *in London* and I have lived *there* ever since[6]

2.1.3.

Symbolic usage (Fillmore 1975; Levinson 1983) is achieved by pointing to an entity not necessarily present at the moment of utterance (cf. Bühler's *deixis am Phantasma*):

(4) *This city* stinks
(5) *That*'s a beautiful view, both from Levinson (1983: 66)

2.1.4.

Discourse deixis (Fillmore 1975; Levinson 1983; Lakoff 1974; Rauh 1983), called "textual deixis" by Lyons (1977) and Ehlich (1982), is close to anaphora in that a demonstrative is used in such instances to refer to a portion of prior or subsequent discourse. Lakoff claims that *this* is more versatile, since it can be used in both cases, whereas *that* is limited to prior discourse only (Lakoff 1974: 346):

(6)   Kissinger made his long-awaited announcement yesterday.
      This/that statement confirmed the speculations of many observers
(7)   *This/*that* is what we must do: round up all the usual suspects...

2.1.5.
Social deixis has only been singled out by Fillmore (1975) and Levinson (1983). Fillmore defines it as the aspects of social situation in which a speech act occurs; this includes the devices for person marking, the methods of separating speech levels, the use of names, titles, kinship terms, etc. Notice how the borderline between pragmatics and sociolinguistics becomes fuzzy in this area of study since it is of concern to both disciplines. This type of deixis is not so frequently encoded in ModE, which has a rather simple address system. However, I have attested some social-deictic usage of *this/that* in the following telephone conversation (overheard during my stay in Palo Alto in 1984/85). Here the interchange of the distal vs. proximal demonstrative indicates, as expected, the distance of the object (Charlotte) from the Origo, i.e. in A's utterance Charlotte is far from A's Origo, hence *that* is employed, whereas in B's reply Charlotte, being the speaker, is at the Origo, hence she uses *this* as referring to herself:

(8)   A: Is *that* Charlotte?
      B: Yes, *this* is Charlotte

Interestingly, on another occasion, Charlotte answered:

      B: Yes, *this* is *she*

where social deixis was combined with empathy so that the speaker referred to herself from the perspective of her interlocutor. All these intricacies of social conditioning of the use of demonstratives might be even more complex as we move backwards in time and look for instances of the ancestors of social deixis in EModE. As already noticed by Jespersen (1961 VI/1: 409ff.), the non-anaphoric *this/that* in speaking of persons "have perhaps at no time been very frequent; now at any rate they are very rare".

2.1.6.
Emotional deixis was first distinguished by Lakoff (1974), and later recognised by Lyons (1977) under the name of empathetic deixis. Other authors either ignore this use of demonstratives completely or, like Levinson (1983: 66),

consider it non-deictic. According to Lakoff (1974: 352), emotional deixis signals the attitude of the speaker towards a given entity by means of *this/that*:

(9)   I see there's going to be peace in the mideast.
       This Henry Kissinger is really something!
(10)   *That* Henry Kissinger sure knows his way around Hollywood!

Note that the proximal/distal distinction normally expressed by the two demonstratives is neutralised in such contexts. Moreover, emotional deixis is limited to colloquial discourse, and its use presupposes that the speaker and the hearer share the knowledge of the facts alluded to, and that there is something remarkable about these facts, hence the oddity of

(11)   ?*That* Poland has big coal resources (Kryk 1987: 94).

2.2. Non-deictic usage of this and that

Most authors have considered the non-deictic usage of deictic categories uninteresting or at least marginal. Some of them have discussed the problem under the rubric of "the neutral usage of *that*", which is unmarked with respect to proximity, as opposed to *this,* which remains marked as [+proximal], cf. Lyons (1977: 647). Levinson (1983: 66) simply considers usages like those below non-deictic:

(12)   Oh, I did *this* and *that*

A much more explanatory account of the history of the neutral usage of demonstratives can be found in Jespersen (1961 II/1: 409ff.). Thus, neuter pronouns *þis and þæt* were employed neutrally already in OE and were carried over through ME to ModE. The abundance of possible contexts to be found both in Jespersen and other grammars of ModE reveals the wide distribution of these forms. Consider the following examples:

(13)   *This* is my brother John
(14)   Is *that* you?

and some formulaic expressions like

(15)   *that's* it/*that*'ll do/at *that*

as well as

(16)   *this* is all/*this* will do/*this* is not true.

The above-mentioned deictic and non-deictic usage of *this* and *that* will now be confronted with examples from my corpus in search for possible correspondences. A reservation must be made at this point concerning the scope of my study. As indicated in the title, for reasons of brevity I will focus here on *this* and *that* in their demonstrative functions. Therefore I will have nothing to say on the relative pronoun *that*, as well as the content clause complementizer *that*, despite an obvious connection between all these categories.[7]

3.   The usage of EModE demonstratives

3.1. *The corpus*

My corpus is based on *The Helsinki Corpus of English Texts* (Kytö 1991) and comprises all the private letters from the last EModE period (labeled EModE III), i.e. 1640-1710. The letters, collected under the file name CEPRIV3, were written by several authors whose names appear under abbreviated headings, like RHADSR (Haddock, Richard, Sr.); RHADDJR (Haddock, Richard, Jr.); CHATTON (Hatton, Charles); ALHATTON (Hatton, Alice), etc. The entire corpus has been scanned for the occurrences of *this* and *that*. These data have then been classified according to the various usages of *this* and *that*. Before the analysis proper is attempted, I would like to formulate the following hypotheses pertaining to the nature of the data and the aim of this study:[8]

a) The majority of the usages of the two demonstratives in EModE will probably coincide with the usages distinguished in ModE and described in 2. above, especially if we accept Romaine's uniformitarian principle concerning the analogies between the linguistic mechanisms operating today and in the past.

b) Letters are a special type of text where a preference of some forms over others is likely to occur. For instance, unlike the participants of a (face-to-face) conversation, the authors of letters would find the gestural deictic usage superfluous, whereas they would rather refer to places or events by means of symbolic pointing, and employ discourse deixis to refer to some elements or larger portions of the text.

c) In EModE certain formulaic expressions and/or idiomatic phrases must have already been present; however, it can be conjectured that certain allegedly very recent usages of English demonstratives did not yet exist at the turn of 17th and 18th centuries.

3.2. *The analysis*

3.2.1. That

My analysis will start with *that* due to the potential multiplicity of its grammatical and pragmatic functions. Firstly, *that* is not only a demonstrative, but can also play the role of other grammatical categories: a (content clause) complementizer and a relative pronoun. It has already been mentioned above that both these grammatical functions will be ignored here. As could be expected, simple statistics applied to my corpus have revealed that the complementizer function of *that* has the highest frequency of occurrence (a total of 93 in all the texts analysed), whereas the relative pronoun and the demonstrative usage have roughly the same frequency of occurrence, i.e. 36 and 29, respectively. Secondly, *that* does not only function as a (distal) demonstrative but also as a neutral form, hence it should occur in a wider range of contexts and be, therefore, amenable to a more multiaspectual investigation (even though, statistically, it turns out to be of lower frequency than *this*, i.e. 29 vs. 64, respectively).

In my analysis of the corpus the following usages of *that* have been attested:

3.2.1.1. *Discourse deixis*

My initial hypothesis as to the high frequency of occurrence of *that* in the discourse function has been confirmed by the fact that almost 50% of instances of *that* are indeed used discourse-deictically. Consider the following examples:

(17) destroying the French shipps to the southwards of Trepassa,
      and consequently you will not come in for your share of *that* capture
      (RHADSR 43)
(18) asked him if hee could object agt mee for learning: hee said hee
      was satifyed in *that* (HOXINDEN 280)
(19) heare yoᵘ see what yoʳ dafter doe write that shee have yoʳ
      writetinges, *that* is true (PINNEY 39)

Notice that in all three instances *that* refers back not so much to an entity mentioned previously in the discourse, but to a larger portion thereof: a description of a wartime event, a concrete personal situation, and the contents of someone's writings, respectively.

Since so many instances of discourse deixis, parallel to the ModE usage, have been attested in my corpus, one could conjecture that a similar parallel could be drawn in the case of pointing.

3.2.1.2. That *in pointing* ~

As could be expected, gestural use of demonstratives in letters would be, at best, very rare. This is what follows from my corpus, since no token of gestural *that* has been found. The only cases of relevance here would be the following occurrences of *that* in symbolic pointing:

(20)   Pray God send you wth ye King of Spaine well out *that*
       place (RHADSR 46)
(21)   intend to be at Kimbolton *that night* (FHATTON I 147)

Both *that place* and *that night* are here being referred to symbolically since in neither of the cases is the sender of the message copresent with these spatio-temporal locations. Consequently, this usage of *that* in EModE has also proved parallel its to present counterparts.

3.2.1.3. *The 'grammatical' cases*

I have called the next two usages 'grammatical cases' since they represent primarily a grammatical rather than a pragmatic phenomenon and are therefore not part of my theoretical framework above. Interestingly, while my corpus contains only one occurrence of a comparative construction *such ... that*, perfectly acceptable in ModE, another construction *that ... which* (now becoming obsolescent, cf. Jespersen 1961 II/1: 412) occurs 4 times, e.g.

(22)   Yours I received and have *such* a Narrative of the Scot from
       your Mother *that* I would have neither of you to have to doe
       with her at all (JOPINNEY 58)
(23)   Pray lett's understand whether *that* letter miscarried *which* I sent
       last week (STRYPE 181)
(24)   ... this is to desire Thee not to be troubled in the least Measure at
       that which joyes me (HOXINDEN 292)

Apparently, *that ... which* was a popular construction at the end of the EModE period, and its decline started only later, whereas *such ... that* either was not so popular yet or its single occurrence is simply an accidental property of my corpus.

Another kind of my 'grammatical cases' are fixed expressions and phrases which have been subsumed under this heading since they are special collocations often formed contrary to the rules of grammar. Two instances of such phrases have occurred in my data, interestingly both coming from the same author (HOXINDEN 275 and 280, respectively):

(25)   I thinke thou wert best send up the silver Tanker to my brother
       to that effect

(26) the business with my Brother barrow without mee, and try what
       might be done *that way*

Another kind of a fixed expression used by the same author is worth noting for
yet another reason: while *no more than that* would freely be used to refer
(back) to a portion of prior discourse, it cannot, according to Lakoff (1974:
350) be used for subsequent discourse deixis. However, this is what we find in

(27) I shall say no more than *that*: no man can have a more real heart
       toward any then hath to Thee and Thine (HOXINDEN 293)

3.2.1.4. *Emotional deixis*

Emotional deixis seems to be a fairly recent phenomenon in English, described
in connection with the notions of solidarity, camaraderie, or emotional closeness
in general (Fillmore 1975, Lakoff 1974). It might, therefore, be worth checking
whether it could be attested in EModE. Surprisingly, two undoubtedly
emotional-deictic usages occur in my corpus, cf.:

(28) only *that Capt. Emes* wth his wife and son (RHADSR 45)
(29) If *that honest Scott*, Mr. Ennis (CHATTON I 161)

It can therefore be hypothesised that emotional deixis is not at all a recent
development of English, but it used to signify solidarity and empathy already in
the EModE period.

3.2.2. This

3.2.2.1. *Direct pointing*

As regards the proximate demonstrative *this* my conjecture is that it will much
more frequently be used for direct pointing than the distal *that*. It follows from
my data that this is indeed the case, since out of 64 occurrences of *this* in my
corpus, as many as 26 involve direct pointing, either to a time span (18
instances) or to objects (8 instances). Consider the following examples of
straightforward direct pointing to a current point or period of time:

(30) I resolved *this Saturday Evening* to trouble you with a letter
       (STRYPE 182)
(31) Crue hath been an hour with mee *this morning* (PHENRY 340)

While there is nothing unusual in these two examples, which are parallel to
modern usage, some peculiarities have nevertheless been detected in my corpus
as regards this type of pointing, cf.

(32) R. James, in Southold Bay, *this 25th May, 1672* (RHADSR 14)

(33) Alicant, *this 31st of July, 1706* (NHADD 50)

As compared to the ModE convention of letter writing, where the date suffices
to mark a particular day, a preceding *this* would be considered superfluous. It
could only be used in situations where a more general term like *Sunday* would
require some specification, hence the acceptability of *this Sunday* nowadays.

    Another peculiar usage of *this* can be noticed in the following example:

(34) I beg they may not faile *this next week* (CHATTON 148)

In a way it is similar to the usage of *this* in (16) above in that it would be
considered optional nowadays (*this* as the forthcoming point of time being
conflated with the more precise *next*). It is possible that the semantics and
pragmatics of EModE required more precision from the speakers so that they
would use additional means of indicating contemporaneity and copresence with
the Origo as we do in ModE, since language has the tendency towards
becoming a more economical system.[9]

    Direct pointing to objects involves either an entity present at the speaker's
Origo, but absent from the addressee's location, e.g.

(35) It is no smal trouble to me to part from *this brave ship*
      (RHADSR 21)

or, more frequently, *this* refers to an object present at the Origo of the sender at
Coding Time (CT), consecutively being present at the Origo of the addressee at
Receiving Time (RT), e.g.

(36) *this bad scrawle and blotted paper*, but I write wth pen
      (NHADD 51)
(37) ...in order to which pray observe my directions in *this letter* at
      the other side of the paper (HOXINDEN 293)

An interesting case of a direct pointing to an unidentified object, apparently sent
along with the letter, can be found in

(38) Cut *this* off and send it to the Scott sealed up (JOPINNEY 59)

All in all, the instances of direct pointing to objects are in no way different from
the ModE counterparts, and I will have nothing more to say on this topic.

3.2.2.2. *Symbolic pointing*

Like in the case of *that*, *this* can also be employed in symbolic pointing,
although only 6 occurrences of such a usage have been found in my corpus, e.g.

(39) Sunday last we took *this place*, attacking it by land (RHADSR 50)

(40) I am suldom trobelled at any thinge of *this worlde*
      (JPINNEY 18)

As can be expected, no differences have been detected between the EModE usage and their ModE equivalents, other examples including such obvious collocations as *this parish, this cold place, this quarter, this country.*

3.2.2.3. *Discourse deixis*

As in the case of *that*, the discourse-deictic usage of *this* has a high frequency of occurrence in my corpus (18 out of 64). Most of the examples do not differ from their modern counterparts, like

(41) *This* is all the account I can give thee as concerning Him
      (HOXINDEN 277)
(42) I do not hear of anny other thing mentioned, but I suppose *this* was not all
      (ANHATTON 212)

Therefore, I will concentrate here on two cases revealing some differences between EModE and ModE. Consider the following data:

(43) *This is to acquaint* of your ingaging wth ye French (RHADSR 41)
(44) My dere beyond all expression, *this is to desire Thee* not to be troubled in the least Measure (HOXINDEN 292)

Notice how the construction *This is to...*, which in ModE is basically reserved for formal and rather stilted formulas employing performatives (e.g. *This is to inform you that...*), serves here a much wider purpose of making someone acquainted and expressing one's desires. It seems that the repertory of performatives was much richer in EModE than it is now. At least, this is what was true of promises (cf. Arnovik 1993).

3.2.2.4. *Problematic usage*

The two remaining cases will be discussed separately, since they do not exactly fit under any of the previously distinguished rubrics. Consider the following examples:

(45) *This day* as I came from Westminster I saw the King and the Queen at dinner (HOXINDEN 278)
(46) *This dinner we had* Beanes and Bacon, Sammon &c. (PHENRY 341)

What is so special about them is that in both cases *this* is used, although the objects referred to are placed in the past (as indicated by the tense forms of the verbs). The possible explanations here could go along two different lines. Either the two usages are the idiosyncrasies of individual styles, or *this* is intended as an emotional deictic and it was favoured over *that* since it expresses more empathy and is in that sense closer to a discourse deictic. I would opt for the latter solution as it seems to have more explanatory power for elucidating the history of the emotional-deictic usage of demonstratives. However, a more extensive study of the area will certainly be needed to clarify the observations presented in this study.

4.   Conclusions and prospects

The analysis has shown that many of the ModE usages of *this* and *that* were already present in EModE. This conclusion, as easy as it is to anticipate, is therefore, on the face of it, not very revealing. Nevertheless, it might be a valuable insight for a pragmatist who attempts to trace back certain patterns of modern language use. S/he would realise that most of the demonstrative usages must have originated in earlier periods of the history of the English language. The remaining usages, which either do not exist anymore nowadays or occur in a limited number of contexts (like, for example, certain speech acts or syntactic constructions of a formulaic type), certainly constitute a challenge to the analyst. They would require an in-depth study of the time span between EModE and ModE in order to establish the time of their becoming obsolescent and then eventually obsolete. This kind of investigation would certainly profit from studying the social and political conditions of those times, so that we will learn not only the *when?* but also the *why?* of the linguistic change, although the reconstruction of language in its social context is an equally difficult task in synchronic studies approached both through a sociolinguistic interview, or through the extant written texts of a language no longer spoken, cf. Romaine (1982: 126).

Notes

1.   The volume contains the papers from the Workshop on Socio-historical Linguistics held at Adam-Mickiewicz-University Poznań, Poland on August 20th, 1983 in conjunction with the Sixth International Conference on Historical Linguistics.

2.   Cf., in particular, the arguments in Bar-Hillel (1970), Benveniste (1971), Brugmann (1904), Frei (1944), Greenberg (1978; 1985), Kryk (1987), Kryk-Kastovsky (in press), Kuryłowicz (1972), Perkins (1992), Rauh (1983), Svorou (1993).

3.   She has also pointed out earlier (Traugott 1972: 135) that once *the* developed from the demonstrative *that*, the former was anaphoric, whereas the latter was almost

exclusively deictic, which can be seen in the infrequency of alternation between *the* and *that* in ME and EModE manuscripts.

4. On impromptu speech as a bundle-concept consisting of a number of situational parameters, like: context-of-situation, the medium (written or spoken, i.e. including letters) and the topic, cf. Östman (1982: 155ff.).

5. A full list of the possible meanings of lexical items as ubiquitous as demonstratives is simply unattainable, both because of their frequency of occurrence and an abundance of relevant literature resulting in an abundance of usages labelled differently by different authors. The present account is largely based on a table juxtaposing many such approaches which I have proposed elsewhere (Kryk 1987: 31).

6. On the controversy concerning the similarities and differences between deixis ~ and anaphora ~ , see e.g. Ehlich 1982; 1983.

7. The early ME relative pronouns, which are the ancestors of the ModE relatives, originate in certain uses of the OE demonstrative and interrogative pronouns, cf. e.g. Romaine (1982: 56); on the role of *that* as complementizer and the general tendency in IE languages to employ neutral pronouns in this role, cf. Frajzyngier (1991:222ff.).

8. The data quoted here includes the source and the pagination. The original spelling has been preserved, although diacritics used in the corpus, like pauses, etc. have been kept to a minimum. I would like to thank Christiane Dalton-Puffer, University of Vienna, for her invaluable help with the corpus.

9. Cf. Hopper and Traugott's remarks on the competing motivations for the maximisation of "economy" or "simplicity" in language, which they summarise as "maximization of efficiency via minimal differentiation on the one hand, and maximization of informativeness, on the other" Hopper and Traugott (1993: 64).

References

Arnovik, Leslie
    1993   "The sociological origins of promissory expansion; or, the linguist as social historian." Paper presented at the International Conference on the History of Language Sciences (ICHoLS VI), Georgetown University, Washington, D.C., August 9-14, 1993.

Bar-Hillel, Yehoshua
    1970   "Indexical expressions." In: Yehoshua Bar-Hillel (ed.). *Aspects of Language*. Jerusalem: The Magnes Press, 69-88.

Benveniste, Emile
    1971   *Problems in General Linguistics*. Coral Gables, Fla.: University of Miami Press.

Brugmann, Karl
    1904   "Die Demonstrativa der indogermanischen Sprachen." *Abhandlungen der
              Sächsischen Gesellschaft der Wissenschaften* 22: 1-144.
Bühler, Karl
    1934   *Sprachtheorie.* Jena: Fischer.
Ehlich, Konrad
    1982   "Anaphora and deixis: same, similar, or different?" In: Robert Jarvella and
              Wolfgang Klein (eds.). *Speech, place and action. Studies on deixis and
              related topics.* Chichester, New York: Wiley & Sons, 315-338.
    1983   "Deixis und Anapher." In: Gisa Rauh (ed.). *Essays on deixis.* Tübingen:
              Gunter Narr, 79-97.
Faarlund, Jan Terje
    1985   "Pragmatics in diachronic syntax." *Studies in Language* 9-3: 363-393.
Fillmore, Charles J.
    1975   "Santa Cruz lectures on deixis 1971." *Indiana University Linguistics Club.*
Frajzyngier, Zygmunt
    1991   "The *de dicto* domain in language." In: Elizabeth Closs Traugott, Bernd
              Heine (eds.). *Approaches to Grammaticalization.* Vol. 1. Amsterdam:
              Benjamins, 219-251.
Frei, Henri
    1944   "Sytemès de déictiques." *Acta linguistica* 4. 111-129.
Fries, Udo
    1994   "Text deixis in Early Modern English." In: Dieter Kastovsky (ed.). *Studies
              in Early Modern English.* Berlin: Mouton de Gruyter, 111-128.
Greenberg, Joseph H.
    1978   "How does a language acquire gender markers?" In: Joseph H. Greenberg
              (ed.). *Universals of Human Language.* Vol. 3. (*Word structure*). Stanford,
              Ca.: Stanford University Press, 47-82.
    1985   "Some iconic relationships among place, time, and discourse deixis." In:
              John Haiman (ed.). *Iconicity in Syntax.* Amsterdam: Benjamins, 271-287.
Hopper, Paul J., and Elizabeth Closs Traugott
    1993   *Grammaticalization.* Cambridge: Cambridge University Press.
Jespersen, Otto
    1961   *A Modern English Grammar on Historical Principles.* London: Allen &
              Unwin.
Kiełkiewicz-Janowiak, Agnieszka
    1992   *A Socio-historical Study in Address: Polish and English.* Frankfurt am
              Main: Lang.

Kopytko, Roman
  1993   *Polite Discourse in Shakespeare's English.* Poznań: Wydawnictwo
            Naukowe UAM.
Kryk, Barbara
  1987   *On Deixis in English and Polish: The Role of Demonstrative Pronouns.*
            Frankfurt am Main: Lang.
Kryk-Kastovsky, Barbara
  in press "Modern approaches to deixis." In: Kurt Jankovsky (ed.). *Papers on the*
            Historical Dimension of Language. Münster: Nodus.
Kuryłowicz, Jerzy
  1972   "The role of deictic elements in linguistic evolution." *Semiotica* 5: 174-
            183.
Kytö, Merja
  1991   *Manual to the Diachronic Part of the Helsinki Corpus of English Texts.*
            Coding Conventions and Lists of Source Texts. Helsinki: Helsinki
            University Press.
Lakoff, Robin
  1974   "Remarks on *This* and *That.*" *CLS* 10: 345-356.
Levinson, Stephen
  1983   *Pragmatics.* Cambridge: Cambridge University Press.
Lyons, John
  1977   *Semantics.* Vol. 2. Cambridge: Cambridge University Press.
Mey, Jacob L.
  1993   *Pragmatics. An Introduction.* Oxford: Blackwell.
Östman, Jan-Ola
  1982   "The symbiotic relationship between pragmatic particles and impromptu
            speech." In: Nils Erik Enkvist (ed.). *Impromptu Speech: a Symposium.*
            Publications of the Research Institute of the Åbo Akademi Foundation NO
            78. Åbo: Åbo Akademi.
Perkins, Revere D.
  1992   *Deixis, Grammar, and Culture.* Amsterdam: Benjamins.
Rauh, Gisa
  1983   "Aspects of deixis." In: Gisa Rauh (ed.). *Essays on Deixis.* Tübingen:
            Gunter Narr, 9-60.
Romaine, Suzanne
  1982   *Socio-historical Linguistics.* Cambridge: Cambridge University Press.
Stein, Dieter
  1985   "Perspectives on historical pragmatics." *Folia Linguistica Historica* VI/2:
            347-355.

Svorou, Soteria
    1993   *The Grammar of Space*. Amsterdam: Benjamins.

Traugott, Elizabeth Closs
    1972   *A History of English Syntax*. New York: Holt, Rinehart and Winston, Inc.
    1982   "From propositonal to textual and expressive meanings: some semantic-pragmatic aspects of grammaticalization." In: Winfred P. Lehmann, Yakov Malkiel (eds.). *Perspectives on Historical Linguistics*. Amsterdam-Philadelphia: Benjamins, 245-271.
    1990   "From less to more situated in language: the unidirectionality of semantic change" In: Sylvia Adamson, Vivien Law, Nigel Vincent, Susan Wright (eds.). *Papers from the 5th International Conference on English Historical Linguistics*. Amsterdam: Benjamins, 497-517.

The Ambiguous Adverbial/Conjunctions *þa* and *þonne* in Middle English
A Discourse-Pragmatic Study of *then* and *when* in Early English Saints' Lives

Brita Wårvik
University of Turku

1. Introduction

The purpose of this paper is to discuss one particular feature of the language of narrative in Middle English: the ambiguous adverbial/conjunctions *þa* and *þonne*, and their successors *then* and *when*. This paper focuses on the merger of the discourse-functionally different forms of the adverbial and the introduction of the disambiguous form for the conjunction in Middle English.

Collections of saints' lives provide nicely comparable materials for a diachronic study of discourse-pragmatic features, because in them we have basically the same stories retold at different times. The earliest texts that have been included in the present study are the lives of saints by Ælfric (dated around 1000; henceforth *ÆLS*). The Middle English collections in this study are the *South English Legendary* (late thirteenth century; *SEL*), Mirk's *Festial* (early fifteenth century; *Mirk*), and Caxton's *Golden Legend* (1483; *GL*).[1]

2. Background: Old English

One of the most prominent features of Old English narrative is the use of the adverbial *þa* 'then'; its frequency in many texts is high enough to have provoked even negative criticism of the style of such texts (cf. Andrew 1940). However, when the use of *þa* is investigated from a text-linguistic perspective, the high frequency is shown to be motivated by its textual functions. As argued by

Enkvist and Wårvik, *þa* functions as a foreground marker in Old English narrative texts, keeping track of the main story-line (Enkvist and Wårvik 1987, Wårvik 1990). Foster maintains that *þa* acts as a marker of discourse units in Old and Middle English narratives (Foster 1975); Enkvist and Wårvik connect this segmentation function of *þa* with other signals of text strategic continuities and suggest that *þa* cooperates with other expressions of temporal continuity to signal unit boundaries in the structure of the narrative (Enkvist and Wårvik 1987, Wårvik 1987). Moreover, textual units are in the focus of the study by Waterhouse, who claims that *þa* serves as a sentence marker in Ælfric's *Lives of Saints* (Waterhouse 1984).

In addition to its multifunctionality, *þa* presents another problem to the student of Old English: it can be used both as an adverbial, 'then', 'after that', and as a conjunction, 'when'. Grammars of Old English generally view this distinction as dependent on word order, so that *þa* followed by subject-verb order is to be interpreted as a conjunction, while *þa* followed by verb-subject order and in non-initial positions is an adverbial (cf. Mitchell 1985: § 2543ff.). The distinction between main and subordinate clauses may be blurred in correlative constructions, that is, pairs of clauses headed by *þa* or *þonne*, for example (on correlation, cf. Mitchell 1985: § 1887ff.). In correlative constructions with *þa*, main and subordinate clauses are typically distinguished by different word orders. Another disambiguation strategy is doubling the word: the form *þa þa* is frequent especially in the works of Ælfric (cf. Mitchell 1985: §1889). Such doubled forms give rise to one question: were they synonymous with the single *þa* used as a conjunction, or were they interpreted as combinations of *þa*$_{\text{adverbial}}$ and *þa*$_{\text{conjunction}}$, that is, as 'then when' or 'when then' (cf. Mitchell 1985: § 2575).

Occasionally, modern readers wish to see correlative pairs of subordinate and main clauses also in strings of *þa*-verb-subject clauses, thus avoiding the repetitive paratactic links which they consider as signs of primitive style (cf. Andrew 1940). However, instead of trying to force *þa*-clauses into two opposed classes, we should consider them in terms of a scale with intermediate degrees from main to subordinate clauses (cf. Mitchell 1985: § 2546; generally on taxis and clause status e.g. Haiman and Thompson 1984, Lehmann 1988).

The following sample exemplifies the use of *þa* in Old English narrative. The text is from the life of St. Eustace from *ÆLS*.

> Hit gelamp sume dæge þæt he ferde ut on huntað mid eallum his werode and his wuldre . þa geseah he micelne floc heorta . and he ða ge-stihte his werod swa him gewunelic wæs . hu hi on þone huntað fon sceoldon . þa hi ealle ymb þone huntað abysgode wæron . þa æteowode him-sylfum an ormæte heort . se wæs

ormætre mycelnysse . ofer ealle ða oþre . and wlitig . and þa gewende he fram þam flocce . and ræsde into þam wudu þær he þiccost wæs . Þa þæt placidas geseah . þa gewilnode he þæt he hine gefenge . and him geornlice æfter ferde . mid feawum geferum . Þa æt nixtan wurdon hi ealle geteorode . and he ana unwerig him æfter fyligde . Witodlice þurh godes fore-stihtunge . ne hors ne he sylf gewergod wæs . ne he for ðæs weges earfoðnysse ablan . ac he lange æfter word . and feor fram his geferum ge-wat . Se heort þa witodlice astah on anne heahne clud . and þær gestod . Placidas ða lange stod . and beheold þone heort . and wundrode his micelnysse . and ablan his æhtan . Him þa god geswutelode þæt he him swilcne dom ne ondrede . ne his mægnes micelnysse ne wundrode. (*ÆLS* XXX, lines 24-41)

'It happened one day that he went out hunting with all his company and array; then he saw a great flock of harts, and disposed his company, as was customary to him, in order to take them by hunting. When they were all busied about the hunting, then there appeared to himself an immense hart, which was of exceeding bigness above all the others, and beautiful; and then he turned from the flock, and rushed into the wood where it was thickest. When Placidas saw that, he desired to take it and zealously went after it with a few companions; then at last they were all tired, and he alone, unweary, followed after it. Verily through God's predestination neither his horse nor himself was wearied, nor did he stop for the roughness of the way, but he went long after (it), and departed far from his companions. Then indeed the hart mounted up on a high rock and there stood. Then Placidas stood long and beheld the hart, and wondered at its size, and ceased his pursuit. Then God revealed to him that he should not fear such power, nor wonder at the greatness of his might.'[2]

After the introduction (*hit gelamp sume dæge þæt..*) we find adverbial *þa* in the clauses depicting foregrounded events that forward the story. *þa* marks discourse units in the sense that a clause containing *þa* is often followed by one or more clauses linked to it by coordination (*and, ac*); generally, these non-initial clauses have the same subject as the *þa*-clause, and this is typically indicated by zero anaphora. By taking the *þa*-clauses in the example we obtain the following skeleton of the story.

þa he (Placidas=Eustace) saw the harts
þa he arranged his company
þa the hart appeared
þa it turned from the herd and rushed into the wood
þa he wanted to catch it and went after it
þa they all got exhausted and he alone followed it

þa the hart climbed on a rock and stood there
þa he stood long and looked at the hart and wondered at its size and
ceased his pursuit
þa God showed him that he should not fear such power...

The conjunction *þa* 'when' occurs twice, both in correlative constructions: 'when they were all busied about the hunting, then there appeared to himself an immense hart' and 'when Placidas saw that, he desired to take it'. Both instances illustrate the typical use of *þa*$_{conjunction}$-clauses in Old English narrative: they depict events that are on the story-line, but serve as background to the events in the accompanying main clause, which may be marked by the adverbial *þa*.

In addition to its text-structuring role, *þa* can also function as a time adverbial similarly to its Modern English counterpart *then* 'at that time', for example

He gebæd eac swylce for eall cristen folc .
and þæt god forgeafe þære eorðan renas .
for þan ðe se hæða þa hynde ða eorðan .
(*ÆLS* XIV, lines 165-168)
'He prayed likewise for all Christian folk,
and that God would give rain to the earth
because the heat was then wasting the land.'

However, there are certain contexts of the Modern English *then* that *þa* does not share, that is, references to habitual and repeated situations, to present and future events, as well as to hypothetical situations. In these contexts Old English uses *þonne*, which, like *þa*, acts both as an adverbial and as a conjunction (cf. Mitchell 1985: §2562), as in the following examples.[3]

and gif seo hringe him folgað æt þam forman tige .
Þonne wat he to soðan þæt ic þe sende to him .
(*ÆLS* XXI, lines 45-46)
'and if the ring yield at the first tug
then shall he know for a truth that I sent thee to him.'

On hwilcum godum tihst þu us to gelyfenne ?
Hu magon hi ahreddan ðe fram frecednyssum .
þonne hi ne mihton hi sylfe ahreddan .
(*ÆLS* XIV, 148-150)
'On what sort of gods persuadest thou us to believe ?

How can they deliver thee from perils,
when they cannot deliver themselves?'

3. Changes in Middle English

During the Middle Englishþonneþa ~ period the use of þa changes radically. Firstly, þa gradually loses its foregrounding function and simultaneously, its frequency decreases. Furthermore, its semantic identity changes: on the one hand, the distinction between þa and þonne practically disappears, and on the other hand, the conjunction þa (as well as þonne) is replaced by the unambiguous *when*.

Let me begin by presenting the frequencies of þa and þonne in the two earlier samples of stories and of *then* in the two later samples.

Table 1: *Frequencies of* þa, þonne *and* then *in samples of* ÆLS, SEL, Mirk *and* GL.

TEXT	þa/1000 words*	then/1000 words*	þonne/1000 words*	size of sample words approx.
ÆLS	20.6		0.6	39,100
SEL	2.7		0.5	29,800
Mirk		15		16,900
GL		8		34,600

* variant forms are subsumed under the main entry

The data in Table 1 show, first, that the frequencies of þa are lower in Middle English narratives than in Old English: there is a great difference between *ÆLS*, on the one hand, and *SEL* and *GL*, on the other hand. *Mirk*, however, has a higher frequency of *then* than the other Middle English samples. Secondly, Table 1 shows that the distinction between þa and þonne is maintained in Early Middle English, but Late Middle English merges them in *then*. On the basis of evidence from the *Helsinki Corpus* and according to the *OED*, the merger of þa and þonne begins in the early fourteenth century, and the distinction disappears. Occasional þa-forms can be found even later, and in some dialects *tho* 'at that time' still occurs.

Let us now turn to the conjunction þa and its descendants. Table 2 shows the different temporal subordinating conjunctions and presents their frequencies in the samples as well as their usage in correlative constructions.

Table 2: *The frequencies of temporal subordinate clauses (*when*) and their use in correlative constructions in samples from* ÆLS, SEL, Mirk, *and* GL.

TEXT	temporal conjunctions*	conjunctions N	conjunctions/ 1000 words	correlatives/ conjunction
ÆLS	þa	22		86%
	þa þa	47		51%
	þonne	16	2.5	6%
	others	14		93%
SEL	þa	155	6.5	2%
	when	40		0
Mirk	when	98		13%
	then when	17	5.5	12%
	others (with then)	5		0
GL	when	170		4%
	then when, when	7	7	0
	then	14		0
	others			

* variant forms of the conjunctions are subsumed under the main entry

The figures in Table 2 show interesting developments in the use of the conjunctions meaning 'when'. To begin with the different types of conjunctions found in the samples, in *ÆLS* we find the ambiguous adverbial/conjunctions *þa* and *þonne*. Further, we find the doubled form *þa þa*, which is, as noted, frequently used by Ælfric; in this sample *þa þa* is the most frequent temporal conjunction. Next, in *SEL*, both *þa* and *when* are used, but the conjunction *þa* is almost four times as frequent as *when*. It is also worth observing that the doubled form *þa þa* does not occur in this sample. Finally, in *Mirk* and *GL*, the conjunction *þa* has given way to *when*. However, we also find temporal subordinate clauses introduced by *then when*, which very much resembles the doubled form *þa þa* (cf. above).

On the basis of these samples of narrative, the conjunctions *þa* and *when* appear to coexist in texts from the late thirteenth century, after which *þa*$_{\text{conjunction}}$ disappears. The doubled form *þa þa* seems to fall out of use by the early thirteenth century: the latest occurrences in the *Helsinki Corpus* are in texts from around 1200. In the late Middle English texts, *Mirk* and *GL*, *when* is the norm, but we also find *then when* and *when then*.

Secondly, the figures in Table 2 reveal differences in the frequencies of temporal conjunctions in the samples. Such differences alone do not, however, indicate any linguistic changes, because the use of temporal subordinate clauses depends on the elaboration and length of the stories in their different versions. Nevertheless, when these frequencies are considered together with those of *þa* and *then* (Table 1) and the proportions of correlation, they suggest differences in the strategies of marking narrative structure.

Thus, *ÆLS* has the highest frequency of *þa*$_{adverbial}$ and the lowest of temporal conjunctions; as expected, the proportion of temporal subordinate clauses in correlative constructions is highest in this sample. These characterisations tally with general tendencies in Old English narratives: a foregrounded story-line marked by adverbial *þa* and a preference for paratactic links.

The Middle English texts display lower frequencies of adverbial *þa* and higher frequencies of temporal subordinate clauses than *ÆLS*. Moreover, the proportions of correlative constructions among temporal subordinate clauses are very low, ranging from 0% to 13% as opposed to 6% to 93% in *ÆLS*. Interestingly, in *Mirk*, where the frequency of temporal subordinate clauses is lower than in the other Middle English texts, adverbial *þa* is considerably more frequent and the proportion of correlative constructions is greater. Further, *Mirk* has a proportionately higher frequency of *then when*, and we even find other temporal subordinating conjunctions in combination with *then*.

On the whole, higher frequencies of adverbial *þa* and *then* appear to go together with lower frequencies of temporal subordinate clauses and greater proportions of correlation. The fact that the later samples show higher proportions of temporal subordinate clauses agrees with the alledged development towards hypotaxis (cf. Rynell 1952; on text types and taxis in the history of English, cf. Wårvik 1994).

Finally, I wish to deal with a more detailed question concerning the changes affecting *þa* and *þonne*: the disappearance of their conjunctive uses. The following discussion concentrates on *SEL*, where we find instances of both *þa*$_{conjunction}$ and *when* (cf. Table 2).

Though the non-narrative counterpart of *þa*, i.e. *þonne*, occurs in *SEL*, there are no instances of *þonne* as a conjunction in this sample. *þa*, however, occurs both as an adverbial and as a conjunction. Comparing the frequencies of *þa* and *þonne* as adverbials in the earlier texts (cf. Table 1), we see that the frequencies of *þa* are much lower in *SEL* than in *ÆLS*, while the frequencies of *þonne* are almost equal. When we consider this difference together with the higher frequency of temporal subordinate clauses in *SEL*, we are rather led to expect that *þonne*$_{conjunction}$ would be fairly frequent in this sample.

As noted above, *þa* and *þonne*, both as adverbial and as conjunction, are distinguished by their different discourse roles: *þa* is used in narrative contexts and *þonne* in non-narrative contexts. The non-occurrence of *þonne*$_{conjunction}$ in *SEL* raises the question of how its discourse roles are realised. Table 3 presents the distribution of *þa*$_{conjunction}$ and *when* in different discourse contexts in *SEL*.

Table 3: *Discourse contexts of* þa$_{conjunction}$ *and* when *in a sample of* SEL

DISCOURSE CONTEXT	*þa*$_{conjunction}$*	*when**
	N	N
NARRATIVE		
past singular event		
simple past	120	2
pluperfect	29	0
past repeated event	0	9
past hypothetical event	0	1
REPORTED SPEECH		
past singular event (narrative)		
simple past	4	0
pluperfect	1	0
present event	0	13
future event	0	2
present hypothetical event	0	3
past event, present perfect	0	3
COMMENTARY		
past situation	1	4
present situation	0	3

* variant forms are subsumed under the main entry

The data in Table 3 suggest that *when* is first introduced in those discourse contexts which were earlier occupied by *þonne*$_{conjunction}$. Later, *when* expands also to the discourse contexts of *þa*$_{conjunction}$; this is the situation in *Mirk* and *GL*.

In *SEL*, we find *þa*$_{conjunction}$ in clauses depicting past singular events; the majority of these events are given in the simple past tense, while the rest (19%) are in the pluperfect. Temporal subordinate clauses introduced by *þa*$_{conjunction}$ occur in narrative passages, usually in the narrative proper but also in stories within reported speeches (3%). Only one *þa*$_{conjunction}$ is found in a clause of commentary, and there, too, it refers to a past event. In sum, *þa*_{conjunction} is used in its traditional discourse contexts: in narrative, foregrounded story-line clauses.

In contrast to *þa*_{conjunction}, *when* does not occur in narrative contexts; there are only two instances of *when* in clauses depicting past singular events. Instead, in narrative passages, *when* is used to introduce clauses depicting past events that are repeated, i.e. habitual, or hypothetical. Within reported speech, *when*-clauses depict present, future, and hypothetical events; there are also three instances of present perfect. Further, *when*-clauses are found in commentary, referring to both past and present events. All of these uses are typical of *þonne*, both as an adverbial and as a conjunction.

The difference in discourse roles between *þa*_{conjunction} and *when* can be illustrated by the following examples from *SEL*:

> Þo Dacian þis isei . is wit him was nei bynome
> Mahon he sede hou geþ þis . war is þi mihte bicome
> Wanne i ne may þis foule þeof . ouercome in none wise
> (*SEL* 33, 73-75)
> 'When Dacian saw this . his reason was almost taken from him
> "Mahon", he said, "how is this happening . where is your might gone
> when I cannot this foul thief . overcome in any way'

> þo hi come hom to his In : he made hom faire chere
> & cortesliche serueþe hom : quinte man as he were.
> ac euer whan he from hom turneþe : þ^e teres ourne of his eie;
> ac fair semblant he made y-nou : euer whan hi him seie.
> (*SEL* 59, 139-142)
> 'When they came home to his inn : he made them a nice feast
> and kindly served them : the courteous man that he was.
> but always when he turned from them : tears ran from his eyes;
> but he showed a good enough appearance : always when they saw him.'

> þis kniȝt stod a-midde þe water : no wonder þe him wo were,
> whan he sei þat þis wilde bestes : his sones awei bere;
> (*SEL* 59, 91-92)
> 'this knight stood in the middle of the water : no wonder that he was in grief,
> when he saw that wild beasts : carried away his sons;'

> Þat folk of þe cite was adrad . to þe duk hi sede
> [... reported speech ...]
> Þo þe duk ihurde þis . adrad he was wel sore

(*SEL* 14, 95-98)
'the people of the city were afraid : to the duke they said
[... reported speech ...]
when the duke heard this he was frightened very badly'

4. Conclusion

This paper has presented an investigation of the changes involving *þa* and *þonne*, and *then* and *when* in Middle English. In Old English *þa* acts in important discourse roles, and the distinction between *þa* and *þonne* is discourse-dependent. The samples of Old and Middle English narrative texts studied for this investigation give us some suggestions about how *þa* begins to lose its prominent role. Obviously, comparable samples of other kinds of texts need to be studied to confirm the generality of the findings.

First, the distinction between *þa* and *þonne* is maintained in Early Middle English, but in Late Middle English the longer form, *then,* prevails. Though the shorter form, *þa,* can occasionally be found in later texts and *tho* still occurs dialectally, the different discourse roles of *þa* and *þonne* are no longer distinguished by the different forms.

Secondly, the frequencies of $þa_{adverbial}$ and *then* are generally lower in Middle English narratives than in Old English. As a third point, concomitantly with this tendency, there appears to exist an inverse relation between the frequency of $þa_{adverbial}$ and the frequency of temporal subordinate clauses introduced by $þa_{conjunction}$, *when* and related conjunctions.

In the fourth place, it seems that the conjunctive use of *þonne* disappears earlier than that of *þa*. Moreover, the distinction between *þa* and *þonne* as adverbials persists longer than the conjunctive use of *þonne*. On the basis of the distribution of $þa_{conjunction}$ and *when* in *SEL* it can be suggested that the discourse roles of $þonne_{conjunction}$ are taken over by *when*. In other words, *when* is first introduced in the discourse contexts of $þonne_{conjunction}$ and only later begins to appear in the contexts of $þa_{conjunction}$.

In conclusion, it appears that the changes involving the uses of Old and Middle English *þa* and *þonne* can be elucidated by considering their different discourse functions. The data reported in this paper give grounds for suggesting that the shorter form, *þa*, which was used in narrative contexts, remained longer in use as a conjunction than the longer form, *þonne*, which typically occurred in non-narrative contexts. In the adverbial uses, however, *þa* gave way to *þonne*, but at the same time, the frequency of this discourse marker in narrative decreased.

From the perspective of their discourse roles, it is interesting to observe that the conjunction associated with story-line materials (i.e. *þa*) persists longer than its non-narrative counterpart *þonne*, while it is the adverbial associated with off-story-line, backgrounded material (*þonne*) that finally prevails over the foreground marker *þa*. In the disappearance of *þa*, the form certainly plays a role, as on the one hand, *þa* has numerous homonyms, and on the other hand, reductions are likely to affect it more heavily than *þonne*. However, the fact that *þonne* is first to adopt unambiguous forms for the adverbial and the conjunction gives reason to suspect that the discourse role of *þa* in narratives may have promoted its longer use as a conjunction compared with *þonne*.

Notes

1. The following lives are included in this study (numbers refer to the editions):

    ÆLS: Agatha (8), Agnes (7), Alban (19), Cecily (34), Denis (29), Edmund (32) Eustace (30), George (14), Lucy (9), Mark (15), Peter (10), Sebastian (5), Swithun (21), Thomas (36)

    SEL: Agatha (14), Agnes (8), Alban (46), Cecily (74), Denis (67), Edmund (77), Eustace (59), George (33), Lucy (82), Mark (34), Peter (48), Sebastian (7), Swithun (50), Thomas (83)

    Mirk: George (31), Jacob (50), Katherine (67), Mark (32), Martin (66), Matthew (18,60), Peter & Paul (45), Philip & Jacob (33), Simon & Jude (63), Stephen (7), Thomas (5)

    GL: Agatha, Agnes, Albon, Cecily, Denis, Edmund, Eustace, George, Lucy, Mark, Peter, Sebastian, Swithun, Thomas

2. Translations of *ÆLS* are from Skeat (ed.) 1966. Other translations are by BW.

3. In this paper I use the form *þa* to refer to all the variants of the shorter form, such as *þo* and *tho*; similarly, *þonne* is used for the longer forms, subsuming *þanne*, *thanne*, *than*, *then*, *thenne*; and *when* refers to all the variants, such as *hwanne*, *whan*, *hwenne*, and *whenne*.

Primary sources

ÆLS

Skeat, Walter W. (ed.)

1966 *Ælfric's Lives of Saints* (Early English Text Society, Original Series, Vols. 76, 82, 94, 114). [first published 1881–1900, reprinted as two volumes 1966] London: Oxford University Press.

GL

Ellis, Frederick S. (ed.)

1892 *The Golden Legend by Master William Caxton*. Facsimile reprint. 3 vols. London.

Mirk

Erbe, Theodor (ed.)

1905 *Mirk's Festial*. (Early English Text Society, Extra Series, 96). London: Kegan Paul, Trench, Trübner & Co.

SEL

D'Evelyn, Charlotte and Anna J. Mill (eds.)

1956 *The South English Legendary* (Early English Text Society, 235, 236). London: Oxford University Press. Lives no: 7, 8, 14, 33, 34, 46, 48, 50, 67, 77, 82, 83.

Horstmann, Carl (ed.)

1887 *The Early South English Legendary* (Early English Text Society, 87). London: Trübner & Co. Lives: 59, 74.

References

Andrew, S. O.

1940 *Syntax and Style in Old English*. Cambridge: Cambridge University Press.

Enkvist, Nils Erik, and Brita Wårvik

1987 "Old English *þa*, temporal chains, and narrative structure". In: Anna Giacalone Ramat, Onofrio Carruba and Giuliano Bernini (eds.). *Papers from the 7th International Conference on Historical Linguistics* (*Current Issues in Linguistic Theory*, 48). Amsterdam: Benjamins, 221-237.

Foster, Robert

1975 " The use of *þa* in Old and Middle English narratives." *Neuphilologische Mitteilungen* 77, 404-414.

Haiman, John, and Sandra A. Thompson

1984 "'Subordination' in universal grammar". *Proceedings of the Tenth International Meeting of the Berkeley Linguistic Society*, 510-523.

Helsinki Corpus

> *The Helsinki Corpus of English Texts: Diachronic Part.* The International Computer Archive for Modern English. Bergen: The Norwegian Computing Centre for the Humanities.

Lehmann, Christian

> 1988   "Towards a typology of clause linkage." In: John Haiman and Sandra A. Thompson (eds.). *Clause Combining in Grammar and Discourse* (*Typological Studies in Language*, 18). Amsterdam: Benjamins, 181-225.

Mitchell, Bruce

> 1985   *Old English Syntax.* 2 Vols. Oxford: Clarendon Press.

Oxford English Dictionary (OED)

> 1989   2nd edition. Prepared by Simpson, J. A. & E. S. C. Weiner. 20 Vols. Oxford: Clarendon Press.

Rynell, Alarik

> 1952   "Parataxis and hypotaxis as a criterion of syntax and style." *Lunds Universitets Årsskrift*, N.F. 1, Bd 48, Nr 3.

Wårvik, Brita

> 1987   "On text strategies in Old English narrative prose". In: Heikki Nyyssönen, Riitta Kataja, and Vesa Komulainen (eds.). *CDEF86. Papers from the Conference of Departments of English in Finland.* Oulu: University of Oulu, 77-92.

> 1990   "On grounding in English narratives: A diachronic perspective." In: Sylvia Adamson, Vivien A. Law, Nigel Vincent, and Susan Wright (eds.). *Papers from the 5th International Conference on English Historical Linguistics* (*Current Issues in Linguistic Theory*, 65). Amsterdam: Benjamins, 559-575.

> 1991   "In search of orality in the history of English: A study in signals of textual organization." In: Svetla Cmejrková, František Daneš, and Eva Havlová (eds.). *Writing vs Speaking: Language, Text, Discourse, Communication* (*Tübinger Beiträge zur Linguistik*, 392). Tübingen: Gunter Narr, 383-388.

Waterhouse, Ruth

> 1984   "Sentence determination in Ælfric's *Lives of Saints*." *Neuphilologische Mitteilungen* 85: 257-272.

Middle English *þo* and other Narrative Discourse Markers

Monika Fludernik
University of Freiburg, Germany

In 1979 Paul J. Hopper presented a ground-breaking analysis of word order in OE prose. He argued that the use of three different word order patterns ~ in OE narrative prose could be explained in terms of relative focus or foregrounding. Changes of the subject receive the greatest emphasis and are structured according to the verb-subject-object pattern (VSO), neutral narrative events are rendered in a SOV pattern, and backgrounded phrases have SVO patterns. The most marked foregrounding structure is that which has a verb-first pattern, and it can be compared with German verb-first patterns at story onset-points (particularly in jokes: *Kommt der Bauer in die Stadt; Trifft der Joseph den Hugo am Marktplatz*). As Riehl (1993) has noted, this pattern is quite common in the history of the German language, and its pervasiveness throws some doubt on the famous verb-second thesis. Recent research has modified and downtoned this hypothesis in any case. Compare, for instance, the discussion of the notorious verb-second thesis in Betten (1987: 121-125) as well as in Ebert (1978: 34-43). Verb-first patterns are fairly rare in contemporary English although they persist in traditional ballads and at the beginning of folktales: *Lived a king in the land of the fairies.* The verb-first pattern is also found in a restricted number of set phrases: *Came a long and weary time.*[1] Unlike the OE pattern, Modern English can employ the verb-first strategy only with presentatives and intransitives. Compare: **Gives John book to Jill;* or **Reads book John.*

A second common structural feature of OE has been discovered by Wårvik and Enkvist. In their 1987 paper on the use of OE *þa* Enkvist and Wårvik noted that major narrative plot-advancing clauses were employing a *þa* + V + NP (=S) pattern and hypothesised that *þa* was used to mark the continuation of the plot, in other words that it served the function of a discourse marker. Hopper's examples of the V + S pattern in fact regularly employ *þa*,

with conjoined narrative clauses using *ond* + NP + O + V (usually without an
explicit subject), and backgrounded subsidiary clauses have the explicit anaphor
he and also a structure of S (=NP) + O + V (1979: 54-55). In the *þa*-clause the
object can be added in clause-final position and some specifying temporal
constituents may be inserted between *þa* and the verb:

> *þa geascode he þone syning*
> ond hine þær berad
> ond þone bur utan beeode
> *ond þa ongeat se syning þæt*
> ond he on þa duru eode
> *ond þa unheanlice hine werede*
> oþ he on þone æpeling locude
> *ond þa utræsde on hine*
> ond hine micle gewundode
> ond hie alle on þone cyninge wæron feohtende
> oþ þæt hie hine ofslægenne hæfdon.

> '*Then he found the king/* And overtook him there/ And surrounded the hut/ *And
> then the king perceived it/* And went out of the door/ *And defended himself
> valiantly/* Until he saw the nobleman/ *And then he rushed out upon him/* And
> wounded him grievously/ And they all began to fight against the king/ Until they
> had slain him.' (Hopper 1979b: 54-55)[2]

In the present paper I will attempt to follow the development of OE *þa* in a
selected number of ME texts[3] and trace the eventual elimination of *þa/þo* and its
replacement by a different set of discourse markersdiscourse markers. The
results of the analysis can be summarised as follows: ME *þo* appears pervasively
in *verse* narrative but has already been supplanted by *þan* in the *Northern
Homily Cycle* and in the fifteenth-century life of Margery Kempe. Chaucer
employs neither *þo* nor *þan* with any frequency. *Þan* occurs regularly in *The
Gilte Legende* but has disappeared as the ruling discourse marker by the time of
Caxton. Malory still uses *þenne*, but also has *so* as a frequent alternative
discourse marker.

The elimination of *þo* appears to relate to the triple function of *þo* as
observable in the *(Early) South English Legendary (ESEL/SEL)*. Curiously, in
ESEL the *þo* + V + S construction is extremely rare: *Þo gan seint Iohan to
weope sore* ("St. John"; *ESEL* 410: 283[4]). The *SEL*, by contrast, has numerous
instances of the old *þo* + V + S pattern:

Þo gan þis holyman to speke ("St. Lawrence"; *SEL* II 364: 167)

Þo let he fecche Katerine ("St. Katherine"; *SEL* II 542: 275)

On the other hand, *þo* frequently appears in postposed position:

Huy crieden ȝeorne on ore louerd þo : and in penaunce huy were,
In fastingue and in oresones : þritti dawes þere.
Þo tur[n]de þat gold bi-fore heore eiȝene : into bowes of treo,
And þe ȝymmes into harde stones : ase huy hadden er i-beo.
("St. John"; *ESEL* 411: 307-10)

Hi cride *þo* in Iesu Crist . and in penance were
In fastinge and in orisons . þritti dawes þere
Þo turnde þat gold biuore hare eiȝene
("St. John the Evangelist"; *SEL* II 603: 309-11)

Glad was þo þis Iustice . of wordes þat he [St. Lawrence] sede
For hope of þe grete tresour ("St. Lawrence"; *SEL* II 361: 74-75)

Note that the last example has expressive preposing, operating much in the same way as the initial *þo*-construction. Compare also "Iredi was þat folk *þo*" ("St. Bartholomew"; *SEL* II 378: 147).

In all these examples, *þo*, although no longer in clause-initial position and no longer triggering the VP + NP word order, nevertheless functions much as a discourse marker ~ *þo*. Compare the German equivalents

Da sprach der König,...
Der König sagte da,...

More syntactic variation occurs in "Lo seide þapostles *þo* . þat ȝe alle iseo" ("St. Simon and St. Jude"; *SEL* II 455: 203).

Discourse-uses of *þo* occur even without any 'preposing' patterns and are marked additionally by the paragraph signal in the manuscript:

¶ Þe oþer ssrewen lowe *þo* . and sede þat hi so spake
For þe duc ssolde al oneiware . of is fon be[o] itake
("Simon and St. Jude"; *SEL* II 452: 109-10)

"¶ Seint Quintin was *þo* at Rome" *(SEL* II 456: 13), on the other hand, in spite of the paragraph marker (the episode incipit[5] is marked instead by the use of the proper name in verse-initial position), needs to be read as 'then' or 'once' without any discourse function. "St. Quentin" has a great choice of such *þo* uses which can be quite ambiguous between discourse readings and readings as temporal adverbials:

¶   Þemperour sende þo . in to eche londe
      To turmenti Cristene men ("St. Quentin"; *SEL* II 457: 21-22)

¶   Wele þat þe iustise . was wroþ & gram þo (Ibid., 457: 41)

This, in context, may be both 'then'/'as a consequence' or discourse-functional
'*da*'.

¶   Þe iustise was þo so wroþ . þat he nuste non oþer dede
      (Ibid., 457: 53)

He let þo walle pich . & gresse & ooylle also (Ibid., 459: 89)

Þe iustise let nyme þo . spites of ire tueye (Ibid., 459: 103)

These are all discourse-functional uses of þo, but the word order does not
conform to the standard pattern.

The most common use of þo in *ESEL*, which is also very frequent in the
SEL, is that in the function of a conjunction:

Þo he couþe gon ant speke : he ne pleide neuere mo,
Ake ȝwane oþur children rageden faste : to churche he wolde go
("St. Brendan"; *ESEL* 240: 9-10).

Þo he was to londe i-come : ase him þouȝte ful longue er,
Þat child he sette a-donn to grounde
("St. Christopher"; *ESEL* 274: 99-100)

A-Morewe, so sone ase hit was day: þe bischop after teofle [Theophilus]
sende,
Þat he to him wel hasteliche : with-oute ani defaute wende.
Merci he criede wel deolfulliche: þo he to him cam
("St. Theophilus"; *ESEL* 290: 73-75)

Compare, in the *SEL*, in the Legend of St. Bartholomew:

Þo þe angel hadde al þis ido . to heuene he flei anhei (*SEL* II 380: 191)

Þo þe king hurde þis . sori he was inou (*SEL* II 381: 233)

As, which frequently occurs in the meaning of 'when', shares most syntactic
environments with the conjunction þo:

As sein Ion þe waungelist . vorþore wende þere
and boþe þis men forþ wiþ him . þat so riche of golde were
A ded man toward buringe . me broȝte up a bere
("St. John"; *SEL* II 602: 277-79)

For *ase* he criede on hire so ӡeorne : þat swete mayde so hende
Cudde hire milde-hede, and fram heouene : to him a-doun gan wende.
("St. Theophilus"; *ESEL* 291: 107-8)

As occurs with particular frequency after "adeictic" (Harweg 1974) temporal specifications:

A-Morewe, *so sone ase* was day ("St. Theophilus"; *ESEL* 290: 73)

In a dai *as* al þis folk . to þis temple was ibroӡt
("St. Bartholomew"; *SEL* II 376: 81)
As he was in churche a day ("St. Giles"; *SEL* II 384: 13)

¶   Þe Sonedai þere after . *as* sein Gile masse song
("St. Giles"; *SEL* II 389: 133)

ESEL also has *so þat* as a discourse marker in the function of 'as':

So þat hi come in þe see .[...] þis gode man his sone sende
("St. Nicholas"; *SEL* II 562: 373-4)

So þat seint Iohan in a time : to þat Bishop cam,
Aftur ӡwam he bi-tok him er in warde : guode ӡeme a-boute he nam.
("St. John"; *ESEL* 414: 395-96)[6]

There are two further uses of *þo*. One of these occurs in expressive constructions:

Þo was þis Quiene sori i-novӡ! : in grete deole and fere
hire sauter heo nam on honde: ("St. Kenelm"; *ESEL* 355: 338-39)

Þo can also be employed as a purely temporal adverbial in the meaning of 'then' where it no longer triggers a discourse-marker reading and co-occurs with an NP + VP word order:

Symon and Iude þat were *þo* . in þe lond alle beie (*SEL* II 451: 86)

He esste anon wat hi were . and wat he þere *þo* soӡt (*SEL* II 451: 88).

ESEL even has anticipations of the Chaucerian *þis*-construction, which reintroduces protagonists at the beginning of new episodes:

Þis ӡongue Man þat was to liue a-rerd: bi-heold þeos oþure tweiӡe
("St. John"; *ESEL* 411: 291)[7]

Compare in Chaucer:

> In Londoun was a preest, an annueleer [...]
> ... I wol procede as now,
> And telle forth my tale of the chanoun
> That broghte this preest to confusioun.
> **This false chanon** cam upon a day
> Unto this preestes chambre
> ("The Canon's Yeoman's Tale" G 1012-1023; Chaucer 1988: 276)
>
> **This Pandarus** gan newe his tong affile [...]
> (*Troilus and Criseyde* II 1681; Chaucer 1988: 512)

To summarise: *þo* occurs in initial position as a discourse marker ~ at foreground episode incipits, equalling the function of OE *þa* in the Hopper examples from the *Anglo-Saxon Chronicle*. Secondly, *þo* is used as a conjunction and in this case follows the 'backgrounded' word order of *þo* + NP + V (*þo Decius hurde þis*). Thirdly, *þo* begins to be used in the meaning of 'then' and comes to be placed *after* the VP.

There are additional *þo* forms which further help to ambiguate the meaning and function of *þo*. Sometimes *þo* appears to be a variant of *þei* ('though'):

> Swete Louerd quaþ þis holyman . ich bidde þe milce and ore
> For *þo* þat ich was acused . i ne uorsok þe noȝt
> Ac þo me asked ich was iknewe . of þe wiþ worde & þoȝt
> ("St. Lawrence"; *SEL* II 362: 124-26)[8]

The same legend also has two uses of *þo* in what appears to be the discourse marker function with non-standard word order.

> Decius *þo* þe emperor . ferde as he were wod (Ibid., 362: 115)

The emperor has been engaged in threatening St. Lawrence for the past fifty lines of the text, but has so far remained unnamed. The question is therefore whether the line should read 'Decius, the then emperor,'[9] or whether this is a post-posed discourse-*þo*. There is a second atypical passage further down which also combines the backgrounded NP + VP pattern with *þo*:

> Oules he let nyme of ire . þat harde were inou
> And is fleiss þat er was bileued . þer wiþ me todrou
> *þo* is fleiss was so todrawe . þat reuþe it was to se[o]
> þeof he sede ȝute þe sselt . in more torment be[o]
> ("St. Lawrence"; *SEL* II 363: 145-48).

Þo can be read both as the discourse marker~ in ME*þo* of *þo ȝan he his eiȝen upcaste* and as resultative 'then'. The latter reading would anticipate uses of *þenne* and *þan* in fifteenth-century prose (Malory and *The Gilte Legende*).

The status of flux that can be observed in the *(E)SEL* can be documented further by the proliferation of other adverbials such as *anone*, and by the accumulation of several discourse markers within one line:

> *Þo* com *þer* a swete uois . adoun fram heuene *anon*
> ("St. Lawrence"; *SEL* II 363: 133)

> Þe ssrewe tolde *þanne* men . þat is wonder miȝte ise[o]
> þat he hadde þe man iheld . wiþ is holy miȝte inou
> ("St. Bartholomew"; SEL II 374: 20-21)

> *Anon so* he sede is orison ("St. Giles"; SEL II 385: 25)

> Glad was þe paintor *þo þerwiþ* . for he ne couþe no such make
> Þe king Abakar was gladdore . *þo* it him was betake.
> ("St. Simon and St. Jude"; SEL II 450: 43-44)

In the last passage postposed discourse-*þo* is followed by *þerwiþ*, and in the second line *þo* is used as a conjunction. Further down one has:

> Glad was þe king *þo* ('when') he him isei . to him he seide *anon*
> (Ibid., 450: 58)

Here *anon* has the function of 'then' as an adverbial, whereas a few lines later one has

> ¶   Sein Iude wende forþ *anon* (Ibid., 451: 71)

This is an episode incipit in which *anon* at least subliminally works as a discourse marker. Note also that in line 58 *anon* comes after an O + S + V structure (*to him he seide anon*), with a preposing construction that echoes that of "Glad was þe king".

Besides *anon* and *so*, *there*-constructions also interact at incipit points:

> Riȝt *as* hi þis dede dude . a voiȝ *þer* com anon
> From heuene ("All Saints"; *SEL* II 460: 119-20)

Incipits in Chaucer and Gower frequently employ an *it befell*-construction or adeictic markers (Harweg 1974), and this already appears in the *SEL*, too:

> A Gyw was while *in a tyme* ("St. Nicholas"; *SEL* II 563: 411)

> *In a tyme* hit biful (Ibid., 563: 417)

So far I have argued that there appears to be an old *þo*-pattern in which *þo* operates as a discourse marker~ in ME and which survives into the late fourteenth- and early fifteenth-century texts. There are some few instances still in Capgrave's *Saint Katherine*, but none in Lydgate, *The Gilte Legende* or in Caxton. In the fifteenth-century texts *then, than, thenne, thanne* predominate, *þo* having already been replaced by different incipit structures as early as Chaucer, Gower and the *Northern Homily Cycle*. The analysis of the *SEL* suggests a development in which *þo* becomes ambiguous between different functions (as a discourse marker~ in ME, adverbial or conjunction) and different syntactic arrangements (clause-initial, post-verbal) and then starts to compete with other conjunctions (*as, so, when, anon*) and adverbials (*anon*). One could therefore argue that *þo* loses its strictness of syntactic application and that, as a consequence, the other discourse markers gain ground. The *when...then* syntagm wins out over all competitors in the fifteenth century, presumably under the influence of French *quand*-clauses, which may have strengthened the *when* and *then* patterns in translations such as *The Gilte Legende*.[10]

> *And whanne* these princes knewe this by the portour that priueli hadd told hem, thei rente her clothes and cried, weping bitterly. *And thanne* Neponcien remembered hym how blessid Seint Nicholas hadde deliuered thre innocentes, and preied his felawes that thei wolde require his helpe. ("St. Nicholas"; *Three Lives* 57: 9-14)

> *And whanne* the holi man wost it he praied these thre princes to come with hym in haste, *and whanne* he come to the place there as thei schuld be biheded he fonde hem on her kneis, thaire eyghen bounde, and the man loftyng up his swerde redi ouer her [hedis]. *And thanne* Seint Nicholas sette afere with the loue of God putte hymselff hardeli bitwene hem and toke the suerde of the mannes honde and caste it fer from hym, and vnbounde her eyghen and ledde the innocentis sauf with hym. (Ibid., 56: 8-15)

This pattern of development, however, does not tell the story quite truthfully since it assumes an easy transition from a situation of uniformity through a turbulent period of competition and ambiguity to another fairly stable distribution of a new set of forms. The story is much more complicated than that. Not only does the evidence from the *St. Katherine* group already hint at the same kind of ambiguity and variation that is documented in the *SEL*; these early texts also already contain incipit structures which are typical of Chaucer's narrative. Nor can a unitary development be postulated for either the prose or the verse writing.

To illustrate. The early thirteenth-century *Seinte Katerine* has a few examples of *þa* as a discourse marker~ in ME

> *Þa* ontswerede þe an swiðe prudeliche þus to þe prude prince
> (*Seinte Katerine* 30-32: 213-14)

but also instances of *þa* as a conjunction in the meaning of 'when':

> *Þa* he [þus hefde] iseid, cleopede an of his men dearnliche to him
> (Ibid., 22: 147-48)

> *Þa* þis wes ido þus, het eft þe keiser þet me schulde Katerine bringe beuoren him
> (Ibid., 74: 527-76: 528)

Compare also, in *Þe Liflade* [...] *of Seinte Iuliene*:

> Þe reue *þa* he herde þis het hire hon up ant hongin biþe toppe. ant swa me dude sone. (*Liflade* Roy. 17 A xxvii; 24: 200-201)

> *Þa* elewsius iseh þis *þ*[111] ha þus feng on to festnen hire seoluen þohte *þ*[t] he walde anan don hire ut of dahene (Ibid., 24: 211-12)

In addition, there are numerous constructions with demonstrative *þis* much on the lines of the later Chaucerian pattern:

> *Þeos meiden* lette lutel of [al] þet he seide (*Seinte Katerine*, 20: 129)

> *This Troilus,* as he was wont to gide

> His yonge knyghtes, lad hem up and down
> In thilke large temple on every side
> (*Troilus and Criseyde* I 183-85; Chaucer 1988: 475)

There are even a fair number of incipits that have a pure S + V pattern:

> *Þe keiser* bistearede hire wið swi[ð]e steape (*Seinte Katerine* 18: 111)

> *Ha* onswerede ant seide (Ibid., 26: 168)

In addition, *þa* occurs in postposed position in the function of a discourse marker:

> [Feng] *þa* Porphire to freinen þis meiden (Ibid., 86: 598)

> Onswerèdé *þa* þe an (Ibid., 69: 603)

As and *þus* also already appear in this early text:

Þus hwil ha wiste hire, ant þohte a to witen hire, meiden i meiðhad, *as* ha
set in a [bur] of hire burde-boldes ha iherde a swuch nurð towart te
aweariede maumetes temple (Ibid., 8: 49-51)

as ha þis iherde ant nuste ʒet [h]wet hit wes, ha sende swiðe forte witen
hwet wunder hit were. (Ibid., 10: 53-54)

As he iseid hefde, bisohten as ha stoden, alle in a steuene, þet tes meiden
moste i þe wurðschipe of Godd wið halwende weattres bihealden ham
alle. (Ibid., 72: 507-9)

In the *St. Margaret* legend *þa* as clause-initial discourse marker occurs a few
times:

[A]s ha biheold, lokinde up-on hire riht-half, *þa* seh ha hwer set an
unsehen unwiht (*Seinte Marherete* 24: 20-21)

Wið þis, *þa* þudde ha o þe þurs feste wið hire fot, wið euch-an of þeose
word (Ibid., 28: 20-21)

[E]fter þeos bone, *þa* beah ha þe swire *t*[12] cweð to þe cwellere
(Ibid., 50: 21-22)

Þa þa can also be found in postverbial position in the function of a discourse
marker~ in ME, most commonly in conjunction with a *verbum dicendi:*

[C]omen lihtin[d]e *þa* þe engles of leome, *t* seten ant sungen on hir bodi
bilehwit, *t* iblesceden hit. (Ibid., 52: 4)

"Wumme! leafdi," quoð he *þa*, "wa me mine liues, bute ich hit am þet
weorri a wið rihtwise" (Ibid., 30: 32-33)[13]

"Ah þu wurchest," quoð ha, *þa*, to Olibrium þe luðere, "þine feader
werkes, þe feondes of helle" (Ibid., 14: 26-28)

þet liht a-lei lutlen, *t* heo biturde hire *þa t* cweð to þet unwhit [sic!]
(Ibid., 30: 4-5)

Another thirteenth-century text, the story of the fox and the wolf in the well,
also employs *þo* regularly, but again in two functions: that of the clause-initial
discourse-marker followed by VP + NP, and in the function of a temporal
conjunction *þo*. Examples of initial discourse markers:

Þo eroust bigon þe vox to erne ("Of þe vox and of þe wolf", 16[14])

And *þo* eroust kom wiit to him (Ibid., 124)

Þo gon þe wolf sore agrise (Ibid., 240)

Þo hede þe wreche fomen I-nowe (Ibid., 288)

Examples of the conjunctive use:

To late þe vox wes biþout,
Þo he wes in þe ginne I-brout (Ibid., 81-82)

Þo he com amidde þe putte,
Þe wolfe þene vox opward mette (Ibid., 241-42)

Þo þat hit com to þe time
Þat hoe shulden arisen Ine (Ibid., 263-64)

Þoþo also once occurs in the discourse-marker function in postponed position:

"Vuolf," quod þe vox him *þo* (Ibid., 221)

The diversity of *þo* in its various uses and functions can, in fact, be traced back even earlier to the twelfth century. In the twelfth-century *Early English Homilies (EEH) þa* occurs not merely in the patterns reserved for OE *þa*, although that use is pervasive:

Þa wearð se cyng to þan swyðe afyrht, $þ^t$ he eall ascranc, 7^{15} man him lædde to þone wytege Daniel. (*EEH* 37: 23-25)

Þa cwæð Darius se cyng to Daniele þan wytega (*EEH* 38: 17)

Þa þohte ic $þ^t$ $þ^t$ wære seo helle, þe ic oft on life embesecgen geherde (*EEH* 116: 28-29)

Additional constituents can be inserted between *þa* and the verb:

Þa æfter sumen fyrste wurden heo ungesome, Philippus 7 Areth (*EEH* 53: 32-33)

Þa æfter þrym dagen com an þæs caseres þeignen, Libanus gehaten, 7 gesohte þæs biscopes fet, fulhtes biddende (*EEH* 51: 20-22)

Þa betwux þysen, gelamp $þ^t$ Herodes, swa we ær cwæden, his wyten gefeormode on þan dæige þe he geboren wæs (*EEH* 54: 27-28)

In the following sentence *þa* appears to have been repeated hypercorrectly both initially and after the main verb, probably because a full subsidiary clause has been inserted before the verb and the syntax might otherwise have become unclear:

Þa for þan intingan þe he cwæð, "Syle for me 7 for þe", wenden *þa* þa oðre apostles $þ^t$ Petrus wære fyrmest, 7 axodan *þa* þone Hælend, hwa wære formest manna on heofona rice. (*EEH* 62: 8-11)

See also the following two examples:

> Ða mid þam þe þæt wif gehyrde þæs mædenes gretynge, *þa* blissode þæt cild Johannes on his moder innoðe, 7 seo moder wearð afylled mid þan Halegan Gaste (*EEH* 148: 14-17)

Þa also occurs regularly, though less frequently, in non-initial position. Most commonly *þa is* placed second after an initial NP, the subject, with the verb either following directly after *þa* or with an adverbial phrase interposed between *þa* and the verb:

> Daniel *þa* worhte þan drace þas lac. (*EEH* 40: 23-24)

> Julianus *þa* ongan to lufigene hæðengeld, 7 his cristendome wiðsoc (*EEH* 50: 14-15)

> Ða ealdres 7 þa boceres *þa* cidden þᵗ Crist mid þan synfullen mannen wæs etende. (*EEH* 60: 10-12)

> Joseph *þa* up stod 7 cwæð to Annam 7 Caipham (*EEH* 81: 37)

> Se cyng *þa* sone swyðe þæs fægenode 7 he(t) up ateon ardlice Daniel 7 þa inn awurpen þe hine wreigdon ær. (*EEH* 38: 27-28)

> Heo *þa* mid glæden mode him to gebrohten goldes, 7 seolfres, 7 deorewurðra gimmen ungerime heapes. (*EEH* 50: 36 - 51: 2)

> Ic *þa*, betwix þan werodan þan ængle folgede (*EEH* 117: 24-25)

A more substantial subsidiary clause is inserted between *þa* and the verb phrase in the following passage:

> Seo dohter *þa*, swa swa we ær cwæden, plegede mid hire mædenen on þan gebeorscipe (*EEH* 54: 30-31)

Þa comes in third place if the clause starts with the discourse marker 7:[16]

> 7 heo *þa* eall þᵗ land to cristendome awænden. (*EEH* 89: 24-25)

> 7 he *þa* mid þan worde him bead swylce lac swylce he sylf breac, þᵗ wæren þreo berene hlafes, for bletsunge. (*EEH* 50: 20-21)

In one case *þa* in this position (as in the earlier examples from the *SEL*) may actually be an adverbial 'then' or 'at that time':

> Darius *þa* se cyng on dæigred aras 7 eode to þan seaðe 7 sarlice clypode (*EEH* 38: 20-21)

Compare the earlier examples from the *SEL* given above.

Þa can also occur in second position after the *verb* and be followed by the noun phrase (subject):

Comen *þa* syððen his frynd, 7 his lic bebyredon. (*EEH* 53: 8-9)

If the subject has been elided, one gets V + *þa* + O:

Ongann *þa* sænden his ættrige wæpnen, *þ*ᵗ synd costnungen, togeanes þan halgen were. (*EEH* 130: 19-20)

Forleas *þa* on þan færelde his ænne scoh, 7 oðerne mid him to his gebedhuse ham gebrohte. (*EEH* 130: 35 - 131: 2)

One even finds the old O + V + S pattern, with *þa* inserted *after* the verb and *before* the subject in third position. The object position is here filled with an indirect object:

Heom com *þa* stefne of heofone þuss cweðende (*EEH* 82: 30)

Þa, in contrast to the OE usage, also occurs in quite atypical positions, particularly after an initial subject and verb (which may also have a clause-initial 7 preceding them):

Heo eodan *þa* ealle ut ætforen þan cynge (*EEH* 39: 33)

7 he æt *þa* sone of þære Godes sande, 7 se ængel ardlice eft Abacuc ferede to his lande ongean ofer swyðe langne weig. (*EEH* 41: 10)

Since the traditional use of *þa* in initial position and in the function of a discourse marker correlates with the incipit point of a narrative episode, it is particularly interesting to observe that the lexical incipit marker *hit gelamp* (which is later replaced by *it befil*) can be combined with *þa*, and that *þa* can be positioned both initially, before this idiom, and in third place after it. The phrase, of course, also occurs without any *þa*:

Hit gelamp eft syððen *þ*ᵗ he on swefne ane gesihðe beo him sylfen geseh (*EEH* 36: 24-25)

Þa betwux þysen, gelamp *þ*ᵗ Herodes, swa we ær cwæden, his wyten gefeormode on þan dæige þe he geboren wæs (*EEH* 54: 27)

Hit gelamp *þa þ*ᵗ he hine gebæd to his deofolgelde, 7 his twegen sunen hine mid swurde acwealden, swa swa se witega þurh Godes Gast gewitegode. (*EEH* 107: 9-11)

Hit gelamp on sume dæge, þa þa Godes ængles comen, 7 on his gesihþe stoden, *þa* wæs eac swylce se scucce heom betwux, to þan cwæð Drihten (*EEH* 123: 19-22)

When placed in clause-second position, *þa* also frequently follows a prepositional phrase or temporal adverbial, in contexts where from a present-day perspective one would tend to talk about preposed or topicalised constituents:

> Eft *þa* on þone seofoðen dæig eode se cyng sarig to þan seaðe 7 beseh into. (*EEH* 41: 12-13)

> Efne *þa* comen feola geferen 7 synfulle mænn, 7 sæten æt þære þenunge mid þan Hælende 7 his leorningenihten. (*EEH* 59: 12-13)

> Onmang þan *þa* stod *þære* sum of þan cæmpen, þe scolden habben gehealden þæs Hælendes byrigene (*EEH* 78: 35-37)

> Onmang þan *þa* com *þær* an scaðe, 7 an rode tacne on his exle bær. (*EEH* 87: 25-26)

Note in the first example how *eft þa* becomes one unit as a sequential discourse marker, with further adverbial specifications inserted before the V + S block. In the third and fourth example the collocation with *þær* is very prominent, to the point where one may start to consider *þa* as having lost its original function and having been absorbed into a presentative 'there'. This kind of use certainly anticipates later *there* constructions. Compare also:

> *Þa* comen *þære* þreo mære weres of Galilea to Jerusalem. (*EEH* 79: 35-36)

> *Þa* wæs *þær* geworden mycel stefne, 7 mycel liht swylc þunreslege 7 þuss cwæð (*EEH* 85: 23-24)

> On þære tide þe Ælfred, Norðhumre king, 7 Æðelred, Myrcene king, wunnen heom betweonan, *þa* æt sumen gefihte wearð an þeign Æðelredes kinges mid oþren cæmpen afelled, se wæs Ymme gehaten. (*EEH* 119: 20-23)

Already in these early homilies *þa* is also regularly used as a conjunction, most commonly in the construction *þa þa ... þa* and *hwæt þa*.
Þa þa ... þa:

> *Ða þa* Joseph hæfde þuss gespecan, *þa* wæs eall *þ*t folc blissigende wið him (*EEH* 82: 12-13)

> *Þa þa* se Hælend ferde on summere byrig, *þa* geseh he sitten ænne mann æt tollsetle, Matheus gehaten, 7 cwæð to him (*EEH* 59: 8-10)

Eft, *þa þa* seo halige cwen hine asænde, swa swa we nun hwon ær sædon, *þa* ferde his gast swiftlice (*EEH* 52: 2-3)

Hwæt þa:

> *Hwæt þa* þa Judeisce ealdres 7 bocheres *þ*^t gesegen, heo *þa* acsoden 7 cwædon to Cristes leorningcnihten (*EEH* 59: 13-15)

Most commonly, however, *hwæt þa* appears to correspond to clause-initial discourse marker *þa:*

> *Hwæt þa*, se cyng Ezechias awearp his purprene reaf, 7 dyde hære to his lice, 7 bær þa gewriten into Godes temple (*EEH* 106: 19-21)

> *Hwæt, þa*, an ængel of þan uplicen werode bebead þan gewæpnodan ængle þe þa sawle gelædde, *þ*^t heo eft heo ongean læden scolden to þan lichame, þe heo of gelædd wæs. (*EEH* 110: 7-10)

> *Hwæt þa* min latðeaw lædde me ongean to þære blostmbære stowe, 7 me befran, hweðer ic wyste hwæt þa þing wæren þe ic gesegen hæfde? (*EEH* 117: 29-32)

> *Hwæt þa* Job aras 7 totær his tunece, 7 his loccas forcearf, 7 feoll to eorðen, 7 cwæð (*EEH* 125:3-4)

> *Hwæt þa* Jobes gebroðre, 7 gesustren, ealle þa þe hine ær cuðen, comen him to, 7 hine gefrefrodan, 7 his mycel wundredan, 7 him geofe geafen. (*EEH* 128: 18-20)

Hwæt appears to operate as an intensifier of *þa* rather than as a separate discourse marker. There are no sentences with clause-initial *hwæt* (*not* followed by *þa*), and OE *hwæt* from *Beowulf* has already died out.

To return to the *þa þa ... þa* construction in the function of a conjunction. Besides the reduplicated *þa þa ... þa* one also finds *þa ... þa* in the meaning of 'as' or 'when'.

> *Þa* heo ham comen, *þa* sæden heo hwu heo gefaren hæfden (*EEH* 80: 30-31)

> *Þa* geherde seo helle *þ*^t hit wæs twygge geclyped, *þa* cleopode heo ongean 7 þuss cwæð (*EEH* 85: 26-27)

> *Þa* Dauid þuss gespecan hæfde, *þa* þær to becom se wulderfulle King on mannes gelicnysse, 7 þa gaten tobræc (*EEH* 85: 32-34)

> *Þa þ*^t folc of þære ceastre *þ*^t geherde *þ*^t Joseph wæs gecumen, *þa* comen heo ealle him togeanes 7 cwædon (*EEH* 81: 9-10)

Þa þa Judees *þ*ᵗ geherdan, *þ*ᵗ Joseph hæfde þæs Hælendes lichame abeden, *þa* sohten heo hine (*EEH* 78: 2-3)

That *þa þa* corresponds to the temporal conjunction *as* is corroborated by the translation of *cum transiret:*

> Se godspellere Matheus, þe we todæig wurðigeð, awrat beo him sylfen hwu se Hælend hine geceas to his geferrædden, þus cweðende, *Cum transiret Jesus, uidit hominem in theloneo sedentem, Matheum nomine. Et reliqua. Ða þa* se Hælend ferde on summere byrig, þa geseh he sitten ænne mann æt tollsetle, Matheus gehaten (*EEH* 59: 5-9)

There are also a few cases of *þa* in the meaning of a temporal conjunction introducing a subsidiary clause and without an anaphoric *þa* in the main clause, a usage which may have developed from a relative clause like the following:

> Ac on þære nihte *þa* se arlease cyng hine on morgen acwellen wolde, com Godes ængel scinende of heofone, 7 gelædde hine ut þurh þa isene geaten, 7 stod eft on morgen *þ*ᵗ cwartern fæste belocan. (*EEH* 108: 7-10)

Here is an example of *þa* as a simple conjunction:

> Þa Judees, *þa* heo *þ*ᵗ geherden, heo leten raðe ealle þa cæmpen heom to gefeccen, þe þæs Hælendes byrigene scolden healden 7 heom to cwæden (*EEH* 79: 10-12)

Besides *þa þa* ... *þa, þa* ... *þa,* and simple *þa,* one additionally comes across reduplicated *þa* as a conjunction which collocates with a main clause that has no initial *þa : þa þa* ..., (S) V.

> Eft *þa þa* heo axoden hwu he mihte swa stearca forhæfdnysse forberen, *he andswerede* (*EEH* 118: 29-30)

> Se Frise *þa þa* he hine gehæften ne mihte, *let hine faren* on his treowðan æfter þan feo þe he for him gesealde (*EEH* 120: 8-9)

From this evidence it would appear that the conjunctive function of *þa/þo* comes about as a consequence of *þa* deletion from earlier *ða þa/þa þa,* and subsequent elimination of the anaphoric *þa* in the main clause: *þa þa* ... *þa > þa* ... *þa > þa* ..., V. However, since the earlier *þa þa* construction usually introduced its main clause with the foregrounded word-order pattern of *þa* + V + S, the later use of *þo* ..., NP + VP as in the *(E)SEL is* not entirely continuous with the earlier evidence. The adverbialisation of *þa,* on the other hand, can be traced to the collocations with *þære.* With the already great variety in word order patterns observable in these texts, later multifunctionality and ambiguity in the *SEL* no longer strike one as a radical departure from the earlier language.

A much more radical hiatus can be observed in the fourteenth century. In the *Northern Homily Cycle (NHC)*, *þo* has disappeared entirely, but *þan(e)* operates in much the same functional and syntactic environments:

þan ware handis wyolent
layd one þat cristis Innocent ("St. Margaret"; *NHC* III 50: 125-126)

þane ansuert scho (Ibid., 51: 158)

olibrius *thane* wes ful thra (Ibid., 51: 138)

þe tyrand *þan*, to se þe flude
þat fra þe maydine ran of blude
had schame (Ibid., 57: 371-73)

Besides these clause-initial and postponed uses of *þan(e)* as a discourse marker~ in ME, *þane* also occurs in the meaning of adverbial 'then' and, in clause-initial position, followed not by the verb-plus-subject construction, but by the NP + VP or O+V+S distribution:

ful wa wes *þane* olybrius (Ibid., 53: 205) – COMPL + V + *than* + S

þane he beheld hyre ink[r]ely (Ibid., 50: 119)   – *than* + S + V

þane margret ger[t] he furth brocht be (Ibid., 53: 230)– *than* + O + V + S

In addition, one also finds *þane sad scho* (Ibid., 57: 359) in the meaning 'and then she in turn said' - with *þane* no longer introducing new information (as *þo* does): the *þa/þo* construction always had a full NP or a full complement since it refocussed attention on a new plot development, introducing a new narrative episode.

Another look at the twelfth-century homilies, however, disabuses us even of this theory of a radical paradigm shift. The final sermon (the Phoenix homily) in several cases employs *þonne* as a clause-initial discourse marker much on the lines of *þa*, and it therefore fully anticipates the usage in the *Northern Homily Cycle*:

Þonne færð eft se fugel fæȝere to his earde emb fiftene wucan, 7 fugeles maniȝe ealle him abuten efne ferden ufene 7 nyðene
(*EEH* 147: 26-28)

7 þonne fealleð Fenix on middan *þ*[t] micele fyr, 7 wurð forbærned eall to duste. *Þonne* on þan þriddan dæʒe ariseð se fæʒere fugel Fenix of deaðe (*EEH* 147: 35-37)

Þo has also disappeared in the fourteenth-century sermons collected in *EETS* 209. Here, too, *than* is all-pervasive and occurs both in syntactic and functional positions of the discourse marker *þo*:

Þan see hure fadre þat he myght not turne hure herte (*Middle English Sermons* [*MES*] 80: 13)

Þan vent þe feend from hym (*MES* 142: 13-14)

and in clause-initial environments with NP + VP word order:

Þan þe kynge vent avey, and he vent to þe dewell as he seid. (*MES* 145: 20-21)

Þan þis mayde answered and seid (*MES* 80: 34)

Þan on a day þe old man com in for to borowe a bushell (*MES* 90: 9-10)

Þan whan þis man saw þat he was brouthe fro is wurshippe vn-to þat myschefe, *þan* he syʒhed and made grett sorowe, and be-þouthe hym-selfe what were þe beste remedie. (Ibid., 90: 6-9)

And when þe daye was sett of hure weddying and all þe lordes were comon, *þan* seid þe kynge to is dowʒtur þat she shuld chese hure an husbond, on of all þoo lordes þat þer were gadered. (*MES* 80: 30-33)

As with the examples from the *SEL*, initial *þan* can be combined with preposed adverbials:

Þan þere sche kneled downe on hure knees and lefte vpe hure eyen to heven and seid on þis manere (*MES* 81: 19-20)

Adverbials and discourse markers also tend to cluster at the beginning of clauses:

Þan anon soþenly and *anon þerr* com to me too blake and horrible persons of sight, and to see hem I was grettely aferd, and on euery halfe I turned me, ʒiff I myght haue hid me fro hem (*MES* 144: 36 - 145: 1)

The sermons make extended use of the demonstrative *þis*, but not clause-initially:

Þan whan þis man saw þat he was brouthe from is wurshippe (*MES* 90: 6-7) and they widely employ clause-initial *and*:

> *And* þe kynge com anoþer tyme vn-to hym (*MES* 144: 27)

> *And whan* þat I sawe hem, me þought þat [I] was all hole. And þei leid beforne me a faire boke for to rede, but it was vondir litill; and þer I founde al þe good dedis þat euer I dud (*MES* 144: 32-35)

> *And whan* þat I saw no noþur bote I ley still. And þei sett hem a-downe and toke forthe a grett boke þat was full blake and horribul, and þer, wold I nold I, þer I rede all myn euyll dedis and all ill þouthes (*MES* 145: 3-6)

Margery Kempe's work, too, has practically only *than* followed by the NP + VP word order:

> *Than* sche ȝaf thankyng & preysing to owr Lord Ihesu Crist for þe hy grace & mercy þat he schewyd vn-to hir vnworthy wrech. (*The Book of Margery Kempe* 90: 31-33)

> Sche, beyng a-basshed þerof, was warnyd in hir sowle no fer to haue, for it was þe sownd of þe Holy Gost. & *þan* owyr Lord turnyd þat sownde in-to þe voys of a dowe, & sithyn he turnyd it into þe voys of a lityl bryd whech is callyd a reedbrest þat song ful merily oftyn-tymes in hir ryght ere. & *þan* schuld sche euyr-mor han gret grace aftyr þat sche herd swech a tokyn. And sche had been vsed to swech tokenys a-bowt xxv ȝer at þe writyng of þis boke. *Than* seyd owr Lord Ihesu Crist to hys creatur (Ibid., 90: 36 - 91: 9)

This can be compared with the *than* sequences in *The Gilte Legende*:

> And *thanne* most they haue foure couple of oxen to drawe hym oute into a gret feelde. And in that same day ther were baptized xx^{ti} thousand men withoute women and children. And *than* the kynge in worship of oure Lady and of Seint George lete make a chirche of mervaylous gretnesse, and fro the auuter of the chirche ther sprange a quicke well that heled of all maner siknesse whoso dranke therof. And *thanne* the kynge offered to Seint George golde withoute nombre, the whiche he refused and comaunded that it shulde be geue to the pore. And *thanne* Seint George taught the kynge of foure thingges, that was that he shulde take gret cure of the chirches of God, and þat he shulde worship prestes, and here goodly the devine seruise, and þat he shuld be almesfull to the pore. And *thanne* he toke his leue of the kynge and went his waye. ("St. George"; *The Gilte Legende* 68: 7-21)

In OE the NP + VP construction used to be employed for backgrounded material, but has now apparently made it to a regular foregrounded construction in which the mere presence of a discourse marker~ in ME (*and, than,* in Malory *so*) serves to signal the foregrounding. One can therefore observe that the predominance of the *þis*-NP construction in Chaucer seems to reflect a general shift towards standardising NP + VP word order as well as a related foregrounding technique which highlights the clause-initial constituent (whether an NP or a discourse marker). This process increasingly allows VP + NP structures to fall into desuetude.

In the fifteenth century, this clause-initial emphasis by means of an NP becomes further extended to accommodate also constructions without the demonstrative pronoun: the proper name alone serves to focus attention on a new agent or a new turn of events. But again, as we have seen, earlier examples can already be found in *Seint Katerine* and of course in the classic texts of the fourteenth century. This construction becomes most pronounced in Bokenham:

> *This Theodosius* had a wyf ful mete
> To hys astate, of whom was born
> A doughtyr fayr, and clepyd Margarete
> ("St. Margaret"; Bokenham 10: 344-46)

> *Thys blessyd Cristyne*, enspyryd wyth grace,
> Thus seyde to hir fadyr ful demurely ("St. Christiana"; 62: 2251-52)

> *Olibrius*, this heryng, feil in a rage ("St. Margaret"; 18: 631)[17]

> *Iulyan þis seying* was sory certeyn ("St. Christiana"; 82: 2995)

Note here already the present participle construction which gains ground in Caxton's prose and becomes the major fare of Elizabethan prose:

> After this she *vnderstanding* how certaine Priests were slayn on the way as they trauailed, by theeues and robbers; *taking* some companions with her, she goeth to gather vp the[ir] bodies. The murdering theeues *vnderstanding* their purpose, determyned among themselues to take them, euerie one, one: and the captaine or cheefe of these fellowes, was called GLUNELACH. The virgin *perceyuing* their intent prayed forthwith to our Lord for ayd [...] (*The Lives of Women Saints of our Contrie of England* 92: 31 - 93: 5)

> And as sone as Cristyn þus entryd was
> In-to þat horribyl & lothful lake,
> þre aungellis aperyd befor hir faas,
> *Bryngyng* hir brede als whyt as lake,

Wyth oþir mete, and anone dyde take
Hir woundis cure; & she, up *lokynge*
To heuenward, began hir preyere make
Wyth deuout corage, þis wyse *seyinge*:
("St. Christiana"; Bokenham 69: 2525-6)

Bokenham also has numerous *(and) when* incipits, but unlike earlier *whan...than*
the *when* clause is regularly followed by a main clause which starts with NP +
VP, with or without another preposed constituent:

And whan kateryn among þese whelys rounde
Set was, wych hyr shuld confounde
Or constreyn hy for feer to sacryfyse,
To god she preyid in secre wyse
That he wold vouchesaf of hys grace,
To wurshyp of hys name in þat place ("St. Katherine"; 194: 7121-25)

Whan Caprasius alle þis sey doon,
Vp-on þe grounde deuouthly knelyng,
From hys preyere he roos up ful soon,
And þankyd god of þys toknyng ("St. Faith"; 104: 3818 - 105: 3821)

But whan þis Quyncyan dede aspye
The purpose of Agas in hyr entent,
By hys offycers for hyr he sent ("St. Agatha"; 228: 8394-96)

And whan þou þus wyth corupcyoun
Defoulyd art, I vdyr-take
The holy gost wyl þe forsake. ("St. Lucy"; 252: 9252-54)

or has subject-verb inversion:

And whan she was brought to swych pouerte
That she ne hadde where hyr heed to leye,
In a tauerners hous in a swyncote lay she
Tyl mydnyht, & þan she took þe weye
To a place of menours, [&] hem dede preye
Te deum laudamus to synge wyth deuocyoun,
That he hyr maad wurthy, er she dede deye,
To suffren despyht & persecucyoun. ("St. Elizabeth"; 276: 10153-60)

And whan she to ʒeris of dyscrescyon
Was comyn, aftyr ther lawes guyse,
Not ouer yonge aftyr myn estymacyon,

But what yer of age I ne can deuyse,
Wedded sche was in ful solenne wyse
Into a cuntre clepyd galyle ("St. Anna"; 44: 1623-28)

And when Cristyn þis gloryus syhte dede se,
Doun plat she fel up-on þe watyr clere [...]
And anone *þe good lord*, cumynge hir nere,
Hyr up lyft, and seyd ("St. Christiana"; 70: 2571 - 71: 2575)   – S+O+V

This can be compared with *The Gilte Legende* (*Three Lives from the Gilte Legende* = GL), where one has:

And *thanne* this bisshop schewed this vision to his felawes and counsailed hem all to be in praiers and he wold kepe the chirche dore. Right as it was schewed vnto hym, *so* it fel that atte the houre of matenys bi purveiaunce of oure Lord Nicholas come furst, and *anone* the bisshop toke hym and asked hym what he hight, and he anone mekely ansuered and said ("St. Nicholas"; *GL*: 52-3)[18]

And *thanne anone* he began to helpe hem in takelyng of her schipp, and *anone* the tempest sesid. And *thanne* he vanisshed away, and *whanne* thei were come to his chirche thei knewe hym anone withoute tellyng of any creature, and yet they hadd neuer sene hym before. And *thanne* they come to hym and gave thankyng[es] to God and to hym of thaire deliueraunce. ("St. Nicholas"; *GL*: 53)

And *thanne* thei said: "What art thou that tellist vs these wordes?" *Thanne* he saide: "I am Nicholas, servaunt of Ihesu Crist, the whiche the Iue hathe so cruelli beten for ye toke awaye his good." And *thanne* thei were gretli aferde and come to the Iue and tolde hym how he hadde done to the ymage and al the miracle, and yalde hym al his good. And *so* the theuis come to the waye of rightwisnesse and the Iue to the faithe of Ihesu Crist. ("St. Nicholas"; *GL*: 62)

[and] *whanne* the fader herde [this] of his sone he made gret wamentacion and pitous sorow, wepte and bere the bodi of his sone to his chaumbre and saide: [...] And *as* he said these wordes the childe *anone* openid his eighen and awoke as though he hadd slept, and arose al hole and sounde. ("St. Nicholas"; *GL*: 62)

Thanne frequently has an adverbial 'and then' meaning which no longer reflects the refocussing function of old *þo* + VP + NP.

The day foluyng George receyued such sentence that he shulde be drawen thorugh all the citee and ***thanne*** his hede to be smiten of. ("St. George"*; GL*: 73)

The Gilte Legende also has an instance of *So as* which uncannily prefigures *so* in Malory.

So as the emperour Peduyk distroied Bonifaunt, and hadde comaunded that all the chirches that were there [were] distroied, and did al his powere to bringe that cite to another place, and that a man fonde and sawe men al in white and shininge, and hym thoght that thei were in a gret counsaile togeder. ("St. Bartholomew"; *Three Lives*: 82)

Anoon and *than* are used widely in Bokenham, again in ambiguous or multifunctional contexts. *Anoon* is followed both by S + V and by V + S word order, and it can collocate with *whan* in the syntactic sequence which is so common in *The Gilte Legende*.

And ***anoon*** Ion to the pryour went
And gan hym tellen euene by and by
("St. Margaret"; Bokenham 34: 1268-69)

And ***anoon*** hir fadir aftyr hir entent,
As hastily as he it coude deuyse,
Ordeynyd hir a neu garnement
And neu encens ek for sacrifyse. ("St. Christiane"; 63: 2299-2302)

Anoon aftyr þat zyon furth was went
Wher goddys rhytwysnes hym wold haue,
From þe emperour ***anoon*** was sent
A neu iuge to Tyre, clepyd Iulyane (Ibid., 78: 2859-63)

And ***anoon was hit*** presentyd ham al þe case
Of cristyne, be þe offycers of þe cyte (Ibid., 73: 2651-52)

Whan þis was doon, ***a-noon*** hastyly
To presoun ageyn he hir send þens (Ibid., 76: 2755-56)

Than, too, is very common, but usually collocates with S + V sequences:

And ***þan*** Cristyn, knelyng on eþir kne,
Thankyd enterly god of his grace;
And vpward wyth þat hir eyne lyft she,
And sey heuyn opyn & ihesu in pas (Ibid., 71: 2587-90)

And *þan* to hyr maydyns she dede seye,
Both for here & hyre owyn consolacyoun
("St. Elizabeth"; 281: 10337-38)

Than comayndyd þis urbane wyth-out let
Off strong yryn a colere ful vnpeteusly
About hir nek fast to be schet,
And aboutyn handis & feet chenys myghty,
And so in presone to be put ful cruelly. ("St. Christiana"; 66: 2395-99)

Capgrave's *Life of St. Katherine* constitutes a meeting ground of earlier and later tendencies. The proper name is quite common in this text as is the construction with demonstrative *þis* – and this seems to be a Chaucerian influence.

Þis phalon was sone on-to þe seyd demetrius (56: 666)

Thys lady answerd on-to þis lord a-geyn (94: 281)

The emperour be-held hir woordis and hir chere,
Wonderynge sore hough she durste be soo boolde
Be-fore swiche puple right in his presens there,
And not considerynge the feste whiche he had holde -
ffor that same tale whiche she hath now toolde
Durste noo man telle, but if he wolde be deed. (281: 603-608)

The mayde answerde right thus to his tale (331: 2164)

However, Capgrave also has remnants of *tho*, various uses of *than(ne)* and a few instances of *thus* in much the same meaning as *than:*

Tho cam our ladye & left hyr up sone;
þus sayd sche te hyr: "be of good comforte!" (Capgrave 230: 1002-03)

Tho sey the emperour there is noon other spede
On-to this mayden whiche is soo stedfast,
But fayre wordes, whiche drawe womanhede
And maketh hem often other thyng to tast
Thanne thei shulde doo if thei wolde be chast. (348: 330 - 349: 334)

Tho spak the mayde swiche woordis on-to hem (365: 820)

Than ros a lord, a man of gret statur,
A rych man eke þei sey þat he was (92: 232-33)

Than made the mayde on-to the emperour
A ful strong chalange, seyenge on this wyse (302: 1275-76)

Thanne was þe emperour ny wood for Ire (358: 603)

Thus arn these ladies euene on-to the trone
Of oure lord almyghty walked foorth a-pace (233: 1016-17)

Thus deyed these men in Nouembre þe xiij. day. (348: 316)

Thus is she bounde & ledde foorth in the toun. (376: 1142)

Both *than* and *tho* occur in non-initial position but in the old discourse-functional use,

An othir duke gan *þan* to approche,
Ser clamadour þei calle his ryth name,
A worthi man & duke of Antioche,
þe qwenes cosyn, a lord of ful grete fame. (134: 932-35)

There stood vp *thanne* with a [full] boold face
A grete clerk, thei called Alfragan (325: 1975-76)

[...] & aftyr hym *þan* roos
A man þei call be name seleucus galericus;
Þer reygned he .xx. wynter & þan ['then'] seleucus garanne
Thre зer bar þe crown. (52: 616-19)

"Gramercy, syr", to hym *þan* seyd þe qween (100: 379)

A gret clerk *þoo* stod up be hym-selue,
þat was fful scharp in wytte, as I wene (122: 715-16)

This same vers was *tho* in hir thought
Whiche our lady hir-self gan make (290: 892-93)

Whan this mayde of this fair processe
had made an ende, there stod vp *tho* a man
Of fers corage, though it were wodnesse–
Maister astenes, soo thei called hym *than;*
ffor very anger of colour was he wan;
with cryenge voys he filled *tho* the place,
Thus spak he *than*: "allas, what is oure grace?" (306: 1401-07)

and *thanne* also appears as an adverbial 'then':

Lordes & ladyes þat wer þer of here kynne,
On-to þat feste come both on & odyr

And all wer þei loggyd in full riall Ine–
Sume wer of here fadyrs syde, summe wer of her modyr.
Of curtesye & gentylnesse, game & non othyr
Was *þan* her carpyng, saue summe spoke of loue;
Euery man spak of þing whech was to hys be-houe. (60: 750 - 62: 755)

There are additional cases of *and thanne* which anticipate *The Gilte Legende*:

She low a lityl whan she herde al this,
And *thanne* she spak with mery countenaunce (352: 421-22)

Remnants of *tho*, though quite rare, can also be discovered in Chaucer:

Tho gan she wondren moore than biforn
A thousand fold, and down hire eyghen caste
(*Troilus and Criseyde* II 141-42; Chaucer 1988: 491)

Tho was I war of Plesaunce anon-ryght,
And of Aray, and Lust, and Curteysie
(*The Parliament of Fowls* 218-19; Chaucer 1988: 388)

Tho gan I walke thorough the mede,
Dounward ay in my pleiyng,
The ryver syde costeiyng.
("The Romaunt of the Rose" 132; Chaucer 1988: 688)

And with that watir, that ran so cler,
My face I wyssh. *Tho* saugh I well
The botme paved everydell
With gravel, ful of stones shene. (Ibid., 688: 124-27)

There are also remnants of the *when ... then* construction:

Whan Ydelnesse had told al this,
And I hadde herkned wel, ywys,
Thanne seide I to dame Ydelnesse (Ibid., 693: 629-31)

Therefore, there appears to be a period of transition throughout the entire fourteenth and early fifteenth century in which older constructions proliferate and become ambiguous, and some of these (like the Chaucerian *this*-construction and the sequential use of *than*), at least temporarily, start to win out over *tho*. At the same time *as, so* and *thus* as well as *anon* occur ever more frequently and start to replace *tho* in its various functions and syntactic positions. Although Chaucer's writing is least affected by the great diversity observable in other texts of the period, his texts, too, retain traces of the competing paradigms.

To round off this survey, let me briefly discuss the situation in Caxton and in Malory. Malory uses a great number of discourse markers~ in ME: *than, so, thus* as well as *also* as a conjunction 'when'. He also employs a great number of *whan*-clauses. *Than* appears to mark major plot developments, but *so* and *thus* seem to be responsible for signalling higher discourse units (the beginning of episodes or the conclusions of discourse units).

> *Thus* he there endured a quarter off a yere, and so at the laste he ran hys way and she wyst nat where he was becom. *And than was he naked*, and waxed leane and poore of fleyshe. And *so* he felle in the felyshyppe of herdemen and shyperdis, and dayly they wolde gyff hym som of their mete and drynke, *and whan* he ded ony shrewde dede they wold beate hym with roddis. And *so* they clypped hym with sherys and made hym lyke a foole.
>
> *And so* uppon a day sir Dagonet, kynge Arthurs foole, cam into Cornwayle with two squyers with hym, and *as* they rode thorow that foreyste they cam by a fayre welle where sir Trystramys was wonte to be. And the weddir was hote, and they alyght to drynke of that welle, and in the meanewhyle theyre horsys brake lowse.
>
> *Ryght so* cam sir Trystramys unto them, and firste he sowsed sir Dagonet in that welle, and aftir that hys squyars, and thereat lowghe the shypperdis. And furthwithall he ran aftir their horsis and brought hem agayne one by one, and ryght so wete as they were he made them lepe up and ryde their wayes.
>
> *Thus* sir Trystramys endured there an halff-yere naked, and wolde never com in towne [ne village]. *So* the meanewhyle the damesell that sir Palomydes sent to seke sir Trystram, she yode unto sir Palomydes and tolde hym off all the myschyff that sir Trystram endured. (IX: 305)

The initial *thus*-clause rounds off Sir Tristram's sojourn with the "damesell" and *so* introduces a new episode, that of his running away. The consequence of *thus* is emphasised by subject-verb inversion after *than*, and his falling in with the shepherds and their treatment of him is emphasised by means of *so*. The two next narrative episodes are also marked by means of *so*, and the conclusion of the interlude has *thus*, with *so* shifting the narrative back to the woman he had fled from.

Malory's pervasive use of *so* has no parallel in Caxton, where *then* prevails over other discourse markers. Caxton also employs many relative constructions. In *The Golden Legend,* for instance, *then* alternates with relative *To whom X said*:

> *And then* the provost, being wroth, commanded her to be put in prison. And the next day following commanded that she should be brought to him, *and then* said to her: O good maid, have pity on thy beauty, and worship our gods, that thou mayest be well. *To whom she said:* I worship him that maketh the earth to tremble, whom the sea dreadeth and the winds and creatures obey. *To whom the provost said:* But if thou consent to me I shall make thy body to be all to-torn. *To whom Margaret said:* Christ gave himself over to the death for me, and I desire gladly to die for Christ. *Then the provost commanded* her to be hanged in an instrument to torment the people, and to be cruelly first beaten with rods, and with iron combs to rend and draw her flesh to the bones, insomuch that the blood ran about out of her body, like as a stream runneth out of a fresh springing well. ("St. Margaret"; Caxton 1973: IV 67-68)

At other places major developments and evaluations are, however, marked by *anon* and *thus*. Whereas the main part of the story continues to alternate between *then* and *To whom* (68-70), the miracle stands out by being framed by means of *but* and *anon*, and the narrative immediately returns to *then* in the recounting of the consequences:

> *But* suddenly the earth trembled, and the air was hideous, and the blessed virgin without any hurt issued out of the water, saying to our Lord: I beseech thee, my Lord, that this water may be to me the font of baptism to everlasting life. *And anon* there was heard great thunder, and a dove descended from heaven, and set a golden crown on her head. *Then* five thousand men believed in our Lord, and for Christ's love they all were beheaded by the commandment of the provost Olybrius, that time in Campolymeath the city of Aurelia. *Then* Olybrius, seeing the faith of the holy Margaret immoveable, and also fearing that others should be converted to the christian faith by her, gave sentence and commanded that she should be beheaded. (Ibid., IV 70)

This use of *anon* corresponds precisely to that in *The Gilte Legende*:

> And whanne George entered into the temple of ydoles to do sacrifice, and alle the peple were there to beholde hym, he kneled downe and praied to oure Lorde that he wolde vtterli destroie al the temple and the ydoles, so

þat atte the preisinge of hym and the conuersion of the peple ther shuld nothinge abyde therof. And *anone* ther descended fyre from heuene and brent the temple and the goddes and the prestes, and sodenly þe erthe opened and swaloued alle so that ther lefte nothinge therof. ("St. George"; Three Lives: 71)

In these contexts *anon* marks the onset of an unexpected event of major proportions.

The final passage relating to St. Margaret's vita has a *thus* which marks the end of the story and signals the onset of an evaluative commentary:

Then Theotinus took up the holy body, and bare it into Antioch, and buried it in the house of a noble woman and widow named Sincletia. *And thus this blessed and holy virgin*, S. Margaret, *suffered death*, and received the crown of martyrdom the thirteenth kalends of August, as is founden in her story; and it is read in another place that it was the third of July. (Caxton 1973: IV 71)

In Caxton's *Paris and Vienne*, on the other hand, the sentences are much longer and paratactic *and*-constructions abound. This foregrounds the *thenne*-clauses and emphasises their function as indicators of major plot development.

The doulphyn wente in grete thouȝt thurgh the paleys hauyng grete Indygnacyon and alle angry in soo moche that none durst speke to hym ne come in his waye/ and he beyng thus in thys manere [b vij^r] he sente for his doughter vyenne & made hyr to come to hym/ and sayd to hyr [direct speech][19] & *whan* vyenne sawe hyr fader in so grete angre ayenst messyre Iaques & hys sone/ she sente for to seche Edward for to come speke to hyr/ & *whan* Edward was come Vyenne sayd to hym [direct speech]. *Thenne* edward Incontynent took leue of vyenne/ & went & sayd to paris all that vyenne had sayd to hym & sayd [direct speech]. *Thenne* ansuerd Parys [direct speech] (Caxton 1957: 33)

By the end of the fifteenth century, one can therefore observe the preponderance of the NP + VP word order, which is infringed only at key points of the narrative and then arguably serves to highlight a narrative turn. *Þo* has disappeared completely and *then* has become the norm, but Malory already diversifies by means of *thus* and *so*. The relative-clause constructions which become common with Caxton multiply in Elizabethan prose, particularly among humanists in the prose of More, Fisher or Lyly, whereas Malory's more 'oral' style persists into the popular writing of Greene and Nashe. The development of narrative prose therefore starts by erasing the reliefing function of *þo*, which had marked a foregrounded level of the narrative macrostructure, and by levelling the narrative to consecutive *(and) then* patterns. However, this levelling tendency is resisted at the same time and counteracted by a number of other devices. In Chaucer - but, as we have seen, already earlier - *þis*-NP constructions serve similar purposes at incipit points of the narrative episode, and present participles are increasingly employed in a backgrounding function. *So* and *thus*, which were present in earlier texts but used only infrequently and in apparently free variation with *as*, *þo* and *than*, begin to signal reliefing points in Caxton and Malory. *Anon*, which earlier had merely been one more variant in the meaning of 'and then', comes to be associated with the climax (incidence point)[20] of the narrative episode and acquires the reading of 'and suddenly'.

Much larger quantities of texts would need to be analysed for a definitive account of discourse markers~ in ME and the narrative structure to which they relate in the late Middle English period. The present sketch merely traces some of the relevant devices and discusses some of the syntactic, functional and semantic relations that need to be taken into account. The functional shift which superficially appears to correlate with the disappearance of *þo* and its replacement by *than* cannot in actual fact be explained in such easy terms. *Than*, it is true, originally occurs much in the same functional and syntactic distributions as *þo*, which explains the eventual disappearance of *þo*. The predominance of *than* and its increasingly sequentialising function may, however be explained rather from the diversity of its original environments and uses. This diversity and its attendant ambiguities may have resulted in the loss of original *þo/than*'s reliefing functions and in a general levelling of the narrative structure. In any case, after the twelfth century ME *þo* no longer occurs exclusively in its OE discourse function. Further research will have to analyse not only many more texts but will also have to come to a better understanding of the episodic structure or pattern of prose and verse narratives. It will additionally need to distinguish between sequentialising and highlighting techniques and devices and will have to present an account of how narrative structures develop, interrelate and fuse in the given period. In any case, the situation appears to be decidedly more complex than has been allowed for and will require dedicated efforts within a pragmatic methodology for some time to come. I therefore invite those more qualified than myself to take over and try to solve the mystery of ME discourse markers.

Notes

1. Note that *Came a boy of seven years* or *Came Felicia, and all our troubles were gone* is perfectly idiomatic, since it marks a major story point. Remnants of the old structure can also be observed in stage directions: *Enter John* or *Exit Gloucester*.

2. Emphases in bold italics are mine.

3. I have analysed the following texts: *Early English Homilies from the Twelfth Century MS Vesp. D.XIV*, *St. Katherine* and *St. Margaret* from the Katherine Group, "Of þe vox and of þe wolf", extracts from the *Early South English Legendary* and from the *South English Legendary*, from the *Northern Homily Cycle* and from the fourteenth-century *Middle English Sermons*, *The Book of Margery Kempe*, Capgrave's *Life of St. Katherine*, three lives from the *Gilte Legende*, parts of Caxton's *Golden Legend* and his *Paris & Vienne*, as well as extracts from Malory's epic.

4. Quotations from the *Early South English Legendary (ESEL)* and the *South English Legendary (SEL)* are cited with the page number first followed by the line number of the particular life. Capital Roman numerals refer to volume number.

5. For the notion of the episode incipit, the onset of a narrative micro-episode, see Fludernik (1991, 1992a, 1992b).

6. See also in *SEL*: "*So þat* sein Ion was icome" ("St. John"; *SEL* II 595: 47).

7. Compare also: "*þis* guode man seint Iulian: to godes seruise him nam" (Ibid., 260: 142).

8. In the following passage *þo* can be read either as 'though' or 'when': "Me specþ of mony stable heorte . ac me þincþ þer was on / þat lou *þo* him stod afure . boþe fleiss and bon" ("St. Lawrence"; *SEL* II 364: 177-78).

9. Compare "þe king of France þat was þo . Charles was is name" (" St. Giles"; *SEL* II 388: 125).

10. Although apparently a translation from Latin, this *whan ... than* pattern occurs also with great frequency in *The Three Kings of Cologne*. See, for example, the passage quoted and discussed by Workman (1940: 151): "*Whan* þes .ij. kynges Melchior and Balthasar were come and abiden in þes plaas aforesayde in þe clowde and in derkenesse, *þan* þis clowde bigan to ascende and to wax clere [...] And *whan* þei þus had mette to-gedir and euerych of hem had tolde to oþir his wille and hys entent, and all her wille and her cause was acordyng in one, *than* þei were moche more gladdere and more feruent in her weye."

11. For typographical reasons *þ*ᵗ represents *that* (ꝥ).

12. For typographical reasons *t* replaces et (ꝸ).

13. Compare also in *Seinte Iuliene:*"Lauerd godd al mihti quoð heo *þa*" *(Liflade* Roy. 17A xxvii; 24: 203).

14. Line numbers only are provided here for this text.

15. For typographical reasons *7* stands for *et* (7).

16. In terms of generative grammar of the X-bar variety, this would support the thesis of CONJ as a separate constituent (Compare Radford 1981: 105).
17. Present participle constructions are italicised in the following.
18. Page numbers only provided for this text.
19. Passages of dialogue have been omitted.
20. Compare Fludernik (1991, 1992a, 1992b).

References

Primary sources:

Butler-Bowdon, W. (ed.)
1940 " The Book of Margery Kempe." *Early English Text Society O.S.*, 212. London: Oxford University Press.

Bokenham, Osbern
1938 " Legendys of Hooly Wummen". In: Mary S. Serjeantson (ed.). MS. *Arundel 327 Early English Text Society O.S.*, 206. London: Oxford University Press.

Capgrave, John
1973 " The Life of St. Katharine of Alexandria [1893]." In: Carl Horstmann (ed.). *Early English Text Society O.S.*, 100. Millwood, New York: Kraus Reprint Co.

Caxton, William
1973 " The Golden Legend." [The Golden Legend or Lives of the Saints as Englished by William Caxton]. In: F. S. Ellis (ed.). *The Temple Classics*. New York: AMS Press. From the edition of 1900, London: J.M. Dent.
1957 " Paris and Vienne." Translated from French and printed by William Caxton. In: MacEdward Leach (ed.). *Early English Text Society*, O. S. 234. Oxford: Oxford University Press.

Chaucer, Geoffrey
1988 *The Riverside Chaucer.* Larry D. Benson (ed.). Third edition. New York: Mifflin.

Hamer, Richard (ed.)
1978 " Three Lives from the Gilte Legende." In: MS. B. L. Egerton 876. *Middle English Texts.* Heidelberg: Carl Winter.

Horstmann, Carl (ed.)
1886 " The Lives of Women Saints of our Contrie of England, also some other liues of holie women written by some of the auncient fathers (c. 1610-

1615)." In: MS Stowe 949. *Early English Text Society O.S.*, 86. London: Trubner & Co.

1887 " The Early South-English Legendary or Lives of the Saints." In: Ms. Laud 108, in the Bodleian Library. *Early English Text Society O.S.*, 87. London: Trubner.

" Þe Liflade ant te Passiun of Seinte Iuliene"

1961 In: S.R.T.O. d'Ardenne (ed.). *Early English Text Society O.S.*, 248. Oxford: Oxford University Press.

Malory, Sir Thomas

1971 " Works." In: Eugene Vinaver (ed.). Second Edition. Oxford University Press.

Metcalfe, W. M. (ed.)

1891 *Legends of the Saints in the Scottish Dialect of the Fourteenth Century.* Part III. Edinburgh and London: William Blackwood and Sons.

" Middle English Sermons"

1940 In: Woodburn O. Ross (ed.). British Museum MS. *Royal 18 B. xxiii. Early English Text Society O.S.*, 209. London: Oxford University Press.

" Of þe vox and of þe wolf"

1913 In: George H. McKnight (ed.). *Middle English Humorous Tales in Verse.* Boston: Heath.

" Seinte Marherete, the Meiden ant Martyr"

1958 In: Frances M. Mack (ed.). Re-edited from MS. Bodley 34, Oxford and MS. Royal 17A xxvii, British Museum, *Early English Text Society O.S.*, 193. London: Oxford University Press, 1934; repr. with corrections.

" Seinte Katerine. Re-Edited from MS Bodley 34 and the other Manuscripts"

1981 In: S.R.T.O. d'Ardenne and E. J. Dobson (eds.). *Early English Text Society S.S.*, 7. Oxford: Oxford University.

Warner, Rubie D.-N. (ed.)

1971 " Early English Homilies from the Twelfth Century MS." *Vesp. D. XIV.* In: *Early English Text Society O.S.*, 152. New York: Kraus Reprint.

Criticism:

Betten, Anne

1987 " Grundzüge der Prosasyntax. Stilprägende Entwicklungen vom Althochdeutschen zum Neuhochdeutschen." *Germanistische Linguistik* 82. Tübingen: Niemeyer.

Ebert, Robert Peter

1978 " Historische Syntax des Deutschen." *Realien zur Literatur* 167. Stuttgart: Metzler.

Enkvist, Nils Erik, and Brita Wårvik
    1987   " Old English *þa*, temporal chains, and narrative structure." In: Anna Giacalone Ramat, Onofrio Carruba, and Giuliano Bernini (eds.). *Papers from the Seventh International Conference on Historical Linguistics.* (Current Issues in Linguistic Theory 48). Amsterdam: John Benjamins, 221-237.

Fludernik, Monika
    1991   " The historical present tense yet again: Tense switching and narrative dynamics in oral and quasi-oral storytelling." *Text* 11.3, 365-398.
    1992a   " The historical present tense in English literature: An oral pattern and its literary adaptation." *Language and Literature* 17, 77-107. (Crosscurrents issue, 1992)
    1992b   " Narrative schemata and temporal anchoring." *The Journal of Literary Semantics* 21, 118-153.

Givón, Talmy Ed.
    1979   *Syntax and Semantics 12. Discourse and Syntax.* New York: Academic Press.

Harweg, Roland
    1974   " Deiktische und adeiktische Zeitstufen." *Zeitschrift für romanische Philologie* 90, 499-525.

Hopper, Paul J.
    1979a   " Aspect and foregrounding in discourse." In: T. Ed. Givón (1979: 213-241).
    1979b   " Some observations on the typology of focus and aspect in narrative language." *Studies in Language* 3.1, 37-64.

Radford, Andrew
    1981   *Transformational Syntax. A Student's Guide to Chomsky's Extended Standard Theory.* (Cambridge Textbooks in Linguistics). Cambridge: Cambridge University Press.

Riehl, Claudia Maria
    1993   *Kontinuität und Wandel von Erzählstrukturen am Beispiel der Legende.* (Göppinger Arbeiten zur Germanistik 576). Göppingen: Kummerle.

Workman, Samuel K.
    1940   *Fifteenth Century Translation as an Influence on English Prose.* (Princeton Studies in English 18). Princeton, NJ: Princeton Univ. Press.

Diachronic Analysis of Japanese Discourse Markers

Noriko Okada Onodera
Sanno College

1. Introduction: diachronic analysis of discourse markers

Many trials and efforts in discourse studies during the past four decades and the increased general interest in the field of pragmatics have resulted in fruitful findings regarding the pragmatics of world languages. Recent synchronic discourse studies have revealed the pragmatic/discourse functions of a large number of linguistic items, whose functions we had known were mainly semantic and grammatical. The discovery of the discourse/pragmatic functions of language have added another important aspect of language to our epistemology. However, this discovery has at times brought a slight misapprehension among the readers of the discourse papers. That is, the recently found discourse/pragmatic functions have sometimes been interpreted to be somewhat *new* functions. Are the pragmatic functions of each linguistic item really new? When did these functions occur in the history of each item? These are my initial questions.

To answer these questions, we need to deal not only with the presently used languages which we have long analysed in our synchronic discourse studies but also with languages used in earlier times. To gain sight into the true relationship between pragmatic functions and time, we need to inspect the functions of past languages for each time stage, and overlook them chronologically. Concerning the diachronic approach to discourse in English, there is already substantial literature that we can depend upon. Researchers generally agree that discourse markers are quite old (Stein 1985, Brinton 1990, Enkvist and Wårvik 1987, etc.). This area was once termed "historical discourse analysis" (Enkvist and Wårvik 1987: 222). However, for the Japanese language, the study of discourse from a historical point of view is still at its dawning (Fujii 1991, Onodera 1993a, 1993b, 1993c). A few other works are now in progress, in relation to the conception of the grammaticalisation process, a diachronic path of language that is of increasing interest in Japan (Suzuki and Ono 1992, Matsumoto 1988, etc.). In respect to 'historical discourse analysis' in Japanese, however, this paper seems to be one of the initial studies in this area.

There were two reasons for my undertaking a diachronic analysis of discourse markers. The first was to answer the question: When did the pragmatic functions first appear in the history of each linguistic item? The second reason was more specifically brought up in my synchronic discourse analyses. That is, the diachrony of the two Japanese words I had been analysing, *demo* and *dakedo*, aroused my curiosity. These two words seemed most interesting in their diachronic perspective, at least in terms of word-formation.

This paper shows a diachronic analysis of some Japanese discourse markers. Synchronic discourse studies have also found several expressions to be discourse markers in the Japanese language (Maynard 1989, 1992, Onodera 1989, etc.). Among such markers, I will examine *demo* and *dakedo*, hitherto so-called adversative conjunctions. I will analyse the functions of these items used in earlier time stages, and explore whether or not there is a shift in their functions in different time stages. If there is a shift, I will illustrate how the functional shift proceeds. The diachronic analysis of the discourse markers would respond to the questions mentioned above; the time when the pragmatic functions appeared in each item in question, and whether or not the pragmatic functions are new.

Following this section, in section 2, three key concepts framing this study will be introduced and defined; "discourse markers" (2.1.), the "pragmatic change" (2.2.), and the "functional-semantic model of language" (2.3.). In section 3, I will analyse the Japanese markers *demo* and *dakedo* diachronically. Their functions in Japanese ranging from their first appearances until the present day will be revealed. I will then discuss, in section 4, the functional change of *demo* and *dakedo*, relating it to Traugott's (1982) hypothesised pragmatic change in *demo* and *dakedo*. In my conclusion (section 5), I will suggest that the functional changes in *demo* and *dakedo* also follow the process of grammaticalisation.

2.   Key concepts of this study

2.1. *Discourse markers*

Discourse markers are elements that express the speaker's judgement/attitude toward the proposition to be informed and at times express the speaker's actions in the course of conversational management. They also contribute to the discourse cohesion by their textual function of linking the prior and upcoming discourse. In the on-going conversation, the markers inform the hearers of the speaker's actions and the relationship between the current utterance and its prior and following text. In doing so, the markers guide the hearers in a more appropriate interpretation of the utterance. They aid the hearers in better understanding of what is currently going on in the interactional conversation. This is why elements of this kind are called 'markers'.

In English, expressions commonly used in conversation such as *and, but, oh, well, y'know, I mean*, etc. have been demonstrated to belong to this group (Schiffrin 1987, Warner 1985, Schourup 1982, Östman 1981, etc.). In French, *mais heu, ben alors voilà, quoi, oh, ah*, etc. have been found to have the same function (Auchlin 1981, Brunet 1983). Also in Japanese, *demo, dakedo, dakara, datte* have been proved so far to be the same elements (Onodera 1989, 1993a, Maynard 1989, 1992), and many more expressions with similar characteristics would be identified as markers. The expressions mentioned here, which look like different grammatical members at a glance, have come to be elaborately defined as one group in Schiffrin (1987).

I will discuss some crucial points concerning the definitions of the markers. Schiffrin has provided two patterns of definitions; one "operational" (Ibid.: 31), and the other a "more theoretical" (Ibid.: 40, 327) definition. The operational definition states that the markers are the "sequentially dependent elements which bracket units of talk". 'Sequential dependence' expresses a feature of the markers, i.e. the level on which the markers function is the discourse level. The second feature is articulated by 'bracket'~ , the notion of which comes from Goffman (1974). Brackets mark "the boundaries of units not only of talk, but of social life and social organization in general" (Schiffrin 1987: 36). Brackets offer frames of interpretation through which the containing utterance or any activity is defined. Although brackets both initiate and terminate units of talk, the symbolism and the predominance of initiating brackets commonly attract more attention. Goffman (1974: 255) suggests that the beginning bracket will establish not only an episode but also a slot for signals informing and defining what kind of transformation is to be made of the material within the episode.

A more theoretical definition was provided after the analysis of eleven English expressions (Schiffrin 1987). That is, markers are "contextual coordinates " (Ibid: 327): they index the containing utterance to the local contexts in which utterances are produced and are to be interpreted (Ibid.: 326). The contexts in this case include participants and text. The participant coordinates to which the marker indexes the containing utterance are the speaker and the hearer. A marker indicates that the utterance is focused on either the speaker (proximal) or the hearer (distal), or both. Likewise, the textual coordinates show whether the utterance focuses more on prior text (proximal) or upcoming text (distal), or both. As contextual coordinates, the markers inform the hearers of the location of the current utterance in the surrounding local context, indicating the relationship between the utterance, and the participants and text.

In this study, the condition which allows an expression to be judged as a marker is the following: an expression has to bear either textual or expressive function of language or both. Although textual and expressive functions will be discussed in detail in the next section, here I just mention that this condition is applied in my analysis to judge when an expression becomes a marker in the diachrony of language. Concerning the time when an item becomes a marker, another point in the analysis will be the fact that an item is used in utterance (sentence)-initial positions. These conditions will be considered when I analyse the linguistic items used in conversation in different time periods and substantiate the point of change of the items into the markers.

2.2. *Pragmatic change*

'Pragmatic change' is a process of meaning/functional change of linguistic items involving shifts from the semantic to the pragmatic domain. This notion is closest to Traugott's "pragmaticization" (1986: 542) and "semantic-pragmatic change/process" (Traugott 1989 and elsewhere).

Traugott's diachronic research into semantic change during the past decade has discovered regularities in many cases of meaning change, which cover various domains of language. The results she obtained were so regular that she developed some predictive hypotheses. Traugott hypothesised the following order of semantic change:

propositional > ((textual) > (expressive)) (Traugott 1982, 1989)

In this hypothesis, meanings with largely propositional content later acquire textual and/or expressive meanings (Traugott 1989: 31). It is suggested that this direction should be interpreted to "represent mere tendencies, not a strictly unidirectional path" (Traugott 1982: 258). However, this order has been widely evidenced within English and in other world languages (e.g. Myhill 1988 in Spanish, Genetti 1986 in Bodic languages, etc.) since Traugott's studies. With this hypothesised direction as a core, Traugott's studies have played a significant role in the field of historical semantic change. The diachronic analysis of discourse markers also owes its framework to these studies.

Another orientation suggested to accompany the semantic-pragmatic change is the shift from "less to more personal" (Traugott 1982: 253) meanings. This orientation should be understood to mean *not* 'more individualised' but 'more interpersonal/interactive'. In this tendency an item starts being used to inject the speaker's point of view/belief-state/attitude into what is stated. Two additional tendencies, suggested in Traugott's other works, may be discussed together. One is a shift to 'more speaker-based' and the other a shift to 'more discourse-based' meanings (Traugott 1986). The first shift is characterised as more "person-based"/"speaker attributed" (Ibid: 541). The second shift is explained as referring "less to the described situation, and more to the discourse situation" (Ibid: 545). Overall, these two additional tendencies in meaning change seem to conform to the shift from 'less to more personal', i.e. the shift to more interpersonal.

As reviewed above, the preceding studies on historical semantic change have added a great deal to our epistemology. However, a problem in these works should be mentioned. That is, there have been discrepancies between some of their data and what they say in the description of their analysis. Since the subject matter is the *pragmatic* change, the analysts refer to the articulation of speaker attitude or the strategic negotiation of speaker-hearer interaction and other pragmatic aspects of language in their analysis. However, in many cases the data they deal with are traditionally-used intuitive and made-up sentences. There is a somewhat crucial gap between their data and the orientation of the study, namely, the analysis of pragmatics of language. It would be very difficult to look into and see the interactional features in made-up sentences.

The current study, then, will be an attempt to supplement the prior works on semantic/pragmatic change by applying a sounder pragmatic viewpoint, in terms of both theory and methodology. If the interactive/pragmatic facet of language is to be examined accurately, an approach which takes a pragmatic viewpoint and treats the pragmatics of language appropriately (such as Schiffrin 1987) should be employed. Such an approach would look at naturally-occurring language (spoken language) for the analysis of present-day languages, and would study approximations for languages in earlier times (cf. the discussion in Jucker 1994). I admit that historical pragmaticians do not have any faithful records of past spoken language. However, language in literature such as play scripts, popular ballads, conversational segments from fiction, or records of meetings, sermons, depositions of witnesses and private diaries (Jucker Ibid.: 535) are available, if we carefully search for examples of each linguistic item in question. The language used in literature of this kind has to be worth exploring as approximations to our spoken language.[1]

Before closing this section, I would like to specify the domain which the pragmatic viewpoint in my study of pragmatic change covers. Taking a broad view of the scope of pragmatics, the pragmatic viewpoint (e.g. I refer to the pragmatic functions on many occasions in my analysis) in this study takes in context-sensitive meanings including meanings negotiated/created interactively by the speaker and the hearer, discourse functions and speaker's actions.

2.3. Functional-semantic model of language

A functional-semantic model of language is used in Traugott's framework of semantic-pragmatic change. It explains the functions of language well, and it seems to be good in explicating functional shifts in linguistic items. For the study of pragmatic change, I will also employ the same model. Here this model and three functions of language that the model comprises will be introduced.

The functional-semantic model illustrated in Traugott (1982) is a modified version of Halliday and Hasan's (1976) linguistic system. It is also affiliated with Silverstein's (1976) similar approach. Within this model there are three functional-semantic components: propositional (ideational in Halliday and Hasan), textual and expressive (interpersonal in Halliday and Hasan) components.

First, the propositional function has to do with the "resources of the language for making it possible to talk about something" (Traugott 1982: 248). It is "concerned with the expression of 'content', with the function that language has of being ABOUT something" (Halliday and Hasan 1976: 26). This function is called, in other words, the ideational (Halliday and Hasan) or referential function. In my study, except for the parts reviewing or discussing Traugott's research *itself*, the "propositional" function – originally so called in Traugott's (1982) proposal – is replaced by the "ideational" function to avoid the terminological confusion. The reason for this in fact comes from my synchronic analyses of Japanese and English conversations (Onodera 1993a). This reason will be provided in the next paragraph.

In the analysis of the English discourse marker *but~* (Schiffrin 1987), a type of contrast which *but* marks, lies between the two propositions. This is considered to be a genuinely referential contrast because a contrast clearly exists in the words or sentences. On the other hand, in my analysis of Japanese conversation, there were not many purely referential constrasts in the examples of *demo* and *dakedo* that are the equivalents of the English *but*. More often, *demo/dakedo* marks a contrast between two pieces of *inference* that are figured out by the hearer from what is said by the speaker. Thus the hearers (in fact, the participants, since the speaker-hearer shift occurs all the time in normal conversations) continuously need to make inferences in order to interpret the speaker's meaning in the on-going talk.

This happens because of a characteristic of Japanese conversations. In such a conversation, expressing 'what the speaker truly wants to say' is very often avoided. Avoidance of direct expressions and straightforward meanings may come from the fact that in Japanese society indirectness or even ambiguity in expressing 'self' is considered to be polite~ and virtuous. This societal tradition is somewhat opposed to the Western notion of politeness in which "avoid ambiguity" (Grice 1975) is evaluated to be cooperative. As a consequence of this tradition in Japanese conversation, we see the speaker's frequent use of indirect expressions and detours, i.e. prolonged utterances, before reaching his/her point. Accordingly, what the speaker means (intends), rather than what the speaker says, is interpreted due to the inference. This is why *demo/dakedo* marks more 'pragmatically inferable contrast' than 'referential contrast' in Japanese conversation.

Since the 'propositional function' seems too strictly semantic to include both referential and pragmatically inferable contrasts, the 'ideational function' replaces the term 'propositional function' in the remainder of my study.

Second, the textual function is served by "the resources available for creating a cohesive discourse" (Traugott 1982). In Traugott's sense, this function refers only to the intersentential linking function. In Halliday and Hasan's approach, the text-forming function is both inside and "outside the hierarchical organization of system" (in terms of sentences and clauses) (1976: 27). That is, the textual function (and also 'cohesion') refers to both intrasentential and intersentential relations. In fact, in my analysis (section 3), we will see examples of the intrasentential linking function. For instance, the clause-connecting function served by the form, *V-te* + *mo*, shows a proper grammatical function of linking prior and upcoming. However, what is clear in the function of linking two utterances (sentences) (e.g. marked by *demo*) is the contribution to discourse cohesion. This is the point in judging only the intersentential linking function as a textual function in Traugott's and my studies.

Lastly, the expressive function is equipped by

> the resources a language has for expressing personal attitudes to what is being talked about, to the text itself, and to others in the speech situation [...] [They] show [...] attitudes toward, even evaluation of, the propositions [...] (Traugott 1982: 248).

This function is also called 'interpersonal' function[2] and is illustrated in Halliday and Hasan (1976: 26-7) to be:

> concerned with the social, expressive and conative functions of language, with expressing the speaker's 'angle': his attitudes and judgements, his encoding of the role relationships in the situation, and his motive in saying anything at all.

Armed with the notions of the three functions of language specified above, I will examine two items for this study, *demo* and *dakedo*, and explore their functions and their change.

3. Diachronic analysis of the Japanese discourse markers *Demo* and *Dakedo* (Markers of contrast)

My recent synchronic analysis of the hitherto so-called adversative connecting elements *demo* and *dakedo*, i.e. the analysis of their use in Present Day Japanese (PDJ for short) conversation (Onodera 1989, and part of Onodera 1993a), has shown that they are markers of contrast. They mark four kinds of contrast: referential contrast, pragmatically inferable contrast, functional contrast and contrastive actions~. Among these four contrasts, *but* in English conversation marks three other than the pragmatically inferable contrast (cf. Schiffrin 1987). *But* and *dakedo/demo* work almost as equivalent markers in conversation. The only difference, i.e. marking pragmatically inferable contrast by *demo/dakedo*, seems to arise from a feature in Japanese conversation, 'avoidance of directness', which is derived from a societal characteristic of Japan, as mentioned above (in 2.3.).

Before we turn to the diachronic analysis of *demo* and *dakedo*, the four types of contrast marked by *demo* and *dakedo* (more precisely, *V-te + mo, V + kedo, demo* and *dakedo*) – referential contrast, pragmatically inferable contrast, functional contrast and contrastive actions – will be briefly introduced.[3] Then the basic relationship between these four contrasts and the three domains identified in the functional-semantic model of language (2.3.) will be discussed.

Referential contrast is the contrast between contraries that are overtly stated in the discourse (e.g. John is *tall*, but Paul is *short*). 'Referential' here has a rather narrow semantic sense: the contrast lies between propositions with semantic content. In this type of contrast, the contrastive meaning resides in the lexical items that are contrasted.

Pragmatically inferable contrast is the contrast between contraries that are inferred. Again, in Japanese conversation there are few purely referential contrasts, but there are many pragmatically inferable contrasts. As already stated, in Japanese conversation, inference (in other words, derived "conversational implicatures" in Grice's (1975) sense) is often required to understand what is meant rather than what is actually 'said' in an utterance.

Functional contrast is the contrast between functionally differentiated portions of discourse. *Demo* and *dakedo* contrast the functional relation between discourse portions. For example, in a question-answer sequence, the relation between the 'request for information' (question), the 'requested information' (answer), and the extra information, etc. is marked by *demo/dakedo*. In discourse such as an argument, we see that discourse portions such as the speaker's 'position' and 'support' (of the position) are related by their functional roles. This kind of relation, i.e. the functional contrast, is marked by *demo/dakedo*.

The last contrast *demo* and *dakedo* mark is contrastive action. It is defined as contrast between actions, which highlights some contrasting aspects of the speaker-hearer interactional dynamics in the on-going discourse. Specific actions include a speaker's 'opening the conversation' and 'changing the topic', which we will see in examples. In each case, the contrast lies between the actions.

The relationship between the four kinds of contrast mentioned above and the three functions organised in the functional-semantic model of language (ideational function, textual function and expressive function) is suggested. When *demo/dakedo* marks referential or pragmatically inferable contrast, it is assumed to have an ideational function. When *demo/dakedo* marks functional contrast, it is considered to have a textual function. When it marks contrastive actions it is suggested to have an expressive function. This relation is basic, but we should bear in mind that this cannot be a clear-cut one-to-one correspondence. There could be functions running between the three functions of language or there could be other kinds of functions of language which do not fall into Traugott's (1982) or Halliday and Hasan's (1976) trichotomy (cf. Jakobson 1960, Lyons 1977). Although the relationship between the four types of contrast and the three functions organised in the functional-semantic model of language is not a clear-cut correspondence, the following table 1 summarises an approximation of the basic relationship.

Table 1: *The basic relationship between the 4 types of contrast and the 3 functions in a functional-semantic model of language*

		Type of Function in Functional-Semantic Model of Language		
		ideational	textual	expressive
Types of contrast	referential/pragmatically inferable contrast	O		
	functional contrast		O	
	contrastive actions			O

It is also possible that a unit-initial marker (*demo* or *dakedo*) denotes more than two types of contrast at the same time (we will see the cases in which it simultaneously marks two or three kinds of contrast in the examples in my data analysis (3.1. and 3.2.)).[4]

3.1. *Diachronic analysis of the Japanese discourse marker* demo

Let us now turn to an analysis of the historical aspect of *demo* and *dakedo*. While I have examined the two conjunctions together in my synchronic analysis, I will look at them individually in the diachronic analysis, because the two items show parallel functions in PDJ, their history must diverge simply because of their morphological difference.

First, I will analyse *demo*. The historical process by which the item first appeared in the Japanese language as a unit-final element *V-te* + *mo* and then develops into the initial *demo* will be described.[5] I assume that *demo* is composed of *de* (a gerundive form of the so-called copula *da*) + *mo* (an adversative clause-final particle). Then I take the position that the conjunction *demo* developed from a clause-final connecting device *V-te* gerundive form + *mo*. This position is based on the conception that *te* is part of a verbal, i.e. gerundive (Hinds 1986: 84, Jorden 1962 part 1: 46, Jorden and Noda 1987 part 1: 94, Kuno 1973: 28 and elsewhere, Martin 1975: 330), and not a conjunctive particle (many studies in *Kokugogaku* (National Language Studies[6])).

There are three time stages for each in which there is somewhat a shift in the functions of the item. For convenience, I will label the three stages Stage I, Stage II and Stage III. Stage I comprises the period which ranges from the 11th century when the item first appeared as a final element *V-te* + *mo* through the 16th century. *V-te* + *mo* is a connecting device which is in frequent use still in

PDJ. However, Stage I is when the item appeared only as the final *V-te + mo.*
Stage II starts when the item first emerged in sentence-initial positions as *demo*
and was realised as a conjunction around the mid 16th century. This stage
continues through the early 20th century. Finally, Stage III covers the uses of
demo after the early 20th century up to the present.

3.1.1. *Stage I: clause-final* V-te + mo *(11th century-16th century)*

One of the earliest examples of the clause-final connecting device *V-te + mo* in
my data is seen in *Genji monogatari*, written presumably between 1002 and
1008.[7] The language used at this time differs substantially from PDJ in several
ways such as in vocabulary, verb inflection and the use of particles. However, a
device which connects two clauses and sets up the adversative relationship
between them, *V-te + mo,* is already used in this story. This device is still
commonly used in PDJ.

(1) illustrates an early use of *V-te + mo*:

(1) *Genji monogatari* (1008)

Nurse: a.   Akekure, mitate matsuri**te mo**,
               Morning and evening see off HUM[8] but,
               'Although I bid farewell to (Ukifune) in the

        b.   akazu oboe tamai, "itsushika
               dear seem HON,   someday
               morning and in the evening, she remains

        c.   kai aru onsama o, mitate
               valuable figure DO, see off
               so dear in my mind." Someday I will bid

        d.   matsuran" to ashitayuube ni
               HUM will QT morning and evening
               farewell to her figure." Only relying on

        e.   tanomi kikoe tsuru ni koso,
               expect HUM   EMP
               this hope, my life can last.'

        f.   inochi mo nobi haberi tsure.
               life   last HUM EMP

(1) is an excerpt from a section where Lady Ukifune (a woman of high birth)
disappeared, but her body was never found. Her nurses and retainers were in
sorrow at their lady's disappearance. In (1a), *mita-te + matsuri-te + mo* (bid

farewell to-HUM-GER + but) is the *V-te* + *mo* connection. This connecting device links the subordinate clause (a) 'Although I bid farewell to her' (*mitate matsurite* + *mo*) and the main clause (b) '(Ukifune) remains so dear' (*akazu oboe tamai*). Notice, however, that the sentence does not end after the main clause, i.e. both (a) and (b) are in the middle of a long sentence.[9] The *V-te* + *mo* device in (a) marks a pragmatically inferable contrast: 'Ukifune leaves' (inferred from 'I bid farewell to her' (a)) vs. 'She remains' (stated) in (b). This pragmatically inferable contrast mostly donates to the ideational component of language.

Other examples of *V-te* + *mo* in *Genji monogatari* all show its ideational function and a clause-connecting function just like (1). Thus, when the unit-final element *V-te* + *mo* first appeared in the 11th century, it carried only an ideational function and an intrasentential connecting function.

(2) illustrates an example of *V-te* + *mo* in the Muromachi period (1336-1573), taken out of *Jinenkoji* (before 1384), a Noo play script. It is an utterance by the main character.

(2) *Jinenkoji* (before 1384)

  a.   Mi o kokkani kudakite **mo**,
         body DO now break   but
         'Although my body would fall apart,

  b.   kano mono o tasuken tame nari,...
         that person DO save purpose COP
         it (my body falling apart) is to save that person ...'

V-te + *mo* in (a) forms a connecting device, but it is again within a sentence. It also marks a contrast pragmatically inferred from (a) and (b): 'it can be a problem that my body would fall apart' vs. 'it is no problem that my body would fall apart (for saving that person)' (b).

All the examples of *V-te* + *mo* between the 11th and the 16th century (i.e. in Stage I) have an ideational and a clause-connecting function. *V-te* + *mo* does not yet gain expressive or textual functions.

3.1.2. *Stage II:* Demo *as a discourse marker (16th century-early 20th century)*

In Stage II, the item first seems to have been used as a unit-initial element *demo*. When *demo* first appeared as an initial element around the 16th century, its textual and expressive functions are seen together. Therefore, *demo* is considered to be not only a conjunction but a discourse marker. We will see that its expressive function during this time stage is accomplished by a particular contrastive action, 'refutation'.

(3) illustrates an early use of *demo* in *Suehirogari*, a *kyoogen* script which was written around the mid 16th century. A *kyoogen* is a comedy which is basically constructed of dialogues (Shiraishi *et al.* 1953). A *kyoogen* is assumed to be presented in contemporary colloquial style.

(3) Noo kyoogen: *Suehirogari* (around the mid 16th century)

Lord: a. Sore wa daidokoro ni
             That TP kitchen   in
             'That is an umbrella,

        b. nan bon mo aru kasa ja.
            several   umbrella COP
            several of which are in our kitchen.

        c. Sore o motomete kuru
            It DO get   come
            You shouldn't have brought

        d. to iu koto ga aru mono ka.
            QT NOM SB   thing
            it back.'

Retainer: e. **Demo** miyako no mono ga,
             But capital LK people SB
             'But, because people in the capital

        f. 'suehirogari' ja to mooshita
            fan   COP QT say-PST
            told me that it was *suehirogari* (a fan),

        g. ni yotte motomete maitta.
            because get-GER come-PST
            I brought it back.'

In (3a-d), the lord says 'It is an umbrella. You shouldn't have brought it back.' The retainer utters *demo* in (e) and tries to refute his lord's idea by giving his reason for getting that article (e-g): 'Because the people told me it was a fan, I got it.'. Here we see a pragmatically inferable contrast marked by *demo*, i.e. 'it is an umbrella' (a-d) vs. 'it is not an umbrella' (e-g). It is noted that while 'it is an umbrella' is stated, 'it is not an umbrella' is a result of an inference. If 'it is not an umbrella' were also stated, the contrast *demo* in (e) marks would be a 'referential contrast', since the contraries appear on the lexical level. Note, also, that *demo* marks the functional contrast between the two positions taken by the lord (a-d) and the retainer (e-g). Finally, a contrastive action~ is marked here: the retainer's refutation of his lord's idea.

Demo in (e) takes part in constructing ideational meaning: it brings about and expresses the adversative meaning between (a-d) and (e-g). It also plays a role in constructing textual meaning by linking the two utterances (a-d) and (e-g): the textual function operates intersententially. *Demo* in (e) also contributes to an expressive function by marking a 'refutation'.

Many other examples of *demo* are seen in different stories in *kyoogen* scripts of this age. The analysis of *demo* in the mid 16th century, when it first emerged in utterance-initial positions, has revealed: First, *demo* marks all the contrasts it can mark, i.e. referential contrast, pragmatically inferable contrast, functional contrast and contrastive actions. Second, *demo*, at its first appearance already, is used to realise ideational, textual and expressive functions. Since it bears textual and expressive functions, *demo* is considered to be a discourse marker. Third, the only contrastive action marked by *demo* in the 16th century is the speaker's refutation.

Two centuries later, we see uses of *demo* in the Edo humorous short stories (*kobanashi-bon*). *Kobanashi-bon* also includes large amounts of conversational segments. (4) illustrates a use of *demo* in Edo literature.

(4) *Kake-suzuri* (1775)

    A: a. Shikashi, aitsu o
           But   that DO
           'But, if (the thief)

       b. motte itte mo, nan
          bring-GER go-GER but, any
          robs it (kake-suzuri), it

       c. no yaku ni tatsu mai.
          be of use   NEG
          will be of no use.'

    B: d. **Demo** omee, kane ga
          But you,   money SB
          'But, there's money in it,

       e. haitte iru jaa nee kai.
          is   TAG
          isn't there? Man.'

In this humorous short story (*kobanashi*), the main character, A, was robbed of his inkstone case (*kake-suzuri*). *Kake-suzuri* is a case to keep money or an account book, as well as an inkstone and brushes. Right before (4), A said, 'Oh, no, my inkstone case is stolen!' Then he continues (a-c), putting on a show of not caring. B then refutes A's idea in (d-e) with *demo*, because he knows that there is money in the case, a fact that would lead B to infer that A *should* care.

In (4), the pragmatically inferable contrast marked by *demo* in (d) is 'The inkstone case will be of no use' (a-c) vs. 'It will be of use' (d-e). Simultaneously, in this argument (4), as explained in section 3 (p. 401), the speaker's positions of A and B ('I don't care' vs. 'I care') are in functional contrast; this contrast is also marked by *demo* in (d). Finally, *demo* also marks B's contrastive action of showing his refutation to A's idea.

Thus, the examples of *demo* in the late 18th century show exactly the same functions as in the mid 16th century. As to the functional-semantic components of language, *demo* in the late 18th century bears all three functions, just as it did in the 16th century.

We will now go on to analyse the Meiji era (1868-1912). In the novels written in Meiji, I found a fairly widespread use of *demo*. (5) is one such example drawn from *Hakai* (1906).

(5)   *Hakai* (1906)

Official: a.   Kazama san no wa
              Mr. Kazama NOM TP
              'In the case of Mr. Kazama,

        b.   juu yo nen to rokkagetsu
              14 years and 6 months
              it's only 14 years and 6

        c.   ni shika nara nai.
              only   is NEG
              months.'

Segawa: d.   **Demo** arimashoo ga,
              But   would be but,
              'It may be so, but,

        e.   wazuka han toshi no
              only a half a year LK
              if an overlooking of only

        f.   koto de kyooikusha o
              thing educator   DO
              half a year could

g.   hitori osukui kudasaru to shitara.
      one   save give HON QT do-if
      save an educator, ...'

(wouldn't it be possible to give pension
to Mr. Kazama?)

When this excerpt occurred, two high school teachers, the main character
Segawa and Kazama, visited a district government official to consult with him
concerning Kazama's pension. Kazama was about to retire. Before (5), the
official announced that it was impossible for Kazama to draw his pension
because he had worked for less than 15 years, and thus had not fulfilled the
condition for eligibility. Following the official's utterance (a-c), Segawa refutes
him by voicing *demo* in (d) to establish his position. Considering also the
official's statement prior to (a-c), there is a pragmatically inferable contrast
between the official's and Segawa's ideas: 'It's impossible to give pension
against the regulations' vs. 'It's possible to give pension.' As is anticipated, the
functional contrast is between the two characters' positions. Again, the
contrastive action marked by *demo* is to show one speaker's refutation of
another's idea.

In the analysis of *demo* in the 18th centruy (in Edo humorous short
stories) and in the Meiji era (1868-1912), I found that *demo* continued to be
used mostly for a particular function, the speaker's refutation. It is noted that in
the Meiji novels, *demo* in other examples may also show other actions, i.e.
claiming the floor and sub-topic change. However, in each case they are only
secondary contrastive actions of *demo*.

The analysis of *demo* in Stage II (mid 16th century-early 20th century)
has shown the following. First, a content word *demo* first emerged in the
utterance (sentence)-initial position in the mid 16th century. Second, the
functions of *demo* recognised at its first emergence all continue during Stage II:
(1) all four types of contrast – referential and pragmatically-inferable contrasts,
functional contrast and contrastive action – are marked by *demo*. (2) By these
functions of contrasting, all three components of language – ideational, textual
and expressive functions – are served. (3) Only the realisation of the expressive
function is 'refutation'. Third, since all the examples of *demo* in this stage carry
textual and expressive functions, this word is used as a discourse marker.

3.1.3. *Stage III:* Demo *as a discourse marker (PDJ)*

In Stage III, in Present Day Japanese conversations, *demo* continues to serve all
three functions of language that are organised in the functional-semantic model

of language. *Demo* is used as a marker. What is salient in this stage is that *demo* marks more diverse kinds of contrastive actions as the realisation of the expressive function. Independently of 'refutation', which was the only contrastive action marked by *demo* between the 16th century and the early 20th century, it designates four additional actions in conversation. They are (1) point-making, (2) claiming the floor, (3) opening the conversation, and (4) changing the topic. I will illustrate, here, examples of 'opening the conversation' and 'changing the topic'.[10]

(6) shows a use of *demo* which marks the speaker's effort to open a conversation. The three female graduate students talked about plans for the summer. Earlier on the same day Mari had brought up plans for the upcoming summer. We already knew that Midori and I were going to visit Japan. Prior to (6), while walking to the student hall, I remember that we were not talking at all, nor were we paying attention to a single topic. When we found seats and sat down, Mari started talking:

(6) Mari: a. **Demo**, nihon ni kaettara tanoshimi desu ne.
              But   Japan to go back fun   COP FP
              'But, it will be fun, won't it, when you go

        b. Minasan. Oishii mono ippai tabete kite
              Guys.   Delicious food much eat come
              back to Japan, guys? Eat a lot of

        c. kudasai.
              give
              delicious food.'

   Noriko: d. Nee. E, kaeranai no?
              Yeh. Well go NEG
              'Yeh. Well, won't you go back?'

Notice that (a) is the first utterance of the entire conversation. By saying *demo*, Mari attempts to enter into a conversation and furnishes the first topic 'it will be good when you go back to Japan (for vacation).' Notice also that there is no ideational contrast. Because (a) is the first utterance in the discourse, we see nothing to refer to in what precedes (a). Even without marking the ideational contrast, *demo* in (a) was clearly heard as a marker to start a conversation by the other two participants. *Demo* in this case marks a contrastive action by connecting no speech activity (silence prior to (a)) and a lively conversation. *Demo* thus contrasts acts, i.e. no speech activity vs. speech activity.

Another contrastive action which *demo* marks in the PDJ conversation is change of topic. This strategy is commonly used in Japanese conversation. (7) shows an example. When the talk in (7) took place, the topic was the comparison between word processors and computers. Under this topic, smaller units of the topic ('what is talked about', i.e. sub-topics) change in this conversation. In (a-b) Mari tries to provide a sub-topic 'people in the MBA program buy their own computers.' However, in (c-h), latching onto (b), Midori also tries to furnish another sub-topic.

(7) Mari: a.   MBA no hito nanka wa jibun de katteru
                       MBA LK people like TP themselves buy
                       'People in MBA seem to buy their own ones.'

              b.   mitai ne.=
                       seem FP

     Midori: c.   =**Demo** ne, gakkoo de kau to sa, ...
                         But   FP school at buy   FP
                       'But, if we buy one at school, ...

              d.   daigaku n naka de aaiu Educational program
                       university inside   that Educational program
                       at university through something like

              e.   mitai n de,
                       like NOM
                       Educational program,

              f.   IBM toka Apple wa nan paasento biki?
                       IBM or   Apple TP what percent discount
                       we can buy IBM or Apple at what percent discount?

              g.   Yonju (p)paasento biki gurai de kaeru n da
                       40   percent discount about buy NOM COP
                       At about 40 percent discount, we can buy

              h.   tte.
                       QT
                       one.'

     Noriko: i.   Honto?
                                                 Really?
                                                 'Really?'

Midori provided a new sub-topic 'we can buy a computer at a discount at school' in (c-h) and we talked on this sub-topic for a while. Therefore, (c) is thought of as a point of changing to a new sub-topic. *Demo* in (c) marks the speaker's sub-topic change. *Demo* (c) does not seem to mark a pragmatically inferable contrast, because nothing in (a-b) is in contrast with what is inferred from (c-h)[11].

(6) and (7) have described two cases of contrastive action that are marked by *demo*. Notice that in the two examples *demo* does not indicate a referential/pragmatically inferable contrast, i.e. *demo* does not contribute to the ideational function. In these cases, *demo* serves an expressive function by marking the speaker's contrastive actions and a textual function by linking prior and upcoming discourse. These examples of *demo* used in PDJ show that, even without involving ideational function, *demo* is still used to serve an expressive function and indicate the speaker's strategic actions in conversation.

In this section (3.1.), I have traced the process, from Stage I to III, in which the final element *V-te* + *mo* developed into the initial element *demo*. The key finding in this analysis is the following: While the item was in unit-final positions, it had only an ideational function with a connecting function *within* a single sentence. When the item became an utterance-initial word, it had more expanded functions as a discourse marker - not only a textual function but also an expressive function, while keeping its ideational function. Therefore, the initial marker *demo* has all three functions noted by Traugott and said to be the basis for a diachronic path which, in the case of *demo*, involves the period from its first appearance in the 16th century until today.

Another finding is that the number of kinds of contrastive action increased when the time stage shifted into Stage III. This, in fact, means the strengthening of the speaker's subjective meaning. Between the first appearance in the 16th century and the early 20th century, *demo* continued to be used only for a particular pragmatic effect of marking the speaker's refutation. In the early 20th century *demo* may have had other contrastive actions (claiming the floor and sub-topic change). Then in Stage III (PDJ), *demo* has a greater variety of contrastive actions – point-making, claiming the floor, opening the conversation, and changing the topic – that occur independently of the 'refutation' action. The expressive function of *demo* has clearly expanded. The following table 2 summarises this expansion of expressive function.

Table 2: *Expansion of Expressive Function in the Change from* V-te + mo *to*
       Demo

	Stage I *V-te + mo* (11th C-16th C)		Stage II *Demo* (16th C-early 20th C)		Stage III *Demo* (PDJ)
Expressive Function	Ø	>	expressive	>	expressive[+]
Realized Expressive Function	Ø	>	only refutation	>	more varieties 1) point-making 2) claiming the floor 3) opening the conversa- tion 4) changing the topic

The expansion of the expressive function is, in other words, the strengthening of
the speaker meaning. The function of *demo* becomes more speaker/discourse-
based, which was first put forward by Traugott (1986). This expressive
strengthening therefore designates the increase in the interpersonal meaning,
which in fact accords with the process of "subjectification" (Traugott 1989,
p.c.).

       The functional change in *demo* will be discussed again in section 4,
relating to Traugott's assumption, integratedly with the results of the diachronic
analysis of *dakedo*.

3.2. *Diachronic analysis of the Japanese discourse marker* Dakedo

In this section, I will observe the process whereby the unit-final element $V +$
kedo changes into the initial *dakedo*, and look at the functions of the item in
different time stages. I assume that *dakedo*, nowadays widely-recognised as a
conjunction (a free morpheme) (Tokieda 1950, Saji 1970, Kyogoku and Matsui
1973, Aoki 1973, NLRI 1955, etc.), is structured as *da + kedo*. *Da* is most
often analysed as a copula (linking verb). *Kedo* is a conjunctive particle which is
strictly required to be attached to a verb (or an adjective) at clause-final
positions; thus it is a bound morpheme. At clause-final positions, *kedo* can in
fact be appended to any verb other than a copula. I suggest that the content
word *dakedo* is derived from the clause-final connecting expression, $V +$ *kedo*.
The view that the source element of *dakedo* is $V +$ *kedo* seems in fact to be
consistent among scholars.

3.2.1. *Motivation for the occurrence of sentence-initial* Dakedo *(Conjunctions prefaced by* D)

Here, again, as in the case of *demo*, some readers may wonder why *kedo* is agglutinated to the element *da* rather than to anything else when the form $V + kedo$ moves to the sentence-initial position. The question may be, in other words: What is the continuity between the gerundive form of a verb and the gerundive form of a copula? I assume that the motivation which led to the occurrence of sentence-initial *dakedo* (or *demo*), a conjunction prefaced by a copula, is greatly ascribed to the replacing function of the copula (*da*, more strictly its stem *d*) (4.4.1 in Onodera 1993a). I will briefly demonstrate where the element *d* comes from to the beginning of the sentence-initial *dakedo* and in fact many other Japanese conjunctions.

While according to the conventional view *da*'s main function was to be a linking verb, Okutsu (1978)[12] pointed out that *da*'s key function was rather to replace some predicate in prior discourse. Indebted to this replacing function, *da* in fact works as an economical and rational strategy in both Japanese grammar and conversation (Onodera 1993b).

The following shows how *da* replaces other verbs. *Da* in (a) replaces the underlined predicates in (b), (c) and (d). (The usual translation of sentence (a) is 'I am an eel', probably based on the conventional conception that *da* is a copula.)

(a) Boku wa unagi *da*.
     I   TP an eel
     'I am an eel.'
     'Concerning myself, it is an eel.'

(b) Boku wa unagi *o tsutta*.
     I   TP an eel DO caught
     'I caught an eel.'

(c) Boku wa unagi *o chuumon suru*.
     I   TP an eel DO (will) order
     'I will order an eel.'

(d) Boku wa unagi *o taberu*.
     I   TP an eel DO (will) eat
     'I will eat an eel.'

(cf. 4.4.1 in Onodera 1993a)

When other verbs are used in what precedes, or even when they are just shared by the speaker and hearer, or presupposed, such verbs do not need to be repeated in the current sentence (utterance). Instead, we can simply use *da* rather than repeat the same predicate, which can be lengthy. The following interchange demonstrates that *da* is used instead of repeating a prior verb. A and B are male speakers who play baseball.

A: a.   Kinoo ame ga futta.
              Yesterday rain SB fell.
              'Yesterday it rained.'

B: b₁.   *Dakedo* boku wa renshuu ni itta.
              But   I   TP training to went
              'But I went to the (baseball) training.' (cf. Okutsu 1978: 33-4)

....

      b₂.   *Futta kedo*,
              Fell (it rained) but
              'Although it rained (yesterday),

              boku wa renshuu ni itta.
              I   TP training to went
              I went to the training.'

When speaker B says *dakedo* as in (b₁), *da* in fact replaces the predicate in (a), *futta* ('fell').[13] If B repeats the predicate *futta* as in (b₂), B can make a statement conveying the same sense in (b₁). The sentences (utterances) (b₁) and (b₂) are both fully grammatical and they carry exactly the same information. The difference is: in (b₁) *da* in *dakedo* replaces the predicate *futta* just given before by another speaker, therefore (b₁) is not redundant. *Da* avoids repetition of the same predicate. And this is *da*'s replacement strategy. I may suggest here that not only the meaning of the predicate 'fall-past' (*futta*) but the whole meaning of A's utterance 'Yesterday it rained.' (*Kinoo ame ga futta.*) is calculated by the hearer and conveyed with the replacing function of *dakedo* in (b₁). This is because the other part of the sentence, rather than only the predicate, is also recovered from the textual context. Thus, by means of *da*'s replacement strategy in Japanese, in many cases, in addition to the replacement of a prior predicate, even the whole meaning of a prior sentence (utterance) can be recovered by the other participant.

    With *da*'s entire function being to replace what is prior to the sentence-initial position, I suggest that *da* contributes to establishing the presupposed condition ('background' event) for the following main clause in which 'foreground' information is often encoded. In other words, this *da* strategy supplies the "frame" or the "topic" of the main clause (cf. Traugott 1985: 295, Schiffrin 1988: 4).

As explained briefly above, the answer to the question where *dakedo* (or *demo*), a conjunction initiated by a copula, comes from seems to owe a clue to the replacement function of *da*. Since the final element $V + kedo$ (or $V\text{-}te + mo$) develops into the initial *dakedo* (or *demo*) rather than any other form in the sentence-initial position, the element *da* (*de*) can replace freely what is prior (centrally a prior predicate). As a result, this replacement function of *da* contributes to many other of the speaker's conversational strategies by realising many conjunctions other than *dakedo* and *demo* (such as *daga*, *dakara*, *datte* and *denakereba*). These conjunctions (sentence-initial expressions) all prefaced by *d* owe their acquisition of a strong textual function as connectives to the replacement function of *d*, too.

Investigating the word-formation of these conjunctions as above, it seems to be rational that the element *d* appears at their beginning. In the sentence-initial positions, *d* in different conjunctions refers to what is prior: e.g. just a preceding predicate in the on-going discourse, what the participants were talking about on the preceding day, and what has just been recalled by the participants, etc. In each case of *d*'s replacing what is prior, *d* focuses on a predicate. However, as stated before, the range to which *d* can refer (replace) is somewhat broad, with a predicate as the centre. We can indeed recover many topics and facts beyond some temporal distance by this function of *d* in Japanese conversation. In fact, many conjunctions in Japanese are prefaced by *d*, and they are strong in terms of both conversational strategic use and textual function.

When the final elements such as $V + kedo$ and $V\text{-}te + mo$ move into sentence-initial positions, no other verb but *d* emerges as an element initiating a conjunction, representing (or replacing) other verbs.

Let us now return to the discussion which preludes to the diachronic analysis of ($V + kedo$ and) *dakedo*. There are two stages recognised in this item's functional change. For convenience, the first and second stages are called Stages I and II. Stage I begins in the 18th century, when item $V + kedo$ seemed to have first appeared in the Japanese language, and goes through the early 20th century. During this stage, we see this item only in clause-final positions. Stage II starts in the early 20th century when the item first emerged in sentence-initial positions as *dakedo*, which is a content word and a conjunction. Stage II covers the period from the early 20th century until the present.

3.2.2. *Stage I: clause-final* V + kedo *(18th century – early 20th century)*

As far as I know, the oldest example of the final connecting device *V* + *kedo* appears in a *jooruri* (ballad drama) book, *Chuushin kana tanzaku* (1732). This occurrence is also reported in Yuzawa (1970) and Uchio and Okamura (1973). (8) illustrates one of the earliest examples of *V* + *kedo*.

(8) *Chuushin kana tanzaku* (1732)

A: a.   Inakamono ja to **iwa nsu kedo,**
             Countrywoman COP QT say HON but,
             'Although (you) call (me) a countrywoman,

    b.   kyoo hazukashii umai sakari,
             capital fine   delicious at (its) best
             since it is at its best,

    c.   hitokuchi kuwazu ni okarenu me nsu.
             a mouthful eat NEG cannot help
             I can't help eating a mouthful of it.'

In the sources only the utterance in (8) is cited, and the preceding and following discourse is not available. In (8), A says, 'Although (you) call a person who eats such a thing a countrywoman, I can't help trying a mouthful of it.' In this example *V* + *kedo* (*iwa-nsu* + *kedo*) marks a pragmatically inferable contrast, i.e. 'You think a countrywoman is something I should mind' (a) vs. 'I don't think a countrywoman is something I should mind' (b–c). *V* + *kedo* in (a) could mark a contrastive action~: if prior to (a) another speaker in fact called A a countrywoman, and in (a) A attempted to refute/challenge what another speaker said. However, since the surrounding textual content is not available (even the subject of the verb 'call' in (a) is ambiguous), any possible contrastive action cannot be discussed further. *V* + *kedo* does not seem to mark a functional contrast. The pragmatically inferable contrast makes a contribution to the ideational function. Thus, in the final connecting element *V* + *kedo* in (8), we see an ideational function and a clause-connecting function.

Another example where *V* + *kedo* shows an ideational function is drawn from a *kabuki* script written later in the 18th century. (9) is such an example.

(9) *Sanjikkoku yofune no hajimari* (1758)

a.   Chitto ome ni wa **irimasu mai kedo,**
      A little eyes in   enter would not but
      'Although it doesn't usually draw

b.   suwa to iwaba donata demo,
      when the time comes anyone (HON)
      (people's) attention, it is a fine

c.   doitsu demo kiri kanenu
      anyone   cut would
      sword which would cut just

d.   wazamono degozarimasu.
      a fine sword COP
      anybody when the time comes.'

In (9), *irimasu* + *mai* (a polite form of *iru* (to enter) + a modal auxiliary expressing the unlikelihood of an affair in the near future) constitute a VP in a subordinate clause (a). *Irimasu-mai* + *kedo* is the clause-final connecting element in (9). Its function is, as in (8), to link a subordinate clause (a) and a main clause (b-d): this clause-connecting device operates only within a sentence. V + *kedo* expresses the adversative relationship between the two clauses and is involved in the transmission of propositional information. There is no full-fledged expressive or textual function. Thus, V + *kedo* maintains an ideational function and the grammatical function of clause-linking.

In this section, I have traced the use of V + *kedo*. In summary, the clause-final connecting device V + *kedo*, which is the source element of the conjunction *dakedo*, contributes to the ideational function of language and serves a clause-connecting function.

3.2.3. *Stage II:* Dakedo~ *as a discourse marker (early 20th century-PDJ)*

In the Taishoo era (1912–1926), the final expression V + *kedo* is in more common use. Upon the more frequent use of its unit-final correspondent, we first meet the initial element *dakedo*. Today *dakedo* is widely recognised as a conjunction (Tokieda 1950, Saji 1970, Kyogoku and Matsui 1973, Aoki 1973, NLRI 1955, etc.). Hence, it is now a content word, consisting of two morphemes *da* and *kedo*, while the final element V + *kedo* contains two separate words. In this section, I will analyse the use of *dakedo* from the

Taishoo era, when this item seems to have appeared first (cf. Aoki 1973[14]) to the present day.

As for *dakedo* in the Taishoo era, it is recognised that in some contexts it has ideational and textual functions and in others ideational, textual and expressive functions: Expressive function is *optional* for *dakedo* at this time stage. I will first illustrate *dakedo* with ideational and textual functions, and next *dakedo* with all three functions.

Dakedo which has ideational and textual functions is considered a discourse marker, since it has the textual function of linking portions of discourse intersententially. (10) is an example. This excerpt is cited from *Anya kooro* (1922), a novel. When this excerpt took place, the main character (Kensaku), whose baby had been sick, had hired a nurse (Nurse H). Kensaku and his wife had been very satisfied with Nurse H. However, considering H's health, another nurse was hired to support H. H did not like the way the other nurse cared for the baby. Nurse H then says:

(10) *Anya kooro* (1922)

Nurse H: a.   Moshi watashi no tame
                     If   me   LK
                     'If it is for me,

               b.   deshitara, dooka moo
                     COP-if   please no more
                               please do not

               c.   otanomi ni naranai de
                     ask-HON   NEG
                     hire another one (nurse) again.

               d.   itadakimasu.
                     receive

               e.   **Dakedo,** watashi hitori de
                     But,   me   alone   COP-GER
                     But, if you think that only me is not

               f.   gofujiyuu da to oboshimesu
                     inconvenient COP QT think HON
                     enough, do it for yourselves, though.'

g.   n deshitara betsu desu kedo.
       NOM COP-if other COP but

In (10), *dakedo* in (e) marks a referential contrast, 'Don't hire another nurse for
me' (a-d) vs. 'Do it for yourselves' (e-g). *Dakedo* also marks a functional
contrast. In (10) H sounds as if she were considering the pros and cons of hiring
another nurse. The pros ('Hire another nurse for yourselves') in (e-g) and the
cons ('Don't hire for me') in (a-d) are contrasting alternating opinions in an
argument, and they are marked as one kind of functional contrast.

As suggested before, when *dakedo* marks a referential contrast, it serves
an ideational function. *Dakedo* also has a full-fledged textual function, i.e. the
function of linking two utterances (a-d) and (e-g). This is an intersentential
linking function. As explained in the discussion on the motivation of the
appearance of the initial *dakedo* in (3.2.1), the element *d* in the word *dakedo*
contributes to this word's textual function because of *d*'s replacement function.

As seen in (10), some instances of *dakedo* at its first emergence in initial
positions contribute to the ideational and textual components of language. I will
now show that other instances also have expressive function. I will look at
dakedo with ideational and textual functions, and also with an expressive
function, which is optional.

The first example is a case in which *dakedo* marks a contrastive action,
'point-making'. With the use of *dakedo*, the speaker sometimes returns to
his/her position to make his/her point in conversation. In (11), we see this use of
dakedo. (11) is an excerpt drawn from an argument between Kensaku and
Naoko in *Anya kooro* (1922). Kensaku and Naoko's baby had been seriously ill.
Prior to (11), Kensaku attempted to persuade Naoko not to worry. Naoko
rebutted by saying that Kensaku's request was an impossibility for her.
Kensaku, then, told her again that her optimistic attitude was indispensable for
their baby. Naoko then says that she knows how she should be, but she also
knows a case in which a baby died of the same disease that their baby has. She
continues:

(11) *Anya kooro* (1922)

Naoko: a.   Sore o shitte iru node,
                  That DO know-GER because,
                  'Because I know it (the more serious case of

           b.   nandaka shinpai de shikata
                  somehow worry COP-GER cannot
                  another baby), somehow I can't

c.   ga nai no.
        help   FP
        help worrying.

d.   **Dakedo**, hontooni watashi,
        But,   really,   I
        But, I will really try to

e.   dekirudake byooki no koto,
        as much as possible disease LK NOM
        forget about (the baby's) sickness

f.   wasureru yoo ni kokorogake masu wa.
        forget   NOM try   FP
        as much as possible.'

Naoko's general position in this exchange is that she will try not to worry about
the baby's sickness. Right before (11), Naoko provided the reason for her
worry, i.e. she knew about a more serious case involving another baby. After
giving this reason to her husband, she says *dakedo* in (d), and tries to return to
her position and says 'I will try to forget the baby's sickness' in (d-f). *Dakedo* in
(d), thus, marks the speaker's contrastive action, point-making and return to her
position. We also recognise the pragmatically inferable contrast between 'I can't
help worrying' stated in (a-c) vs. 'I will try not to worry' inferred from (d-f).
Since *dakedo* here marks a contrastive action, this *dakedo* has an expressive
function in addition to its ideational and textual functions.

I will examine one more example in which *dakedo* serves an expressive
function. In (12), *dakedo* marks the speaker's contrastive action of 'changing
the sub-topic'. (12) is again quoted from *Anya kooro*. When (12) took place,
Kensaku was meeting his two younger sisters after a long time. The sisters
asked about Kensaku's wedding which was to be held soon. Preceding (12), the
youngest sister, Taeko, said, 'I would like to go to Kyoto, then (to attend the
wedding).'

(12) *Anya kooro* (1922)

Kensaku: a.   Oniisan ni tsurete kite
                    Brother   take-GER come-GER
                    'You can ask your brother

b.   morau sa.
        receive FP
        to take you.'

Taeko: c.   Ee, sono tsumori.
                Yes, that intention
                'Yes, I'm planning to do that.

        d.   **Dakedo**, itsu na no?
            But,   when COP FP
            But, when will it be?

        e.   Gakkoo ga oyasumi de
            School SB off   COP
            It's impossible unless

        f.   nai to dame na no yo.
            NEG impossible COP FP FP
            I have a holiday from school.'

Kensaku suggests in (a-b) that Taeko ask the elder brother to take her to the wedding. In (c), Taeko shows her agreement with this suggestion and thus maintains the same sub-topic as in (a-b). However, after this, Taeko says *dakedo* and provides a request for information concerning the time when the wedding will be. *Dakedo* here seems to mark Taeko's action of changing the sub-topic. Since sub-topics (and topics) are referentially different information chunks, *dakedo* also marks a referential contrast. Therefore, in (12), *dakedo* is involved in the expressive and ideational components of language as well as in the textual component.

In the Taishoo period, the expressive function of *dakedo* was realised by contrastive actions, 'point-making' (11), 'changing the sub-topic' (12) and 'claiming the floor'.

Following the Taishoo period, in PDJ conversation, we recognise almost the same functions in the uses of *dakedo*. It serves all ideational, textual and expressive functions. The only difference with regards to *dakedo* in PDJ from that in *Taishoo* consists in the expansion of the expressive function. More recently, we in fact see a more widespread use of *dakedo*. In those examples, *dakedo* shows strengthened expressive function by marking contrastive actions more frequently. In addition to the above three contrastive actions seen in *Taishoo*, *dakedo* marks at least one further variety 'opening the conversation'.

Above, I have traced the diachronic process in which the clause-final V + *kedo* came to be used as the utterance-initial *dakedo*. The primary finding is the following: First, as a final connecting element, V + *kedo* carries only an ideational function and an intrasentential connecting function. When this element emerged in utterance-initial positions, as *dakedo*, it began to be used as a discourse marker with ideational and textual functions and, optionally, an expressive function. Armed with expressive function, the marker *dakedo* started articulating the speaker's own evaluation/point of view in *Taishoo*.[15] Still, more recently, it has been recognised that the expressive function has been strengthened. The expressive (interpersonal) strengthening is realised in the process of *dakedo*, as well as in that of *demo*. Second, as for the connecting function, this function of the final V + *kedo* and that of the initial *dakedo* differ in the scope within which this function is realised: V + *kedo* is only a clause-connecting device, while *dakedo* serves an intersentential linking function. Thus, the scope of the connecting function is enlarged (sentence → discourse). This increase in scope allows the textual function of *dakedo*, but not V + *kedo*.

4.   Pragmatic change in the Japanese discourse markers *Demo* and *Dakedo*

In the following section, the diachronic analyses of *demo* (3.1.) and *dakedo* (3.2.) will be reviewed, and I will discuss the direction of their functional change, focusing on Traugott's assumption. The diachronic process in the functions of *demo* is summarised in (A). In (A), "+" superscribed on "expressive" in Stage III indicates that the expressive function has expanded, in comparison to the preceding time stages.

(A) Pragmatic Change in *Demo*

Stage I		Stage II		Stage III
V-te + *mo* (11th C–16th C)		*Demo* (16th C–18th C–early 20th C)		*Demo* (PDJ)
ideational	>	ideational textual expressive	>	ideational textual expressive[+]

The ideational function seems to have been maintained throughout the course of *demo*'s history. The item keeps this function both in unit-final and initial positions.

The textual function arises when the item first emerges in the initial positions in the mid 16th century. Although *V-te* + *mo* had a connecting function, it worked only within a sentence. It is not a full-fledged textual function. The connecting function of *demo*, on the other hand, works beyond the sentence level. This is indeed such a strong linking power that it connects at least two sentences, i.e. two portions of discourse. This textual function creates cohesion.

The expressive function also emerges at the first appearance of *demo*. The examples of *demo* from its first appearance in the 16th century through the early 20th century show its expressive function by marking mostly the speaker's action of refuting the other's idea. The expressive function, however, expands at some point, because *demo* in PDJ is observed to have at least four more varieties of expressive function.

I suggest that the diachronic process of *demo* follows the general direction in meaning/functional changes that has been hypothesised in Traugott (1989: 31): propositional (ideational) > ((textual) > (expressive)). This direction has been in fact attested to in different word classes in several world languages (Traugott 1986, 1988a, 1988b, 1989, Genetti 1986, Myhill 1988 and elsewhere).

The diachronic process of *demo* is also put forward to follow another tendency in meaning shift from "less personal to more personal" proposed in Traugott (1982: 253). The path along which the item developed from *V-te* + *mo* into *demo* experienced a meaning shift from ideational to more speaker − and interaction − based. While *V-te* + *mo* is concerned only with "the expression of content" (=ideational), *demo* is concerned with "expressing the speaker's 'angle'" (Halliday and Hasan 1976: 267).

One thing should be noted. I proposed the direction of the pragmatic change of *demo* as (A), and further suggested that it pursued the tendency of functional change: ideational > ((textual) > expressive). However, the change in *demo* in (A) does not occur in an abrupt linear fashion, but the process is rather gradual, i.e. the change in *demo* is multi-functional. Traugott's (1982: 256) original idea also seems to agree that this is not a linear, but a gradual process.

The diachronic process of the functional shift in *dakedo* is, in summary schematised as (B).

(B)   Pragmatic Change in *Dakedo*

Stage I   Stage II

$V + kedo$ (18th C – early 20th C)   *Dakedo* (early 20th C – PDJ)

ideational   >   ideational
                                             textual (> expressive)

The ideational function is sustained in the whole historical process of *dakedo*. When the original final element $V + kedo$ evolved to emerge as *dakedo* in initial positions, we saw that *dakedo* had ideational and textual functions, and optionally expressive function. In PDJ, *dakedo*'s expressive function is strengthened both in frequency and variety. Accordingly, I tentatively suggest the direction 'textual (> expressive)' in the course of change of *dakedo*, as illustrated in (B). Thus the diachronic process in *dakedo* has been revealed to be a semantic-pragmatic change, and it also conforms to the two tendencies in meaning change in general which *demo* follows.

In conclusion, the pragmatic change in both *demo* and *dakedo* seems to follow Traugott's hypothesised directions:

ideational > ((textual) > (expressive))
less personal to more personal

In Japanese as well as in English, Spanish (Myhill 1988), Bodic (Genetti 1986) and other languages, cases that support Traugott's hypothesis with regard to functional change have also been discovered.

One more thing is briefly mentioned, concerning the motive for the positional shift, i.e. the process in which the final V-$te + mo/V + kedo$ move into sentence-initial position. This issue may be somewhat related to a typological characteristic of Japanese. In such a shift, first, the subordinate clauses V-$te + mo$ and $V + kedo$ are detached from the rest of the sentence by 'postposing'[16] which occurs often in Japanese conversation. Then, those subordinate clauses which have become movable start being used in utterance-initial positions. In initial positions, as opening brackets (see 2.1.), the items then start working as markers with expanded pragmatic functions. This positional shift in the items observed above appears to be plausible in our naturally-occurring simultaneous discourse.

5. Conclusion: Pragmatic change and grammaticalisation

I now answer one of the questions posed at the beginning of this paper: Are the pragmatic functions newly-found in recent studies really new? In short, the answer is no. The Japanese discourse markers *demo* and *dakedo* were first discovered to be markers in Present Day Japanese. However, through a diachronic analysis, their pragmatic functions as markers have been found to have first appeared not in our present-day language, but in the language of much earlier days. *Demo*'s appearance as a marker in fact dates back to the 16th century, and it started serving its expressive and textual functions then. And *dakedo*'s appearance as a marker dates from the early 20th century. The development of discourse studies occurred during the last half century, and their contribution to our epistemology by newly finding the pragmatic functions of language seems to have been appreciated. However, we should bear in mind that those pragmatic functions themselves are not always new. They are newly-found in the synchronic analysis of language, but once they are approached diachronically their true history will be clearly revealed. To suggest the importance of holding this diachronic viewpoint in the study of pragmatics may be one of the main purposes of this book. I also hope that the field of pragmatic studies with a diachronic perspective will grow in the future.

Concluding this paper, I suggest that the diachronic process which *demo* and *dakedo* undergo follows another kind of diachronic process, grammaticalisation, as well as semantic-pragmatic change which has been just found in what precedes. Grammaticalisation is defined in Traugott and König (1991: 189) to

> refer(s) primarily to the dynamic, unidirectional historical process whereby lexical items in the course of time acquire a new status as grammatical, morphosyntactic forms, and in the process come to code relations that either were not coded before or were coded differently.

Although a statement such as "there is no full agreement on definitions of grammatical forms" (Hopper and Traugott 1993: 4) suggests that ambiguity and disputability still exist in this field, I attempt to show that the diachronic process of *demo* and *dakedo* involves not only a pragmatic change, but a grammaticalisation process.

Here I focus on the process which *dakedo* underwent. As seen in (3.2.) and section 4, the functional change in *dakedo* is schematised as:

Stage I	Stage II
V + *kedo* (18th C-early 20th C)	*Dakedo* (early 20th C-PDJ)
ideational >	ideational
	textual (> expressive)

Now, attention is paid to *dakedo*'s change in form, and I will focus on the element *da*.

    V + *kedo* is a clause-final connecting phrasal construction (Stage I). As well as any other verb, a copula *da* can occur preceding a connecting particle *kedo*. In this stage, *da* carries full semantic content as a linking verb (i.e. 'A *is* B.' In Japanese, 'A wa B *da*.') (The first step). When this element first appears in sentence-initial positions as *dakedo* (in Stage II), the element is recognised as an independent word and a conjunction. Recall that on its first appearance, *dakedo*'s expressive function was only optional. When *dakedo* serves an ideational function, we have seen that *dakedo* marks either referential or pragmatically inferable contrast. In the operation of marking referential/pragmatically inferable contrast, *da*'s main function is not to be a copula, but to replace a predicate stated in prior discourse. This is the 'replacing function' of *da* which I explained in (3.2.1.). Because of this function of replacing a prior verb, *da* (or its stem *d*) can be called a pro-predicate or an auxiliary (The second step). After its first appearance in the early 20th century, we saw that *dakedo* served an expressive function even without serving an ideational function. In this case of independently operating expressive function, *da*'s replacing function is not seen. In my data, some examples of 'starting conversation' and 'point-making' show such cases. With these uses of *dakedo*, the speaker's own subjective point of view/attitude/belief-state is expressed (The final step). The above three steps in the formal change of *dakedo* are summarised as (A):

(A)   da + kedo   > da|kedo   >   dakedo
      (clause-final)   (sentence-initial)   (sentence-initial)

Let us compare this change of *dakedo* with another change in an English expression analysed in Hopper and Traugott (1993: 13). They look at the widespread use of *lets* to show that grammaticalisation is an everyday fact of language. The case of change in *lets*, often regarded as peripheral, illustrates an interesting semantic change. The first use is shown in (a).

    (a)   Let us go. (i.e. release us.) (Ibid.: 11)

It is a second-person imperative, and the subject of *let* is 'you'. Then the second use, sometimes called 'adhortative', is exemplified in (b).

(b)   Let's go to the circus tonight. (Ibid.)

This use involves urging or encouraging. It is an ordinary use of a 'first-person imperative'. Now, the third use (c) is noticed in very colloquial English.

(c)   Lets give you a hand. (Ibid.)

While the use of *let's* continues being distributed in conversation, it spreads even to non-first person plural subjects. This use can be described as "no more than an introductory particle" (Quirk *et al*. 1973: 404).

The formal change in the element *us* is now summarised. A first person pronoun *us* becomes cliticised in the transition from (a) to (b). Then *us* even loses its status as a separate morpheme and becomes a simple phonemic constituent of a monomorphemic word in (c) (Hopper and Traugott 1993: 13). This formal change:

(A')   (let) us > (let)'s > (let)s

explains a more general shift of

(B')   word > affix > phoneme (Ibid.)

If we appraise the formal change in *dakedo* as in (A)

(A)   *da* + kedo   >   *da*|kedo   >   *da*kedo
              (clause-final)(sentence-initial)(sentence-initial)

parallel to the case of *let's*, the path which the element *da* follows also illustrates a more general shift of

(B)   word > auxiliary > syllable
              (verb)

While *da* serves a replacing function, it works as a pro-predicate (like an auxiliary) (The second step). However, when *dakedo* is employed in more strategic uses by a speaker, for example 'starting conversation' and 'point-making', *da*'s replacing function, i.e. its function as an auxiliary, is no longer seen (The final step). *Da* becomes one syllabic constituent of the monomorphemic word *dakedo*. Here, *da* is a syllable,[17] rather than a phoneme, as the element *us* ended up in the grammaticalisation process of *lets*. In either case of *lets* or *dakedo*, however, the element in the final step (*s* and *da*) becomes just a phonemic element which has lost or is in the process of losing its semantic content. In the process of *da*, there is a clear gradual loss in semantic complexity. The sense of *da* becomes less specific and more general.

In Hopper and Traugott (1993: 13), the new function of *lets* (c) is said to be "provisional [...] rather than permanent and absolute; *lets* may not survive". However, this new grammatical resource is also regarded to have "entered the language and to be available to speakers for the building of interactive discourse" (Ibid.). In our analysis of *dakedo* (3.2.), it has also been recognised that the first emergence of unit-initial *dakedo* in language is ascribed to strategic convenience in interactional discourse. As can be seen, with its replacing function, *da* in the sentence-initial position contributes considerably to conversational strategies. By freely replacing (referring to) yesterday's topics or shared topics beyond the temporal distance, *dakedo* is used for specific strategies such as 'changing the topic' and 'opening the conversation'. But the frequent use of this discourse strategy has led eventually to the establishment of a free morpheme, a conjunction *dakedo*. The view is recalled here that discourse frequency indicates the emergence of new grammatical patterns (Givón 1984, Hopper 1987).

I have suggested that the diachronic paths which *demo* and *dakedo* have undergone involve grammaticalisation. In addition to the change in *lets*, the cases of *demo* and *dakedo* share the characteristics commonly seen in grammaticalisation processes: "(a) earlier forms may coexist with later ones [...], (b) earlier meanings may constrain later meanings [...]" (Hopper and Traugott 1993: 17).

With respect to formal change, it is true that the cases of *demo* and *dakedo* follow tendencies somewhat opposite to many other examples of grammaticalisation. Such tendencies are (1) the change from clitics (*-mo* and *-kedo*) to independent words (*demo* and *dakedo*), and (2) the enlargement of the scope of an item (also analysed in Matsumoto 1988). As for (2), the connecting function in *demo/dakedo*, which is intersentential, is larger than the same function in unit-final *V-te* + *mo/V* + *kedo*, which is intrasentential: this is the reverse process of the typical examples. Although these two directions in the changes of *demo* and *dakedo* are still disputable, further analyses of linguistic typology which may have an influence on the changes in *form* should be proposed. In the study of grammaticalisation, analysts treat both functional/meaning change and formal change in items of concern. With respect to formal change, the Japanese cases of *demo* and *dakedo* have showed some opposition to other examples discovered in languages such as English. However, this kind of difference in the direction of formal change might occur according to typological differences in language; for example word-order, pre-/post-positional languages, and so forth.[18]

There is another characteristic which proves that the processes which *demo* and *dakedo* undergo take part in grammaticalisation. That is, words belonging to an open class, like that of nouns and verbs, develop into closed class words such as adverbs and conjunctions (Heine, Claudi and Hünnemeyer 1991: 3). Sankoff (1988: 17) also states that an instance of grammaticalisation is constituted when "the once content-words or open-class morphemes of the language have become function words, or closed class morphemes". In conclusion, the diachronic process of *demo* and *dakedo* fulfils the definition of grammaticalisation (Traugott and König 1991) mentioned at the beginning of section 5, in addition to some other common features in the grammaticalisation process.

Lastly, the discovery that the diachronic process of some Japanese discourse markers involves grammaticalisation is suggested to cover the whole group of discourse markers. Schiffrin (1992: 363) writes that the English discourse marker *then* undergoes a semantic-pragmatic change and it also figures in "grammaticalisation, the historical process whereby lexical items acquire a new status as grammatical, morphosyntactic forms". This finding in English, a language typologically quite different from Japanese, advances the following. Discourse markers may be a synchronic reflection of both semantic-pragmatic change and grammaticalisation, whereby the elements come to express more the speaker's subjective evaluation in meaning and capture a novel status as grammatical figures.

Notes

* I wish to express my sincere gratitude to my doctoral thesis committee: Deborah Schiffrin, Deborah Tannen and Senko K. Maynard. A special thank-you is due to Elizabeth C. Traugott, who gave invaluable comments on the earlier version of this paper, especially on the issue of grammaticalisation. I am also grateful for the useful comments of Andreas Jucker, Ryoko Suzuki, Peter Ackermann and Jo Eitington. I am of course solely responsible for any errors of fact or interpretation.

1.   The examples in this paper are drawn from the following literature as approximations to our spoken language.

Genji monogatari, 1008: a novel

Jinenkoji, before 1384: a *noo* script

Suehirogari, around the mid 16th C: a *kyoogen* script

Chuushin kana tanzaku, 1732: a *jooruri* script

Sanjikkoku yofune no hajimari, 1758: a *kabuki* script

Kake-suzuri, 1775: a *kobanashi* (humorous short story)

Hakai, 1906: a novel

Anya kooro, 1922: a novel

I extracted conversational segments from novels and a *kobanashi*. *Noo, kyoogen, jooruri* and *kabuki* are all Japanese traditional plays with long histories. (*Kyoogen* originated in around the 12th century, so did *noo* in the 14th century, and *jooruri* and *kabuki* in the 16th century.) The play scripts are comprised primarily of the performers' lines that should be close to the spoken language of those days. For the analysis of the PDJ for which the naturally-occurring language is available, I also looked at tape-recorded conversations.

2.   I appreciate a useful discussion with Sachiko Ide and Tetsuo Kumatoridani on the terminology of this function. My current view is that when the language is trichotomised, as in a functional-semantic model, into ideational, textual and expressive functions, part of the 'expressive function' evinces interpersonal and social meanings.

3.   For a fuller explanation and definition of each type of contrast, see (3.2.) *Referential Contrast and Pragmatically Inferable Contrast*, (3.3.) *Functional Contrast* and (3.4.) *Contrastive Actions* in Onodera (1993a).

4.   We will see soon that when unit-final elements (V-*te* + *mo* and V + *kedo*) mark contrast, they mark only referential or pragmatically inferable contrast. This is because they still do not bear an intersentential linking function which allows a textual function and they do not bear an expressive function as markers. In comparison, since unit-initial markers (*demo* and *dakedo*) are conjunctions with an intersentential linking function, they always seem to show the textual function. This textual function is recognised in the connection of something prior and something upcoming beyond the sentence-level.

5.   Some readers may wonder why V-*te* + *mo* (the *te* gerundive form of *any* verb + *mo*) develops into *demo* (composed of the gerundive form of the *copula* + *mo*). I will answer this question in (section 3.2.1.) when I explain why the final V + *kedo* changes into the initial *dakedo*. See (3.2.1).

6.   National Language Studies (*Kokugogaku*) is one branch in the study of the Japanese language that has a long history. For instance, the grammar taught in school in Japan is mainly influenced by *Kokugogaku*.

7.   My basic standpoint towards the concept of "the first appearance" of an item is provided in note 14. Please see note 14 as for "the first appearance". This standpoint is valid throughout this paper.

8.   In my transcript, a word-for-word (morpheme-for-morpheme) gloss is given on the line between the Japanese utterance and the free translation. The following abbreviations are used in my examples:

COP   copula
DO   direct object
EMP   emphatic
FP   sentence-final particle
GER   gerundive form
HON   honorific
HUM   humble
LK   linker
NEG   negative
NOM   nominaliser
PST   past/perfect tense
QT   quotative marker
SB   subject marker
TAG   tag-question-like expressions such as auxiliary verb forms (e.g.
           desho, daro, ja-nai) and the interjection and FP *ne(e)*
TP   topic marker

9.   In the Japanese of those days, a sentence presumably tended to be long, consisting of many successive clauses.

10.   For examples and discussions on other contrastive actions which *demo* marks, see Chapter 3 in Onodera (1993a).

11.   If a topic is considered to be an ideationally different information piece (Schiffrin p.c.), (a-b) and (c-h) would be regarded as referentially different units. In this view, there is a pragmatically inferable contrast between (a-b) and (c-h).

12.   The discussion on the functions of the copula *da* is fully developed in Okutsu's *"I am an eel" grammar ("Boku wa unagi da" no bunpoo*, 1978).

13.   In Japanese, the equivalent expression to 'It rained' is *Ame ga futta* (Rain SB fell). In this structure, *futta* 'fell' is the predicate.

14.   Aoki (1973) also reports the first appearance of *dakedo* in the Taishoo era. Regarding the 'first appearance' of an item, Aoki (1973: 210) states that it is not something which provides strong evidence for " no existence of the item in the preceding time stages". Here 'first appearance' rather means " the emergence of the item is first recognised in that time stage" (Ibid.). I basically agree with Aoki's treatment of the term. This is because it seems almost impossible for anybody to obtain exactly the *first* use of an item both in written and spoken language. That is, it seems ultimately impossible to prove or substantiate the first appearance of an item.

15.   The possibility exists that the same kind of speaker's evaluation/point of view has been
      expressed by different words in our earlier time stages. For example, back in the 11th
      century, in the text of *Genji monogatari*, a conjunction *saredo*, which is equivalent to
      'but', was in common use in the conversational segments. It seems quite possible that
      saredo functioned as a marker, as well as similar words such as *saraba* ('then'),
      saritomo and *saritotemo* ('although you say so') in *Genji monogatari*. (It is noticeable
      that this set of words is initiated with the element *sa*, which corresponds to the modern
      deictic word *soo/sore*.)

16.   Because of space limitations, I am not giving any example here regarding this
      characteristic. A fuller explanation of this matter is provided in (7.2.1) in Onodera
      (1993a).

17.   Japanese and English have different phonological structures. While Japanese is a
      mora-counting language and is called a CV-patterned language, English is a syllable-
      counting or a CVC-patterned language. In Japanese, a mora, instead of a phoneme, is
      often perceived as a minimum phonological unit. Each Japanese alphabet
      (*hiragana/katakana*) expresses a mora, and it consists of a CV sequence, namely a
      consonant and a vowel. *Da*, for example, is a mora and it also conforms to a syllable,
      consisting of two phonemes, a consonant *d* and a vowel *a* (Ootsuka and Nakajima
      1982: 650, Amanuma *et al.* 1978: 47-8, 135)

18.   The Japanese examples of *demo/dakedo* (and also Matsumoto's (1988: 340-1)
      examples of *ga* and *dakara*) in fact raise a question about what to or not to include
      under the name 'grammaticalisation'. The question may be related to the issue of
      extending the notion of grammaticalisation. However, in the broad sense of
      grammaticalisation which is the starting point here, now interpreted, the Japanese
      cases of *demo*, *dakedo*, *dakara* and *ga* should count as illustrations of this process (cf.
      Traugott p.c., Hopper and Traugott 1993).

References

Amanuma, Yasushi, Kazuo Ootsubo, and Osamu Mizutani
      1978   *Nihongo onseigaku*. (Japanese phonetics). Tokyo: Kuroshio Shuppan.
Auchlin, Antoine
      1981   " Mais heu, pis bon, ben alors voilà, quoi! Marqueurs de structuration de la
                conversation et completude." *Cahiers de linguistique Française*. Les
                differents types de marqueurs et la determination des fonctions des actes de
                langage en contexte (part 2). Unité de linguistique Française.
Aoki, Reiko
      1973   " Setsuzokushi oyobi setsuzokushiteki goi ichiran." (List of conjunctions
                and conjunctive items). In: Kazuhiko Suzuki and Ooki Hayashi (eds.).

Setsuzokushi, kandooshi (Hinshibetsu nihonbunpoo kooza 6). Tokyo: Meiji Shoin, 210-53.

Brinton, Laurel J.

1990   " The development of discourse markers in English." In: Jacek Fisiak (ed.). *Historical Linguistics and Philology.* Berlin: Mouton de Gruyter, 45-71.

Brunet, Jean-Paul

1983   " L'interjection: son rôle et son impact dans une classe de français." *Canadian Modern Language Review* 40.1, 88-93.

Enkvist, Nils Erik, and Brita Wårvik

1987   " Old English *þa*, temporal chains, and narrative structure." In: Anna G. Ramat *et al.* (eds.). *Papers from the 7th International Conference on Historical Linguistics.* Philadelphia: John Benjamins, 221-37.

Fujii, Noriko

1991   *Historical Discourse Analysis: Grammatical Subject in Japanese.* Berlin: Mouton de Gruyter.

Genetti, Carol

1986   " The development of subordinators from postpositions in Bodic languages." *BLS* 12, 387-400.

Givón, Talmy

1984   *Syntax: A Functional-Typological Introduction.* Vol. 1. Philadelphia: John Benjamins.

Goffman, Erving

1974   *Frame Analysis.* Cambridge, MA: Harvard University Press.

Grice, H. P.

1975   " Logic and conversation." In: Peter Cole and Jerry L. Morgan (eds.). *Speech Acts. Syntax and Semantics.* Vol. 3. New York: Academic Press, 41-58.

Halliday, M. A. K., and Ruqaiya Hasan

1976   *Cohesion in English.* London: Longman Group.

Heine, Bernd, Ulrike Claudi, and Friederike Hünnemeyer

1991   *Grammaticalisation: A Conceptual Framework.* Chicago: University of Chicago Press.

Hinds, John

1986   *Japanese.* London: Croom Helm.

Hopper, Paul J.

1987   " Emergent grammar." *BLS* 13, 139-57.

Hopper, Paul J., and Elizabeth C. Traugott

1993   *Grammaticalisation.* (Cambridge Textbooks in Linguistics.) Cambridge: Cambridge University Press.

Jakobson, Roman
    1960   " Closing statement: Linguistics and poetics." In: Thomas A. Sebeok (ed.).
              Style in Language. Cambridge, MA: MIT Press, 350-77.
Jorden, Eleanor Harz
    1962   *Beginning Japanese*. Part 1. New Haven, CT: Yale University Press.
Jorden, Eleanor Harz, and Mari Noda
    1987   *Japanese: the Spoken Language*. Part 1. Tokyo: Kodansha International.
Jucker, Andreas H.
    1994   " The feasibility of historical pragmatics." *Journal of Pragmatics* 22, 533-
              536.
Kuno, Susumu
    1973   *The Structure of the Japanese Language*. Cambridge, MA: MIT Press.
Kyogoku, Okikazu, and Eiichi Matsui
    1973   " Setsuzokushi no hensen." (The change of conjunctions). In: Kazuhiko
              Suzuki and Ooki Hayashi (eds.). *Setsuzokushi, kandooshi (Hinshibetsu
              nihonbunpoo kooza* 6). Tokyo: Meiji Shoin, 89-136.
Lyons, John
    1977   *Semantics*. Vol. 1 & 2. Cambridge: Cambridge University Press.
Martin, Samuel E.
    1975   *A Reference Grammar of Japanese*. New Haven, CT: Yale University Press.
Matsumoto, Yo
    1988   " From bound grammatical markers to free discourse markers: History of
              some Japanese connectives." *BLS* 14, 340-51.
Maynard, Senko K.
    1989   " Functions of the discourse marker *dakara* in Japanese conversation". *Text*
              9.4, 389-414.
    1992   " Speech act declaration in conversation: Functions of the Japanese
              connective *datte*." *Studies in Language* 16.1.
Myhill, John
    1988   " The grammaticalisation of auxiliaries: Spanish clitic climbing." *BLS* 14,
              352-63.
National Language Research Institute (Kokuritsu kokugo kenkyuujo)
    1955   *Danwago no jittai*. (The current situation of the language of discourse).
              NLRI Report 8. Tokyo: Shuuei Shuppan.
Okutsu, Keiichiro
    1978   *'Boku wa unagi da' no bunpoo*. ('I am an eel' grammar). Tokyo: Kuroshio
              Shuppan.

Onodera, Noriko Okada
 1989 " Multi-planed functions of the Japanese discourse connective *demo*." Paper presented at the *LSA Annual Meeting*, Washington, D.C., December 1989.
 1993a *Pragmatic Change in Japanese: Conjunctions and Interjections as Discourse Markers*. Ph.D. dissertation, Georgetown University.
 1993b " Pragmatic change in Japanese: The cases of conjunctions and interjections as discourse markers." Paper presented at the *4th International Pragmatics Conference*, Kobe, Japan, July 1993.
 1993c " Discourse markers no kyoojiteki, tsuujiteki bunseki." (Synchronic and diachronic analyses of discourse markers). Paper presented at the symposium on 'Sociolinguistic Perspectives on Discourse Analysis' at the *11th National Conference of the English Linguistic Society of Japan*, Kyoto, November 1993.

Ootsuka, Takanobu and Fumio Nakajima (eds.)
 1982 *The Kenkyusha Dictionary of English Linguistics and Philology*. Tokyo: Kenkyusha.

Östman, Jan-Ola
 1981 *'You know': A Discourse Functional Approach*. Philadelphia: John Benjamins.

Quirk, Randolph, Sidney Greenbaum, Geoffrey Leech, and Jan Svartvik
 1973 *A Concise Grammar of Contemporary English*. New York: Harcourt Brace Jovanovich.

Saji, Keizo
 1970 " Setsuzokushi no bunrui." (Classification of conjunctions). *Bunpoo* 2.12, 28-39.

Sankoff, Gillian
 1988 " The grammaticalisation of tense and aspect in Tok Pisin and Sranan." Paper presented at the *Symposium on Grammaticalisation*, University of Oregon, Eugene, May 1988.

Schiffrin, Deborah
 1987 *Discourse Markers*. Cambridge: Cambridge University Press.
 1988 " Sociolinguistic approaches to discourse: topic and reference in narrative." In: K. Ferrera, B. Brown, K. Walters, and J. Baugh (eds.). *Linguistic Contact and Variation*. Austin: University of Texas Press, 1-28.
 1992 " Discourse markers." In: W. Bright (ed.). *International Encyclopedia of Linguistics*. Vol. I. Oxford: Oxford University Press, 361-4.

Schourup, Lawrence Clifford
 1982 *Common Discourse Particles in English Conversation*. (Working Papers in Linguistics 28). The Ohio State University Department of Linguistics.

Shiraishi, Daiji, Shinichi Niima, Eitaroo Hirota, and Akira Matsumura (eds.)
    1953   *Koten dokkai jiten.* (Dictionary for interpreting classical literature). Tokyo: Tokyodoo.

Silverstein, Michael
    1976   " Shifters, linguistic categories, and cultural description." In: Keith M. Basso and Henry A. Selby (eds.). *Meaning in Anthropology.* Albuquerque: University of New Mexico Press, 11-55.

Stein, Dieter
    1985   " Discourse markers in Early Modern English." In: R. Eaton *et al.* (eds.). *Papers from the 4th International Conference on English Historical Linguistics.* Philadelphia: John Benjamins, 283-302.

Suzuki, Ryoko, and Tsuyoshi Ono
    1992   " Word order variability in Japanese conversation: motivations and grammaticization." *Text* 12.3, 429-45.

Tokieda, Motoki
    1950   *Nihonbunpoo koogohen.* (Japanese grammar. Vol. for spoken language). Tokyo: Iwanami.

Traugott, Elizabeth Closs
    1982   (1980) " From propositional to textual and expressive meanings: Some semantic-pragmatic aspects of grammaticalisation." In: Winfred P. Lehmann and Yakov Malkiel (eds.). *Perspectives on Historical Linguistics.* Philadelphia: John Benjamins, 245-71.
    1985   " Conditional markers." In: J. Haiman (ed.). *Iconicity in Syntax.* Philadelphia: John Benjamins, 289-307.
    1986   " From polysemy to internal semantic reconstruction." *BLS* 12, 539-50.
    1988a   " Is internal semantic-pragmatic reconstruction possible?" In: Caroline Duncan-Rose and Theo Vennemann (eds.). *On Language: Rhetorica, Phonologica, Syntactica.* New York: Routledge, 128-44.
    1988b   " Pragmatic strengthening and grammaticalisation." *BLS* 14, 406-16.
    1989   " On the Rise of Epistemic Meanings in English: An Example of Subjectification in Semantic Change." *Language* 65, 31-55.

Traugott, Elizabeth C., and Ekkehard König
    1991   " The Semantics-Pragmatics of Grammaticalisation Revisited." In: Elizabeth C. Traugott and Bernd Heine (eds.). *Approaches to Grammaticalisation.* Vol. 1. Philadelphia: John Benjamins, 189-218.

Uchio, Kumi, and Kazue Okamura
    1973   "Joshi sooran." (List of particles). In: Kazuhiko Suzuki and Ooki Hayashi (eds.). *Joshi (Hinshi betsu nihonbunpoo kooza* 9). Tokyo: Meiji Shoin, 249-88.

Warner, Richard G.
   1985.   *Discourse Connectives in English.* New York: Garland.
Yuzawa, Kookichiro
   1970   *Tokugawa jidai gengo no kenkyuu.* (A study of the language of the
             Tokugawa period). Tokyo: Kazama Shoboo.

Interjections in Early Modern English
From Imitation of Spoken to Conventions of Written Language

Irma Taavitsainen
University of Helsinki

1. Introduction

Interjections have received increasing attention in theoretical discussions (see the special issue of the *Journal of Pragmatics*, Vol. 18, 2/3, Sept. 1992). Traditionally they were characterised as belonging to the purely emotive level of language (Quirk *et al.* 1985: 853), but the issue is much more complicated, and the old views have been challenged. Interjections have not previously been discussed in a historical perspective from a pragmatic point of view.

Interjections have been defined as linguistic gestures which express a speaker's mental state, action or attitude, or reaction to a situation. They range from onomatopoetic *ad hoc* formations to fixed one-word utterances and set phrases; such secondary interjections merge with routines and other adjoining groups. Sometimes interjections have been included in the class of particles because they are uninflected. The borderlines between various categories of routines, emphatics, and particles are fuzzy and, if the pragmatic use of interjections is taken into account, they can be considered a subgroup of pragmatic markers. Interjections encode speaker attitudes and communicative intentions and are context-bound, whereas routines consist of fixed formulae as stereotyped reactions to a situation, e.g. *how do you do, bye-bye* (Ameka 1992: 102, 106).

Besides being self-oriented expressions of emotions, attitudes and mental processes, interjections may also be directed at someone to acquire a desired reaction, for example to stop an action, or they may serve communicative intentions more broadly. Because of their situational dependence, they can only be interpreted relative to their context. In spoken language, intonation plays an important role in the interpretation of interjections as pitch, lengthening, loudness and non-verbal sounds all add to the expressiveness and convey specific nuances of meaning. This information is absent from the material discussed below, which makes the interpretation of interjections in historical texts different from that of their modern counterparts.

The aim of the present study is to chart the use of interjections in Early Modern English (hereafter EModE) texts in the light of examples and to assess how their use differs, on the one hand, from that of their modern counterparts and, on the other hand, from their predecessors in Late Middle English. I shall attempt to place interjections along the spoken vs. written dimension of language and relate them to written conventions of genres and records of spoken language in older texts.

The material of the present study has been gathered from the EModE section (1500-1710) of the *Helsinki Corpus* (hereafter HC) and it concentrates on primary interjections. The following lexical forms were found in the EModE subsection of the HC: *Ah!* (*A!*) *Alas!* (*Allas! Alack!*) *Eh! Fie!* (*Fy! Fye!*) *Ha! Ho! Hoa! Hush!* (*Husht!*) *Lo! Loe! O! Oh! Pshaw! Tush!* (*Tushe!*) *Tut! Welaway! Wough!* Some items in the list are 'natural utterances' that imitate sounds, some have their origins in foreign phrases (*alas* < Fr; for *lo* see below). Words like interrogative pronouns that have come to be used as exclamations *Why! What! How!* pose different problems and are not included in the present assessment. *Pardee* and *benedicitee* represent utterances that merge with secondary interjections; swearing in general has not been included.

2. Between Present-day spoken and Late Middle English written interjections

Modern assessments have concentrated on spoken language, but when interjections are considered from a historical perspective the dichotomy of spoken vs. written language becomes important. Genres defined by external criteria of purpose, audience and situation provide a key to the assessment as their distance from spoken language varies. Interjections in writing may have been produced in imitation of spoken language, but still under the constraints of the written medium, and their meaning has to be interpreted without the help of intonation; expressions in drama are different in this respect as their speech acts are recreated on stage in each performance (see below). In contrast to the immediate situation that provides a clue to the interpretation in spontaneous speech, a wider context has to be considered in order to detect the textual function. It may be that the older use of interjections was different from modern usage, but on the other hand, there may be similarities, and it is of interest to see how the different genres make use of interjections and whether the interjections can be scaled accordingly.

In contrast to the traditional view of interjections according to which they belong to the purely emotive level of language, three functional categories have been distinguished in the analysis of Present-day spoken interjections (Ameka 1992: 113-4):

1. Focus on the speaker's mind, with two subgroups: the first is the emotive level that has been mentioned as the primary or only category in earlier grammars; the second is the cognitive function reflecting the speaker's mental processes.
2. The conative function focuses on the interaction between the participants of the speaking situation. Such interjections are directed at an auditor, and they demand an action or response in return.
3. In some cases interjections have a purely phatic function. They are used for contact, or to keep the conversation going; in contrast to the previous group, they do not demand an action or response.

Of the interjections under scrutiny, *oh* and *ah* are the only ones that have received a detailed assessment in Present-day English (Aijmer 1987). Her material consisted of 34 informal, spontaneously recorded conversations from the London-Lund Corpus of Spoken British English, totalling 170 000 words. *Oh* is one of the most frequent lexical items in her material, with 716 examples; *Ah* was found 77 times. These interjections were more frequent in telephone conversations than in face-to-face discussions, they did not occur in radio interviews, and only 3 occurrences were found in courtroom proceedings. Reported speech had 64 examples of *oh* and 5 of *ah*. In these quotations they were used to create a funny, dramatic or ironic effect, and they often signalled the speaker's change from one role to another, or a change in footing or style (Aijmer 1987: 61, 81, 83).

According to my earlier assessment of the functions of interjections in the Late Middle English subcorpus of the HC and parts of *The Canterbury Tales* with the help of the *Chaucer Concordance*, some of the uses were clearly focused on the speaker, narrator or author with an emotive or cognitive meaning; some had their focus on the addressee, reader or audience in general as they were used in the vocative or conative meaning. The phatic function belongs to the spoken language, and in its place, purely textual functions had been developed in written fiction. Turning points in the plot are marked by collocations and cumulative lists of interjections, and foregrounding in narration is evident in some texts. Turn-taking in the performance of a text was marked by the vocative use of interjections at the openings of speech acts. The marking of turn-taking was especially obvious in romances and medieval drama, while the other textual functions were most prominent in Chaucer's works, and he seems to have developed their use to a culmination (Taavitsainen, forthcoming b). Narrative conventions in EModE must have been influenced by Chaucer's usage as he must have set a model to be imitated by later story-tellers. The examination of interjections may illuminate the persistence of such conventions in later periods as well (see below).

3. Occurrences of interjections in Early Modern English genres

In an attempt to place EModE interjections along the dimension spoken vs. written, genres provide the starting point. Drama imitates speech; direct quotations in fiction and some adjoining non-literary genres, such as autobiography, history, and travelogue, are produced in imitation of various levels of speech; handbooks, educational and philosophical writings may employ dialogue form, but the speech acts serve an educational purpose and are designed accordingly. The dialogue form may be partly in imitation of speech in handbooks, but in philosophy and education it was produced in imitation of classical models, and the style must have been influenced by classical rhetoric doctrines. Sermons were designed primarily for oral delivery on formal occasions, but writing them down may have involved various degrees of editing. Trial records are written accounts of speech in court rooms but, again, the process of writing them down may have included editing. The range of these writings is from spontaneous speech to semi-formal and formal oral presentation in the written form. The formatting conventions and recording practices are not known in detail.

The following list gives the absolute numbers of occurrence of interjections according to genres in the EModE section of the HC.[1] Individual texts are also given because there is a great deal of variation within the genres.[2]

EModE1 1500-1570:

Handbooks:	*O!* (1 Turner)
Educational treatises:	*O!* (3 Elyot)
Philosophy:	*O!* (2 *Boethius*)

Sermons:	*Alas!* (4 Fisher), *Lo! Loo!* (2 Fisher), *O!* (4 Fisher, 1 Latimer), *Oh!* (1 Latimer)
Trials:	*Ah!* (1 Throckmorton), *Oh!* (2 Throckmorton)
History:	*Alas!* (1 Fabyan), *Loe!* (1 More)
Autobiography:	*Fye!* (2 Mowntayne), *O!* (4 Mowntayne)
Fiction:	*Alas!* (3 *Mery Talys*, 3 Harman), *Benedicite!* (1 *Mery Talys*, 1 Harman), *Fye!* (5 Harman), *Lo!* (3 *Mery Talys*), *O!* (1 *Mery Talys*, 1 Harman), *Tushe!* (1 Harman)
Comedy:	*Ah!* (10 Udall, 2 Stevenson), *Alas!* (1 Udall, 9 Stevenson), *Fy!* (4 Udall, 10 Stevenson), *Lo!* (2, Stevenson), *Oh!* (1 Udall), *O!* (2 Udall, 1 Stevenson), *Pardee!* (1 Udall), *Tut!* (2 Udall), *Welaway!* (1 Stevenson), *Wough!* (1 Udall)
Bible (Tyndale):	*Ah!* (1), *O!* (1), *Loo!* (6), *Tush* (1)
Letters, private:	*Loe!* (1, More)

EModE2 1570-1640:

Handbooks:	*Ah!* (1 Gifford), *Alas!* (1 Gifford), *Fie!* (1 Gifford), *O!* (2 Gifford),
Philosophy:	*O!* (2 *Boethius*)
Sermons:	*Alas!* (1 Hooker), *O!* (5 Hooker)
Trials:	*Ah!* (1 Raleigh), *O!* (1 Raleigh), *Oh!* (9 Raleigh, *Tush!* (1 Essex)
Diary:	*Fy!* (1 Madox)
Fiction:	*Ah!* (3 Armin, 1 Deloney), *Alas!* (4 Deloney), *Fie!* (1 Deloney), *O!* (7 Armin, 8 Deloney), *Tush!* (3 Deloney)
Comedy:	*Ah!* (1 Shakespeare), *Alas!* (3 Shakespeare), *Fie* (3 Middleton, 3 Shakespeare), *Ha!* (3 Middleton, 3 Shakespeare), *Hoa!* (3 Shakespeare), *Husht* (1 Middleton), *O!* (22 Middleton, 7 Shakespeare), *Oh!* (2 Shakespeare), *Tut!* (1 Shakespeare)
Letters:	*Allas!* (1 Harley), *Oh!* (1 Knyvett)
Bible (Authorized Version):	*Lo!* (3), O! (1)

EModE3 1640-1710:

Handbooks:	*Oh!* (2 Walton)
Philosophy:	*O!* (3 *Boethius*)
Sermons:	*O!* (1 Tillotson)
Trials:	*Oh!* (1 Lisle)
Autobiography:	*Oh!* (1 Fox)
Biography:	*Oh!* (1 Burnet)
Fiction:	*Ah!* (1 *Penny*), *Alas!* (2 *Penny*, 1 Behn), *Fie!* (6 *Penny*), *Lo!* (1 *Penny*), *O!* (25 *Penny*, 2 Behn), *Oh!* (7 *Penny*, 3 Behn)
Comedy:	*Ah!* (5 Vanbrugh, 2 Farquhar), *Alack!* (1 Farquhar), *Alas!* (2 Vanbrugh), *Eh!* (2 Vanbrugh, 1 Farquhar), *Ha!* (3 Vanbrugh, 5 Farquhar), *Ho!* (2 Vanbrugh), *Hush* (1 Vanbrugh, 1 Farquhar), *O!* (27 Vanbrugh, 1 Farquhar), *Oh!* (3 Vanbrugh, 1 Farquhar), *Pshaw!* (2 Farquhar)

	Total	E1	E2	E3
Comedy	158	47	52	59
Fiction	94	19	27	48
Sermons	19	12	6	1
Trials	17	3	13	1
Bible	13	9	4	–
Handbooks	8	1	5	2
Autobiography	7	6	–	1
Philosophy	7	2	2	3
Education	3	3	–	–
Letters	3	1	2	–
History	2	2	–	–
Biography	1	–	–	1
Diary	1	–	1	–

4.   The use of interjections

One of the difficulties in assessing interjections from a historical perspective lies in their semantic interpretations. In the following, the meanings and emotional colourings given in the *Middle English Dictionary* and the *Oxford English Dictionary* provide a starting point for the analysis. Frequencies of occurrence in various genres are given, together with selected examples. It is evident that interjections are mostly found in direct speech quotations; those in narrative passages are few, but they are of special relevance for the assessment of the scale from spoken to written language. These cases are mentioned separately; all other examples are from direct quotations.

AH: formerly *A* (29 examples: 20 in Comedy; 6 in Fiction, 1 in the Bible, 1 in Handbooks and 1 in Trials)

This interjection is most frequent in the vocative function, accompanied by a noun of address. In some examples it is repeated, which lends an emotional colouring to the address:

> *Ah*! good Lady, you could mean her no Good. (Raleigh, p.208)

> *Ah* sir, (George) now is the time to perform ... (Deloney, p.82)

> *Ah* master, so kind ... (*Penny*, p.267)

> ... and then sayde as heere ensueth, *Ah, ah* Maister (Cholmely), will this foule packing neuer be left? (Throckmorton, p.64)

> For one madde propretie these women haue in fey, When ye will, they will not: Will not ye, then will they. *Ah* foolishe woman, *ah* moste vnluckie Custance, *Ah* vnfortunate woman, *ah* pieuishe Custance, Art thou to thine harmes so obstinately bent ... (Udall, lines 1131-5)

It is also used by itself, in some cases perhaps to mark the beginning of a speech act without a noun of address:

> "*A* god rewarde you" ... (Harman, p.39)

> ... I heard part of her wordes. *Ah* (quod she) you haue an honest man to your husband ... (Gifford, B2v)

It seems to have a cognitive meaning in Armin's text in the following examples, or the first instance may be a vocative as well:

> ... at vide ruffe (for that was the game he ioyed in) and as he spied a knaue - *Ah*, knaue, art there? quoth he. When he spide a king - King, by your leaue, quoth he ... (Armin, p.8)

> *Ah*! sayes hee, this must haue, must haue a good showre to clense it; ... (Armin, p.45)

In the first instance of the following passage *ah* marks the opening of the speech, and it seems to be a reaction to the shrieking of the women. Once it is used as an outcry in pain.

> (They draw and fight. The Women run shrieking for Help.)
> Aman.: *Ah*! What has my Folly done? Help; Murder, help: Part 'em for Heaven's sake.
> Lord Fop.: (falling back, and leaning upon his Sword) *Ah* - quite thro'
> (Vanbrugh, p.39)

In some cases the emotional colouring is explicit. Sympathy is involved in the following examples in which *ah* occurs in collocation with the adjective *poor*. In the third example it stands alone and has a strong emotional loading, expressing admiration as the speaker indicates the object of love among a crowd:

> Nurse: *Ah* the poor Thing, see how it's melts; it's as full of good Nature ...
> (Vanbrugh. p.60)
>
> Sir Tun: *Ah* poor Girl, she'll be scar'd out of her Wits ...(Vanbrugh, p.60)
>
> R. Royster: Mistresse *ah*. (Udall, line 140)

Consent with the previous speaker is signalled in an example in which the reply adds another detail to the first statement:

> ... But it will not be, our mouth is so drie.
> Tib Talk.: Ah, eche finger is a thombe to day me thinke, ...(Udall, lines 331-2)

Once *ah* is used to introduce a conditional clause that expresses a regretful event. In this case it conveys shades of sorrow and lamentation. In contrast, the next sentence employs *oh* in an expression of wishful thinking:

> M. Mery: Ah that ye would in a letter shew such despite.
> R. Royster: Oh I would I had hym here, the which did it endite
> (Udall, lines 1113-4)

For the collocation *ah ha* expressing a mental process, see *ha*.

ALAS: (37 examples: 16 in Comedy, 13 in Fiction, 5 in Sermons, 1 in History,
        1 in Handbooks, and 1 in Letters)

Sermons employ this interjection in the vocative function in collocation with *man*. It addresses the hearer with a strong emotional plea and is often accompanied with imperative forms and second person singular pronouns. The collocation *alas man* is also found in Handbooks at the beginning of speech acts telling about misfortunes or unfortunate circumstances.

Alas man where is thy shame? Thincke with thy selfe how many abhominable sinnes thou hast done ... (Fisher, p.400)

Alas man, heare what the King and Prophet sayth ...(Fisher, p.401)

Alas man learn to be ashamed and saye with the Prophet Esdras ... (Fisher, p.402)

Dan: If you haue such cunning men and women, what neede you be so much afraide?
Sam: *Alas man*, I could teeme it to goe, and some counsell me to goe ... (Gifford, B1v)

In comedies *alas* is used in the vocative and it may have comical connotations. It occurs in expressions of sympathy, sometimes in collocation with emotive adjectives such as *poor* or *good:*

Alas my neele we shall neuer meete, adue, adue for aye. (Stevenson, p.13)

Alas poore soule, this reward ... (Deloney, p.73)

Alas, good Woman, ... (*Penny*, p.149)

Alas occurs frequently in emotional passages of regret and lamentation. In some cases it seems to be the very stereotype of such feelings:

Inso moche that lamentably he sayd *alas* what haue we done we haue now put to deth hym that hath ben our Soueraygne and drad lorde ... (Fabyan, 170R)

... sayd to ye maltman *alas* I haue let my boget fal into ye water ... (*Mery Talys*, p.148)

how Gods iudgement for their times come so swiftly vpon them, that they haue not the leasure to crie, *Alas*? how their life is cut off like a threed in a moment? how they passe like a shadow? how they open their mouthes to speake, ... (Hooker, p.38)

Bayly: ... And goodwife Chat he set to scole, till both partes cried *alas*, (Stevenson, p.64)

Tyb: She is vndone she sayth (*alas*), her ioye and life is gone (Stevenson, p.8)

Gammer: *Alas* hoge, *alas* I may well cursse and ban
This daie that euer I saw it, ... (Stevenson, p.10)

Mist. Ford: How might we disguise him?
Mist. Page: *Alas*, the day I know not, there is no womans gowne bigge enough
for him: (Shakespeare, p.54)

In some cases this interjection is repeated for greater emphasis. Such cumulative
use seems to echo Chaucer's way of marking turning-points in the plot by
cumulative lists of interjections.[3] In some instances the effect may be comical:

... and ran all nakyd to london agayne and sayde *alas alas* helpe or I shall be
stolen. For my capons be stolen. My hors is stolen. My money and clothys ...
(*Mery Talys*, p.149)

... but in the starting vp, seeing it was a woman, cryed out, *alas, alas*. (Deloney,
p.80)

Once it occurs in the middle of narration. It is a side remark directed at the
readers to provoke their emotions, and it contributes to the overall emotional
tone of the text.

... his old heart, like an extinguish'd brand, most apt to take fire, felt new sparks
of love, and began to kindle; and now grown to his second childhood, long'd with
impatience to behold this gay thing, with whom, *alas*! he could but innocently
play. (Behn, p.157)

Once it occurs in a private letter, and its use is somewhat different from all
other examples. It is a strong expression of personal affect; an appeal to the
addressee. The previous sentence concerns a totally different matter, and the
interjection serves as a topic shift to the expression of personal feelings:

...and it may any thinge at all seet forward your biusnes, I pray you deleuer it to
him. If you do deleuer it to my father, I pray you seale it first. *Allas*! my dear Sir,
I knowe you doo not to the on halfe of my desires, desire to see me, that loues
you more then any earthly thinge. (Harley, p.4)

BENEDICITE: (2 examples in Fiction)

Benedicite is found twice in the present material, in direct quotations. In the
first example, it has preserved some of ist original connotations, but in the
second example it is used to express surprise and wonder:

... when they had causyd hym to sey *Benedicite* ye curat bad hym cry god mercy
& shew his synnys (*Mery Talys*, p.30)

"Benedicite!" quoth this good wife, "and haue they so in dede?" (Harman, p.40)

EH: (3 examples in Comedy)

In the present examples this interjection occurs after a marked pause, introducing a side remark. It may imply surprise, or hesitation before adding a comment. In the third instance *Eh*! is an ejaculation marking the mental process of recognition.

> (Exit running)
> Nurse: *Eh* - the Lord succour thee, how thou art delighted (Exit after her)
> (Vanbrugh, p.60)

> ... and you had seen how the poor thing suck't it - *Eh*, God's Blessing on the sweet Face on't; ... (Vanbrugh, p.63)

> Arch: Come hither, Brother (Scrub), don't you know me? Scrub: *Eh*! my dear brother, let me kiss thee. (Farquhar, p.61)

FIE, FY, FYE: (37 examples: 21 in Comedy, 12 in Fiction, 2 in Auto-
> biography, 1 in Diary, and 1 in Handbooks)

This interjection is often used in swearing, either by itself or with a prepositional phrase with *on*. In several cases it is repeated for emphasis. Popular phrases of folk wisdom, swearing phrases, and other colloquial markers are often incorporated in the same passages (see below). The collocation *fy for shame* is common, and it is used to express strong repulsion, disgust, contempt, or accusation, but it may also be used jokingly.

> ... and I wold God I had such an aunt. *Fy*, quoth he, wold I had your land on condicion you had xxty such aunts. (Madox, p.88)

> Sam: I defie the deuill, worship him? *fie vpon him*, I hate him with all my hart. (Gifford, B2R)

> What neuer a great belly yet? now *fie*, by my fa ... (Deloney, p.69)

> *Oh fie* no, I will not ask him ... (*Penny*, p.119)

> MM: What is hir name. R. Royster: Hir yonder. MM: Whom; RR: Mistresse *ah*.

> MM: *Fy fy for shame*. Loue ye, and know not whome; but hir yonde, a Woman. (Udall, lines 139-141)

R. Royster: By the armes of Caleys it is none of myne.
R. Royster: *Fie* you are fowle to blame this is your owne hand. (Udall, lines 1110-1)

M. Mery: What weepe; *fye for shame*, and blubber; for manholds sake ... (Udall line 1125)

Chat: *Fie on the villaine, fie, fie*, yt makes vs thus agree.
Gramer: *Fie on him knaue*, with al my hart, now *fie*, and *fie* againe.
D. Rat: Now *fie on him* may I best say, whom he hath almost slaine.
Bayly: Lo where he commeth at hand, belike he was not fare ... (Stevenson, p.64)

Page: I will about it, better three houres too soone, then a mynute too late: *fie, fie, fie*: Cuckold, Cuckold, Cuckold. (Shakespeare, p.47)

Violent expression of emotions is found in Mowntayne's autobiography. The interjection is repeated and followed by an exclamatory sentence:

> "Ye," sayed he. "And ys thys the beeste servys that yow can doo my lorde your master? *Fye, for shame, fye*! wyl you folowe now the bludye stepes of that wyckyd man your master! (Mowntayne, p.201)

The collocation *fye, for shame, fye* provides the turning-point of one of the short comic tales in Fiction. It is a watch word, and when uttered at the wrong moment it provides the jest of the story around which the narration is built. The choice of a phrase like this to mark the culmination of a comic tale is in accordance with the conventions derived from medieval fabliaux and Chaucer's use of cumulative lists of interjections at the turning-points of such stories (see note 3).

> ... geue me a watche worde a loud when hee goeth aboute to haue his pleasure of the, and that shall be *"fye, for shame, fye"* ... (Harman, p.70)

> ..."And are you not ashamed? neuer a whyte, "sayth he, "lye downe quickely."
> "Now, *fye, for shame, fye*," sayth shee a loude, whyche was the watche word. At the which word, these fyue furious, sturdy, muffeled gossypes ... (Harman, p.72)

HA: (13 examples in Comedy)

Ha seems to be used in five principal ways in these texts: in imitation of laughter, to express the mental process of recognition, or defining the quality of the experience of wine tasting, insight (in collocation with *ah*), and as a tag to demand an answer:

> ... you are merry, so am I: *ha*, *ha*, then there's more simpathie ... (Shakespeare, p.43)

> *Ha*! By Heavens the very woman. (Vanbrugh, p.34)

> (filling it out) your Worship's Health; *ha*! delicious, delicious ... (Farquhar, p.2)

> Fal: Call him in: such (Broomes) are welcome to mee, that ore'flowes such liquor: *ah ha*, Mistresse (Ford) and Mistresse ... (Shakespeare, p.46)

> Well, what do you make such a Noise for, *ha*? What do you ... (Vanbrugh, p.59)

HO, HOA: (5 examples in Comedy)

This interjection is used to express astonishment, and to request confirmation of what has been said before. In one example it is used in the conative function to attract attention.

> Mis. Ford: Hees a birding sweet Sir Iohn.
> Mis. Page: What *hoa*, gossip Ford: what *hoa*. (Shakespeare, p.54)

> ... Horses into your Body.
> Lord Fop.: *Ho-*
> Ser.: Why, what the devil, have you ... (Vanbrugh, p.40)

> Lo: Igad, Sir, I think y'are in the right on't. *Ho*, Mr. What d'ye ... (Vanbrugh, p.57)

HUSH, HUSHT: (3 examples in Comedy)

In all three examples this interjection is found in side remarks that give information to the audience. It seems to be used as a signal of confidentiality.

> (Enter a Man with Meat in a Basket)
> 2 Prom: *Husht*, stand close (Middleton, p.23)

> (Knocks again)
> Y. Fash.: *Hush*; they come.
> (From within) Who is there? (Vanbrugh, p.57)

> Arch: Hush - I see a dark Lanthorn coming thro, the Gallery ... (Farquhar, p.61)

LO: (19 examples: 9 in the Bible, 4 in Fiction, 2 in Comedy, 2 in Sermons, 1 in History, and 1 in Letters)

The dictionaries point out that the interjection *lo* has two distinct sources of origin. One derives from OE *la*, indicating surprise, grief or joy, as used in vocatives. According to the second source, *lo* may be an abbreviated form of 'look', used in the sense 'look', 'behold'. These two sources lead to two distinct usages, which can be verified in the present material.

In translations of the Bible, *lo* renders the Vulgate Version *ecce*, the Latin translation of the Hebrew particle used to attract attention. In Late Middle English this use is regular, and it is also found in the present material:

> ... and causedest me to take hyr to my wyfe? But now *loo*, there is the wife, take hir and be walkynge. (Bible, Tyndale Ph XII:19)

Yet the correspondence is not regular. No doubt the use of *lo* was so well established in biblical style by this time that the device spread to other passages and to the adjoining genres. There are instances in which *lo* is added for emphasis though the source language does not have it. It is also found in sermons:

> And God loked vpon the erth, and *loo* it was corrupte: (Latin: *qumque vidisset deus terram esse corruptam*) (Bible, Tyndale IV: 12)

> Than sayd God to Noe: the end of all flesh is come before me, for the erth is full of there myschefe. And *loo*, I wyll destroy them with the erth. (Latin: *et ego disperdam eas*) (Bible, Tyndale IV:13)

> Simon Simon *lo* Sathanas hath coueyted gretly to syft you as a man syfteth his whete. (Fisher, p.319)

Once it occurs in a historical piece of writing and once in a personal letter, both examples by the same author. In these cases it seems to have a more emotional tone of lamentation, or it may have been used for emphasis only.

> ... much harme, and you to gret reproche. For loe here is (quod she) ... (More, p.41)

> yet it thinketh me, *loe*, that if I may not declare the causes without perill, than to leaue them vndecared is no obstinacy. (More, letters, p.505)

Lo is used in vivid narration in fiction, perhaps as an equivalent to 'look' in cases with a clear indication of space. It has a deictic function in these cases. The same use is found in Comedies.

And whenne the husbande lokyd vp and sawe the Potte stande there on hyght he sayde thus. *Lo* now standyth the pot there as I wolde haue it This wyfe herynge that sodenly pouryd the hote potage on his hed & sayd thus ... (*Mery Talys*, p.115)

The scoller toke one of ye chykyns in his hand & sayd. *Lo* here is one chykyn/ and incontynent he toke both ye chykyns in his hand ioyntly & sayd here is ... (*Mery Talys*, p.120)

Then the fader toke one of the chykyns to hymselfe and gaue another to his wyfe & sayd thus. *Lo* I wyll haue one of ye chykyns to my parte ... (*Mery Talys*, p.120)

unto thy Master; O how the number of the Ungodly increase? come forth I say.
Ma.: *Lo*, thy Hand-maid is even here
Dame: Look, look, I say, nay, again I sa unto thee, look ... (*Penny*, p.150)

Ganmer: Chil shew you his face, ich warrant the, *lo* now where he is.
Bailie: Come on fellow it is tolde me thou art a shrew (Stevenson, p.57)

D. Rat: Now fie on him may I best say, whom he hath almost slaine.
Bayly: *Lo* where he commeth at hand, belike he was not fare ...(Stevenson, p.64)

O: (141 examples; 70 in Comedy, 44 in Fiction, 11 in Sermons, 4 in Philosophy, 4 in Autobiography, 3 in Handbooks, 3 in Education, 1 in Trials, and 1 in the Bible)

This is the most common interjection in the present material. It is found most frequently in the vocative in a wide range of genres from the Bible, Philosophy and Education to Comedies. This interjection, together with a noun of address, is often prefixed to an exclamatory sentence. The first two examples are from sermons: the first is a reference to the crucifixion scene in the Bible, the second to the Canticles. In sermons the vocative is also used in direct address to the hearer. In the examples from philosophical and educational writings it occurs with a noun of address in direct quotations.

O my God, my God why haste thou forsaken me? (Hooker, p.7)

How faire art thou, and how pleasant art thou, *O my loue*, in these pleasures! (Hooker, p.37)

Furthermore, if sinne was so greuously punished in him that neuer did sinne, how bytterly shall it be punished in thee *O sinfull creature*, the which haste done so may great outragious sinnes. (Fisher, p.399)

O my child Boece ... *O* my norished child ... (E1, *Boethius*, pp.71, 81)

"*O scholler myne*, happy art thou for this opinion, yf thou wilt ad one thing withall." "What's that?" quoth I ... (E2, *Boethius*, p.59)

"*O* my Pupil ..." (E3, *Boethius*, p.128)

O noble Codrus, howe worthy had you ben ... (Elyot, p.153)

O sir, from hensforthe loke that ye take me for a man of great substaunce. (Elyot, p.154)

O Master Master, (*Penny*, p.149)

O Lorde (sayth she than) what a goodly man it is, Woulde Christ I had such a husbande as he is. *O Lorde* (say some) that the sight of his face we lacke ... (Udall, lines 203-5)

It may also be used without the noun of address at the opening of an exclamatory sentence or a wish:

O then to fly vnto God by vnfained repentance, to fall downe before him in the humilitie of our soules, ... (Hooker, p.39)

... and sayde, "*O* wreche that I ham, ..." (Mowntayne, p.202)

O that I were a young wench for thy sake ... (Deloney, p.79)

O were I made of wishes, I went with thee. (Middleton, p.8)

O if my Dame should know on't! (*Penny*, p.148)

... crying out, in their language (Live, *O* King! Long live, *O* King!) and kissing his feet, paid him even divine homage ... (Behn, p.187)

O how glad cham ... (Stevenson, p.70)

O what a happy man shall I be, what a good housewife thou (*Penny*, p.116)

O, a little of the noise and bussle of the World, (Vanbrugh, p.32)

It is often used in mild swearing, or at the beginning of a negative remark or violent protestation:

O barbarous! if they, like unnatural Villains, should use those words, shall I be charged with them? (Raleigh, p.213)

O for Gods sake (quoth he) let me go, for Christs sake let me goe ... (Deloney, p.75)

O fie! take away thy hand, what is't thee dost? (*Penny*, p.148)

O dear! 'tis a relation I have not seen this five years. (Vanbrugh, p.34)

O Lord, O Lord, O Lord, we are both dead men. (Vanbrugh, p.58)

O Heavens, Madam (Vanbrugh, p.36)

O wicked, wicked world (Shakespeare, p.43)

O, no matter, Sir (Vanbrugh, p.61)

O, don't you trouble your Head about that; (Vanbrugh, p.59)

What ist you lack?
T.I.: *O* nothing now, all that I wish is present (Middleton, p.7)

Lady: Thou ly'st breuitie.
S. OI: *O* horrible, dar'st thou call me breuitie? Dar'st thou be so short with me? (Middleton, p.17)

Dan: Is it any trouble of conscience for sinne? If it be, that may turne to good.
Sam: *O*, no, no. I know no cause why. (Gifford, A4R)

It may signify consent as well. In some examples it expresses wondering about something and reflects the mental process of thinking. The collocation *O wel*! is found only once in the present material as a reaction to a previous announcement.

O yes, who knowes this woman, who? (Deloney, p.81)

O you vndoe me Sir, (Middleton, p.24)

To home the hye shyryffe sayd that he had forgotyn to brynge yt with hyme.

"*O wel*! (sayed he), syr Olyver, you are a good man ... (Mowntayne, p.207)

In some passages in fiction it seems to be used to create an emotive tone and adds to the vividness of narration. Its frequent use is especially marked in *Penny Merriments*. In Armin's text the use of this interjection is more complicated as it is used to achieve a special effect of vividness together with a shift in viewpoint:

> The pyper and the minstrel, being in bed together, one cryed *O*! his backe and face; the other, *O*! his face and eye: the one cryed *O* his pype! the other, *O* his fiddle! Good mussicke or broken consorts, they agree well together; (Armin, p.11)

OH: (16 examples: 3 in Trials, 7 in Comedy, 2 in Handbooks, 1 in Sermons, 1 in Letters, 1 in Autobiography, and 1 in Biography)

Besides Comedy, this interjection is most frequent in Trials. It occurs in violent outbursts with an emotional colouring and it is often found in exclamations with a noun of address:

> Hare: You haue hearde Reason and the Lawe, if you will conceyue it.
> Throckmorton: *Oh mercifull God*! *Oh eternall Father*, which seest all things, what maner of Proceedings are these? To what purpose serueth ...
> (Throckmorton, p.76)

> ... and after brake forth into these Speeches: *Oh Villain*! *Oh Traitor*! I will now tell you all the Truth ... (Raleigh, p.210)

> ... he desired to see the Letter again, and then said, *Oh Wretch*! *Oh Traitor*! whereby I perceiv'd you had not perform'd that Trust he had reposed in you. (Raleigh, p.210)

> ... he cry'd out, *Oh Traitor*! *Oh Villain*! now will I confess the whole Truth. (Raleigh, p.210)

Sometimes it is used as an uptaker to express uncertainty and to expose the previous speech to doubt. It may imply irony if the speaker was certain that the previous utterance was a lie. There are two almost identical passages in Raleigh's text in which the preceding statement is the same. The reaction to it in the first case is a counter-question, and in the second case an exclamation of reproach, indignation, or doubt. In the third instance *oh* is used as an exclamation before a personal question, and it may be an ironical remark.

Raleigh: To whom speak you this? You tell me News I never heard of.
Attorney: *Oh* Sir, do I? I will prove you the notoriousest Traitor that ever came to the Bar ...
Raleigh: You tell me News, Mr. (Attorney).
Attorney: *Oh* sir! I am the more large, because I know with whom I deal: For we have to deal to-day with a Man of Wit. (Raleigh, p.208)

... you shall answer every Particular.
Attorney: *Oh* do I touch you?
Lord Cecil: Mr. Attorney, when you have done ... (Raleigh, p.208)

This interjection occurs in mild swearing in several genres. It is found in exclamatory sentences and in wishful thinking:

Oh me, all the Horse are got over the River, what shall ... (Walton, p.211)

Oh dear he will keep such a do ... (*Penny*, p.119)

Oh sad, how Drunk was I last night ... (*Penny*, p.270)

Mi. Ford: Nay, I wil consent to act any villany against him, that may not sully the charinesse of our honesty: *oh* that my husband saw this Letter: it would giue eternall food to his iealousie. (Shakespeare, p.44)

Once it implies disagreement, a protest against the suggestion put forth in the previous speech.

... and dress it for our dinner.
Venat: *Oh* Sir, a Chub is the worst Fish that swims ... (Walton, p.215)

It occurs in the vocative in a rhetorical passage in a sermon by Latimer. The emotive use is further enforced by repetitions and an appeal to God's judgement:

Oh London London, repente repente, for I thynke God is more displeased wyth London than euer ... (Latimer, p.23)

It may also give evidence of the mental process of weighing the argument and coming to a conclusion when used at the opening of a speech act, and it may have an emotional colouring.

Oh sayde hee this is a rationall man I will talke with him ... (Fox, p.156)

His Answer was: *Oh* that Language of Fiends, which was ... (Burnet, p.154)

Oh signals a topic shift in a personal letter:

... but the next day the case was altered. Thus we see what wrangling ther is for the things of this world, which, if god had seen good for vs, might have been ours, but his will be done. *Oh* god sweet harte heer fell out on sunday last the lamentablest accident ... (Knyvett, p.61)

Personal feelings find a vivid expression in a dramatic monologue describing the inner fight between good and evil in a Quaker's conscience:

What a War is there even now, betwixt the Inward and the Outward man! Satan, Satan, I say unto thee, avoid, by Yea and by Nay, I charge thee tempt me not: *Oh*! how the Outward Man prevails! and I can hold no longer; nay, ... (*Penny*, p.147)

In Aphra Behn's text it occurs as an exclamation in a monologue, but besides expressing personal affect, it is directed at the reader and serves as an explicit marker of reader involvement. In her fiction *oh* is used to create the emotional tone of the narrative at other points as well.

He cou'd not be convinc'd he had no cause to sigh and mourn for the loss of a mistress, he cou'd not with all his strength and courage retrieve. And he would often cry, *Oh*, my friends! were she in walled cities, or confin'd from me ...
... Imoinda is as irrecoverably lost to me, as if she were snatch'd by the cold arms of death: *Oh*! she was never to be retriev'd. (Behn, p.160)

PARDEE: (1 example in Comedy)

This interjection is found once as a swearword:

M. Mery.: What shoulde I else sir, it is my dutie *pardee*. (Udall, line 222)

PSHAW: (2 examples in Comedy)

This interjection is used in mild swearing as an expression of rejection, and as a whisper to mark silence:

Arch: *Pshaw*! damn your Onions (Farquhar, p.8)

Arch: Your Lips must seal the Promise.
Mrs Sull: *Pshaw*!
Arch: They must, they must (Kisses her) (Farquhar, p.59)

TUSH/E: (4 examples in Fiction, 1 in the Bible and 1 in Trials)

In the Biblical example it expresses a strong objection to the previous statement, in the Serpent's speech tempting Eve to taste the forbidden fruit.

... lest ye dye.

Then sayd the serpent vnto the woman: *tush* ye shall not dye: But God doth knowe, that whensoever ye shulde eate of it, yours eyes shuld be opened ... (Bible, Tyndale, III:4)

In the trial record it is used in the same sense. In fiction it expresses impatience or contempt, and disagreement:

wherto he replyed, *tush* Sir Wa. this is not a tyme of goinge ... (Essex, p.10)

"Alas!" saith she, "but one old woman and a boy, he hath no occupying at al: *tushe.*" (Harman, p.38)

Tush, what will you haue a greene thing quoth shee (Deloney, p.79)

Tush woman, what talke you of that? thankes be to God (Deloney, p.70)

TUT: (4 examples in Comedies)

Tut expresses impatience or reproach. In the last example it indicates that the piece of news was already known:

There it lieth, the worste is but a curried cote,
Tut I am vsed therto, I care not a grote. (Udall, lines 340-1)

M.M. Who can blame this woman to fume and frette and rage; *Tut*, *tut*, your selfe nowe haue marde your owne marriage. Well, yet mistresse Custance, if ye can this remitte, This gentleman otherwise may your loue requitte (Udall, lines 1119-22)

Page: I have heard the French-man hath god skill in his Rapier.
Shal: *Tut* sir: I could haue told you more, (Shakespeare, p.45)

WELAWAY: (1 example in Comedy)

It may be that this interjection had already become archaic in this period; it does not occur by itself in Late Middle English though several examples can be found in the earlier periods. Chaucer uses it only in collocation with other interjections (see Taavitsainen, forthcoming b). Its use may have lent a special tone to this lamentation.

Gammet: My neele alas ich lost it hodge, ...
But *welaway*, all was in vayne, my neele is neuer the nere ... (Stevenson, p.12)

WOUGH: (1 example in Comedy)

This interjection is found once in a lamentation:

> C. Custance: No God be with you both, and seeke no more to me. (Exeat)

> R. Royster: *Wough*, she is gone for euer, I shall hir no more see. (Udall, lines 1123-4)

5. Scaling interjections according to EModE genres

In Early Modern English, genres differ greatly from one another concerning the frequency and use of interjections. Comedy shows the widest range of interjections in the present material. The discourse form of comedy is based on dialogue, and the characters in these plays represent the middle layers of society; thus the language imitates the normal speech of common people. This is the nearest approximation to everyday spoken language in historical texts. Utterances that imitate sounds like *Pshaw*, *Hush*, *Tut* are found in this genre only, and they resemble modern interjections in many respects. The range of these onomatopoetic formations is, however, fairly limited.

Interjections occur frequently in fiction as well. According to my previous statistical inquiry, they are a distinctive feature of imaginative narration, i.e. fiction, when compared with the adjoining non-literary genres, such as biography, autobiography, history and travelogue, which all belong to non-imaginative narration. This convention dates from Late Middle English (see Taavitsainen, forthcoming a).

Nearly all interjections in fiction are found in direct speech quotations. The examples are especially numerous in *Mery Talys* and *Penny Merriments*, which are both collections of short, funny stories. The characters depicted in them are middle class or lower down on the social scale, and the quotations imitate the colloquial use of language, with swearing and phrases of folk wisdom often present. In Armin's work the use of interjections is somewhat more elaborate. The passage with the most marked use takes an outsider's angle with third person pronouns, and yet it uses *O!* several times as direct speech quotations to shift the angle. This conflict of viewpoints is effective and original. Aphra Behn's text is different from the others of this genre. It is a long narration that can be considered a forerunner of romantic fiction. The use of interjections seems to be consciously targeted at manipulating the readers' emotions by embedding these exclamations in long monologues.

It is somewhat surprising that private letters contain very few interjections, though they include texts by women and the topics include the domestic sphere. *Oh* and *alas* are used in letters as topic shifters: *alas* marks a shift to the personal level of emotions and *oh* to more neutral matters. The distribution of interjections in fiction and private letters is interesting in view of the later development of fiction. Early novels employ the letter-form, but their style may have been more influenced by the conventions of fiction than private letters, at least in this respect.

Genres that represent the formal end of the scale, which are totally based on the written tradition, are Philosophy and Education. The only interjection in these is *o*. Its frequent use in the vocative in all three translations of *Boethius* and in Educational treatises follows the Latin exemplars and obeys the rhetorical rules that served as a model of writing.

The EModE versions of the Bible show a limited range of interjections. Their stylistic marking is explicit and shows transfer from other languages. *Lo* is the equivalent of the Vulgate Latin *ecce*, which corresponds to the Hebrew emphatic particle; *lo* is also used in fiction, but in these texts it is equivalent to 'look' rather than the biblical interjection, and it is likely to belong to a totally different tradition. *Tush*, which otherwise occurs in fiction (and once in trials), is found in the speech of the serpent.

6.   A summary of functions of interjections in EModE

The present assessment may give indications of the place of various interjections on the scale from colloquial to solemn uses of language. It is evident that the use of interjections from a historical perspective is very different from its modern counterpart, although a comparison is complicated owing to the lack of detailed studies of Present-day interjections. According to Aijmer (1987: 61) *oh* is one of the most frequently occurring lexical items in the *London-Lund Corpus* of Spoken British English. In the present material *o* is much more common and seems to be used in the functions taken over by *oh* in Present-day conversations. In Aijmer's material, *ah* was much less common than *oh,* and it always had positive connotations, whereas *oh* was more neutral. In the present material such differences cannot be established.

When compared with the Late Middle English textual functions of interjections, the marking of turn-taking is not evident. It was especially clear in Late Middle English Drama and Romances, in which the use of interjections at the beginning of each speech act is almost regular. This use had the practical function of aiding the hearer in distinguishing the speakers' turns in the performance of the text when read aloud. This issue is connected with several important changes concerning the consumption of these texts. With the spread of literacy reading habits changed, and with cheaper production methods and materials, books or booklets became more readily available to a wider audience.

Creating reader involvement is an important function of interjections in the present material. An emotive loading is often present in speech quotations that employ interjections. The audience is supposed to live with the characters and their emotions. In Aphra Behn's text the appeal to readers is even more direct as the interjections in the middle of long monologues seem to be directed to the audience; such use became common later in romantic fiction.

When the functions of the Early Modern interjections are compared with their modern counterparts, differences become obvious:

EARLY MODERN ENGLISH	PRESENT-DAY
Focus on the speaker/ narrator/ author:	
Emotive:	Emotive:
Ah! Alas! Fy! O! Oh!	*Yak! Wow!*
Pshaw! Tush! Tut!	
Welaway!	
Cognitive:	Cognitive:
Ah! Ah ha! Eh! Ha! O! Oh!	*A ha!*
Focus on the addressee/ reader/ audience:	
Vocative:	
Ah! Alas! O! Oh!	
Conative:	Conative:
Ha! Ho! Hoa! Hush! Lo	*Sh! Eh?*
Textual function:	**Phatic function:**
Reader involvement: *Alas*	*mm*
Turning points in the plot:	
Alas! Fy, for shame, fy!	
Vividness of narration: *O!*	
Topic shift: *Alas! Oh!*	

7. Conclusion

In the light of the present material, there are several important differences between interjections in written texts of past periods and in modern conversation. It has recently been argued that primary interjections do not have addressees; "the conative or phatic ones may be directed at people, but they are not addressed to people" (Ameka 1992: 109). In the present material various interjections are used in addressing people: the vocative function is the most common one. Thus, in contrast to the definition based on Present-day conversation, interjections are not only reactions to situations but are used to appeal to addressees. In addition, they are deliberate devices in manipulating reader involvement. Emotional involvement is often prominent, especially in fiction, and echoes of earlier writings in the fabliaux tradition can be discerned. Genre conventions seem to be an important factor in the use of interjections in written texts, and interjections have developed textual meanings in several genres. Thus interjections in written texts are far removed from purely emotive cries recorded as reactions to situations in conversation.

Notes

1. For a statistical assessment, the occurrence of interjections per 1000 words in individual texts, and the function of interjections in distinguishing between adjoining genres in the HC, see Taavitsainen forthcoming a and forthcoming b.

2. Genres that contained no interjections were Law, Travelogue, and Non-private letters. Brief titles of the works in which interjections are found are given below. For the principles of compilation and bibliographical references of editions, see Rissanen *et al.* 1993.

EModE1 1500-1570:
Handbooks: Turner, *A New Boke of* [...] *All Wines*
Educational treatises: Elyot, *The Boke Named The Gouernour*
Philosophy: Colville, *Boethius*
Sermons: Fisher, *Sermons by John Fisher*; Latimer, *Sermon on the Ploughers*
Trials: The Trial of Sir Nicholas Throckmorton
History: Fabyan, *The New Chronicles of England and France;* More, *The History of King Richard III*
Autobiography: Mowntayne, *The Autobiography*
Fiction: A Hundred Mery Talys; Harman, *A Caveat* [...] *for common Cursetors*
Comedies: Udall, *Roister Doister*; Stevenson(?), *Gammer Gvrtons Nedle*
Bible (Tyndale)
Letters, private: More, *Original Letters*

EModE2 1570-1640:

Handbooks: Gifford, *A Dialogue Concerning Witches*
Philosophy: Elizabeth I, *Boethius*
Sermons: Hooker, *Two Sermons upon Part of S. Judes Epistle*
Trials: The Trial of Sir Walter Raleigh; The Trial of the Earl of Essex
Diary: Madox, *An Elizabethan in 1582: The Diary* [...]
Fiction: Armin, *A Nest of Ninnies*; Deloney, *Jack of Newbury*
Comedy: Shakespeare, *The Merry Wives of Windsor*; Middleton, *A Chaste Maid in Cheapside*
Letters: Harley, *Letters of the Lady Brillana Harley*; Knyvett, *The Knyvett Letters*
Bible: The Authorized Version

EModE3 1640-1710:

Handbooks: Walton, *The Compleat Angler*
Philosophy: Preston, *Boethius*
Sermons: Tillotson, *Sermons*
Trials: The Trial of Lady Alice Lisle
Autobiography: Fox, *The Journal of George Fox*
Biography: Burnet, *Some Passages of the Life and Death of* [...] *Earl of Rochester*
Fiction: Penny Merriments; Behn, *Oroonoko*
Comedy: Vanbrugh, *The Relapse*; Farquhar, *The Beaux Stratagem*

3.   In Chaucer's fabliaux the cumulative use of interjections is used to mark important turning points in the plot, e.g. *"Out! Help! Allas! Harrow! he gan to crye"* is found in the Merchant's Tale (line 2366) and *"Fy! allas! what have I do?" "Tehee!"* in the Miller's Tale. (line 3740)

References

Aijmer, Karin
    1987   *"Oh* and *ah* in English conversation." In: Willem Meijs (ed.). *Corpus Linguistics and Beyond.* Amsterdam: Rodopi, 61-86.
Ameka, Felix
    1992   "Interjections: The universal yet neglected part of speech." *Journal of Pragmatics* 18, 101-118.
Kurath, Hans *et al.* (eds.)
    1954   *MED = Middle English Dictionary.* Ann Arbor, Michigan: University of Michigan Press; London: Geoffrey Cumberlege, Oxford University Press.

Oxford English Dictionary (OED)
  1989   James A. H. Murray *et al.* (eds.). XVII (second edition). Oxford: Clarendon
           Press.
Quirk, Randolph, Sidney Greenbaum, Geoffrey Leech, and Jan Svartvik
  1985   *A Comprehensive Grammar of the English Language.* London: Longman.
Rissanen, Matti, Merja Kytö, and Minna Palander-Collin
  1993   *Early English in the Computer Age: Explorations through the Helsinki
           Corpus.* Berlin, New York: Mouton de Gruyter.
Taavitsainen, Irma
  forthc. a "Genre Conventions: Personal Affect in Fiction and Non-Fiction in Early
             Modern English." In: Matti Rissanen, Merja Kytö and Kirsi Heikkonen
             (eds.). *English in Transition. Diachronic Corpus Studies in Variation.*
  forthc. b "Exclamations in the Late Middle English Period." In: Jacek Fisiak (ed.).
             Studies in Middle English. Berlin, New York: Mouton de Gruyter.

Part III: Diachronic function-to-form mappings

Topics in the History of Dialogue Forms

Gerd Fritz
University of Gießen, Germany

1. Introduction

1.1. *Stages in the development of historical dialogue analysis*

The main objective of the present paper is to give an outline of some of the questions involved in research on the evolution of dialogue forms.[1] The study of the evolution of dialogue forms is the third and most ambitious stage in the development of historical dialogue analysis. These three stages can be described as follows in terms of typical activities:

(i)   The first stage is characterised by the analysis of individual historical texts with the aim of showing the pragmatic structure of dialogues represented in these texts. This has recently been done for several literary texts (e.g. Schlieben-Lange 1979 on the Old Provençal *Flamenca* novel, Weigand 1988 on the *Nibelungenlied*).

(ii) The second stage is characterised by the comparison of earlier dialogue forms with later dialogue forms, e.g. the comparison of procedures of proof in Germanic legal practice and in later Roman law, or the comparison of the practice of swearing in Switzerland in the 16th century and today (cf. Lötscher 1981). This type of contrastive historical analysis is a natural extension of contrastive pragmatics, which has also been an active concern in the last few years (cf. Oleksy 1989).

(iii) The third and most comprehensive approach is the study of the evolution of dialogue forms. This approach is still in its infancy, and it is characterised by the systematic analysis of historical developments of dialogue forms. Its basic objective is to address general and systematic questions of the type we know from historical syntax or historical semantics. Such questions include the following:[2]

–   What types of changes in dialogue forms are there?
–   Are there types of dialogues or aspects of dialogues that are more prone to change than others?
–   How do certain families of dialogue forms develop in the course of time?
–   How does the overall repertoire of dialogue forms in a given society develop in the course of time?
–   How does the diffusion of innovations work in the case of dialogue forms?
–   What counts as an explanation of a change of dialogue forms?
–   Are there universals of dialogue?

If the evolution of dialogue forms is to become a serious field of enquiry, future research will have to venture upon these systematic topics. Research of this kind presupposes both a theory of dialogue structure and a theory of evolution. Take the first question from the above list: What types of changes in dialogue forms are there? A basic assumption for a theory of change could be the following: Dialogue forms may change in any aspect of their structure. Now, in order to clarify what we understand by 'an aspect of their structure' we need a theory of dialogue structure. Let us assume that such a theory specifies several components of dialogue structure and their interrelation (e.g. construction rules for basic utterance forms, principles of local and global sequencing, turn-taking principles, topic structure).[3] In this case we could focus on exactly these components and their interrelations as possible aspects of change. This would also provide us with a first empirical hypothesis, i.e. the hypothesis that changes in one aspect tend to have repercussions in other aspects; for instance, a tightening of rules of politeness may lead to the adoption of new polite forms of utterance, and the introduction of new topics may coincide with changes in vocabulary. Although a full-fledged theory of dialogue structure is not yet available, the outlines of relevant theories have been developed during the last 20 years to such a point that empirical work can be reasonably conducted within the frameworks provided (cf. Fritz 1994a).

As for the theory of evolution, it should deal with the following problems, amongst others:

–   In which ways do dialogue patterns become stabilised within certain speaker communities as accepted forms for certain periods (the questions of conventionalisation, standardisation, or formalisation)?

- How do variants of dialogue forms emerge, how do they coexist and possibly compete (the question of innovation and selection)?
- Which factors are conducive to change and which to continuity?
- How are the organising principles for dialogues learned and how are they transmitted to different groups of speakers (the question of diffusion)?

Again, there is so far no specific theory of the evolution of dialogue forms available; however, the basic ideas of a theory of linguistic evolution could be profitably applied to our field as well (cf. Strecker 1987, Keller 1990).

In the present paper I shall concentrate on a number of basic aspects of dialogue forms and the ways dialogue forms change with regard to these aspects. But before I start on this, I have to remove two objections which might be fatal to the whole enterprise. The first objection concerns the status of dialogue forms. If the critics are right who hold the concept of dialogue form to be of dubious status, there might be no subject matter to our investigations. So we have to clarify our concept of dialogue form. The second objection comes from the sceptics who hold that the programme of a history of dialogue forms is not feasible on empirical grounds. If these sceptics are right, our investigations will come to nothing. So we have to try and get rid of this objection as well. Therefore, the next two paragraphs will deal with these objections.

1.2. On the status of the concept of dialogue form

So far I have taken for granted that there *are* such things as dialogue forms or types of dialogue or genres of dialogue, as some people might prefer to call them. This position accords with our everyday practice. In everyday language we use expressions like *interview*, *debate*, or *quarrel* to refer to stretches of dialogue which are characterised by certain features, including certain types of speech act sequences like question and answer, argument and counterargument, insult and retort. Similar expressions for referring to dialogue forms can also be found in earlier stages of many languages. So obviously members of communities of speakers recognise this kind of pragmatic regularity as a reality of their communicative lives. Dialogue forms can be considered solutions to recurrent communicative problems. Now what is it that raises doubt in the status of this kind of concept? What authors like Davidson, Searle and others really doubt is that dialogues are generally regulated by conventions or constitutive rules. They do not deny that dialogues show regularities and that they are *sometimes* regulated by conventions. This stronger proposition would be plainly false anyway, since in many institutions there are quite obviously highly formalised conventions for conducting dialogues. Both Davidson and

Searle expressly concede this point (Davidson 1985: 24; Searle 1992: 10). And
even many less formalised everyday dialogues – or portions of these dialogues –
have the characteristics of Lewis-type conventions: We expect our partners in
dialogue to make their contributions according to given patterns, and it is
common knowledge among speakers of our community of speakers that we
have these expectations and so on (cf. Lewis 1969: 78). On the other hand,
many dialogues – or portions of dialogue – seem to proceed in a fairly ad-hoc
fashion. So different types of dialogue differ as to the way in which they are
organised, i.e. whether they are loosely or tightly organised, or even
standardised in their utterance forms. What emerges is that we really have two
questions, which are both of an empirical nature and which can therefore not be
solved in the philosopher's armchair: (i) What is the nature and degree of the
regularities involved? (ii) What are the sources of these regularities
(conventions, routines, functional needs, and/or dialogue principles)? As for the
concept of dialogue form, it should be considered a family concept covering
regularities in dialogue which are produced by different types of organising
principles, including both conventions and functional principles (e.g. Gricean
maxims).[4] Historical studies in dialogue forms are one of the means of
increasing our awareness of different degrees of conventionalisation and
standardisation and thereby improving the quality of our present theories of
dialogue.

1.3. *Is an evolutionary history of dialogue forms feasible?*

The first problem that comes to mind when one considers the feasibility of such
a programme is the problem of adequate data, i.e. the problem of historical
sources. This problem concerns both the difficulties presented by the nature of
the data available and the lack of relevant material for most historical periods
apart from the recent past. As soon as we have to rely on written sources, i.e.
dramatic representations of dialogues, narratives of dialogues, descriptions of
dialogue forms, or normative statements as to how dialogues should be
conducted, we are at least one step removed from actual dialogues as data.
Representations of dialogue are themselves products of intentional action and as
such always embody a certain view of their subject. So we may have to perform
difficult hermeneutical operations in order to provide a reconstruction of what
the actual communicative practice may have been like that forms the
background of a particular representation. And the further we move into the
distant past the less numerous even this kind of data becomes. And, of course,
for most historical dialogue forms we also lack another important resource for
dialogue analysis, i.e. our own competence to participate in dialogues of the

relevant type.[5] This lack of material is no doubt a problem one has to take seriously, but it is not generally as hopeless as one might think. In the first place, there is a vast amount of research on literary history, social history, ethnology, the history of philosophy, etc. from which relevant secondary information can be drawn and which leads to more direct sources. Secondly, there are many primary sources which have not yet been systematically used under this particular perspective (cf. Gloning 1993). It is a well-known phenomenon that a clear-cut programme opens one's eyes for the location of useful sources. If, for example, we are interested in the history of planning dialogues, we soon realise that there is an immense amount of material available for this type of dialogue. We find people deliberating on what to do in classical epics from Homer's *Iliad* to the French *Chanson de Roland* and the German *Nibelungenlied*, in historical texts like Thucydides' *Peloponnesian War*, in medieval chronicles (e.g. Marignoli's *Bohemian Chronicle*, dated about 1355), and in didactic works like Barclay's *Argenis* (1621) or Fénelon's *Télémaque* (1699), etc. Furthermore, there is an important lesson to be learned from the various fields of historical linguistics: There is no reason why historical research should be confined to the distant past. Historical changes of dialogue forms are going on around us in our presence, where access to adequate sources is much easier. So why should a systematic history of dialogue forms not start with present-day developments like the ones caused by the introduction of new media. And finally, the evolutionary perspective does not necessarily commit a practitioner to the idea of a complete and continuous history of the dialogue forms in a certain society. On the contrary, it seems advisable to start off with well-chosen fragments from the macrocosm of dialogue forms. And even so one will at times have to have recourse to methods like the reconstruction of missing links for which there is no direct evidence or to forms of "conjectural history" or "rational reconstruction" (cf. Ullmann-Margalit 1978: 276f.) in order to compensate for gaps in the available data. It is true that such methods have to be used very judiciously, but they are not to be excluded on principle, as the example of historical linguistics shows quite clearly. So the upshot of these reflections seems to be: At the present stage, the evolutionary perspective is mainly a guiding principle for research, but in the long run an evolutionary history of dialogue forms may actually prove a successful enterprise.

2.   Organising principles of dialogues and types of historical change

As a basic framework for the description and classification of types of change in the history of dialogue forms I shall use a system of elementary aspects of dialogue forms which includes the following items:

(i)   patterns of speech act sequencing, including the choice of alternative strategies,
(ii)   topics and topical networks,
(iii)   characteristic utterance forms,
(iv)   conversational principles or maxims.

This list may easily be extended and specified in more detail. In order to illustrate this system of aspects I shall now present a few examples of how dialogue forms may change with respect to these aspects. These examples will be mainly taken from the history of German, but of course similar examples could be given for other languages as well.

2.1. *Patterns of speech act sequencing and strategies*

In the introductory section of this paper I accepted the assumption that many dialogue forms are built around certain basic sequences of speech acts; planning dialogues, for example, typically contain suggestions and evaluations of suggestions, etc. So it is in fact these sequences which are the basic building blocks of dialogues, not individual speech acts. Individual speech act types can be defined in terms of the role they play in sequences of this kind. Even if one does not accept this theoretical assumption, which is part of a game-theoretical version of speech act theory (cf. Carlson 1983: 107), one will still find that in many cases it is types of sequences – and not primarily individual speech acts – which show interesting developments over time.

By way of illustration I should like to examine an everyday pattern of dialogue which has interesting connections with formal dialogues in legal procedure, i.e. the elementary sequence of accusation and response to an accusation. Well-known sources for observations on this type of dialogue are Austin's famous paper *A plea for excuses* (Austin 1961) and Goffman's remarks on "remedial interchanges" (Goffman 1971: 138ff.). Descriptions of the present-day basic structures of this kind of dialogue can be found in Fritz/Hundsnurscher (1975) and in recent publications on accounts and apologies (cf. Owen 1983, Olshtain 1989).

Basically, if I accuse someone of having done something wrong (or blame her/him for a certain action), he or she may react to this accusation by employing a number of standard responses like denying the charge, excusing the action by quoting mitigating circumstances, justifying the action by giving reasons for this action, and, finally, apologising. A third move in this language game may consist in an attempt at proving that the defendant was in fact guilty. Now, in a historical perspective it is interesting to see how each component of such a basic pattern can be the locus of change. Changes might occur concerning:

- the typical content of an accusation (accusing someone of touching a lady's hand, accusing a woman of going for a walk on her own, accusing a person of spoiling her/his children, etc.),
- the typical linguistic form an accusation can take (e.g. forms like *why didn't you ...?*),
- the types of responses that are actually practised, including standardised linguistic forms (e.g. for apologies: *I am sorry*; *please accept my apologies*),
- the preferences for certain types of responses (e.g. a preference for justifications as compared to apologies or vice versa),
- common assumptions concerning accepted norms and their hierarchies (that one should not touch a lady's hand; that religious duties are more important than household duties or vice versa, etc.),
- the attitudes to responsibility and to extenuating circumstances, etc.,
- what counts as proof and how proofs are performed.

As for relevant historical developments in legal procedure, there is a large amount of information available in research on legal history. (In Fritz/Muckenhaupt 1981 we attempted a brief reconstruction of some of the historical changes in legal proof procedures in Germany from the late Middle Ages to early modern times.) But it might also be rewarding to trace developments in the everyday versions of this basic pattern. As an example I should like to give a few extracts from a German treatise on matters of marriage published in the year 1472, the so-called *Ehebüchlein* written by Albrecht von Eyb. In the third paragraph of this treatise there is a passage on misdemeanours of which a husband might accuse his wife and the responses his wife might give to such accusations. (*Was aber hübscher wort die fraw gebraucht so sie vn recht wider iren man gethan hat vnd sich entschuldigen will.*) In the case of a grave misdemeanour the wife may react as follows:

(i)   My dear husband I realise that I did wrong and I confess my misdeed. I want to ask you lovingly to forgive what I have done. I shall never do it again, and if I do give offence again, you may kill me.

If a wife has stayed away too long from home at night, her husband may call her names (*du pöse haut* 'you evil hide') and threaten to beat her. In this case she may answer as follows:

(ii)   I felt uneasy all evening and I decided to go to church to confess my sins. As there were so many women there taking up the priests' time with their confessions, I had to wait very long, and I did not realise that such a long time had passed. However you should forgive me, as it was done with the best of intentions.

If her husband suspects her of being 'burdened with someone else's love' (*beladen mit fremder lieb* – a somewhat ambiguous expression) and blames her for it, she may answer:

(iii)   My dear husband, you know I am more than twenty years old, and I am made of flesh and blood as other women are. I am young and proud, and I can't help it if other people find me attractive. Apart from that you have been away for a long time. Is it not natural that I should be moved to desire and mirth like other women? One has to give in to nature at times, but it shall not happen again.

Now if the wife was out dancing or at some other amusement or going for a walk, her husband might give her a sermon on moral behaviour. In this case she could smile and say:

(iv)   Dear husband, you would make a wonderful preacher. What you say is perfectly correct, but it is easier to preach than to act on. ... These wise words would make sense in a monastery where there is nothing else to do.

If this repartee does not help, the wife should ask forgiveness and say:

(v)   Dear husband, I confess that I did wrong, but in your wisdom you may forgive me what I said or did unwisely. I shall no more do anything against your will and I shall submit myself unto you and I shall be obedient in all things. I commend myself to your trust. Do with me as you like.

Now if these sweet words do not subdue her husband's anger – the author suggests – the wife can still sigh deeply, bow her head, start crying and embrace him and kiss him. If all this is of no avail, she should get angry and turn the tables on him and accuse him of all kinds of things he has never done. – The paragraph closes with the enumeration of several classical instances of angry women.

Albrecht von Eyb was a humanist, who freely quoted from classical sources and Italian Renaissance authors, but he was also a lawyer, who is known to have written several legal expertises in cases of marriage conflicts in the city of Nuremberg. We must further keep in mind that his treatise was meant both to instruct and to entertain. Therefore, if we want to use this kind of text as a historical source for the history of dialogue forms we have to try and 'peel off' layers of classical lore and poetic licence and uncover the elements of realistic description. In the case of the present passage the retort (i) is actually introduced as a quotation from an Italian author. But it does not appear as an unlikely reaction in Eyb's own time. Even the remark about killing the culprit is in consonance with contemporary law. Likewise, the suggestion that women should resort to tears is a classical topos, but not necessarily irrelevant to 15th century practice. So it looks as if this passage could be taken to contain some elements of a realistic picture of dialogue patterns used by 15th century citizens.

Closer analysis of this fairly sophisticated passage shows a number of noteworthy features: it is the husband who does the accusing, a fact which reflects the standard division of roles in late medieval ideology of marriage.[6] However, the remarkable array of countermoves seems to indicate that the husbands' authority was not necessarily undisputed. A recurring topic of accusations is the wife's freedom of movement outside the house, which is obviously considered dangerous. As for the justificatory moves, mentioning religious activities seems to be an accepted strategy on the part of the wife. Generally speaking, the moves in this dialogue game reveal a background of religious and legal discourse (the model of confession and asking forgiveness, the act of submission). The latter fact makes this an interesting case of the influence of formal, institutional talk on an everyday dialogue form. Some of the moves presented in Eyb's description contrast quite notably with what we know about present-day dialogues of a similar kind. There are also certain moves missing which recur in present-day dialogues, e.g. arguments disputing the validity of certain norms. These features could form the subject of a contrastive study. What would have to be shown in an evolutionary study is the presumed element of innovation in comparison to typical medieval practice and (some of) the stages of development that lead to modern Central European middle class practice in this type of conflict talk. In order to pursue this development from the 16th century onwards one would have to collect documents of disputes between married persons in novels, dramatical works, pedagogical texts, private letters and documents of divorce suits, just to name a few relevant text types.

As far as the earlier history of this dialogue form is concerned, the better-known late-medieval German texts dealing with the subject of marriage are unfortunately not as informative as the exceptionally detailed and explicit passage from Eyb (cf. Dallapiazza 1981). The same is true of 16th century works like Fischart's famous *Ehezuchtbüchlein* (1578). But it is quite unlikely that the massive literature on marriage in the 15th and 16th centuries in Germany should not provide us with many more pieces of the historical puzzle we have before us (cf. Taylor 1939, Holenstein 1991). So what we have at the moment is at least a starting point for a (partial) history of the basic sequence 'accusation and response to accusation'. This small segment of dialogue is just one element of the large family of types of conflict talk. This family ranges from types of argumentation to swearing and verbal duelling. Therefore, the history of accusation and excuses could be embedded in a more comprehensive history of conflict talk.

As a second example I should like to mention declarations of love. This dialogue form also contains a core sequence, viz. declaring one's love and reciprocating this declaration. In describing historical changes in this dialogue form we could start by comparing the form of this adjacency pair, e.g. by comparing medieval versions like (1) or (2) – the famous passage from Gottfried's *Tristan* – with a modern version like (3). The Middle High German utterances are given together with a transliteration:

(1)   A: Ich minne dich.
           I   love   you.
       B: Als tuon ich dich.
           So do   I   you.
(2)   "in al der werlde enist mir niht
        In all the world not-is to me anything

       in minem herzen liep wan ir."
       in my heart (as) beloved as you

       Isot sprach: "herre, als sit ir mir."
       Isolde said: "Sir, so are you to me."
(3)   A: Ich liebe dich.
       B: Ich dich auch.

These changes in the form of utterance are certainly worth noting. But from the point of view of the dialogue structure the focal point seems to lie elsewhere. It is the strategies used in leading up to the pivotal statements that make declarations of love an interesting type of dialogue. If we try to determine which aspects of declarations of love are likely to change in the course of time, it is the solutions to problems like the following which come to mind: Who is supposed to make the opening move and by which means? What are the intermediate steps that have to be negotiated? How can one phrase a rejection without hurting the respective person's feelings? How can one let the other person know one's feelings without saying too much and without violating social restrictions and thereby taking the risk of being snubbed? The famous ambiguity in one of Isolde's utterances – she uses the Old French word *lameir* which can mean 'the sea', 'bitter', and 'love' (*Tristan* 11986) – is obviously not intended by the author as a sign of her confusion, as some commentators think (cf. Schwarz 1984), but rather as a sophisticated move by which she gives Tristan a hint without having to commit herself at this point of the proceedings. Now, from a historical point of view it is exactly the changing kinds of problems the lovers have to solve in this situation and the changing strategies they use that are worth paying attention to. No doubt, 17th century noblemen, Victorian citizens and present-day students have different problems to solve in this situation and also have different resources at their disposal for the solution of these problems.

The final example of this section shows how a new dialogue type was developed by emphasising one particular type of strategy. At a certain point in planning communications people usually make a suggestion and this suggestion will then be clarified, discussed and evaluated. And after this procedure, which at times can be quite lengthy, the next suggestion will be made and will be dealt with in the same fashion. This strategy is very useful if you want to find out the pros and cons of a certain course of action. But it has one big disadvantage. It prevents a quick survey of the suggestions available and may thereby cause the loss of particularly helpful suggestions. In order to increase the efficiency of the explorative phase of planning talks, American managers in the 1930s developed a particular strategy which expressly excluded the discussion of suggestions and encouraged the collection of as many suggestions as possible. This strategy later became a distinct dialogue form and was called 'brainstorming'.

One aspect of sequencing which has been closely analysed during the last 20 years is turn-taking (cf. Sacks/Schegloff/Jefferson 1974). But it is only recently that emphasis has been placed on the fact that turn-taking mechanisms are culture-specific and that we often find special conventions for turn-taking within institutions. Both these facts provide topics for historical analysis. We could, for instance, ask how the assumptions concerning rank and precedence of certain speakers which determine turn-taking conventions develop in the course of time. In the special case of institutions one would have to show how special turn-taking conventions could have developed to suit the function of a particular institution.

Generally speaking, the invention of completely new speech act patterns seems to have been rather rare in historical times for which we have records. By the time written documents were produced, all the basic patterns known to us today already seem to have been in practice. What is obviously much more frequent is the modification of strategies and the adaptation of existing basic patterns to specific purposes. I shall return to this point later.

2.2. *Forms of utterance*

The history of utterance forms is the classical domain of historical linguistics. It is therefore not surprising that many of the results of historical phonology, historical syntax or historical semantics are directly relevant to the history of dialogue forms. However, within the framework of the history of dialogue forms certain aspects of linguistic form which have so far not been at the centre of interest in historical linguistics – especially aspects of spoken language – will receive extra attention, e.g.:[7]

(i)   the form and use of syntactic patterns like dislocation or ellipsis,
(ii) the conventional form of certain speech acts (requests, greetings, swearing),
(iii) interjections, particles (e.g. modal particles in spoken German), forms of address,
(iv) idiomatic phrases, sayings, and other routine formulas.

A few examples taken from Middle High German, more specifically from early 13th century German, and present-day German will indicate the kind of historical developments I have in mind:[8]

In Middle High German there is a type of ellipsis in question/answer-patterns which has not come down to our time. The following example is taken from the *Nibelungenlied*, verses 827, 4f.:

(4)   A: ob er sin innen wurde, so torste in nieman bestan.
          if he of it aware became (i.e. the attack), then could dare him nobody confront.
      B: nein er.
          no he.

The answer of B could be paraphrased as '(But) he will not become aware of it.' This kind of strong ellipsis is not possible in Modern German, no more than in Modern English.

On the other hand, we find continuity of certain types of dislocation which occur both in medieval German and in present-day spoken German, e.g. (5) and (6):

(5) din rede diu ist mir leit. (*Nibelungenlied* 56,1)
     your talk that is to me loathsome
(6) diese Sprüche, die höre ich nicht gern.

In Middle High German one could give precedence to a person by uttering (7), whereas in Modern German one could use a related form (8); but the standard expression would be (9), which is probably a French loan:

(7) Herre, welt ir füre gan.
     Sir, would you first go.
(8) Bitte, gehen Sie voran.
(9) Bitte nach Ihnen.

In Middle High German there were at least two idiomatic forms available to express the idea that talking to someone is a waste of breath, (10) and (11). In present-day Standard German, two different metaphorical expressions, (12) and (13), are conventionally used, of which (12) is formed on a pattern very similar to the medieval idioms:

(10) deist gehärpfet in der mül
      that is (like) playing the harp in the mill
(11) deist gerüefet in den walt
      that is (like) shouting into the forest
(12) das ist in den Wind gesprochen
      that is (like) talking to the wind
(13) tauben Ohren predigen
      to preach to deaf ears

2.3. *Topics and networks of topics*

It is one of the merits of ethnomethodology to have shown that topics of dialogues are a respectable subject of conversation analysis (cf. Adato 1971). In a way, the history of topics and networks of topics is a natural extension of work done in this tradition. In doing topic talk, speakers rely on their knowledge, which is contextually bound, socially distributed and historically determined. Therefore, it is not surprising that one important aspect of the change of dialogue forms is the change of topics. In order to show that topics are not external to the structure of dialogues, one can draw attention to the fact that many kinds of discourse actually rely on the existence of certain topics, e.g. in religious discourse. Often it is new concepts that provide new topics and sometimes even completely new forms of dialogue. Without the concept of sin there could probably be no dialogue form of confession. And without the concept of the subconscious there could probably be no psychoanalytical dialogue. In the 19th century, the discovery (or invention) of the concept of the subconscious was the basis for a new type of scientific explanatory discourse, and this topic was later diffused to non-scientific contexts so as to constitute an everyday pattern of explanation for psychological problems (cf. Pörksen 1986: 150ff.).

The central issue in this field of enquiry is changes in conventional topics and the relationships between topics in topical networks. A case in point is the topic of natural energy resources, especially the sub-topic of fuel consumption, which has been a topic both in the media and in private discussions for the last thirty years. In the sixties – my own experience extends mainly to England, France and Germany – the topic of fuel consumption of motor cars tended to be discussed as a matter of personal economy. In the early seventies, especially after the so-called first oil crisis (1973), the topic acquired closer connections with questions like political and economic crises, the limits of natural resources, alternative energies, etc. Although the topic of environmental protection had been discussed since the late sixties – *Umweltschutz* became a household word in Germany in 1970 –, it was only after the possible impacts of the combustion of fossil fuels on the world's atmosphere and climate became widely known that the topic of fuel consumption became firmly integrated into the environmental topic. Apart from illustrating the structure and development of networks of topics, this example also shows an unexpected relationship between fairly distant fields of research: In this particular area, historical dialogue analysis can draw inspiration from public opinion research, especially research on 'agenda setting', which has developed methods for the description of so-called 'careers of topics', including the introduction and diffusion of new topics (cf. Schönbach 1982, contributions to Protess/McCombs 1991).

I shall conclude this section by listing a number of relevant aspects of the history of topics:

(i)   How is thematic knowledge distributed amongst speakers of a community?

(ii)   How are new topics invented, introduced and diffused (e.g. from scientific discourse to everyday discourse)?

(iii)   How does the evaluation of topics change? (Some topics are considered important at a certain time, later on they are 'out'.)

(iv)   How do norms governing the acceptability and treatment of topics change (e.g. norms concerning talk about sexuality and death)?
(iv)   Do topic careers show typical profiles?
(v)   How is the continuity of topics within certain societies or groups to be explained (e.g. traditions of religious topics)?

2.4. *Communication principles*

The last group of organising principles I shall deal with are conversational maxims or, as I prefer to call them, communication principles. Whereas philosophers tend to view basic conversational maxims as universally valid, sociologists, ethnologists, and historians of dialogue forms tend to emphasise the fact that many specific principles and their modes of application are not historically invariable and therefore not universally valid at all. For example, the principle of comprehensibility, which can be considered a very basic principle for many forms of dialogue, is applied in completely different ways in courtly conversations of the 17th century and in present-day small talk. Courtly conversation often required a high degree of indirectness, and therefore suggesting and deciphering hidden meaning was all-pervasive (cf. Schmölders 1986: 29). So, at least at surface level, comprehensibility did not have priority in this type of conversation. It is even less prevalent in many forms of religious discourse, where the laymen often do not even understand the language in which the discourse is conducted.[9]

A second example is the maxim of politeness – a long-time favourite of students of pragmatics (cf. Brown/Levinson 1987, Watts/Ide/Ehlich 1992). Its general status and the linguistic means of applying the maxim are quite obviously subject to historical change. One case in point is the history of forms of address. In the German language, for example, there was only one pronoun of address used in the early middle ages, namely *Du*. By the end of the 17th century there is a system of four different pronouns of address which are employed according to fairly subtle social rules (*du*, *ihr*, *er*, *sie* (plur.)). In the 19th century this system is gradually reduced to the binary system we know in German today (*Du* and *Sie*; cf. Metcalf 1938). Another case of historical change in the system of politeness is the changing attitude towards the use of compliments in the course of the 18th century. Whereas during the 17th century polite people throughout Europe insisted on long and frequent compliments, this practice was increasingly criticised in the course of the 18th century. For Germany, this has been convincingly shown by Beetz in his book on early modern politeness (Beetz 1990). It is also rewarding to compare this description

484   Gerd Fritz

of the early modern practice of compliment exchanges with descriptions of different types of present-day compliments and compliment responses (e.g. Herbert 1989).

Principles guiding individual types of speech acts are also historically variable, and we often find conflicting principles stemming from different traditions. As examples one could adduce the principles concerning self-praise and asking questions. For Germanic knights it was obviously perfectly acceptable to indulge in self-praise, whereas the Christian principle of humility strictly forbade self-praise. Today the Christian tradition seems to prevail in western cultures, although violations of this principle are quite common amongst politicians, artists, and academics.[10] As for question-asking, there is evidence in 12th century German epic texts of rules of etiquette that forbid asking too many questions. (Of course, there are also excellent strategic reasons why one should not ask to many questions. But these reasons do not seem to be mentioned in 12th century texts.) Contemporaneous didactic texts, however, give young persons the advice to ask questions freely in order to overcome their ignorance. This dilemma of principles looks like a universal communicative problem, but quite obviously different aspects of the dilemma come to the fore in different cultures, and different solutions to the problem evolve in different historical periods.

In order to further indicate the variety of principles which govern dialogue forms I shall add some more examples with a few comments. This list could be continued almost indefinitely.

(i)   The principle of silence, which has a long tradition not only in monastic life (cf. Luhmann/Fuchs 1989, Hahn 1991, Burke 1993: 123ff.), contrasts with the principle of 'conversability', which is propagated by courtly conduct books (cf. Strosetzki 1978: 55).

(ii)   In the 17th and 18th centuries, the principle of brevity was often adhered to in talk between princes and servants. However, the reasons legitimising this principle are different for the two groups of speakers: By restricting himself to short statements the prince shows his majesty, whereas the servants make their contributions short in order to express their respect towards their master (cf. Braungart 1988: 18).

(iii) In a society where new information is a scarce commodity, the Gricean principle of informativity (Grice 1989: 26) may be limited in its application or even inverted to a principle of information restriction, as in Malagasy narratives (cf. Keenan 1976). Francis Bacon, in his essay *Of negotiating* (1597), recommends that "in dealing with cunning persons" one should "say little to them".

(iv) Flattery has been the object of criticism ever since Theophrast's *Charakteres*, but several authors suggest a moderate dose of praise as a means of creating an agreeable atmosphere (e.g. Hunold 1716: 82f.)

(v)   Contradicting one's partners in conversation is considered bad style by some authors (e.g. Hunold 1716: 52f.); on the other hand, contradiction is recommended as a powerful means of extracting information from one's opponents (Gracián 1653/1990: 106).

The history of communication principles is probably one of the most fruitful topics in historical pragmatics. And, of course, there is a wealth of sources of information available on such principles, from personal letters and novels to conduct books and other forms of instructional literature. Recent work on the history of communication principles includes Schmölders' useful introduction to her selection of texts *Die Kunst des Gesprächs* (Schmölders 1986) and chapters from Burke's *The art of conversation* (Burke 1993).[11] As in the other areas of historical dialogue analysis, further progress in the history of communication principles will depend on the degree to which researchers will focus on systematic and general questions like the following:

(i)   How does the extension or restriction of the range of application (including the conditions of application) come about (e.g. the extension of a principle restricting the giving of commands to the performance of *all* directives, or the restriction of the number of topics to which the principle of silence applies)?

(ii) How do different forms of application of a certain principle develop (e.g. competing forms of politeness)?

(iii) How does the diffusion from one particular group to a major segment of a society come about (e.g. the diffusion of politeness principles from the courts to the middle classes)?

(iv) How does the interaction of principles influence the development of dialogue forms (e.g. simultaneous pressure of the principle of brevity and the principle of explicitness)?

(v)   Are there principles which favour changes in dialogue forms and others which favour continuity (e.g. the principles of efficiency and originality as motors of change and the principle of comprehensibility as a factor of stability)?

(vi) How are instrumental principles and deontic principles historically related (i.e. principles guiding successful action vs. principles specifying duties)?

(vii) How do clusters of principles build up to form coherent systems (e.g. the ideal of gentleman, or pietistical systems of rules for conversation)?

(viii) Does the history of dialogue forms indicate particularly stable principles? (In other words: Are there hopeful candidates for universal principles?)

3.   The evolution of dialogue forms in institutional contexts

Special purposes of dialogues call for specialised dialogue forms. This simple assumption guides the historian of dialogue forms to the analysis of dialogues in institutional contexts~ . In a way, dialogue forms are themselves institutions, but they often become embedded in what we normally call institutions, i.e. in legal institutions, religious institutions, medical institutions, etc. By being thus embedded, everyday dialogue forms acquire special structures, special principles, and often also special types of problems.[12] Take for instance dialogues between doctors and patients during the doctors' visit in a hospital ward. Their basic function is to provide information for diagnosis and therapy. Dialogues conducted in this context rely on elementary patterns like question and answer, requesting, describing, and story-telling. However, within this particular functional context these patterns appear in fairly characteristic constellations: it is the doctor who exercises special rights in uttering requests, in turn-taking, in initiating relevant topics, in giving or withholding information, and in introducing the proper vocabulary, and the patient has to adapt her descriptions and narrative attempts to what is expected of her in this particular setting. This constellation generally leads to fairly frequent interruptions on the part of the doctor and to problems of comprehension on the part of the patient.[13] As a solution to the functional problem of gaining necessary information, this asymmetrical form of dialogue seems to be fairly well-established. But at least from the point of view of the patient, it is definitely less than optimal. Therefore, one might consider it not a really stable pattern in a long-term perspective. However, it is interesting to see that some of the relevant complaints of patients are historically quite old, e.g. the complaint that the doctors' pronouncements are incomprehensible to the layman. Gloning (1993) gives a rather amusing example from the 17th century, but the type of complaint is certainly much older.

From an evolutionary point of view it is the process of institutionalisation which is of particular interest.[14] For historically distant periods we may have to reconstruct this process by contrasting everyday patterns and institutional variants and by showing functional reasons for the development of the institutional variants. As an illustration of this method I shall describe some of the basic structures of 17th century court audiences as special versions of an everyday dialogue pattern. This activity type is well-documented in different kinds of contemporary texts. The first periodical newspapers, i.e. the early 17th century weeklies, are full of reports on legations to the emperor and other princes and the audiences given by these high personages (e.g. *Aviso 1609*, *Relation 1609*). We also have personal reports by envoys to their principals on audiences granted by the emperor (e.g. von Czepko 1658/1980). And finally, there are books with instructions on how ceremonial actions like audiences should be properly conducted (e.g. von Rohr 1733).

Generally speaking, the structure of an audience is a highly complicated and ritualised version of the basic pattern 'request and response to request'. In its everyday version, for instance in our family lives, this basic pattern has the following structure: A child addresses her father and asks if she can go and play with her friend. In most cases the father will decide on the spot and either give permission or reject the request. Now, in an audience these basic elements are separated and enriched with other elements. These extra elements mainly belong to the following categories:

(i)   Access to the audience has to be gained by a complicated procedure, which includes presenting one's credentials, giving presents to various persons, soliciting through intermediaries, and waiting in the antechamber. Strict rules of precedence regulate the date of admission.

(ii)   Once the audience has been granted, the actual request – the so-called *proposition* – has to be embellished with compliments, and it has to be presented with a backing of legal or historical arguments and in good rhetorical form – both orally and in writing.

(iii)   The answer to the request – the so-called *resolution* – is normally not given during the audience at all, but is deferred to a later moment, when it is given in writing.

The function of this total procedure is quite obviously to preserve distance between the envoy and the court, to diminish the surprise element of requests, and to allow the emperor and his surroundings to gain time for their decisions. The function of the written form is to make the proceedings legally valid. Giving the answer to the request at a later moment minimises the chances of the requestor's arguing and uttering dissatisfaction in the presence of the emperor, which spares the court much embarrassment in the case of a negative answer. So what we find is a very sophisticated type of communicative activity which is attuned to the delicate tasks of a complex administration. When we compare this procedure to descriptions of representatives' visits to royal courts in medieval texts, we certainly find an amount of polite ritual in the earlier period, but in general, the access to the royal personages is much more direct. So, during the medieval period, the dialogue form corresponding to the later form of audience is still rather close to the basic pattern. A detailed historical analysis would have to show how the characteristic traits of the 17th century pattern developed in response to the demands of an increasingly complex task of administration.

4.   Historical explanation

The last example already paved the way to a final question, the question of explanation in the history of dialogue forms. As everyone knows, historical explanation is an extremely difficult topic, and I shall only give a few hints as to how this question might be approached.

The first idea is that, for several reasons, the historical explanation of a dialogue form is not a monolithic enterprise. It is good to remind oneself that the various aspects of dialogue forms may very well call for separate explanations. We cannot necessarily expect the history of dialogue topics to run parallel to the history of politeness rules for turn-taking or to the history of preferences for certain strategies. Apart from this, the emergence of a dialogue form within a certain group will possibly call for explanatory devices that differ from the ones we need for the explanation of the diffusion of an established dialogue form to other social groups.

As for the emergence and transformation of dialogue forms, a useful explanatory framework could be inspired by Lewis's theory of convention. If we consider dialogue forms to be solutions to recurring problems of communication, at least part of an historical explanation will consist in showing which communication problem is solved by the dialogue form in question and how it is solved. This kind of explanation could be termed a functional explanation. To give an example: the dialogue form of bargaining could be shown to be a solution to the problem of finding an adequate price for goods for which there is no value fixed in advance. It is worth mentioning that the problem-solving conception does not commit us to the view that these solutions are intentionally sought. In many cases they are "the result of human action but not of human design" (Ullmann-Margalit 1978: 263). What humans are usually after is the solution of their local practical problems and not, as a rule, the creation of new dialogue forms. I shall not embark on a discussion of the merits and problems of this type of explanation. I shall, however, at least indicate one type of dialogue form for which a straightforward functional explanation may not be sufficient, i.e. forms of 'empty ritual'. In the words of a prominent representative of the evolutionary view of institutional history, Stephen Toulmin:

> Within any actual human community, the mere existence of any social institution, custom, or procedure will not be explicable in functional terms alone; since it may have survived a long sequence of historical changes, only because no better-adapted alternative was available, or because the institutional selection process was unusually conservative - so that it kept its place in spite of having lost its original significance, or adaptive advantage (Toulmin 1972: 350f.).

As a final illustrative example which could count as an interesting candidate for a functional explanation I should like to mention the exchange of ritual insults. This type of dialogue is known in different present-day cultures and is also represented in earlier historical periods. A well-known description of one variant of this practice was given by Labov in his classical paper on ritual insults (Labov 1972). In this paper he describes the patterns and the social significance of exchanges of this kind, which are practised by boys living in the black ghettos of New York. The following is an example of such an exchange (Labov 1972: 161):

(14) David: Your father got brick teeth.
      Boot: Your father got teeth growin' out his behind.

The basic insight of Labov's analysis is the following: Ritual insults are no real insults. Whereas real insults lead to fights, ritual insults are a means of giving vent to aggressions without having to resort to actual fighting. As I said, similar patterns of verbal duels can be found in different societies today but also in early medieval societies in different European countries. The following Old Norse example, taken from the beginning of the *Hárbarðzlióð*, shows how two speakers - in fact two gods in disguise - playfully provoke each other by casting doubt on each other's social status (cf. Bax 1991: 205):

(15) Thor: Hverr er sá sveinn sveinna, er stendr fyr sundit handan?
                       'Who is this youngster standing beyond the sound?'

      Hárbarð (Odin): Hverr er sá karl karla, er kallar um váginn?
                       'Who is this common man shouting across the sea?'

This kind of dialogue belongs to a family of dialogue forms some of which were so well established that they deserved special descriptive expressions. The following are some of the original Germanic names for forms of verbal duels:

(16)   Old Norse: *hvöt*   'provocation'
                            senna   'verbal duel'
        Anglo-Saxon: *gylpcwide,*   'boasting speech'
                            gylpspraec
        Middle English: *flyting*   'quarrel', 'verbal contest'
        Middle High German: *gelpf*   'boasting', 'challenge'

Among this group of dialogue forms, at least two related patterns seem to have
coexisted during the early medieval period: One consisted of boasts and mutual
insults which functioned as challenges preparing an actual fight. The other one
was more like a contest of ritual insults, functioning as a substitute for fighting.
More detailed information on these dialogue types is available in articles by Bax
and in Hughes' book on swearing (cf. Hughes 1991, under the heading of
flyting). Now it looks as if the challenge pattern was the original, archaic
dialogue form, and the pattern of ritual insults was a later invention. If so, a
functional explanation would have to show how the later form could have
developed from the earlier one and what functional meaning the new form had.
This is certainly not a simple task, and I shall not attempt such an explanation
here, but probably Labov's analysis of ritual insults would provide a useful point
of departure for a functional explanation of the history of these dialogue forms.

Notes

1.   The ideas presented in this paper ultimately go back to a seminar on the history of
        forms of communication which I conducted at the University of Tübingen in 1979. In
        the meantime, I had the opportunity of discussing my views with several groups of
        colleagues at the Universities of Tübingen and Gießen and at the 5th Congress of
        Dialogue Analysis at the Sorbonne, Paris 1994. I am particularly grateful for objections
        and suggestions made by Madeleine Elam, Jacek Fisiak, Thomas Gloning, Franz
        Hundsnurscher, Andreas Jucker, Manfred Muckenhaupt, Hans Ramge, and Bruno
        Strecker.
2.   A more detailed list is given in Fritz 1994b: 545f.
3.   Some people might prefer to think in terms of organising principles rather than in
        terms of dialogue structure.
4.   This position is compatible with the view presented in Dascal (1992). It avoids both the
        mistakes of radical functionalism and of radical constitutivism.
5.   It is also important to keep in mind the many connections between oral and written
        communication, of which I shall mention just a few: Speeches and sermons will often

be delivered in a form very close to the written text; on the other hand, letters or written narratives and plays may imitate spoken language. In the 17th century we find the advice given to writers to improve their style by means of conversation with polite people. ("Mich dünckt/ wer etwas gutes schreiben will/ der muß mit galanten Leuten conversieren", Christian Weise 1691: 292; quoted by Nickisch 1990: 122).

6.   As Brook (1994: 212f.) reminds us, the portrayal of a domineering wife, a frequent topic of medieval satirical literature, is a reversal of the normal role of husbands and wives in medieval society.

7.   Recent work in this sector includes: Grosse (1985) and Sonderegger (1990) for spoken language in medieval German, Lebsanft (1988) for greetings in Old French, Hughes (1991) for the history of swearing and swearwords in English, just to mention a few titles. Of course, prospects are much better for a history of idioms or a history of the syntax of spoken language than for a history of prosody.

8.   I shall give a transliteration of the medieval German utterances.

9.   Göttert (1991) gives some interesting details of the history of the principle of comprehensibility.

10. Malinowski reports remarkable self-praise communication from the inhabitants of the Trobriand Islands (Malinowski 1923).

11. The kind of perspective that is being advocated here can also be found in one of the classics of social history, i.e. in Elias's book on the process of civilization (Elias 1978).

12. Recent literature on this topic includes Rolf (1994) and contributions to Drew/Heritage (1992).

13. This description is based on the findings in Bliesener (1982) and on, fortunately rather restricted, personal experience.

14. Berger and Luckmann (1967) give a useful characterisation of the essential features of institutionalisation.

Bibliography of primary sources

Der Aviso des Jahres 1609
    1939   In Faksimiledruck herausgegeben und mit einem Nachwort versehen von Walter Schöne. Leipzig: Otto Harrassowitz.
Bacon, Francis
    1958   " Of negotiating". In: Oliphant Smeaton (ed.). *Francis Bacon's Essays*. London: J. M. Dent & Sons, 144-145. (Original written in 1597).

Czepko, Daniel von
  1980   " Gesandschaffts-Relation" (1658). In: Daniel von Czepko. *Sämtliche Werke*. Herausgegeben von Hans-Gert Roloff und Marian Szyrocki. Vierter Band. Prosa-Schriften I. Berlin/New York: De Gruyter, 116-195.
Eyb, Albrecht von
  1472   *Ob einem manne sey zunemen ein eelichs weyb oder nicht*. Nuremberg. Reprinted Darmstadt: Wissenschaftliche Buchgesellschaft 1993.
Straßburg, Gottfried von
  1967   *Tristan und Isold*. Herausgegeben von Friedrich Ranke. 11. unveränderte Auflage. Dublin/Zürich: Weidmann.
Gracián, Balthasar
  1990   *Handorakel und Kunst der Weltklugheit*. Translated by Arthur Schopenhauer. Edited by Arthur Hübscher. Stuttgart: Reclam. (Original written in 1653).
" Hárbarðzlióð"
  1962   In: *Edda. Die Lieder des Codex Regius nebst verwandten Denkmälern. I. Text*. Vierte, umgearbeitete Auflage von Hans Kuhn. Heidelberg: Winter, 78-87.
Hunold, Christian Friedrich
  1716   *Die Beste Manier In Honneter Conversation, Sich höflich und Behutsam aufzuführen/ und in kluger Conduite zu leben*. Von Menantes. Hamburg: Fickweiler.
Das Nibelungenlied
  1961   Nach der Ausgabe von Karl Bartsch herausgegeben von Helmut de Boor. 16. Aufl. Wiesbaden: Brockhaus.
Die Relation des Jahres 1609
  1940   In Faksimiledruck herausgegeben und mit einem Nachwort versehen von Walter Schöne. Leipzig: Otto Harrassowitz.
Rohr, Julius Bernhard von
  1733   *Einleitung zur Ceremoniel-Wissenschaft der Grossen Herren*. Berlin: Johann Andreas Rüdiger. Reprinted with an introduction by Monika Schlechte. Weinheim: VCH 1990.

References

Adato, Albert
  1971   *On the Sociology of Topics in Ordinary Conversation: An Investigation into the Tacit Concerns of Members for Assuring the Proper Conduct of Everyday Activities*. Los Angeles: University of California Ph. D. Thesis.

Austin, John L.
1961   " A plea for excuses". In: John L. Austin. *Philosophical Papers*. Oxford: Oxford University Press, 175-204.

Bax, Marcel
1991   " Historische Pragmatik: Eine Herausforderung für die Zukunft. Diachrone Untersuchungen zu pragmatischen Aspekten ritueller Herausforderungen in Texten mittelalterlicher Literatur." In: Dietrich Busse (ed.). *Diachrone Semantik und Pragmatik. Untersuchungen zur Erklärung und Beschreibung des Sprachwandels*. Tübingen: Niemeyer, 197-215.

Beetz, Manfred
1990   *Frühmoderne Höflichkeit. Komplimentierkunst und Gesellschaftsrituale im altdeutschen Sprachraum*. Stuttgart: Metzler.

Berger, Peter L., and Thomas Luckmann
1967   *The Social Construction of Reality. A Treatise in the Sociology of Knowledge*. Harmondsworth: Penguin.

Bliesener, Thomas
1982   *Die Visite - ein verhinderter Dialog*. Tübingen: Narr.

Braungart, Georg
1988   *Hofberedsamkeit. Studien zur Praxis höfisch-politischer Rede im deutschen Territorialabsolutismus*. Tübingen: Niemeyer.

Brook, Christopher N. L.
1994   *The Medieval Idea of Marriage*. Oxford: Clarendon Press.

Brown, Penelope, and Stephen C. Levinson
1987   *Politeness. Some Universals in Language Usage*. Cambridge: University Press.

Burke, Peter
1993   *The Art of Conversation*. Oxford: Polity Press.

Carlson, Lauri
1983   *Dialogue Games. An Approach to Discourse Analysis*. Dordrecht: Reidel.

Dallapiazza, Michael
1981   *Minne, husere und das ehlich leben. Zur Konstitution bürgerlicher Lebensmuster in spätmittelalterlichen und frühhumanistischen Didaktiken*. Frankfurt am Main/Bern: Lang.

Dascal, Marcelo
1992   " On the pragmatic structure of conversation." In: John R. Searle *et al.* (eds.). *(On) Searle on Conversation*. Amsterdam/Philadelphia: John Benjamins, 35-56.

Davidson, Donald
    1985   " Communication and convention." In: M. Dascal (ed.). *Dialogue – an Interdisciplinary Approach*. Amsterdam/Philadelphia: John Benjamins, 11-25.

Drew, Paul, and John Heritage (eds.)
    1992   *Talk at work. Interaction in Institutional Settings*. Cambridge: Cambridge University Press.

Elias, Norbert
    1978   *Über den Prozeß der Zivilisation*. 2 Vols. 5th ed. Frankfurt a. M.: Suhrkamp.

Fischart, Johann
    1578   Das philosophisch Ehzuchtbüchlin. Straßburg. In: Adolf Hauffen (ed.). *Johann Fischarts Werke. Dritter Teil*. Stuttgart: Union Deutsche Verlagsgesellschaft. (n.d.).

Fritz, Gerd
    1994a   " Grundlagen der Dialogorganisation." In: Gerd Fritz and Franz Hundsnurscher (eds.). *Handbuch der Dialoganalyse*. Tübingen: Niemeyer, 177-202.

    1994b   " Geschichte von Dialogformen." In: Gerd Fritz and Franz Hundsnurscher (eds.). *Handbuch der Dialoganalyse*. Tübingen: Niemeyer, 545-562.

Fritz, Gerd, and Franz Hundsnurscher
    1975   " Sprechaktsequenzen. Überlegungen zur Vorwurf/Rechtfertigungs-Interaktion". *Der Deutschunterricht* 27, 81-103.

Fritz, Gerd, and Manfred Muckenhaupt
    1981   " Beweisen - Kommunikationsformen und ihre Geschichte." In: Gerd Fritz and Manfred Muckenhaupt, *Kommunikation und Grammatik*. Tübingen: Narr, 196-207.

Gloning, Thomas
    1993   " Sprachreflexive Textstellen als Quellen für die Geschichte von Kommunikationsformen." In: Heinrich Löffler (ed.): *Dialoganalyse IV*. Tübingen: Niemeyer, 207-217.

Göttert, Karl-Heinz
    1991   " Ringen um Verständlichkeit. Ein historischer Streifzug". *Deutsche Vierteljahresschrift für Literaturwissenschaft und Geistesgeschichte* 65, 1-14.

Goffman, Erving
    1971   *Relations in Public. Microstudies of the Public Order*. Harmondsworth: Penguin.

Grice, H. Paul
    1989   *Studies in the Way of Words. Cambridge*, Mass./London: Harvard University Press.

Grosse, Siegfried
    1985   " Reflexe gesprochener Sprache im Mittelhochdeutschen". In: *Sprachgeschichte. Ein Handbuch zur Geschichte der deutschen Sprache und ihrer Erforschung*. Bd. 2. Berlin/New York: Mouton de Gruyter, 1186-1191.

Hahn, Alois
    1991   " Rede- und Schweigeverbote." *Kölner Zeitschrift für Soziologie* 43, 86-105.

Herbert, Robert K.
    1989   " The ethnography of English compliments and compliment responses: A constrastive sketch." In: Wieslaw Oleksy (ed.). *Contrastive Pragmatics*. Amsterdam/Philadelphia, 3-36.

Holenstein, Pia
    1991   *Der Ehediskurs der Renaissance in Fischarts Geschichtklitterung*. Bern: Lang.

Hughes, Geoffrey
    1991   *Swearing. A Social History of Foul Language, Oaths and Profanity in English*. Oxford: Blackwell.

Keenan, Elinor Ochs
    1976   " The universality of conversational postulates." *Language in Society* 5, 67-80.

Keller, Rudi
    1990   *Sprachwandel. Von der unsichtbaren Hand in der Sprache*. Tübingen: Francke.

Labov, William
    1972   " Rules for ritual insults." In: David Sudnow (ed.). *Studies in Social Interaction*. New York: Free Press, 120-169.

Lebsanft, Franz
    1988   *Studien zu einer Linguistik des Grusses. Sprache und Funktion der altfranzösischen Grußformeln*. Tübingen: Niemeyer.

Lewis, David K.
    1969   *Convention: A Philosophical Study*. Cambridge, Mass.: Harvard University Press.

Lötscher, Andreas
 1981 "Zur Sprachgeschichte des Fluchens und Beschimpfens im Schweizerdeutschen." *Zeitschrift für Dialektologie und Linguistik* 48, 145-159.

Luhmann, Niklas, and Peter Fuchs
 1989 *Reden und Schweigen.* Frankfurt am Main: Suhrkamp.

Malinowski, Bronislaw
 1923 "The problem of meaning in primitive languages." In: C. K. Ogden and I. A. Richards (eds.). *The Meaning of Meaning. Supplement I.* London: Routledge & Kegan Paul, 296-336.

Metcalf, George Joseph
 1938 *Forms of Address in German (1500-1800).* St. Louis: Washington University Studies.

Nickisch, Reinhard M.G.
 1990 "Die Allerneueste Art Höflich und Galant zu Schreiben. Deutsche Briefsteller um 1700: Von Christian Weise zu Benjamin Neukirch". In: Paul Valentin and Klaus J. Mattheier (eds.). *Pathos, Klatsch und Ehrlichkeit.* Tübingen: Stauffenberg, 117-138.

Oleksy, Wieslaw
 1989 *Contrastive Pragmatics.* Amsterdam: Benjamins.

Olshtain, Elite
 1989 "Apologies across languages." In: Shoshana Blum-Kulka, Juliane House and Gabriele Kasper (eds.). *Cross-Cultural Pragmatics: Requests and Apologies.* Norwood, N.J.: Ablex, 155-173.

Owen, Marion
 1983 *Apologies and Remedial Interchanges. A Study of Language Use in Social Interaction.* Berlin/New York: Mouton.

Pörksen, Uwe
 1986 *Deutsche Naturwissenschaftssprachen. Historische und kritische Studien.* Tübingen: Narr.

Protess, David L., and Maxwell McCombs (eds.)
 1991 *Agenda Setting. Readings on Media, Public Opinion, and Policymaking.* Hillsdale, N.J.: Lawrence Erlbaum.

Rolf, Eckard
 1994 "Dialoge in Institutionen." In: Gerd Fritz and Franz Hundsnurscher (eds.). *Handbuch der Dialoganalyse.* Tübingen: Niemeyer, 321-355.

Sacks, Harvey, Emanuel A. Schegloff, and Gail Jefferson
 1974 "A simplest systematics for the organization of turn-taking in conversation". *Language* 50, 696-735.

Schlieben-Lange, Brigitte
 1979   " Ai las - que planhs! Ein Versuch zur historischen Gesprächsanalyse am
          Flamenca-Roman". *Romanistische Zeitschrift für Literaturgeschichte* 3, 1-
          30.
Schmölders, Claudia (ed.)
 1986   *Die Kunst des Gesprächs. Texte zur Geschichte der europäischen
          Konversationstheorie.* 2nd ed. München: Deutscher Taschenbuchverlag.
Schönbach, Klaus
 1982   " The issues of the seventies. Elektronische Inhaltsanalyse und die
          langfristige   Beobachtung   von   Agenda-Setting-Wirkungen   der
          Massenmedien." *Publizistik* 28, 129-140.
Schwarz, Alexander
 1984   *Sprechaktgeschichte. Studien zu den Liebeserklärungen in mittelalterlichen
          und modernen Tristan-Dichtungen.* Göppingen: Kümmerle Verlag.
Searle, John R.
 1992   " Conversation." In: John R. Searle *et al.* (eds.). *(On) Searle on
          Conversation.* Amsterdam/Philadelphia: John Benjamins, 7-29.
Sonderegger, Stefan
 1990   " Syntaktische Strukturen gesprochener Sprache im älteren Deutschen." In:
          Anne Betten (ed.). *Neuere Forschungen zur historischen Syntax des
          Deutschen.* Tübingen: Niemeyer, 310-323.
Strecker, Bruno
 1987   *Strategien des kommunikativen Handelns.* Düsseldorf: Schwann.
Strosetzki, Christoph
 1978   *Konversation. Ein Kapitel gesellschaftlicher und literarischer Pragmatik im
          Frankreich des 17. Jahrhunderts.* Frankfurt am Main/Bern: Lang.
Taylor, Archer
 1939   *Problems in German Literary History of the Fifteenth and Sixteenth
          Centuries.* London: Oxford University Press.
Toulmin, Stephen
 1972   *Human Understanding. The Collective Use and Evolution of Concepts.*
          Princeton, N.J.: Princeton University Press.
Ullmann-Margalit, Edna
 1978   " Invisible-hand explanations." *Synthese* 39, 263-291.
Watts, Richard J., Sachiko Ide, and Konrad Ehlich (eds.)
 1992   *Politeness in Language. Studies in its History, Theory and Practice.*
          Berlin/New York: Mouton de Gruyter.

Weigand, Edda
    1988   "Historische Sprachpragmatik am Beispiel: Gesprächsstrukturen im Nibelungenlied". *Zeitschrift für deutsches Altertum* 117, 159-174.

"Then I saw to antique heddes"
Discourse Strategies in Early Modern English Travelogues

Tuija Virtanen
Åbo Akademi University

1. Introduction

As any text producer, the writer of a travelogue has a linearisation problem: in view of her/his communicative goal, s/he will have to choose an appropriate order for presenting the information s/he wishes to include in the piece of writing. The textualisation process may be hypothesised to involve recursive choices from a number of alternatives, and the product of that process, the resulting text, may be assumed to reflect such underlying strategies. This suggests that we may get at discourse strategies through a study of authentic texts.

In this paper I shall focus on discourse strategies in Early Modern English travelogues. I use the concept 'discourse strategy' in Enkvist's (1987) sense, i.e. 'a goal-oriented weighting of decision criteria'. In other words, the communicative goal affects the text producer's weighting of linguistic parameters (cf. also Enkvist 1985). Some discourse strategies may be characterised as more prototypical than others in a particular genre. Prototypicality thus here refers to abstractions of intertextual conventions valid for the genre in question at the time of writing, and peripheral or innovative choices may, accordingly, contribute to the development of the genre.

An important motivation for the choice of linearisation strategies is 'experiential iconicity' (Enkvist 1981) – a notion referring to instances where the linear ordering in the text forms an icon of our experience of the world. This notion has usually been dealt with in the context of the ordering of clause constituents, or clauses in a sentence. It is, however, evident that discourse-related iconicity is a strong motivating force behind a number of decisions concerning textualisation. (For iconicity, see also e.g. Firbas 1979; Givón 1985; Levelt 1981; Virtanen 1993).

Iconic strategies may be expected to appear in travelogues, where the writer records, reports, narrates, or describes the highlights of her/his journey, focusing on what s/he finds worth communicating to readers. Iconicity may be reflected in the order in which the text producer presents various activities and observations connected with the journey. S/he may, for instance, choose to follow the chronological order of her/his itinerary or that of a series of events as experienced and later recalled by her/him. Iconically motivated discourse strategies may be assumed to facilitate discourse processing.

The data for this study originates in the diachronic part of the *Helsinki Corpus of English Texts* (see Kytö 1991), which contains samples of Early Modern English travelogues, totalling some 40,000 running words (see p. 491). The texts have been classified in the corpus as instances of a text category entitled 'non-imaginative narrative'.

In what follows, I shall discuss manifestations of the temporal, locative, and participant/topic-oriented strategies in the light of examples from these texts. The discussion will be related to differences in discourse types that these strategies evoke in the modern reader and are assumed to have evoked at the time of writing. Although there is variation between the text fragments listed above, they will not be specifically compared with one another in this study. Finally, to examine the development of the travelogue genre, more data would obviously be necessary.

2.   Temporal discourse strategy

The travelogue texts under investigation have been classified as narrative and they manifest an underlying temporal discourse strategy. In other words, these texts seem, to a large extent, to conform to a chronologically ordered series of events as experienced by the traveller. It is, however, not possible to see from the text fragments included in the corpus whether the texts, in fact, manifest a global temporal strategy. Still, there are metatextual indications of narrative in the titles of the texts and in the texts themselves, such as *account, report, narrative, diarie*; *there befell a strange accident, which I thinke worth the relating* (TAYLOR 1, 31).

Coherent temporal sequentiality is generally regarded as the basic criterion for narrative – so basic that it can be left unmarked as long as the text is temporally iconic (for a discussion, see e.g. Enkvist 1981, 1987; Labov 1972;

Longacre 1983; Wårvik 1992; Werlich 1976; Virtanen 1992a). Obviously, texts may manifest other temporally iconic relations, such as those of duration, frequency, or adjacency (see Genette 1972; Givón 1983), not considered in this context. Coherent temporal sequentiality may also be interpreted in terms of causality (for a discussion, see e.g. Enkvist 1981; Wårvik 1992). Travelogue texts show variation in terms of reports or chronicles vs. stories, all of which can be classified as narrative on the grounds that they display temporal succession. However, while stories clearly depict a causally related series of events leading to a situation which is different from the one at the outset of the narrative, reports or chronicles may be mere records of what happened and in which order.

In (1) below we find a series of explicit markers of the temporal discourse strategy. While two events coded in the form of the simple past tense are normally interpreted as temporally sequential on the basis of expectations raised by experiential iconicity, the temporal text strategy is usually signalled through a chain of clause-initial or sentence-initial adverbials of time. Such a chain of adverbials and other temporal markers referring to a common temporal frame creates cohesion and coherence in the text. (For a discussion of tense in narrative, see Fleischman 1990; for the temporal discourse strategy, see e.g. Enkvist 1987; Grimes 1975; Longacre 1983; Virtanen 1992a).

(1)   *The next Morn* we were waited on by the Country Women bringing us Cheese, and Butter made before our Eyes, with no other Churn than a Goatskin, in which they shook the Milk till Butter came; [...]

        The Day after, as soon as we heard the Waters were abated, we set forward, and found it true what had been reported [...]

        The rest of this day's Journy was between the Mountains, where we were encounter'd by strange Flashes of Lightning, [...]

        The following Day we continued going between two Chains of Dry and Burnt Hills, through a stony Valley, [...] (FRYER 2, 185-7)[1]

Further, initial placement of strategically important adverbials signalling a new stage in the narrative facilitates text segmentation. The reader is given a signal of a shift from the 'unity of time' of one episode to the temporal setting of the following one, and hence, this signal functions as a marker of a textual boundary. As the new episode thus only starts once the textual shift has been clearly indicated, the reader has, at that point, an opportunity to drop from her/his working memory many of the aspects that have been kept activated over minor boundaries within the preceding unit of text. Contrary to content, signals of text structure need not enter the longer-term memory systems (cf. e.g. Chafe 1987).

Then, denoting 'after that', is the prototypical adverbial marker of the temporal strategy; it is also the one that can be left out in a temporally sequential text if no other lexical content is intended. Consider the following example, in which we can easily insert another implicit 'then', as indicated in square brackets.

(2)   *Then* we asked them, if there were any Portugals in the Iland, ['then'] they
         said no, for they had banished them all because [...] (COVERTE 1, 12)

The two events of asking a question and answering it are presented in a temporally and causally iconic order. Clauses such as these, coding temporally adjacent, sequential events, can thus be interpreted as iconic, and explicit markers of the temporal discourse strategy are not needed at the outset of every single action or event constituting the narrative. If, however, the implicit 'then' surfaces in a temporally sequential narrative, apparently 'redundantly', it tends to have important discourse-pragmatic functions, such as the signalling of grounding relations (Wårvik 1990, 1992, this volume) or the peak profile of a climactic narrative (Longacre 1983; Virtanen 1992a). An abundant use of *then* in a narrative may point to an oral residue in the text (see e.g. Ong 1982; Wårvik 1990, 1994). *Then* is often a signal of a minor textual boundary (cf. Virtanen 1992a, 1992b).

Deviations from temporal succession (in terms of simultaneous, previous, or future events) must obviously be explicitly signalled once the reader's expectations of a temporal discourse strategy have been activated. Similarly, deviations from temporal adjacency usually demand lexically weighty signals, cf. e.g. *the Day after* in (1) above. Such signals are often adverbials, placed at the outset of the relevant textual unit, as the following marker of simultaneity of events.

(3)   *In the meane time*, our Pinnis came on shore, which had beene at an other
         place of the Iland for Cattell, according to appointment, but were deferred of, till
         they might get fitter opportunity for their intended treacherie. (COVERTE 1, 12)

When two or more adverbials signalling the temporal discourse strategy cluster at the outset of a new textual unit, these may appear in a chronological order:

(4)   *And hauing viewed and seen this great and rich Citie of Agra with the*
         pleasures and Commodities thereof; on the 18. day of Ianuarie, my selfe with
         Ioseph Salcbancke and Iohn Frenchan, went to the King and craued his Passe for
         England, who very courteously demanded of vs if we would serue him in his wars
         [...] (COVERTE 2, 41)

The first adverbial clause in this example summarises the previous episode while the second adverbial indicates the temporal setting of what follows in the narrative (for lexical overlap in sentence-initial adverbial clauses, see Thompson and Longacre 1985). The ordering may also be from a more general marker to a more specific one, as in (1) above: *The Day after, as soon as we heard the Waters were abated.*

3.   Locative discourse strategy

A chain of temporal markers indicating the route of the traveller in these texts may also include locative elements, e.g.

(5)   *A bowte ij of the cloke at Aftyr none,* we toke our assis at Betlehem, *ffyrst* we come to the Sepulcre of the vij prophetis. [...]
        And from thense we com to the howse of Zacharie, in the Mowntayns of Jude whych ys v myle from Betlehem, and v from Jherusalem, [...]
        Thanne next aftyr we come to the howse of Symyonis Justi et Timorati, [...]
        In ower way home wardys, ij myle from Jherusalem, we com vnto a cloyster of Grekkys monkes, [...] (TORKINGTON 2, 50-1)

The effect of a spatio-temporal chain on discourse processing relies on the activated temporal discourse strategy allowing the reader to infer the sequentiality of the stops. It is beyond the scope of the present paper to address the question which of these two notions, temporality or spatiality, in fact implies the other in instances like these where the role of the discourse type is crucial in determining the interpretation that the text receiver is likely to give to the underlying strategy. (For discussion, see e.g. Enkvist 1981, 1987; Fleischman 1990, 1991; Lyons 1977; Levinson 1983; Virtanen 1993.) Some of the now temporal markers appear in a spatial form in the corpus, e.g.

(6)   [...] so being landed, we went vp and downe and could finde nothing but stones, heath and mosse, and wee expected Oranges, Limonds, Figges, Muske-millions, and Potatoes: *in the meane space* the wind did blow so stiffe, and the Sea was so extreme rough, that our Ship-boate could not come to the land to fetch vs, [...] (TAYLOR 1, 31)

Sentence-initial adverbials of place indicate a stop on the route and, occasionally, the distance of a stop from some other location (e.g. *in ower way home wardys, ij myle from Jherusalem* in (5) above). Conforming to iconicity, the text-strategically important locatives in these data often also indicate 'source' (e.g. *from thense* in (5); *thens; thence; from this bridge; from*

Colchester) and they may be directly, or later on in the sentence, followed by the new goal, the next stop or an intermediate point on the route, e.g.

(7)   *From Barnardes Castelle over the right fair bridge on Tese of 3. arches* I enterid straite into Richemontshire, that stil streaccith up with that ripe to the very hed of Tese.
         From this bridge I ridde a mile on the stony and rokky bank of Tese to the bek caullid Thuresgylle, a mile from Barnardes Castelle, and there it hath a bridge of one arche and straite enterith into Tese. (LELAND 1, 77)

Once a stop has been indicated, existential constructions tend to appear, to present sights and give information about them.

(8)   *Ther* ys also the place wher David Slew Golyas. (TORKINGTON 2, 51)

(9)   *Ther* is a meatly good wood on eche side of Tese about Barnardes Castel. (LELAND 1, 78)

Locative markers may obviously form a discourse-strategic chain of their own. They are then usually adverbials indicating position, and this position is a new stop on the route to which the reader is first led, to be subsequently told more about the site. The locative discourse strategy thus allows the writer to take the reader on a tour from one place to another (cf. Enkvist 1981, 1985, 1987; Linde and Labov 1975). Consider the following passage.

(10)   *In the ploughid feeldes hard by thys village* hath and be founde Romaine coynes, and other many tokens of antiquite.
         Betwixt Akeland and Bincester is an exceding fair bridg of one arch apon Were. There is another a litle above Duresme caullid Thunderland Bridge.
         From Binchester to Branspeth 4. miles, al by mountaine ground, as is about Akeland, and not fertile of corne, but welle woddid. (LELAND 1, 71)

The traveller following the route and reporting the course of his journey is not explicitly present in this passage. This absence, together with the locative discourse strategy, makes the text descriptive. Compare with (5) and (7), above, where the traveller appears on the scene, making the text more narrative.

In a passage such as (10) above, iconicity lies in the strategy of first leading the reader from one stop to another with the help of the initial locative and only then presenting her/him with the sight that the writer has chosen to focus on. The travelogue writer here gives a description of what anyone going to the same place may see. Passages like these may have a general purpose and thus resemble a modern travel guide, addressed to a generic 'you', the tourist who will buy it and use it on the spot. The generic 'you' may surface in these travelogues, too:

(11)   On the Castle hill *you* see the whole Citty at once, being built round it, its a
              vast place and takes up a large tract of ground its 6 miles in compass;
              (FIENNES 148)

The writer of this kind of text seems to view her/his communicative goal as one
of recording what is to be found on and around the particular itinerary that s/he
once followed. The goal of recording distances and observations is sometimes
explicitly stated in metatextual comments, e.g. *this I put in only to know the
number of miles that I went in one yeare* (FIENNES 141); [...] *the City and the
Castle, which as my poore vnable and vnworthy pen can, I will truly describe*
(TAYLOR 1, 129).

       The use of the temporal discourse strategy connected with the presence of
an agentive participant in the text makes the passage narrative, and some of the
travelogue samples, in fact, resemble stories. But even in a report or a chronicle,
the writer using these strategies focuses on the series of events that took place
on the journey: although the sights may be identical on the next trip, the events
will most probably not be so. Clearly, then, the choice of discourse strategy in
these and other travelogue texts is highly indicative of the writer's
communicative goal. In one text or at one stage in a text, it may be more
expedient to tell what happened on the way and/or to record observations, in
another text (unit), again, to describe what the reader will see if s/he goes to the
very same places.

       Travelogues thus manifest variation between narrative and descriptive
passages, between the narrative of past events and the generic present of their
descriptive parts. Further, the presence or absence of explicit mentions of the
traveller in the discourse also suggests a discourse-type difference: on the one
hand, we find agentive, or more generally, participant-oriented discourse, and
on the other hand, topic-oriented discourse, and it is to these that we shall now
turn our attention.

4.   Participant/topic-oriented discourse strategy

A basic difference between narrative and non-narrative texts is the temporal
discourse strategy implicitly or explicitly present in the former. Furthermore,
narratives tend to be about characters participating in the chain of actions and
events presented in the discourse. Non-narrative texts, again, often deal with
concrete or abstract topics, rather than animate participants. A topic-oriented
strategy thus gives the text a descriptive or expository flavour.

The writer of a travelogue may choose to present her/his observations in a narrative or non-narrative form, as illustrated by (12) and (13), respectively, from one and the same text. The narrative in (12) is like a report or a chronicle, a list of what the writer/traveller (*I*) saw, probably following the order of the itinerary and observations, as recalled at the time of writing; by contrast, the narrative in (17), p. 489 below, resembles a story. The non-narrative passage in (13) opens with an existential construction introducing the topic of the subsequent discourse, the two baths to be dealt with in the passage. In this example we first find what Daneš (1974) calls a 'split rheme'. The baths form two (sub)topics/themes, which are devoted a section each and then brought together again in the last paragraph.

(12)   Then I saw a braunch with leves foldid and wrethin into circles.
         Then I saw ij. nakid imagis lying a long, the one imbracing the other.
         Then I saw to antique heddes with heere as rofelid yn lokkes.
         Then I saw a grey-hound as renning, and at the taile of hym was a stone engravid with great Romane letters, but I could pike no sentence out of it.
         Then I saw another inscription, but the wether hath except a few lettres clere defacid.
         Then I saw toward the west gate an image of a man embracid with 2. serpentes. I took, it for Laocoon.
         Betwixt the weste and the north gate.
         I saw 2. inscriptions, of the wich sum wordes were evident to the reader, the residew clene defacid.
         Then I saw the image of a nakid man. (LELAND 2, 141)

(13)   There be 2. springes of whote wather in the west south west part of the towne. Wherof the bigger is caullid the Crosse Bath, bycause it hath a cross erectid in the midle of it. This bath is much frequentid of people deseasid with lepre, pokkes, scabbes, and great aches, and is temperate and pleasant, having a 11. or 12. arches of stone in the sides for men to stonde under yn tyme of reyne.
         Many be holp by this bathe from scabbes and aches.
         The other bathe is a 2. hunderith foote of, and is lesse in cumpace withyn the waulle then the other, having but 7. arches yn the waulle. This is caullid the Hote Bathe; for at cumming into it men think that it wold scald the flesch at the first, but after that the flesch ys warmid it is more tolerable and pleasaunt.
         Both these bathes be in the midle of a litle streat, and joine to S. John's hospitale: so that it may be thought that Reginalde Bisshop of Bathe made this hospitale nere these 2. commune bathes to socour poore people resorting to them. (LELAND 2, 141-2)

Travelogue writers may follow the taxonomy of a topic, as in the following description of Edinburgh castle. The passage is structured with the help of a taxonomic strategy making use of different parts of the Castle.

(14) [...] but hauing rested two houres and refreshed my selfe, the Gentleman and I walked to see the City and the Castle, which as my poore vnable and vnworthy pen can, I will truly describe.

The Castle on a loftie Rocke is so strongly grounded, bounded, and founded, that by force of man it can neuer be confounded; *the Foundation and Walls* are vnpenetrable, *the Rampiers* impregnable, *the Bulwarkes* inuincible, no way but one to it is or can be possible to be made passable. (TAYLOR 1, 129)

When the topic is locative, as in (14), we often find a blend of the two strategies. Consider (15), where the locative topic, Euston Hall, is first described in general terms, followed by a taxonomically and sequentially organised tour. The various stops on this tour are realised through locative noun phrases and adverbials. Having thus 'zoomed in' the house in its large park, the text producer goes on to focus on the entire building and then on parts of it, proceeding from the outside to the inside. Once entered into the house, the reader would probably also first find a staircase and then a long gallery hung with pictures at length, as this is the order of the description. The route goes on to cover the sides of the gallery one after the other, then the middle square, and finally the end of the room.

(15)   Next day I went to *Euston Hall which* was the Lord Arlingtons and by his only daughters marriage with the Duke of Grafton is his sons by her, *its* two mile from Thetford; *it* stands in a large parke 6 miles about, *the house* is a Roman H of brick, *4 towers* with balls on them, *the windows* are low and not sarshes else *the roomes* are of a good size and height; *a good staircase* full of good pictures, *a long gallery* hung with pictures at length - *on the one side* the Royal family from K. Henry the 7th by the Scottish race his eldest daughter down to the present King William and his Queen Mary, *the other side* are forreign princes from the Emperour of Moroccoe the Northern and Southern princes and Emperour of Germany; there is *a square in the middle where* stands a billiard table hung with outlandish pictures of Heroes, there is Count Egminton Horn Counts Egmont and Hoorn etc., *at the end of the roome* is the Duke and Dutchess of Graftons pictures at length also; (FIENNES 150)

After this passage, the underlying narrative again surfaces as the text producer recalls having proceeded from the long gallery to other rooms: *thence I enterd into* [...]. However, as she does not seem to remember exactly where in the house the different rooms and paintings were, we get indications such as *in one of the roomes was* [...], or *in another place there is* [...], where the tense again changes into the generic present of a description. This description finally leads the reader out of the house into the different courts and eventually to the back gate, where the text producer once more appears on the scene to continue her travelling: *at the back gate I crossed over the river Waveny* [...]. Embedded in a narrative 'frame', the description thus makes use of the taxonomic structure of the house while at the same time conforming to the chronology of the visit to various parts of the place.

Narratives are usually accounts of a series of actions performed by a character or a group of characters. In addition to the temporal strategy, they thus also manifest another, co-occurring discourse strategy: an agent-oriented or, more generally, participant-oriented strategy. This kind of strategy is exposed through a chain of references to the participant(s) of the narrative, consisting of full noun phrases, proper names, pronouns, and zero anaphora. Third-person narratives may exhibit a full range of linguistic manifestations of participant coding; in first-person narratives this is obviously not the case. (For discussions of the participant-oriented discourse strategy, see e.g. Björklund 1993; Björklund and Virtanen 1991; Enkvist 1987; Fox 1987; Givón 1983, 1984, 1990; Grimes 1975; Longacre 1983; Virtanen 1991, 1992a.)

In the travelogue texts under investigation here, participant orientation is mostly created through a chain of references to the text producer, alone (*I*) or included in a group (*we*). In narrative passages, participant(s) often appear in agentive contexts or are affected by various events that take place during the journey, as shown in most of the examples presented above. Evaluative and metatextual material containing first-person references also contributes to coherence in a text centred on the first-person participant(s), e.g. *I much doubte wither these antique workes were sette in the tyme of Romans dominion in Britayne in the walles of Bath* [...] (LELAND 2, 141); *by enquiry* [*I*] *found it to be thro' pride and sloth* (FIENNES 143); *as I hard; as I remembre* (LELAND 1,76).

Sometimes the reader is informed of the past of a sight through a narrative built around a historical person: The following passage is structured with the help of references to agentive participants and may be assumed to follow the chronology of the constructions.

(16)   There was of very auncient a manor place logging to the Bisshop of
         Duresme at Akeland. *Antonius de Beke* began first to encastellate it, *he* made the
         greaut haulle, there be divers pillors of black marble spekelid with white, and the
         exceding fair gret chaumbre with other there.

He made also an exceding goodly chapelle ther of stone welle squarid, and a college with dene and prebendes yn it, and a quadrant on the south west side of the castell for ministers of the college.

Skerlaw, Bisshop of Duresme, made the goodly gate house at entering ynto the castelle of Akeland. (LELAND 1, 70)

In other narrative passages, again, such as (17), the text producer's 'we' group is confronted with one or more other participants. Even when the participants of one or both of these groups are individualised, as in this climactic passage, group continuity is normally preserved throughout the text (fragment).

(17) [...] The Kings brother being then on the sands, commanded a Negro to gather Coquonuts to send to our General, and made choise of Edward Churchman one of our men, to fetch the same, whom we neuer saw after, nor could euer know what became of him; But when they saw that none of vs would come a shore, but stood vpon our gard, they gaue the watchword and sounded a horne, and presently set vpon our men at the watering place and slew Iohn Harrington, the boat-swaines man, and wounded Robert Buckler, Master Ellanors man very sore, with 8. or 10. seuerall wounds, and had killed him, but that we discharged a Musket or two, which (as it seemed) hurt some of them; for then they retired and cried out: and so (though weake and faint) he did at length recouer our boat. (COVERTE 1, 15)

5. Conclusion

The discourse strategies presented in this paper may appear globally or locally in a text and they are often combined in specific ways. Hence, prototypically, the temporal and participant-oriented strategies are associated with narratives, the topic-oriented strategy, again, with non-narrative discourse. As the choice of discourse strategies may thus evoke a particular discourse type, the text producer can help the receiver by making use of shared intertextual knowledge. Prototypical strategies make the discourse easier to process, allowing the text receiver to fully focus on its content.

The travelogue genre is expected to display narrative text organisation. Yet the texts under investigation here are not necessarily instances of the (near-)prototypical narrative, i.e. a story; they are often more like reports or chronicles. Further, we find descriptions and expository passages structured with the help of locative and/or topic-oriented strategies. Although the use of the locative discourse strategy, especially if combined with present tense verbs, evokes the descriptive type of discourse, references to a participant and past events in the text activate a narrative schema. Implicit temporality is easily associated with journeys, and discourse-strategic chains of adverbial markers here often consist of both temporal and spatial elements.

Temporality is also involved in the locatively structured passages recording observations that the text producer recalls having made along the itinerary: the locative discourse strategy has the effect of taking the reader on a tour. When the first-person narrator disappears from the textual surface, the tense may easily change into the generic present typical of the descriptive and expository types of discourse, and the content may be organised around a topic rather than a participant.

Obviously, these texts also display discourse strategies other than the ones considered above. Furthermore, evaluative elements may be found throughout the texts – sometimes giving the impression of 'spokenness' in the sense that they seem to reflect the text producer's thought processes. However, the strategies under investigation here give the text a backbone and hence, facilitate discourse processing. They contribute to coherence and text segmentation. Explicit markers of these strategies help the reader to structure the text into units of various sizes. Changes in major discourse strategies often indicate important boundaries in the text.

The temporal and locative discourse strategies rely on iconicity, both on the clause level and the level of the entire text (unit). Also, starting clauses with activated participants or topics helps to relate these to the discourse topic and hence makes the text easier to process. Iconic strategies are, in a sense, basic or unmarked: they go unnoticed in a culture unless you choose to go against them, which demands explicit signalling.

Note

1.   'FRYER 2, 185-7' refers to the second sample from John Fryer in the *HC*, pp. 185-187 in the text used in the corpus; for full reference, see Kytö 1991.

Data

Leland, John. *The itinerary of John Leland in or about the years 1535-1543.* (2 samples; LELAND)

Torkington, Richard. *Ye oldest diarie of Englysshe travell: Being the hitherto unpublished narrative of the pilgrimage of Sir Richard Torkington to Jerusalem in 1517.* (2 samples; TORKINGTON)

Taylor, John. *The pennyles pilgrimage,* 1630. (3 samples; TAYLOR)

Coverte, Robert. *A trve and almost incredible report of an Englishman,* 1612. (2 samples; COVERTE)

Fiennes, Celia. *The journeys of Celia Fiennes,* 1698. (1 sample; FIENNES)

Fryer, John. *A new account of East India and Persia, being nine years' travels,* 1672-1681 (2 samples; FRYER)

References

Björklund, Martina
　　1993　　*Narrative Strategies in Čechov's The Steppe: Cohesion, Grounding and Point of View.* Åbo: Åbo Akademi University Press.

Björklund, Martina, and Tuija Virtanen
　　1991　　"Variation in narrative structure: A simple text vs. an innovative work of art." *Poetics* 20. 4, 391-403.

Chafe, Wallace L.
　　1987　　"Repeated verbalizations as evidence for the organization of knowledge." *Preprints of the Plenary Session Papers: XIVth International Congress of Linguists, Berlin/GDR, August 10-15, 1987.* Berlin: Akademie der Wissenschaften der DDR, 88-110.

Daneš, František
　　1974　　"'Functional sentence perspective' and the organization of the text." In: František Daneš (ed.). *Papers on Functional Sentence Perspective.* Prague: Academia, 106-128.

Enkvist, Nils Erik
　　1981　　"Experiential iconicism in text strategy." *Text* 1. 1, 97-111.
　　1985　　"A parametric view of word order." In: Emel Sözer (ed.). *Text Connexity, Text Coherence: Aspects, Methods, Results.* Hamburg: Helmut Buske, 320-336.
　　1987　　"A note towards the definition of text strategy." *Zeitschrift für Phonetik, Sprachwissenschaft und Kommunikationsforschung* 40. 1, 19-27.

512   Tuija Virtanen

Firbas, Jan
    1979   "A functional view of 'Ordo Naturalis'." *Brno Studies in English* 13, 29-60.
Fleischman, Suzanne
    1990   *Tense and Narrativity: From Medieval Performance to Modern Fiction.*
            London: Routledge.
    1991   "Discourse as space/Discourse as time: Reflections on the metalanguage of
            spoken and written discourse." *Journal of Pragmatics* 16. 4, 291-306.
Fox, Barbara
    1987   "Anaphora in popular written English narratives." In: Russell S. Tomlin
            (ed.). *Coherence and Grounding in Discourse.* Amsterdam & Philadelphia:
            John Benjamins, 157-174.
Genette, Gérard
    1972   *Figures III.* Paris: Seuil.
Givón, Talmy (ed.)
    1983   *Topic Continuity in Discourse: A Quantitative Cross-Language Study.*
            Amsterdam & Philadephia: John Benjamins.
Givón, Talmy
    1984-90 *Syntax: A Functional-Typological Introduction.* Vol. I 1984, vol. II 1990.
            Amsterdam & Philadelphia: John Benjamins.
    1985   "Iconicity, isomorphism and non-arbitrary coding in syntax." In: John
            Haiman (ed.). *Iconicity in Syntax.* Amsterdam & Philadelphia: John
            Benjamins, 187-219.
Grimes, Joseph E.
    1975   *The Thread of Discourse.* The Hague & Paris: Mouton.
Kytö, Merja
    1991   *Manual to the Diachronic Part of the Helsinki Corpus of English Texts.*
            Department of English, University of Helsinki. [2nd ed. 1993]
Labov, William
    1972   *Language in the Inner City: Studies in the Black English Vernacular.*
            Philadelphia: University of Pennsylvania Press.
Levelt, W. J. M.
    1981   "The speaker's linearization problem." *The Psychological Mechanisms of
            Language.* London: The Royal Society and The British Academy, 91-101.
Levinson, Stephen C.
    1983   *Pragmatics.* Cambridge: Cambridge University Press.
Linde, Charlotte, and William Labov
    1975   "Spatial networks as a site for the study of language and thought."
            Language 51. 4, 924-939.

Longacre, Robert E.
    1983   *The Grammar of Discourse*. New York & London: Plenum Press.
Lyons, John
    1977   *Semantics*. Cambridge: Cambridge University Press.
Ong, Walter J.
    1982   *Orality and Literacy: The Technologizing of the Word*. London & New York: Methuen.
Thompson, Sandra A., and Robert E. Longacre
    1985   "Adverbial clauses." In: Timothy Shopen (ed.). *Language Typology and Syntactic Description. Vol. II: Complex Constructions*. Cambridge: Cambridge University Press, 435-454.
Virtanen, Tuija
    1991   "On participant reference in the narrative: A text-linguistic approach to a literary text." *Parlance* 3.1, 20-41.
    1992a   *Discourse Functions of Adverbial Placement in English: Clause-Initial Adverbials of Time and Place in Narratives and Procedural Place Descriptions*. Åbo: Åbo Akademi University Press.
    1992b   "Given and new information in adverbials: Clause-initial adverbials of time and place." *Journal of Pragmatics* 17. 2, 99-115.
    1993   "Adverbial placement and iconicity." Paper presented at the 3rd International Cognitive Linguistics Conference in Leuven, Belgium, July 18-23, 1993. To appear in the proceedings.
Wårvik, Brita
    1990   "On the history of grounding markers in English narrative: Style or typology?" In: Henning Andersen and Konrad Koerner (eds.). *Historical Linguistics 1987*. Amsterdam & Philadelphia: John Benjamins, 531-542.
    1992   *On Grounding in Narrative: A Survey of Models and Criteria*. Unpublished thesis. Department of English, Åbo Akademi University, Finland.
    1994   "In search of orality in the history of English." In: Světla Čmejrková, František Daneš and Eva Havlová (eds.). *Writing vs. Speaking: Language, Text, Discourse, Communication*. Tübingen: Gunter Narr, 383-388.
    1995   "The ambiguous adverbial/conjunctions *þa* and *þonne* in Middle English: A discourse-pragmatic study of *then* and *when* in Early English Saints' Lives." In this volume.
Werlich, Egon
    1976   *A Text Grammar of English*. Heidelberg: Quelle & Meyer.

Linguistic Politeness Strategies in Shakespeare's Plays

Roman Kopytko
Adam Mickiewicz University, Poznań

1. Aims and scope

This paper has both theoretical and descriptive aims. The theoretical objective consists in showing that the analysis of politeness in terms of the social variables (P) - *power*, (D) - *social distance* and (R) - *ranking of impositions* is inadequate and that some other variables have to be postulated to account for Shakespearean data (e.g. (Ap) - *positive affect*, (I) - *intimacy*, (C) - *cunning*, (Im) - *importance*, (An) - *negative affect*).

The descriptive aims of the present analysis focus on the interactional style~ or 'ethos' of the society represented in Shakespeare's tragedies and comedies. The interactional style, reflecting the affective quality of social interaction, will be analysed in terms of 'negative' and 'positive' politeness strategies (cf. Brown and Levinson 1987) correlated with the social and psychological variables mentioned above. It will be shown that the 'ethos' of the society reflected in Shakespeare's plays is predominantly that of in-group positive politeness rather than that of negative politeness associated customarily with the native speakers of Modern English in contemporary Great Britain.

The data on Shakespeare's English is drawn mainly from the four major tragedies, i.e. *Hamlet, Macbeth, Othello, King Lear*, and from four comedies: *The Taming of the Shrew, A Midsummer Night's Dream, The Merchant of Venice* and *Twelfth Night*, abbreviated respectively as follows: *Ham., Mcb., Oth., KL, TSh, MND, MV, TN*. Occasionally, data from other plays will be referred to.

Shakespearean quotations in the present study are based on D. Bevington's 1988 edition of Shakespeare's four tragedies and four comedies. New York: Bantam Books.

For the sake of space each linguistic strategy of politeness will be illustrated by one or two typical instances only, and analysed in the 'immediately relevant context', i.e. defined in terms of social/psychological variables (P, D, A, etc.). Shakespeare's use of the strategies of politeness in his comedies will be summarised briefly in the final section of this article, (for details cf. Kopytko 1993).

The scope of linguistic politeness is so vast that it would be a breach of Leech's Modesty Maxim (cf. Leech 1983) to attempt to present it exhaustively in one study (or paper). Therefore, some topics have been marginalised, reduced or excluded from this account, especially forms of address (e.g. names, titles, pronouns of address *you/thou*). Because of the high frequency of occurrence they deserve a separate study.

An analysis of the interactional style in Shakespeare's English will be presented in terms of Brown and Levinson's (1987) strategies of negative and positive politeness, so far, in my view, the best available descriptive framework for politeness phenomena. However, in contrast to Brown and Levinson (1987) the present approach to verbal interaction is social-cognitive rather than sociolinguistic. (For a critique of Brown and Levinson's theoretical assumptions cf. Kopytko 1993 and in press).

The present analysis of polite discourse in Shakespeare's tragedies is based on the dramatic text of four major tragedies: *Hamlet*, *King Lear*, *Macbeth*, and *Othello*. Brown and Gilman (1989) justified the selection of the four tragedies for their analysis by stressing the fact that (1) dramatic texts provide the best information on the colloquial speech of the period; (2) the psychological soliloquies in the tragedies provide the access to inner life, which is necessary for a proper test of politeness theory; and, (3) the tragedies represent the full range of society in a period of high relevance to politeness theory. Salmon (1987: 265) justified her use of plays in the study of the sentence structures of colloquial Elizabethan English by claiming that "the more skillful the dramatist the more skillful he will be, in presenting the normal life of his time in authenticating the action by acceptable version of contemporary speech." Similarly, Blake (1983) and Hulme (1962) stressed Shakespeare's skill and genius rather than the use of constructions not shared by his contemporaries.

2.   Positive politeness

Positive politeness is oriented towards the addressee's positive face, i.e. his positive self-image or personality, which imposes on S (although informally) the requirement of satisfying H's positive self-image, at least to some degree (especially when S wishes to maintain a good relationship, cooperation etc., with H).

A taxonomy of positive politeness proposed by Brown and Levinson (1987: 102) includes fifteen strategies. A slightly modified version, also consisting of fifteen strategies is offered by Brown and Gilman (1989: 167). The substrategies of positive politeness will be referred to by the symbol P with an ordinal number, e.g. P1, i.e. the first strategy of positive politeness.

P1 — *notice admirable qualities, possessions, etc.*

A typical instance of P1 consists of a form of address preceded by the name of one or more of his/her unusual or admirable qualities, as in the following examples:

(1) *Duke* (to Othello)Valiant Othello, we must straight employ you
     Against the general enemy Ottoman. (*Oth.* 1.3.50-51)

A more complex type of P1 is that of an extended compliment as in the following example:

(2) *Albany* (to Edgar) Methought thy very gait did prophesy
     A royal nobleness. I must embrace thee. (*KL* 5.3.178)

It should be noticed that the attitude of S to H or *affect* (A) may be favourable (positive) or unfavourable (negative). If necessary the subscript (p) for 'positive' and (n) for 'negative' will be added after (A) to stress the difference, i.e. (Ap) and (An) respectively. As can be expected, positive politeness will be analysed in terms of (Ap). Thus, it may be suggested that *positive affect* (Ap) of S to H is mainly responsible for Shakespeare's use of P1. The formulation of P1 by Brown and Gilman as "notice admirable qualities, possessions etc." is problematic because it is an open-ended list of items, thus admitting some kind of arbitrariness as to what does and what does not belong to the set of items that can make up the list. Therefore, any kind of 'essentialist' approach (or definition) must be abandoned in favour of intuitive judgments about *Y's* belonging to *X* (which unfortunately may be fallible). The same is true in the case of other positive and negative politeness strategies.

For the purpose of the present description, P1 may be formulated as follows:

P1 — *notice admirable qualities, achievements of H.*

In conclusion, the following observations seem to be crucial for politeness theory: (1) P1 is offered preponderantly by S high *power* (P) to H lower *power* (P); (2) *affect* (A) is closely correlated with P1.

P2 — *exaggerate sympathy, approval, etc.*

P2 is not a particularly popular strategy with Shakespeare. Some representative examples from *King Lear* are the following:

(3)   *Goneril* (to Lear) Sir, I love you more than words can wield the matter,
                            Dearer than eyesight, space and liberty,
                            Beyond what can be valued, rich or rare,
                            No less, than life, with grace, health, beauty, honor;
                            As much as child e'er loved, or father found;
                            A love that makes breath poor and speech unable.
                            Beyond all manner of so much I love you.
                            (*KL* 1.1.55-61.)

(4)   *Kent* (to Lear)   Royal Lear,
                            Whom I have ever honored as my king,
                            Loved as my father, as my master followed,
                            As my great patron thought on in my prayers -
                            (*KL* 1.1. 139-142)

As can be seen in (3) and (4), P2 is used by S lower *power* (P) to H high *power* (P). (Ap) is present in (4), i.e. Kent's sincere affection for Lear. Goneril's and Regan's use of 'faked' P2 must be accounted for in terms of *cunning* (this variable will be discussed below).

P3 — *intensify interest to H*

P3 intensifies the interest of the hearer in the speaker's contribution, as in the following example:

(5)   *Horatio* (to Bernardo and Marcellus)
                            In the most high and palmy state of Rome
                            A little ere the mightest Julius fell,
                            The graves stood tenantless and the sheeted dead
                            Did squeak and gibber in the Roman streets;
                            (*Ham*. 1.1.117-120)

P3 is usually used to establish or maintain closer affective ties between S and H.

P4 — *use ingroup identity markers in speech*

Affect (Ap) is involved in the use of in-group address forms in P4, as in the following examples:

(6)   *Othello* (to Desdemona) All's well now, *sweeting;*
                                                Come away to bed. (*Oth.* 2.3. 246-247)

P5 — *seek agreement*

Seeking agreement with H is another form of satisfying his positive face, strengthening a good relationship, securing cooperation, etc.
       The following is an example:

(7)   *Duke*   There is no composition in these news
                               That gives them credit.
       First Senator Indeed, they are disproportioned.
                               My letters say a hundred and seven galleys.
                               (*Oth.* 1.3. 1-4)

Usually it is the case that S lower *power* (P) seeks agreement with H higher *power* (P) (or with equals) rather than vice versa. Closely related to P5 is P6.

P6 — *avoid disagreement*

P6 - the desire to agree or appear to agree – may be exemplified by the following instances:

(8)   *Queen*   Let not thy mother lose her prayers Hamlet.
                         I pray thee, stay with us, go not to Wittenberg
       Hamlet   I shall in all my best obey you, madam.
                         (*Ham.* 1.2.118-120)

As can be seen, some form of imposition on the part of S is linked to a promise, acceptance, or a sincere or pretended agreement on the part of H.
       A variant of P6 – avoid possible disagreement by hedging your statements – is illustrated in (9) below:

(9)   *Knight* (to King Lear) My lord, I know not what the matter is,
                               but to my judgment [...] (*KL* 1.4.56-57)

The important social variables correlated with P5 and P6 seem to be *power* (P) and *intimacy* (I) rather than *affect* (Ap), though the scarcity of data does not allow for any conclusive claims.

P7 — *assert common ground*

P7 is a strategy usually used for softening requests for favours. S can stress his/her general interest in H by indicating that they share similar opinions, attitudes, experiences, etc., which strengthen their good relationship, cooperation, etc. The typical instances of P7 in Shakespeare's tragedies are the following:

(10) *Hamlet* (to Rosencrantz and Guildenstern)
               But let me conjure you, by the rights of
               our fellowship, by the consonancy, by
               the obligation of our ever-preserved love,
               and by what more dear a better proposer
               could charge you withal, be even and direct
               with me whether you were sent for or no.
               (*Ham.* 2.2.284-289).

In Shakespeare's tragedies the use of P7 is usually associated with a request for a 'big' favour. The crucial variable characteristic of P7 seems to be *intimacy* (I). That is, the invoked *intimacy* of S with H is to diminish *social distance* (D) between them and as a result minimise the weightiness of the Face Threatening Act (FTA). Furthermore, another parameter referred to (above) as *cunning* also seems to be involved in P7. This is the case because S's skillful playing on *intimacy* (I) is to induce H to do him a favour. Generally, it may be suggested that the element of *cunning* (C) is in correlation with a strategy when the primary motive of using a strategy (P) of politeness is not satisfying H's positive face but inducing H to satisfy S's wants. So far, it may be claimed that P2 and P7 are potentially associated with the social/psychological variable (C) *cunning*.

P8 — *joke*

Strategy P8 – joke to put the hearer at ease – is not too frequently used in Shakespeare's tragedies. The strategy of joking may be useful in diminishing the *social distance* between S and H because jokes can be used to stress the fact that there must be some mutual background knowledge and values that S and H share.
       Two illustrative examples come from *Macbeth:*

(11) *Macduff* (to Porter) Was it so late, friend, ere you went to bed
                           That you do lie so late? (*Mcb.* 2.3. 21-22)

(12) *Macduff* (to Porter) I believe drink gave thee the lie last night.

Porter (to Macduff) That it did, sir, i' the very throat on me.
(*Mcb*. 2.3. 36-37)

There is too little data to come to any conclusion about the use of P8 in Shakespeare's plays. However, as can be seen in (11) and (12), S high *power* (P) offers P8 to H low *power* (P) to put him at ease. As a result of using P8, the value of *intimacy* (I) may increase and the distance between S and H decrease, as can be observed in Porter's growing 'joking disposition' in his encounter with Macduff, (this in a humorous scene directly preceding the dramatic discovery of Duncan's murder).

P9 — *assert S's knowledge of and concern for H's wants*

P9 is used to indicate that S is taking account of H's wants as in the case of requests, offers, etc. The example of P9 presented by Brown and Levinson (1987: 125) is the following: "I know you can't bear parties, but this one will really be good – do come". P9 seems not to be very popular with Shakespeare. In concise form P9 is present in (13) below:

(13) *Regan* (to Oswald of himself and Goneril)
         I know you are of her bosom. (*KL* 4.5. 26.)

P9 is closely related to P7. With P9 again some motive of *cunning* (C) must be involved, because S, in using P9, attempts to induce H to do him a favour by playing on *intimacy* (I) or *affect* (A) between S and H.

P10 — *offer, promise*

P10 describes one of the most frequently used strategies of positive politeness in Shakespeare's plays. P10 stresses the fact that S and H are good cooperators, that they share some goals, or that S is willing to help to achieve those goals.
         For instance:

(14) *Desdemona* (to Cassio) Be thou assured, good Cassio, I will do
         All my abilities in thy behalf. (*Oth*. 3.3.1-2)

In terms of social variables P10 seems to be frequently correlated with *affect* (A) and *cunning* (C).
         The variable (P) does not seem to constrain the use of P10, although obviously those in *power* may be particularly prone to making promises (and not keeping them). Users of P10 in Shakespeare's tragedies, however, are characterised, preponderantly, by high *power* (P).

P11 — *be optimistic*

P11 - be optimistic that the hearer wants what the speaker wants (that the Face Threatening Act is slight) – is used by Shakespeare as follows:

(15) *Polonius*   You shall do marvelous wisely, good Reynaldo,
                     Before you visit him, to make inquire
                     Of his behavior.
     Reynaldo   My lord, I did intend it. (*Ham.* 2.1.3-6)

P11 implies some form of imposition of values, points of view, etc. and presumptuousness of S towards H.

P12 — *include both S and H in the activity*

The inclusive form 'we', frequently used in the construction *let's*, when S really means 'you' or 'me', in fact appeals to a good, cooperative relationship between S and H, often redressing Face Threatening Acts.
      Shakespeare's instances of P12 include the following:

(16) *Horatio* (to Bernardo and Marcellus): Well, sit we down,
                             And let us hear Bernardo speak of this.
                             (*Ham.* 1.1. 37-38)

A double P12 expressed by means of *let us* and verb (V) followed by inclusive 'we', e.g. *sit down,* appears in (16) above. In this example, the social variable involved in P12 is *intimacy* (I) rather than *affect* (A).

P13 — *give (or ask for) reasons*

P13 belongs to the most frequently used strategies of positive politeness in Shakespeare's plays. According to P13, S should give reasons for why s/he wants what s/he does so that it will seem reasonable to the hearer, as in the following example:

(17) *King*   Sweet Gertrude, leave us too,
                     For we have closely sent for Hamlet hither,
                     That he as 'twere by accident, may here
                     Affront Ophelia. (*Ham.* 3.1. 28-31)

P13 is usually offered by S high *power* (P) to H lower *power* (P); however, there are also instances of P13 offered by S lower *power* (P) to H higher *power* (P).

Characteristically, in the majority of the instances *social distance* in P13 is diminished by *cunning* (C) rather than *intimacy* (I) or *affect* (Ap). Sometimes P13 assumes the form of a long explanatory speech, e.g. the King's explanation of his decision to dispatch envoys to Norway (*Ham*. 1.2.1-32); or Hamlet's speech to the players about the art of acting (*Ham*. 3.2.1-45); or even a whole scene as in the Ghost's accounting for its appeal to Hamlet: "Revenge his foul and most unnatural murder" (*Ham*. 1.5.26-110).

P14 — *assume or assert reciprocity*

Cooperation between S and H may be secured when S claims that s/he will do X for H if H does Y for S. Or, it briefly asserts reciprocal exchange, as in the following example:

(18) *Macbeth* (to Banquo) If you shall cleave to my consent, when 'tis,
          It shall make honor for you. (*Mcb*. 2.1.25-26)

P14 takes the form of a conditional statement (*if...*, *then...*) which must be pragmatically interpreted as an offer or promise. Therefore, it might be claimed that P14 is, in fact, a subtype of P10 – offer, promise.

P15 — *give something desired: gifts, position, sympathy, understanding*

P15 is used when S wants to satisfy some of H's psychological or social needs, e.g. to be liked, admired, cared about, understood, etc. P15 belongs to the most frequently used strategies of positive politeness in Shakespeare's plays.
      A characteristic use of P15 in Shakespeare's tragedies is the following:

(19) *Hamlet* (to Players) You are welcome masters, welcome, all. I am glad to
          see thee well. Welcome good friends. O, old friend!
          Why, thy face is valanced since I saw thee last.
          (*Ham*. 2.2. 421-423)

P15 is usually used for the benefit of H and is then correlated with *affect* (Ap) rather than *intimacy* (I) or *cunning* (C).

P16 — *satisfy H's informational deficit*

P16 is a strategy I have formulated on the basis of Shakespearean data. It was not postulated in Brown and Levinson 1987.
      In a more extensive formulation P16 could be restated as follows: *satisfy H's informational deficit by offering information or an explanation of a state of affairs,* as in the following examples:

(20) *Horatio*   What does this mean, my lord?
     Hamlet   The King doth wake tonight and takes his rouse,
                           Keeps wassail, and the swaggering upspring reels; And as
                           he drains his drafts of Rhenish down,
                           The kettledrum and trumpet thus bray out
                           The trumph of his pledge.
     Horatio   Is it a custom?
     Hamlet   Ay, marry, is't,
                           But to my mind...it is a custom
                           More honored in breach than the observance...
                           (*Ham.* 1.4. 7-16)

P16 in (20) above seems to be strongly correlated with *intimacy* (I) between Hamlet and Horatio. Other instances show that (Ap) and (C) are also associated with P16.

3.   Negative politeness

Negative politeness is oriented towards (partially) satisfying H's negative face, that is his/her preference for freedom of action and self-determination and reluctance to impose. The function of the strategies of negative politeness is to minimise the force of impositions of the FTAs. It should be recalled that in Western cultures negative politeness is the most conventionalised set of linguistic strategies for FTA redress.

According to Brown and Levinson (1987), negative politeness is realised linguistically by means of ten strategies. The main topic of the present section will be the presentation of Shakespeare's use of the strategies of negative politeness in his tragedies. These strategies will be referred to in abbreviated form as (N), standing for negative politeness, followed by a number.

N1 — *be conventionally indirect*

In N1 S wishes to minimise imposition through indirectness and going 'on record' at the same time. Indirect speech acts (e.g. *Can you (please) answer the phone?*) are the most significant forms of conventional indirectness. Shakespeare does not seem to take advantage of N1 (a strategy frequently used in Modern English) too often.

Data include the following instance:

(21) *Horatio* (to Queen) 'Twere good she were spoken with, for she may
strew Dangerous conjectures in ill-breeding minds.
(*Ham.* 4.5. 14-15)

In (21) above N1 appears in an act of advice for the benefit of H which makes it strongly related semantically to P15, a strategy of positive politeness. Thus, any claim or assumption about discrete boundaries between the strategies of positive and negative politeness seems to be unjustified.

N2 — *question, hedge*

Brown and Gilman (1989: 168) formulate N2 as follows: "Do not assume willingness to comply. Question, hedge." A 'hedge' is a particle, a word or phrase that modifies the degree of membership of a predicate or a noun phrase in a set. That is, the presence of a 'hedge' implies that that membership is partial or true only in certain respects, etc. Hedges frequently used in Modern English include: *sort of* (e.g. *He is sort of a politician*), *rather, true, pretty, quite,* etc. Shakespeare uses N2 quite often as in the following example:

(22) *Cassio* (to Emilia)   Yet I beseech you,
If you think fit, or that it may be done,
Give me advantage of some brief discourse
With Desdemona alone. (*Oth.* 3.1. 54-57)

The choice of a linguistic strategy correlated with the weightiness of a Face Threatening Act calculated in terms of Brown and Levinson's (1987: 76) formula: $W_x = D(S,H) + P(H,S) + R_x$ (where W_x is the numerical value that measures the weightiness of the FTA_x, D(H,S) is the value that measures the *social distance* between S and H, P(H,S) is the measure of the *power* that H has over S, and R_x is the value that measures the degree to which the FTA_x is rated an imposition in that culture (cf. Brown and Levinson 1987: 76)) seems to be incomplete and inadequate for accounting for some significant Shakespearean uses of N2 and N1. Specifically, the use of N2 in (22) above cannot be explained in terms of high (P), (D) or high (R) because (a) H's (P) is lower than S's, and (b) (D) and (R) also seem to be low.

Therefore, it appears that another variable may be involved in some instances of N1 and N2. The postulated variable (Im) – *Importance* may be briefly characterised as follows:

> *Importance* (Im) refers to the degree of *importance* that S attaches to an act (X) that is requested of H, or is to be performed by H for S.

Thus, for Cassio in (22) above the question of talking to Desdemona is so important that despite his (relative) high *power* (P) in relation to Emilia and low ranking of imposition (R), and despite of low *social distance* (D) he offers her a deferential *I beseech you* and two 'hedges' *If you think fit* or *that it may be done*.

N3 — *be pessimistic*

N3 – be pessimistic about ability or willingness to comply. Use the subjunctive. N3 is exemplified in Shakespeare's tragedies as follows:

(23) *Macbeth* (to Doctor)   If thou couldest, Doctor, cast
                                   The water of my land, find her disease,
                                   And purge it to a sound and pristine health,
                                   I would applaud thee to the very echo,
                                   That should applaud again. (*Mcb.* 5.3. 52-56)

It happens that in (23) above *importance* (Im) seems to be directly involved, i.e. Macbeth's desire to cure his wife.

N4 — *minimise imposition*

One way of diminishing the weight of an FTA is to indicate that (R), i.e. the seriousness of the imposition, is low. In Modern English a range of expressions may be used to minimise imposition, e.g. *a little, a bit, a drop, a sip, just,* etc. Shakespeare's use of N4 is rather frugal.

N4 is present in the following examples:

(24) *Guildenstern* (to Hamlet) Good my lord, vouchsafe me word with you.
                                  (*Ham.* 3.2. 294)
(25) *Edgar* (to Albany)   Hear me one word. (*KL* 5.1. 39)

(R) in both (24) and (25) is low (S wishes to deliver a message to H). *Importance* (Im) for S in (24) is moderate but high in (25). The relationship of *power* (P) is in favour of H; (D) is high, especially in (25). The data related to N4 are too scarce to come to any definite conclusion.

N5 — *give deference*

Basically, there are two variants of N5 because an act of deference may be realised (a) when S humbles and abuses himself or (b) when S raises H by satisfying his/her want to be treated as superior. An act of deference offered by

S to H usually indicates that H is of higher social status than S, i.e. H's *power* (P) is high.

Shakespeare uses N5 as follows:

(26) *Othello* (to the Duke and Venetian Senators):
                    Most potent, grave, and reverend signiors,
                    My very noble and approved good masters.
                    (*Oth.* 1.3.76-77)

The instances of N5 are numerous in Shakespeare's plays. However, most of them are strictly associated with, or rather realised by, a number of forms of formal address, which have been excluded from the present study.

As can be seen in (26) above it is high *power* (P) and *social distance* (D) that trigger N5. Additionally, in (26) *importance* (Im) is clearly involved, i.e. Othello's defense of face against Brabantio's accusations.

N6 — *apologise*

S can express his reluctance to impinge on H's negative face by apologising, asking forgiveness, admitting the impingement.

A characteristic example of N6 used by Shakespeare is the following:

(27) *Hamlet* (to Horatio) I am sorry they offend you, heartily;
                    Yes, faith, heartily. (*Ham.* 1.5. 139)

The dominating form of N6 in Shakespeare is begging forgiveness for something that happened or is about to happen to H. N6 seems to be triggered off by *affect* (Ap) or *cunning* (C).

N7 — *impersonalise S and H*

Phrasing an FTA as if the agent were other than S and the addressee other than H or only inclusive of H is one way of avoiding a direct form of imposition on H. In Shakespeare, N7 appears in the following examples

(28) *Knight* (to Lear)   ...Your Highness is not entertained with
                    that ceremonious affection as you were wont.
                    (*KL* 1.4. 57-58)
(29) *Hamlet* (to Horatio) Does it not, think thee, stand me now upon...
                    (*Ham.* 5.2. 63)

In Shakespeare, N7 appears in two forms: (a) in passive constructions without agents as in (28) and (b) in impersonal verbs as in (29). (For an account of impersonal verbs in Shakespeare cf. Kopytko 1988).

The use of N7 in Shakespeare seems to be governed, first of all, by *affect* (Ap) or *cunning* (C).

N8 — *state the FTA as a general rule*

To soften the offence of an FTA and dissociate S and H from a particular imposition, it is possible to state the FTA as an instance of some general social, (psychological) rule, regulation or obligation. N8 is exemplified by the following instances:

(30) *Gloucester* (to Kent) I am sorry for thee friend.
'Tis the Duke's pleasure,
Whose disposition, all the world well knows,
Will not be rubbed nor stopped. (*KL* 2.2. 155-158)

(31) *Gloucester* (to Lear)   My dear lord,
You know the fiery quality of the Duke,
How unremovable and fixed he is
In his own course. (*KL* 2.4. 90-93)

Both instances of N8 above seem to result from S's (i.e. Gloucester's) *affect* (Ap) towards H, i.e. Kent and Lear, who fall victim to the Duke's psychological problems that "all the world well knows".

N9 — *nominalise*

Nominalisation is used in N9 to distance the actor and add formality. In effect, the progressive removal of the active 'doing' part of an expression in favour of an impersonal, distanced actor may diminish the potential danger of an FTA, as in the following example:

(32) *King* (to Hamlet)   But to persever
In obstinate *condolement* is a course
Of impious stubborness. (*Ham*. 1.2. 92-94)

As can be seen, the use of N9 is associated with (relatively) high use of *power* (P) of S in relation to H. Furthermore, in Shakespeare's use of N9 in his tragedies, the strategy is correlated with an increase in formality and *negative affect* (An) of S towards H, which is clearly visible in (32) above.

N10 — *go on record as incurring a debt*

As in the following instances S can redress an FTA by explicitly claiming his indebtedness to H:

(33) *Queen* (to Rosencrantz and Guildenstern)
          Your visitation shall receive such thanks
          As fits a king's rememberance. (*Ham.* 2.2. 25-26)

It may be tentatively claimed that N10 is closely correlated with (a) *importance* (Im) as in (33), i.e. the *importance* of Rosenkrantz and Guildenstern's mission for the queen; (b) *cunning* (C), and (c) *positive affect* (Ap) associated with S's gratitude for H's favours for him.

4.   A Quantitative Account

Brown and Levinson's formula calculating the weightiness of an FTA as: $W_x = D(S,H) + P(H,S) + R_x$ (see above) has been found inadequate because it does not account for social/psychological variables such as *importance, cunning, affect,* etc., i.e. it does not represent adequately all the contextual (pragmatic), social and psychological factors contributing to an actual FTA in a discourse. Accounting for all those factors on a summative basis seems to be rather unrealistic. (For a critique of Brown and Levinson's 1987 quantification formula cf. Kopytko 1993, and in press).

The quantification approach used in the present study is less ambitious than Brown and Levinson's (1987) but it is at least feasible. The occurrences of particular strategies will simply be enumerated and correlated with social/psychological variables.

An approximate quantitative account of Shakespearean data analysed in four tragedies (*Hamlet, Macbeth, Othello* and *King Lear*) and four comedies (*The Taming of the Shrew, A Merchant of Venice, A Midsummer Night's Dream* and *Twelfth Night*) includes, in sum, 637 occurrences of the use of politeness strategies in Shakespeare's English. Of that number, 418 occurrences appear in tragedies and 219 in comedies. Thus, an approximate ratio of the use of politeness strategies in tragedies in comparison to comedies is 1.9 to 1. However, taking into account the fact that the total number of verses in the tragedies, is about two thousand greater than in comedies, a more realistic claim will be that the above-mentioned ratio is 1.5 to 1 in favour of the tragedies.

A detailed distribution of the occurrence of the use of negative and positive politeness strategies in Shakespeare's tragedies and comedies are presented in tables. Each strategy of negative and positive politeness is assigned a number (for occurrences) and correlated with social/psychological variables typical of its use. The variables include the following:

Table 1: *Tragedies*

Negative Politeness		Positive Politeness	
N1 –	5 (Ap)(C)(Im)	P1 –	18 (Ap)(C)
N2 –	18 (P)(Im)(D)	P2 –	3(Ap)(C)
N3 –	4 (P)(Im)	P3 –	6 (Ap)
N4 –	2 (P)(Im)(D)	P4 –	5 (Ap)
N5 –	9 (P)(Im)(D)(Ap)	P5 –	3 (P)(I)
N6 –	20 (Ap)(C)	P6 –	9 (P)(I)
N7 –	5 (Ap)(C)	P7 –	5 (I)(C)
N8 –	2 (Ap)	P8 –	2 (I)
N9 –	4 (D)(Ap)	P9 –	2 (I)(C)
N10 –	11 (Ap)(Im)(C)	P10 –	108 (Ap)(C)
		P11 –	14 (Ap)(C)(P)
		P12 –	27 (Ap)(I)
		P13 –	63 (Ap)(I)(C)
		P14 –	2 (I)(C)
		P15 –	58 (Ap)(I)(C)
		P16 –	14 (Ap)(I)(C)
Total: 80		Total: 338	

(P) – *power*, (D) – *social distance* (in the present analysis (D) has been broken down into a number of subvariables, e.g. (I), (Ap), (C), etc., which (D) seems to subsume; in the tables below (D) refers to the occurrences in which low (I) – *intimacy* between S and H appears), (I) – *intimacy*, (Ap) – *positive affect*, (An) – *negative affect*, (C) – *cunning* and (Im) – *importance*.

As can be seen in table 1, 338 instances of positive politeness strategies and 80 of negative politeness have been identified in the four tragedies analysed, which makes an approximate ratio of 4.2 to 1 in favour of the strategies of positive politeness. The respective numbers for the comedies in table 2 are 162 and 57, and the approximate ratio 2.8 to 1 in favour of positive politeness strategies. The total number of instances of positive politeness strategies in both tragedies and comedies is 500, and the respective number of negative politeness comes to 137, which makes the approximate ratio 3.6 to 1 in favour of positive politeness. This is perhaps the most significant finding of the present analysis.

Table 2: *Comedies*

Negative Politeness		Positive Politeness	
N1 –	5 (D)(I)(Ap)	P1 –	4 (Ap) (C)
N2 –	23 (D)(P)(Im)	P2 –	0---
N3 –	0---	P3 –	0---
N4 –	1 (P)(Im)	P4 –	2 (I)
N5 –	1 (P)	P5 –	1 (I)
N6 –	17 (D)(Ap)	P6 –	0---
N7 –	0---	P7 –	0---
N8 –	0---	P8 –	0---
N9 –	0---	P9 –	2 (Ap)
N10 –	10 (Ap)	P10 –	90 (Ap) (C) (P)
		P11 –	0---
		P12 –	10 (I)
		P13 –	13 (I) (Ap)(C)
		P14 –	1 (Ap)
		P15 –	30 (Ap) (I) (C)
		P16 –	9 (Ap) (I) (C)
Total: 57		Total: 162	

Unexpectedly, social relations between members of the upper class (presented in tragedies) and the middle class (presented in comedies) are characterised by low *social distance* (D), a friendly display of positive politeness strategies, and a marginal use of negative politeness strategies induced by high *power* (P) and high *social distance* (D) relations between S and H.

The analysed evidence in our Shakespearean corpus of data is too scarce to say anything conclusive about politeness strategies among the lower classes. However, it may be claimed that in general the social relations within the lower classes may be characterised by Bald-on-record strategies (BRS) and positive politeness strategies reflecting in-group solidarity. The strategy of politeness offered to the upper classes (by the lower class) is that of negative politeness, i.e. deference induced by high *power* (P) and high *social distance* (D) of H.

I tentatively assume that the high rate of occurrence of positive politeness strategies in Shakespeare's plays characterises the interactional style or 'ethos' of Elizabethan society. It should be stressed, however, that this assumption is valid for in-group politeness only. There is no reason to believe that Shakespeare created an 'artificial' society in his plays rather than reflected the one he belonged to. This is surprising, especially in view of popular claims about the interactional style of modern British society which is associated instead with high *social distance* (D), i.e. negative politeness culture.

If both claims, i.e. about the Elizabethan society and modern British society, are at least to some degree true, it may be tentatively proposed that the interactional style or 'ethos' of British society has evolved from the dominating positive politeness culture in the 16th century towards the modern negative politeness culture.

Obviously, the form of that domination, the social distribution, the quantified account, etc. of the two co-existing interactional styles require more research. However, as presented above, the ratio of positive to negative politeness strategies in Shakespeare's plays (3.6 to 1) cannot be easily dismissed.

What strategies of positive and negative politeness are most frequently used in the plays analysed? As can be seen in the tables above, for both tragedies and comedies three strategies of positive politeness account for the greatest number of instances, i.e. P10 – *offer, promise* – 108 in tragedies and 90 in comedies; the respective numbers for P13 – *give reasons* – are 63 vs. 13; and P15 – *give something desired* – 58 vs. 30, i.e. they account for 229 instances out of 338 in tragedies, and 133 out of 162 in comedies.

The most frequently used strategies of negative politeness include N2 – *question, hedge* (18 vs. 23); N6 – *apologise* (20 vs. 17) and N10 – *Go on record as incurring a debt* – (11 vs. 10). Those three strategies of negative politeness account for 49 instances out of 80 in tragedies and 50 out of 57 in comedies.

One might ask why there are more instances of politeness in tragedies than in comedies (the ratio mentioned above is 1.5 to 1). There is no easy answer to such a question, unless it is a guess or trivial statement, e.g. because the exigency of the plot, or a character delineation, etc., require it to be so. A more reasonable approach would be to replace the question *why* something happened by asking *how* something happened. A question formulated in the latter way stands a better chance of receiving a rational answer. Namely, it may be claimed that the more frequent use of politeness in tragedies is closely associated with the numerical increase of some social/psychological variables correlated with particular strategies of politeness in tragedies, specifically (Ap), (C), (Im) and (I), in comparison with comedies. A detailed, generalised account of the correlation of social/psychological variables with the strategies of negative and positive politeness in comedies, tragedies, and both comedies and tragedies are presented in tables 3 – 5. The eight variables are respectively the following: (P) – *power*, (D) – *social distance*, (I) – *intimacy*, (Ap) – *positive affect*, (An) – *negative affect*, (C) – *cunning*, (Im) – *importance*.

Table 3: *Comedies*

Strategies	Social/Psychological variables						
	(P)	(D)	(I)	(Ap)	(An)	(C)	(Im)
Negative Politeness	3	3	1	3	0	0	2
Positive Politeness	1	0	6	7	0	5	0
Total:	4	3	7	10	0	5	2

Table 4: *Tragedies*

Strategies	Social/Psychological variables						
	(P)	(D)	(I)	(Ap)	(An)	(C)	(Im)
Negative Politeness	4	4	0	6	1	4	6
Positive Politeness	3	0	9	10	0	10	0
Total:	7	4	9	16	1	14	6

Table 5: *Comedies and tragedies*

Strategies	Social/Psychological variables						
	(P)	(D)	(I)	(Ap)	(An)	(C)	(Im)
Negative Politeness	7	7	1	9	1	4	8
Positive Politeness	4	0	15	17	0	15	0
Total:	11	7	16	26	1	19	8

It is to be understood that the social variable *power* (P) has been identified as correlated with three strategies of negative politeness and one of positive politeness. The variable (D) is correlated with three strategies of negative politeness and no positive politeness strategies and so on.

In sum, the frequency of correlation of social/psychological variables with the strategies of negative politeness (based on tables 3 and 4 above) is ordered in the following way:

Negative Politeness Strategies:
(Ap) – 9, (Im) – 8, (P) – 7, (D) – 7, (C) – 4, (I) – 1, (An) – 1

It is to be understood that the largest number of negative politeness strategies is correlated with (Ap), then (Im), and so on.

A parallel ordering for the strategies of positive politeness is the following:

Positive Politeness Strategies:

(Ap) – 17, (I) – 15, (C) – 15, (P) – 4

Finally, the overall ordering for the strategies of negative and positive politeness based on table 5 above may be represented as follows:

Positive and Negative Politeness Strategies:
(Ap) – 26, (C) – 19, (I) – 16, (P) – 11, (Im) – 8, (D) – 7, (An) – 1

As can be seen, the variables most frequently correlated with strategies of politeness in Shakespeare's plays are: (Ap) – 26, (C) – 19 and (I) – 16. Thus, Brown and Gilman's (1989: 192) claim that "interactive *intimacy* (I) is of little *importance*" is true only for strategies of negative politeness.

The crucial observation about of politeness and variables is that negative politeness strategies are correlated with seven variables (i.e. (Ap, Im, P, D, C, I, An) and those of positive politeness with four variables (Ap, I, C, P). That is, (Im), (An) and (D) (representing (I_L) low *intimacy*) are variables associated with the strategies of negative politeness only.

It is the approach here to the variable (D) that differs significantly from those of Brown and Levinson (1987) and Brown and Gilman (1989). According to the former, *social distance* – (D) is a complex variable, perhaps subsuming some other variables; but for their universalist claims (and aims) formulated at a high level of abstraction, it is not necessary to analyse (D) in terms of its possible constituents.

Brown and Gilman (1989) have broken *social distance* (D) down into two independent variables, (I) – interactive *intimacy* and (A) – *affect*.

For descriptive purposes three independent variables have additionally been proposed in the present analysis of Shakespearean data, i.e. (1) (An) – *negative affect*; (2) (C) – *cunning* viewed as a premeditated act of S to deceive H by making him believe that an act X performed by S for H is sincere, unselfish or simply for the benefit of H; and finally (3) (Im) – *importance*, which is to be understood as the degree of *importance* that S attaches to an act X that is requested of H or is to be performed by H for S.

Thus, a generalised representation of the complex variable subsuming other independent variables is the following:

(a)

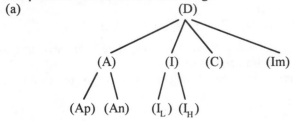

(I_L) and (I_H) stand for low and high *intimacy* between S and H. (I_L) is correlated with the strategies of negative politeness (in the tables represented as (D)); (I_H) on the other hand is correlated with the strategies of positive politeness.

An alternative and perhaps conceptually more adequate representation of the variable (D) is the following:

(b)

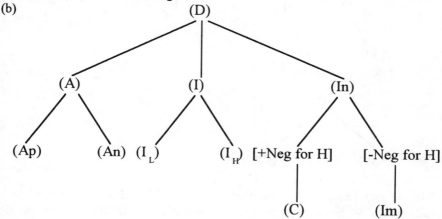

In (b) above, *cunning* (C) and *importance* (Im) have been subsumed under the psychological category (variable) of *Intent* (In). I assume that this variable will account for S's use of a politeness strategy for some (usually covert) intent, which in the case of *cunning* (C) is marked as [+Neg for H], i.e. marked positively for the negative consequences of S's intent for H. For the *importance* (Im) variable *Intent* (In) is marked as [-Neg for H] indicating the lack of negative consequences for H.

Although the representation of the social variable (D) in (a) is definitely more complex than those of Brown and Levinson (1987) and Brown and Gilman (1989), it is quite probable that new data on politeness phenomena will suggest the necessity for postulating other independent variables.

A representation of the complex variable (D) correlated with the strategies of negative and positive politeness respectively is the following:

Negative politeness

(c)

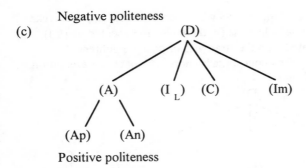

Positive politeness

(d)

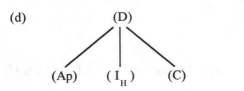

Thus, it may be concluded that *social distance* (D) analysed in terms of such independent variables as *affect* (A), *cunning* (C), or *importance* (Im) and (I) *intimacy*, i.e. changeable and unpredictable entities, is not a deterministic (predictive) category or concept. Therefore, the descriptive part of this paper seems to support the non-deterministic view of politeness phenomena.

5.   Brown and Levinson's strategies vs. Leech's maxims

A set of six maxims of politeness proposed by Leech (1983) may be claimed to subsume their more specific manifestations, i.e. the 15 positive and 10 negative politeness strategies. Thus, I suggest that the *Tact maxim* – (a) Minimise cost to *other* [(b) Maximise benefit to *other*] subsumes all ten strategies of negative politeness as well as: P9 – assert knowledge of the hearer's wants, and indicate that you are taking account of them; P11 – be optimistic that the hearer wants what the speaker wants, that the FTA is slight; P12 – use an inclusive form to include both S and H in the activity; P13 – give reasons why S wants what he does so that it will seem reasonable to H; P16 – satisfy H's informational deficit – most likely fits the above set of Brown and Levinson's strategies of positive politenes.

    Generosity maxim – (a) Minimise benefit to *self* [(b) Maximise cost to *self*] subsumes: P10 – offer, promise; P14 – assert reciprocal exchange; P15 – give something desired: gifts, position, understanding, etc.

Approbation maxim – (a) Minimise dispraise of *other* [(b) Maximise praise of *other*] is manifested in: P1 – notice admirable qualities, possessions, etc.; P2 – exaggerate sympathy, approval, etc.

Agreement maxim – (a) Minimise disagreement between *self* and *other* [(b) Maximise agreement between *self* and *other*] subsumes: P5 – seek agreement; P6 – avoid possible disagreement.

Sympathy maxim – (a) Minimise antipathy between *self* and *other* [(b) Maximise sympathy between *self* and *other*] is manifested in: P4 – use ingroup identity markers in speech; P3 – intensify the interest in H of the speaker's contribution; P7 – assert common ground; P8 – joke to put the hearer at ease.

Modesty maxim – (a) Minimise praise of *self* [(b) Maximise dispraise of *self*] has no equivalents (manifestations) in Brown and Levinson's strategies of politeness.

Which of the six maxims of politeness proposed by Leech (1983) may be claimed to characterise the interactional styleof the society represented in Shakespeare's plays? On the basis of the data presented in the tables 1 and 2 and the correlations of maxims and strategies of politeness presented above, it may be deduced that two maxims of politeness, i.e. the *Tact maxim* and *Generosity maxim*, are decisive for the characterisation of the interactional style of the Shakespearean society.

Thus, *Tact maxim* appears in 199 instances in tragedies and 91 in comedies; the respective numbers for *Generosity maxim* are 168 and 121. Altogether, the two maxims of politeness account for 367 instances out of 418 in tragedies and 212 out of 219 in comedies. Jointly, both in tragedies and comedies they account for 579 instances out of 637 (i.e. for over 90 per cent of the instances). Which of the two maxims is more frequently used in Shakespeare's plays? On the basis of our data (i.e. 579 instances) the *Tact maxim* is responsible for 290 and the *Generosity maxim* for 289 instances. As a result, a view of a balanced use of the two major maxims of politeness in the Elizabethan society, i.e. *Tact* and *Generosity*, seems to be well justified.

6.   Final remarks

An overall quantitative analysis of politeness phenomena in Shakespeare's plays (i.e. one including a quantitative account of the forms of address) could possibly change the ratio of occurrence of the positive vs. negative politeness strategies presented above in favour of one or the other strategy. Such an analysis, however, would be an extremely difficult task to perform due to the high frequency of occurrence of address forms and difficulties with their pragmatic interpretation, i.e. a decision whether a given instance is intended to appeal to the positive or negative face of the addressee.

In the present study the two closely related aspects of politeness, forms of address and strategies of politeness, have been separated both for practical and methodological reasons. Thus for those who believe that the type of social interaction or 'ethos' of a society is characterised best by the forms of address used in that society, the present study needs to be supplemented by a quantitative account of address forms in Shakespeare's plays. On the other hand, those who view forms of address (especially of the formal type), among other things, as ritualised openings of discourse, i.e. pragmatically 'empty' instances of pure form, may consider such an account inconclusive.

Furthermore, as the following quotation indicates, the cases of ironic interpretation require a special treatment in pragmatics:

> My good Lord! God give your lordship good time of day! I am glad to see *your lordship* abroad. I heard say your *lordship* was sick. I hope your *lordship* goes abroad by advice. *Your lordship*, though not clean past to your mouth, hath yet some smack of age in you, some relish of the saltness of time, and I most humbly beseech *your lordship* to have a reverend care of your health. (*2H4* 1.2.93-100)

Appendix

References to Shakespearean data analysed in this study.

Positive Politeness

P1–	Oth. 1.3.50, 2.1.45, 2.1.180, 3.4.170, 3.4.124; Mcb. 1.5.54, 1.4.14; Ham. 1.2.87, 2.2.225, 3.2.53, 3.3.15, 5.2.331; KL 1.1.254, 2.1.113, 2.4.171, 5.3.178.
P2–	KL 1.1.55, 1.1.70, 1.1.139.
P3–	Ham. 1.1.117, 1.2.197, 1.2.193, 1.3.144, 5.1.15, 5.1.40.
P4–	Oth. 2.3.246, 3.3.98, 3.4.48, 4.2.25; Ham. 1.2.163.
P5–	Oth. 1.3.1; Ham. 1.1.108, 1.1.178; KL 1.2.149.
P6–	Ham. 1.2.40, 1.2.118, 1.3.45, 1.3.137, 3.1.38, 3.2.331, 5.2.93; Oth. 3.2.4; KL 1.4.56.
P7–	Ham. 1.2.45, 1.2.51, 2.2.10, 2.2.284; KL 3.1.17.
P8–	Mcb. 2.3.21, 2.3.36.
P9–	KL 4.5.26, 4.5.31.
P10–	Ham. 1.2.20, 1.2.175, 1.2.256, 1.2.258, 1.3.86, 1.5.152, 2.1.103, 2.2.25, 2.2.84, 2.2.157, 2.2.268, 2.2.389, 2.2.527, 3.2.86, 3.3.29, 3.3.29,

3.3.344.5.150, 4.7.69, 4.7.156, 5.2.91; Oth. 1.1.187, 1.2.48, 1.3.126, 1.3.282, 1.3.376, 1.3.383, 2.1.267, 3.3.1, 3.4.131, 2.1.275, 2.1.282, 2.3.44, 2.3.248, 2.3.308, 3.1.37, 3.1.57, 3.2.6, 3.3.1, 3.3.5, 3.3.19, 3.3.19, 3.3.91, 3.3.95, 3.3.228, 3.4.132, 3.4.166, 4.1.151, 4.1.209, 4.2.245, 4.2.247, 4.3.11, 5.1.3, 5.1.103; KL 1.1.29, 1.1.31, 1.1.103, 1.2.103, 1.2.172, 1.3.11, 1.4.70, 1.4.308, 1.5.6, 1.5.32, 2.1.118, 2.2.157, 2.4.171, 2.4.221, 3.5.25, 3.6.2, 4.1.74, 4.1.180, 4.3.52, 4.5.22, 4.6.168, 5.1.32, 3.3.8, 4.6.180, 4.6.186, 4.6.191, 4.6.193, 4.7.57, 4.7.74, 4.7.290, 5.1.35, 5.1.41, 5.1.50, 5.1.57, 5.2.4, 5.3.10, 5.3.12, 5.3.17, 5.3.31, 5.3.103, 5.3.167, 5.3.248, 5.3.325; Mcb. 1.2.69, 1.3.150, 1.4.32, 1.4.45, 1.6.29, 2.3.46, 3.1.16, 3.1.128, 3.2.32, 3.6.51, 5.8.50, 5.8.60.

P11–   Ham. 1.2.106, 1.2.251, 2.1.3; KL 1.1.211; Oth. 1.3.223, 3.3.43, 3.3.53, 3.3.83, 3.3.92, 3.3.260, 4.1.253, 4.1.267, 4.3.1.

P12–   Ham. 1.1.35, 1.1.37, 1.1.175, 1.1.181, 1.5.199, 4.7.149, 4.7.192, 5.2.338; KL 3.7.106, 5.1.34; Mcb. 1.4.56, 1.3.154, 2.3.125, 2.3.135, 2.3.137, 4.3.1, 4.3.214; Oth. 2.1.42, 2.1.179, 2.3.1, 2.3.105, 2.3.114, 2.3.276, 5.1.127.

P13–   Ham. 1.2.1-32, 1.5.26-110, 2.1.38, 2.2.1, 3.1.28, 3.1.44, 3.2.1-45, 3.2.37-45, 3.2.108, 3.2.171, 3.2.223, 3.2.347, 3.3.1, 3.3.24, 3.4.180, 4.1.34, 4.3.34, 4.3.41, 4.4.1, 4.5.101, 4.7.108, 5.2.345, 5.2.40, 5.2.331, 5.2.397, 1.2.88, 1.2.115; Oth. 1.1.43, 1.1.87, 1.1.98, 1.1.110, 1.1.149, 1.2.36, 1.2.83, 1.3.117, 1.3.117, 1.3.262, 1.3.263, 2.1.97, 2.1.120, 2.3.30, 3.3.32, 3.3.157, 3.3.211, 3.4.51, 3.4.113, 4.1.75; KL 1.2.36, 2.1.27, 2.2.70, 2.2.143, 2.2.130, 2.4.233, 3.4.23, 4.1.41, 4.5.18, 4.6.226, 4.7.48, 5.1.42, 5.3.130; Mcb. 1.4.44, 2.3.23, 3.1.14, 3.4.118, 4.2.22-28.

P14–   Mcb. 2.1.25; Oth. 1.3.178.

P15–   Ham. 1.2.62, 1.2.68, 1.2.75, 1.2.160, 1.2.165, 2.1.76, 2.2.26, 2.2.29, 2.2.42, 2.2.43-50, 2.2.171, 2.2.371, 2.2.421, 3.1.39, 3.1.92, 3.2.52, 3.2.91, 4.5.41, 4.5.152, 5.2.180; Oth. 1.2.10, 1.3.67, 1.3.202, 2.1.183, 2.3.184, 2.3.253, 2.3.293, 2.3.318, 3.1.22, 3.1.37, 3.1.44, 3.3.78, 3.3.298, 3.3.305, 3.4.111, 3.4.171, 4.2.115, 3.4.479, 4.2.143; KL 1.1.185, 1.2.162, 2.1.26, 2.1.104, 3.2.61, 3.4.146, 3.6.33, 4.1.63, 4.2.22, 4.7.82, 5.3.4, 5.3.41; Mcb. 1.4.22, 1.4.29, 2.4.39, 3.1.11, 3.4.16, 4.3.215, 4.3.209.

P16–   Ham. 1.3.111, 1.3.114, 1.4.7, 1.4.12, 1.5.173, 2.1.79, 2.2.131, 3.2.349, 4.7.1, 5.2.15; Oth. 1.3.19, 2.3.212; KL 1.1.36, 1.1.94, 2.4.26, 5.3.46.

Negative Politeness

N1–   J.C. 4.3.256; Ham. 3.4.195, 4.5.14; Oth. 1.2.29; Mcb. 1.3.150.

N2–   Ham. 1.3.90, 2.2.21, 1.3.286; KL 1.2.81, 2.2.522, 3.2.314; Oth. 1.1.123, 1.1.182, 1.2.92, 4.7.18, 4.7.26, 4.7.87, 1.2.27; Mcb. 2.1.23, 3.1.76, 3.4.40, 3.4.44.

N3–   Ham. 2.2.540, 5.2.90; KL 5.1.40; Mcb. 5.3.52.
N4–   Ham. 3.2.294; KL 5.1.39.
N5–   Ham. 1.3.82, 2.2.213; Oth. 1.3.54, 1.3.76, 1.3.238, 1.3.248, 2.1.86; Mcb.
         4.2.66.
N6–   Oth. 1.3.54, 2.3.183, 3.3.147, 3.3.225, 3.3.250, 3.3.407, 3.4.177, 5.1.95,
         5.2.307; KL 1.1.209, 1.2.36, 1.4.64, 1.4.272, 4.7.8, 5.3.75; Mcb. 4.3.21,
         4.3.201.
N7–   KL 1.4.57, 4.7.20; Oth. 3.4.90; Ham. 5.2.63; R 3 3.1.63.
N8–   KL 2.2.155, 2.4.90.
N9–   Ham. 1.2.92, 5.2.127; Oth. 1.1.37, 3.3.272, 4.2.210.
N10–   Ham. 2.2.25, 2.2.35, 2.2.273, 5.2.83; Oth. 1.3.72, 3.1.41, 3.4.168, 4.3.3; Mcb.
         1.6.15, 5.8.75.

References

Blake, Norman F.
    1983   *Shakespeare's Language: An Introduction*. New York: St. Martin's.
Brown, Penelope, and Stephen C. Levinson
    1987   *Politeness: Some Universals in Language Usage*. Cambridge: Cambridge
             University Press.
Brown, Roger, and Albert Gilman
    1989   "Politeness theory in Shakespeare's four major tragedies." *Language in
             Society* 18, 159-212.
Hulme, Hilde M.
    1962   *Explorations in Shakespeare's Language: Some Problems of Word Meaning
             in the Dramatic Text*. New York: Longman.
Kopytko, Roman
    1988   "The impersonal use of verbs in William Shakespeare's plays." *Studia
             Anglica Posnaniensia* 21, 41-51.
    1993   *Polite Discourse in Shakespeare's English*. Poznań: Adam Mickiewicz
             University Press.
    in press "Against rationalistic pragmatics." *Journal of Pragmatics*.
Leech, Geoffrey N.
    1983   *Principles of Pragmatics*. New York: Longman.
Salmon, Vivian, and Edwina Burness (eds.)
    1987   *A Reader in the Language of Shakespearean Drama*. Amsterdam:
             Benjamins.

Constraints on Politeness
The Pragmatics of Address Formulae in Early English Correspondence

Terttu Nevalainen and Helena Raumolin-Brunberg
University of Helsinki

1. Introduction

Letters furnish one of the most useful sources for English social history and sociohistorical linguistics. Many outstanding letter collections have been preserved from the fifteenth and early sixteenth centuries, and an increasing number survive from later periods. In his history of the English family, Houlbrooke (1984) highlights one of the key issues of our study when he describes letter-writing in Early Modern England:

> The growth of literacy and the improvement of postal services facilitated correspondence. The increasing readiness of members of the propertied classes to write rather than dictate their letters made possible a new epistolary privacy. This in turn encouraged a loosening of formalities, a fuller expression of intimate feelings and a more discursive treatment of personal pleasures. (Houlbrooke 1984: 4)

What intrigues us is how this loosening of formalities manifests itself and how it can be accounted for in pragmatic terms. We propose to explore it in one particular section of personal letters in the Late Medieval and Early Modern periods: the form of address used in the salutation at the beginning of a letter. Looking at forms of address over an extended period of time gives rise to some fundamental questions. Did the growth of literacy and privacy lead to an increase in what Brown and Levinson (1987) call positive politeness, with a simultaneous decrease in negative politeness? Assuming that these distinctions are historically valid, is there, in other words, a shift away from deference towards greater intimacy? Or could address forms perhaps signal a long-term trend away from, as Kopytko (1993: 107) finds, dominantly positive linguistic politeness in Shakespeare's time, towards a more negative politeness culture today?

Our topic is diachronic in that we examine forms of address over a period of about two hundred and fifty years (1420-1680). We relate our descriptions of address forms to the specific social conditions of the time along the lines suggested in Nevalainen and Raumolin-Brunberg (1989). Our framework is hence sociopragmatic in the general sense Leech (1983: 10) gives to the term. It should perhaps be emphasised that we expect to be dealing with changing conventions that reflect new circumstances in letter-writing rather than some permanent changes in personal relations across time. Some such social changes might, of course, have taken place, but we have not based our study on that premise.

We have restricted ourselves to salutations for two reasons. Firstly, the form of address in the salutation is an integral part of a personal letter, just like the superscription on the back of it. The difference between these speaker-addressee and speaker-referent forms, as Brown and Levinson (1987: 180) call them, is particularly relevant to letters. As opposed to the superscription, the form in the salutation is the private form of address, meant for the eyes of the addressee only and not for the bearer of the letter or any strangers who might happen to see it. In the introduction to his popular letter-writing manual, *The Secretary in Fashion* (1640), de la Serre warns his readers that kinship terms should not be expressed in the superscription: 'for sometimes it is not fitting that those who carry the Letters should know there is any alliance between the parties which write to one another".

The other reason for limiting the topic of our study to forms of address in letter salutations is methodological. They form a conventional but socially motivated selection from a set of forms available at any given time. More than a hundred different forms of address, excluding Christian names and pronouns, appear in the four Shakespearian tragedies (*Hamlet, King Lear, Macbeth, Othello*) studied by Brown and Gilman (1989), for instance. In order to be able to make diachronic generalisations, it is important that the forms of address in letters represent authentic contexts of use, whose main determinants can be identified and interpreted in sociopragmatic terms. Since personal letters are available from the Late Middle English period onwards, it is possible to trace changes in address forms over an extended period of time.

Our article is organised as follows. An overview of previous work on the topic is followed by a discussion of the sources of English letter-writing conventions in section 2. The social factors connected with letter-writing in

Late Medieval and Early Modern England – social stratification, literacy and postal services – are introduced in section 3. In sections 4–6 we describe the changing usage of address forms in some thirty collections of correspondence dating from 1420 to 1680. A large part of this material is drawn from the *Helsinki Corpus of Early English Correspondence,* which is in the process of being computerised (see References, p. 73ff.). In section 7 we relate our findings to the social realities of the period under investigation and evaluate diachronic changes in the light of the theory of politeness suggested by Brown and Levinson (1987). We finish by discussing the methodological implications of our study to the quantitative model proposed by Brown and Gilman (1989: 175-176) of scoring forms of address for politeness.

2.   Background issues

2.1. *Previous approaches*

Set against the volume of research on second-person pronouns in English, work on titles and other forms of address is scanty. To our knowledge, the only book-length study in the history of English titles and forms of address is Böhm (1936). The thesis supplies concise histories of titles of honour and respect based on secondary sources and a limited sample of drama and correspondence from the late fifteenth century onwards.

Forms of address have for a long time primarily interested literary historians, particularly Shakespearian scholars, including Breuer (1983) and Replogle (1987). Both are socially oriented. Replogle (1987) makes frequent use of contemporary sixteenth-century commentary to account for Shakespeare's address forms, and Breuer (1983) relies on social historians' reconstruction of titles and forms of address in Early Modern England. His main source is Laslett's (1965) classic *The world we have lost.* Both studies conclude that Shakespeare was well aware of the conventions of his time but could also exploit them for dramatic purposes.

Recent studies dealing with the linguistic evolution of titles and address forms similarly draw on sociohistorical research. Williams (1992) discusses titles of address in a manuscript listing London renters of several parishes in 1638. His data show the spread of *Mr/master* and the demise of *goodman* in London. Nevalainen's (1994) study of the generalisation of titles in the seventeenth century is based on a trial for high treason in 1688. The examination records suggest that *Mr* had not yet been extended to labourers in the countryside at the time. Social ranks could also differ in their use of titles. People from the lower ranks tended to upgrade the titles of their social superiors, and use *lady* instead of *mistress*, for instance, while social peers were found to retain traditional terms such as *Mrs/mistress* and *goodman* more often than people separated by greater social distance.

Address forms are also included in two recent studies on linguistic politeness, Brown and Gilman (1989) and Kopytko (1993). Both apply the Brown and Levinson (1987) politeness theory to Shakespeare's usage in order to test the claims to universality made by the theorists. Brown and Levinson base their approach on the notion of face, people's emotionally invested self-image. Face consists of personal freedom of action (negative face) and appreciation by others (positive face). Face must be constantly attended to in interaction because it can be lost, maintained or enhanced. People will normally co-operate in maintaining each other's face, because "everyone's face depends on everyone else's being maintained" (Brown and Levinson 1987: 61). As some acts intrinsically threaten face, it is argued that the politeness levels in discourse are determined by the seriousness of a face-threatening act (FTA). It involves three factors: the relative power (P) and social distance (D) of the speaker and the hearer, and the ranking of impositions (R).

The results of both Brown and Gilman (1989) and Kopytko (1993) largely agree with the predictions of the theory. Although the universality of face has been challenged, for instance, by research on the Japanese language and culture (e.g. Matsumoto 1988), it does appear to apply to the past stages of English, at least to Shakespearean language. Brown and Gilman (1989: 192-196) argue, however, that the social distance factor (D) subsumes interactive closeness and affect, and while affect (personal liking) strongly influences politeness, intimacy has little or no effect. Kopytko (1993: 113-114) similarly breaks D down into a number of independent variables.

Unfortunately, the contribution made by forms of address to the quantitative comparisons cannot be evaluated in either case. Brown and Gilman (1989: 175-176) do include address form scores in their overall politeness scores, but do not discuss their share of the figures. Kopytko (1993: 53), on the other hand, finds these forms too unwieldy to quantify in his material of eight plays and omits them altogether. As pointed out above, both studies nevertheless furnish us with interesting hypotheses which are worth testing. Methodologically we shall take the middle course between the two and present our data in terms of their quantitative prototypicality, relative commonness or rareness, but without exact quantification. We shall return to the issue of quantifying politeness strategies diachronically in the final sections of this paper after having presented our own evidence.

2.2. *Forms of address as conventional politeness*

In the Middle Ages the principles of *ars dictaminis,* or the art of letter-writing, were a matter of conventional rhetoric rather than free choice. They were propagated by dictaminal treatises and formularies of model letters, which instructed their readers in the correct form and appropriate style of letters written for different occasions. In particular, letters had to observe the etiquette of social hierarchy (Henderson 1993).

There is evidence to show that the *dictamen* was also a significant factor in the spread of English letter-writing. Richardson (1984) argues, however, that the format most commonly used in late medieval England was not so much the humanist letter than the *ars notaria,* the model for drawing up legal, business, and diplomatic documents. The most visible official model for the late medieval epistolary form was no doubt the documents issued – after 1420 in English – by the King's Chancery. Chancery letters were normally structured along the following lines (Hall 1908: 270-280, Richardson 1984: 213-214):

1. Address (*Right trusty and wellbeloved*)
2. Salutation (*We greet you well/after hearty commendations*)
3. Notification (*And we let you wit that*)
4. Exposition (*Whereas*)
5. Disposition/Injunction (*We are pleased with these presents to grant*)
6. Final clause (Injunction: *For it is our pleasure*; Proviso: *Provided that/and these letters shall be a sufficient warrant*)
7. Valediction and Apprecatio (*And so we bid you heartily farewell, which knoweth Almighty God, who have you ever in keeping*)
8. Attestation (*Written under our seal at; written at*)
9. Date

According to Richardson (1984), this Chancery model was also followed in private correspondence in the fifteenth century more closely than the Anglo-Norman models that had appeared in formularies throughout the previous century (cf. Davis 1965). Hall (1908: 271-273) points out that English vernacular letters also partly reproduced mere oral conventions, especially with respect to the everyday salutations, forms of address and valediction. One of the main differences between the *Stilus Anglicus* and the earlier Latin models is the use of a direct vocative address instead of the Latin dative (see further

Svennung 1958: 19-32). Both Richardson (1984) and Davis (1965) show that in the fifteenth century the forms of address usually consisted of complex noun phrases premodified by the intensifier *right*.

In the Renaissance, letter-writing became a method of teaching classical rhetoric. Elementary-level model letters in English have survived from the fifteenth century, a hundred years before the printing of the first English letter-writing manuals (Voigts 1981). Some researchers argue that Renaissance humanism left its impact especially on private letter-writing. Houlbrooke (1984: 32) notes that while medieval letters had emphasised the distance between superiors and subordinates in the family, humanists revived the simpler epistolary forms of antiquity. They also encouraged writers to employ a more intimate style and to express their feelings.

The earliest letter-writing manuals printed in English prescribed forms of address less narrowly than some of the later ones. Compare the two extracts cited in (1), which come from the first printed English letter-writer (Fulwood 1568) and one of the most widely circulated seventeenth-century handbooks (de la Serre 1640); both are anglicised from French originals. William Fulwood dedicated *The Enemie of Idlenesse* to "the right worshipfull the Maister, Wardens, and Company of the Marchant Taylours of London", and John Massinger, de la Serre's translator, dedicated his work to "the worthily admired for Learning and Good Parts M. Thomas Berney, Gent. of Grayes-Inn". It appears from both works and the model letters they print that a form of address in the salutation formed an essential part of personal letters.

(1a) Note also that most comonly in Epistles & Letters, there be three necessary points. The firste is the salutation or recommendation, whych is made in sundrie maners, according to the pleasure of the enditer, as may well be perceiued by diuers styles hereafter following. (Fulwood 1568 [1571]: 1-2)

(1b) The inward Superscription is that which is set within side of Letters, using the Titles of Lord or Master, Lady or Mistress, at the beginning in a line apart with a great distance between that and the second line, as

> Sir,
> I have received your Letter, &c.

But those whom we will not shew so much respect unto, we joyn it with the body of the Letter in this manner, *Sir, I have understood, &c.* Those who are of Kin, add after the Title of Master, or Mistress, their degree of Kindred; as *Sir, and most loving uncle,* or *Mistress, and most loving Cousen.* (de la Serre 1640 [1654]: n.p.)

Letter-writing manuals repeatedly emphasise that the main point to bear in mind in both superscriptions and forms of address elsewhere is the social standing of the addressee. Fulwood and de la Serre can again be quoted here:

(2a)   We haue to consider these poyntes following: to wit the estate dignitie or qualitie of him vnto whome we write: whyther he bee a publike person or a priuat, whyther he be rich or poore, a friend or an enemie: also whither he bee well knowen vnto vs, or but little. (Fulwood 1568 [1571]: 4v.)

(2b)   But the chief thing we must take care of herein, are his titles, to give everie one such as befit him, or he desires to have; otherwise his Letters are not well accepted of and breed distast. (de la Serre 1640 [1654]: n.p.)

Forms of address reveal a carefully graduated scale of social hierarchy, thus reflecting the power relations of Late Medieval and Early Modern English society. Whether the use of these differentiated forms of address could be looked upon as anything more than expressions of conventional politeness is one of the key issues of our inquiry. Can we, in other words, consider them as predictable as Brown and Gilman (1989: 179) claim the use of the second-person pronouns *you* and *thou* to be in the majority of cases? Following the status rule, these pronouns of address would be an obligatory aspect of speech, automatic and ever-present, and hence would no longer serve as a strategy of politeness. The answer to our question would appear to be in the negative. At no point in our historical material is the choice of address form totally predictable. In Brown and Levinson's theory of politeness, redressing a potential face-threat to the addressee is the main motivation for the use of different politeness strategies. A letter may perform a variety of functions, most of them potentially threatening either to the positive or the negative face of the addressee.

2.3. *Letter types*

As we have seen, the organisation of public and private letters was quite similar in the fifteenth century. Nor were the two sharply distinguished in the classifications of letter types proposed by Renaissance humanists, who taught letter-writing as an exercise in rhetoric (Henderson 1993: 146). In *De conscribendis epistolis* (1522 [1985]: 71), Erasmus divides letters into three principal rhetoric-functional kinds: persuasive, demonstrative and judicial. Love letters, for instance, are included in the first. Familiar letters form a separate category for Erasmus. They may be informative, announcing public or private news, or narrative, congratulating, lamenting, instructing, expressing gratitude, offering assistance, or joking. As Henderson (1993: 151) points out, familiar letters cannot be said to persuade. That is why many letters that a modern reader might consider familiar come under the first three categories in Erasmus' classification.[1]

In reality most personal letters are mixed. This was pointed out by Erasmus himself (1522 [1985]: 70) and many other authors of letter-writing manuals, including de la Serre (1640 [1654]): "Mixt Letters, which treat of several matters ... are the commonest of all: for we seldom write any Letters upon one onely subject." As manuals were usually meant for writers without the benefit of a classical education, they provided what was needed in terms of both function and content. Fulwood specifies:

(3)   Domesticall or houshold letters are more in vse than any other, forsomuch as of their nature they are very necessarye, to let our frendes vnderstande of our estate, and of our businesse, be it of helth, prosperitie, sicknesse, aduersitie, or any other domesticall and familiar things ... (Fulwood 1568 [1571]: 69v.)

The letters included in our *Corpus of Early English Correspondence* are mostly of the mixed kind, both in terms of their main functions or speech acts and their subject matter. As to subject matter, they largely deal with family business of various kinds and news. Some specimens of pure news letters occur in most of our collections but few are dominated by news; the news letters of John Chamberlain and Richard Verstegan are exceptions in this respect. The other frequently found kind deals with household business.

The more professional letters were written by the merchant families of the Celys and the Johnsons in the fifteenth and sixteenth centuries, and the wide circle of business associates of the Marescoes in the seventeenth. John Browne, a Bristol merchant, was the first to publish a letter-writer for the specific needs of young businessmen. Obviously, there was an audience for his slender publication, as *The Marchants Avizo* (1589) ran to several editions.

Reflecting the many roles and duties of individuals, correspondence pertaining to the realms of the church, law and government is also included. Not infrequently it provides us with letters variously known as suitor's letters, petitions, or supplications – a subgenre of particular interest from the point of view of politeness. Whigham (1981: 865) classifies them as letters of *negotium*, which aim at creating a community of author and addressee in pursuit of a specific and local goal. A case in point here are requests for patronage. Practical advice on how to write requests could be gleaned from the manuals ranging from Fulwood's (1568) section on "how a noble man writeth Letters for the promotion of a man", to Breton's (1602) "Letter to his Mistress, desiring marriage" (to "Courteous Mistress Amy, the only joy of my heart"). Requests for money were already contained in the earliest surviving English model letters (Voigts 1981: 577). They continue to be a recurrent topic in personal correspondence throughout our period.

3.   England 1420-1680: Social order, literacy and postal services

3.1. *Social order*

The two hundred and fifty years this study covers is a period that witnesses a transition from the medieval social order with three estates to a more modern type of 'class' society, which is assumed to originate in the eighteenth century. The medieval three estates, clergy, warriors (lords, knights) and labourers, were differentiated by social function, the later classes primarily on economic criteria (Wrightson 1991: 30-31). Tudor and Stuart social analysts, like William Harrison (1577), Sir Thomas Wilson (c. 1600) and Gregory King, emphasised the hierarchical order of their society. The division of people into different 'degrees' varied from one writer to another, but it was common at least to distinguish between four groups: the gentry (nobility included), citizens and merchants, yeomen, and labourers (Laslett 1965 [1983]: 23-52, Wrightson 1991).

   Table 1 is a description of the hierarchical social order prevailing in Early Modern England (based on Laslett 1965 [1983]: 38, Breuer 1983: 56, Nevalainen and Raumolin-Brunberg 1989: 90, and Nevalainen 1994). In the countryside the social structure was rather uncomplicated. A person's social status was connected with wealth, which in an agricultural society meant landownership. The main dividing line was between gentlemen and non-gentlemen, i.e. between people who did not work manually for their living (gentlemen) and those who did (yeomen and all degrees below). Yeomen were mostly substantial freeholders, while lesser farming people were called husbandmen. Towns had hierarchical structures of their own, with citizens, burgesses, aldermen, and wealthier merchants enjoying a high status in these relatively independent communities. Below them in the social scale were craftsmen and lesser tradesmen. Both in country and town, a very large proportion of the population worked in the service of others (for further information on social order, see e.g. Laslett 1965 [1983], Stone 1966, Wrightson 1982, 1991; Palliser 1983, Boulton 1987, Keen 1990).

Table 1 also gives us the conventional titles of different social ranks. This list of titles serves as a frame of reference for our discussion in sections 5 and 6. The titles did not remain unchanged during the early modern era. The title given to the wives of knights (*Dame*), for instance, was replaced by *Lady*, and the polite *Sir* for clergymen disappeared. One aspect of our research here is to trace the development of these changes in letters.

Table 1: *Rank and status in Tudor and Stuart England*

Estate		Grade	Title
GENTRY	Nobility	Royalty, Duke, *Archbishop* Marquess, Earl, Viscount Baron, *Bishop*	**Lord, Lady**
	Gentry (proper)	Baronet 1611-, Knight Esquire Gentleman	**Sir, Dame** **Mr, Mrs**
	Professions	Army Officer (Captain, etc.), Government Official, (Secretary of State, etc.), Medical Doctor (Doctor), Merchant, Lawyer, Clergyman, etc.	
NON-GENTRY		Yeoman, Merchant, Husbandman	**Goodman, Goodwife**
		Craftsman, Tradesman, Artificer	(Name of Craft: Carpenter, etc.)
			none
		Labourer; Servant, Cottager	(Labourer, etc.)
		Pauper	(none)

(Note: occupational titles given in brackets)

We would like to emphasise that the impression given by a schematic table like our Table 1 is too rigid and stable. In reality the social structure was by no means rigid, and changes took place during the early modern era. Especially during Elizabethan and Early Stuart times social mobility was marked (Stone 1966, Wrightson 1982). The channels which led to gentility were the professions: the church, law, government office, military forces, commerce. Writing in 1577, William Harrison has this to say:

> [...] Who soeuer studieth the lawes of the realme, who so abideth in the vniuersitie giuing his mind to his booke, or professeth physicke and the liberall sciences, or beside his seruice in the roome of a capteine in the warres, or good counsell giuen at home, whereby his common-wealth is benefited, can liue without manuell labour, and thereto is able and will beare the port, charge, and countenance of a gentleman, he shall for monie haue a cote and armes bestowed vpon him by heralds (who in the charter of the same doo of custome pretend antiquitie and seruice, and manie gaie things) and therevnto being made so good cheape be called master, which the title that men giue to esquiers and gentlemen, and reputed for a gentleman euer after [...] (*Holinshed's Chronicles. England, Scotland and Ireland.* Vol. I: 273).

Harrison's words indicate that there was no authoritatively defined system of social degrees, but the principles of ranking people were more or less conventional. Apart from the professions, one could be elevated to a higher status by means of a good marriage or by the acquisition of land. The status of gentleman was also easily lost by impoverishment or simply by being a non-inheriting younger son. In fact, many younger sons of gentle families were recruited as apprentices for different craftsmen and tradesmen (for London, see e.g. Rappaport 1989).

Finally, we would like to point out that the proportion of the ranks of nobility and gentry was always very small, less than 5% of the total population (for the somewhat variable figures, see e.g. Laslett 1983: 36-39). The growth of the professions was significant during the early modern period, but it must nevertheless be acknowledged that our corpus, mostly consisting of letters exchanged between the highest echelons of society, and consequently this study, only covers the language of a small proportion of people who lived in England between 1420 and 1680.

3.2. *Literacy*

Although on an international scale Late Medieval and Early Modern England ranked high in terms of literacy, the fact remains that during these centuries the country only underwent a development from an oral to a semi-literate society. The assessments of the range of literacy vary to a great deal (for an overview, see Cressy 1980: 42-61), often reflecting the different views on the phenomenon as such. We should bear in mind that the level of literacy varies, ranging from a poor ability to read to fluency in reading and from poor writing skills to total fluency in both reading and writing. Unfortunately, not all writers on the subject are quite accurate about the level they are referring to.

Since there is no direct evidence of the range of literacy in past times, such indirect proofs as book production and book ownership and the extent of educational facilities have been utilised. The ability or inability to sign one's name has become one of the most powerful tools in testifying to a person's reading skills. There is plenty of evidence that reading was taught before writing in early modern schools (Schofield 1968: 317, Cressy 1980: 19-41, Spufford 1981 [1989]: 19-44). This allows us to draw the conclusion that the ability to write one's name instead of inscribing a mark was an indication of a person's ability to read.

Cressy's extensive study (1980) of Tudor and Stuart literacy is based on the occurrence of signatures as opposed to marks in different types of documents, such as indications of loyalty in the form of oaths (e.g. the Protestation Oath in 1642), wills, marriage bonds, and depositions in ecclesiastical courts. According to Cressy (1980: 176), illiteracy was very high in 1500; only 10% of men and 1% of women could sign their names. In the middle of the sixteenth century, the corresponding figures were 20% and 5%, at the time of the Civil War (1642) 30% and 10%. The above figures represent a national estimate, and the actual level of literacy varied a great deal, depending on local circumstances. On the whole, literacy was more common in towns than in the countryside, and the figures for London exceeded the national ones, although variation existed between different London parishes (Cressy 1980: 73-75).

There was a clear social hierarchy of literacy: at the top were professional people, like lawyers and clergymen (100% literacy), followed by nobility and gentry (97-98% literacy), yeomen and wealthier merchants, tradesmen and craftsmen, husbandmen, servants, labourers, and women (cf. Table 1, above). It is noteworthy that the overall literacy of women was at the same level as that of men of the lowest social ranking. However, London was an exception even in this respect, as at the end of the seventeenth century almost half of London's female population could read, and 70% of servants could sign their names (Cressy 1980: 118-141).

Cressy's study covers a period starting in 1500. As regards late medieval literacy, opinions, based on sources which are less reliable than Cressy's, seem to diverge to a considerable extent. There are scholars who advocate quite widespread literacy, e.g. Kingsford (1925 [1962]: 34-35), Lester (1987: 216) and Keen (1990: 224). Graff (1987: 106), on the other hand, gives the following estimate on late medieval literacy: urban male population 25%, men in general

6-12%, and women less than half of this figure. However, extensive variation must be taken into account since there is evidence of London merchants scoring as high as 40% (Graff 1987: 99).

Illiteracy as such and the general oral or semi-literate nature of society are factors that set limits to the study of correspondence. In this context, on the sender's side, literacy refers to a relatively demanding level of literacy, viz. the ability to write. The recipient's role requires reading skills. These requirements could be relaxed, however, by reliance on local assistance or even professional amanuenses. Despite the social hierarchy of literacy, it is probable that every local community had at least one or two members who could read and write. These people were able to help their neighbours where literacy was needed (Wrightson 1982: 194). On the other hand, this type of assistance of course prevented the correspondence from being private. Hence, as Houlbrooke (1984: 4) notes, the growth of literacy is a major factor in the development of epistolary privacy, which in turn could lead to the loosening of formalities and to more intimate discourse in the exchange of personal letters.

The social hierarchy of literacy automatically leads to a bias in the representativeness of our letter corpus. Due to illiteracy, the lower ranks are automatically excluded, and the female correspondents represent only the highest echelons of society. A partial remedy to this problem, i.e. the inclusion of letters where assistance has been used, leads to another problem: inauthentic data. It is often impossible to know whether the sender of a letter dictated his or her letter to the amanuensis or whether only general instructions were given. Especially in the latter case the linguistic choices were not made by the sender but by the amanuensis. Although our general policy in the *Helsinki Corpus of Early English Correspondence* is to focus on autograph letters, for reasons of social representativeness non-autograph data have been included as supplementary material. The study of the forms of address, which in broad terms represent a selection of conventions, may not suffer so much from lack of authenticity as does research into more unconscious linguistic behaviour. The form chosen, no matter whether by the amanuensis or the sender, should in any case be appropriate for the relationship between the sender and the recipient.

3.3. *Postal services*

Apart from literacy, another important factor affected the volume of letter writing – namely, the facilities for transmitting letters. A considerable change took place in postal communications during the Tudor and Stuart times. The irregular services that had been created to meet the needs of the State, supplemented by private messengers and carriers, developed into a postal monopoly with fixed rates providing service to private citizens and administrative bodies alike (Walker 1938, Crofts 1967).

The organisation of postal services in the Tudor era had to face two major obstacles: poor roads and lack of horses. Only in the South did the roads gradually become so good that wheeled traffic was possible; elsewhere packhorses were used (Crofts 1967: 8-9). In the middle of the sixteenth century road repairs were made the responsibility of local parishes, but improvement was slow (Walker 1938: 64-69, Crofts 1967: 14-15).

The other main problem facing the Tudor postmaster generals, the availability of horses, was solved by establishing local posts, 'standing posts by pay', whose masters were responsible for providing necessary horses and men to ride them. The new system still embraced two ways of transporting official dispatches: the 'through' post and the packet. The former meant that one and the same messenger continued from post to post, only changing horses and receiving a new guide. The packet consisted of letters to be immediately relayed from one postmaster to another, with the date and hour of arrival endorsed on the cover (Crofts 1967: 71-76, Walker 1938: 113-114).

Private letters, also called 'bye letters', were transported along with the packets from the earliest times of postal service (Walker 1938: 110, Brayshay 1991). Their transport could be very slow, because usually they were carried in the same bag as the packet; in other words, the postmaster did not forward them alone but had to wait until an official packet arrived, unless he had so many horses that he could always have one available for the official mail (Crofts 1967: 97). In the first half of the seventeenth century the mail service was finally improved. A regular weekly transport for all letters was organised along six main roads to different parts of the country, the main directions being Scotland in the North and Dover in the South. The new system was a combination of horse transportation on the main roads and footmen carrying the letters further to the countryside (Walker 1938: 157-161, Clay 1984 I: 182). The reform meant that the postboy in a red jacket, with a bag and a horn, became a common sight even in the remotest villages (Walker 1938: 173). At the same time the conveyance of private letters became a state monopoly, though there was no effective control on private entrepreneurs (Crofts 1967: 55).

All through the early modern era, mail secrecy was a special concern for letter writers. Letters were occasionally opened by local postmasters, representatives of the Privy Council, or even rivalling court factions. Especially during the Civil War it was not uncommon for letters to be intercepted (Walker 1938: 59-60; 124-127). The need for special consideration concerning the contents of one's message, of course, affected the style of writing, and real familiarity may only be expected when postal secrecy can be taken for granted. With the stabilisation of society and the increasing volume of correspondence, the public postal services gradually reached a high level of reliability and replaced the use of private transport by servants, carriers, friends, business associates and such like, who had previously been employed by the letter-writing population.

4.   The forms of address 1420-1680

4.1. *Vocabulary*

The core vocabulary constituting the forms of address underwent surprisingly few changes during the two hundred and fifty years this study covers. It is quite natural that the words denoting kinship and family ties were widely used as nouns of address. *Father, mother, son, daughter, brother, sister, husband, wife, nephew, cousin, bedfellow, uncle* and *aunt* formed the stock of headwords in the address noun phrases in family letters. Names, both Christian and surnames, and the word *friend* also occur in address forms. Words denoting social status, such as *lord, lady, master, mistress, sir, madam*, form a further group of nouns that is found all through the period examined here. This group is complemented by professional titles, such as *secretary, doctor, captain*, and *chancellor*. In addition, there are occurrences of address phrases which contain no nominal headword at all, like the formal *trusty and well-beloved* and the deferential *right worshipful*.

Many of the nouns listed above were also used as modifiers of proper names or other nouns. The most frequent noun modifiers found throughout the data are *master, brother* and *cousin*, out of which *master* and *cousin* modify a surname, while *brother* occurs with both a given name and a surname, like in the Cely letters "Brothir Jorge" and in the Oxinden letters "Bro: Oxinden".[2] The use of the terms of near kinship, like *brother, son* and *sister*, as modifiers of surnames persists all through Early Modern English. Although there are forms like "Sister Jackson", by which Samuel Pepys addresses his married sister Pauline, most of the cases appear to refer to relatives by marriage, so that it is not his father but his father-in-law who addresses Sir Thomas Wentworth as "Sonne Wentworth". It is also important to notice that *master* often modifies a professional title, as in *master secretary* and *Mr dean*.

The inventory of adjectives and participles used as honorifics and terms of endearment is somewhat larger than that of nouns, and it is here that changes also took place during our period. Let us begin by listing those words that persist throughout the data: *good, reverent/reverend, honourable, loving* and *kind*, the latter two being rare before 1550. The early collections make ample use of the words *worshipful, trusty* and *(well-)beloved*, and the intensifying adjectives *singular* and *especial*. Similarly, adjectives like *own, old* and *faithful* occur, though rarely in the later collections. The repertoire expanded in the late sixteenth century, when we find the first examples of *noble, worthy* and *honoured*, which gradually gained great popularity. The first instances of the present-day ubiquitous *dear* appear in the fifteenth century, but it increased in popularity much later. *Sweet* often collocated with the noun *heart* and with names.

Two intensifiers, *right* and *most*, are popular all through the data. *Well* and other intensifiers of the participle *beloved*, such as *entirely, dearly* and *heartily*, become rare after 1550, with the structural simplification of the address form. *Very*, first appearing in the first half of the sixteenth century, gains broader currency as time wears on. Finally, it may be mentioned that the possessive pronoun *my/mine* is often added to the forms of address. On the one hand, it appears to have been used to intensify the intimacy and affection prevailing between the correspondents (*OED*, s.v. *dear*) but, on the other, may simply delimit the described reciprocal relationship between two persons, the sender and the recipient. The possessive pronoun was gradually established as an obligatory element in forms such as *my lord*, possibly under French influence (cf. *ma dame, mon sieur*). No examples of the Shakespearean word order *good my lord* occur in our data (e.g. Barber 1976: 233-234).

A comparison of the actual-letter data with the recommendations of letter-writing manuals creates an interesting picture. The earliest printed manual, *The Enemie of Idlenesse* (1568), William Fulwood's translation from French, offers a choice of adjectives and participles that seems relatively conservative. Along with *well-beloved*, it includes *dearly* and *entirely beloved, worshipful, trusty, loving, dear* and *honourable*. Only the last three maintained wide currency during the following generations. Flemming's translation from Latin, *The Panoplie of Epistles* (1576), also contains the receding forms *well-beloved* and *worshipful*, along with *beloved, good, loving, dear, reverend* and *sweet*. It also gives adjectives which do not occur in the letter corpus examined for this study, such as *careful, natural* and *comfortable*. Breton's seventeenth-century *A Post with a Packet of Mad Letters*, with *dear, honest, kind, noble, sweet, good, fair, gentle, worthy* and *honourable*, appears to comply with current usage as evidenced in contemporary letters. The only word missing here is *honoured*, which is frequent in actual data, usually intensified by *much* or *most*.

Although we shall not carry out any quantitative analysis of the data in terms of positive vs. negative politeness, as Brown and Gilman (1989) have done, a general characterisation of the core vocabulary is illuminating. Instead of separating the two face redressing policies, we suggest a continuum on a sliding scale of values. At the negative end of the scale we place the honorific titles indicating a person's social status (Negative strategy (5), *Give deference*; Brown and Levinson 1987: 178-187), while nicknames and terms of endearment are placed at the other end of the scale. This extreme accommodates several of Brown and Levinson's (1987: 102) strategies of positive politeness: (4) *Use in-group identity markers*, (8) *Joke*, and (15) *Give gifts* (sympathy, understanding). On a more general level, superstrategies also provide useful tools for analysis, such as 'Convey that X is admirable, interesting', especially in Brown and Gilman's (1989: 167) formulation: *Notice admirable qualities*. Another superstrategy, 'Convey that Speaker and Hearer are co-operators', with two substrategies ('claim reflexivity' and 'claim reciprocity'), may lead to diverging interpretations. The choice of a relational noun, which indeed kinship terms and some status nouns are, implies the existence of a reciprocal relationship, which may either be one of power, and hence of negative politeness (*father/child, master/servant*), or may express positive reciprocity only (*sweetheart*).

Most address nouns can be placed at various points along the politeness scale. The professional or occupational titles, for instance, are not far from the negative extreme, whereas kinship terms and the noun *friend* are placed close to the positive end. Names may have a position near both poles, since their use may reveal the addressee's non-titled low social status (cf. Table 1, above). On the other hand, names can be in-group identity markers.

It seems to us that the variability of placement needs special emphasis, since the interpretation of the use of a given term depends on the context. Although the use of an occupational title may serve to raise the addressee's social status as part of a deference strategy, it is not necessarily so. Similarly, although we believe that kinship nouns are predominantly positive terms, claiming 'a common ground' shared by the interlocutors (Brown and Levinson 1987: 102-103), at times their unmodified use appears rather to be a neutral choice of form of address.

The characterisation of honorific and endearing adjectives is perhaps more problematic. Besides clear cases, a surprising number of the adjectives discussed above have multiple meanings, of which at least one is connected with social status. *Generous, gentle, honest, honourable, kind, noble, reverent/reverend, worshipful* and *worthy* are all adjectives for which the *Oxford English*

Dictionary gives at least one sense, often characterised as archaic or obsolete, that contains a description of social status, such as 'high-born' (s.v. *generous*), 'well-born' (s.v. *gentle*, s.v. *kind*), 'holding a honourable position' (s.v. *honest*), 'of distinguished rank', (s.v. *honourable*), 'illustrious by rank, title, or birth' (s.v. *noble*), 'worthy of deep respect or reverence on account of (rank), age, or character' (s.v. *reverent/reverend*), 'distinguished in respect of character or rank' (s.v. *worshipful*) and 'holding a prominent place in the community' (s.v. *worthy*). It is especially in the earlier letters that this connection with social status may have been relatively strong. Breuer (1983: 59) goes so far as to argue that the adjectives *noble, honourable* and *gracious* should be understood as concepts of rank as late as Shakespeare's time.[3]

It appears to us, however, that most of the above-mentioned adjectives came to develop parallel new senses by metaphorical extension relatively early on. The process of semantic change was from the representative of a rank, like *noble* for the nobility, to the appreciated qualities of the people of this rank. It seems that these new meanings, positive in their politeness orientation (see above, positive strategy *Notice admirable qualities*, Brown and Gilman 1989: 167), are the predominant ones in the letters, although some ambiguity may have been felt. Those adjectives that did not develop the new meanings, such as *honourable, reverent/reverend* and *worshipful*, were conventionalised in status use, remaining honorifics used in the negative politeness strategy. It is interesting that these three near-synonyms in structurally similar address phrases underwent specification to a particular social rank or use, *right honourable* to the nobility, *right reverend* to the clergy and *right worshipful* to official language, usually with reference to the gentry.

There are problems even with the adjectives *dear* and *good*, which Brown and Gilman (1989: 207-208) characterise as especially positive. According to the *Oxford English Dictionary*, apart from having been a synonym of *noble* and *honourable, dear* had the sense 'esteemed, valued' along with 'loved' (cf. German *teuer* vs. *lieb*). Although the later usage, especially in family letters, is in harmony with the second meaning, some of our early instances (e.g. *Dere in God*, Paston) point rather to the first sense. There are no examples of adjectives developed from the Old English *leof* in our corpus.

The *Oxford English Dictionary* also gives a rank-induced definition for the adjective *good*: 'a term of indefinite commendation; in early use chiefly implying distinguished rank or valour' (s.v. *good*). It became one of the conventional epithets for the nobility (*good lord/lady*, even *goodlordship*, 'patronage') and yeomen (*goodman, goodwife* and *goody;* see Table 1). Our feeling is that among conventional address forms this word may basically be interpreted as positive, but its semantic content is depleted (for terms of endearment, see also Tiusanen 1968).

What has been said above of the adjective *good* is by no means irrelevant to the other lexemes either. The conventionalisation of collocations into forms of address necessarily leads to semantic fading, and the fact that new items are introduced while old ones fall into disuse testifies to a need for expressions with more semantic import. For the purposes of this study, however, it is sufficient to interpret each lexeme as to its principal orientation on the politeness scale instead of exploring the different phases of semantic change.

4.2. *Structure*

Late Medieval English, attested by the Paston, Stonor and Cely letters, favoured complex address forms. As described in section 2.2, early Chancery letters were compiled in accordance with a conventional epistolary pattern, and the earliest private and semi-private letters appear to have followed this model. Nevertheless, we should not forget that simple forms of address, such as *sir, brother* + surname, and *my old friend*, also occur – though rarely – in these letters, possibly reflecting the oral tradition mentioned by Hall (1908: 271-273; see 2.2., above). Hall also mentions that unmodified *sir*, although rare in English before the seventeenth century, was common in Latin and French.

Most of the forms of address used in the late medieval letters have at least one modifier; the majority of them have two or more. The examples in (4) document increasing complexity, from one modifier (4a) to intensified (4b) and coordinated modification (4c) with further intensification (4d, 4e). Examples (4f) and (4g) consist of more than one head noun, possibly reflecting a practice of indicating both the social status and the relationship to the writer (cf. the quotation from de la Serre in section 2.2., above). Example (4h) without a head noun is the standard formula – well preserved throughout the Tudor and Stuart eras – by which the Monarch and the Privy Council addressed their subjects.

(4a) Worshipful Sir
(4b) Right worshipful Sir
(4c) Right honourable and worshipful Sir
(4d) Right worshipful and my right singular good master
(4e) "Right enterly and my moste speciall belovyd husband" (Stonor)
(4f) "Ryght trusty syr and brother" (Cely)
(4g) "Reuerent and worschepffull syr ande my speceall ffrende and gossep" (Cely)
(4h) (Right) trusty and (right) well-beloved

Letters from the first half of the sixteenth century follow the medieval pattern in broad terms. Although simpler forms like *master/brother* + surname and *my lord* begin to be frequent, complex phrases prevail, even in such an intimate relationship as existed between Sir Thomas More and his daughter Margaret Roper (examples 5a and 5b). Example (5c) represents a typical formula in exchanges between noblemen, while (5d) is an example of extreme complexity, written by a clergyman.

(5a) "Myne owne good Doughter"(More)
(5b) "Myne owne most entierlie beloued Father"(More)
(5c) My very good Lord
(5d) "Right honorable, and my owne most trusty & hartely beloved goode Lord in our Saveyor Christe Jhesu" (Clifford)

Collections dating from the late sixteenth century and the beginning of the seventeenth witness an increased use of one unmodified noun alone. *Sir* has become so widespread that in the Wentworth collection (1597-1628) it covers almost half of all address forms. *Madam, cousin, brother, son* and proper names also appear on their own as forms of address. Nominal modifiers, such as *cousin* and *master*, are also favoured, but the most common forms are a combination of one adjective and a noun (examples in 6a). The cases in (6b) indicate that intensified forms still occur. Example (6c) has a co-ordinate modifier, while (6d) illustrates the traditional formula consisting of adjectives without a head noun. Example (6e) represents the most complex usage of this period, a form by which a bishop is addressed. Example (6f), from a letter by Sir Thomas Wentworth to his friend Christopher Wandesford written in 1623, shows that the standard formulae by no means restricted the creativity of individual letter writers.

(6a) Dear Brother; Worthy Sir; Good Sister; My sweet Will
(6b) My much honoured Lady; My most honoured Lord
(6c) "Most louing and gentle ffather" (Gawdy)
(6d) Right honourable and truly honoured
(6e) Right reverend father in God and my very good Lord
(6f) "My diligent and expedite Ambassadore resident with his Maiestie of greate Brittaine" (Wentworth)

The contemporary printed letter-writers testify to similar developments as the actual-letter data. While Fulwood still offers complex forms of address with ample modification, the works by Flemming, Breton, and especially de la Serre provide simpler models. Breton's works also contain copious examples of the kind of imaginative use between friends illustrated in example (6f) above.

The latest collections in the corpus testify to continued simplification. Unmodified *sir* is very popular. If any modification occurs, it usually consists of only one noun or adjective. The most complex forms of this period are intensified or co-ordinate phrases like *"Most ever honoured Sir"* (Pepys) and *"My ever most Honour'd and most Dear Lord"* (Conway).

The scoring system developed by Brown and Gilman (1989: 175) for deference in Shakespearean drama accounts for address forms with at most one adjective. Without arguing for any direct parallelism between address forms in drama and correspondence, let alone spoken language, we may suggest that this pattern simply reveals its temporal context: it was in Shakespeare's time when single-adjective address forms also gained currency in personal letters. Any straightforward quantification of the diachronic process is, however, frustrated by the changing prototypes of address phrases. The most we can say is that the early complex modification structure with several adjectives and intensifiers gave way to unintensified single-adjective phrases and forms with no modification at all.

In politeness terms, the early system offered advantages over the later simple forms: the complex phrases could accommodate both positive and negative strategies simultaneously. *Right worshipful and my good kind brother* contains adjectives that not only express deference to the addressee but also highlight his positive qualities. It was also possible to combine two nominal heads representing different strategies, such as *right reverent sir and my speciall good friend*. The routinisation of simple forms forced the writer to make a choice, although the possibility of using mixed phrases remained in the sense that the modifier and the head could represent opposite strategies, as in *dear* (positive) *sir* (negative). Conventionalisation soon neutralised these semantic mixtures.

4.3. Non-use of address form

Although the focus of this paper is on the development of the form of address in the salutation at the beginning of a letter, it is important to bear in mind that many letters did not contain any direct address form at all. No-naming, as Ervin-Tripp (1972) calls the choice, does not usually mean, however, that no conventional salutation opened the letter (see the examples in 7). No-naming is also a phenomenon which undergoes a change during the period studied. While the early collections, and especially those with a large amount of official correspondence, like Cromwell (see Ellis), More and Wyatt, include a fair number of letters with no form of address, they are practically non-existent in the latest collections.

(7a) I greet you well
(7b) After reverent/humble recommendation
(7c) In as humble wise as I can I recommend your good mastership
(7d) My duty promised unto your Lordship in my humblest manner
(7e) After my humble duty remembered, desiring your blessing
(7f) After my (very) hearty commendations
(7g) "Aftyr moste humbyl comendacions with lycke desyre of your helth and perfygth recouery, pleasyth yowr good lordshyp to vndyrstand" (Fox)
(7h) "Pleasithe yt your right honorable lordship to be advertised, my humble dewty unto the same lowly remembryd" (Clifford)
(7i) It may like your good Grace to understand/to be advertised
(7j) Please it your mastership
(7k) May it please you, Sir
(7l) "The Holy Spirite of God be with you" (More)
(7m) Salutem in Christo
(7n) With my very hearty commendations, Brother, and like thanks

A choice of no-naming opening formulae from different collections is given in examples (7a) to (7n). All examples except for (7l) and (7m) in fact go back to the salutations and notifications of early Chancery letters (Richardson 1984: 213-214; see section 2.2., above). Most of the examples represent either a salutation (7a-7f) or a notification (7i-7k), while some (7g-7h) include both components. It is interesting to observe how the notification formula gradually becomes opaque: (7j) and (7k) do not contain the semantic element of notification at all. Example (7l) illustrates an opening of religious content found in Sir Thomas More's letter to his daughter Margaret. Latin phrases like (7m) can also be found in clerical letters, and many letters also include, before the form of address, an invocation like *Jesus* and *Emanuel* (example (11b), section 6.2.; Hall 1908: 272). In example (7n) the opening salutation is interrupted by a form of address. This usage is especially common in the correspondence of the Johnsons, a sixteenth-century merchant family.

The letter-writing manuals also include no-naming openings, especially when the recommendations are directed to merchants. John Browne (1589) and Angel Day (1586) give model letters without any address forms (see section 6.2., below). The most complex openings illustrated in examples (7c-7e) and (7g-7i) above are not included in these manuals, perhaps because they were becoming less fashionable at the time the manuals were compiled. Finally, it is important to point out that some manuals, especially Breton (1602), contain models for good friends to open their letters with no address form or conventional salutation at all. Occasional examples of this usage can be found in our corpus.

5. The social organisation of address forms

In order to test the findings of Brown and Gilman (1989) and Kopytko (1993), we base our discussion of the social organisation of address forms on the social distance (D) between the correspondents. D is derived from stable social attributes, such as kinship. According to Brown and Levinson (1987: 77), the reflex of social closeness is generally the reciprocal giving and receiving of positive face. As opposed to negative face – the basic claim to territories and freedom of action – positive face represents the desire that our self-image be appreciated and approved of by others. As shown in detail in section 4, the linguistic strategies adopted to cater for the two in address forms are different. Negative face wants are redressed by giving deference, by using titles and honorific adjectives, and positive face wants, for instance, by claiming in-group membership by using terms of endearment.

For the purposes of discussion we divide our data into four broad categories which are distinguished by increasing distance: nuclear family, friends, extended family, and no kinship. Within each category, differences of relative power (P), the degree to which the writer can exercise control – material or otherwise – over the addressee, are systematically related to the use of address forms. Because most of our letters have mixed functions and contents, the third parameter, gravity of imposition (R), will not be systematically assessed in this study.[4] The dozen letter-writing manuals that we have consulted agree on the overriding relevance of power as a factor determining the choice of address form. Distance is also explicitly mentioned by writers like Fulwood, as in (2a), but the manuals do not appear to connect the gravity of imposition with address forms.

5.1. Nuclear family

In Late Medieval and Early Modern England, the term 'family' often referred to the body of persons living in one house or under one head, including children, relatives and servants. Nonetheless, it was the nuclear family of two generations in the modern sense of the term that was the prevailing type of household in England in our period. The husband was the head of the family, and his strongest personal obligations were to his spouse and children. Within the family, the closest bond was between husband and wife. They had shared responsibilities towards their children and servants, who were in turn expected to obey them. It was similarly the scriptural duty of the wife to obey her husband. The performance of familial duties was based on affection and obedience (Houlbrooke 1984: 18-21).

Both obedience and affection are recorded in the forms of address used by family members in their mutual correspondence. Contemporary courtesy books, too, make a difference between "reverend" and "mild and loving" speech (Finkenstaedt 1963: 125). We may start by looking at how address forms are used by siblings, as they could be expected to show relatively smaller contrasts of power than the other family relations. An exception is the eldest brother, who was always more privileged than the younger ones (Stone 1966: 37-38).

5.1.1. *Brothers and sisters*

Brotherhood is usually recognised in address forms. Forms denoting affection commonly occur in letters from fifteenth-century gentlemen to their younger brothers (*right well-beloved brother*), but they are never very elaborate. Both younger and elder brothers of this rank write plain *brother* to each other, elder brothers also *brother* followed by the first name of the recipient (*brother John, brother Edmund*). *Right (entirely) well-beloved brother* is also common in merchants' correspondence in the fifteenth century. In terms of modification, the most positively polite forms in their letters are *right entirely well-beloved and my singular good brother* and *right heartily beloved and mine especiall good brother*.

Among the gentry, younger brothers commonly give deference by resorting to the appropriate honorifics, such as *right worshipful brother*, or even *right reverent and worshipful brother*. The latter respectful form is also incidentally used by a merchant requesting money of his younger brother, whom he elsewhere in the letter calls *brother George*. Affection and respect are occasionally mixed in forms such as *right worshipful sir and my special good brother* (gentleman) and *right reverent and heartily well-beloved brother*, or *reverent sir and brother* (merchant). When the elder brother has been knighted, his brothers commonly show reverence by addressing him as *sir* or *right worshipful sir*. The Paston correspondence also contains some isolated instances of younger brothers addressing their elders as *good lord, your good mastership*, or even as *lansman* or *myn heer* ('sir') – the latter two borrowed from Dutch (Mikkola 1984: 76).

In the course of the sixteenth century the most elaborate forms of showing deference largely give way to *brother*, or *brother* premodified by adjectives of the affectionate kind. *Right worshipful brother* still occurs in a letter written by a gentlewoman to her brother. Towards the end of the century, a young gentleman may variably address his elder brother either as *sweet brother, my good brother* or *my only sweetest and best beloved brother*. On the respectful side, he may use a mixture such as *Mr sheriff and my best beloved brother* or, to a brother who has been knighted, *sir*. *Well-beloved brother* continues in our early sixteenth-century merchant letters, but plain *brother* is perhaps more common, as is no-naming at the beginning of the letter.

In the seventeenth century, further simplification takes place. Plain *brother* is common among both the higher and the lower ranks. The old use of *brother* followed by first name continues to occur with reference to a younger brother (*brother Richard, brother Nath*). Simple positive forms are generalised: *(my) good brother, dear(est) brother*, and *loving brother*. The most complex affectionate forms found in our data are *most loving brother, my most dear brother*, and *my dear and loving brother*. There is an occasional deferential instance of *my most honoured brother* from a younger brother. *Sir* and *my lord* continue to be used by younger brothers writing to their titled elders; even *honoured sir* is once used by a sister, who nevertheless usually opts for *good brother*.

Although our evidence here is scanty, it appears that sisters never receive as many deferential forms of address as their brothers. In the early sixteenth century sisters may address each other as *sister* followed by their married name (*sister Roper*). Some hundred years later we find the gentry addressing their sisters as *good sister, (my) dear sister* or *dearest sister*. At the end of our period both plain *sister* and the older form, *sister* plus married name (*sister Jackson*), are found in brothers' letters. A gentleman shows his respect by writing *most honoured sister*. He may also convey his affection by calling his sister *dearest dear*.

5.1.2. *Husband and wife*

Although ideally the relationship between husband and wife was founded on mutual love and respect, it was not an equal one. Nor was it, however, as predictable as one might expect (Wrightson 1982: 92). Our fifteenth-century data, largely representing the usage of the gentry, show a great deal of variation in the use of address forms. In the early letters no-naming commonly occurs in husbands' letters, but it is also found in wives'. When an address form appears, a gentleman does not make use of the relational term *wife*, but refers to his wife by her first name, either together with her title (*mistress Margery*) or with an adjective showing positive politeness (*my own good Jane*). The two could also be combined to yield a more deferential form (John Paston I from the Fleet to Margaret Paston: *mine own dear sovereign lady*).

A typical phrase used by gentlewomen to address their husbands in the fifteenth century is the formulaic *right worshipful husband*. Deferential terms vary from the simple status indicator *sir* to elaborate formulations, including *right reverent and worshipful husband* and the 'mixed' form *right reverent and worshipful and entirely best beloved cousin*. The term *cousin* appears in the superscriptions of husbands' letters to their wives, but in address forms it is only used by some gentlewomen in our fifteenth-century data. It must have persisted longer in speech, however, as its use by wives is condemned by W. Gouge in his treatise *Of Domestical Duties* (1626) as inappropriatly suggesting equality between husband and wife or the husband's inferiority (Finkenstaedt 1963: 125).

There is next to no evidence of the address forms used by lower-ranking women in our fifteenth-century letters. Our meagre data suggest that a wealthy merchant's wife could use a highly deferential form to address her husband and elevate him to the gentry by referring to him as *right reverend and worshipful sir*.

The positive terms used by gentlewomen around this time vary a great deal in complexity from the rare *dear husband* to *my best beloved husband* and *right entirely and my most speciall beloved husband*. The term *cousin* also occurs in these formulations. Affection and respect can be mixed in one and the same person's letters, as in those from Margery Paston to her husband John Paston III. John was addressed by the form in (8a) when they were engaged, and by both (8b) and (8c) some years after their marriage (Paston 662-665).

(8a) "Ryght reuerent and wurschypfull and my ryght welebeloued Voluntyne"
(8b) "Right reuerent and worshipfull ser"
(8c) "Myne owyn swete hert"

As we move on to the sixteenth century, the data become socially more varied and numerous. Some aristocratic letters suggest a rare degree of equality between husband and wife in terms of endearment. The favourite form of address used by Lord and Lady Lisle in the 1530s is the reciprocal *mine own sweetheart*. Arthur Lisle also addresses Honor Lisle as *my very heart root and entirely beloved bedfellow* as well as *gentle bedfellow and my very heart root*. Occasionally we find the simple *sweetheart* or *entirely beloved wife*. Honor Lisle's terms include *mine own sweet heart root* and *good mine own*, as well as *mine own sweet good lord*. Another common term of endearment used by noblewomen and gentlewomen is *dear heart*.

At the same time, gentlewomen continue to address their husbands formally according to their social status as plain *sir* or *right worshipful sir*. The earlier practice of gentlemen referring to their wives by *mistress* and first name similarly continues in the sixteenth century (*mistress Alice*). This also occurs in our merchants' letters (*mistress Sabine*), on a par with *well-beloved wife*. The corresponding term *well-beloved husband* may be returned by the wife, or she may show more affection by addressing her husband as *entirely and well beloved bedfellow*. Sabine Johnson, the wife in question, however, objects to her husband's use of *mistress Sabine*, and writes in reply in 1545:

(9) In moest loving wise, welbeloved husbond (master I shold saye, because yet doyth becom me baetter to call yu master than you to call me mystres), you letter of 15 of this present I have receyved this day ... (Johnson 515)

Mistress may be considered too high a title by Sabine, or her repartee may be part of the mutual teasing of the couple. John Johnson opens one of his letters by greeting his wife as follows:

(10) With all my herte, good wyf (but sometyme a shrowe), I comend me unto you, being glad to hear of your helthe with our ij jewellis, the Lord contynew it and send us a mery meating. (Johnson 250)

Status terms continue to be employed to some extent by the higher social ranks in the seventeenth century. A plain gentleman may be addressed as *(good) master* plus surname (*Mr Thynne*). Appropriate status terms are also used by wives writing to their titled husbands. They may appear by themselves (*sir, my lord*) or be combined with *dear* (*my dear(est) sir, my dear lord*). The corresponding *(dear) madam* occurs only rarely in our sources.

Seventeenth-century letter-writing manuals and courtesy books suggest that the terms *husband* and *wife* continued as forms of address. Our evidence for them is scanty. For what it is worth, the usage of John Wilmot, the Earl of Rochester, ranges from the respectful *madam* to the simple or premodifed *wife* (*wife, dear wife*). He also has one apologetic instance of *my most neglected wife*.

In the social ranks that we have evidence for, the address forms used by married couples were simplified in favour of positive terms earlier than those used by siblings or, for that matter, children writing to their parents. The common terms used reciprocally in the seventeenth century vary from the old *dear(est) heart* to the superlative *my dearest dear*. The most common forms in our data are variants of *(my) dear(est)*. Husbands also employ other simple terms such as *endeared, sweetheart,* and *sweet love*. This course of development points to extensive generalisation of the positive politeness strategy in marital correspondence.

As suggested above in section 4.1., first names and nicknames may serve as in-group identity markers in address forms. An early instance of unadorned familiarity of this kind is Thomas Cromwell addressing his wife by her first name alone (*Elizabeth*). We have a number of cases involving either plain nicknames or nicknames premodified by terms of endearment from the latter part of our period. Writing to his wife at the beginning of the seventeenth century, Captain Thomas Stockwell addresses her as *good Hester*. John Hoskyns calls his wife Benedicta *Ben* and *my best deserving Ben*. John Holles addresses his wife Ann as *Nan*, and John Thynne his wife Joan as (*my*) *good Pug*. Joan Thynne remains more deferential, and replies (*good*) *Mr Thynne* or *my good husband*, but her young daughter-in-law Maria calls her husband Thomas *my fair Thomken, mine own sweet Thomken* and, with erotic undertones, *my best beloved Thomken and my best little Sirrah*. Thomas Thynne replies *good sweet*. A later seventeenth-century instance of the use of nicknames in marital correspondence is Captain Richard Haddock's *my dear Betty*. Insofar as we can draw some conclusions from this evidence on first-name usage in the seventeenth century, it seems to be restricted to the ranks below the nobility.

5.1.3. *Parents and children*

Kinship was usually recognised in the address forms selected by parents and children throughout our period. The politeness strategies are largely predictable: parents receive terms of negative politeness while children are addressed by relatively simple positive or neutral terms. No-naming is also common in letters from parents in the fifteenth and sixteenth centuries. In our fifteenth-century data the most elaborate form received by a gentleman from his mother is *right well-beloved son,* and plain *son* is the simplest. *Son* and full name also occurs in a father's letter from the turn of the century (*son Robert Plumpton*).

With the exception of one occurrence of plain *mother* in a son's letter, fifteenth-century gentlemen and gentlewomen address their mothers with respect (*right worshipful mother, right reverend and worshipful mother*), or with a mixture of respect and affection (*right worshipful and my most entirely beloved mother*; *right worshipful and my right tender mother*; *right worshipful and my most kind and tender mother*). Both among the gentry and high-ranking merchants, fathers only receive varying degrees of respect, most commonly *right reverend and worshipful father*. The status term *sir* appears in *right worshipful sir*.

Two trends characterise the sixteenth and seventeenth centuries: a simplification of negative politeness terms and an increased use of positive ones. The early sixteenth-century data continue the use of *right worshipful sir, right worshipful father* and *right worshipful mother*. From the late sixteenth century onwards, we find gentlemen's sons commonly addressing their fathers as plain *sir*. *Honoured sir* and *honoured father* both appear in letters by (young) sons and daughters in the seventeenth century, and a teenage daughter also calls her noble father *my lord*. At the same time the general term *madam* is extended to mothers, as is the 'mixed' form *dear madam*. A young boy may write to his mother *most honoured and dear mother*.

Our first evidence for the mutual use of positive politeness terms comes from the correspondence of Sir Thomas More and his daughter Margaret Roper in the 1530s. Margaret writes *my own good father* or *mine own most entirely beloved father*, and her imprisoned father returns *my own good daughter* or *my dearly beloved daughter*. Gregory Cromwell also calls his father *most dear father*. The positive terms used for parents in the late sixteenth century include *my (very) good mother, my very good father* and *my loving and gentle father*.

Our seventeenth-century data suggest an increased use of positive terms, especially of mothers. The collocations *dear mother* and *my dear mother* occur, but they are perhaps not so common as the more adorned forms, *most dear mother, most dear and loving mother, loving and kind mother*. Fathers may be addressed as *kind* or *dear father*. The unadorned *son* is very common in letters from both fathers and mothers, but sons are also referred to as *good son, dear son* and *my good child*, daughters similarly as *my dear child*. Some more complex positive forms are occasionally found in parents' letters (*my most dear and beloved son; my dear and worthy daughter; my dearest dear*).

Parents may also address their children nonreciprocally by their first names. We find instances of this strategy from the first half of the sixteenth century onwards (Wyatt to his son: *Thomas*; Rochester to his: *Charles*; Holles to his daughter: *Arbella*). First names often combine with kinship terms. A son is referred to by *son* plus his first name (*son Daniel*), and a daughter by *daughter* and her first name (*daughter Hester*). A daughter may have *daughter* followed by her married name (*daughter Oxinden*).

Nicknames, a more positive strategy, are used among the gentry from the late sixteenth century onwards. Thus, John Holles calls his sons John and Denzell *Jack* and *Den*, respectively. Katherine Oxinden calls her son *Harry*, and Katherine Lady Zouch hers *Jake*. John Hoskyns addresses his married daughter Elizabeth as *Bess* or *daughter Bess*. An accumulation of positive politeness strategies is shown by Lady Katherine Paston's habit of calling her teenage son *my good Will* or *my sweet Will.* The modern stereotype appears in Elizabeth Smith's *dear Tom.*

5.2. Friends

Apart from members of the nuclear family, it is between close friends that we find the least social distance (D) and its component affect (personal liking) at its greatest. We shall next examine the address forms used in letters between some persons who, either according to the editor or to our own observations, appear to have been close personal friends.

In the late fifteenth century John Dalton, a young wool merchant, addresses his friend George Cely with different forms, including the Christian name *(brother George)*, positively modified phrases, *(right entirely and) well-beloved brother,* and respectful forms like *right worshipful brother* and *right worshipful sir and brother.* The use of *brother* probably corresponds to the usage within the same guild or company and can hence only be interpreted as a conventionalised in-group term and not as a particular indicator of intimacy.

In the seventeenth century we find first names, nicknames and phrases with *friend* in correspondence between gentlemen and clergymen *(honest/loving Harry, honest/good John, John, loving friend, my dear and true friend).* A friend is greeted with *Ah Harry, Harry* in distress, and intimate and occasionally jocular forms like *dear twin, Sir my friend* and *heroic sir* also occur. It is obvious that socially equal friends preferred terms of positive politeness, although the neutral and routinised *sir* was also an acceptable variant.

The Wentworth collection includes letters exchanged between two friends, Sir Thomas Wentworth and George Wandesford, esquire. This relation is of special interest owing to the social imbalance between the persons. Sir Thomas, baronet, addresses his friend, along with the ordinary *sir*, as *gentle Mr Wandesford* and the jocular *my ambassador resident* (see also example (6f) in section 4.2., above). He is called *sir* by Wandesford up to 1628, when Wentworth is made baron and viscount. After this date the form used is the socially correct *my lord.* A similar change of address form is found in the Hatton collection, where Sir Charles Lyttleton, having saluted his childhood friend Charles Hatton with *dearest Kytt,* uses *my lord* after the elevation of the latter to the nobility (for further cases, see Replogle 1973 [1987]: 106-107).

On the other hand, differences in social rank did not always hinder the use of intimate forms between friends. An outstanding example is the correspondence between James I and the Duke of Buckingham. It may not be surprising that the King, the social superior, uses a nickname, *(My sweete) Steenie,* to address Buckingham, but the latter's *Dere Dad, Gossope and*

Steward to the King is astonishing in its familiarity (see further, Ellis III: 146, 158).

At the end of the seventeenth century we have the example of two friends of different sex and rank. In their prolific correspondence Doctor Henry More invariably addresses Lady Conway as *madam*, while her variants for him consist of *sir, dear sir* and *dear doctor* (for friendship between two women, see section 6.1., below).

Letter-writing manuals offer a great deal of advice on how to write letters to friends. Fulwood's *dear and well-beloved friend* is succeeded by Breton's selection of simpler forms, such as *kindest of friends, honest/dear* + first name, even *cousin*. More complex jocular forms also occur along with plain *sir*. The latter is the only choice given by de la Serre.

5.3. Non-nuclear family

This section covers address forms employed in letters exchanged between relatives outside the nuclear family, viz. uncles, aunts, nephews, nieces, cousins, in-laws and other relatives by marriage or otherwise further removed. The few instances of letters to grandparents are illustrated in section 6.1. The importance of extended kinship appears to have varied a great deal, both individually and socially. The letters reveal the significance of extended kinship in the establishment of personal contacts with influential people or in questions of patronage and help in different kinds of need. According to Wrightson (1982: 44-51), kinship outside the nuclear family was of less significance for people lower down the social scale and outside the special conditions of gentlemanly, professional and mercantile life (see, however, Cressy 1986). Our informants, stemming from the ranks for which kin mattered, to a large extent indicate kinship relations in the address forms, especially among social equals.

The closest members of non-nuclear families – uncles, aunts, nephews and nieces – were usually addressed by the term designating the relationship, such as *right worshipful and my heartily beloved nephew* and *most trusty and well-beloved niece* in the fifteenth-century Paston letters. Later examples, much simpler in structure, include *nephew* + surname (*nephew Oxinden*), *uncle* + Christian name (*uncle Edward*), unmodified *uncle, (most) loving uncle, dear aunt* and *my (very) good aunt*. The husbands and wives of relatives could use the same forms as their spouses. In the earliest collections kinship terms do not necessarily correspond to their present-day equivalents, so that an uncle may address his nephew as *cousin* (cf. Houlbrooke 1984: 40). *Sir* appears as an address form from nephew to uncle and vice versa at the turn of the seventeenth century, and at the same time an uncle's wife is called *madam* by her nephew.

Although examples are scanty, social inequality seems to override this pattern, since Henry Oxinden (gentleman) addresses his uncle (knight) as *noble sir*, but is referred to as *nephew Oxinden* and *good nephew* by him.

As regards in-laws, the main principle was to adopt the kinship term used by the marriage partner, so that a father-in-law called his son-in-law *son*, a daughter-in-law her mother-in-law *mother*, brothers-in-law called each other *brother*, sisters-in-law addressed each other as *sister*, and so on. This practice was extended even further, for instance, to the in-laws of one's children. Most of our examples come from letters exchanged between sibling families, with brothers- and sisters-in-law involved.

Our data from the fifteenth century contain deferential elements, like *right worshipful son* from a father-in-law, and combine them with terms of affection *ryght worshipful and my good kind brother*. In the letters from the turn of the seventeenth century the terms are chosen from the vocabulary of positive politeness, such as *son* + surname, *good brother, good sister, my dear sister, my beloved good sister* and even the northern in-group *maugh*. It is noteworthy that both his aristocratic fathers-in-law address Thomas Wentworth as *son Wentworth*, even after he was created viscount. Only after the death of Wentworth's second wife Arbella, which his father-in-law, Lord Clare, blames on him, is the form of address changed to the more formal *my lord*. Late seventeenth-century correspondents use the forms *daughter, (loving) brother, my dear brother, dear sister* and *brother* + nickname, as with the nuclear family. As the examples show, the data are scanty as regards letters to parents-in-law.

As usual during our period studied, the addressee's social superiority takes precedence over kinship, manifesting itself in the selection of status nouns. Consequently, in the fifteenth century a wealthy merchant addresses his mother-in-law, whose husband was a knight, as *right honourable and my (right) singular good lady*. Similarly, in the early seventeenth century a gentleman salutes his knighted brother-in-law with *(noble) sir*, while gentlemen brothers-in-law are called *(good) brother*. The difference between the nobility and gentry is coded in all cases, so that a baronet opens his letters to his nobleman brother-in-law *my (much) honoured lord*, but receives *my dear brother*. Continuity of this practice is witnessed at the end of the century, when a knight addresses his aristocratic brother-in-law with *my dear lord* and even with the complex *my ever most honoured and dear lord* and is reciprocated with *my dearest brother*.

The next group of kin to be discussed, cousins, is more vague. As regards families with well-established pedigrees, socially equal first cousins in the early sixteenth century addressed each other as *cousin, cousin* + surname (*cousin Pettit*), or *loving/honoured/good/worthy cousin*, sometimes intensified by *most* (especially with *honoured, worthy*). A female cousin is saluted by her male cousin as *my most dear cousin* and also as *honoured cousin*. At end of the century *dear cousin* also appears between male persons. In the same way as earlier, the addressee's higher social rank is indicated in the form of address: a mere gentleman addresses a knight or baronet as *sir*, and a baronet uses *my much honoured lord* with a nobleman. Both are called *(my) good cousin* by their social superior.

As mentioned above, the noun *cousin* is by no means limited to usage among first cousins. Instances of this term, indicating kinship of a most general kind, abound in the medieval collections of Paston and Stonor letters. Social equals use this word when there is some kind of distant relationship, not only lateral but also any relationship contracted by marriage, e.g. *right worshipful and my tender/heartily well-beloved cousin* is used between gentlemen and knights. This convention holds throughout the data, later with simple phrases, like *cousin, good/honoured cousin* and *cousin* + surname. The word *kinsman* is occasionally also used to indicate remote kinship. As with in-laws, social inequality intervenes, and the noun *cousin* is not used as an address form to a social superior. This practice is well documented in the fifteenth-century Cely letters, where a kinsman, William Cely, works as a factor for his relatives. His address forms are very respectful and there are no instances of reference to the kin relation.

Finally, it may be worth mentioning that especially in the early letters one finds nouns denoting close kinship, such as *right worshipful brother* and *right trusty and heartily well-beloved son,* used as address forms with no obvious motivation except benevolent patronage or spiritual kinship (Houlbrooke 1984: 39). They may reflect in-group usage, or may be based on relations which the editors have not been able to trace.

5.4. *Non-kin relations*

Our previous discussion has already shown the sensitivity of the address forms to social stratification, even in relations of kinship and friendship. This section will provide an overview of the forms of address used in the correspondence of people who are not connected by any kinship ties or close friendship. We shall first discuss social equals at different levels, then look at the address forms employed by social inferiors upwards, and finally by superiors downwards. Although we will not be dealing with it directly, one should bear in mind that the no-naming strategy was widespread in official correspondence.

5.4.1. *Social equals*

Let us begin with the topmost stratum, the nobility. Unfortunately, the limits of the data prevent any differentiation between the different titles (see Table 1). Male aristocrats mostly used the noun *lord* (*my lord, my (very) good lord*) among themselves. In some cases *right honourable* is used alone or combined with a phrase headed by *lord*, like *right honourable and my singular good lord* in the early sixteenth century. This practice corresponds to the instructions given by the contemporary letter-writing manuals.

As Table 1 also shows, bishops enjoyed a status comparable to that of the nobility. The few occurrences in the data of mutual address forms by bishops would indicate that, both among themselves and in addressing members of the nobility, they employed the same phrases as noblemen (*my very/singular good lord*) along with *right honourable*. Examples of women in the highest rank are scanty, but Lady Lisle is referred to as *madam* by a bishop.

In the few Paston-letter examples of the upper layer of the gentry, knights addressed each other as *right worshipful sir/cousin*. The noun *cousin* may have in-group connotations here. In the seventeenth century knights, and from 1611 onwards baronets, saluted each other mostly with plain *sir*, or *sir* modified by either *worthy* or *noble*. Again, examples of women are few, but *madam* appears (see section 6.2., below).

The largest number of our informants, ordinary gentlemen, salute each other with modified *sir, master*, or a surname. The complex phrases found in the medieval collections often combine the first two nouns, as in *right worthy and worshipful sir and mine right good master*. Occasionally, *sir* also occurs alone, even in the earliest data, though complex forms are more frequent. Another important strategy is to combine the title *master* with a surname (*master Ros, master Paston*). This latter pattern is on the increase in the data in the early sixteenth century (*master Wilson, Mr Boner*). As mentioned above (section 4), *master* was also used as the premodifier of professional titles held by gentlemen, as in *master secretary* and *master vice-chancellor*. In the sixteenth century a further strategy was possible, i.e. the use of *right worshipful*, which was also recommended by Fulwood.

Both main patterns, unmodified or modified *sir* on the one hand, and *master* + surname on the other, were current in the seventeenth century. In the Oxinden collections we find both *(worthy/good) sir* and *(worthy) Mr Oxinden*. By the latter half of the century, however, the use of *sir*, without modification or modified by a single adjective (*worthy, noble, honourable, honoured*, and *dear*), underwent an expansion at the expense of the *Mr* + surname model. There is little evidence about the kind of address forms that were used in the case of several recipients. In the seventeenth century *gentlemen* was chosen by a baronet as an address form to two knights, and also by a gentleman to a mayor and aldermen, thus interestingly revealing the gentlemanly status of high city administrators. There are examples of gentlewomen being addressed as *madam* and *mistress* + surname in the seventeenth century. Finally, we may point out that the adjective *reverend* occurs in letters written to members of the clergy, but among ordinary clergymen we mostly find the same forms as between gentlemen, viz. *(good) sir* and *Mr* + surname (*Mr Cosin*).

It is unfortunate that our corpus contains only a small number of letters exchanged by non-kin social equals below the gentry. Nevertheless, we have enough data for a glimpse of merchants' language. The great variety of address nouns is conspicuous in the Cely collection. Apart from *sir*, medieval wool-merchants greeted each other with nouns like *brother, friend, cousin,* and even *lover*. It is worth noticing that the noun *master* does not occur among equals. It has already been mentioned that *brother* was a conventional address form among members of guilds and companies, or even among people of the same profession (*OED*, s.v. *brother*, 4).

By way of contrast we may present merchants' language from the seventeenth century (Lowther and Marescoe-David). At the beginning of the century we find forms like *kind/loving partner, Mr* + surname and *honest* + full name. At the end of the century, not unexpectedly, simple *sir* and *madam* were the typical forms of address, but modified forms also occur, such as *worthy/esteemed/honoured sir* and, of more positive orientation, *worthy/loving/esteemed friend*. Although the evidence is scanty, there seems to be some continuation in the use of the noun *friend* among merchants. The temporal gap of missing data can be partly filled with information gathered from letter-writing manuals. Fulwood (1568) suggests that merchants should open their letters with *trusty and well-beloved* and *right trusty*.

5.4.2. *Social inferiors upwards*

Although no systematic study of royal letters has been carried out for this study, the sporadic data included in the present corpus indicate that monarchs were approached with different no-naming conventions. The literature analysed in this study contains occasional address forms, such as *sir(e)* in the late Middle Ages and late seventeenth century, and *Most mercyfull king and most gracyous souerayng lorde* in Thomas Cromwell's plea for mercy in 1540. In his manual of 1576, Flemming quotes actual letters as models and illustrates address forms with Erasmus' *Moste high and mightie King* (to Henry VIII) and Roger Ascham's *Most excellent Ladie Elizabeth* (to Queen Elizabeth).

Noblemen almost invariably received an address form headed by the noun *lord* throughout the data. Faithful to the convention of the time, the fifteenth-century instances are complex, combining positive politeness with adjectives expressing deference, e.g. *right worshipful and my right good lord; right high and mighty prince; my right good and gracious lord*. The earliest examples of the simple *my lord* date from the first half of the sixteenth century, but in contemporary practice, the more complex *my very/singular good lord* and especially *right honourable and my singular good lord* were common. *Right honourable* alone, an exception to the *lord* pattern, is occasionally found from the early sixteenth century onwards. About a hundred years later noblemen were addressed with *my most/much honoured lord,* and occasionally with *right honourable (and truly honoured)*. At the end of the century the simple *my lord* gained general currency.

Noblewomen often received a form of address with *lady,* as in the early sixteenth-century *right honourable and my singular good lady*. Later forms include *my much/most honoured lady*. On the other hand, *madam* was a valid alternative from the sixteenth century onwards, and its use became more widespread as time wore on.

Bishops were usually addressed by phrases headed with *lord*. The modifier *reverend* came to be attached to clerical titles, so that in the seventeenth century we find a baronet saluting an archbishop with *most reverend father in God, and my very good lord,* while a bishop receives the same phrase with the intensifier *right* instead of *most*. It is noteworthy though that, along with *my lord,* a bishop also receives *right reverend sir,* hence proving that the use of *lord* was not the only alternative. We may also include in this social stratum people in high administrative offices, such as Lord Keeper and Lord Treasurer, who were also addressed by their inferiors with a phrase headed *lord*.

Moving on to the gentry proper, at the end of the fifteenth century knights usually received from their social inferiors an address form that included either the noun *sir* or *master,* or both, e.g. *right worshipful sir; right honourable and singular good master;* and *right worshipful sir and my good master*. A few examples of *master* + surname (*master Stonor*) also survive. It appears that in a clear servant/master relation the employer is called *master* more often than *sir*. In the early seventeenth century, letters to knights and baronets usually opened with a *sir* phrase, either unmodified or modified with *noble, good, honourable* and *worthy*. The form *noble cousin* in the Oxinden letters forms an interesting exception to this pattern. Instances of adjectival phrases like *right worshipful* also occur, especially in official contexts. *Dear/honoured/noble sir* comprise the alternatives in the latest letters in the corpus. Persons holding influential administrative offices were always addressed with reverent forms. Thomas Cromwell, Henry VIII's principal secretary, for instance, received *most singular good master* and *right worshipful* from knights in the King's service.

Wives and widows of knights received address forms headed by *lady* or *madam* throughout the centuries covered by this study. In the late Middle Ages the wife of Sir William Stonor was addressed as *right reverent and worshipful lady* by an apprentice and as *right worshipful and reverent madam* by a merchant. The first half of the seventeenth century witnesses forms like *madam*, *my very good lady*, and *noble lady*. At the end of the century letters to spouses of knights opened with *(honoured) madam* and *ever honoured*.

As described in section 3.1., the borderline between gentry and non-gentry was by no means self-evident and diachronically stable. We shall mainly discuss letters received by gentlemen from people who were in a service relation to a gentleman master, including clerks, bailiffs, stewards, chaplains, tenants, lawyers and doctors, although they themselves may have been entitled to the title of gentleman (for the status of servants, see e.g. Wildeblood and Brinson 1965: 93-110). We shall also include here lower clergy and gentlemen in lower administrative positions writing to their gentleman superiors. It is obvious that merchants selling their produce to gentlemen also belong to this group. The picture that emerges here is not very different from the one given above of knights. The early forms of address contained *master* or *sir* or both, e.g. *right reverend and worshipful sir* (written by a chaplain), *right worshipful master* (lawyer) and *right worshipful sir and my good master* (clerk) in the early collections. Unmodified *sir* also occurs. In the sixteenth century we find forms like *right worshipful sir* (merchant) and *my master* (servant). In the seventeenth century the unmodified *sir* increses in use, but forms like *worthy sir* and *(most) honoured sir* (servants, merchants) also occur. Again, evidence about salutations given to women is scanty. The early usage seems to involve the noun *mistress* (e.g. *right worshipful and myn right honourable and good mistress* from a servant). Later usage preferred *madam*.

In the merchant community, factors and agents used deferential language towards their masters and principals. Apart from no-naming, the manuals recommend forms like *right worshipful sir* (Fulwood) and plain *sir* (Breton) for these relationships. In actual letters an early form is *right worshipful sir and my good master*. In the sixteenth century a younger merchant addresses his elder companion with a high administrative position as *right worshipful*. The end of the seventeenth century witnesses the surprisingly complex form *kind sir and my (very) loving friend* from a representative to his principal.

5.4.3. Social superiors downwards

From the medieval days to the end of the seventeenth century the standard form of address used by the kings and queens of England in their official dispatches was *(right) trusty and (right) well-beloved*. The word *cousin* was added as a headword in the letters sent to the highest levels of the nobility (*OED*, s.v. *cousin*). On the other hand, in private writing the royal family enjoyed a freedom that surpassed all others', and it was widely utilised by James I's daughter Elizabeth, later Queen of Bohemia. Courtiers and family friends could receive from her mocking phrases like "*Honest fatte Thom*" (Sir Thomas Rowe) and "*Thou ugly, filthy camel's face*" (the Earl of Carlisle).

Noblemen and bishops address their inferiors with a similar formula of positive orientation (*(right) trusty and (right) well-beloved*) as the monarchs, either without a noun or with *friend, cousin, servant* or *sir* as head of the phrase. Occasional instances of the full name (*John Paston*) and of the surname modified by *cousin* also occur. In the first half of the sixteenth century a nobleman addresses knights and gentlemen with *right honourable (sir)* or *master* + surname. The latter pattern is the choice that holders of high church offices seemed to prefer. A century later, the data contain instances where a gentleman is addressed by a nobleman as *Mr* + surname, while a baronet is called *(noble) sir, sir* + full name and *noble friend* by his superiors. The few occurrences of female members of the nobility addressing their social inferiors testify to similar conventions as in men's letters.

In the fifteenth century knights open their letters to gentlemen and merchants with phrases including *cousin, right worshipful cousin* or *cousin* + surname. Holders of higher administrative offices often greet those with a lower position with either *Mr* + surname or a phrase with *sir*. There are instances of knights and ordinary gentlemen addressing their inferiors, for instance bailiffs, tenants or even merchants, with the noun *friend* (*my old friend*) or the recipient's full or surname (*Richard Croft; Aubrey*). One hundred years later, the bailiff Captain Thomas Stockwell is addressed by his master Sir Oliver Lambert with a great variety of forms, mostly indicating positive politeness: "*Tom Stockwell*", "*frind Stockwell*", "*Ca: Stocwell*", "*Tom*" and "*Honest Tom*". It is noteworthy that Lambert's wife Elizabeth also uses similar forms: "*Friend Stockwell*", "*onist Stockewall*", "*Stockewall*" and "*Tom Stockwell*". Around the same time, we find Nathaniel Bacon addressing a craftsman as *goodman*. In the first half of the seventeenth century a baronet addresses his bailiff by his full name, *Richard Marris*, but a gentleman salutes his tailor with *Mr* + surname (*Mr Hadnam*), which shows that the status noun *master* had come to embrace craftsmen as well. The use of the Christian name as an address form is rare, but at times servants are addressed in this way, for instance in the Cely collection in the fifteenth century and in the Holles letters in the seventeenth century. Among merchants, the address forms given to inferiors include *brother (brother George Cely), cousin (cousin Johnson)* and name *(honest Archie Millan)*.

6. Two case studies on individual variation

Some of our generalisations in the previous section can be illustrated by looking at the range of address forms received by single individuals. For this purpose we have selected two people, contemporaries of Shakespeare, with a large number of connections both within the family and outside of it. This kind of material provides essential information on the multiple roles occupied by individuals in Early Modern English society.

6.1. *Lady Joan Barrington*

Lady Joan Barrington (d. 1641) was seventy years of age when her husband, Sir Francis, died in 1628. Most of the letters in *Barrington Family Letters 1628-1632* are addressed to her.[5] As Arthur Searle (1983: vii), the editor of the collection, points out, the quantity of these letters, as well as their content, indicate that Lady Joan Barrington was the focal point of the extended family, the dowager and respected matriarch on a recognisable early seventeenth-century pattern. The Barringtons were old Essex gentry with a prominent role in county politics and a long tradition in Puritanism.

As elsewhere, one would expect the form of address given to Lady Joan to be selected on the basis of relative rank, relative age and personal relationship. Lady Joan's correspondents range from the nobility, the Earls of Bedford and Warwick, down to her own household steward and tenants. There are also a number of clergymen, many of them directly patronised by the family, but the majority consists of Lady Joan's extended family. As she represents the oldest surviving generation, most of her correspondents are younger than her and thus unequal in terms of age. The youngest generation is that of her grandchildren, nephews and nieces.

There is perhaps less variation in the forms by which Lady Joan is addressed than might be expected, and the immediate family cannot always be distinguished from outsiders. The most common term of address applied to her by kin and non-kin alike is *madam*. Simple *madam* begins the letter by Francis Russell, the fourth Earl of Bedford, as well as that by Tobias Bridge, Lady Joan's steward. It is used exclusively by her two elder sons, her daughter-in-law (the wife of her eldest son Thomas), her eldest son-in-law, and certain clergymen.

It is noteworthy that none of Lady Barrington's daughters calls her *madam*, except the eldest once. More positively polite terms are regularly used instead. Lady Joan is *most dear mother* to her two elder daughters, and *dear mother* to her youngest. Her impecunious youngest son also calls her *dear mother* except in his last three letters, where he adopts the use of *madam* (not, as far as one can judge, because of any serious imposition, though). Lady Joan's two brothers call her *good sister* and *dearest sister*.

The mixed form *good madam* is preferred by two of Lady Joan's four sons-in-law. The husband of her youngest daughter uses *madam* or *dear mother*. *Good madam* further occurs in letters by her niece and two nephews by marriage; the third nephew calls her *dear aunt*. Outside the family, *good madam* is the term favoured by the Earl of Warwick, some clergymen enjoying the Barringtons' patronage, and one of Lady Joan's tenants.

Increasing elaboration is shown by the mixed forms *good madam and loving sister* used by Lady Joan's sister-in-law and by *my honourable and most worthy lady sister* written by her brother-in-law. Mostly negative politeness is conveyed by the variety of forms ranging from *much* or *most honoured madam* to *most dear and much honoured madam* employed by Oliver St. John, the husband of her granddaughter Joan (who herself writes to Lady Joan simply *dear grandmother*). One of the few surviving letters by Lady Barrington is her reply to Oliver St. John, whom she addresses as *good son*. Lady Joan's goddaughter calls her either *dear lady mother* or *much honoured lady mother*.

Negative politeness terms vary most in the letters written by the clergy. Besides the simple and premodified *madam (good/worthy/much honoured madam)*, which are common, the older respectful forms *honourable and right worshipful/worthy* occur in one vicar's letters of duty. A much more frequent term is *lady* premodified by honorific adjectives (*honourable/noble/worthy lady; noble and worthy lady; my honourable good lady*). Premodified forms of *lady* (*honourable/honoured/noble lady*) are also used by male members of the higher-ranking gentry. The use of the term records the conventionalised elevation of gentlewomen to ladies.

As Lady Joan does not have any noblewomen correspondents, we do not know how they would have addressed her. Her contemporary, Jane Lady Cornwallis, is alternatively called *dear madam, dear lady* or simply *dear Cornwallis* by her friend Lucy, Countess of Bedford. The Queen greets Lady Cornwallis, later Lady Bacon, with the traditional form *right trusty and right well beloved*.

The data show that *madam* has been adopted as the standard form of address by most people outside Lady Joan's family circle as well as by her elder sons. This is also the form advocated by seventeenth-century letter-writing manuals translated from French, such as Du Bosque (1638) and de la Serre (1640). As it neutralises degrees of deference, however, other means to convey respect are resorted to in the body of the letter. *Your ladyship* often replaces *you* not only in the letters written by clergymen and other non-kin writers from the highest to the lowest but by Lady Joan's extended family, nephews and nieces, and occasionally by her brother-in-law and sons-in-law.

6.2. *Mr Nathaniel Bacon*

Nathaniel Bacon (?1546-1622) belongs to Lady Barrington's generation, but his correspondence dates from 1559–1595. The Bacons represent Norfolk gentry. Nathaniel was the second surviving son of Sir Nicholas Bacon, Lord Keeper to Elizabeth I, and his first wife Jane. Through his family he had close connections with many prominent people of his time, which can be seen from his correspondence, but he himself remained largely a county figure, holding the office of Justice of the Peace in Norfolk for fifty years (Hassell Smith 1978: xvi).[6]

Kinship terms are systematically used by Nathaniel's immediate family circle when they write to him. His father and stepmother Ann usually address him as *son*, his full brothers and brothers-in-law as *brother*. Rarer forms used by his father are the plain *Nathaniel* and *son Nathaniel* and, by his brothers, *good brother*, *brother Nathaniel*, *my brother* and *brother Bacon*. This range of variation is nicely captured by the two letters from Nathaniel's half-brother Anthony Bacon, who calls him plain *brother* as well as *my very good brother*. Nathaniel's two sisters and his daughter never use either his first name or surname, but normally resort to positively modified kinship terms, typically *my good brother* and *most dear father*.

The positively polite *good brother* and *(good) brother Nathaniel* appear in letters by his brothers-in-law and *brother Bacon* in those by his sister-in-law. They all represent gentry. *Son* followed by surname is typically employed by Nathaniel's father-in-law (*son Bacon*). His cousins' strategies vary from the positively polite *cousin Nath* and *my very good cousin* to the negative-neutral *sir*. As we have seen in section 5.3., the use of the term *cousin* does not always refer to consanguinity. This may also be the case with Mistress Jane Tuttoft, who calls Nathaniel Bacon *cousin,* but whose connection with the Bacons the editors of the letters are unable to establish.

No-naming is the strategy selected by Nathaniel's (natural) mother-in-law, who begins her letter by the conventional phrase *after my hartie comendacyons to you and my good doughter your bedfellowe*. She closes her letter in a more positively polite manner, *your loving mother Wenefred Dutton*. For no apparent reason, the address form may also occasionally be left out by Nathaniel's next of kin, including his father, full brothers, and brothers-in-law. The traditional invocation *Jesus* followed by *after my hearty commendations* is once found in a letter by Nathaniel's first cousin, Robert Blackman, who more often gives him the familiar-sounding *cosen Nath*. On the strength of this evidence we must conclude that no-naming is not necessarily a sign of lack of familiarity or even distance. It is doubtful whether it could be analysed further in terms of affect, following the lead of Brown and Gilman (1989).

No-naming was also an established convention in late sixteenth-century officialese, as Angel Day demonstrates in *The English Secretorie* (1586: 23). This is shown by the correspondence received by Nathaniel Bacon in his capacity as a local magistrate from the central administration, including the Privy Council, the Lord Chancellor, and the Secretary of State. These letters regularly begin with the phrase *after our/my hearty commendations*. This formula was also common at the local level, but with more variation. On occasion it could be expanded to include a form of address, as in a petition by the Mayor and Aldermen of King's Lynn, who write *right worshipfull, our humble commendations to yow remembred*. While fellow magistrates could sometimes omit such formal markers of politeness, officials of a humbler sort (customers, surveyors) were in the habit of combining a suitably respectful form of address with a formulaic discharge of their duty, as in *right worshipful, my duty done* or *sir, my duty remembered*, fully in accordance with Angel Day's precepts.

Right worshipful also begins a few letters coming from the higher ranks, including such a variety of people as Robert Dudley, Earl of Leicester, Stephen Drury, Attorney, and John Percival, Rector of Stiffkey, Nathaniel Bacon's manor. According to the letter-writing manuals of the day, it is the usual form of address that one gentleman is supposed to give to another, and *right worshipful sir*, a factor's salutation to his master (Fulwood 1568 [1571]: 117, 120r.). Compared with the recommendations of Fulwood (1568) and Flemming (1576), Bacon's correspondents show more variation. Except for administrative business letters, *right worshipful* has given way to plain *sir* among gentlemen.

Although not so common as *madam* in the case of Joan Barrington, *sir* occurs across the social spectrum. It is equally used by William Cecil, Baron Burghley, Sir William Butts, the merchant Clement Hyrne, and the yeoman John

Mounford. The modified *worshipful sir* also occurs. *Sir* is particularly favoured by the legal profession from the Attorney General downwards. This moderately upgrading term is the typical address form in letters written to Nathaniel Bacon by the gentry, especially by esquires and gentlemen.

The address forms in letters written by the clergy vary from no-naming and *right worshipful* to *Mr (Nathaniel) Bacon*. The appropriate status term *Mr*, in full and abbreviated form, is employed by the higher clergy, including the Bishop of Norwich (*Mr Bacon, after my veri hertye salutations in Christ*), as well as occasionally by the nobilty (*good Mr Bacon*) and higher-ranking gentry (*Good Master Bacon; Mr Nathaniel Bacon*). It hardly ever appears in letters written by vicars and rectors, the lesser gentry, or by the few people representing the ranks below them.

The negatively polite *right worshipful* and no-naming both appear in merchants' letters. Similar formulae are found in John Browne's guide *The Marchants Avizo* (1589), where the young merchant's model letters never include a direct form of address. Compare the examples in (11) and (12).

(11a) Right worshipfull my bound dutye remembrid, maye it please yowe to understond ... (Francis Johnson 1577)
(11b) Emanuell. My humble dutye remembred unto your woorship and also to your bedffellowe. (John Braddock 1587)
(11c) Pleaseth it youe righte worshipfull to be advertized that ... (Richard Clarke 1589)

(12a) After my duetie remembred, I pray for your good health & prosperitie, &c. (*The Marchants Avizo* 1589: 13)
(12b) After my very hartie comendations vnto you: I pray for your good health and prosperitie. (*The Marchants Avizo* 1589: 18)

As in (11b), some merchants refer to Nathaniel Bacon as *your worship* in the body of their letters, as do systematically some vicars and rectors. The practice is also common in the few letters written by (or in some cases on behalf of) yeomen, shipmasters, and servants who corresponded with him. They, too, begin by discharging their duty in formulaic terms, and the form of address used, if any, is usually the traditional *right worshipful*.

7. Summary and discussion

The vast amount of data discussed in sections 5 and 6 calls for a summary. The following generalisations are made on the basis of what appear to us to be the prototypical cases in our corpus.

7.1. Nuclear family and friends

Whenever power is unequally distributed, it overrides social closeness even within the nuclear family. Parents receive more deferential forms from their children, elder brothers from their younger brothers, and husbands from their wives, than vice versa. In the course of time, the recognition of mutual affection increases within the family circle, especially between husband and wife.

The forms and substrategies used change with time. The following generalisations mostly apply to the gentry. Among siblings, the negative strategies typically simplify from *right worshipful sir* and *right worshipful brother* to plain *sir*. *Brother* remains the neutral choice throughout our 250-year period, and plain *sister* is also attested at the end of it. *Brother* plus first name occurs throughout our period, as does *sister* and surname. The former is no doubt more intimate than the latter. Typical positive forms evolve from *right well-beloved brother* both among the gentry and among merchants to *brother* premodified by *good, dear* or *loving. Dear(est) sister* is similarly attested at the end of our period.

From wife to husband, the early negative formula is commonly *right worshipful husband* or *right worshipful sir*, but plain *sir* is also used by gentlewomen. Status terms continue to be used of husbands throughout our period, but wives are hardly ever addressed as *madam*. In our earliest data, husbands use either neutral or positive terms or, more commonly, resort to no-naming. The positive terms used by wives in the early letters tend to be more complex than those of their husbands. Very early on, the nobility uses reciprocal terms of endearment such as *mine own sweetheart*. The typical form adopted in the seventeenth century by couples from all the ranks we have evidence for is the reciprocal *my dear(est)*. The use of first names and nicknames both alone and combined with adjectives of endearment is also well-attested among the ranks below the nobility.

The early negative politeness terms used by children vary from *right worshipful mother* to *right reverend and worshipful mother/father* and *right worshipful sir*. Plain *sir* and *madam* are generalised towards the end of our period. Mixed forms including positive and negative terms occur from the beginning. Positive terms appear on their own from the sixteenth century onwards and gain ground in the seventeenth. They appear to be more frequently given to mothers than to fathers (typically: *(most) dear mother*). Names are never used by children.

Parents prefer neutral and positive terms. No-naming is very common, especially in the fifteenth and sixteenth centuries. Plain *son* occurs throughout our period. Increasingly, first names combine with *son* and *daughter*. A married daughter may also be designated by *daughter* plus her married name. The use of nicknames is attested from the turn of the seventeenth century onwards. The other positive politeness strategy, terms of endearment, changes from the early *right well-beloved son* to *son* premodified by *good* or *dear*. Nicknames and first names also combine with positive adjectives.

Socially equal friends rely on terms of positive politeness. Apart from adjectives like *dear* and *loving*, they use in-group terms, especially nicknames, and joke a great deal. At the same time, the increasingly routinised forms *sir* and *madam* offer a more neutral choice. In relations of social inequality, power usually overrides close distance and hence affection, so that inferiors do not choose terms from the positive end of the politeness scale but from among the more neutral status nouns, like *my lord, sir* and *madam*. There are only few exceptions to this power pattern, and the changes in address forms that take place along with a person's social advancement testify to continued sensitivity to social differences.

7.2. *Non-nuclear family*

Among social equals and from superiors downwards there is a strong tendency to indicate kinship, even a distant one, by choosing a specific kinship noun or, with remote kin, the word *cousin*. Husbands and wives use the same forms of address as their spouses. Uncles, aunts, nephews and nieces mainly give and receive forms of positive politeness, such as *(most) loving uncle* and *good nephew*. The earliest forms are structurally more complex and also contain respectful elements. Unmodified phrases and names like *uncle Edward* and *nephew Oxinden* occur later. *Sir* and *madam* are also used along with kinship terms. The address forms given to brothers-, sisters- and sons-in-law, of which we have extensive coverage in our data, are very much like those used in the nuclear family, documenting a development towards simpler forms and more positive politeness strategies. Unmodified first names and nicknames are, however, not found among in-laws.

It is obvious throughout the data that social status – power in terms of politeness theory – overrides kinship relations. If the addressee's rank is higher than the sender's, no kinship terms are chosen. Gentlemen address their knighted brothers-in-law as *(noble) sir* but are called *good brother* by them; and they use address phrases containing *lord* for their noble brothers-in-law baronets and knights but are reciprocated with *brother*. The same is true of other in-laws, cousins, and more distant relatives, and our scanty evidence points to the same practice even within closer family members, i.e. uncles, aunts, nephews and nieces.

Our data include one extreme case where affect, strong anger, played a decisive role in the choice of the address form. Lord Clare, father of Viscount Wentworth's second wife Arbella, blamed her untimely death on his son-in-law and consequently changed his address form from *son Wentworth* to *my lord*. This example shows that affect, along with power, could influence the politeness strategies selected.

7.3. *Non-kin relations*

As we have seen, social equals and superiors behave similarly in that they indicate kinship even with non-nuclear kin. Writing to non-kin, social equals, however, follow the practice of social inferiors. This usage consists of negative face-redressing strategies, deferentially coding the addressee's social status. Table 2, below, shows that a conspicuous borderline exists in the choice of address forms between the peerage and the gentry on the male side. A nobleman's status is indicated either by *my lord* alone, *(my) lord* premodified by honorific adjectives, or by the phrase *right honourable*.

Below the nobility, the medieval alternatives are *sir* and *master*, often combined into a complex phrase. From the sixteenth century onwards, we can distinguish between two rivalling patterns: the use of *sir*, premodified by adjectives, e.g. *worthy/honourable/noble sir*, and the use of *master* + surname, e.g. *(good) master Wilson, Mr Denne*. The latter gradually gave way to the former, which with time became neutralised to plain *sir*, although modified forms always existed. In the sixteenth century *right worshipful* was another common alternative, especially in official correspondence.

Below the gentry, the information we have about merchants' letters provides evidence of a wider range of nouns: along with *sir*, nouns like *friend*, *cousin* and *brother* are used in the early letters, hence reflecting strategies of positive politeness and possibly also the fact that no conventional titles existed. Later letters follow the models of the gentry, although the noun *friend* is found even at the end of the seventeenth century.

As regards women, the development is different. There is no borderline between the nobility and the gentry, but the noun *lady* is also given to knights' wives from the late Middle Ages onwards (see Table 2). *Dame*, according to

Table 1 reserved for wives of the upper gentry, is not found in our corpus as an address form in letter salutations. *Mistress* was given to gentlewomen and merchants' wives, but *madam* soon became the form of general applicability.

In contrast with social equals and inferiors, social superiors often adopt strategies of positive politeness, choosing in-group nouns like *cousin* and *friend* even where no actual kinship exists. The standard formula *(right) trusty and (right) well-beloved* also consists of adjectives of positive orientation. The use of the recipient's name could serve two purposes: on the one hand, it supported in-group identity, but on the other hand, especially as regards servants, it rather revealed the recipient's lower social position. However, it is important to notice that status nouns were also used by social superiors. As a matter of fact, we may say that from the seventeenth century onwards the two neutral forms, *sir* and *madam*, could be used in any kind of relationship between the sender and the recipient, *sir* below the nobility and *madam* for all ranks included in our study. The use of the terms *sir, madam, lord* and *lady* among the upper social ranks is summarised in Table 2.

Table 2: *Social ranks and nouns of address in Early Modern England*

Rank/Term	lord	lady	sir	madam
Nobility	x	x	–	x
Knights and baronets	–	x	x	x
Gentry	–	–	x	x

The early policy of combining adjectives of both positive and negative orientation, terms of endearment and honorifics, was lost with the simplification of the address phrase. Social superiors often chose benevolent positive adjectives, while inferiors could either reinforce their status-bound strategy by using an appropriate adjective (*worshipful sir, honoured lord*) or refer to the addressee's positive qualities in combination with a status noun (*my very good lord, dear sir*). These forms gradually underwent a process of semantic bleaching.

7.5. *Diachronic trends*

There are a number of generalisations that we would like to suggest on the basis of sections 5 and 6. Our key findings are summarised and discussed below.

(1) Overall, address forms in letter salutations become more regular, as no-naming diminishes in personal correspondence in the course of time. These speaker-addressee forms are also simplified structurally. It is difficult to say

whether we are here witnessing a change in the diachronic perception of the Gricean maxim of quantity ('make your contribution as informative as is required but do not make it more informative than is required') or simply another process of routinisation in letter-writing conventions. One could be the prerequisite of the other.

(2) Of the three factors (P, D, R) that are expected to correlate with the choice of address form, power is the decisive one. Power normally equals social status, either inherited, or acquired by office or occupation. It is regularly encoded in address forms between people of unequal status and often between equals, too. Power operates asymmetrically. Higher status, and hence greater P, licenses the selection of a positive politeness strategy in the address form, such as the use of an in-group term, which cannot be reciprocated by an addressee with a lower status. The reciprocal use of positive terms presupposes equal social status, close distance (D) and, presumably, mutual affection. Even severe impositions (R) need not alter the form of address. This is also recognised by Brown and Levinson (1987: 18), who are now prepared to accept the fact that a given address form may occur with an FTA of any R-value.

(3) The politeness strategies recorded in address forms evolve with time, both with respect to the overall strategy and to individual substrategies. The negative strategy of giving deference is simplified not only structurally but also socially. The spread of *sir* neutralises power distinctions among the ranks below the nobility, and *madam* throughout the rank hierarchy (see Table 2, above). Positive substrategies, ranging from terms of endearment to marking in-group identity by the use of first names and even nicknames, simplify and diversify. Although positive terms are gaining ground among intimates in the course of our period, close distance does not absolutely predetermine the orientation of the address form.

According to Coulmas (1979: 254), routine formulae in general help to maintain orderliness of communication by regulating emotional situations and reducing the complexity of social interactions. If a possible face-threat to the addressee qualifies as an emotional situation, with routine address forms its redress would have to be attended to elsewhere in the letter. The forms of address in the body of the letter and in subscriptions are the obvious points of comparison and a good topic for further inquiry.

On the other hand, routine formulae, such as *sir* and *madam*, certainly reduce the complexity of social interaction and minimise the risk of face loss on the part of the writer. Seen in this light, the diachronic trend towards simplification in address forms is perhaps more speaker-oriented than hearer-oriented. The improvement in literacy increased the number of letter writers, many of whom lacked the benefit of traditional education. These people formed an expanding market for letter-writing manuals and other conduct books. These manuals may or may not have contributed to the process of routinisation, but at least they testify to a desire for rules. Another social factor in the process would appear to be the fluidity of the social hierarchy towards the end of our period, especially the increase in the number of professional people (Stone 1966, Wrightson 1991). It was also reflected in the generalisation of *Mr* and *Mrs* to refer to people below the gentry proper in all spoken and written communication.

If what we are witnessing were merely routinised social indexing, we could hardly speak of a selection of politeness strategies in the Brown and Levinson sense of the term. This is where the options at the positive end of our politeness continuum come in. While deference is routinely encoded in address forms with distants, a whole range of positive substrategies opens up to intimates of comparable social standing. Positive orientation is also available to social superiors regardless of distance. As we have seen, the set of positive address forms is practically open-ended, ranging from *my own sweetheart* to *thou ugly, filthy camel's face.* Contrary to Brown and Gilman's (1989) findings, the distance factor is relevant to the choice of orientation. Although it may be personal affect and changing moods that in the end decide the choice of a given positive address form, their mutual selection is only licensed by close distance in the first place.

Moreover, affect need not be decisive. We were most of the time unable to associate a change in address forms, say, within the family, either with absolute distance or with changes in personal affect. Some of this 'free variation' might be accounted for by situational factors unknown to us. Another factor is no doubt individual variation. As Green (1989: 145-146) points out, there are great differences in individual estimates of distance and the gravity of imposition, as well as in personal styles. The writer may also wish to vary the address form in order to alter the distance to the addressee. The selection of a term with a positive orientation may serve the purpose of a "social accelerator", indicating that a person wants to "come closer" to the addressee (Brown and Levinson 1987: 103). Some shifts of the opposite kind can be explained by changed affect. Our corpus contains some clear-cut instances of positive terms changing to negative after the correspondents have fallen out with each other. It is questionable whether these cases count as redressive action on the part of the writer; on the contrary, a shift towards more negative politeness may be intended as an intrinsic FTA (cf. Brown and Levinson 1987: 65-67).[7]

Our findings have methodological implications that go beyond the material considered in this study. As the choice of address form need not reflect the gravity of imposition, it should not prejudice our judgement of the weightiness of the FTA in question. Thus, the formula suggested by Brown and Levinson (1987: 76) for calculating the weightiness of the FTA ought not automatically to include the choice of address form. This view is further supported by the way in which distance operates in the selection of address form. Politeness does not necessarily increase with distance. What we have witnessed diachronically is a process of both social and structural simplification of deferential address forms, and hence decreased negative politeness between distants. It follows from the asymmetry of the status rule that we also cannot assume that distance necessarily correlates with deference, as the Brown and Levinson formula would predict – distants were entitled to use positive and neutral terms with their social inferiors.

The other problem associated with the study of address forms also has to do with precise quantification. Brown and Gilman (1989: 175-176) assign one point for negative politeness for any single deferential term and two points for two terms, and one point for positive politeness for the use of Christian names with royalty. If the two scores were kept separate, they could tell us something about the complexity of the strategies employed, including the mixtures of positive and negative terms so common in our data. If they are added up to make up a total score, however, as Brown and Gilman do, these mixed strategies become irrecoverable. Preferring to place address forms on a qualitative scale, we would argue, *contra* Brown and Gilman (1989: 175), that *my dread lord* and *sweet lord*, for instance, do not convey the same amount of negative politeness.

Overall, we doubt that the simple additive model suggested by previous studies for deciding the degree of politeness could be directly applicable to real-time diachronic investigations of address forms. All it could record would be shifts in the structural complexity of address form noun phrases. But the simple scoring of the number of forms could not distinguish between *right worshipful husband* and *my dearest dear*, for instance, as both have one adjectival premodifier. We therefore suggest that simplification should be discussed in terms of quantitative prototypes on the politeness continuum (*sir* vs. *right worshipful sir*). Even prototypes do not solve the diachronic problem of interpretation (see above, point 1). At the moment we feel that the issue could best be broached at the level of basic orientation, positive as opposed to negative, and the substrategies used. From this vantage point we can observe the proliferation of positive substrategies in letters – partly no doubt due to the changed circumstances in letter writing in the course of time.

8. Conclusion

To return to the basic issues motivating this study, the answer to our first question is in the affirmative. The growth of literacy and privacy do coincide with an increase in the use of positive politeness strategies in address forms in letters. The use of nicknames between close friends and within the family is one of them. Whether this could be a sign of a more positive politeness culture in the Shakespearean period in terms suggested by Kopytko (1993: 107), is a more complicated issue to assess. As Houlbrooke (1984: 2) points out, the primary sources that have come down to us are uneven in both their social and their temporal coverage. This is certainly true of our materials, which do not reach the lowest social ranks and hence are not representative of the Late Medieval and Early Modern English society as a whole.

Our data nevertheless suggest that if there was a general process towards a more negative politeness culture, it was not uniform. In the mid-seventeenth century the negatively oriented prototypes were plain *sir* and *madam*. It is a sign of cyclicity in the evolution of address forms that their functional equivalents today are divided between the complex *dear sir/dear madam* and *dear Mr X/dear Ms/Mrs/Miss X*. Plain *sir* and *madam* have in turn retreated to the negative end of the politeness continuum. The new strategically mixed alternatives incorporate the adjective *dear* and should hence be considered more positive than the plain forms despite the fact that the collocations must have lost part of their semantic force in the process of routinisation.

In view of both materials and methods, it is too early to make any far-reaching generalisations about the Late Medieval and Early Modern English politeness cultures. Representative comparisons between the past and the present cannot be based on Shakespeare's plays alone, nor on the correspondence of the topmost ranks of the changing English society. Drama and letters will both furnish indispensable evidence of the actual complexities of use, but letters have the advantage of offering an uninterrupted flow of authentic information. They may hence contribute more to our understanding of the sociopragmatic realities of the past. But the whole range of extant sources, both literary and non-literary, should be tapped in order to gain as wide a perspective as possible.

Notes

1.   The persuasive category includes letters of conciliation, reconciliation, encouragement, discouragement, persuasion, dissuasion, consolation, petition, recommendation, admonition, and the amatory letter. Erasmus' demonstrative letters comprise "accounts of persons, regions, estates, castles, springs, gardens, mountains, prodigies, storms, journeys, banquets, buildings, and processions". The judicial category consists of letters of accusation, complaint, defence, protest, justification, reproach, threat, invective, and entreaty (Erasmus 1522 [1985]: 71). Many similar rhetorical-functional classifications can be found in early modern letter-writers (see e.g. Flemming 1576, 'An epitome of preceptes', Day 1586, Gainsford 1616).

2.   In the interest of clarity, address types (= forms appearing in several writers' letters) have been modernised. Individual examples are given in inverted commas, in which case the source is indicated by the family name appearing in the title of the collection. A complete list of collections is given under References.

3.   We may point out that *noble* often occurs in the collocation *noble sir*, which is not an address form given to the nobility but to various members of the gentry.

4.   To be exact, the forms included in our survey consist of the direct forms of address at the very beginning of a letter before the salutation, if there is one. No-naming refers to absence of such a form at this point. Interesting though they are, the forms of address within the body of the letter would go beyond the limits of an already crowded paper (see, however, section 6).

5.   The number of letters included in the collection is 252 and the number of correspondents is 48. With few exceptions, the letters are holograph.

6.   The collection consists of three volumes of letters and papers. Most of the letters are holograph, but there are also a number of secretarial copies especially among those sent to and by crown officials. Unfortunately, some letters are reproduced in calendar-form. The number of correspondents is close to 140.

7.   It is interesting to observe that the great majority of the new *nomina appellativa* introduced into Early Modern English were in fact pejorative (see Nevalainen, forthcoming). The use of invective and hence overt face-threatening acts involving forms of address were common, for instance, in courtrooms in the Early Modern period.

References

Primary sources

The collections marked by an asterisk (*) have been extensively sampled for the pilot version of the computerised *Helsinki Corpus of Early English Correspondence*, and provide the core corpus of this study (see Nevalainen and Raumolin-Brunberg 1994). The other texts listed serve as supplementary material.

*Bacon
    1978-1988   *The Papers of Nathaniel Bacon of Stiffkey.* Vols. I-III. (Norfolk Record Society 46, 49, 53.) Eds. A. Hassell Smith – Gillian M. Baker – R. W. Kenny. Norwich.

*Barrington
    1983   *Barrington Family Letters, 1628-1632.* (Camden Fourth Series 28.) Ed. Arthur Searle. London.

*Brereton
    1976   *Letters and Accounts of William Brereton of Malpas.* (The Record Society of Lancashire and Cheshire 116.) Ed. E. W. Ives. Old Woking, Surrey: The Gresham Press.

*Cely
    1975   *The Cely Letters, 1472-1488.* (Early English Text Society 273.) Ed. Alison Hanham. London – New York – Toronto: Oxford University Press.

*Clifford
    1962   *Clifford Letters of the Sixteenth Century.* (Publications of the Surtees Society 172.) Ed. A. G. Dickens. Durham – London.

    1992   *Letters of the Cliffords, Lords Clifford and Earls of Cumberland, c.1500-c.1565.* (Camden Miscellany 31, Camden Fourth Series 44.) Ed. R. W. Hoyle. London.

*Conway
    1992   *The Conway Letters: the Correspondence of Anne, Viscountess Conway, Henry More, and Their Friends 1642-1684.* [Rev. ed.] Eds. Marjorie Hope Nicholson – Sarah Hutton. Oxford: Oxford University Press.

*Cornwallis
    1842   *The Private Correspondence of Jane, Lady Cornwallis, 1613-1644.* Ed. Lord Braybrooke. London: S. & J. Bentley, Wilson & Fley.

*Elizabeth, Queen of Bohemia
    1953   *The Letters of Elizabeth Queen of Bohemia.* Ed. L. M. Baker. London: Bodley Head.

*Ellis
    1825   *Original Letters Illustrative of English History; Including Numerous Royal Letters.* Vols. II–III. Ed. Henry Ellis. 2nd edition. London: Harding, Triphook, and Lepard.

*Ferrar
    1938   *The Ferrar Papers.* Ed. B. Blackstone. Cambridge: Cambridge University Press.

*Fleming
    1904-1924 *The Flemings in Oxford, Being Documents Selected from the Rydal Papers in Illustration of the Lives and Ways of Oxford Men 1650-1700.* Vols. I-III. (Oxford Historical Society 44, 62, 79.) Ed. John Richard Magrath. Oxford.

*Gawdy
    1906   *Letters of Philip Gawdy of West Harling, Norfolk, and of London to Various Members of His Family 1579-1616.* Ed. Isaac Herbert Jeayes. London: Roxburghe Club.

*Haddock
    1965 [1883] *Correspondence of the Family of Haddock, 1657-1719.* (Camden Miscellany 8, Camden New Series 31.) Ed. Edward Maunde Thompson. New York – London.

*Hatton
    1878   *Correspondence of the Family of Hatton, 1601-1704.* Vols. I-II. (Camden Society 22, 23) Ed. E. M. Thompson. London.

*Holles
    1975-1986 *Letters of John Holles, 1587-1637.* Vols. I-III. (Thoroton Society Record Series 31, 35, 36.) Ed. P. R. Seddon. Nottingham.

*Hoskyns
    1937   *The Life, Letters and Writings of John Hoskyns, 1566-1638.* (Yale Studies in English 87.) Ed. Louise Brown Osborne. New Haven: Yale University Press, London: Humphrey Milford – Oxford University Press.

*Johnson
    1953   *The Johnson Letters, 1542-1552.* Ed. Barbara Winchester. Unpublished doctoral dissertation. University of London.

*KPaston
    1941   *The Correspondence of Lady Katherine Paston, 1603-1627.* (Norfolk Record Society 14.) Ed. Ruth Hughey. Norwich.

Lisle
    1981   *The Lisle Letters*. Ed. Muriel St. Claire Byrne. Chicago: The University of Chicago Press.

Lowther
    1977   *Commercial Papers of Sir Christopher Lowther 1611-1644*. (Publications of the Surtees Society 189.) Ed. D. R. Hainsworth. Durham – London.

*Marescoe-David
    1987   *Markets and Merchants of the Late Seventeenth Century; The Marescoe-David Letters, 1668-1680*. (Records of Social and Economic History New Series 12.) Ed. Henry Roseveare. Oxford: Oxford University Press for the British Academy.

*More
    1947   *The Correspondence of Sir Thomas More*. Ed. Elizabeth Frances Rogers. Princeton: Princeton University Press.

*Oxinden
    1933   *The Oxinden letters, 1607-1642. Being the Correspondence of Henry Oxinden of Barham and His Circle*. Ed. Dorothy Gardiner. London: Constable & Co. Ltd.

Paston
    1971   *Paston Letters and Papers of the Fifteenth Century*. Parts I-II. Ed. Norman Davis. Oxford: Clarendon Press.

*Pepys
    1955   *The Letters of Samuel Pepys and His Family Circle*. Ed. Helen Truesdell Heath. Oxford: Clarendon Press.

*Plumpton
    1968 [1839] *Plumpton Correspondence. A Series of Letters, Chiefly Domestick, Written in the Reigns of Edward IV. Richard III. Henry VII. and Henry VIII.* (Camden Society Old Series 4.) Ed. Thomas Stapleton. New York – London: AMS Press

Rochester
    1927   *John Wilmot Earl of Rochester his Life and Writings, with his Lordship's Private Correspondence*. (Palaestra 154, Untersuchung und Texte aus der deutschen und englischen Philologie.) Ed. Johannes Prinz. Leipzig: Mayer & Müller.

Smyth
    1982   *Calendar of the Correspondence of the Smyth Family of Ashton Court, 1548-1642*. (Bristol Record Society Publications 35.) Ed. J. H. Bettey. Gloucester.

*Stockwell
  1932-1933   *The Miscellaneous Papers of Captain Thomas Stockwell, 1590-1611.* Vols.
              I-II. (Southampton Record Society 32, 33.) Ed. J. Rutherford. Southampton.
*Stonor
  1919   *The Stonor Letters and Papers, 1290-1483.* Vols. I-II. (Camden Society
              Third Series 29, 30.) Ed. Charles Lethbridge Kingsford. London.
  1924   *Supplementary Stonor Letters and Papers, 1314-1482.* (Camden Miscellany
              XIII, Camden Third Series 34.) Ed. Charles Lethbridge Kingsford. London.
Thynne
  1983   *Two Elizabethan Women: Correspondence of Joan and Maria Thynne,
              1575-1611.* (Wiltshire Record Society.) Ed. Alison D. Wall. Stoke-on-
              Trent.
*Wentworth
  1973   *Wentworth Papers, 1597-1628.* (Camden Fourth Series 12.) Ed. J. P.
              Cooper. London.
*Wyatt
  1963   *Life and Letters of Sir Thomas Wyatt.* Ed. Kenneth Muir. Liverpool:
              Liverpool University Press.

Secondary sources

Barber, Charles
  1976   *Early Modern English.* London: André Deutsch.
Böhm, Annemarie
  1936   *Entwicklungsgeschichte der englischen Titel und Anreden seit dem 16.
              Jahrhundert.* PhD Dissertation. Berlin: Brandenburgische Buchdruckerei.
Boulton, Jeremy
  1987   *Neighbourhood and Society: a London Suburb in the Seventeenth Century.*
              (Cambridge Studies in Population, Economy and Society in Past Time 5.)
              Cambridge: Cambridge University Press.
Brayshay, Mark
  1991   "Royal posthorse routes in England and Wales: the evolution of the
              network in the later-sixteenth and early-seventeenth century." *Journal of
              Historical Geography* 17/4, 373-389.
Breton, Nicholas
  1602 [1669] *A Post with a Packet of Mad Letters.* London.
Breuer, Horst
  1983   "Titel und Anreden bei Shakespeare und in der Shakespeare-Zeit." *Anglia*,
              101 1/2, 49-77.

Brown, Penelope and Stephen C. Levinson
    1987   *Politeness: Some Universals in Language Usage.* Cambridge: Cambridge
          University Press.

Brown, Roger and Albert Gilman
    1989   "Politeness theory and Shakespeare's four major tragedies." *Language in*
          Society 18, 159-212.

B[rowne], J[ohn]
    1589 [1957] *The Marchants Avizo.* Ed. Patrick McGrath. Cambridge, MA: Baker
          Library, Harvard Graduate School of Business Administration – London:
          St. Catherine's Press.

Clay, C.G.A.
    1984   *Economic Expansion and Social Change, England 1500-1700. I-II.*
          Cambridge: Cambridge University Press.

Corfield, Penelope J. (ed.)
    1991   *Language, History and Class.* Oxford: Basic Blackwell.

Coulmas, Florian
    1979   "On the sociolinguistic relevance of routine formulae." *Journal of*
          Pragmatics 3, 239-266.

Cressy, David
    1980   *Literacy and Social Order: Reading and Writing in Tudor and Stuart*
          England. Cambridge: Cambridge University Press.
    1986   "Kinship and kin interaction in Early Modern England." *Past and Present*
          113, 38-69.

Crofts, J.
    1967   *Packhorse, Waggon and Post: Land Carriage and Communication under*
          the Tudors and Stuarts. London: Routledge and Kegan Paul.

Davis, Norman
    1965   "The *Litera Troili* and English letters." *Review of English Studies*, N.S.
          16/63, 233-244.

Day, Angel
    1586 [1967] *The English Secretorie, 1586.* (English Linguistics 29.) Menston: The
          Scolar Press.

de la Serre, Puget
    1640 [1654] *The Secretary in Fashion.* Transl. John Massinger. London.

Du Bosque, M.
    1638   *The Secretary of Ladies.* Transl. I[erome] H[ainhofer]. London.

Erasmus, Desiderius
    1522 [1985] *De conscribendis epistolis.* In: J.K. Sowards (ed.), *Collected works of Erasmus,* Vol. 25, *Literary and educational writings* 3. Toronto – Buffalo – London: University of Toronto Press.
Ervin-Tripp, Susan M.
    1972   "Sociolinguistic rules of address." In: J.B. Pride and J. Holmes (eds.). *Sociolinguistics.* Harmondsworth: Penguin, 225-240.
Finkenstaedt, Thomas
    1963   *You und thou: Studien zur Anrede im Englischen.* Berlin: Walter de Gruyter.
Flemming, Abraham (transl.)
    1576   *A panoplie of Epistles, or a Looking Glasse for the Vnlearned.* London.
Fulwood, William (transl.)
    1568 [1571] *The Enemie of Idlenesse.* London.
Gainsford, Thomas
    1616 [1974] *The Secretaries Studie, 1616.* (The English Experience 658.) Amsterdam – Norwood, N.J: Walter J. Johnson, Theatrum Orbis Terrarum.
Goody, Jack (ed.)
    1968   *Literacy in Traditional Societies.* Cambridge: Cambridge University Press.
Graff, Harvey J.
    1987   *The Legacies of Literacy: Continuities and Contradictions in Western Culture and Society.* Bloomington – Indianapolis: Indiana University Press.
Green, Georgia M.
    1989   *Pragmatics and Natural Language Understanding.* Hillsdale, N.J.: Lawrence Erlbaum.
Hall, Hubert
    1908   *Studies in English Official Historical Documents.* New York: Franklin.
Harrison, William
    1577 [1965] "The Description of England." In: *Holinshed's Chronicles; England, Scotland and Ireland, I, England.* London: AMS Press, 221-421.
Henderson, Judith Rice
    1993   "On reading the rhetoric of the Renaissance letter." In: Heinrich F. Plett (ed.). *Renaissance-Rhetorik/ Renaissance Rhetoric.* Berlin – New York: Walter de Gruyter, 143-162.
Houlbrooke, Ralph A.
    1984   *The English Family 1450-1700.* London – New York: Longman.
Keen, Maurice
    1990   *English Society in the Later Middle Ages 1348-1500.* Harmondsworth: Allan Lane, the Penguin Press.

Kingsford, C.L.
    1925 [1962] *Prejudice and Promise in Fifteenth Century England.* London: Frank Cass & Co.
Kopytko, Roman
    1993   *Polite Discourse in Shakespeare's English.* Poznań: Adam Mickiewicz University Press.
Laslett, Peter
    1965 [1983] *The World We Have Lost – Further Explored.* London: Routledge.
Leech, Geoffrey
    1983   *Principles of Pragmatics.* London: Longman.
Lester, G.A.
    1987   "The books of a fifteenth-century gentleman, Sir John Paston." *Neuphilologische Mitteilungen* 88/2, 200-217.
Matsumoto, Yoshiko
    1988   "Reexamination of the universality of face: politeness phenomena in Japanese." *Journal of Pragmatics* 12, 403-426.
Mikkola, Tellervo
    1984   *Forms of Address and Subscriptions in the Paston Letters of the Fifteenth Century.* Unpublished MA Thesis. University of Helsinki, Department of English.
Nevalainen, Terttu
    1994   "Ladies and gentlemen: the generalization of titles in Early Modern English." In: Francisco Fernández, Miguel Fuster, and Juan José Calvo (eds.). *English Historical Linguistics 1992.* (Current Issues in Linguistic Theory 113.) Amsterdam – Philadelphia: John Benjamins, 317-327.
    forthc.   "Early Modern English lexis and semantics." In: Roger Lass (ed.), *The Cambridge history of the English language*, Vol. 3, *Early Modern English 1476-1776.* Cambridge: Cambridge University Press.
Nevalainen, Terttu and Helena Raumolin-Brunberg
    1989   "A corpus of Early Modern Standard English in a socio-historical perspective." *Neuphilologische Mitteilungen*, 90/1, 67-111.
    1994   "Sociolinguistics and language history: The Helsinki Corpus of Early English Correspondence." *Hermes, Journal of Linguistics* 13, 135-143.
Palliser, D. M.
    1983   *The Age of Elizabeth. England under the Late Tudors 1547 – 1603.* London – New York: Longman.

Rappaport, Steve
    1989   *Worlds Within Worlds: Structures of Life in Sixteenth-Century London.*
        (Cambridge Studies in Population, Economy and Society in Past Time 7.)
        Cambridge: Cambridge University Press.

Replogle, Carol
    1987   "Shakespeare's salutations: a study in stylistic etiquette." In Vivian
        Salmon and Edwina Burness (eds.). *A Reader in the Language of*
        Shakespearean Drama. Amsterdam, Philadelphia: John Benjamins, 101-
        115. [Reprinted from *Studies in Philology* 70 (1973): 172-186.]

Richardson, Malcolm
    1984   "The *dictamen* and its influence on fifteenth-century English Prose."
        Rhetorica 2, 207-226.

Schofield, R.S.
    1968   "The measurement of literacy in pre-industrial England." In: Jack Goody
        (ed.), 311-325.

Spufford, Margaret
    1981 [1989]*Small Books and Pleasant Histories: Popular Fiction in Seventeenth-*
        Century England. London: Methuen.

Stone, Lawrence
    1966   "Social mobility in England, 1500-1700." *Past and Present* 33, 16-55.

Svennung, J.
    1958   *Anredeformen: vergleichende Forschungen zur indirekten Anrede in der*
        dritten Person und zum Nominativ für den Vokativ. (Acta Societatis
        Litterarum Humaniorum Regiae Upsaliensis 42.) Uppsala: Almqvist &
        Wiksell – Wiesbaden: Otto Harrassowitz.

Tiusanen, Ritva
    1968   *Shakespeare's and Chapman's Terms of Endearment: A Study in Sense,*
        Stylistic Value, and Background. Unpublished Lic.Phil. thesis. University of
        Helsinki, Deparment of English.

Voigts, Linda Ehrsam
    1981   "A letter from a Middle English dictaminal formulary in Harvard Law
        Library MS 43." *Speculum* 56/3, 575-581.

Walker, George
    1938   *Haste, Post, Haste! Postmen and Post-roads Through the Ages.* London:
        George G. Harrap & Co.

Whigham, Frank
    1981   "The rhetoric of Elizabethan suitor's letters." *PMLA* 96/5, 864-882.

Wildeblood, Joan and Peter Brinson
    1965   *The Polite World; A Guide to English Manners and Deportment from the Thirteenth to the Nineteenth Century.* London: Oxford University Press.

Williams, Joseph M.
    1992   "'O! When degree is shak'd': sixteenth-century anticipations of some modern attitudes toward usage." In: Tim William Machan and Charles T. Scott (eds.). *English in its Social Contexts: Essays in Historical Sociolinguistics.* New York, Oxford: Oxford University Press, 69-101.

Wilson, Thomas
    c.1600   *The State of England, Anno Dom. 1600.* (Camden Society 52). Ed. F.
    [1936]   J. Fisher. London: Royal Historical Society.

Wrightson, Keith
    1982   *English Society 1580-1680.* London: Hutchinson.
    1991   "Estates, degrees, and sorts: changing perceptions of society in Tudor and Stuart England." In: Penelope J. Corfield (ed.), 30-52.

Index of Names and Sources

Index of Subjects

—Y—

21. STARKE, James et al. Tropical Rainforests: A Disappearing Treasure. Washington: Smithsonian Institution, 1990.

22. ALLER, P. ... and Size (1981) ...

23. PORTMANN, Richard. PAYNE, and Lars KUSTOWSKI ...

24. MAYNARD, Smith ...

25. COOPER, ...

26. STYVAALI, Gus. Tree Ecology ...

27. STINE, John. The Wallace ...

28. VAN, J. WOLD, Herts. ...

29. DARWIN, Robert T. ...

30. WORTHAM, Scott. ...

31. WILLIAM, Wallace. ...

32. SHNAEL ...

33. COOPER, ...

34. WARREN, Richard ...

35. RICHIE, ...

36. HILLIS, ...

37. CARLSON, ...

38. REITHER ...

39. HILLIS, ...